The Employee-Organization Relationship
Applications for the 21st Century

SERIES IN APPLIED PSYCHOLOGY

Series Editors
Jeanette N. Cleveland, Colorado State University
Kevin R. Murphy, Landy Litigation and Colorado State University

Edwin A. Fleishman, Founding Series Editor (1987–2010)

Gregory Bedny and David Meister
The Russian Theory of Activity: Current Applications to Design and Learning

Winston Bennett, David Woehr, and Charles Lance
Performance Measurement: Current Perspectives and Future Challenges

Michael T. Brannick, Eduardo Salas, and Carolyn Prince
Team Performance Assessment and Measurement: Theory, Research, and Applications

Jeanette N. Cleveland, Margaret Stockdale, and Kevin R. Murphy
Women and Men in Organizations: Sex and Gender Issues at Work

Aaron Cohen
Multiple Commitments in the Workplace: An Integrative Approach

Russell Cropanzano
Justice in the Workplace: Approaching Fairness in Human Resource Management, Volume 1

Russell Cropanzano
Justice in the Workplace: From Theory to Practice, Volume 2

David V. Day, Stephen Zaccaro, and Stanley M. Halpin
Leader Development for Transforming Organizations: Growing Leaders for Tomorrow's Teams and Organizations

Stewart I. Donaldson, Mihaly Csikszentmihalyi, and Jeanne Nakamura
Applied Positive Psychology: Improving Everyday Life, Health, Schools, Work, and Safety

James E. Driskell and Eduardo Salas
Stress and Human Performance

Sidney A. Fine and Steven F. Cronshaw
Functional Job Analysis: A Foundation for Human Resources Management

Sidney A. Fine and Maury Getkate
Benchmark Tasks for Job Analysis: A Guide for Functional Job Analysis (FJA) Scales

J. Kevin Ford, Steve W. J. Kozlowski, Kurt Kraiger, Eduardo Salas, and Mark S. Teachout
Improving Training Effectiveness in Work Organizations

Jerald Greenberg
Organizational Behavior: The State of the Science, Second Edition

Jerald Greenberg
Insidious Workplace Behavior

Edwin Hollander
Inclusive Leadership: The Essential Leader-Follower Relationship

Jack Kitaeff
Handbook of Police Psychology

Uwe E. Kleinbeck, Hans-Henning Quast, Henk Thierry, and Hartmut Häcker
Work Motivation

Laura L. Koppes
Historical Perspectives in Industrial and Organizational Psychology

Ellen Kossek and Susan Lambert
Work and Life Integration: Organizational, Cultural, and Individual Perspectives

Martin I. Kurke and Ellen M. Scrivner
Police Psychology into the 21st Century

Joel Lefkowitz
Ethics and Values in Industrial and Organizational Psychology

Manuel London
Job Feedback: Giving, Seeking, and Using Feedback for Performance Improvement, Second Edition

Manuel London
How People Evaluate Others in Organizations

Manuel London
Leadership Development: Paths to Self-Insight and Professional Growth

Robert F. Morrison and Jerome Adams
Contemporary Career Development Issues

Michael D. Mumford, Garnett Stokes, and William A. Owens
Patterns of Life History: The Ecology of Human Individuality

Michael D. Mumford
Pathways to Outstanding Leadership: A Comparative Analysis of Charismatic, Ideological, and Pragmatic Leaders

Kevin R. Murphy
Validity Generalization: A Critical Review

Kevin Murphy
A Critique of Emotional Intelligence: What Are the Problems and How Can They Be Fixed?

Susan E. Murphy and Ronald E. Riggio
The Future of Leadership Development

Susan E. Murphy and Rebecca J. Reichard
Early Development and Leadership: Building the Next Generation of Leaders

Kevin R. Murphy and Frank E. Saal
Psychology in Organizations: Integrating Science and Practice

Margaret A. Neal and Leslie Brett Hammer
Working Couples Caring for Children and Aging Parents: Effects on Work and Well-Being

Robert E. Ployhart, Benjamin Schneider, and Neal Schmitt
Staffing Organizations: Contemporary Practice and Theory, Third Edition

Steven A.Y. Poelmans
Work and Family: An International Research Perspective

Erich P. Prien, Jeffery S. Schippmann, and Kristin O. Prien
Individual Assessment: As Practiced in Industry and Consulting

Robert D. Pritchard, Sallie J. Weaver, and Elissa L. Ashwood
Evidence-Based Productivity Improvement: A Practical Guide to the Productivity Measurement and Enhancement System

Ned Rosen
Teamwork and the Bottom Line: Groups Make a Difference

Heinz Schuler, James L. Farr, and Mike Smith
Personnel Selection and Assessment: Individual and Organizational Perspectives

John W. Senders and Neville P. Moray
Human Error: Cause, Prediction, and Reduction

Lynn M. Shore, Jacqueline A-M. Coyle-Shapiro, and Lois E. Tetrick
The Employee-Organization Relationship: Applications for the 21st Century

Kenneth S. Shultz and Gary A. Adams
Aging and Work in the 21st Century

Frank J. Smith
Organizational Surveys: The Diagnosis and Betterment of Organizations Through Their Members

Dianna Stone and Eugene F. Stone-Romero
The Influence of Culture on Human Resource Processes and Practices

Kecia M. Thomas
Diversity Resistance in Organizations

George C. Thornton III and Rose Mueller-Hanson
Developing Organizational Simulations: A Guide for Practitioners and Students

George C. Thornton III and Deborah Rupp
Assessment Centers in Human Resource Management: Strategies for Prediction, Diagnosis, and Development

Yoav Vardi and Ely Weitz
Misbehavior in Organizations: Theory, Research, and Management

Patricia Voydanoff
Work, Family, and Community

Mark A. Wilson, Winston Bennett, Shanan G. Gibson, and George M. Alliger
The Handbook of Work Analysis: Methods, Systems, Applications, and Science of Work Measurement in Organizations

The Employee-Organization Relationship

Applications for the 21st Century

Edited by

Lynn M. Shore
San Diego State University

Jacqueline A-M. Coyle-Shapiro
London School of Economics and Political Science

Lois E. Tetrick
George Mason University

Routledge
Taylor & Francis Group
New York London

Routledge
Taylor & Francis Group
711 Third Avenue
New York, NY 10017

Routledge
Taylor & Francis Group
27 Church Road
Hove, East Sussex BN3 2FA

© 2012 by Taylor & Francis Group, LLC
Routledge is an imprint of Taylor & Francis Group, an Informa business

Printed in the United States of America on acid-free paper
Version Date: 20111209

International Standard Book Number: 978-0-415-88077-0 (Hardback)

For permission to photocopy or use material electronically from this work, please access www.copyright.com (http://www.copyright.com/) or contact the Copyright Clearance Center, Inc. (CCC), 222 Rosewood Drive, Danvers, MA 01923, 978-750-8400. CCC is a not-for-profit organization that provides licenses and registration for a variety of users. For organizations that have been granted a photocopy license by the CCC, a separate system of payment has been arranged.

Trademark Notice: Product or corporate names may be trademarks or registered trademarks, and are used only for identification and explanation without intent to infringe.

Library of Congress Cataloging-in-Publication Data

The employee-organization relationship / editors, Lynn M. Shore, Jacqueline A-M.Coyle-Shapiro, Lois E. Tetrick.
  p. cm. -- (Series in applied psychology)
  Includes bibliographical references and index.
  ISBN 978-0-415-88077-0 (hardcover : alk. paper)
  1. Industrial relations. 2. Psychology, Industrial. 3. Organizational behavior. I. Shore, Lynn M. II. Coyle-Shapiro, Jacqueline A-M. III. Tetrick, Lois E.

HD6971.E553 2012
331--dc23   2011047971

Visit the Taylor & Francis Web site at
http://www.taylorandfrancis.com

and the Psychology Press Web site at
http://www.psypress.com

To all of the creative people who have contributed to the EOR literature, most especially Lyman Porter, Denise Rousseau, Bob Eisenberger, and Anne Tsui, who inspired me with their ideas and insights. And, to my patient and neglected coauthors and friends, Jim Dulebohn and Sandy Wayne, who allowed me to complete this book and put their manuscripts on the back burner (temporarily!).

— **Lynn M. Shore**

To Riccardo Peccei, whose inspiration has continued far beyond my days as a student.

— **Jacqueline A-M. Coyle-Shapiro**

To inspiring colleagues, be they my coeditors, coauthors, students, coworkers, or friends, who have stretched my thinking about the EOR. Without such challenges, we can't hope to enhance the world of work for all of us currently engaged and those who will follow.

— **Lois E. Tetrick**

Contents

Series Foreword xix
Preface xxiii
About the Editors xxv
About the Contributors xxix

Chapter 1 Expanding the Boundaries and Challenging the Assumptions of the Employee–Organization Relationship Literature 1

Lynn M. Shore, Jacqueline A-M. Coyle-Shapiro, and Lois E. Tetrick

Current Status of EOR Theory 2
How the Book Is Organized: Gaps in the Literature 10

PART 1 New Ways of Thinking About the Employee–Organization Relationship

Chapter 2 Is the Employee–Organization Relationship Misspecified? The Centrality of Tribes in Experiencing the Organization 23

Blake E. Ashforth and Kristie M. Rogers

The Organization as Context 25
The Roles of Tribe Members: Focal Individual, Manager, and Peers 29
The Psychological Convergence of Tribe and Organization 39
Discussion 41

Chapter 3 The Employee–Organization Relationship and Ethics: When It Comes to Ethical Behavior, Who Is the Organization and Why Does It Matter? 55

Marshall Schminke

xi

Top Management, Supervisor, and Coworker
Influences on Employee Ethics 56
Top Management, Supervisors, and Coworkers: Who
Exerts the Strongest Influence? 61
Implications for EOR and Ethics Researchers 64
Looking to the Future 72
Conclusion 79

Chapter 4 Social Identity-Based Leadership and the
Employee–Organization Relationship 85
Daan van Knippenberg
Leadership and the Employment Relationship: Social
Exchange or Social Identity? 86
Advantages of Social Identity–Based Leadership 94
Leaders as Entrepreneurs of Identity: Motivating by
Shaping Who We Are 99
Where Do the Cultural Universals Stop and the
Cultural Specifics Begin? 105
Conclusion 106

Chapter 5 Resource Commensurability and Ideological
Elements of the Exchange Relationship 113
Judi McLean Parks and faye l. smith
Introduction 113
Theoretical Development 115

Chapter 6 Perceived Organizational Cruelty: An Expansion of
the Negative Employee–Organization Relationship
Domain 139
Lynn M. Shore and Jacqueline A-M. Coyle-Shapiro
Definition of Perceived Organizational Cruelty 140
Comparison of POC and Other Negative EOR
Concepts 141
A Model of POC 146
Antecedents of POC 148
Outcomes of POC 154

Moderators 157
Conclusion and Future Research 161

Chapter 7 Assumptions in Employee–Organization
Relationship Research: A Critical Perspective From
the Study of Volunteers 169

Jone L. Pearce
A Few Things Volunteers Can Teach Us About
Employee–Organizational Relationships............................ 169
Volunteer–Organization Relationships................................ 171
Assumption 1: The EOR Is Clear to Employees 173
Assumption 2: The EOR Is Driven by How the
Organization Treats Participants... 175
Assumption 3: Participants Are Dependent on Their
Organization 177
Assumption 4: The Organization Is Not Understaffed 179
Assumption 5: Participants Understand Their
Participation as an Inducement–Contribution
Exchange 181
Conclusions.. 185

PART 2 Putting the "R" Back in the EOR

Chapter 8 Can the Organizational Career Survive? An
Evaluation Within a Social Exchange Perspective........ 193

David E. Guest and Ricardo Rodrigues
Introduction 193
The Career From a Social Exchange Perspective 195
The Changing Context of Careers and Career
Management... 199
The Case for Retaining the Organizational Career 203
The New Career 207
Have Organizational Careers Survived? 210
Separating the Rhetoric From the Reality: The Future
of Organizational Careers Through the Lens of
Exchange Theory 214

Chapter 9 Work–Family Flexibility and the Employment Relationship 223

Ellen Ernst Kossek and Marian N. Ruderman

Growing Diversity and Intensity of Work–Family Demands 224
Commonalities in the Transformation of Work, Family, and the Employment Relationship 226
Work–Family Boundary-Blurring Flexibility Practices 234
EOR Linkages to Work–Family Flexibility: Theory and Hypotheses 238
Conclusions and Future Directions 248
Acknowledgment 250

Chapter 10 Rethinking the Employee–Organization Relationship: Insights From the Experiences of Contingent Workers 255

Daniel G. Gallagher and Catherine E. Connelly

Defining the Domain 257
Contingent Employee–Organization Relationships 260
Direct Hires 261
Research Implications 271
Cultural Influences 273
Practical Implications 274
Conclusion 276
Acknowledgment 277

Chapter 11 Virtual Employee–Organization Relationships: Linking in to the Challenge of Increasingly Virtual EOR 281

Kathryn M. Bartol and Yuntao Dong

Human Resource and Virtuality Architecture 282
Translating Mechanisms and Psychological States 288
Outcomes 295
Discussion 297

Chapter 12 A Relational Perspective on the Employee–
Organization Relationship: A Critique and
Proposed Extension 307

Riki Takeuchi
Theoretical Overviews and Critique 309
Relational View of Social Exchange Relationships 314
Discussion 324

PART 3 Creation, Maintenance, and Completion of the Employee–Organization Relationship

Chapter 13 Fostering Anticipatory Justice: A New Option
for Enhancing the Employee–Organization
Relationship? 335

Debra L. Shapiro and Mel Fugate
Objectives and Motivation for Including Anticipatory
Justice in EOR Research and Practice 336
Revisiting the Inducements–Contributions Model
and Other Social Exchange–Based Concepts as
Explanations for the Quality of EOR 341
Illustrations of Anticipatory Justice and How It Might
Increase EOR Quality 345
Are There Boundaries of Anticipatory Justice Effects? 349
Implications of Broadening EOR to Include
Anticipatory Justice 354
Conclusion 359

Chapter 14 Applicant–Organization Relationship and
Employee–Organization Relationship: What Is the
Connection? 363

Ann Marie Ryan
AOR Elements 364
Dynamic Nature of AORs 377
AOR as a Signal of EOR 378
Breach or Violation 380
Practical Implications 383
Conclusions 384

Chapter 15 Employee–Organization Relationships: Their Impact on Push-and-Pull Forces for Staying and Leaving 391

Peter W. Hom
EOR Framework on Push-and-Pull Forces for Staying and Leaving 392
Mutual Investment EOR 398
Overinvestment EOR 404
Quasi-Spot Contracts 407
Underinvestment EOR 409
EOR Multilevel Effects 412
Further Model Refinements 413
International Implications 414
Practical Implications 416

Chapter 16 Employee–Organization Relationship in Older Workers 427

Mo Wang and Yujie Zhan
The Meaning of Aging to the EOR 428
EORs and Retirement 435
Conclusions 447

PART 4   Organizational and Strategic Implications

Chapter 17 Strategic Human Resource Management and Employee–Organization Relationship 455

David Lepak and Wendy R. Boswell
Evolving Issues 458
Conclusion and Future Research Directions 473

Chapter 18 Emotions: The Glue That Holds the Employee–Organization Relationship Together (or Not) 485

Lois E. Tetrick
Social Exchange in the EOR 487
Emotions 495

Aggregation of Individual-Level Effects to
Organizational-Level Effects: Emotional Contagion 499
Implications and Conclusions 502

Chapter 19 Managing Diversity Means Managing Differently:
A Look at the Role of Racioethnicity in Perceptions
of Organizational Support 509

Derek R. Avery, Patrick F. McKay, and Quinetta M. Roberson

Current Diversity Trends 510
How Racioethnic Diversity Influences Perceptions of
Organizational Support..511
Research Implications...523
Managerial Implications 525
Conclusion...527

Chapter 20 Why Work Teams Fail in Organizations: Myths and
Advice 533

Eduardo Salas and Stephen M. Fiore

Teamwork, Team Theories, and the EOR 534
The Myths of Teamwork..537
Advice: Fostering Effective Teamwork.............................. 548
Conclusion...551

Chapter 21 The Employee–Organization Relationship and the
Scholar–Practitioner Divide.. 555

Wayne F. Cascio and Robert J. Greene

The Scholar–Practitioner Divide...559
Integrating the Organization's and the Employee's
Perspectives 566
Conclusion...572

Chapter 22 Conclusion and Directions for Future Research.......... 577

Lynn M. Shore, Jacqueline A-M. Coyle-Shapiro, and Lois E. Tetrick

Examining Established Viewpoints................................... 577
The EOR and Its Impact 585

Future Research 587
Conclusion.. 588

Author Index 591
Subject Index 607

Series Foreword

Jeanette N. Cleveland
Colorado State University

Kevin R. Murphy
Landy Litigation and Colorado State University
Series Editors

There is a compelling need for innovative approaches to the solution of many pressing problems involving human relationships in today's society. Such approaches are more likely to be successful when they are based on sound research and applications. Our Series in Applied Psychology offers publications that emphasize state-of-the-art research and its application to important issues of human behavior in a variety of social settings. The objective is to bridge both academic and applied interests.

Understanding the relationships between employees and organizations has emerged as one of the most important issues in the study of behavior in organizations. Shore, Coyle-Shapiro, and Tetrick, in *The Employee-Organization Relationship: Applications for the 21st Century*, bring together leading edge scholarship and a keen appreciation for the interplay between science and practice in this vital area. We are very glad to welcome this book to the Applied Psychology Series.

There are four overriding themes to this volume. The first seven chapters deal with expanding our understanding of employee–organization relationships (EORs). Shore, Coyle-Shapiro, and Tetrick lay out the challenges inherent in building coherent theories and models of the EOR and relating those theories and models to the large literature dealing with related concepts. Ashforth and Rogers ask the critical question of whether employees have meaningful relationships with organizations and conclude that it is the "tribe" (i.e., small, cohesive groups who interact regularly and who share common identity, values, and assumptions) and not the organization that is the center of employee–organizational linkages. Schminke extends the notion that there are multiple loci to the EOR and examines in particular links with supervisors that might have implications for ethical behavior. In the chapter that follows, van Knippenberg examines two theories that attempt to explain the ways leaders influence the EOR. He concludes that social identity theories provide more explanatory power than social exchange theories, and he shows how successful leaders can represent prototypes of the organization to their subordinates. McLean Parks and smith take a somewhat different tack, examining how ideological resources can be a critical part of the leader–member exchange. They note that ideological similarities and differences are likely to be an increasingly critical element in multinational organizations. Shore and Coyle-Shapiro explore the dark side of the EOR, focussing specifically on perceptions of organizational cruelty. The distinguishing feature of organizational cruelty is its perceived intentionality; as Shore and Coyle-Shapiro show, perceptions of cruelty on the part of an organization are particularly damaging to the EOR. Finally, Pearce examines a unique EOR, the relationship between organizations and volunteers. Substantial differences in the exchange relationship with organizations exist for voulnteers and regular employees, and Pearce shows how these differences help to establish quite different EORs.

The next five chapters ask readers to take the "relationship" component of the EOR seriously. Guest and Rodrigues challenge the current assumption that careers are becoming more individually focused, but they note the challenges to the continuation of the long-term EOR that served to define the traditional one-organization career. Kossek and Ruderman note that most workers have important relationships, in particular with family, which can compete with the EOR. They show that even organizations that attempt to implement family-friendly policies sometimes fail because they fail to fully appreciate the sometimes competing interests of employers and employees. Gallagher and Connelly explore the nature of the relationship between organizations and their temporary employees. They note that current theories of the EOR are not fully appropriate for contingent workers and argue convincingly that it is important and useful to understand how temporary workers and organizations view their relationships. Bartol and Dong examine EOR in virtual organizations. They note that virtual organizations require human resource policies and networks that can be quite different from those of more traditional organizations, and that these virtual HR policies are an important part of the link between individuals and virtual organizations. Takeuchi notes that there is a great deal to be gained by taking the "social" aspect of social relationships seriously. In particular, he illustrates the importance of understanding the perspectives of both parties in the social relationship that EOR theory attempts to explore.

The four chapters that follow ask how the EOR is built, maintained, and repaired. Shapiro and Fugate draw attention to the role of future-oriented assessments of organizations in building and maintaining the EOR. They introduce the concept of anticipatory justice to help organize relevant theory and research. Ryan considers the perceived relationships between applicants and organizations and argues that at least part of the EOR is defined well before employees ever enter the organization. Hom shows how the EOR influences employees' decision to stay in or to leave jobs and organizations. Wang and Zhan note that the nature and the content of the EOR is likely to change as individuals and careers mature, and that the perspectives of older workers are inadequately considered in current EOR research.

The final six chapters examine the organizational and strategic implications of the EOR. Lepak and Boswell argue that strategic human resources theory has not yet taken the relationship between employees and organizations seriously. They suggest that a more balanced approach that considers both parties in the EOR would help expand the utility of strategic human relationship approaches. Tetrick argues that the EOR has a significant emotional component that has been ignored in most research and that can critically affect the strength, direction, and outcomes of relationships between individuals and organizations. Avery, McKay, and Roberson argue that research on the EOR has largely ignored issues of race and ethnicity and that perceptions of the degree to which an organization is providing support are often viewed through the lenses of race and ethnicity. Salas and Fiore show how the relationship between individuals and organizations both shapes and is shaped by team relationships. They argue that teams are increasingly important in organizations and (like Ashforth and Rogers) that teams are likely to be critical mediators between the individual and the organization. Cascio and Greene show how perceptions that managers are making fair and sound decisions influence the EOR, and they provide sound advice for increasing the likelihood that managers *will* make such decisions and that employees will perceive them to be good decisions. In their summary chapter, Shore, Coyle-Shapiro, and Tetrick identify particularly promising avenues for future research.

The Employee-Organization Relationship: Applications for the 21st Century will be invaluable to students, researchers, and managers. It pushes organizational researchers to do work that is more inclusive and more likely to be relevant to the problems faced by both employees and organizations. It provides a set of frameworks for students and managers to understand the critical issues in EOR research and their relevance for understanding behavior in organizations. Finally, it shows how psychology and psychological research can be used to better understand organizations and the experience of work. *The Employee-Organization Relationship* fills an extremely valuable role in the Applied Psychology Series.

Preface

Research on the employee–organization relationship (EOR) continues at a fast clip, building on a voluminous body of knowledge. Even so, in the spring of 2009, we concluded that the time was ripe for expansion. Luckily, we persuaded some talented and creative scholars to join us on this journey! Authors were invited to raise questions, challenge existing theoretical assumptions, and make novel connections with other literatures. Most importantly, we urged them to share a perspective on the EOR literature that reflected their own expertise and opinions. Each of our contributors did so with great enthusiasm, making for a set of exciting and thought-provoking chapters.

The book is divided into four parts, but it is important to know that these were not created a priori, but instead were constructed post hoc. This is largely because of our missive to authors to "say something new and interesting about the EOR," resulting in great variety as well as interesting connections within and across these parts. While encouraging diversity and innovation, we also provided some structure to create common themes across the chapters in this volume. Each contributor was asked to integrate existing EOR definitions, concepts, and theories as reflected in the chapter by Shore et al. (2004) published in *Research in Personnel and Human Resources Management* that provided a comprehensive review of the literature. In addition, authors were encouraged to offer some ideas about the influence of culture and implications for practice. However, as you will see, each of the chapters reflects the unique voices of our contributors. So get ready for a stimulating read!

This book offers perspectives on the EOR that are useful to scholars, practitioners, and graduate students. For scholars, many of our contributors provide new perspectives and tackle thorny theoretical issues (see, in particular, Part 1, "New Ways of Thinking About the Employee–Organization Relationship"). Likewise, there are a number of chapters focusing on the changing world of work and the implications for the EOR (see Part 2, "Putting the 'R' Back in the EOR"). Part 3, "Creation, Maintenance, and Completion of the Employee–Organization Relationship," emphasizes processes in the EOR and Part 4, "Organizational and Strategic

Implications," provides some new ways of thinking about the impact of the EOR. Scholars and students alike will find food for thought across all the chapters and will discover a stimulating variety of perspectives and opinions that not only inform thinking but encourage future research.

Some of our chapters were written with the practitioner in mind, most notably, Chapters 20 (Salas & Fiore) and 21 (Cascio & Greene). However, as mentioned earlier, all contributors wove in some implications for practice so that readers who are interested in applying the EOR research to solve organizational problems will have some thought-provoking ideas at hand.

We would like to thank the contributors for agreeing to join us on this journey and for working so conscientiously to accomplish the goals of this volume. We would also like to thank Jan Cleveland, our series editor. It was Jan who first suggested the book to us at a surprise dinner celebration honoring Lois Tetrick during her presidential year at the Society for Industrial and Organizational Psychology in San Francisco. Jan's encouragement and support for our concept was instrumental in helping us facilitate an exceptional volume. Anne Duffy, our editor at Psychology Press/Routledge, has been a delight to work with, and we thank her for her patience and wise counsel. We would also like to thank the reviewers, Carol Kulik (University of South Australia), Tammy Allen (University of South Florida), and Jeanette Cleveland (Pennsylvania State University), who helped us refine our ideas and sharpen our book concept.

June, 2011

Lynn M. Shore
San Diego, California, USA

Jacqueline A-M. Coyle-Shapiro
London, England, UK

Lois E. Tetrick
Fairfax, Virginia, USA

REFERENCE

Shore, L. M., Tetrick, L. E., Taylor, M. S., Coyle-Shapiro, J., Liden, R., McLean Parks, J., ... Van Dyne, L. (2004). The employee-organization relationship: A timely concept in a period of transition. In J. Martocchio (Ed.), *Research in personnel and human resources management* (Vol. 23, pp. 291–370). Greenwich, CT: JAI Press.

About the Editors

Lynn M. Shore is Professor of Management at San Diego State University and Co-Director of the Institute for Inclusiveness and Diversity in Organizations. She received her PhD in industrial/organizational psychology from Colorado State University. Previously she was on the faculty at Georgia State University and University of California, Irvine. She has been a Visiting Scholar at London School for Economics and Political Science, University of Toulouse, Dauphine University, and The Chinese University of Hong Kong. Dr. Shore has held leadership roles in the Academy of Management, having served as Human Resources Division Chair (2000–2001), on the HR Executive Committee (1995–1998), as Professional Development Workshop Chair for the Diversity and Inclusion Theme Committee (2010–2011), and on the GDO Executive Committee (2011–2014). Her research areas are the employment relationship and workforce inclusion and diversity. In the area of employment relationships, she has researched such topics as perceived organizational support, psychological contracts, leader–member exchange, and international aspects of employment relationships. Dr. Shore's work on inclusion has studied factors that facilitate high-functioning groups, and her work on diversity has examined the impact that composition of the work group and employee/supervisor dyads has on the attitudes and performance of work groups and individual employees. Her articles have appeared in *Academy of Management Journal, Academy of Management Review, Journal of Applied Psychology, Personnel Psychology,* and *Journal of Management*. Dr. Shore is a former Associate Editor of the *Journal of Applied Psychology* and serves on the editorial boards of the *Journal of Applied Psychology, Journal of Management,* and *Journal of Organizational Behavior*. She is a Fellow of the American Psychological Association and the Society for Industrial and Organizational Psychology.

Jacqueline A-M. Coyle-Shapiro is Professor in Organizational Behaviour at the London School of Economics and Political Science (LSE) where she received her PhD in 1996. Prior to joining the LSE, she was a Lecturer at the School of Management, University of Oxford. She has published in such journals as the *Academy of Management Journal, Journal of Applied*

Psychology, Journal of Organizational Behavior, and *Journal of Vocational Behavior.* She is currently Senior Editor at the *Journal of Organizational Behavior* and serves on the editorial boards of the *Journal of Management, Journal of Applied Behavioral Science,* and *Journal of Managerial Psychology.* Her research focuses on studying relationships in organizational settings, and their antecedents, mechanisms, and consequences. Specifically, her research interests include employee–organization relationships, psychological contracts, perceived organizational support, social exchange theory, organizational justice, organizational citizenship behavior, and communal relationships. She is also a member of the Innovation Co-Creation Lab (http://icclab.com), where she conducts research on how relationships within groups facilitate or hinder the innovation process. She has been elected to the leadership track of the Organizational Behavior Division of the Academy of Management 2011–2015.

Lois E. Tetrick received her doctorate in industrial and organizational psychology from Georgia Institute of Technology in 1983. Upon completion of her doctoral studies, she joined the faculty of the Department of Psychology at Wayne State University and remained there until 1995 when she moved to the Department of Psychology at the University of Houston. She joined the faculty at George Mason University in 2003, where she is the Director of the Industrial and Organizational Psychology Program. Professor Tetrick is currently a consulting editor for the *Journal of Applied Psychology* and is on the editorial boards of the *Journal of Organizational Behavior and Management* and *Organization Review: The Journal of the International Association for Chinese Management Research.* She is a former editor of the *Journal of Occupational Health Psychology* and a former associate editor of the *Journal of Applied Psychology.* Dr. Tetrick is a coeditor with Jacqueline A-M. Coyle-Shapiro, Lynn M. Shore, and Susan Taylor of *The Employment Relationship: Examining Psychological and Contextual Perspectives* (Oxford University Press, 2005). Recently, she and Jim Quick edited the second edition of the *Handbook of Occupational Health Psychology* (American Psychological Association, 2010). Dr. Tetrick is a fellow of the American Psychological Association, the Society for Industrial and Organizational Psychology, the American Psychological Society, and the European Academy of Occupational Health Psychology. She has served as President of the Society for Industrial and Organizational Psychology and as Chair of the Human Resources Division of the Academy of

Management. Dr. Tetrick has two areas of research. One area focuses primarily on the employment exchange relationship, including psychological contracts and the employee–organization relationship. The other area is occupational health psychology including such topics as safety, occupational stress, and the work–family interface. A common underlying interest in both of these lines of research is incorporating a global perspective in understanding employees' experiences of the work environment.

About the Contributors

Blake E. Ashforth is the Horace Steele Arizona Heritage Chair in the W. P. Carey School of Business, Arizona State University. He received his PhD from the University of Toronto and was previously a faculty member at Wayne State University and Concordia University. His research concerns the ongoing dance between individuals and organizations, including identity and identification, socialization and newcomer work adjustment, and the links among individual-, group-, and organization-level phenomena. Recent specific projects have focused on dirty work, ambivalence, organizational dualities, respect, and organizational sacralization and sacrilege. He is a fellow of the Academy of Management and a Senior Editor for *Organization Science*.

Derek R. Avery is an associate professor of human resource management in the Fox School of Business at Temple University. He received his PhD in industrial/organizational psychology from Rice University in 2001. Broadly speaking, his research examines the antecedents and consequences of organizational diversity and seeks to identify strategies for maximizing productivity and minimizing employee withdrawal in heterogeneous workplaces. He has won several research awards including the Saroj Parasuraman Award for best published paper on diversity and the Dorothy Harlow Distinguished Paper Award, both from the Gender and Diversity in Organizations division of the Academy of Management. He is an active member of the Society for Industrial/Organizational Psychology and the Academy of Management.

Kathryn M. Bartol is the Robert H. Smith Professor of Management and Organization and Co-Director of the Center for Leadership, Innovation, and Change at the Robert H. Smith School of Business, University of Maryland, College Park. She received her PhD in organizational behavior and human resource management from Michigan State University. She has previously served as President of the Academy of Management and Dean of the Academy's Fellows Group. She is also a Fellow of the American Psychological Association, the American Psychological Society, the International Academy of Management, and the Society for Industrial/

Organizational Psychology. Her numerous publications have appeared in major journals in management and psychology. Her research centers on leadership, knowledge creation and sharing, networks, and virtual teams and work.

Wendy R. Boswell is the Rebecca U. '74 and William S. Nichols III '74 Associate Professor of Management and outgoing Director of the Center for Human Resource Management in Mays Business School, Texas A&M University. Professor Boswell received her PhD in industrial and labor relations, human resource studies from Cornell University. Her research focuses on employee attraction and retention, job search behavior, workplace conflict, and the work-family interface. Professor Boswell's work has appeared in such journals as *Academy of Management Journal, Academy of Management Review, Journal of Applied Psychology, Personnel Psychology, Human Resource Management,* and *Journal of Management.* She serves on the editorial boards of the *Academy of Management Review, Journal of Applied Psychology,* and *Personnel Psychology,* and has recently completed a term as an Associate Editor for *Journal of Management.*

Wayne F. Cascio holds the Robert H. Reynolds Chair in Global Leadership at the University of Colorado, Denver. He received his PhD in industrial and organizational psychology from the University of Rochester. He has published 24 books and more than 135 articles and book chapters, including *Investing in People* (with John Boudreau, 2nd ed., FT Press, 2011), *Managing Human Resources: Productivity, Quality of Work Life, Profits* (8th ed., McGraw-Hill, 2010), and *Applied Psychology in Human Resource Management* (with Herman Aguinis, 7th ed., Prentice Hall, 2011). A former president of the Society for Industrial and Organizational Psychology, Chair of the Society for Human Resource Management Foundation, and member of the Academy of Management's Board of Governors, he is an elected fellow of the National Academy of Human Resources, the Academy of Management, and the Society for Industrial and Organizational Psychology. He received the Distinguished Career award from the Human Resources Division of the Academy of Management in 1999, an honorary doctorate from the University of Geneva in 2004, and the Society for Human Resource Management's Losey Award for Human Resources Research in 2010.

About the Contributors • xxxi

Catherine E. Connelly is an Associate Professor at the DeGroote School of Business at McMaster University in Hamilton, Ontario, Canada. She received her PhD in management from Queen's University in Kingston, Ontario, Canada. Her research focuses on the attitudes and behaviors of nonstandard workers (e.g., temporary workers, part-time workers, independent contractors, board members, volunteers, mobile workers) and ways in which employees' communication is affected by their perceptions and attitudes. Her research has been published in a number of journals, including the *Journal of Applied Psychology*, the *Journal of Management*, *Journal of Organizational Behavior*, *Journal of Vocational Behavior*, *Journal of Management Information Systems*, *Information & Management*, *IEEE Transactions on Engineering Management*, *Human Resource Management Review*, *Career Development International*, *Group Decision & Negotiation*, *Leadership & Organization Development Journal*, and *Journal of Curriculum Theorizing*. She serves on the Editorial Board of *Human Relations*.

Yuntao Dong is the PhD candidate of Management and Organization at the Robert H. Smith School of Business, University of Maryland, College Park. She received her master's degree in organizational behavior and human resource management from Peking University, China. She has presented papers on multilevel impacts of leadership as well as virtual human resources (HR) and turnover at Academy of Management and Society for Industrial/Organizational Psychology annual meetings. Her research interests include leadership, empowerment, virtual HR practices, and multilevel research.

Stephen M. Fiore is faculty with the University of Central Florida's (UCF) Cognitive Sciences Program in the Department of Philosophy and Director of the Cognitive Sciences Laboratory at UCF's Institute for Simulation and Training. He earned his PhD degree in Cognitive Psychology from the University of Pittsburgh, Learning Research and Development Center. He maintains a multidisciplinary research interest that incorporates aspects of the cognitive, social, and computational sciences in the investigation of learning and performance in individuals and teams. He is coeditor of recent volumes including *Macrocognition in Teams* (Ashgate, 2008), *Toward a Science of Distributed Learning* (American Psychological Association, 2007), and *Team Cognition* (American Psychological Association, 2004), xxxii • *About the Contributors*

and he has coauthored more than 100 scholarly publications in the area of learning, memory, and problem solving at the individual and the group level. As principal investigator and co-principal investigator, he has helped to secure and manage approximately $15 million in research funding from numerous federal sponsoring organizations.

Mel Fugate is an Associate Professor of Management and Organizations in the Cox School of Business at Southern Methodist University. His primary research interests involve employee reactions to organizational change and transitions (e.g., downsizings, mergers and acquisitions, restructurings, and plant closings). He investigates employees' change-related cognitive appraisals, emotions, coping efforts, and withdrawal. Other research interests include leadership, organizational culture, employability, and performance. Dr. Fugate has published in and reviewed for several top journals, such as the *Academy of Management Journal, Academy of Management Review, Journal of Applied Psychology, Journal of Occupational and Organizational Psychology, Journal of Vocational Behavior,* and *Personnel Psychology* (also served on editorial board). Dr. Fugate earned his PhD in organizational behavior at Arizona State University and a BS in engineering and business administration at Michigan State University. His previous professional lives included work as a consultant and multiple positions in health care and the pharmaceutical industry.

Daniel G. Gallagher is the CSX Corporation Professor of Management at James Madison University. He earned his PhD at the University of Illinois. He has been a member of the faculty at the University of Iowa, Michigan State University, the University of Pittsburgh, and Queen's University, Canada. Professor Gallagher's research has focused on a range of topics including impasse resolution procedures, union commitment and participation, nonstandard employment arrangements, and the career challenges of independent contracting. He is also currently pursuing a research agenda in the areas of rule bending and ethical behavior. His work has been published in the leading journals in the areas of management, labor relations, psychology, and organizational behavior. He continues to serve as an editorial board member for a number of journals including *Industrial Relations, Human Relations, Labour & Society,* and the *European Journal of Work and Organizational Psychology.*

Robert J. Greene received his PhD in applied behavioral science from Northwestern University and his MBA from the University of Chicago. He is the CEO of Reward Systems, Inc., a consultancy specializing in human resource (HR) management strategies and programs. He has consulted with private and public sector organizations for more than 30 years, specializing in HR strategy, performance management, and rewards management. Robert Greene was instrumental in developing the PHR and SPHR certification programs for Society for Human Resource Management (SHRM) and the CCP and GRP certification programs for the American Compensation Association (ACA; now World at Work). He was the first recipient of the Keystone Award, bestowed by ACA (World at Work), for achieving the highest level of excellence in the field of rewards management. He has authored almost 100 articles and book chapters and the book *Rewarding Performance: Guiding Principles and Custom Strategies* (Routledge/Taylor & Francis Group, 2010). He is a faculty member for DePaul University's MBA and MSHR degree programs and serves on the advisory board of the Management Department in the School of Commerce. He has taught globally for DePaul, SHRM, and the World at Work.

David E. Guest is Professor of Organizational Psychology and Human Resource Management in the Department of Management, King's College London. He received his PhD in occupational psychology from Birkbeck College, University of London. He has written and researched extensively in the areas of employment relations; human resource management, performance, and employee well-being; the psychological contract; and careers. He sits on a number of editorial advisory boards. He is currently Managing Director and Programme Director, Workforce Programme, for the King's National Institute for Health Research Patient Safety and Service Quality Research Centre. He recently coedited *Employment Contracts, Psychological Contracts, and Employee Well-Being* (with Kerstin Isaksson and Hans De Witte, Oxford University Press, 2010).

Peter W. Hom is a Professor of Management at the WP Carey School of Business, Arizona State University (Tempe, AZ). He received his PhD from the University of Illinois. Dr. Hom has developed and tested theories of employee turnover and designed realistic job previews to reduce reality shock. He has authored scholarly articles and books on this topic. He and Drs. Griffeth, Prussia, and Caranikas-Walker won the 1992 Scholarly Achievement Award from the Human Resource Management Division of the Academy of Management for best academic article in human resources. Dr. Hom serves on Editorial Boards for the *Journal of Applied Psychology*, *Academy of Management Journal*, and *Journal of Management*.

Ellen Ernst Kossek is University Distinguished Professor at Michigan State University's School of Human Resources & Labor Relations. She received her PhD from Yale University. A popular keynote speaker both in the United States and internationally, Dr. Kossek has trained, conducted research, and consulted on workplace issues related to the changing workplace and organizational effectiveness with managers and university students at all levels. She was elected to the Board of Governors of the National Academy of Management, Gender and Diversity in Organizations Division Chair, and a Fellow of the American Psychological Association and the Society of Industrial and Organizational Psychology. Her research involves managing organizational change on workplace flexibility, work and family/nonwork relationships, work processes, and the employment relationship; international human resources management; workplace inclusion; and gender and diversity. She has published widely in referred journals on these topics and served on many editorial boards. She has won awards for her research for advancing understanding of gender and diversity in organizations. She has received major funding from foundations, governments, and employers. Dr. Kossek is Associate Director of the Center for Work, Family Health and Stress of the U.S. National Institutes of Health National Work, Family, and Health Network. She has authored or edited nine books including *CEO of Me: Creating a Life That Works in the Flexible Job Age* (Prentice Hall, 2007) on work–life patterns. Recently she has published the work style profile assessment with the Center for Creative Leadership. She has worked and conducted research and training in the United States, Asia, and Europe on employment issues.

David Lepak is Professor of Human Resource Management and Associate Dean for the School of Management and Labor Relations at Rutgers University. His research focuses on strategic human resource (HR) management with particular interests in understanding the mediating mechanisms by which HR systems impact individual and organizational outcomes. His research has appeared in such journals as *Academy* of Management Review, Academy of Management Journal, Journal of Applied Psychology, Personnel Psychology, and Journal of Management. He has served as Associate Editor of the Academy of Management Review and British Journal of Management and serves on a number of editorial boards. He is currently program chair for the Strategic Human Capital interest group of the Strategic Management Society.

Patrick F. McKay is an Associate Professor of Human Resource Management in the School of Management and Labor Relations at Rutgers University. Professor McKay received his PhD in industrial-organizational psychology in 1999 from the University of Akron. His primary research interests are diversity, recruitment, selection, work attitudes, retention, and individual-level and organizational-level performance. He has published articles in respected research outlets such as the *Journal of Applied Psychology, Personnel Psychology,* and *Organization Science.* Professor McKay has won several research awards including the Academy of Management's 2009 Saroj Parasuraman Award, which recognizes the best published article on gender and diversity within organizations, and the 2007 Dorothy Harlow Distinguished Paper Award for the top diversity paper presented at the Academy of Management conference. He serves on the editorial boards of the *Academy of Management Review, Journal of Applied Psychology, Journal of Management, Organizational Behavior and Human Decision Processes,* and *Personnel Psychology.*

Judi McLean Parks holds the Taylor Chaired Professorship of Organizational Behavior at Olin Business School at Washington University. She received her PhD in organizational behavior from the University of Iowa. Her research focuses on psychological contracts between workers and organizations, including the impact of perceived injustice on work behaviors, workplace conflict, revenge, and more recently, positive effects of rule breaking at work. Her work also explores resource allocations and ethics in negotiations, as well as the impact of organizational identity and "incongruent" identities (e.g., a company known for environmental abuses hiring "green" workers) on work attitudes and behaviors. Dr. McLean Parks was founding editor of *Negotiation & Conflict Management Research,* the official scholarly publication of the International Association for Conflict Management. In addition, she previously was editor of the *International Journal of Conflict Management* and *SSRN Negotiations Papers,* Two Party

Negotiations series. She also has served on editorial boards of the *Academy of Management Review* and *Journal of Organizational Behavior.*

Jone L. Pearce is Dean's Professor of Leadership in The Paul Merage School of Business, University of California, Irvine. She received her PhD in administrative sciences from Yale University in 1978. She conducts organizational behavior research on interpersonal processes, such as trust and status, and how these processes may be affected by political structures, economic conditions, and organizational policies and practices. Her work has appeared in more than 90 scholarly articles in such publications as the *Academy of Management Journal, Academy of Management Review, Journal of Applied Psychology,* and *Organization Science.* She has edited several volumes and written five books, including *Volunteers: The Organizational Behavior of Unpaid Workers* (Routledge, 1993), *Organization and Management in the Embrace of Government* (Erlbaum, 2001), *Organizational Behavior: Real Research for Real Managers* (Melvin & Leigh, 2006, revised and expanded in 2009), and *Status in Management and Organizations* (Cambridge University Press, 2010). She currently serves on several editorial boards and is a Fellow of the Academy of Management, the International Association of Applied Psychology, the American Psychological Association (Div 14, SIOP), and the Association for Psychological Science.

Quinetta M. Roberson is a Professor of Management in the Villanova School of Business at Villanova University. Prior to her current position, she was an Associate Professor of Human Resource Studies at Cornell University. Professor Roberson earned her PhD in organizational behavior from the University of Maryland. Her research interests center on contextual investigations of organizational justice issues (specifically, fairness in teams) and strategic diversity management. Her research has appeared in such journals as the *Academy of Management Review, Journal of Applied Psychology, Organizational Behavior and Human Decision Processes, Organizational Research Methods,* and *Personnel Psychology.* Dr. Roberson is an Associate Editor at the *Journal of Applied Psychology* (2008–2014) and is currently working on a book, *Handbook of Diversity in the Workplace* (Oxford University Press, in press). Professor Roberson teaches courses globally on human resource management and diversity at the undergraduate, graduate, and executive levels.

Ricardo Rodrigues is a Senior Lecturer in Human Resource Management at Kingston Business School. He has recently completed a PhD in Management Studies at King's College London. His research interests center on career orientations and career boundaries as a basis for understanding contemporary career dynamics. His research attempts to go beyond the dominant rhetoric on contemporary careers, namely the idea of the boundaryless career, and offers an evidence-based and theoretically grounded perspective of the nature of career boundaries and of the domains that structure the direction of people's careers.

Kristie M. Rogers is a fifth-year doctoral student at the W. P. Carey School of Business, Arizona State University. Her research focuses on social interactions and relationships in organizational life. Her dissertation explores the role of respect in organizations. Specifically, she seeks to understand how employees come to feel respected, how respect is behaviorally enacted, and how respect influences employee outcomes such as engagement, identification, and performance. To gain these insights, she combines several research designs including a grounded theory approach in a prison-based labor setting and a quantitative study in a hospital.

Marian N. Ruderman has broad expertise with 25 years in the field of leadership development. At the Center for Creative Leadership, she has held a variety of research and management positions. Marian has written several books and developed several assessments and products including the *Global Leader View* and the *WorkStyle Profile*. Marian is currently a Senior Fellow and Director, Americas & EMEA (Europe, Middle East, and Africa) Research at the Center for Creative Leadership (CCL). She holds a BA from Cornell University and an MA and a PhD in organizational psychology from the University of Michigan.

Ann Marie Ryan is a professor of organizational psychology at Michigan State University. Her major research interests involve improving the quality and fairness of employee selection methods and topics related to diversity and justice in the workplace. In addition to publishing extensively in these areas, she regularly consults with organizations on improving assessment processes. She is a past president of the Society of Industrial and Organizational Psychology and past editor of the journal *Personnel Psychology*. Ann Marie has a long record of professional service on association committees and National Academy of Science panels, and she currently serves on the Defense Advisory Committee on Military Testing. She received her BS with a double major in psychology and management from Xavier University, Ohio, and her MA and PhD in psychology from the University of Illinois at Chicago.

Eduardo Salas is University Trustee Chair and Pegasus Professor of Psychology at the University of Central Florida. He received his PhD in industrial/organizational psychology from Old Dominion University. He has coauthored more than 350 journal articles and book chapters; has edited 20 books; has served or is serving on 18 editorial boards; is past Editor of the *Human Factors* journal and current Associate Editor of *Journal of Applied Psychology* and *Military Psychology*. He is past President of the Society for Industrial and Organizational Psychology (SIOP). He was editor of SIOP's Professional Practice Book Series and is now editor of the Organizational Frontier Book Series. He is a Fellow of Divisions 14 (three-time recipient of Division's applied research award), 19 (recipient of Division's Gersoni award for scientific contributions to the field), 21 (recipient of Division's Taylor award for scientific contributions to the field), and 49 of the American Psychological Association.

Marshall Schminke is the BB&T Professor of Business Ethics at the University of Central Florida. He received his doctorate from Carnegie Mellon University and has served as a Visiting Scholar at Oxford University. He is an Academic Fellow at the Ethics Resource Center in Washington, DC, and his work has appeared in the *Academy of Management Journal*, *Journal of Applied Psychology*, *Organizational Behavior and Human Decision Processes*, *Journal of Management*, *Business Ethics Quarterly*, and other scholarly outlets. He has edited two books on managerial ethics, and he has served as associate editor for *Academy of Management Journal*, *Journal of Management*, and *Business Ethics Quarterly*. Beyond these academic pursuits, he has served as an advisor to organizations ranging from family businesses to Fortune 500 firms, the U.S. Strategic Command, the U.S. Army, and a number of universities and professional organizations. He has served as an expert witness in U.S. District Court Proceedings. His strategic planning process for policing has received national awards and has been featured at the FBI Training Academy. His thoughts on business ethics, strategy, and management have appeared in more than

50 newspapers and magazines, including *The New York Times, Newsday*, and the *Chicago Tribune*.

Debra L. Shapiro is the Clarice Smith Professor of Management and PhD Program Director at the University of Maryland's Robert H. Smith School of Business, and formerly the Willard J. Graham Distinguished Professor of Management and Associate Dean of PhD Programs at University of North Carolina-Chapel Hill's Kenan-Flagler Business School (1986–2003). She received her PhD in organization behavior from Northwestern University. A past Chair of the Conflict Management Division, executive board member, and elected Fellow of the Academy of Management (AOM) and past Associate Editor of *The Academy of Management Journal* (2005–2008), her research centers on how to manage conflict (e.g., change resistance, perceived injustice, conflict in teams, and cross-cultural challenges) in organizations. She is a four-time recipient of Best Paper Awards from the AOM (1991, 1992, 1996, and 2007) and from the International Association for Conflict Management (in 1999). She has published in *Administrative Science Quarterly, The Academy of Management Journal, The Academy of Management Review, Organizational Behavior and Human Decision Processes, Journal of Applied Psychology, Journal of Personality and Social Psychology, Journal of Experimental Social Psychology, Organizational Dynamics*, and other journals. She is coeditor of *Managing Multinational Teams: Global Perspectives* (Elsevier, 2005) and the forthcoming SIOP Frontier Series book, *The Psychology of Negotiation in the 21st Century Workplace* (Psychology Press/Taylor & Francis Group, forthcoming). Citations of Shapiro's work in Web of Science are approximately 2,000 and more than double this number in Google-Scholar.

faye l. smith earned her PhD from the University of Iowa in the discipline of strategic management. Her research in strategic management assesses competitive dynamics and cooperative strategies. She is also interested in organizational identity and work–life balance issues, as well as systems effects within organizations. Her research has been published in journals such as the *Strategic Management Journal, Academy of Management Review, Administrative Science Quarterly, Academy of Management Executive, Canadian Journal of Administrative Science, Journal of Leadership and Organizational Studies, Human Resource Development Review, Management Communication Quarterly*, and *Sex Roles*, and she had contributed chapters in multiple academic editions. She has business work experience in the social expression and banking industries. She is a professor at the Steven L. Craig School of Business at Missouri Western State University and has also held academic positions at Oklahoma State University, University of Wisconsin–Milwaukee, and Emporia State University.

Riki Takeuchi is an Associate Professor in the Department of Management at the School of Business and Management, Hong Kong University of Science & Technology. He received his PhD from the Robert H. Smith School of Business, University of Maryland at College Park in December 2003. His research theme revolves around understanding social exchange relationships among various organizational constituents. As part of this theme, he is interested in understanding international assignment experiences for expatriates and spouses through multiple theoretical lenses. His second research area relates to macro/strategic human resource management with particular focus on employer–employee relationships and examines the role of human resource systems at multiple levels, including firm, business unit, and individual levels. Finally, the third research stream broadly focuses on social exchange relationships with an emphasis on organizational justice and organizational citizenship behaviors.

Daan van Knippenberg is Professor of Organizational Behavior at the Rotterdam School of Management, Erasmus University Rotterdam, the Netherlands. He received his PhD in psychology from Leiden University, the Netherlands. His research interests include leadership, teams, social identity, and creativity and innovation. His work has been published in such outlets as *Academy of Management Journal, Journal of Applied Psychology,* and *Organizational Behavior and Human Decision Processes.* He is founding editor of *Organizational Psychology Review,* associate editor of *Journal of Organizational Behavior,* and former associate editor of *Organizational Behavior and Human Decision Processes.* He is also director and cofounder of the Erasmus Center for Leadership Studies and cofounder and co-organizer of the New Directions in Leadership Research conference.

Mo Wang, a tenured Associate Professor in the Warrington College of Business Administration at the University of Florida, specializes in research and applications in the areas of older worker employment and retirement, occupational health psychology, cross-cultural human resource management, and advanced quantitative methodologies. He received his PhD in industrial/organizational psychology and developmental psychology from Bowling Green State University in 2005. He has received numerous awards for his research in these areas. He currently serves as an associate editor of the *Journal of Applied Psychology*. He is also the editor for the *Oxford Handbook of Retirement* (Oxford University Press, forthcoming) and *Mid and Late Career Issues* (Routledge, forthcoming) with Wang-Olson-Shultz.

Yujie Zhan is an assistant professor of organizational behavior/human resource management in the School of Business & Economics at Wilfrid Laurier University, Canada. She received her PhD in industrial/organizational psychology from the University of Maryland. Her research interests include older worker employment and retirement, emotion regulation at work, and organizational climate. Her research has appeared in top-tier academic journals, such as *Journal of Applied Psychology*, *Personnel Psychology*, and *Academy of Management Journal*.

1

Expanding the Boundaries and Challenging the Assumptions of the Employee–Organization Relationship Literature

Lynn M. Shore
San Diego State University

Jacqueline A-M. Coyle-Shapiro
London School of Economics and Political Science

Lois E. Tetrick
George Mason University

Remarkable progress has been made since the 1980s in the study of the employee–organization relationship (EOR), and the interest in understanding this fundamental aspect of organizational life shows no sign of slowing down. The EOR is "an overarching term to describe the relationship between the employee and the organization" (Shore et al., 2004, p. 292) and encompasses psychological contracts, perceived organizational support, and the employment relationship. Social exchange (Blau, 1964) and the inducements–contributions model (March & Simon, 1958) have provided the dominant theoretical foundation to understanding the employee–employer exchange relationship.

Given the large body of research that has evolved as evidenced by meta-analyses on psychological contracts (Zhao, Wayne, Glibkowski, & Bravo, 2007) and perceived organizational support (Rhoades & Eisenberger, 2002), as well as multiple books on the topic of the EOR (Conway & Briner, 2005; Eisenberger & Stinglhamber, 2011; Rousseau, 1995), our readers might be forgiven for asking, do we need another book? To this, we say, read on and you will find a series of innovative and thought-provoking chapters that will set the foundation for the next phase of the EOR literature.

This book is organized into four parts in addition to this opening chapter and the closing chapter, both written by the editors. First, we review the current state of the EOR literature prior to outlining how the chapters in this book advance our understanding and push the boundaries forward in the EOR domain.

CURRENT STATUS OF EOR THEORY

Our starting point is to review existing frameworks that capture the EOR prior to examining their underlying mechanisms and associated outcomes. Given the theoretical importance of social exchange theory and the inducements–contributions model to these frameworks, we begin with a brief historical review.

Social Exchange Theory and Inducements–Contributions Model

The inducements–contributions model (March & Simon, 1958) has its origins in Barnard's (1938) idea of "exchange of utilities" (p. 240) and focused on the resources exchanged in the EOR. This was expanded upon in later work by Blau (1964), who took a broader focus on the type of exchange relationship that develops between employees and their organization. March and Simon (1958), in their inducements–contributions model, viewed the employment relationship as an exchange of organizational inducements for employee contributions. An important element in their model is the notion of balance. From the employee's perspective, satisfaction is enhanced when there is a greater difference between the inducements provided by the organization and the contributions required in return. From the organization's perspective, its continued existence depends on whether the contributions from employees are sufficient to generate the necessary inducements. Subsequent work by Blau added greater specification to the nature of the resources exchanged.

Social exchange theory owes much to the work of Blau (1964) who distinguished between two types of relationships: economic and social exchange. Blau defines economic exchange as one where the nature of the exchange is specified and the method used to assure that each party fulfills its specific obligations is the formal contract upon which the exchange is based. In contrast, social exchange involves unspecified obligations— "favors that create diffuse future obligations, not precisely specified ones, and the nature of the return cannot be bargained about but must be left to the discretion of the one who makes it" (p. 93). Therefore, social and economic exchanges differ in the extent to which each party's obligations are specified as part of the exchange.

Because social exchange relationships involve unspecified obligations, trust plays an important role in the process of the exchange: One party needs to trust the other to discharge future obligations (i.e., to reciprocate) in the initial stages of the exchange, and it is the regular discharge of obligations that promotes trust in the relationship. However, Blau (1964) argues that the timing of reciprocation is important: "posthaste reciprocation of favors, which implies a refusal to stay indebted for a while and hence an insistence on a more businesslike relationship is condemned as improper" (p. 99). The underlying rationale is that remaining obligated for a period of time to another party and the trust that the obligations will be discharged serve to strengthen the social exchange. Furthermore, the social exchange process takes time to develop, beginning with minor transactions in which little trust is required. If the recipient returns the small benefits received, this acts as a demonstration of their trustworthiness, facilitating the ongoing conferring of benefits and discharging of obligations. Consequently, the norm of reciprocity and the importance of trusting the exchange partner to reciprocate distinguish social exchange from economic exchange. Thus, social exchange is characterized by investment in the relationship that carries an inherent risk that the investment will not be repaid.

Another difference between economic and social exchange is the time orientation of the relationship. Economic exchanges are time limited, whereas in social exchange relationships, there is a long-term orientation where the exchange is ongoing and indefinite. The long-term horizon is necessary for the development of trust and for a pattern of predictability to develop between giving and receiving of benefits between the exchange partners. Therefore, the key elements that distinguish social exchange from economic exchange are the unspecified obligations, norm of reciprocity, trust, and the long-term horizon of the relationship.

Although social exchange theory has provided the conceptual basis for research in the EOR, it is only recently that measures of social and economic exchange have been developed (Shore, Tetrick, Lynch, & Barksdale, 2006). The authors found empirical support for the distinctiveness of social and economic exchange, and their findings suggest that both types of exchange relationships can operate concurrently. Consistent with the tenets of social exchange theory, the empirical findings support the positive effect of social exchange relationships on outcomes such as performance and altruism as well as affective commitment, suggesting that compared to economic exchange, social exchange relationships yield more desirable benefits for organizations.

Employment Relationships

Drawing on the inducement–contribution model and social exchange theory (March & Simon, 1958), Tsui, Pearce, Porter, and Tripoli (1997) outline four types of employment relationships that differ on two dimensions: the degree of balance/imbalance in each party's contributions and whether the focus of these contributions is economic or social. Briefly, a balanced economic exchange (quasi-spot contract) occurs when the employer offers short-term purely economic inducements in return for highly specified outcomes. A balanced social exchange (mutual investment) takes place when both parties offer an open-ended and long-term investment to each other. The underinvestment approach occurs when the employer expects open-ended commitment and long-term investment from employees in return for short-term economic inducements. The overinvestment approach is characterized by the employer offering long-term investment in return for highly specified employee outcomes. Rather than focusing on particular individuals, the unit of analysis is the job level. Subsequent work examined the nature of the EOR between the organization and groups of employees (Song, Tsui, & Law, 2009). A distinguishing feature of this framework is that it captures the EOR from the organization's perspective vis-à-vis the more employee-centered perceived organizational support and psychological contract frameworks.

Psychological Contracts

The historical development of the psychological contract includes the seminal works of Argyris (1960), Levinson, Price, Munden, Mandl, and Solley (1962), and Schein (1965). Argyris viewed the psychological contract as an implicit understanding between a group of employees and their foreman and argued that the relationship could develop in such a way that employees would exchange higher productivity and lower grievances in return for acceptable wages and job security (Taylor & Tekleab, 2004). Subsequently, Levinson et al. (1962) influenced by the work of Menninger (1958) introduced a more elaborate conceptualization of the psychological contract. Menninger suggested that in addition to tangible resources, contractual relationships also involve the exchange of intangibles. Furthermore, the exchange between the two parties needs to provide mutual satisfaction in order for the relationship to continue (Roehling, 1997). Levinson et al. defined the psychological contract as comprising mutual expectations between an employee and the employer. These expectations may arise from unconscious motives, and thus each party may not be aware of their own expectations let alone the expectations of the other party. Although Schein's (1965) definition shares some similarities with Levinson et al., he placed considerable emphasis on the matching of expectations between the employee and organization. The matching of expectations and their fulfillment are crucial to attaining positive outcomes such as job satisfaction, commitment, and performance. Rousseau's (1989) seminal article is credited with reinvigorating research on psychological contracts. Rousseau defined the psychological contract as "an individual's belief regarding the terms and conditions of a reciprocal exchange agreement between that focal person and another party. Key issues here include the belief that a promise has been made and a consideration offered in exchange for it, binding the parties to some set of reciprocal obligations" (Rousseau, 1989, p. 123). This reconceptualization of the psychological contract emphasized obligations rather than expectations and gave less emphasis to matching between the employee and organization in favor of perceived agreement from the employee's perspective. Therefore, the psychological contract shifted from capturing the two parties to the exchange and their contingent interplay to an individual's perception of both parties' obligations in the exchange.

Perceived Organizational Support

Perceived organizational support (POS) was developed by Eisenberger, Huntington, Hutchison, and Sowa (1986) to capture an individual's perception concerning the degree to which an organization values his/her contributions and cares about his/her well-being. Employees make attributions about the organization's benevolence and form a global belief concerning the favorability of the organization's judgment of him/her and the expectancy that he/she would be treated beneficially in a variety of circumstances (Eisenberger & Stinglhamber, 2011). In forming this global belief, employees personify the organization, reflecting that organizational agents do not simply act as individuals with their own motives in their actions but are rather strongly influenced by the values of upper level managers. Therefore, employees "view the organization as having a personality, using their everyday understanding of personality to try and understand why the organization acts as it does, ascribing persisting traits and motives to the organization" (Eisenberger & Stinglhamber, 2011, p. 41). As such, employees think of their exchange relationship as one with a more powerful entity with human-like qualities.

Favorable treatment from the organization has been demonstrated to lead to perceptions of organizational support and more so if this treatment is interpreted as under the discretion of the organization. Organizational fairness is thought to have a cumulative effect on POS, reflecting a concern for the welfare of employees and, in particular, procedural justice. This is consistent with Tyler and Lind's (1992) relational model, which posits that individuals want to feel good about themselves and inclusion within a group contributes to affirming individuals with a sense of self-worth and identity. As Tyler and Lind note, "people are sensitive to procedural nuances because procedures are viewed as manifestations of basic process values in the group, organization, or institution using the procedure" (p. 140). Therefore, procedural justice is likely to signal to employees their relative standing in the eyes of the organization. In addition, Shore and Shore (1995) identify human resource practices that recognize employee contributions as enhancing employee perceptions of organizational support. These practices include training and developmental experiences (Wayne, Shore, & Liden, 1997), job security (Rhoades & Eisenberger, 2002), and job autonomy (Eisenberger, Rhoades, & Cameron, 1999). According to organizational support theory, when employees perceive that the organization is supportive, they will reciprocate by helping the organization achieve its goals (Eisenberger, Armeli, Rexwinkel, Lynch, & Rhoades, 2001).

Underlying Explanatory Mechanisms

The dominant explanations underlying the employee–organization exchange relationship are the norm of reciprocity and the extent to which balance exists in the relationship.

Reciprocity

The norm of reciprocity is central to explaining why psychological contract breach/fulfillment and POS are related to outcomes. Gouldner (1960), in his seminal work, suggested that "(1) people should help those who have helped them, and (2) people should not injure those who have helped them" (p. 171). Gouldner distinguished between two types of reciprocity: heteromorphic and homeomorphic reciprocity. Heteromorphic reciprocity occurs when the content of the exchange between two parties is different but equal in perceived value. Homeomorphic reciprocity occurs in exchanges where the content or the circumstances under which things are exchanged are identical. Regarding how the norm of reciprocity operates, Gouldner argues that the strength of an obligation to repay is contingent upon the value of the benefit received. Benefits are more valued when (a) the recipient is in greater need, (b) the donor cannot afford to give the benefit (but does), (c) the donor provides the benefit in the absence of a motive of self interest, and (d) the donor was not required to give the benefit. Therefore, highly valued benefits create a stronger obligation to reciprocate.

Although Gouldner (1960) distinguished between two different forms of reciprocity, this was later extended by Sahlins (1965, 1972) who conceptualized reciprocity based on three dimensions: (a) immediacy of returns—the timing by which the recipient needs to reciprocate in order to discharge the obligation, and this could range from simultaneous reciprocation to indefinite; (b) equivalence of returns—the extent to which exchange partners return the same resource; and (c) interest—the degree to which exchange partners are other-interested, mutually interested, or self-interested in the exchange process. From these three dimensions, Sahlins (1972) outlines three forms of reciprocity: generalized, balanced, and negative. Generalized reciprocity is altruistic in orientation where there is a lack of concern over the timing and the content of the exchange. According to Sahlins, repayment may be conditional upon what the recipient can afford and when the recipient can reciprocate, but this does not preclude the situation where reciprocation never occurs. Hence, this form of reciprocity is viewed as "sustained one-way flow" (Sahlins, 1972, p. 194). Balanced reciprocity is characterized by quid pro quo, and a perfectly balanced exchange is one where there is a simultaneous exchange of an equivalent resource. However, Sahlins states that "balanced reciprocity may be more loosely applied to transactions which stipulate returns of commensurate worth or utility within a finite period of time" (pp. 194–195). Finally, negative reciprocity is characterized by a taking orientation in which exchange partners have opposite interests and attempt to maximize their own utility at the expense of the other.

Both POS and psychological contract theory rely on the norm of reciprocity to explain why POS and psychological contract breach/fulfillment affect employee attitudes and behavior. However, as noted by Coyle-Shapiro and Conway (2005), the basis of the reciprocation differs such that in organizational support theory, employees based their reciprocation on the perceived *level* of organizational support. In contrast, psychological contract theory predicts that it is not treatment per se but the *discrepancy* between what is promised and what is fulfilled that provides the basis upon which employees reciprocate. Although reciprocity is rarely tested explicitly, the empirical evidence supports the contention that employees reciprocate POS and psychological contract fulfillment through enhanced attitudes and positive behaviors.

Level of Investment and Balance/Imbalance

A complementary explanatory mechanism underpinning the EOR is that employees strive to maintain balance and match the investment of their exchange partner. Thus, individuals in the process of reciprocating favorable treatment will attempt to match the level of the investment of the donor to obtain balance in the exchange. Empirical evidence seems to support the idea of "matching" in exchange relationships. The most positive outcomes occur when employees and employers have high mutual obligations (Shore & Barksdale, 1998) or high mutual investments (Tsui et al., 1997). Not surprisingly, underinvestment by the employer, in which the inducements were short term and monetary with no commitment to the long term while the employee was expected to fulfill broad and open-ended obligations (imbalance favoring the organization), yields the worst results. Taken together, these results broadly support the norm of reciprocity and individuals' desire for balance in exchange relationships. That said, there is evidence that individuals differ in terms of their equity sensitivity and hence their desire to maintain balance in exchange relationships (Coyle-Shapiro & Neuman, 2004).

Outcomes Associated With the EOR

The empirical evidence is supportive of the contention that relationships that are supportive, where obligations have been fulfilled and employees are the recipients of organizational investment, lead to more favorable outcomes (i.e., positive employee attitudes and behavior).

Attitudes

Empirical evidence supports the negative relationship between psychological contract breach and employee attitudes such as trust in the organization (Robinson, 1996), organizational commitment (Turnley & Feldman, 1999), job satisfaction (Tekleab & Taylor, 2003), and cynicism toward the organization (Johnson & O'Leary-Kelly, 2003). POS has been positively linked to affective commitment, trust, and work engagement (Eisenberger & Stinglhamber, 2011), and the overinvestment and mutual investment approaches resulted in higher employee affective commitment and greater trust in coworkers (Tsui et al., 1997).

Behaviors and Performance

A similar picture emerges in looking at the effects of the EOR on employee behaviors and performance. A meta-analysis (Zhao et al., 2007) found that psychological contract breach was negatively related to organizational citizenship behavior (OCB) and employee performance. Psychological contract fulfillment was positively associated with OCB (Coyle-Shapiro, Kessler, & Purcell, 2004; Robinson & Morrison, 1995). POS has been positively linked to job performance (Armeli, Eisenberger, Fasolo, & Lynch, 1998) and citizenship behavior (Chen, Eisenberger, Johnson,

Sucharski, & Aselage, 2009). More recently, POS has been linked to a broader set of employee behaviors to include safety-related behaviors, creativity and innovation, and acceptance of new technology (Eisenberger & Stinglhamber, 2011). Tsui et al. (1997) found that overinvestment and mutual investment approaches were more strongly and positively related to job performance and OCB.

Summary

Looking back at the research conducted on the EOR, one is struck by the consistency and clarity of the findings. Relationships matter in the context of the EOR, and more positive relationships yield more positive outcomes whether these relationships are characterized by the amount of support, the level of investment, the degree of balance, or the fulfillment of obligations. Irrespective of the framework adopted, the findings are remarkably consistent in terms of eliciting more positive outcomes and minimizing negative behaviors. With such a clear and consistent message, one could be forgiven for thinking that there is little left to be covered in the EOR.

HOW THE BOOK IS ORGANIZED: GAPS IN THE LITERATURE

Although a great deal of research has been conducted on the EOR, there has been a somewhat narrow focus in the literature, both theoretically and empirically. The goal of this volume is to enlarge the EOR literature in multiple ways in order to create a much richer area with a broader array of concepts, variables, and connections with other literatures. When the editors invited each of the authors, it was with the missive to "do something creative" that expanded upon the EOR literature, raised questions about underlying assumptions or theories, linked the EOR with other literatures, or had implications for research and/or practice. Thus, this book was an intentional departure from many edited books by encouraging a wide diversity of chapters with a view of broadening the field of inquiry associated with the EOR. Following is a description of each part of the book in which authors tackled a gap or opened new terrain in the EOR literature.

New Ways of Thinking About the EOR

The first part in the book presents several theoretical innovations to the literature. In this part, the authors argue that several themes in the EOR literature need careful reexamination in order to move to the next phase of research. A theme that is apparent in the summary of the EOR literature in this introductory chapter is that social exchange theory and the norm of reciprocity have predominated theoretically. However, as yet there has been fairly narrow theorizing about the source of employee perceptions of the organization as a personified entity (for exceptions, see Eisenberger et al., 1986). Three chapters in this part posit that there is a need to focus on the individuals and groups that personify the organization and in turn form the basis of EOR perceptions. First, Ashforth and Rogers pose that these perceptions are developed through social construction and identification processes that are located in *the tribe*—the local work group including peers and supervisor. Second, Schminke uses the ethics literature as a lens to point to the importance of the supervisor as a representative of the organization and thus questions whether the relationship with the supervisor should be treated as a component of the EOR rather than as a distinct relationship. Furthermore, van Knippenberg argues eloquently for the important role of the leader in enhancing the EOR through inspiring strong organizational identification.

Likewise, three chapters advocate for the value of incorporating social identity theory and associated identification processes in the EOR. Ashforth and Rogers argue that identification and attachment to the tribe lead to identification and attachment to the organization, raising questions as to whether relationships the employee has with the tribe and organization should be treated separately in the EOR literature. Similarly, van Knippenberg discusses the importance of delineating the limitations of exchange theory for understanding the EOR. He makes the case that although the EOR literature has been dominated by social exchange theory, in light of the evidence of the importance of social identification processes, it is critical for research on the EOR to further compare the roles of social identity–based leadership and social exchange–based leadership. Also highlighting the significance of identification processes, McLean Parks and smith point out that the focus on exchange in the EOR has been primarily on tangible and socioemotional resources, with limited theorizing about organizational inducements consisting of ideological exchange elements in which identity, both personal and organizational, is important. Such inducements can be identity affirming or disconfirming and hence play a vital function in determining the fulfillment and violation of the work relationship. Importantly, McLean Parks and smith also highlight the value of nontangible resources as reflected in ideological exchange for understanding the EOR.

Another area of development in this book is shown in Shore and Coyle-Shapiro's chapter on perceived organizational cruelty, focusing on extreme negative relationships between employees and organizations. The empirical literature on the EOR has focused chiefly on ways to build positive relationships between employees and organizations and secondarily on determinants of broken or problematic relationships through studying breach and violation of psychological contracts or unbalanced relationships such as overinvestment and underinvestment employment relationships (Shore et al., 2004). Shore and Coyle-Shapiro argue for the need to understand employees' perceptions of the EOR when they believe they have been severely mistreated and point out that social exchange theory may have some limitations for understanding negative EORs.

In the final chapter of the first part, Pearce revisits the implicit assumptions of EOR research by examining studies of the volunteer–organization relationship. Such assumptions include the view that EORs are clear to the parties involved, the relationships are principally motivated by how the organization treats employees, employees are dependent on their organizations, the organizations are not understaffed, and the participants perceive their organizational involvement in inducement–contribution terms. Pearce concludes with points about the overreliance on the inducements–contributions and social exchange frameworks, highlighting, along with the other chapters in this part, the importance of further developing nonutilitarian conceptualizations of the EOR.

Putting the "R" Back in the EOR

In the second part of the book, chapters are focused on the nature of the EOR. These chapters highlight the *relationship* aspect of the EOR and how the relationships may have changed due to the changing nature of work and organizations or how the relationships should be viewed differently in the EOR literature.

Several chapters focus on whether the literature has adequately dealt with the changes in the world of work that may influence the EOR and, in particular, whether social exchange theory needs to be revisited as the core theoretical foundation of this literature. Guest and Rodrigues examine evidence pertaining to the debate in the literature that careers are changing from traditional (high degree of trust, fairness, social support, long-term duration, and fulfillment of the psychological contract) to boundaryless (protean, self-oriented, and self-managed). They discuss social exchange theory and potential elaborations in light of current career trends. Similarly, Kossek and Ruderman point out that early work and family policies were adopted by organizations based on the assumption of a long-term social exchange in which such opportunities would yield organizational benefits over time such as employee loyalty and hard work. However, they raise questions as to whether organizational leaders continue to view work–family flexibility in this way given the assumed reduced duration of work relationships, boundarylessness of careers, and desire of organizational leaders to maintain control of work conditions. Furthermore, Gallagher and Connelly propose that there is a need to explore the extent to which existing theoretical frameworks in the EOR, which have been built in permanent employment contexts, are fully applicable to the understanding of contingent work. They also examine elements of the contingent relationship that have implications for permanent employment such as volition (choice) and multiple employment relationships. In sum, all three chapters provide much needed discussion about the extent to which social exchange theory applies in present-day employment relationships and some suggestions for development and elaboration.

Bartol and Dong's chapter on virtual relationships incorporates the concept of psychological connectivity, the adequacy of social ties to the organization, and how the EOR can enhance the sense of connection. While psychological connectivity is clearly essential for virtual relationships, social networks also may be important, although rarely studied, elements of the EOR domain (c.f., Lai, Rousseau, & Chang, 2009). Building on the theme of social embeddedness, the final chapter in this part by Takeuchi discusses the value of examining both parties to an exchange as well as including multiple stakeholders (supervisors, coworkers, and subordinates) who have a social exchange relationship with the employee and who may impact the quality of the EOR. Takeuchi argues that examining the broader social context in which the EOR is embedded is an important next step in conceptualizations of the EOR. Like chapters in the prior part of this volume (e.g., Ashforth & Rogers; Schminke; van Knippenberg), Bartol and Dong, and Takeuchi argue for the need to examine the broader social domain within the organization that may contribute to the EOR and also the importance of incorporating the socially embedded nature of the EOR into research and theory.

Creation, Maintenance, and Completion of the EOR

In the third part of the book are four chapters that discuss changes in the nature of the EOR over time as well as work and life stages. These include during recruitment (preentry) and both personal and work-related experiences that are associated with the maintenance and dissolution of the EOR (turnover and retirement).

All four chapters in this section discuss the role of expectations in various stages of the EOR, including the development, maintenance, and dissolution of the EOR, but in distinct ways. Shapiro and Fugate depict ways to foster positive EORs through anticipatory justice. They propose that EOR research would profit from including social exchange measurements that are anticipatory in nature in addition to the present- or past-oriented assessments that have been the primary focus of EOR research. This recommendation is based on research showing that justice expectations that communicate hope for the future have a positive influence on attitudes and behavior. In addition, Ryan's chapter focuses on the applicant–organization relationship (AOR) during recruitment and discusses the role of expectations in the development and progression of this relationship. She presents the utility of many EOR concepts to the recruitment context such as transactional and relational elements of the relationship, mutuality in obligations, reciprocity in the exchange, and breach and violation. Furthermore, Hom discusses expectations of employees and employers that are associated with various employment relationships (using Tsui et al.'s [1997] framework) and links these with both push-and-pull forces for leaving as well as staying. He argues that each type of EOR has associated expectations from both the employee and employer that influence the likelihood of turnover. Finally, Wang and Zhan discuss the perspective of older workers who are approaching retirement age, positing that they compare their EOR with their organization and their expected postretirement life and that this comparison influences the decision to retire. In sum, these chapters pose that employees engage in relational sense-making based on the expectations set forth by the organization through the EOR, which in turn affects employee decisions to go forward or leave the relationship.

Organizational and Strategic Implications

The final part of this volume includes chapters on the EOR that have broader organizational and strategic implications. In particular, each chapter makes important points about the need to integrate the EOR into activities viewed to be important for group and/or organizational success.

The first two chapters explore the influence of the EOR using a predominantly organization-level focus. Lepak and Boswell examine how understanding the link between human resources practices and organizational performance can benefit from taking a more balanced view of the exchange between individuals and their organization. Likewise, they posit that the EOR literature can benefit by paying greater attention to the strategic perspective embraced in the strategic human resources management literature. In a related vein, Tetrick argues that organizational health and employee health are interdependent. In a departure from most prior EOR literature, she proposes that the inducements provided to employees contribute to employee emotional responses, which then affect employees and organizations through emotional contagion processes. Emotional contagion creates an emotional climate that can be either positive or negative, which represents the "glue" that links the EOR with both employee and organization health.

The next two chapters spotlight two important contextual elements that need more attention in the EOR literature, specifically diversity and teams. Avery, McKay, and Roberson point out the importance of considering the strategic implications of an increasingly global economy involving people from a broad array of groups, and thus contend that incorporating diversity into thinking about the EOR is critical. They point out that limited attention has been given to diversity in the EOR literature and, importantly, to the different expectations and preferences that may be associated with membership in various groups. Based on their review of the racioethnicity literature, they conclude that (a) perceived organizational obligations differ for minority and majority employees, and (b) many minority employees pay particular attention to what they perceive to be diversity promises and are especially sensitive to their fulfillment. Salas and Fiore point out the increasing prevalence of the use of teams as a critical organizational structure. They present a new concept that they refer to as team-centric EOR, a meso-level organizational structure in which the interconnections within the team moderate the connections between the employee and the organization as a whole. They argue that understanding how teams fit into the EOR is critical to organizational success, suggesting that the EOR literature and teams literature can benefit from greater conceptual development of these interconnections.

This part ends with a chapter by Cascio and Greene on the EOR and the scholar–practitioner divide. They discuss how the EOR as a multilevel phenomenon is likely to be influenced by a number of contextual factors, including organizational stresses, group and organizational norms and culture, and employees' personal circumstances. Within this complex context, Cascio and Greene argue that managers should familiarize themselves with the research evidence on the EOR and interpret it so they can integrate it into their decisions. Likewise, they suggest that managers must also convince employees of the soundness of their decisions, both by sharing the evidence that supported those decisions and by engaging in a dialogue to ensure employees understand how the decisions were made. They then illustrate positive EORs by presenting two practical examples that reflect these essential principles. They conclude by pointing out that there is substantial research evidence that can be valuable to human resources practitioners in showing employees that they are being treated fairly and in a manner consistent with the perceived employment relationships they have with their employers.

As noted earlier in this introductory chapter, we end the book by presenting a concluding chapter that looks for common themes and issues across the chapters and suggests some future research directions that are apparent across many of the chapters. We believe each of the chapters in this volume raises challenging or novel ideas that help move the EOR literature forward, and we hope that you agree!

REFERENCES

Argyis, A. (1960). *Understanding organizational behavior*. Homewood, IL: The Dorsey Press, Inc.

Armeli, S., Eisenberger, R., Fasolo, P., & Lynch, P. (1998). Perceived organizational support and police performance: The moderating influence of socioemotional needs. *Journal of Applied Psychology, 83*, 288–297.

Barnard, C. I. (1938). *The functions of the executive*. Cambridge, MA: Harvard University Press.

Blau, P. M. (1964). *Exchange and power in social life*. New York, NY: John Wiley & sons.

Chen, Z., Eisenberger, R., Johnson, K. M., Sucharski, I. L., & Aselage, J. (2009). Perceived organizational support and extra-role performance: Which leads to which? *Journal of Social Psychology, 149*, 119–124.

Conway, N., & Briner, R. (2005). *Understanding psychological contracts at work: A critical evaluation of theory and research*. Oxford, UK: Oxford University Press.

Coyle-Shapiro, J., & Conway, N. (2005) Exchange relationships: Examining psychological contracts and perceived organizational support. *Journal of Applied Psychology, 90*, 774–781.

Coyle-Shapiro, J. A.-M., Kessler, I., & Purcell, J. (2004). Exploring organizationally directed citizenship behaviour: Reciprocity or "It's my job"? *Journal of Management Studies, 41*, 85–106.

Coyle-Shapiro, J., & Neuman, J. (2004). Individual dispositions and the psychological contract: The moderating effects of exchange and creditor ideologies. *Journal of Vocational Behavior, 64*, 150–164.

Eisenberger, R., Armeli, S., Rexwinkel, B., Lynch, P. D., & Rhoades, L. (2001). Reciprocation of perceived organizational support. *Journal of Applied Psychology, 86*, 42–51.

Eisenberger, R., Huntington, R., Hutchison, S., & Sowa, D. (1986). Perceived organizational support. *Journal of Applied Psychology, 71*, 500–507.

Eisenberger, R., Rhoades, L., & Cameron, J. (1999). Does pay for performance increase or decrease perceived self-determination and intrinsic motivation? *Journal of Personality and Social Psychology, 77*, 1026–1040.

Eisenberger, R., & Stinglhamber, F. (2011). *Perceived organizational support: Fostering enthusiastic and productive employees*. Washington, DC: American Psychological Association Books.

Gouldner, A. W. (1960). The norm of reciprocity: A preliminary statement. *American Sociological Review, 25*, 161–178.

Johnson, J. L., & O'Leary-Kelly, A. M. (2003). The effects of psychological contract breach and organizational cynicism: Not all social exchange violations are created equal. *Journal of Organizational Behavior, 24*, 627–647.

Lai, L., Rousseau, D. M., & Chang, K. T. (2009). Idiosyncratic deals: Coworkers as interested third parties. *Journal of Applied Psychology, 94*, 547–556.

Levinson, H., Price, C., Munden, K., Mandl, H., & Solley, C. (1962). *Men, management, and mental health*. Cambridge, MA: Harvard University Press.

March, J. G., & Simon, H. A. (1958). *Organizations*. New York, NY: Wiley.

Menninger, K. (1958). *Theory of psychoanalytic technique*. New York: Basic Books, Inc.

Rhoades, L., & Eisenberger, R. (2002). Perceived organizational support: A review of the literature. *Journal of Applied Psychology, 87*, 698–714.

Robinson, S. L. (1996). Trust and breach of the psychological contract. *Administrative Science Quarterly, 41*, 574–599.

Robinson, S. L., & Morrison, E. W. (1995). Psychological contracts and OCB: The effect of unfulfilled obligations on civic virtue behavior. *Journal of Applied Psychology, 16*, 289–298.

Roehling, M. V. (1997). The origins and early development of the "psychological contract" construct. *Journal of Management History, 3*, 204–217.

Rousseau, D. M. (1989). Psychological and implied contracts in organizations. *Employee Responsibilities and Rights Journal, 2*, 121–139.

Rousseau, D. M. (1995). *Psychological contracts in organizations: Understanding written and unwritten agreements.* Thousand Oaks, CA: Sage Publications.

Sahlins, M. (1965). On the sociology of primitive exchange. In M. Banton (Ed.), *The relevance of models for social anthropology.* London, UK: Tavistock Publications.

Sahlins, M. (1972). *Stone age economics.* New York, NY: Aldine De Gruyter.

Schein, E. H. (1965). *Organizational psychology.* Englewood Cliffs, NJ: Prentice Hall.

Shore, L. M., & Barksdale, K. (1998). Examining degree of balance and level of obligations in the employment relationship: A social exchange approach. *Journal of Organizational Behavior, 19*, 731–744.

Shore, L. M., & Shore, T. H. (1995). Perceived organizational support and organizational justice. In R. Cropanzano & K. M. Kacmar (Eds.), *Organizational politics, justice, and support: Managing social climate at work* (pp. 149–164). New York, NY: Quorum Press.

Shore, L. M., Tetrick, L. E., Lynch, P., & Barksdale, K. (2006). Social and economic exchange: Construct development and validation. *Journal of Applied Social Psychology, 36*, 837–867.

Shore, L. M., Tetrick, L. E., Taylor, M. S., Coyle-Shapiro, J., Liden, R., McLean Parks, J., ... Van Dyne, L. (2004). The employee-organization relationship: A timely concept in a period of transition. In J. Martocchio (Ed.), *Research in personnel and human resources management* (pp. 291–370). Greenwich, CT: JAI Press.

Song, L. J., Tsui, A. S., & Law, K. S. (2009). Unpacking employee responses to organizational exchange mechanisms: The role of social and economic exchange perceptions. *Journal of Management, 35*, 56–93.

Taylor, M. S., & Tekleab, A. G. (2004). Moving forward with psychological contract research: Addressing some troublesome issues and setting research priorities. In J. Coyle-Shapiro, L. Shore, M. S. Taylor, & L. Tetrick (Eds.), *The employment relationship: Examining psychological and contextual perspectives* (pp. 253–283). Oxford, UK: Oxford University Press.

Tekleab, A. G., & Taylor, M. S. (2003). Aren't there two parties in an employment relationship? Antecedents and consequences of organization-employee agreement on contract obligations and violations. *Journal of Organizational Behavior, 24*, 585–608.

Tsui, A. S., Pearce, J. L., Porter, L. W., & Tripoli, A. M. (1997). Alternative approaches to the employee-organization relationship: Does investment pay off? *Academy of Management Journal, 40*, 1089–1121.

Turnley, W. H., & Feldman, D. C. (1999). The impact of psychological contract violations on exit, voice, loyalty, and neglect. *Human Relations, 52*, 895–922.

Tyler, T. R., & Lind, E. A. (1992). A relational model of authority in groups. *Advances in Experimental Social Psychology, 25*, 115–191.

Wayne, S. J., Shore, L. M., & Liden, R. C. (1997). Perceived organizational support and leader-member exchange: A social exchange perspective. *Academy of Management Journal, 40*, 82–111.

Zhao, H., Wayne, S. J., Glibkowski, B. C., & Bravo, J. (2007). The impact of psychological contract breach on work-related outcomes: A meta-analysis. *Personnel Psychology, 60*, 647–680.

Part 1

New Ways of Thinking About the Employee–Organization Relationship

2

Is the Employee–Organization Relationship Misspecified? The Centrality of Tribes in Experiencing the Organization[1]

Blake E. Ashforth and *Kristie M. Rogers*
Arizona State University

Research on the employee–organization relationship (EOR) has focused largely on the nature of the exchange process between the employee and organization (Coyle-Shapiro & Shore, 2007). An exchange-based relationship forms when the employee and organization reciprocally bestow benefits on one another, leading to an ongoing sense of "mutual obligation" (Coyle-Shapiro & Shore, 2007, p. 167). The notion of exchange in the EOR has sparked a great deal of research over the last 20 years, particularly on psychological contracts, perceived organizational support, leader–member exchange, and the employment relationship (Shore, Tetrick, Taylor, et al., 2004). Individuals' attitudes toward the quality of the EOR are reflected in such concepts as organizational commitment, loyalty, organizational identification, and withdrawal cognitions.

But what does it really mean to say an employee has a "relationship" with his or her organization? How might an employee have a direct tie to something as abstract as an organization? A major clue can be found in the literatures on exchanges with, attitudes toward, and perceptions of the organization. Examples abound. Brandes, Dharwadkar, and Wheatley (2004) found that "local social exchanges" (p. 279; i.e., relationships with one's supervisor and employees in other areas) had a greater impact on extra-role behavior and employee involvement behavior (but not in-role

---

[1] This chapter is greatly expanded from an initial thought piece (Ashforth, 2008). We thank Lynn M. Shore, Jacqueline A-M. Coyle-Shapiro, and Lois E. Tetrick for their helpful comments.

23

behavior) than did "global social exchanges" (p. 280; i.e., relationships with the organization and top management). Ashforth, Harrison, and Corley (2008) concluded that although research on identification has focused overwhelmingly on the organization as the referent, individuals tend to identify less strongly with the organization than with more proximal entities, such as the workgroup and occupation.[2] And three studies by Eisenberger, Stinglhamber, Vandenberghe, Sucharski, and Rhoades (2002) found that individuals perceived greater supervisory support than organizational support, perhaps because "supervisors have greater daily contact with most employees than do upper level managers [and] may be able to more readily convey positive valuations and caring" (p. 572). In short, perhaps the relationship between the employee and his or her organization is largely mediated by relationships with more proximal and tangible entities (cf. Shore, Tetrick, Coyle-Shapiro, & Taylor, 2004; Silva & Sias, 2010).

To couch the matter more provocatively, we contend that *what scholars and managers attribute to the EOR is actually often a misspecification of individual–tribe relationships*. In all but the smallest of organizations, the tribe not only substantially mediates the impact of the organization on the individual and vice versa, but is also the locus and crucible for most of the individual's sensemaking, behavior, and attitudes. Millions of years of evolution have predisposed us toward the exclusiveness and immediacy of tribes (e.g., Kurzban & Neuberg, 2005); conversely, the recent ascent of large-scale organizations and their distal quality means that they simply do not exert the same innate tug upon us.

We mean "tribe" in the colloquial sense of a relatively small, interactive, and cohesive group whose members know and care about one another and who share a particularized identity along with certain goals, values, and norms (e.g., Symons, 1986). The term "tribe" is intended to convey the primal quality of localized attachments to one's role, peers, and immediate manager. A tribe has very high entitativity, that is, a strong sense of itself as a group (Yzerbyt, Judd, & Corneille, 2004). Entitativity may be fostered by clear boundaries, low permeability (i.e., difficult to join or leave), relatively small size, member similarity, shared mission and goals, group-based rewards, task interdependencies, regular interaction, intergroup competition, and length of existence (i.e., duration of group)

---

[2] It should be noted that occupations are not fully nested within the organization (e.g., many organizations employ financial analysts).

(cf. Lickel et al., 2000). The more of these qualities a group has, the more tribe-like it tends to be. The prototypical example of a workplace tribe is a workgroup (many workgroups, of course, lack some of the tribal attributes noted above), although occupational communities, friendship cliques, networks, entry cohorts, departments, and so on can certainly have tribal qualities.

Our discussion proceeds as follows. First, in the section "The Organization as Context," we argue that the organization becomes known primarily through expectations and interactions that are grounded and decoded in the tribe and that tribes have necessarily particularistic views of "the organization." Second, in the section "The Roles of Tribe Members," we discuss how one's role situates one in the organization and provides the basis for interacting with the tribe, how one's immediate manager represents and enacts the organization for the tribe and directly supervises tribe members—thereby shaping individuals' views of the organization and their roles within it—and how one's peers help one socially construct the organization and one's relationship with it. Third, in the section "The Psychological Convergence of Tribe and Organization," we argue that tribe members' views of the tribe tend to converge with their views of the organization, although the latter is still understood to be a discrete entity. Finally, in the "Discussion" section, we discuss the implications of our analysis for theory and practice.

THE ORGANIZATION AS CONTEXT

For the individual, organizational life is experienced locally. A typical individual performs a specific set of tasks, linked more or less with a bounded and specific set of coworkers and a manager, while based in a specific physical setting. Most of her interactions within the organization are with her peers and manager, and much of her time is spent at "her" work station. It is a highly grounded, particularized, and personalized existence; that is, one that is rooted in a rich and necessarily unique, localized setting, peopled with particular relationships. It is, in short, a *tribal* existence.

Consider measures of two constructs that purport to describe important elements of "the organization" writ large: organizational culture and organizational climate. For example, the *Organizational Culture Inventory* asks respondents, "the extent to which people are expected or implicitly required to...point out flaws" and "involve others in decisions affecting them" (Human Synergistics International, 2010). Such items are grounded in interpersonal interactions. Conversely, an *Organizational Climate Measure* item such as "this company tries to look after its employees" (Patterson et al., 2005, p. 406) asks respondents to evaluate a highly abstract statement about the workplace. Whether questions are highly grounded or highly abstract, how does a person formulate answers? Research on cognition indicates that when the stimulus is novel or when mindful processing is deliberate or socially facilitated, one is apt to rely more on "bottom-up" inductive processes—decoding "critical incidents" (Gundry & Rousseau, 1994, p. 1065)—than "top-down" deductive processes (Louis & Sutton, 1991; Walsh, 1995). That is, the person is more likely to reflect on his relevant experiences in the organization and essentially aggregate them into a modal response (e.g., my manager often criticizes my work, so I guess people are expected to point out flaws), than to deduce his response from abstract clues (e.g., my organization has a reputation for high quality, so I guess people are expected to point out flaws). If induction and deduction collide, the former will tend to have more sway because individuals trust in their actual experiences to reveal the way things "really work." As Rentsch (1990) put it, "small events carry big messages" (p. 678).

To be sure, some experiences may involve communications from "the organization," such as reading a company policy or hearing a senior manager's perspective during a meeting. These experiences, however, are largely abstract in the sense that they remain unanchored and unproven—a textbook-only description. Further, because organizations often espouse the wished-for rather than describe the actual, particularly in recruiting and socializing newcomers (Wanous, 1992), their communications may be taken with a grain of salt. Conversely, an individual is likely to have considerably more experiences of a grounded nature, whether direct (it happened to them) or indirect (they observed or heard of it). Because these experiences are *visceral*—they are real in the sense that they engage the individual more fully in a rich and revealing encounter—they tend to carry more weight than occasional company pronouncements.

In short, from the mélange of highly particularized, grounded occurrences, the person infers a more abstract and general quality about the nature of the organization at large. Having been often treated in particular ways and/or witnessing and hearing about others, she infers certain stable attributes about the context. As Ostroff, Kinicki, and Tamkins (2003) observe about organizational culture: "Culture has been treated almost exclusively as a construct that resides at the organizational level. Yet, the conceptualization of culture rests upon shared meaning... [A] multilevel process takes place in culture, moving from individual constructions of the situation and sensemaking to the creation of shared meanings across people" (p. 577). Our point, then, is that the abstract entity called the organization is actually *known* largely through a series of micro-level encounters, and these occur primarily within tribes.

Moreover, the individual's intrinsic needs and motives are substantially addressed at the tribal level. Research on work adjustment suggests that role transitions such as organizational entry and transfers trigger motives for identity (What is my role here?), meaning (What is going on, and why does it matter?), control, and belonging (Ashforth, 2001), and Masterson and Stamper (2003) introduced the concept of "perceived organizational membership" (p. 475), arguing that it arises from a sense of need fulfillment, of mattering, and of belonging. As will become evident later, these various needs and motives tend to be fulfilled by immersing oneself in the rhythms of the tribe, learning from one's manager, connecting to other members, internalizing the tribe's perspectives, and enacting one's role.

So, then, what *is* the role of the wider organization in the life of the individual? The organization sets the *context* (Johns, 2006). The mission statement, strategy, structure, physical setting, human resource management practices, espoused values and norms, and so on set the framework for subunits and individuals (Shore, Tetrick, Taylor, et al., 2004), particularly the role parameters (e.g., what to do, whom to interact with). However, we argue below that the enactment of that framework and the meaning that is imputed are largely mediated by one's tribe.

The Tribe as Mediator

As crucial as context-setting is for the organization, tribe, and individual, the context is nonetheless abstract and even impoverished. Because all but the smallest organizations contain quite differentiated subunits, the mission, culture, strategy, and so forth tend to be couched in fairly simple, overarching terms. It falls to lower levels of the organization to successively flesh out what those terms mean. Thus, as one travels down the organizational hierarchy, the goals, culture, and so on tend to become more tactical and grounded. Generally, the mission, culture, and other attributes of the organization are consistent with those of the tribes precisely because the tribes are created to realize the organization's mission and enact its culture and other attributes (Ashforth, Rogers, & Corley, 2011).

At the same time, *within* a given level of the hierarchy, structural differentiation leads to subunits that fulfill different functions (e.g., marketing, operations), with concomitant differences in goals, interaction styles, time horizons, and so forth (Lawrence & Lorsch, 1967). The upshot is that while organizations generally have an identifiable overarching context (in the sense that individual perceptions can be reliably aggregated), different subunits are likely to flesh out elements of that context in different ways. Thus, an espoused value of integrity may mean "being honest with customers" to the sales department and "providing fault-free products" to the operations department. Indeed, research on countercultures (Martin, 1992) and identity foils (Ashforth, Rogers, & Corley, 2011) indicates that some tribes may deliberately define themselves in *opposition* to another tribe or what they perceive as the prevailing organizational context. For example, in a study of a natural foods co-op, Ashforth, Reingen, and Ward (2011) found that an informal group of pragmatists coalesced in opposition to an informal group of idealists who were, in the pragmatists' eyes, driving the co-op to bankruptcy through their unwillingness to compromise on certain principles.

Further, even where groups at the same level are ostensibly the same in terms of function and design, there are likely to be discernible differences in how the groups enact and socially construct the context. Two examples will suffice. Gamson, Fireman, and Rytina (1982) ran an experiment on "unjust authority" (from their book's title). They created a bogus company and recruited participants, through newspaper ads, for a 2-hour "research session" (p. 42). Eighteen groups of participants were exposed to the same encounter: A company representative asked some group members to express opinions that were counter to their own views and taped their "testimony" for use in court as evidence of community standards. Using the pretext of technical difficulties, groups had downtime to discuss what was happening. The actual purpose of the experiment was to observe what the groups would subsequently do in the face of this unethical company behavior. The researchers found that, despite the common context, the groups reacted in very different ways; group dynamics took on a life of their own such that it was difficult to predict the process and eventual outcome from the initial composition of the group. Similarly, Barley and Knight (1992) discuss how communities of doctors and of nurses differentially embraced rhetoric on stress. The authors posit that occupational subcultures develop, and the extent to which a subculture embraces rhetoric on stress affects self-reports of stress by its members. Thus, it is not the stimulus of a stressor per se that determines whether or not an individual will report experiencing stress, but the extent to which those around him also report feeling stress. Nurses exposed to the same stimulus as doctors were argued to report far more stress. The stark between-group differences revealed by these two studies clearly indicate that groups that share a common context are capable of creating their own more or less unique world. This is the world of the tribe.

In sum, although the organization establishes the context for tribal dynamics, that context is necessarily enacted and socially constructed locally. In the following section, we examine what each of the key elements of the tribe—one's role, immediate manager, and peers—contributes to these localized dynamics.

THE ROLES OF TRIBE MEMBERS: FOCAL INDIVIDUAL, MANAGER, AND PEERS

The Role of the Focal Individual

Individuals are typically hired by the organization to perform a specific job. Thus, their very reason for organizational membership, and the basis of the EOR and the member–tribe relationship, is necessarily their bundles of assigned tasks. More broadly, individuals fulfill certain "roles," by which we mean a formal position in the tribe and organization along with the expectations that they and their "role set" (others with whom they interact) attach to the position (Ashforth, 2001; Katz & Kahn, 1978). Indeed, one's role may expand to include various idiosyncratic elements that are only tangentially related to the specific job for which one was hired (e.g., one may be the informal leader or the humorist of a tribe).

One's role is the center of one's organizational universe. One's role strongly shapes where one is located in the organization, what one does, what one attends to and how one makes sense of the tribe and organization, who one interacts with and how one is perceived, what stressors and affective states one experiences, and how much impact one may have on the tribe and organization. One's role, in short, largely defines one and provides the basis for involvement with others. Thus, roles are central to the experience of the tribe and the wider organization (Sluss, van Dick, & Thompson, 2010). For example, a meta-analysis by Kristof-Brown, Zimmerman, and Johnson (2005) indicates that perceived fit with one's job is strongly correlated with perceived person–group fit ($r = .49$), perceived person–organization fit ($r = .72$), and organizational commitment ($r = .47$).

Further, because roles are largely enacted within the proximal confines of the tribe, individuals are inclined to see their tribal experience as essentially their "organizational" experience and thus extrapolate or generalize from their localized experiences to the organization as a whole. For instance, if a person feels efficacious within her tribe, she is likely to feel efficacious within "the organization" as a whole, even if her actual impact does not extend much beyond the tribe. Her daily reality is that she is having an important impact on her role and those around her. Using Firebaugh's (1980) memorable term, the tribe is essentially a "frog pond" (p. 46), and the smaller the pond, the bigger one feels (Brass, 2000).

The Role of the Immediate Manager

Coyle-Shapiro and Shore (2007) note that "there is no research that explicitly asks employees who they have in mind (i.e., which organizational agents) when they answer questions about the EOR" (p. 168). However, it seems likely that individuals tend to think first of their immediate manager. Immediate managers represent and enact the organization and are the individuals' direct supervisors; thus, they exert a huge influence on individuals' perceptions of the organization, tribe, and their EOR.

Representing the Organization

As arguably the most salient day-to-day agent of the organization, the immediate manager is effectively seen as representing the organization

(Tekleab & Taylor, 2003). As Ferris et al. (2009) observe, "Individuals do not, in reality, enter into an exchange agreement with the 'organization,' as the EOR model would suggest. Rather, the representative of the organization (i.e., typically the immediate supervisor) is the dyadic partner with whom the employee interacts" (p. 1382). Even if more senior managers and human resource specialists determine elements of the employment relationship at the "strategic level (pay, career development, job security)" (Coyle-Shapiro & Shore, 2007, p. 173), it is the immediate manager who is the face of the organization in a day-to-day sense and executes the strategy. Thus, the immediate manager serves as a "linking-pin" (Sparrowe & Liden, 1997, p. 526) that connects individuals to the organization: As the manager is seen to act, so the organization is seen to act. For example, Eisenberger et al. (2002) found that perceived supervisory support (PSS) at Time 1 predicted change in perceived organizational support (POS) at Time 2, whereas POS at Time 1 did not predict change in PSS at Time 2, suggesting that individuals infer POS from the way their managers treat them. Thus, "According to OST [Organizational Support Theory], support from the supervisor results in a favorable relationship between the employee and the *organization*" (Eisenberger, Jones, Aselage, & Sucharski, 2004, p. 211, their emphasis; see also Sluss, Klimchak, & Holmes, 2008). Moreover, the effect of PSS on POS was greater when the supervisor had high status (Eisenberger et al., 2002), presumably in part because the supervisor was seen to more fully represent the organization.

Indeed, managers may even be seen to *personify* the organization (Coyle-Shapiro & Shore, 2007; Eisenberger et al., 2004). Organizations are not people, yet they are routinely endowed with human-like characteristics to make them more comprehensible to insiders and outsiders alike (e.g., Davies & Chun, 2002). This process is called anthropomorphization (Sluss & Ashforth, 2008). It seems likely that employees, particularly newcomers, make attributions about the "character" of the organization based on the behavior of their immediate manager. Further, once an anthropomorphic image becomes more or less institutionalized (e.g., Southwest Airlines is a friendly company), the image may color how managers are perceived—a process called personalization (Sluss & Ashforth, 2008). Anthropomorphization and personalization are thus complementary: Individuals make sense of the organization in terms of human-like characteristics, and they may make sense of their manager (and tribe) in terms of those characteristics. The result is that the manager (and tribe) may be seen to personify the organization, embodying and enacting the characteristics ascribed to the organization.

On a 7-point scale that measured the extent to which one's immediate manager was seen to personify the organization (sample item: "My supervisor is characteristic of [name of organization]"), Eisenberger et al. (2010) found a mean of 4.8 in a sample from a U.S. organization (Study 1) and 5.3 in a sample from diverse Portuguese organizations (Study 2). These relatively high values suggest that such personifying may indeed be quite common. Further, the researchers found that managers who expressed favorable attitudes toward their organization were more likely to be seen by subordinates as personifying the organization. In addition, the greater the perceived personifying, the stronger was the relationship between employees' leader–member exchange (LMX) and affective organizational commitment. In other words, because one viewed one's manager as representing the organization, one's relationship with the manager was seen as tantamount to one's relationship with the organization, thereby strengthening the impact of the manager's behaviors on one's attachment to the organization.

Enacting the Organization

Immediate managers are responsible for enacting the organization vis-à-vis their subordinates. "Enactment" is the process by which individuals act in and on their environment and in so doing generate feedback for sensemaking about that environment and their place within it (Weick, 1995). By enacting the organization via their role as agents of the organization, managers put into play their perspectives on what the organization is all about and how it should work. They instantiate the organization and thus "produce part of the environment they face" (Weick, 1995, p. 30). The organization gains flesh and life through enactment and is thus made "real" for tribe members. Moreover, complementing the sensemaking role of enactment is the sense*giving* role of providing interpretations to the tribe so that some degree of consensus may be achieved (Gioia & Chittipeddi, 1991; Smith, Plowman, & Duchon, 2010).

Of course, managers are not simply mechanical conduits of organizational interests and edicts. As Coyle-Shapiro and Shore (2007) argue, managers have their own agendas and interpretations, which may strongly affect the way they enact the organization. The result is that no two managers are likely to enact the organization in quite the same way, even if they play functionally equivalent roles (e.g., project leaders). Thus, each tribe gains some particularistic coloring as the recurring cycles of action–feedback–sensemaking/sensegiving play out over time. In short, how a manager enacts the organization strongly shapes not only what the organization is seen to be by the tribe's members, but the particularism of the tribe itself (as evidenced through its subculture, subclimate, practices, relationships, and so on).

Directly Supervising

The final source of immediate managers' influence is direct supervision. Managers are responsible for assigning tasks, providing guidance, monitoring performance, providing constructive feedback, being supportive, and so on. They help tribe members fulfill their respective roles and in so doing, link individuals to the tribe and the wider organization. Managers may also be responsible for helping to socialize and mentor members (Ashforth, Sluss, & Harrison, 2007; Liden, Bauer, & Erdogan, 2004). This involves helping individuals to become effective members of the organization by acting as a role model and guiding their development and their learning about the organization. Further, through *leader relational behavior* (i.e., encouraging open communication, collaboration, and trust among group members), managers help foster an individual's interpersonal and intragroup relationships (Carmeli, Ben-Hador, Waldman, & Rupp, 2009, p. 1553; Baker & Dutton, 2007).

Although preemployment experiences, recruitment practices, and newcomer orientation and training provide general notions of the EOR, it is largely through direct supervision within the nuanced setting of the tribe that substantial portions of one's EOR take specific form (cf. Rousseau, 2001).[3] Notions of what one is expected to do, what constitutes a reasonable day's work, what kinds of support and rewards one will receive, how fair the system is, and so forth become crystallized through interacting with one's immediate manager. For example, De Vos, Buyens, and Schalk's (2005) review of psychological contract operationalizations indicates five

---

[3] We strongly suspect that when the signals from these sources disagree, the individual places more weight on those from the direct supervisor because the supervisor is the most proximal, salient, and ongoing representative of the organization.

content domains: career development, job content, financial rewards, social atmosphere, and respect for private life. Day-to-day supervision bears directly on job content, social atmosphere, certain kinds of rewards, and respect issues, while mentoring bears on career development. Further, research suggests that the extent to which the employee and manager have a common understanding of the psychological contract is positively associated with the employee's performance (Dabos & Rousseau, 2004), and the extent to which the psychological contract is actually fulfilled positively affects the employee's organizational commitment and negatively affects turnover intentions (Zhao, Wayne, Glibkowski, & Bravo, 2007), as well as the evolution of the contract to a more relational basis (e.g., open-ended, rewards loyalty) (Lester, Kickul, & Bergmann, 2007).

In sum, by representing and enacting the organization and directly supervising individuals, immediate managers shape how individuals conceive of the organization and their role within it. Research on leadership attests to the powerful role that managers play in shaping the EOR. For example, Loi, Mao, and Ngo (2009) found that the perceived quality of LMX predicted the perceived quality of individuals' socioemotional exchange with the organization itself, which in turn predicted organizational commitment and intentions to quit. Indeed, Loi et al. describe LMX as "*the* building block" (p. 408, our emphasis) of the EOR. Walumbwa and Hartnell (2011) found that transformational leadership predicted relational identification (defining oneself in terms of the leader–subordinate relationship), which Sluss (2006) in turn found to predict organizational identification. In other words, certain leader behaviors draw individuals into defining themselves partly through their relationship with their manager, which then provides a bridge to defining themselves partly in terms of the organization.

The Role of Peers

As important as one's immediate manager is, "most employees undoubtedly spend more time interacting with peers, and also have multiple peer group members with whom to interact" (Seers, 1989, p. 132). Although immediate managers instantiate the organization and thus help shape the tribal climate and cohesion, peers tend to complement this influence, as suggested by Seers' findings that LMX and team-member exchange (TMX) were correlated at .42 and that TMX explained variance in work satisfaction, coworker satisfaction, and general satisfaction (although not supervisory and pay satisfaction) beyond that explained by LMX (see also Chiaburu & Harrison, 2008).[4] In terms of the EOR, we argue that the primary influence of peers is in helping the individual socially construct her understanding of the situation. Indeed, Louis, Posner, and Powell (1983) found that newcomers rated interactions with peers as the most available and important socialization aid in becoming an effective employee, and Korte (2009) concluded from a study of newly hired engineers that "the *work group was the primary context* for socialization—not the organization" (p. 293, his emphasis).

The Importance of Social Construction

Research on social learning theory, social information processing theory, symbolic interactionism, social comparison theory, and relative deprivation theory clearly indicates that individuals socially construct the meaning of work and its context. For example, experimental research by Bateman, Griffin, and Rubinstein (1987) found that perceptions and attitudes regarding tasks were subsequently influenced by group discussion about those tasks, and a field study by Klein, Conn, Smith, and Sorra (2001) indicated that the greater the social interaction among group members, the less variability there was in their perceptions of elements of the work environment.

Why does social construction occur? Work contexts are inherently complex, ambiguous, and dynamic, suggesting that there is seldom only one way to interpret a given context. Individuals look to those around them—their peers (and manager)—to help make sense of the context and their role and relative standing within it. This process occurs at both the tribal and interpersonal levels (cf. Postmes, Spears, Lee, & Novak, 2005). Each tribe is more or less unique (because it is embedded in a particular local context), and its members are highly personalized in one another's eyes (i.e., Jane has particularized relationships with Susan, her manager, and Ravi and Gloria, her coworkers, that are not readily transferable to another tribe). Thus, the individual puts great stock both in the prevailing consensus of the tribe and in what its particularized members think, feel, and do.

---

[4] In cases where the quality of LMX (and, therefore, perceived EOR) is poor, peers may instead serve as a bulwark against the manager and, by extension, the wider organization (Sias, 2009).

At the tribal level, the greater the sense of entitativity (again, as fostered by shared goals, clear boundaries, task interdependencies, etc.), the more one will tend to see fellow tribe members as interchangeable exemplars of the tribe (Crawford, Sherman, & Hamilton, 2002), and therefore credible referents for sensemaking. One then internalizes what appear to be the collective beliefs of the tribe. Thus, research indicates that an important function of groups and subcultures in organizations is to provide consensual clarity, allowing members to approach the daunting complexity, ambiguity, and dynamism they face in a shared, and seemingly manageable, way (Martin, 1992). Further, tribal endorsement of a set of perceptions gives them a *normative* weight, fueling pressures for group conformity (Barker, 1993; Meyer, 1994).

At the interpersonal level, individuals are likely to see peers as highly credible referents because they tend to be: (a) similar (individuals doing similar work tend to have similar backgrounds, interests, skills, and so on; Lawrence & Lorsch, 1967); (b) valued (individuals tend to care what their peers think and what their peers think of them); (c) salient (when the individual thinks of the "organization," it is largely the world of the tribe that comes to mind); and (d) accessible (given physical proximity and task interdependence) (Ashforth, 1985; Salancik & Pfeffer, 1978). Accordingly, one may internalize the more or less idiosyncratic beliefs of other individuals in addition to the shared beliefs of tribe members.

These tribal and interpersonal influences are likely to strongly shape the social construction of the EOR, such as psychological contract fulfillment (Henderson, Wayne, Shore, Bommer, & Tetrick, 2008; Ho, 2005), the various forms of justice (Spell & Arnold, 2007), and organizational support (Rhoades & Eisenberger, 2002). The informational contributions of peers typically complement that of the immediate manager: Peers have a somewhat different vantage point on the tribe, they are actually doing rather than supervising the work, and individuals are less concerned with appearing knowledgeable and competent with their peers than with their manager (Morrison, 1993).

The Process of Social Construction

How does social construction operate? Research on socialization and social learning theory suggests various overlapping avenues: by instruction, including narratives; by asking questions; by observation; by scanning website and other repositories of information; and by direct experience coupled with feedback (e.g., Bandura, 1977; Morrison, 1993). Individuals engage, both proactively and reactively, in discussions and socially mediated experiences to make sense of their role, tribe, organization, and EOR. In so doing, they develop increasingly complex schemas that reflect a meld of their own impressions and the expressed beliefs of credible referents (Rousseau, 2001). Given the socially mediated nature of this learning, tribe members are apt to reach more or less agreement on at least the most central issues.

However, the challenge for the individual is to develop not only a *generalized* sense of the EOR—the prototypical tribal member's relationship with the organization—but also a *particularized* sense of the EOR—the individual's own more or less idiosyncratic relationship with the organization. The latter is constructed via social comparison processes whereby the individual contrasts the treatment he expects and receives relative to that of other tribe members (Shore, Tetrick, Taylor, et al., 2004).[5] For instance, Henderson et al. (2008) found that individuals who had a more positive relationship with their manager (high LMX) than did their average coworker were more likely to perceive psychological contract fulfillment. Ho (2005) notes that social information serves "associative" and "comparative" functions. In the former, information about the nature of a peer's EOR provides a signal about how the organization is likely to treat one. In the latter, information provides a standard against which one's own treatment is compared. Putting the two together, information about, say, a training opportunity offered to a peer sends a positive (associative) signal about the organization's investment in its employees, thereby enhancing the quality of one's EOR; however, if that opportunity is denied to oneself, it (comparatively) indicates a possible inequity that may undermine one's EOR. Ho argues that the comparative function is more likely to dominate when the information concerns scarce resources that will provide a relative advantage for the recipient (e.g., compensation, job security, mentoring by top performers).

---

[5] Although such comparisons may also involve non–tribe members, social comparison theory indicates that individuals prefer to contrast themselves with similar and salient others, suggesting that fellow tribe members will tend to be the first choice (Festinger, 1954).

It is important to note that actual unanimity within the tribe is not necessary for sensemaking regarding either the generalized EOR or a given particularized EOR. Indeed, it's likely that variance will exist on the latter because of self-serving biases about the relative status and deservingness of tribe members. As long as individuals feel a sense of groupness (entitativity), they may tolerate and even appreciate some diversity of opinions; also, as suggested by the false consensus effect (e.g., Krueger & Clement, 1994), they may simply assume that other members think like them. That said, tribes whose members differ *widely* in their perceptions of the work environment, indicating a failure of social construction to achieve consensus, are likely to be less cohesive, experience more conflict among members, and have poorer work adjustment (see the review by Klein et al., 2001); in short, they are likely to lose a sense of entitativity.

It is also important to note that the perceptions that emerge from social construction may or may not be valid in any objective sense, but the (assumed) consensus provides the normative weight alluded to above. Indeed, the power of social construction and the resulting social validation is demonstrated by groups that cling to beliefs that outsiders regard as patently wrong, such as the denial practiced by some workers at a failing plant studied by Illes (1996). Over time, social constructions often come to be seen as simply "the way things are" rather than as the more or less arbitrary constructions that they inherently are, and newcomers are strongly encouraged to accept them as self-evident conclusions. Indeed, what was *descriptive* may even become *prescriptive* as individuals internalize the constructions, adapt to their implications, and thereby develop a stake in perpetuating them. "Is" thus becomes "must be" and perhaps "ought to be." Barker (1993) describes how self-managing teams developed overarching values that soon morphed into behavioral norms and then formalized rules (e.g., "a team member should be able to do all the work roles on the team" morphed into "specific guidelines for how long new members had to train for a specific function…and…would have to work in assembly before rotating to a new team job, such as repair" [p. 429]). The social constructions had become social constraints.

In sum, through social construction processes, the individual's perceptions of the EOR are likely to be strongly influenced by the prevailing views of the tribe, and subsequent events are likely to be filtered through this tribal prism.

THE PSYCHOLOGICAL CONVERGENCE OF TRIBE AND ORGANIZATION

Research on identification and commitment indicates that attachments to one's manager and workgroup or department tend to be positively correlated with attachment to one's organization (e.g., Carmeli, Atwater, & Levi, 2011; Riketta & van Dick, 2005). Why might this be? We argue that in addition to the tribe mediating the EOR, one's perceptions of and attitudes toward the tribe will tend to converge with one's perceptions of and attitudes toward the organization.

Sluss and Ashforth (2008) describe various cognitive, affective, and behavioral mechanisms through which identification with one target (they use the supervisor–subordinate relationship as their example) may "converge" with organizational identification. Cast in terms of tribe–organization convergence, these mechanisms include: (1) *social influence*, where, as one identifies with the tribe, one is predisposed to accept the views of tribe members, which tend to be positive toward the wider organization; (2) *anthropomorphization*, as noted, where one develops a perception of the otherwise abstract and distal organization by ascribing to it characteristics of the tribe and its members; (3) *personalization*, as also noted, where one's sense of the organization may be used to make sense of a new tribe (the reverse of anthropomorphization), and where identification with the organization predisposes one to like and get to know one's tribe members; (4) *affect transfer*, where the psychological association between the tribe and organization (the former is nested within the latter) causes a nonconscious transference of feelings from one to the other; and (5) *behavioral sensemaking*, where, given the nested nature of tribe and organization, actions that reflect on one tend to reflect on the other, fostering the sense that one must therefore be psychologically attached to both.

The result of these five processes is that one's perceptions of and attachment to the tribe tend to inform one's perceptions of and attachment to the organization, and vice versa. Given our earlier argument that the tribe tends to be far more salient than the organization (even while the organization sets the context for the tribe), we suspect the tribe→organization influence is typically stronger than the reverse. For example, we mentioned earlier that Eisenberger et al. (2002) found that perceived supervisory support (PSS) predicted change in perceived organizational support (POS), whereas POS did not predict change in PSS. The bottom-up convergence is very important because it suggests that: (a) the member–tribe relationship strongly colors the EOR, such that (b) on the practical side, fostering the member–tribe relationship is a major route toward simultaneously fostering the EOR, and (c) rather than develop separate models of the two relationships, scholars might develop a more inclusive model of both (cf. Ashforth et al., 2008).

Eisenberger et al. (2002) further found that the impact of PSS on voluntary turnover was mediated by POS, suggesting that, following the norm of reciprocity, POS created a "felt obligation toward the organization" (p. 570). Eisenberger, Armeli, Rexwinkel, Lynch, and Rhoades (2001) in fact documented that such a felt obligation, engendered by POS, predicted affective organizational commitment, organizational citizenship behavior ("organizational spontaneity"), and in-role performance (but not withdrawal behavior). In other words, although individuals' perceptions of and attitudes toward the organization are strongly shaped by tribal dynamics (in this case, PSS), these perceptions and attitudes nonetheless trigger a sense of obligation to the wider organization and subsequently have a real impact on organizationally oriented behavior.

Our point is not that the EOR as perceived by the individual is simply an artifact or epiphenomenon of her relationship with the tribe. To be sure, as noted, the tribe strongly influences perceptions of and attitudes toward the organization, generally leading to convergence. And the organization is experienced and becomes known to the individual through the nature of the micro-level encounters within the tribe such that, in a visceral sense, the tribe *is* the organization. That said, the organization is nonetheless seen as a discrete entity, as the home within which the tribe dwells, and the individual is likely to realize that at least some organizational policies and practices (concerning, for example, compensation, job security, and health and safety) are largely beyond the tribe's control. Thus, the individual is able to have a sense of the organization per se and how she relates to it, even if that relationship is mediated by the tribe. Consequently, she is willing and able to act toward the organization beyond the tribe. Indeed, at times she may even act in ways that benefit the organization at the expense of the tribe (e.g., volunteering the tribe for a disliked assignment; working to overcome tribal resistance to organizational change; cf. positive deviance, Spreitzer & Sonenshein, 2004).

In sum, beyond the tribe mediating the EOR, the members' perceptions of and attitudes toward the tribe are apt to converge with their perceptions of and attitudes toward the organization. Nonetheless, the organization continues to be seen as a discrete entity, albeit one that is heavily colored by members' tribal experiences.

DISCUSSION

We began by asking what it really means to say that an employee has a "relationship" with something as abstract as an organization. We argued that what scholars and managers attribute to the EOR largely represents the relationship between the employee and her tribe. Although the organization sets the context for the EOR, both the context and EOR remain rather abstract and generic until given flesh through more grounded experiences. First, an individual comes to know the organization largely via expectations and interactions that are based and decoded in the unique local context of her tribe. Second, the key components of the tribe for constructing the EOR are the individual's role, immediate manager, and peers: The role provides the basis for interacting with the tribe; the manager represents and enacts the organization and directly supervises the tribe; and the peers help socially construct the organization and their generalized (shared) and particularized (unique) relationships with it. Third, an individual's perceptions and attitudes regarding the tribe tend to converge with her perceptions and attitudes regarding the organization, although the organization is still understood to be a discrete entity. Thus, the tribe mediates the impact of the organization on the individual (and, to a lesser extent, vice versa).

Implications for Theory

Our analysis suggests that the tribe is the pivot of the EOR: To understand the EOR, one must understand what occurs within the tribe. This has three major implications for theory. First, because perceptions of the EOR emerge from the grounded experiences and interactions of tribe members, it is very difficult to predict the perceived EOR from a static set of predictors, no matter how comprehensive they may be. Earlier, we noted studies by Gamson et al. (1982) and Barley and Knight (1992) indicating that despite a seemingly common context, different groups can socially construct the context very differently and act accordingly. Thus, the *process* by which tribe members construct and enact the EOR has a major impact on the perceived EOR (and its trajectory), suggesting the utility of developing models and studies that map these complex dynamics over time.

Second, process variables such as organizational support and psychological contract fulfillment, outcome variables such as organizational commitment and organizational identification, and macro variables such as organizational culture and organizational climate may misspecify the level of the referents. Rather than tapping into the individual's relationship with (or perceptions and attitudes regarding) the organization per se, assessments of these constructs may spuriously reflect his relationship with (or perceptions and attitudes regarding) the tribe. Thus, studies that measure organizational support, organizational commitment, organizational culture, and so forth, but not their tribal counterparts, may be doomed to wrongly attribute tribal-level referents to the organization.

That said, outcome variables such as job performance and intentions to quit confound the tribe and organization because performance facilitates the goals of both and when one quits the organization one simultaneously quits the tribe. Organizational citizenship behaviors (OCBs) present an interesting case because OCB measures, such as Lee and Allen's (2002), often include some items that are more relevant to the tribe and some that are more relevant to the organization. Not surprisingly, then, when Masterson, Lewis, Goldman, and Taylor (2000) divided OCBs into organizationally directed and supervisor-directed subscales, they found that POS predicted the former, whereas LMX predicted the latter.

Thus, to avoid the misspecification of variables, it is important for scholars to think about: (a) the likely mediating mechanisms by which tribal dynamics affect certain outcomes and macro variables; (b) whether the individual can meaningfully distinguish between the tribal and organizational levels; and (c) the appropriate level of referents rather than reflexively including organizationally oriented variables. Regarding the last, a study by Howes, Cropanzano, Grandey, and Mohler (2000) provides an example of the gains to be realized. Howes et al. (2000) disaggregated POS into organizational support for the individual, team support for the individual, and organizational support for the team. Whereas organizational support for the individual was the strongest predictor of organizational commitment and intentions to quit the organization, team support for the individual was the strongest predictor of team commitment and intentions to quit the team, and organizational support for the team was the strongest predictor of team performance.

Third, we believe that the distinction between the generalized EOR (i.e., the prototypical tribal member's relationship with the organization) and the particularized EOR (i.e., the individual's own more or less idiosyncratic relationship) is very important. Research on LMX, perceived organizational support, justice, and psychological contract fulfillment typically focuses on how the individual was treated (and its effects), implicitly speaking to the particularized EOR. However, the generalized EOR matters to the individual because it serves as: (a) a foundation for the development of the particularized EOR (what she should expect); and (b) a baseline against which her own treatment can subsequently be compared. As equity theory and relative deprivation theory clearly indicate, an individual's absolute treatment tends to matter less than her relative treatment. That said, for some aspects of the EOR—particularly justice and LMX—individuals likely also have what can be termed an *idealized EOR*, that is, a general standard about what is right and reasonable to expect that *transcends* any given tribe or organization (e.g., performance appraisals should focus on criteria one can influence; a manager should be supportive). Like the generalized EOR, an idealized EOR provides a baseline for the development of one's particularized EOR and for gauging one's own treatment. Provocative research questions, then, concern the interactions among these three forms of EOR (e.g., What elements of the EOR are most likely to exist in idealized form? How consensual are tribe members' idealized EORs? How might consensual idealized EORs affect the emergence of the generalized EOR, and vice versa? Under what conditions might the generalized EOR matter more than the idealized EOR?).

Boundary Conditions

Various factors may mitigate the formation, dynamics, and influence of tribes in organizations. We will briefly consider the nature of the organization and the national culture.

Nature of the Organization

Situational strength refers to "implicit or explicit cues provided by external entities regarding the desirability of potential behaviors" (Meyer, Dalal, & Hermida, 2010, p. 121). A strong situation exists where individuals are induced to perceive and respond in the same manner. Thus, strong situations tend to mitigate the role of tribes. For example, mechanistic organizations tend to be highly centralized, with top-down (versus lateral) communication, clear and fixed tasks, and an emphasis on employee obedience. Similarly, a hierarchical organizational culture (as per the competing values framework; Cameron, Quinn, Degraff, & Thakor, 2006) emphasizes efficiency and tight control at the expense of collaboration and empowerment. Such organizational structures and cultures appear to their members to be institutionalized in the sense meant by Zucker (1977), namely objective (versus socially constructed), external to any one person or group, and persistent. By disempowering groups and providing a seemingly immutable perspective on the organization, the role of tribes is curtailed. Finally, many elements of the context that affect the EOR may be amenable to objective assessment (e.g., relative compensation in the industry), determined by extraorganizational dynamics (e.g., labor law), and anchored in outsiders' perceptions (e.g., organizational image), further reducing the tribe's mediation of the EOR.

However, even under such conditions, we nonetheless envisage a major role for tribes. First, even seemingly institutionalized organizations, objective assessments, extraorganizational factors, and outsiders' perceptions are at least somewhat amenable to localized social constructions. For instance, research on dirty work indicates that managers actively work to neutralize the societally imposed stigma that is associated with jobs that are physically, socially, or morally tainted (Ashforth, Kreiner, Clark, & Fugate, 2007). As Ho (2005) concluded, "the social influence phenomenon is so robust and dominant that it occurs even in the presence of diagnostic, objective information and standards guiding one's evaluation" (p. 114). Second, as hinted earlier in our discussion of countercultures and identity foils, tribes may coalesce in direct opposition to a strong and oppressive organizational structure and culture (Ashforth & Mael, 1998). For example, Weeks (2004) describes "the ritual of complaint" (from the book's title) in a bank and how employees viewed the organization as a negative foil for their own subunits, which they saw more positively. Third, organizations and their tribes are apparently becoming increasingly organic (e.g., Sisaye, 2005). In the face of dynamic, complex, and ambiguous environments, organizations are flattening their hierarchies and delegating complex work to highly interactive groups and teams. Thus, we suspect that tribes are becoming ever more important in organizational life.

National Culture

Certain cultural values, particularly collectivism and power distance, may make tribes more or less crucial to the EOR. Research indicates that individuals in collectivistic cultures see groups as more entitative and agentic than do those in individualistic cultures (Kashima et al., 2005). Additionally, collectivists tend to have interpersonal rather than institutional loyalties (Chen, Tsui, & Farh, 2002) and base trust on the likelihood of sharing interpersonal links rather than sharing membership in a group (Yuki, Maddux, Brewer, & Takemura, 2005). Due to the perception of entitativity and the interpersonal nature of attitudes, the tribe may be seen as a stand-alone group, undermining the convergence processes through which we suggested the tribal experience comes to represent the EOR. In short, collectivism may lead to perceptions of the tribe and the organization being somewhat decoupled. Further, one may view membership in the tribe as more important than membership in the wider organization. In a study of reactions to team fluidity, Harrison, McKinnon, Wu, and Chow (2000) found that managers in collectivistic national cultures perceived ingroup relationships as very important and reacted to changes in team membership or leadership with more negative attitudes than did managers in individualistic cultures.

Power distance, on the other hand, may mitigate tribal influence on the individual and leave the power to guide the individual's relationship with the organization to those with higher status. In cultures of high power distance, individuals lower in the hierarchy accept status differences and power centralization without question (Hofstede, 1983), and high-status members are seen as more important than lower status members to the success of the group (Earley, 1999). We suggested earlier that when top-down messages from the organization collide with an inductive understanding acquired through tribal experience, the latter will prevail. However, the importance placed on higher status individuals in high power distance cultures may lead employees to instead defer to the top-down messages.

Implications for Practice

Our analysis suggests that one's relationship with the organization is mediated by one's tribe. The major implication is that a strong employee–"tribe" relationship is a prerequisite for a strong EOR for virtually everyone who is not structurally or dispositionally isolated (e.g., a night security guard, a loner).[6] Thus, initiatives directed at the EOR per se may have less impact than initiatives directed at the employee–tribe relationship, as well as the tribe–organization relationship. The literature on group and team dynamics is replete with practices that enhance the employee–group bond, such as selecting on person–group fit and utilizing collective socialization (e.g., Ashforth, Sluss, et al., 2007; Werbel & Johnson, 2001). Further, the notion of tribe–organization convergence suggests that a managerial focus on fostering a healthy tribe will go far in simultaneously fostering a healthy EOR.

What is less clear is: (a) how to enhance the tribe–organization relationship; (b) whether a tribal focus might come at the expense of the organization; and (c) what the role of senior management should be. The tribe–organization relationship can be enhanced by negotiating group goals and performance-contingent group rewards, establishing clear performance metrics, and providing copious support to the tribe and its manager, including information, teamwork training, resources, and autonomy (e.g., Kennedy, Loughry, Klammer, & Beyerlein, 2009). For example, we noted Howes et al.'s (2000) finding that organizational support for teams was associated with team performance, and Erdogan and Enders (2007) found that high-LMX supervisors who felt supported by their organization had a greater positive impact on the performance and satisfaction of their subordinates.

Might an emphasis on tribes come at the expense of the organization? Research on the dual identity model indicates the utility of simultaneously valuing both lower order (the tribe) and higher order (the organization) identities (e.g., Richter, West, van Dick, & Dawson, 2006), and Boisnier and Chatman (2003) argue that organizational subcultures can complement a strong overarching culture. Thus, the challenge for management is to harness a given tribe to the organization in such a way that both entities are recognized and respected—in short, by focusing on the

---

[6] We recognize that collectives may fall short of constituting a full-blown tribe; hence, the quotation marks around "tribe."

tribe–organization relationship. To illustrate, Whole Foods makes extensive use of overlapping teams within and between stores (such that no one tribe becomes an end in itself), with each highly accountable to the organization via regularly publicized metrics (Fishman, 1996). In addition, Gittell, Seidner, and Wimbush (2010) document how cross-functional boundary spanners, meetings, conflict resolution, and other cross-functional practices enabled "relational coordination" (p. 491) across tribes in hospitals, facilitating their overarching mission of patient care. Thus, as Brandes et al. (2004) recommend, "Effective managers will be able to balance both local and global ties simultaneously to enhance individual job performance" (p. 296).

Beyond harnessing tribes to the organization, what is the role of senior management? Senior managers must establish a general context in which highly differentiated tribes can flourish. Senior managers are in a position to establish the overarching mission and goals of the organization, as well as the broad parameters of the culture and climate and to provide tribes with a common experience of the organization by facilitating social interactions between tribes and communicating unambiguous messages to all organizational members (Hartnell & Walumbwa, 2011). That said, we argue that senior managers should not attempt to mitigate the differentiation of the tribes, but instead recognize the importance of the tribal experience and encourage lower level managers to enact top-down messages in such a way that the intended mission, goals, and so on become the tribal experience. The role of lower managers (tribal leaders) in facilitating the EOR is to then work within these parameters, fleshing out the general context in accord with local conditions and the particular needs and wants of tribe members.

In closing, we contend that the proximal tribe is more salient in a day-to-day sense than is the distal organization. To truly understand the connection between an employee and her organization, one must first understand the connection between the employee and her tribe.

REFERENCES

Ashforth, B. E. (1985). Climate formation: Issues and extensions. *Academy of Management Review, 10,* 837–847.

Ashforth, B. E. (2001). *Role transitions in organizational life: An identity-based perspective.* Mahwah, NJ: Erlbaum.

Ashforth, B. E. (2008). "Organizational" behavior is largely tribal behavior. In D. Barry & H. Hansen (Eds.), *The Sage handbook of new approaches in management and organization* (pp. 538–539). Los Angeles, CA: Sage.

Ashforth, B. E., Harrison, S. H., & Corley, K. G. (2008). Identification in organizations: An examination of four fundamental questions. *Journal of Management, 34,* 325–374.

Ashforth, B. E., Kreiner, G. E., Clark, M. A., & Fugate, M. (2007). Normalizing dirty work: Managerial tactics for countering occupational taint. *Academy of Management Journal, 50,* 149–174.

Ashforth, B. E., & Mael, F. A. (1998). The power of resistance: Sustaining valued identities. In R. M. Kramer & M. A. Neale (Eds.), *Power and influence in organizations* (pp. 89–119). Thousand Oaks, CA: Sage.

Ashforth, B. E., Reingen, P. H., & Ward, J. C. (2011). *Friend and foe? Duality and relational pluralism in a natural food cooperative.* Manuscript under review.

Ashforth, B. E., Rogers, K. M., & Corley, K. G. (2011). Identity in organizations: Exploring cross-level dynamics. *Organization Science, 22,* 1144–1156.

Ashforth, B. E., Sluss, D. M., & Harrison, S. H. (2007). Socialization in organizational contexts. *International Review of Industrial and Organizational Psychology, 22,* 1–70.

Baker, W., & Dutton, J. E. (2007). Enabling positive social capital in organizations. In J. E. Dutton & B. R. Ragins (Eds.), *Exploring positive relationships at work: Building a theoretical and research foundation* (pp. 325–345). Mahwah, NJ: Erlbaum.

Bandura, A. (1977). *Social learning theory.* Englewood Cliffs, NJ: Prentice-Hall.

Barker, J. R. (1993). Tightening the iron cage: Concertive control in self-managing teams. *Administrative Science Quarterly, 38,* 408–437.

Barley, S. R., & Knight, D. B. (1992). Toward a cultural theory of stress complaints. *Research in Organizational Behavior, 14,* 1–48.

Bateman, T. S., Griffin, R. W., & Rubinstein, D. (1987). Social information processing and group-induced shifts in responses to task design. *Group & Organization Studies, 12,* 88–108.

Boisnier, A., & Chatman, J. A. (2003). The role of subcultures in agile organizations. In R. S. Peterson & E. A. Mannix (Eds.), *Leading and managing people in the dynamic organization* (pp. 87–112). Mahwah, NJ: Erlbaum.

Brandes, P., Dharwadkar, R., & Wheatley, K. (2004). Social exchanges within organizations and work outcomes: The importance of local and global relationships. *Group & Organization Management, 29,* 276–301.

Brass, D. J. (2000). Networks and frog ponds: Trends in multilevel research. In K. J. Klein & S. W. J. Kozlowski (Eds.), *Multilevel theory, research, and methods in organizations* (pp. 557–571). San Francisco, CA: Jossey-Bass.

Cameron, K. S., Quinn, R. E., Degraff, J., & Thakor, A. V. (2006). *Competing values leadership: Creating value in organizations.* Cheltenham, UK: Edward Elgar.

Carmeli, A., Atwater, L., & Levi, A. (2011). How leadership enhances employees' knowledge sharing: The intervening roles of relational and organizational identification. *Journal of Technology Transfer, 36,* 257–274.

Carmeli, A., Ben-Hador, B., Waldman, D. A., & Rupp, D. E. (2009). How leaders cultivate social capital and nurture employee vigor: Implications for job performance. *Journal of Applied Psychology, 94,* 1553–1561.

Chen, Z. X., Tsui, A. S., & Farh, J.-L. (2002). Loyalty to supervisor vs. organizational commitment: Relationships to employee performance in China. *Journal of Occupational and Organizational Psychology, 75,* 339–356.

Chiaburu, D. S., & Harrison, D. A. (2008). Do peers make the place? Conceptual synthesis and meta-analysis of coworker effects on perceptions, attitudes, OCBs, and performance. *Journal of Applied Psychology, 93*, 1082–1103.

Coyle-Shapiro, J. A.-M., & Shore, L. M. (2007). The employee-organization relationship: Where do we go from here? *Human Resource Management Review, 17*, 166–179.

Crawford, M. T., Sherman, S. J., & Hamilton, D. L. (2002). Perceived entitativity, stereotype formation, and the interchangeability of group members. *Journal of Personality and Social Psychology, 83*, 1076–1094.

Dabos, G. E., & Rousseau, D. M. (2004). Mutuality and reciprocity in the psychological contracts of employees and employers. *Journal of Applied Psychology, 89*, 52–72.

Davies, G., & Chun, R. (2002). Gaps between the internal and external perceptions of the corporate brand. *Corporate Reputation Review, 5*, 144–158.

De Vos, A., Buyens, D., & Schalk, R. (2005). Making sense of a new employment relationship: Psychological contract-related information seeking and the role of work values and locus of control. *International Journal of Selection and Assessment, 13*, 41–52.

Earley, P. C. (1999). Playing follow the leader: Status-determining traits in relation to collective efficacy across cultures. *Organizational Behavior and Human Decision Processes, 80*, 192–212.

Eisenberger, R., Armeli, S., Rexwinkel, B., Lynch, P. D., & Rhoades, L. (2001). Reciprocation of perceived organizational support. *Journal of Applied Psychology, 86*, 42–51.

Eisenberger, R., Jones, J. R., Aselage, J., & Sucharski, I. L. (2004). Perceived organizational support. In J. A.-M. Coyle-Shapiro, L. M. Shore, M. S. Taylor, & L. E. Tetrick (Eds.), *The employment relationship: Examining psychological and contextual perspectives* (pp. 206–225). Oxford, UK: Oxford University Press.

Eisenberger, R., Karagonlar, G., Stinglhamber, F., Neves, P., Becker, T. E., Gonzalez-Morales, M. G., & Steiger-Mueller, M. (2010). Leader-member exchange and affective organizational commitment: The contribution of supervisor's organizational embodiment. *Journal of Applied Psychology, 95*, 1085–1103.

Eisenberger, R., Stinglhamber, F., Vandenberghe, C., Sucharski, I. L., & Rhoades, L. (2002). Perceived supervisor support: Contributions to perceived organizational support and employee retention. *Journal of Applied Psychology, 87*, 565–573.

Erdogan, B., & Enders, J. (2007). Support from the top: Supervisors' perceived organizational support as a moderator of leader-member exchange to satisfaction and performance relationships. *Journal of Applied Psychology, 92*, 321–330.

Ferris, G. R., Liden, R. C., Munyon, T. P., Summers, J. K., Basik, K. J., & Buckley, M. R. (2009). Relationships at work: Toward a multidimensional conceptualization of dyadic work relationships. *Journal of Management, 35*, 1379–1403.

Festinger, L. (1954). A theory of social comparison processes. *Human Relations, 7*, 117–140.

Firebaugh, G. (1980). Groups as contexts and frog ponds. In K. H. Roberts & L. Burstein (Eds.), *New directions for methodology of social and behavioral science*, vol. 6: *Issues in aggregation* (pp. 43–52). San Francisco, CA: Jossey-Bass.

Fishman, C. (1996). Whole Foods is all teams. *Fast Company*. Retrieved from http://learning.fastcompany.com/online/02/team1.html

Gamson, W. A., Fireman, B., & Rytina, S. (1982). *Encounters with unjust authority*. Homewood, IL: Dorsey Press.

Gioia, D. A., & Chittipeddi, K. (1991). Sensemaking and sensegiving in strategic change initiation. *Strategic Management Journal, 12*, 433–448.

Gittell, J. H., Seidner, R., & Wimbush, J. (2010). A relational model of how high-performance work systems work. *Organization Science, 21*, 490–506.

Gundry, L. K., & Rousseau, D. M. (1994). Critical incidents in communicating culture to newcomers: The meaning is the message. *Human Relations, 47*, 1063–1088.

Harrison, G. L., McKinnon, J. L., Wu, A., & Chow, C. W. (2000). Cultural influences on adaptation to fluid workgroups and teams. *Journal of International Business Studies, 31*, 489–505.

Hartnell, C. A., & Walumbwa, F. O. (2011). Transformational leadership and organizational culture: Toward integrating a multilevel framework. In N. M. Ashkanasy, C. P. Wilderom, & M. F. Peterson (Eds.), *Handbook of organizational culture and climate* (2nd ed., pp. 225–248). Thousand Oaks, CA: Sage.

Henderson, D. J., Wayne, S. J., Shore, L. M., Bommer, W. H., & Tetrick, L. E. (2008). Leader-member exchange, differentiation, and psychological contract fulfillment: A multilevel examination. *Journal of Applied Psychology, 93*, 1208–1219.

Ho, V. T. (2005). Social influence on evaluations of psychological contract fulfillment. *Academy of Management Review, 30*, 113–128.

Hofstede, G. (1983). The cultural relativity of organizational practices and theories. *Journal of International Business Studies, 14*, 75–89.

Howes, J. C., Cropanzano, R., Grandey, A. A., & Mohler, C. J. (2000). Who is supporting whom? Quality team effectiveness and perceived organizational support. *Journal of Quality Management, 5*, 207–223.

Human Synergistics International. (2010). *Organization culture inventory.* Retrieved from http://www.humansyn.com/products/documents/OCI_hand_scored.pdf

Illes, L. M. (1996). *Sizing down: Chronicle of a plant closing.* Ithaca, NY: ILR Press.

Johns, G. (2006). The essential impact of context on organizational behavior. *Academy of Management Review, 31*, 386–408.

Kashima, Y., Kashima, E., Chiu, C.-Y., Farsides, T., Gelfand, M., Hong, Y.-Y., ... Yzerbyt, V. (2005). Culture, essentialism, and agency: Are individuals universally believed to be more real entities than groups? *European Journal of Social Psychology, 35*, 147–169.

Katz, D., & Kahn, R. L. (1978). *The social psychology of organizations* (2nd ed.). New York: Wiley.

Kennedy, F. A., Loughry, M. L., Klammer, T. P., & Beyerlein, M. M. (2009). Effects of organizational support on potency in work teams: The mediating role of team processes. *Small Group Research, 40*, 72–93.

Klein, K. J., Conn, A. B., Smith, D. B., & Sorra, J. S. (2001). Is everyone in agreement? An exploration of within-group agreement in employee perceptions of the work environment. *Journal of Applied Psychology, 86*, 3–16.

Korte, R. F. (2009). How newcomers learn the social norms of an organization: A case study of the socialization of newly hired engineers. *Human Resource Development Quarterly, 20*, 285–306.

Kristof-Brown, A. L., Zimmerman, R. D., & Johnson, E. C. (2005). Consequences of individuals' fit at work: A meta-analysis of person-job, person-organization, person-group, and person-supervisor fit. *Personnel Psychology, 58*, 281–342.

Krueger, J., & Clement, R. W. (1994). The truly false consensus effect: An ineradicable and egocentric bias in social perception. *Journal of Personality and Social Psychology, 67*, 596–610.

Kurzban, R., & Neuberg, S. (2005). Managing ingroup and outgroup relationships. In D. M. Buss (Ed.), *The handbook of evolutionary psychology* (pp. 653–675). Hoboken, NJ: Wiley.

Lawrence, P. R., & Lorsch, J. W. (1967). *Organization and environment: Managing differentiation and integration.* Boston, MA: Harvard University.

Lee, K., & Allen, N. J. (2002). Organizational citizenship behavior and workplace deviance: The role of affect and cognitions. *Journal of Applied Psychology, 87*, 131–142.

Lester, S. W., Kickul, J. R., & Bergmann, T. J. (2007). Managing employee perceptions of the psychological contract over time: The role of employer social accounts and contract fulfillment. *Journal of Organizational Behavior, 28*, 191–208.

Lickel, B., Hamilton, D. L., Wieczorkowska, G., Lewis, A., Sherman, S. J., & Uhles, A. N. (2000). Varieties of groups and the perception of entitativity. *Journal of Personality and Social Psychology, 78*, 223–246.

Liden, R. C., Bauer, T. N., & Erdogan, B. (2004). The role of leader-member exchange in the dynamic relationship between employer and employee: Implications for employee socialization, leaders, and organizations. In J. A.-M. Coyle-Shapiro, L. M. Shore, M. S. Taylor, & L. E. Tetrick (Eds.), *The employment relationship: Examining psychological and contextual perspectives* (pp. 226–250). Oxford, UK: Oxford University Press.

Loi, R., Mao, Y., & Ngo, H.-Y. (2009). Linking leader-member exchange and employee work outcomes: The mediating role of organizational social and economic exchange. *Management and Organization Review, 5*, 401–422.

Louis, M. R., Posner, B. Z., & Powell, G. N. (1983). The availability and helpfulness of socialization practices. *Personnel Psychology, 36*, 857–866.

Louis, M. R., & Sutton, R. I. (1991). Switching cognitive gears: From habits of mind to active thinking. *Human Relations, 44*, 55–76.

Martin, J. (1992). *Cultures in organizations: Three perspectives.* New York: Oxford University Press.

Masterson, S. S., Lewis, K., Goldman, B. M., & Taylor, M. S. (2000). Integrating justice and social exchange: The differing effects of fair procedures and treatment on work relationships. *Academy of Management Journal, 43*, 738–748.

Masterson, S. S., & Stamper, C. L. (2003). Perceived organizational membership: An aggregate framework representing the employee-organization relationship. *Journal of Organizational Behavior, 24*, 473–490.

Meyer, G. W. (1994). Social information processing and social networks: A test of social influence mechanisms. *Human Relations, 47*, 1013–1047.

Meyer, R. D., Dalal, R. S., & Hermida, R. (2010). A review and synthesis of situational strength in the organizational sciences. *Journal of Management, 36*, 121–140.

Morrison, E. W. (1993). Newcomer information seeking: Exploring types, modes, sources, and outcomes. *Academy of Management Journal, 36*, 557–589.

Ostroff, C., Kinicki, A. J., & Tamkins, M. M. (2003). Organizational culture and climate. In W. C. Borman, D. R. Ilgen, R. J. Klimoski, & I. Weiner (Eds.), *Handbook of psychology: Industrial and organizational psychology* (Vol. 12, pp. 565–593). New York: Wiley.

Patterson, M. G., West, M. A., Shackleton, V. J., Dawson, J. F., Lawthom, R., Maitlis, S., ... Wallace, A. M. (2005). Validating the organizational climate measure: Links to managerial practices, productivity and innovation. *Journal of Organizational Behavior, 26*, 379–408.

Postmes, T., Spears, R., Lee, A. T., & Novak, R. J. (2005). Individuality and social influence in groups: Inductive and deductive routes to group identity. *Journal of Personality and Social Psychology, 89*, 747–763.

Rentsch, J. R. (1990). Climate and culture: Interaction and qualitative differences in organizational meanings. *Journal of Applied Psychology, 75*, 668–681.

Rhoades, L., & Eisenberger, R. (2002). Perceived organizational support: A review of the literature. *Journal of Applied Psychology, 87*, 698–714.

Richter, A. W., West, M. A., van Dick, R., & Dawson, J. F. (2006). Boundary spanners' identification, intergroup contact, and effective intergroup relations. *Academy of Management Journal, 49*, 1252–1269.

Riketta, M., & van Dick, R. (2005). Foci of attachment in organizations: A meta-analytic comparison of the strength and correlates of workgroup versus organizational identification and commitment. *Journal of Vocational Behavior, 67*, 490–510.

Rousseau, D. M. (2001). Schema, promise and mutuality: The building blocks of the psychological contract. *Journal of Occupational and Organizational Psychology, 74*, 511–541.

Salancik, G. R., & Pfeffer, J. (1978). A social information processing approach to job attitudes and task design. *Administrative Science Quarterly, 23*, 224–253.

Seers, A. (1989). Team-member exchange quality: A new construct for role-making research. *Organizational Behavior and Human Decision Processes, 43*, 118–135.

Shore, L. M., Tetrick, L. E., Coyle-Shapiro, J. A.-M., & Taylor, M. S. (2004). Directions for future research. In J. A.-M. Coyle-Shapiro, L. M. Shore, M. S. Taylor, & L. E. Tetrick (Eds.), *The employment relationship: Examining psychological and contextual perspectives* (pp. 351–364). Oxford, UK: Oxford University Press.

Shore, L. M., Tetrick, L. E., Taylor, M. S., Coyle-Shapiro, J. A.-M., Liden, R. C., McLean Parks, J., ... Van Dyne, L. (2004). The employee-organization relationship: A timely concept in a period of transition. *Research in Personnel and Human Resources Management, 23*, 291–370.

Sias, P. M. (2009). *Organizing relationships: Traditional and emerging perspectives on workplace relationships.* Los Angeles, CA: Sage.

Silva, D., & Sias, P. M. (2010). Connection, restructuring, and buffering: How groups link individuals and organizations. *Journal of Applied Communication Research, 38*, 145–166.

Sisaye, S. (2005). Management control systems and organizational development: New directions for managing work teams. *Leadership & Organization Development Journal, 26*, 51–61.

Sluss, D. M. (2006). *Generalizing relational identification to and from organizational identification.* Unpublished doctoral dissertation, Arizona State University, Tempe.

Sluss, D. M., & Ashforth, B. E. (2008). How relational and organizational identification converge: Processes and conditions. *Organization Science, 19*, 807–823.

Sluss, D. M., Klimchak, M., & Holmes, J. J. (2008). Perceived organizational support as a mediator between relational exchange and organizational identification. *Journal of Vocational Behavior, 73*, 457–464.

Sluss, D. M., van Dick, R., & Thompson, B. S. (2010). Role theory in organizations: A relational perspective. In S. Zedeck (Ed.), *APA handbook of industrial and organizational psychology: Building and helping the organization* (Vol. 1, pp. 505–534). Washington, DC: American Psychological Association.

Smith, A. D., Plowman, D. A., & Duchon, D. (2010). Everyday sensegiving: A closer look at successful plant managers. *Journal of Applied Behavioral Science, 46*, 220–244.

Sparrowe, R. T., & Liden, R. C. (1997). Process and structure in leader-member exchange. *Academy of Management Review, 22*, 522–552.

Spell, C. S., & Arnold, T. J. (2007). A multi-level analysis of organizational justice climate, structure, and employee mental health. *Journal of Management, 33*, 724–751.

Spreitzer, G. M., & Sonenshein, S. (2004). Toward the construct definition of positive deviance. *American Behavioral Scientist, 47*, 828–847.

Symons, G. L. (1986). Coping with the corporate tribe: How women in different cultures experience the managerial role. *Journal of Management, 12*, 379–390.

Tekleab, A. G., & Taylor, M. S. (2003). Aren't there two parties in an employment relationship? Antecedents and consequences of organization-employee agreement on contract obligations and violations. *Journal of Organizational Behavior, 24*, 585–608.

Walsh, J. P. (1995). Managerial and organizational cognition: Notes from a trip down memory lane. *Organization Science, 6*, 280–321.

Walumbwa, F. O., & Hartnell, C. A. (2011). Understanding transformational leadership-employee performance links: The role of relational identification and self-efficacy. *Journal of Occupational and Organizational Psychology, 84*, 153–172.

Wanous, J. P. (1992). *Organizational entry: Recruitment, selection, orientation, and socialization of newcomers* (2nd ed.). Reading, MA: Addison-Wesley.

Weeks, J. (2004). *Unpopular culture: The ritual of complaint in a British bank*. Chicago, IL: University of Chicago Press.

Weick, K. E. (1995). *Sensemaking in organizations*. Thousand Oaks, CA: Sage.

Werbel, J. D., & Johnson, D. J. (2001). The use of person-group fit for employment selection: A missing link in person-environment fit. *Human Resource Management, 40*, 227–240.

Yuki, M., Maddux, W. W., Brewer, M. B., & Takemura, K. (2005). Cross-cultural differences in relationship- and group-based trust. *Personality and Social Psychology Bulletin, 31*, 48–62.

Yzerbyt, V., Judd, C. M., & Corneille, O. (Eds.). (2004). *The psychology of group perception: Perceived variability, entitativity, and essentialism*. New York, NY: Psychology Press.

Zhao, H., Wayne, S. J., Glibkowski, B. C., & Bravo, J. (2007). The impact of psychological contract breach on work-related outcomes: A meta-analysis. *Personnel Psychology, 60*, 647–680.

Zucker, L. G. (1977). The role of institutionalization in cultural persistence. *American Sociological Review, 42*, 726–743.

3

The Employee–Organization Relationship and Ethics: When It Comes to Ethical Behavior, Who Is the Organization and Why Does It Matter?

Marshall Schminke
University of Central Florida

Daily headlines underscore the challenges managers face in creating and sustaining ethical organizations. Accounts of scandals at companies like AIG, Goldman Sachs, Countrywide Financial, and Lehman Brothers appear alongside equally troubling stories of misdeeds in political, religious, and not-for-profit settings. Ethics researchers have explored both individual and organizational influences on ethics, and this research has increased our understanding of ethical behavior in organizations. This chapter seeks to expand our knowledge even further by considering not just the individual and the organization, but the relationship between the two—the employee–organization relationship (EOR)—as an important factor in determining ethical outcomes. In addition, it seeks to enhance our understanding of the EOR by demonstrating how organizational ethics research might inform our thinking about the EOR. In particular, it describes the role that organizational ethics play in creating a powerful contextual influence, providing both opportunities and constraints on the multiple connections that exist between employees and their organizations.

To date, little research has linked the EOR and ethics. This is surprising. Substantial research demonstrates the influence of the EOR on a host of important individual and organizational outcomes, including organizational citizenship (Bell & Menguc, 2002), commitment (Shore, Bommer,

Rao, & Seo, 2009; Tsui, Pearce, Porter, & Tripoli, 1997), trust (Shore et al., 2009; Zhang, Tsui, Song, Li, & Jia, 2008), turnover (Shaw, Dineen, Fang, & Vellella, 2009; Shore et al., 2009) performance (Tsui et al., 1997), service quality (Bell & Menguc, 2002), and even corporate entrepreneurship (Ribeiro-Soriano & Urbano, 2010). It is reasonable to believe that connecting ethics and EOR research has the potential to benefit both streams of work.

Social exchange has provided the dominant framework for understanding the EOR, and as Shore and Coyle-Shapiro (2003) observed, a critical issue in understanding the influence of the EOR involves the question of who represents the organization in the exchange relationship with the employee. This is especially relevant for understanding the role of the EOR in ethics. The ethics literature demonstrates that top managers (e.g., Schminke, Ambrose, & Neubaum, 2005), supervisors (e.g., Brown, Treviño, & Harrison, 2005), and coworkers (e.g., Zey-Ferrell & Ferrell, 1982) all exert important influences on employee ethics. Therefore, a central issue in understanding the impact of the EOR involves understanding which of these contact points represents the organization as the dominant exchange relationship with the employee. Doing so has the potential to enhance our understanding of the EOR, organizational ethics, and the relationship between them.

This chapter unfolds in four sections. The first briefly reviews the literature on the influence of top management, supervisors, and coworkers on employee ethics. The second presents some initial empirical evidence that among these groups, supervisors exert the strongest influence. The third section discusses implications for both EOR and ethics research. The final section outlines a research agenda that may serve to answer some of the questions raised by the chapter.

TOP MANAGEMENT, SUPERVISOR, AND COWORKER INFLUENCES ON EMPLOYEE ETHICS

To understand how ethics emerge and develop in organizational settings, researchers have explored the impact of top management, supervisors, and coworkers on the ethical decisions and actions of employees. Results suggest each plays an important role.

Top Management Influences

Upper level management may influence organizational ethics in several ways. One of these suggests that organizational reward and punishment systems, which are implemented and enforced by senior managers, have the potential to shape the organizational ethos with respect to ethics by sending a message about whether ethical behavior is something valued and supported by the organization. Both theoretical and empirical research points to the importance of a proper "tone at the top" for influencing the ethical behavior of employees through the messages sent by the organizational reward system (Ashkanasy, Windsor, & Treviño, 2006; Jones, 1991; Treviño & Youngblood, 1990; Weaver, Treviño, & Cochran, 1999).

Additional research points to other paths by which top management actions may influence employee ethical behavior. For example, Armstrong, Williams, and Barrett (2004) found that risky shift and escalation of commitment among top managers influenced ethical violations among employees. Bowen (2004) also identified several factors that reflect the influence of top managers in shaping organizational ethics, including a supportive ethical culture, a collaborative management style, and a strong commitment to ethics training. Similarly, Ghosh (2008) demonstrated that corporate values, which are shaped and emphasized by top management teams, exert powerful influence on employee decisions regarding ethics.

In all, scholars have uncovered multiple processes by which top management shapes organizational ethics. The literature often points to the importance of the "tone at the top" in establishing ethical organizations (Schwartz, Dunfee, & Kline, 2005; Weber, 2010). However, additional evidence identifies limitations top managers face in affecting organizational ethics.

For example, Ashkanasy et al. (2006) found that the influence of reward and punishment systems implemented by top managers was mitigated by the level of cognitive moral development (CMD) of employees. Low-CMD employees, those using self-focused reasoning, reacted in a manner congruent with reward system expectations. That is, in organizations with reward systems that condone unethical behavior, pragmatic (low-CMD) employees made less ethical decisions. However, high-CMD employees, those using other-focused reasoning, responded differently. In organizations with reward systems that condone unethical behavior, other-focused employees actually exhibited more ethical decision making.

Similarly, Treviño, Weaver, and Brown (2008) suggested that top managers differ from lower level employees in terms of roles, identities, and perceptions. They hypothesized that these differences may lead top managers to view organizational ethics in fundamentally different ways. Results supported their predictions, as top managers were significantly more positive than lower level employees about the state of ethics in their organizations. These results suggest a second form of limitation on the power of top managers to shape ethics effectively. That is, if top managers are unable to detect or to understand the ethical issues, challenges, and concerns faced by lower level employees, they are unlikely to exert effective influence over them. Further, the relationship between top managers and employees is often distant. Therefore, even if top managers do grasp the day-to-day concerns of employees accurately, even good-faith attempts to communicate the importance of sound ethical principles and to act upon those principles may either dissipate or fail to resonate with average employees.

In all, evidence suggests that top management shapes organizational ethics in a variety of ways. However, a variety of limitations exist on top management's ability to understand and respond effectively to the ethical concerns of employees. Therefore, it is clear that despite their formal roles as broad-based organizational leaders, top managers may not effectively represent the organization in the EOR, at least with respect to ethics.

Supervisor Influences

The ethics literature often points to supervisors as an important driver of employee ethics (Drake, Meckler, & Stephens, 2002). Although some work has singled out supervisors per se as an important influence on employee ethics (Fraedrich & Iyer, 2008), much of what we know is drawn from research on ethical leadership (Brown et al., 2005), where the focal leaders have mostly occupied supervisory roles.

Brown et al. (2005) define ethical leadership as "the demonstration of normatively appropriate conduct through personal actions and interpersonal relationships, and the promotion of such conduct to followers through two-way communication, reinforcement, and decision-making" (p. 120). As such, ethical leadership is a broad-based construct that captures a range of ethics-related activities. Ethical leaders do not simply talk about ethics; they behave ethically and work actively to spread ethical practices.

Most empirical research involving ethical leadership has focused on supervisory leadership. This work has demonstrated the power of supervisors in shaping the ethical environment and the ethical behavior of employees. For example, Walumbwa and Schaubroeck (2009) established a link between supervisor ethical leadership and outcomes including psychological safety and employee voice. Mayer, Kuenzi, Greenbaum, Bardes, and Salvador (2009) demonstrated a relationship between supervisory ethical leadership and the level of citizenship behavior and deviance activities in a work group. Others have shown ethical leadership to exert even broader impacts on the ethical context of organizations by affecting ethical climate as well (Neubert, Carlson, Kacmar, Roberts, & Chonko, 2009).

One especially compelling piece of evidence of the potential for supervisors to play a prime role in representing the organization in the EOR is the robust impact of ethical leadership on outcomes beyond those specifically focused on ethics. For example, studies demonstrate a relationship between ethical leadership and employees' willingness to report problems, willingness to exert extra effort on the job, ratings of satisfaction with supervisor, ratings of supervisor effectiveness, and perceptions of organizational culture (Brown et al., 2005; Toor & Ofori, 2009).

In all, research points to supervisors—and supervisor ethics—as exerting a powerful influence on employee ethics and beyond. Combined with—or perhaps due to—the more proximal relationship supervisors have with employees, supervisors represent an attractive candidate for representing the organization in the EOR.

Coworker Influences

The relationship between employees and coworkers is also often a proximal one, so it is not surprising that research confirms the influence of coworkers on the ethical decision-making process of employees. For example, the second of Kohlberg's (1984) three levels of CMD—conventional reasoning—is the level at which most working adults operate (Treviño, 1986; Weber, 1990). It reflects ethical decision making as part of a collective moral entity. What is right depends on the norms, values, and expectations of one's social setting and therefore involves an understanding of the ethical beliefs of others. In an organizational setting, this includes (although is not limited to) the behavior and expectations of one's coworkers. Although supervisors—and perhaps to a lesser extent top managers—participate as active members of the organizational social setting for most employees, many jobs entail more frequent, interactive, and lengthy interactions with coworkers than either supervisors or top managers.

Early research into the influence of coworkers on employee ethics pointed to the potential for coworkers to affect employee ethics. Zey-Ferrell, Weaver, and Ferrell (1979) found that marketing managers' perceptions about the behavior of their peers was a stronger predictor of their own behavior than either their perceptions of top management beliefs or their own personal ethical beliefs. Similarly, Zey-Ferrell and Ferrell (1982) found the ethical behavior of advertising account executives to be most strongly predicted by the behavior of their peers.

Other work also suggests the power of peer influences on ethical decision making and behavior. O'Leary and Pangemanan (2007) found that coworkers exerted considerable peer pressure on individuals facing ethical dilemmas, typically leading to less extreme (either ethical or unethical) acts on the part of individuals. Likewise, Schmidtke (2007) demonstrated coworker influences on employee theft.

Recent conceptual work lays an even stronger foundation for considering the impact of coworkers. Husted and Allen (2008) proposed a cross-cultural model of business ethics that suggests an important role for coworkers as well. This model conceptualizes societal culture, as revealed in individualism and collectivism, as a group-level construct. Group-level cultures suggest an important role for coworker influences, as cultural group values impact individual values and, in turn, individual ethical decision making.

Other work suggests that peers other than coworkers may also influence employee ethics. Fraedrich and Iyer (2008) discovered that peers such as business associates and friends also impact ethical decision making. In this study, friends exerted a stronger influence on the ethical decision-making process than either superiors or business associates. These results suggest that our thinking about peer influences might benefit from extending the concept to include peers inside and outside the organization.

In all, considerable research has explored the impact of top managers, supervisors, and coworkers on the ethical decision making and actions of employees. Results suggest each has the potential to influence employee ethics in meaningful ways. However, little is known about the relative importance of each of these sources of influence. As a result, we are left to wonder about an important question for understanding the EOR with respect to ethics: In the eyes of employees, who represents the organization? That is, who is the "O" in the EOR when ethics are involved? The next section explores some preliminary evidence about the relative impact of top managers, supervisors, and coworkers on ethical outcomes that may shed some light on the issue.

TOP MANAGEMENT, SUPERVISORS, AND COWORKERS: WHO EXERTS THE STRONGEST INFLUENCE?

Extant research does not explicitly address the question of which organizational contact point—top managers, supervisors, or coworkers—exerts the strongest influence on employee ethics. However, I recently had the opportunity to partner with the Ethics Resource Center (http://www.ethics.org) in Washington, DC, in exploring data that may provide some preliminary answers. The data, owned by the Ethics Resource Center, include responses from 6,765 employees representing four firms engaged in technology development and manufacturing. The data allow us to examine the relative impact of the ethical activities of top management, supervisors, and coworkers on the pressure employees feel to violate ethical standards.

Data were gathered via on-site surveys. Respondents averaged 34 years of age, with 2 years of college and 4 years of experience with their current firms. Sixty-four percent were male. Employees provided responses to questions about a variety of ethical issues in their organizations, including their perceptions of the organization's ethical practices, ethics training, and ethical culture. I explored these data for insights on two fronts: (1) whether the ethical activities of top management, supervisors, or coworkers exert the most powerful impact on employee ethics, and (2) if one of these is dominant, what particular aspect of behavior plays the most significant role in that influence?

The outcome of interest in these analyses was the extent to which employees feel pressured to commit unethical actions on the job. Pressure to behave unethically was measured in two ways. The first assessed whether employees felt pressured to violate the company's ethical standards. (Item:

"How often do you feel pressured by other employees or management to compromise your company's standards of ethical business objectives?") The second assessed whether employees felt pressured to violate their own personal ethical standards. (Item: "In this job I have to do things that really go against my conscience.")

The predictors of these two outcomes are what the Ethics Resource Center refers to as ethics-related actions (ERAs) at multiple levels of the organization. ERAs reflect a constellation of ethics-related conduct on the part of top management, supervisors, and coworkers, such as communicating about the importance of ethics, setting a good example, and being supportive in upholding ethical standards. Four-item scales assessed the ERAs of each.

Top management ERAs were assessed with the following four items: (1) I am satisfied with the information I get from top management about what's going on my company; (2) I trust that top management in my company will keep their promises and commitments; (3) Top management in my company talks about the importance of ethics and doing the right thing in the work we do; and (4) Overall, the head of my company sets a good example of ethical business behavior.

Supervisor ERAs were assessed with the following four items: (1) I trust that my supervisor will keep his or her promises and commitments; (2) My supervisor talks about the importance of ethics and doing the right thing in the work we do; (3) Overall, my supervisor sets a good example of ethical business behavior; and (4) My supervisor supports me in following my company's standards of ethical behavior.

Coworker ERAs were assessed with the following four items: (1) My coworkers carefully consider ethical issues when making work-related decisions; (2) My coworkers talk about the importance of ethics and doing the right thing in the work we do; (3) Overall, my coworkers set a good example of ethical business behavior; and (4) My coworkers support me in following my company's standards of ethical behavior.

Employees responded to each item on a five-point (1 = strongly disagree, 5 = strongly agree) Likert-type scale. Responses for each of the three ERA scales were averaged to create ERA scores for top management, supervisors, and coworkers. Reliabilities (coefficient α) were above .70 for all scales.

The first research question asked whether top management, supervisor, or coworker ERAs exert the strongest influence on employee perceptions of being pressured to behave unethically. Ordinary least squares regression analyses revealed that all three ERAs exerted a significant impact on perceived pressure to violate both organizational and personal ethical standards. That is, the conduct of top management, supervisors, and coworkers all matter.

However, standardized betas revealed that supervisor ERAs exerted the strongest impact on both pressure to violate company ethical standards and pressure to violate personal ethical standards. (Standardized betas for top management, supervisor, and coworker ERAs were .17, .25, and .03, respectively, for pressure to violate company ethical standards, and .15, .26, and .12 for pressure to violate personal ethical standards.) In all, although all three groups' ERAs influenced individual ethical outcomes, the impact of supervisors was felt most strongly.

The second research question asked which aspect of the supervisor ERAs exerts the strongest impact on pressure to violate ethical standards. The four supervisor ERA items may be viewed as reflecting (roughly) trust, ethics communication, ethical modeling, and ethical support. This regression analysis examined the impact of each of these components on perceived pressure to violate standards.

Three of the four supervisor ERA items (trust, modeling, and support) were significantly related to pressure to violate both organizational and personal ethical standards. (The second item, communication, was not significantly related to either.) For both types of ethical pressure, the fourth item, which reflects ethical support on the part of the supervisor, exerted the strongest impact. (Standardized betas for trust, modeling, and support, respectively, were .09, .11, and .23 for pressure to violate company ethical standards, and .12, .16, and .26 for pressure to violate personal ethical standards.) In all, these results suggest that of the supervisor ERAs, the ability to create an ethically supportive situation for an employee appears to be the most potent tool.

Of course, these results do not prove that when employees think about organizational ethics, they are thinking only of supervisory ethics. Likewise, they do not prove that when it comes to ethics, the "organization" in the EOR is captured only by the actions of supervisors. The results indicate that a variety of organization members exert an impact on the ethical pressures experienced by employees. The actions of top managers, supervisors, and coworkers all have the potential to shape employee ethics. However, among these influences, supervisors matter most. In addition, among the things supervisors do, providing a supportive ethical environment for employees is more powerful than being trusted, communicating about the importance of ethics, or even modeling proper ethical behavior. In all, these results suggest that with respect to organizational ethics, the relationship between the employee and the organization is important. Further, these results suggest that for many employees dealing with ethical pressures, the "O" in the EOR has the face of a supervisor.

IMPLICATIONS FOR EOR AND ETHICS RESEARCHERS

Implications for EOR Research

The discussion and evidence thus far have implications for scholars involved in both EOR and ethics research. For EOR scholars, at least four issues emerge.

The Role of Supervisors in the EOR

The first implication involves the role of supervisors in the EOR. The analyses performed on the Ethics Resource Center data were exploratory in nature and were not driven by a theoretical prediction of the importance of supervisory support in the evolution of organizational ethics. However, they are nonetheless consistent with evidence from the organizational support literature that supervisors provide an important foundation for the EOR. This requires a closer look at perceived supervisory support (PSS), perceived organizational support (POS), and the EOR.

EOR research typically focuses on the exchange relationship between the employee and the organization. At the individual level, these exchange relationships include psychological contracts (Rousseau, 1995), POS (Eisenberger, Huntington, Hutchison, & Sowa, 1986), and leader–member exchange (LMX) (Graen & Uhl-Bien, 1995). Each points to the importance of understanding who represents the organization in the exchange relationship (Shore & Coyle-Shapiro, 2003). Because the implications of this are similar across the three domains, we will consider the case of POS as an illustration of the role of supervisors in the EOR.

The POS literature describes a process by which employees assess whether their organization values the contributions they make and cares about their well-being. Early research focused on POS as a global representation of organizational support. However, even this early work emphasized that perceptions of support must emanate from the actions of organizational actors, and employees may draw inferences from the favorable or unfavorable actions of their supervisors as indicative of support on the part of organizations (Eisenberger et al., 1986). Thus, early research paved the way for considering the role of supervisors in the EOR.

More recently, POS researchers have turned their attention explicitly to PSS and its relationship to POS. Evidence suggests PSS serves as an antecedent to POS (Eisenberger, Stinglhamber, Vandenberghe, Sucharski, & Rhoades, 2002; Shanock & Eisenberger, 2006). In doing so, it confirms the role immediate supervisors play in developing perceptions of general organizational support (POS), which, in turn, is viewed as a foundation of the EOR. This structured relationship between PSS and POS—that PSS serves as a foundation for POS—in conjunction with the Ethics Resource Center results presented earlier suggest supervisors might play a more central and explicit role in conceptualizing and modeling the EOR.

Some EOR scholars have recently integrated the role of supervisors into their work. For example, Zhang et al. (2008) explicitly integrate the role of supervisory support into research involving the EOR. However, one aspect of this research is noteworthy. Rather than PSS serving as a foundation for, a component of, or an indicator of the EOR, supervisory support and EOR were conceptualized as being distinct from one another. Zhang et al. proposed (and found) that supervisory support and an organization's EOR approach independently influence the level of trust that develops among middle managers. Further, they proposed (and found) that supervisory support moderates the relationship between the organization's EOR approach and trust.

One especially promising avenue for research on the role of supervisors in the EOR involves the concept of supervisor's organizational embodiment (SOE). Eisenberger et al. (2010) describe SOE as a belief by the individual employee that his or her supervisor's identity is shared with that of the organization. That is, a high-SOE employee believes praise or criticism from a supervisor reflects praise or criticism from the organization. Eisenberger et al. demonstrate that SOE moderates the relationship between LMX and affective commitment to the organization such that the relationship is stronger for high-SOE employees. However, perhaps as importantly for advancing our understanding of the central role played by supervisors in the EOR, Eisenberger et al. provide thoughts both about the processes by which SOE should operate (through both socioemotional and instrumental paths) and the levels at which it operates (both individual and collective).

In all, placing supervisors—and in particular the role of supervisory support—into models of the EOR is potentially both interesting and valuable. However, EOR scholars might benefit even more from considering supervisory support as an integral component of the EOR, rather than distinct from it.

The Structure of Multiple Psychological Contracts

Implications for EOR research exist beyond those focused on supervisors and supervisory support. They also include issues related to psychological contracts and the possible role of ethics as a more general foundation for thinking about the EOR from this perspective.

For example, the social exchange literature acknowledges that individuals establish exchange relationships with multiple others in organization settings. Establishing multiple exchange relationships implies individuals also establish psychological contracts with each of these exchange partners (Rousseau, 1989). To date, little research has explored the structure and importance of these multiple exchange relationships and multiple psychological contracts that result from them. Therefore, we do not know much about their implications for modeling the EOR.

More complex theorizing on the part of EOR scholars is needed in order to accommodate the existence of these multiple psychological contracts and their varied—and perhaps unstable—level of influence on employees. Theorizing about the conditions under which multiple relationships (and thus, multiple contracts) are likely to emerge, theorizing about the pattern of strong and weak relationships (and contracts) and the processes by which those patterns emerge, and theorizing about the conditions that would give rise to a dominant relationship (and contract) may all help to understand the EOR more fully.

Our earlier examination of ethics data reveals clues that may provide a preliminary foundation for such theorizing. For example, results showed that top management, supervisors, and coworkers each exerted a significant influence on the ethical pressures felt by employees. However, those influences differed depending on whether the outcome of interest was pressure to violate company standards or pressure to violate personal standards. Coworkers exerted a very modest impact on the pressure employees felt to violate company standards (standardized beta of .03, versus .17 and .25 for top management and supervisors, respectively). However, coworker influences were considerably stronger when predicting pressure to violate personal standards (standardized beta of .12), which was on par with the impact of top management (standardized beta of .15).

If part of the psychological contract between employees and organizations involves organizational ethics, these outcomes might be viewed as reflecting distinct components of the psychological contract. For example, the employee may view maintaining organizational ethical standards as an obligation to the organization, whereas organizational assistance in maintaining the employee's ethical standards may be viewed as an obligation on the part of the organization to the employee. These results suggest that potentially interesting asymmetries may emerge with respect to the importance of different relationships—and thus, different contracts—for different aspects of organizational ethics. As such, they provide a foundation for speculating about the process by which, and conditions under which, stronger and weaker contractual relationships might be expected to emerge.

Greenbaum, Folger, and Ford (in press) have formalized the notion of moral contracts in organizations. They argue that employees expect organizations to uphold obligations beyond those that relate only to the employee's well-being. In particular, employees expect organizations to uphold more general moral obligations as well. These expectations comprise a moral contract, and a breach of the moral contract may lead employees to experience psychological violation similar to that experienced as a result of violation of other psychological contracts.

The Role of Ethics as a Foundation for the EOR

A third implication for EOR research lies in considering organizational ethics not simply as an exemplar of the EOR process at work, but rather as a foundational component of the EOR in its own right, one reflecting an important aspect of the organizational context. Scholars point to the importance of context as a key influence on EOR. Tetrick et al. (2004) have taken up the issue of context explicitly, arguing that recent increases in the diversity of types of linkages between individuals and organizations make it increasingly important that scholars recognize the potential impact of context on the EOR. They suggest that EOR research should explore context as a primary research question, in that it has the potential to influence the locus of obligations in EORs.

Ethics scholars have long pointed to the ethical context of organizations, whether in the form of ethical climate (Schminke, Arnaud, & Kuenzi, 2007; Victor & Cullen, 1988) or ethical culture (Treviño, 1990), as an important contextual influence on employee behavior. The ethical context of organizations represents a prime candidate for such a contextual consideration of the EOR. As Tetrick et al. (2004) note, context surrounds the locus of obligations and contains the terms and conditions of the relationship. It provides both constraints and opportunities that influence the connections between individuals and their organizational contact points. Organizational ethics represent a key determinant of such constraints and opportunities, in that they represent normative judgments about appropriate social conduct (Green, 1994), "the principles, norms and standards of conduct governing an individual or group" (Treviño & Nelson, 1995, p. 12).

One path by which organizational ethics may influence the EOR, therefore, lies in the nature of the exchange relationships between the employee and the organization. Social exchange theory notes that work relationships emanate from reciprocal, ongoing interactions between employees and organizations. In these interactions, employees reciprocate the treatment they receive from others, including the organization (Cropanzano & Mitchell, 2005). When organizations treat employees well (e.g., ethically), the positive norm of reciprocity (Gouldner, 1960) dictates that employees will respond in kind (e.g., ethically), leading to high-quality relationships. However, Gouldner notes that negative behavior is reciprocated as well. Mistreatment of employees on the part of organizations (e.g., unethical treatment) activates the negative norm of reciprocity, prompting employees to respond to unethical treatment with unethical behavior of their own.

Cross-Cultural Effects

The chapters in this volume raise a number of intriguing issues with respect to the potential impact of culture on the EOR. Similarly, it is impossible to discuss ethics—and the potential for ethics to inform our thinking about the EOR—without considering cross-cultural issues as well. At a general level, the relative influence of coworkers, supervisors, and top managers on employee ethics and the EOR will depend on cultural differences like power distance (Hofstede, 2001). However, cultural issues pertaining to ethics present additional unique challenges as well.

One prominent approach to thinking about ethics from a cross-cultural perspective is known as integrative social contracts theory (ISCT) (Donaldson & Dunfee, 1994). ISCT seeks to balance the tension between localized ethical norms and universalistic ethical principles (hypernorms). Local norms are reflected in what Donaldson and Dunfee refer to as community-specific microcontracts, which represent shared understandings of the ethical norms relevant to a particular community. Hypernorms reflect a more general set of principles that apply across communities, thereby placing a higher order set of constraints on those responsible for establishing local norms. As such, hypernorms comprise a macrocontract that serves as a guide for evaluating lower level microcontracts. Although a single, unequivocal list of hypernorms has yet to emerge, Donaldson and Dunfee argue that the convergence of religious, cultural, and philosophical beliefs has allowed scholars to identify a foundational set of norms (often cast in the language of rights) that may be viewed as universal. These include the rights to physical security and well-being, political participation, informed consent, the ownership of property, the right to subsistence, and the obligation to respect the dignity of all individuals.

ISCT provides four basic principles for guiding the relationship between local and universal ethical norms: (1) Local communities may specify ethical norms for their members; (2) these microsocial contracts must be grounded in informed consent and supported by a right of exit; (3) in order to be valid, a microsocial contract must be compatible with hypernorms; and (4) if conflicts exist among norms that satisfy the first three principles (1 through 3), they are to be resolved by applying rules consistent with the spirit and letter of the macrosocial contract.

ISCT provides adequate flexibility for communities to establish different norms with respect to ethical issues, yet constrains the moral free space of those communities within certain parameters. As an illustration, consider the issue of gift-giving in business settings. Some communities may embrace gifts between parties, while others may prohibit it (so long as informed consent and right of exit are present). However, substantial gifts from a businessperson to a political official, which may intentionally or unintentionally subvert the political process, would not be considered valid in a microsocial contract because they violate the hypernorm of political participation in the macrosocial contract. That is, they negate the validity of others' participation in the open political system (Donaldson & Dunfee, 1994).

Because of this flexibility in allowing variation in local ethical norms while holding fast to a more macro-level set of ethical hypernorms, ISCT may provide a useful platform to consider cross-cultural issues in the EOR as well. This is especially true if, as suggested earlier, ethics may serve as a general foundation for thinking about the EOR, at least from a psychological contracts perspective.

In all, ethics—and the contextual manifestations of ethics in the form of ethical climate and ethical culture—represent a potentially important contextual factor in defining the terms and conditions of relationships and the constraints and opportunities facing each party in the relationship. The issue of how ethical theory and research might be integrated more directly into contextual considerations of the EOR is revisited below.

Implications for Ethics Research

Ethics researchers have not embraced fully the concept of the EOR and the role it might play in improving and expanding ethics research. Karnes (2009) is a partial exception, exploring from a historical perspective the changing relationship between employees and employers as a function of changes in the social contract between them. But even Karnes does not explicitly embrace the EOR as presented in this volume. Nowhere in the ethics literature do the basic building blocks of EOR research (e.g., social exchange, psychological contracts, and the employment relationship) appear center stage. Nor does the work of the EOR scholars that populate this volume appear prominently in theory development papers related to ethics. That should change. Embracing the EOR as a potential foundation of one or more streams of ethics research presents two considerable opportunities for ethics scholars.

Extending the Reach of Ethics Research

From a purely practical perspective, the apparent link between organizational ethics and the building blocks of EOR research presents a prime opportunity for ethics researchers to extend the impact of their work. Business ethics reflect normative judgments about what constitutes acceptable behavior in organizational settings. It is difficult to imagine how these standards of conduct could not be closely tied to the employee's organizational experiences and, thus, to the employee's relationship with the organization. This places business ethics squarely at the foot of the EOR.

A challenge often faced by ethics researchers is a tendency to be insular, often speaking to each other about issues that are of interest primarily to other ethics scholars and participating in scholarly give-and-take primarily among other ethics scholars. The EOR, its established conceptual frameworks, and its established record of scholars and scholarship offer ethics scholars a prime opportunity to adopt new ways of thinking, while at the same time taking their work to a broader audience to touch on issues of importance outside their immediate domain.

Insights From the Building Blocks of EOR

Beyond the practical implications of a broader impact for the work of ethics researchers, the EOR presents scholarly implications as well. The most significant of these may be that it opens access to the well-established family of concepts and constructs that provides the foundation for EOR research, including social exchange, psychological contracts, LMX, POS, and the employment relationship.

For example, the most comprehensive recent review of the organizational ethics literature (Treviño, Weaver, & Reynolds, 2006) makes no mention of the EOR per se. Further, it makes only passing reference to social exchange and no reference at all to the concepts typically viewed as representing the exchange relationship (e.g., psychological contracts, POS, LMX, and the employment relationship). This is not the fault of the review. A review cannot shine light on research that does not exist. It is rather a comment on the extent to which ethics scholars have failed to draw upon well-developed models and concepts that have great promise for adding to our understanding of organizational ethics. Each of these constructs holds potential for ethics research and researchers, for extending both the power and reach of models of organizational ethics.

Social exchange is the only component of EOR research that appears to occupy a significant role in current ethics research. Research on ethical leadership builds on the premise that it matters, at least in part, due to norms of reciprocity (Blau, 1964), employees will react to caring and fair leaders in positive ways. However, although social exchange has found its way into conversations about organizational ethics, neither of its primary indicators—POS and LMX—plays a significant role in current ethics research. Yet as indicators of quality of social exchange (and thus, of the EOR), both present opportunities for ethics researchers to develop a more refined picture of the interplay between ethics and the quality of the relationship individuals have with their organizations. In the next section, we look at these and other issues as potential avenues for future research.

LOOKING TO THE FUTURE

For authors and readers alike, one of the most significant benefits of a volume like this is its ability to juxtapose interesting and important—but often unconnected—concepts with one another. In doing so, new connections may initiate ideas for creative and useful research that were previously overlooked. Overlaying ethics research on the EOR has the potential to do that. Several potentially interesting research ideas emerge as a result.

For example, each of the topics outlined in the earlier Implications for EOR and Ethics Researchers section represents a potentially productive stream of research. As noted there, research has not yet fully integrated the role of the supervisor into models of EOR. Scholars have not yet come to grips with how best to think about and to model the multiple psychological contracts any one employee wrestles with. EOR scholars have not embraced the potential importance of ethics into their EOR frameworks, and ethics scholars have not recognized the potential value of thinking about how the foundational concepts of EOR could inform thinking about organizational ethics. Each of these represents potentially useful paths for additional work. But beyond these broad strokes, the material covered in this chapter raises several more specific opportunities for meaningful research.

Looking Deeper Into the Ethics Literature

If, as argued earlier, ethics provide a basic foundation for the relationship employees experience with their organizations, then EOR scholars might benefit from looking deeper into the ethics literature for inspiration about the next generation of EOR research. Both traditional and emerging approaches to studying organizational ethics could provide relevant foundations. We explore two possibilities here: multidimensional models and the role of emotion.

Multidimensional Models of Moral Behavior

Rest's (1986) four-component model of ethical behavior changed the face of ethics research. Rest noted that four factors are necessary for the emergence of moral behavior: (1) moral sensitivity, (2) moral judgment, (3) moral motivation, and (4) moral character. Moral sensitivity allows an actor to recognize a situation as involving a moral issue. Moral judgment provides an individual with the tools for assessing the correct course of action. However, knowing what to do is not the same as actually doing it. Although an actor might identify the correct course of action from a moral perspective, other values (e.g., safety, economic, power) may be deemed more important than one's moral values in a given situation. When that occurs, motivation to pursue the morally correct course of action diminishes. Finally, even if an individual recognizes a moral event exists, selects the moral course of action, and values moral outcomes, most situations require a level of moral character to ensure follow-through. Such character reflects an individual's moral courage and ability to overcome obstacles in seeing intentions through to outcomes.

Considerable ethics research and even reviews of ethics research (see the review by Treviño et al. [2006] of the behavioral ethics literature as an example) have embraced Rest's (1986) multidimensional perspective on the sources of ethical action as a general organizing framework. It may be possible that a similar structure could apply to the EOR. A multidimensional model of the EOR would allow scholars to break the EOR into component parts—EOR sensitivity, EOR judgment, EOR motivation, and EOR character—each of which might provide scholars with a finer-grained picture of the processes by which the EOR emerges and the impacts it exerts on employees and the organization.

For example, EOR sensitivity may represent an important individual-difference variable. Certain individuals may enter the workplace with more sensitive "radar screens" for issues relating to their relationship with their organization. As such, they would be more likely to notice, and to react to, issues related to the EOR such as quality of exchange relationship, contract violations, and so on.

Even if an employee is sensitive to EOR issues (e.g., LMX, POS, or contract violation), the employee may not have well-considered, well-defined positions on what constitutes an appropriate EOR or an appropriate response to a faltering EOR. Such an employee may be thought of as being deficient on EOR judgment. Likewise, an employee might notice EOR issues when they emerge (sensitivity) and might even harbor thoughtful positions about appropriate responses to those issues (judgment), but if the importance of other factors such as economic security, serious health issues, or a burning passion for a nonwork hobby or political cause has pushed EOR issues to the back burner, motivation to respond to EOR issues will be low. Finally, even if an employee is sensitive to EOR issues, has thoughtful responses prepared, and EOR concerns are among his or her top priorities, the issue of EOR character—perhaps better framed as EOR efficacy in this context—would remain. Does the employee have the tools, courage, ability, or other contingencies necessary to respond to the EOR relationship in the manner in which the employee would prefer?

EOR scholars might benefit from such a multidimensional approach. For example, research shows large, unexplained variation in the strength of the relationship between LMX and various outcomes (Gerstner & Day, 1997). To date, reasons for such variation have been largely speculative. However, a four-component model like this offers four distinct paths through which scholars might probe the causes of such ambiguities it the literature. Are some individuals—or perhaps more importantly, types of individuals—simply not sensitive to EOR issues? Are some lacking in understanding of what constitutes appropriate responses to various EOR states? Are some motivated by events beyond those reflected in the EOR? And do some wish to react to their EOR situation but find they cannot, due to a lack of tools, courage, or training? The answer to all four of these questions is undoubtedly yes. The challenge for EOR scholars is to unpack the processes by which each might influence the development of—and reactions to—the EOR.

The Role of Emotion

Recent neuroscience research on ethical judgments and behavior points to emotion as a critical component of the ethical decision-making process

(Greene, Nystrom, Engell, Darley, & Cohen, 2004; Greene, Sommerville, Nystrom, Darley, & Cohen, 2001; Koenigs et al., 2007; Moll & de Oliveira-Souza 2007). The importance of emotion in ethics has not been of interest only to neuroscience scholars. Ethics research based in psychology (Krettenauer & Eichler, 2006; Moore, Clark, & Kane, 2008; Valdesolo & DeSteno, 2006; Vélez García & Ostrosky-Solís, 2006), organizational studies (Gaudine & Thorne, 2001; Sekerka & Bagozzi, 2007), and moral education (Morton, Worthley, Testerman, & Mahoney, 2006; Walker, Pitts, Henning, & Matsuba, 1995) has offered theoretical and empirical perspectives on the critical role emotion plays as a part of the moral judgment and behavior process as well.

By contrast, the EOR literature is largely silent on the role of emotion as a component of the EOR or its development. EOR scholars are aware of the role emotion may play in how employees interact with and respond to their organizations. For example, a meta-analysis by Zhao, Wayne, Glibkowski, and Bravo (2007) reveals that psychological contract breach is related to the affective reactions of violation and mistrust. Further, in Chapter 6 of this volume, Shore and Coyle-Shapiro reference the potential negative emotional reactions employees may experience as a result of distrust that may emanate from negative EORs. Similarly, in Chapter 18 of this volume, Tetrick notes potential health issues that may arise from employees' emotional reactions to their relationship with their organization.

All of these efforts consider emotion as a reaction to the EOR, rather than its role in the formation of the EOR, its underlying psychological contracts, and so on. The modest emphasis placed on emotion in research concerning the development of the EOR is surprising in that it plays such a central role in the theoretical foundations of the EOR. For example, Rousseau's early work on psychological contracts (e.g., Rousseau, 1990; Rousseau & McLean Parks, 1993) emphasizes the importance of emotion in social contracts by framing relational contracts as exhibiting a socioemotional focus.

Of course, modeling the role of emotion as a component of the EOR would not be a straightforward transfer of its role in the ethical decision-making literature. EOR research does not rest as heavily on understanding a specific decision-making process as does ethics research. However, research shows emotion plays a critical role in the formation of judgments more broadly (Damasio, 1994; Etzioni, 1988; Pizarro, 2000), and employee judgments certainly comprise an important component of the process by which the EOR comes into focus. Thus, exploring the role of emotion in the EOR may provide an important extension of current EOR research.

POS, PSS, and Ethics

Results from the Ethics Resource Center data point to supervisors, and in particular to supervisory support, as a critical component in understanding the relationship between the organization and employee and the impact of that relationship on ethical outcomes. Initial results focused on the pressure employees feel to behave unethically. One extension of this work would be to explore the impact of top management, supervisors, and coworkers on a broader array of ethical outcomes. Understanding the factors that exert pressure on employees to violate ethical standards is valuable. But ethics officers and ethics scholars are interested in more than just whether employees feel pressure. They are interested in whether that pressure converts to unethical action. They are interested in whether employees develop a greater awareness of the ethical issues that surround them. They are interested in whether employees are willing to report unethical behavior when they encounter it. Considerable additional research is needed to determine whether supervisors play the leading role in determining these and other ethics-related outcomes or whether other organizational contact points (top management, coworkers) exert more profound influences on other types of outcomes.

In addition, the data suggest supervisory support plays a strong role in influencing ethical outcomes. But the data do not provide a clear picture of what supervisory support with respect to ethics really means. Is supervisory ethical support distinct from general PSS? If so, it suggests a potentially complex relationship between the employee and the organization with respect to support. It suggests not only that employees may experience generalized perceptions of supervisory and organizational support (PSS and POS, respectively), but also that ethics-specific support may exist and may matter, at both levels. Therefore, we could conceive of four distinct types of support (PSS, PSS-Ethics, POS, and POS-Ethics), all of which could play a role in shaping the EOR.

Researching these issues—whether ethics-specific forms of support exist alongside general POS and PSS assessments, and whether they influence different ethical outcomes differently—would be challenging but straightforward. Existing measures of POS and PSS could be employed alongside modified versions that tap employee perceptions of ethics-specific support. Paired with a broader array of ethical outcome variables (e.g., ethical awareness, ethical behavior, reporting behavior, and so on), researchers could assess whether PSS and POS generalize to ethical support and the extent to which different types of support are related to different outcomes. Doing so would provide direct insights for ethics scholars interested in the role played by support in shaping organizational ethics. It would also provide an indirect view into the relationship between global and facet-specific (e.g., ethical) support that may contribute to a deeper understanding of the relationship between support and the EOR.

Ethics and the Employment Relationship

This chapter has not delved into the portion of EOR research that explores employment relationships from the perspective of the employer. For example, Tsui et al. (1997) propose a typology of four employment relationships organizations may create, each of which reflects a particular set of expectations on the part of both employer and employee.

Two of these approaches reflect balanced exchanges between employers and employees. A *quasi-spot contract* relationship reflects a closed-ended, short-term, nearly purely economic exchange between employer and employee. The employer offers short-term economic rewards for performing specific tasks, and neither party expects additional contributions or inducements beyond those specified in the employment agreement. As a result, employees are not expected to perform tasks beyond those specified, nor are they expected to demonstrate concern for the welfare of other organization members or even the organization itself. A *mutual investment* relationship is also a balanced relationship, but reflects a more open-ended, long-term social exchange relationship. Employer inducements go beyond short-term economic payoffs, extending to longer term employee well-being and development. Employees in turn contribute beyond formal job requirements and are willing to invest in learning firm-specific skills that may not be marketable outside the firm.

Two other approaches reflect unbalanced exchanges. An *underinvestment* approach exists when employees are expected to embrace broad and open-ended obligations to the employer, who responds with only short-term, economic inducements. An *overinvestment* approach exists when employees perform only a limited, well-specified, job-specific set of activities, while the organization offers open-ended, long-term, broad-ranging inducements (Tsui et al., 1997).

Interestingly, although a mutual investment approach leads to high performance on the part of both individuals and firms, research reveals it appears in only about 30% of firms studied. Why that is true remains a puzzle, but such employment relationship choices on the part of employers may have significant implications for understanding organizational ethics.

As an illustration, consider the issue of ethics training. Scholars and practitioners alike devote enormous attention to the question of how to develop effective ethics training. Research has focused on the characteristics of the trainee, the design of the training program, the transferability of training back to the job, and the challenges of evaluating training effectiveness as all contributing to the ethics training effectiveness (Wells & Schminke, 2001). However, the role of the employment relationship itself, as an important component of the context in which the ethics training occurs, has not been considered, and its impact could be considerable.

For example, in a quasi-spot contract arrangement, ethics training would be expected to be of limited effectiveness, regardless of the characteristics of the trainee, design of the program, transferability of the training, and evaluation of training effectiveness. Rather, ethical behavior would be likely to result only by integrating explicit, legalistic behavioral rules into the performance assessment system, rules capable of translating specific behaviors into specific economic rewards. However, even if precise behavioral guidelines could be developed, implemented, and accurately assessed, research shows compliance-based ethics programs to be of limited use (Weaver & Treviño, 1999).

In contrast, a mutual investment relationship may represent rich soil for the type of values-based programs shown to be effective in creating and maintaining ethical organization environments. Effective ethics programs emphasize a constellation of ethical values as a guide for ethical behavior. Once internalized, these values then set the stage for continued ethical activity on the part of employees who are committed to upholding organizational ideals (Weaver & Treviño, 1999).

This example of ethics training also reiterates an important point made earlier, that an organization's ethics may influence how it treats its employees in terms of the EOR. For example, the Tsui et al. (1997) framework suggests the nature of the employment relationship is a choice to be made by employers. Ultimately, that is true. Organizations do dictate the type of employment relationships they engage in with their employees. However, previous actions on the part of the employer may serve to constrain the choices it has with respect to employment relationship types.

As noted earlier, the negative norm of reciprocity (Gouldner, 1960) suggests employees will respond to negative treatment on the part of their organization with negative behavior of their own. Thus, unethical organizational treatment will lead to unethical behavior on the part of employees. Repeated instances may result in a spiral of unethical treatment and reactions, reflecting Masuch's (1985) concept of vicious circles, in which discrete negative organizational actions in organizations may lead to harmful, structurally persistent conditions in the organization. As Masuch notes, "once caught in a vicious circle, human actors continue on a path of action that leads further and further away from the desired state of affairs" (p. 23). In the case of unethical treatment of employees, and subsequent unethical reactions on the part of employees, an organization may find its choices limited with respect to the type of employment relationship to pursue. More specifically, the deterioration of trust, liking, and respect that may result from such a downward ethical spiral may remove social exchange as a possibility for organizing the EOR. Rather, the organization may view economic exchange relationships as the only viable option for coping with unethical employees (which they have, perhaps unknowingly, produced).

To date, ethics researchers have done an admirable job of considering a variety of contextual factors capable of shaping the ethical environment of organizations, including ethical culture, ethical climate, leadership, reward systems, and codes of ethics (Treviño et al., 2006). However, a focus on the structure of the EOR as implemented by the employer has not yet been considered as an important component of the ethical environment. Evidence suggests it should be.

CONCLUSION

The goal of this chapter has been to explore the potential benefits of integrating EOR and ethics research. Doing so allows us to address the important question of who represents the organization in the EOR. Ethics research provides evidence that multiple organizational contact points have the potential to influence the relationship between the employee and the organization; top management, supervisors, and coworkers may all play a role. But among these, preliminary evidence suggests supervisors may be more likely to occupy that role than other organization members.

The conversation in this chapter has implications for EOR and ethics scholars alike. It encourages EOR scholars to consider more closely the role supervisors play. Further, it argues that ethics may represent one of the foundations of the EOR, and as such, what constitutes an attractive ethical context may be applied directly to understanding what constitutes an attractive EOR as well. However, beyond these specific applications of ethics research to the issues of EOR, this chapter has argued that a more general consideration of how the thinking, models, and constructs that comprise both ethics and EOR research might fruitfully be brought to bear on issues and problems faced by the other. Each has the opportunity to gain useful insights from the other.

REFERENCES

Armstrong, R. W., Williams, R. J., & Barrett, J. D. (2004). The impact of banality, risky shift and escalating commitment on ethical decision making. *Journal of Business Ethics, 53*, 365–370.

Ashkanasy, N. M., Windsor, C. A., & Treviño, L. K. (2006). Bad apples in bad barrels revisited: Cognitive moral development, just world beliefs, rewards, and ethical decision making. *Business Ethics Quarterly, 16*, 449–473.

Bell, S. J., & Menguc, B. (2002). The employee-organization relationship, organizational citizenship behaviors, and superior service quality. *Journal of Retailing, 78*, 131–146.

Blau, P. (1964). *Exchange and power in social life.* New York, NY: John Wiley.

Bowen, S. A. (2004). Organizational factors encouraging ethical decision making: An exploration into the case of an exemplar. *Journal of Business Ethics, 52*, 311–324.

Brown, M. E., Treviño, L. K., & Harrison, D. A. (2005). Ethical leadership: A social learning perspective for construct development and testing. *Organizational Behavior and Human Decision Processes, 97*, 117–134.

Cropanzano, R., & Mitchell, M. S. (2005). Social exchange theory: An interdisciplinary review. *Journal of Management, 31*, 874–900.

Damasio, A. (1994). *Descartes' error: Emotion, reason and the human brain.* New York, NY: Penguin Books.

Donaldson, T., & Dunfee, T. W. (1994). Toward a unified conception of business ethics: Integrative social contracts theory. *Academy of Management Review, 19*, 252–284.

Drake, B. H., Meckler, M., & Stephens, D. (2002). Transitional ethics: Responsibilities of supervisors for supporting employee development. *Journal of Business Ethics, 38,* 141–155.

Eisenberger, R., Huntington, R., Hutchison, S., & Sowa, D. (1986). Perceived organizational support. *Journal of Applied Psychology, 71,* 500–507.

Eisenberger, R., Karagonlar, G., Stinglhamber, F., Neves, P., Becker, T. E., Gonzalez-Morales, M. G., & Steiger-Mueller, M. (2010). Leader-member exchange and affective organizational commitment: The contribution of supervisor's organizational embodiment. *Journal of Applied Psychology, 95,* 1085–1103.

Eisenberger, R., Stinglhamber, F., Vandenberghe, C., Sucharski, I. L., & Rhoades, L. (2002). Perceived supervisor support: Contributions to perceived organizational support and employee retention. *Journal of Applied Psychology, 87,* 565–573.

Etzioni, A. (1988). *The moral dimension: Toward a new economics.* New York, NY: Free Press.

Fraedrich, J., & Iyer, R. (2008). Retailers' major ethical decision making constructs. *Journal of Business Research, 61,* 834–841.

Gaudine, A., & Thorne, L. (2001). Emotion and ethical decision-making in organizations. *Journal of Business Ethics, 31,* 175–188.

Gerstner, C. R., & Day, D. V. (1997). Meta-analytic review of leader-member exchange theory: Correlates and construct issues. *Journal of Applied Psychology, 82,* 827–844.

Ghosh, D. (2008). Corporate values, workplace decisions and ethical standards of employees. *Journal of Managerial Issues, 20,* 68–87.

Gouldner, A. (1960). The norm of reciprocity. *American Sociological Review, 25,* 161–178.

Graen, G. B., & Uhl-Bien, M. (1995). Relationship-based approach to leadership: Development of leader-member exchange (LMX) theory of leadership over 25 years. *Leadership Quarterly, 6,* 219–247.

Green, R. M. (1994). *The ethical manager.* New York, NY: Macmillan.

Greenbaum, R. L., Folger, R., & Ford, R. (in press). Moral psychological contract. In S. Gilliland, D. Steiner, & D. Skarlicki (Eds.), *Organizational justice and ethics: Research in social issues in management* (Vol. 7). Charlotte, NC: Information Age Publishing.

Greene, J. D., Nystrom, L. E., Engell, A. D., Darley, J. M., & Cohen, J. D. (2004). The neural bases of cognitive conflict and control in moral judgment. *Neuron, 44,* 389–400.

Greene, J. D., Sommerville, R. B., Nystrom, L. E., Darley, J. M., & Cohen, J. D. (2001). An fMRI investigation of emotional engagement in moral judgment. *Science, 293,* 2105–2109.

Hofstede, G. (2001). *Culture's consequences* (2nd ed.). Thousand Oaks, CA: Sage.

Husted, B. W., & Allen, D. B. (2008). Toward a model of cross-cultural business ethics: The impact of individualism and collectivism on the ethical decision-making process. *Journal of Business Ethics, 82,* 293–305.

Jones, T. M. (1991). Ethical decision making by individuals in organizations: An issue-contingent model. *Academy of Management Review, 16,* 366–395.

Karnes, R. E. (2009). A change in business ethics: The impact on employer-employee relations. *Journal of Business Ethics, 87,* 189–197.

Koenigs, M., Young, L., Adolphs, R., Tranel, D., Cushman, F., Hauser, M., & Damasio, A. (2007). Damage to the prefrontal cortex increases utilitarian moral judgments. *Nature, 446,* 908–911.

Kohlberg, L. (1984). *The psychology of moral development.* San Francisco: Harper & Row.

Krettenauer, T., & Eichler, D. (2006). Adolescents' self-attributed moral emotions following a moral transgression: Relations with delinquency, confidence in moral judgment and age. *British Journal of Developmental Psychology, 24*, 489–506.

Masuch, M. (1985). Vicious circles in organizations. *Administrative Science Quarterly, 30*, 14–33.

Mayer, D. M., Kuenzi, M., Greenbaum, R., Bardes, M., & Salvador, R. (2009). How low does ethical leadership flow? Test of a trickle-down model. *Organizational Behavior and Human Decision Processes, 108*, 1–13.

Moll, J., & de Oliveira-Souza, R. (2007). Moral judgments, emotions and the utilitarian brain. *Trends in Cognitive Science, 11*, 319–321.

Moore, A. B., Clark, B. A., & Kane, M. J. (2008). Who shalt not kill? Individual differences in working memory capacity, executive control, and moral judgment. *Psychological Science, 19*, 549–557.

Morton, K. R., Worthley, J. S., Testerman, J. K., & Mahoney, M. L. (2006). Defining features of moral sensitivity and moral motivation: Pathways to moral reasoning in medical students. *Journal of Moral Education, 35*, 387–406.

Neubert, M. J., Carlson, D. S., Kacmar, K. M., Roberts, J. A., & Chonko, L. B. (2009). The virtuous influence of ethical leadership behavior: Evidence from the field. *Journal of Business Ethics, 90*, 157–170.

O'Leary, C., & Pangemanan, G. (2007). The effect of groupwork on ethical decision-making of accountancy students. *Journal of Business Ethics, 75*, 215–228.

Pizarro, D. (2000). Nothing more than feelings? The role of emotions in moral judgment. *Journal for the Theory of Social Behaviour, 30*, 355–376.

Rest, J. R. (1986). *Moral development: Advances in research and theory.* New York, NY: Praeger.

Ribeiro-Soriano, D., & Urbano, D. (2010). Employee-organization relationship in collective entrepreneurship: an overview. *Journal of Organizational Change Management, 23*, 349–359.

Rousseau, D. M. (1989). Psychological and implied contracts in organizations. *Employee Responsibilities and Rights Journal, 2*, 121–139.

Rousseau, D. M. (1990). New hire perceptions of their own and their employer's obligations: A study of psychological contracts. *Journal of Organizational Behavior, 11*, 389–400.

Rousseau, D. M. (1995). *Psychological contracts in organizations: Understanding written and unwritten agreements.* Thousand Oaks, CA: Sage Publications.

Rousseau, D. M., & McLean Parks, J. (1993). The contracts of individuals and organizations. In L. L. Cummings & B. M. Staw (Eds.), *Research in organizational behavior* (pp. 1–47). Greenwich, CT: JAI Press.

Schmidtke, J. M. (2007). The relationship between social norm consensus, perceived similarity, and observer reactions to coworker theft. *Human Resource Management, 46*, 561–582.

Schminke, M., Ambrose, M. L., & Neubaum, D. (2005). The effect of leader moral development on ethical climate and employee attitudes. *Organizational Behavior and Human Decision Processes, 97*, 135–151.

Schminke, M., Arnaud, A. U., & Kuenzi, M. (2007). The power of ethical work climates. *Organizational Dynamics, 36*, 171–186.

Schwartz, M. S., Dunfee, T. W., & Kline, M. J. (2005). Tone at the top: An ethics code for directors? *Journal of Business Ethics, 58*, 79–100.

Sekerka, L. E., & Bagozzi, R. P. (2007). Moral courage in the workplace: Moving to and from the desire and decision to act. *Business Ethics: A European Review, 16*, 132–149.

Shanock, L. R., & Eisenberger, R. (2006). When supervisors feel supported: Relationships with subordinates' perceived supervisor support, perceived organizational support, and performance. *Journal of Applied Psychology, 91*, 689–695.

Shaw, J. D., Dineen, B. R., Fang, R, & Vellella, R. F. (2009). Employee-organization exchange relationships, HRM practices, and quit rates of good and poor performers. *Academy of Management Journal, 52*, 1016–1033.

Shore, L. M., Bommer, W. H., Rao, A. N., & Seo, J. (2009). Social and economic exchange in the employee-organization relationship: The moderating role of reciprocation wariness. *Journal of Managerial Psychology, 24*, 701–721.

Shore, L. M., & Coyle-Shapiro, J. A.-M. (2003). New developments in the employee-organization relationship. *Journal of Organizational Behavior, 24*, 443–450.

Tetrick, L. E., Taylor, M. S., Coyle-Shapiro, J., Liden, R., McLean Parks, J., Morrison, E. W., … Van Dyne, L. (2004). The employee-organization relationship: A timely concept in a period of transition. In J. Martocchio (Ed.), *Research in personnel and human resources management* (pp. 291–370). Greenwich, CT: JAI Press.

Toor, S., & Ofori, G. (2009). Ethical leadership: Examining the relationships with full range leadership model, employee outcomes, and organizational culture. *Journal of Business Ethics, 90*, 533–547.

Treviño, L. K. (1986). Ethical decision making in organizations: A person-situation interactionist model. *Academy of Management Review, 11*, 601–617.

Treviño, L. K. (1990). A cultural perspective on changing and developing organizational ethics. In R. Woodman & W. Passmore (Eds.), *Research in organizational change and development* (pp. 195–230). Greenwich, CT: JAI.

Treviño, L. K., & Nelson, K. A. (1995). *Managing business ethics: Straight talk about how to do it right.* New York, NY: John Wiley & Sons.

Treviño, L. K., Weaver, G. R., & Brown, M. E. (2008). It's lovely at the top: Hierarchical levels, identities, and perceptions of organizational ethics. *Business Ethics Quarterly, 18*, 233–252.

Treviño, L. K., Weaver, G. R., & Reynolds, S. J. (2006). Behavioral ethics in organizations: A review. *Journal of Management, 32*, 951–990.

Treviño, L. K., & Youngblood, S. A. (1990). Bad apples in bad barrels: A causal analysis of ethical decision-making behavior. *Journal of Applied Psychology, 75*, 378–385.

Tsui, A. S., Pearce, J. L., Porter, L. W., & Tripoli, A. M. (1997). Alternative approaches to the employee-organization relationship: Does investment in employees pay off? *Academy of Management Journal, 40*, 1089–1121.

Valdesolo, P., & DeSteno, D. (2006). Manipulations of emotional context shape moral judgment. *Psychological Science, 17*, 476–477.

Vélez García, A., & Ostrosky-Solís, F. (2006). From morality to moral emotions. *International Journal of Psychology, 41*, 348–354.

Victor, B., & Cullen, J. B. (1988). The organizational bases of ethical work climates. *Administrative Science Quarterly, 33*, 101–125.

Walker, L. J., Pitts, R. C., Hennig, K. H., & Matsuba, M. K. (1995). Reasoning about morality and real-life moral problems. In M. Killen & D. Hart (Eds.), *Morality in everyday life: Developmental perspectives* (pp. 371–407). Berkeley, CA: Cambridge University Press.

Walumbwa, F. O., & Schaubroeck, J. (2009). Leader personality traits and employee voice behavior: Mediating roles of ethical leadership and work group psychological safety. *Journal of Applied Psychology, 94*, 1275–1286.

Weaver, G. R., & Treviño, L. K. (1999). Compliance and values oriented ethics programs: Influences on employees' attitudes and behavior. *Business Ethics Quarterly, 9*, 315–335.

Weaver, G. R., Treviño, L. K., & Cochran, P. L. (1999). Corporate ethics programs as control systems: Influences of executive commitment and environmental factors. *Academy of Management Journal, 42*, 539–552.

Weber, J. (1990). Managers' moral reasoning: Assessing their responses to three moral dilemmas. *Human Relations, 43*, 687–702.

Weber, J. (2010). Assessing the "tone at the top": The moral reasoning of CEOs in the automobile industry. *Journal of Business Ethics, 92*, 167–182.

Wells, D. L., & Schminke, M. (2001). Ethical development and human resources training: An integrative framework. *Human Resource Management Review, 11*, 135–158.

Zey-Ferrell, M., & Ferrell, O. C. (1982). Role-set configuration and opportunity as predictors of unethical behavior in organizations. *Human Relations, 35*, 587–604.

Zey-Ferrell, M., Weaver, K. M., & Ferrell, O. C. (1979). Predicting unethical behavior among marketing practitioners. *Human Relations, 32*, 557–569.

Zhang, A. Y., Tsui, A. S., Song, L. J., Li, C., & Jia, L. (2008). How do I trust thee? The employee-organization relationship, supervisory support, and middle manager trust in the organization. *Human Resource Management, 47*, 111–132.

Zhao, H., Wayne, S. J., Glibkowski, B. C., & Bravo, J. (2007). The impact of psychological contract breach on work-related outcomes: A meta-analysis. *Personnel Psychology, 60*, 647–680.

4

Social Identity-Based Leadership and the Employee–Organization Relationship

Daan van Knippenberg
Rotterdam School of Management
Erasmus University Rotterdam

The psychological linkage between individuals and their employing organization plays an important role in motivating organizational behavior. Recognition of this fact continues to invite academic as well as managerial attempts to understand and manage this relationship. These attempts typically revolve around the strength of the employee–organization relationship: Stronger psychological linkage is seen as yielding more positive outcomes in terms of employee performance, extra-role behavior, retention, and the like (Meyer, Stanley, Herscovitch, & Topolnytsky, 2002; Rhoades & Eisenberger, 2002; Riketta, 2005). Yet, there is more to the psychology of the employee–organization relationship than its strength. Comparison of the two major theoretical perspectives on the psychology of the employment relationship, the social exchange perspective (Blau, 1964; Shore et al., 2004) and the social identity perspective (Ashforth & Mael, 1989; Hogg & Terry, 2000), suggests that a comprehensive understanding of the psychology of the employee–organization relationship should include a consideration of not only its strength but also of its basis in social exchange or in social identification. In addition, a social identity analysis also points to the importance of considering employees' understanding of organizational identity—an understudied issue to say the least, but one that may have great importance for the way the psychological linkage between employee and organization expresses itself in behavior.

Whereas the dominant understanding of the employment relationship is one of a social exchange relationship in which employee and organization are distinct partners (Shore et al., 2004), a social identity analysis understands this relationship in terms of self-conception in which the sense of self and organization are merged (Ashforth & Mael, 1989; Pratt, 1998; Tyler & Blader, 2000; van Knippenberg, 2000a). Social exchange and social identity conceptualizations are not in opposition but represent different forms the psychological linkage of employee and organization may take (van Knippenberg & Sleebos, 2006; van Knippenberg, van Dick, & Tavares, 2007). Even so, an understanding of the employee–organization relationship may benefit from closer consideration of these differences in the nature of the psychological linkage between individual and organization, as they are likely to have both different causes and different consequences.

The strong focus on the strength, or quality, of the employment relationship is also associated with relatively little attention to individuals' understanding of the entity they have a relationship with. A social identity analysis points to cognitive representations of the organizational identity as an important source of influence on individuals' attitudes and behavior (Hogg & Terry, 2000; Turner, Hogg, Oakes, Reicher, & Wetherell, 1987), and this too is an issue that warrants fuller consideration in developing our understanding of the employment relationship.

These, then, are the issues that assume center stage in the current analysis. Although these issues concern the employee–organization relationship more generally, I adopt the perspective of leadership in developing this analysis. Consistent with the notion that the relationship with the organization is first and foremost played out "locally" in the immediate work environment (van Knippenberg & van Schie, 2000; Ashforth & Rogers, Chapter 2, this volume), leaders as representatives of the organization fulfill an important role in shaping the psychological experience of the employment relationship. The advantage of this leadership perspective is that leadership is the arena in which these social identity issues have been most extensively studied, making leadership the natural angle on the matter at hand—an issue that will become more apparent as I elaborate on it below.

LEADERSHIP AND THE EMPLOYMENT RELATIONSHIP: SOCIAL EXCHANGE OR SOCIAL IDENTITY?

It has long been recognized that individuals develop a psychological linkage with their employing organization and that this bond may motivate behavior that serves the organization in one way or the other. This begs the question of both theoretical and applied relevance of how this bond may be influenced to reap the benefits of a strong psychological linkage between the individual and the organization. Leadership is an obvious angle in this respect because leadership may be the most direct and flexible way in which management can influence employees (i.e., as compared to, for instance, more institutionalized human resource practices). Indeed, the essence of leadership is influence, and leadership effectiveness is typically understood in terms of leaders' success in influencing followers (e.g., Kaiser, Hogan, & Craig, 2008; van Knippenberg, 2012a).

Clearly, leaders are not "the organization"; they are its representatives. Because "the organization" is an abstraction, a social construction, however, the relationship with the organization is often understood through the relationship with its representatives (Levinson, 1965). Leaders thus may play a key role in shaping the psychological relationship between employee and organization (Sluss & Ashforth, 2007), especially the more they are perceived to be its representatives (Sluss & Ashforth, 2008; Sluss, Ployhart, & Cobb, 2010; cf. van Knippenberg et al., 2007). Not surprisingly then, there is a wealth of evidence that leadership can have a positive influence on indicators of the psychological bond between employee and organization (Meyer et al., 2002; Rhoades & Eisenberger, 2002; van Knippenberg, van Knippenberg, De Cremer, & Hogg, 2004). There are two distinct conceptual perspectives on the psychology of the employee–organization relationship, however, and these are associated with rather distinct leadership perspectives.

The first is the social exchange perspective. With its long-running tradition (e.g., Blau, 1964; Levinson, 1965; Shore et al., 2004) and strong presence in research in employee–organization relationships, it can easily be classified as the dominant perspective in the field. Core in the social exchange perspective is the assumption that the relationship between employees and their employer is built on the trade of effort and loyalty for benefits such as pay, support, and recognition (Rhoades & Eisenberger, 2002; Rousseau & McLean Parks, 1993). This exchange is proposed to flow from a norm of reciprocity: Benefits received hold an obligation to repay in kind (Eisenberger, Armeli, Rexwinkel, Lynch, & Rhoades, 2001; Gouldner, 1960). Therefore, the more one "gets" from the organization, the more one is under the obligation to "give." Put differently, higher quality exchange relationships with the organization should be reflected in more motivation to exert oneself on behalf of the organization and to remain within the organization. Note that social exchange is not limited to the exchange of materials goods, but also includes the exchange of such immaterial goods as respect, recognition, and friendship. The issue remains, however, that in the social exchange perspective relationship quality is contingent on reciprocity in exchange (Sparrowe & Liden, 1997).

Support for the social exchange perspective on the employment relationship is abundant. For instance, the concept of perceived organizational support, the extent to which the organization is perceived to value the individual's contribution and to care about the individual's well-being (Eisenberger, Huntington, Hutchison, & Sowa, 1986), was proposed to reflect the individual's evaluation of the organization's role in the exchange relationship. In support of the social exchange analysis, meta-analytic evidence shows that perceived organizational support is strongly related to organizational commitment, the most widely studied indicator of the psychological linkage between individual and organization (Meyer & Allen, 1997; Mowday, Porter, & Steers, 1982). One way of paraphrasing this is to say that if the organization shows its commitment to the employee, the employee repays in kind (Eisenberger et al., 1986; also see Rousseau & McLean Parks, 1993). Perceived organizational support is also associated with a range of outcomes such as performance and extra-role behavior that organizations would be keen to foster (Rhoades & Eisenberger, 2002).

Leader–follower relationships can also be understood from this social exchange perspective (cf. Sparrowe & Liden, 1997; Wayne, Shore, & Liden, 1997). Whether labeled leader–member exchange or perceived supervisor support, the underlying notion is the same (Graen & Uhl-Bien, 1995; Kottke & Sharafinski, 1988; Shore & Tetrick, 1991): Better quality social exchange relationships between leader and follower are associated with more positive outcomes (e.g., Gerstner & Day, 1997). Consistent with the notion that individuals in leadership positions fulfill a role as representatives of the organization, and thus of one's relationship with the organization, the quality of the exchange relationship with the leader predicts perceptions of the quality of the exchange relationship with the organization (Eisenberger, Stinglhamber, Vandenberghe, Sucharski, & Rhoades, 2002; Sluss, Klimchak, & Holmes, 2008). One straightforward conclusion thus is that by building high-quality exchange relationships with followers, leaders may strengthen the psychological bond between the individual and the organization and thus motivate efforts on behalf of the organization.

The second perspective on the psychological linkage between individual and organization is the social identity perspective (Ashforth & Mael, 1989; Haslam, van Knippenberg, Platow, & Ellemers, 2003; Hogg & Terry, 2000). The volume of social identity research in organizational behavior is no match for that in social exchange, but the social identity perspective has strong and well-supported roots in social psychology, and the social identity analysis of the employment relationship is well supported, for instance in meta-analytic evidence linking organizational identification to a range of outcome variables (Riketta, 2005). Core to the social identity perspective is the notion that social group memberships are to a greater or lesser extent self-definitional: Individuals may conceive of the self not only as "I," but also as "we" (Tajfel & Turner, 1986; Turner et al., 1987). For the employee–organization relationship, this aspect of self-definition is captured by the concept of organizational identification, the perceived oneness between self and organization (Ashforth & Mael, 1989; Pratt, 1998). The psychological merging of self and organization leads individuals to conceive of the organization's interest as the self-interest (i.e., "our interest"), and thus intrinsically motivates individuals to pursue the organization's best interest not as another party's interest but as the interest of the extended or collective self ("we"; Dutton, Dukerich, & Harquail, 1994; van Knippenberg, 2000a). Where the social exchange analysis identifies a key role for reciprocity and felt obligation in the employee–organization relationship as a motivator of employee behavior (Eisenberger et al., 2001), the social identity analysis thus points to the internalization of the organization's interest as part of the self-interest as a motivation underlying employee behavior.

This is not to say that the social exchange analysis does not propose that individuals will take the organization's interest into account. In the social exchange analysis as most commonly applied to the employee–organization relationship (cf. Rhoades & Eisenberger, 2002), however, this is understood to reflect an eye for the organization's interest from the perspective that the self is best served by striving for mutually beneficial outcomes (cf. trade and buy–sell agreements; Sparrowe & Liden, 1997). Sparrowe and Liden (1997) also suggest that there may exist *generalized reciprocity* in exchange that may lead individuals to strive to serve the organization's interest out of altruistic concerns (even when this does not seem to be reflected in empirical research in the employment relationship). However, neither of these forms of reciprocity captures the psychological relationship implied by social identity: Reciprocity identifies the organization as the *other party* in an exchange relationship, whereas in social identity, *there is no other party*—the organization is included in an extended sense of self. To delineate social identity and social exchange perspectives, the issue thus is not what is being exchanged or what form of reciprocity is followed in exchange (cf. Sparrowe & Liden, 1997), but whether the employment relationship is experienced psychologically as an exchange relationship between different parties or as a merging of self and organization into an extended sense of self (cf. van Knippenberg & Sleebos, 2006; van Knippenberg et al., 2007).

Despite their markedly different conceptualizations of individual–group relationships, social identity and social exchange perspectives need not be in opposition and may in fact complement each other in advancing our understanding of the employee–organization relationship. For many employees, their relationship with the organization will have both elements of social exchange and social identification, and the question is not whether employees have a social exchange or a social identity relationship with the organization, but rather how social identity and social exchange processes may differ in their antecedents and consequences and may influence each other. Indeed, research suggests that organizational identification and indicators of the employment relationship associated with social exchange such as perceived organizational support and organizational commitment are positively correlated (e.g., van Knippenberg & Sleebos, 2006) and, at least to some extent, a social exchange relationship may lead up to organizational identification (Sluss et al., 2008). Even so, there is reason to believe that social identification and social exchange are complementary mechanisms—the one reduces the influence of the other (van Knippenberg et al., 2007).

The rationale behind the proposition that social identity and social exchange attenuate each other's influence is perhaps easiest to see when taking it to the hypothetical extreme of complete organizational identification, where the self is understood purely in terms of the "we" that is the organization. In this case, a social exchange relationship between individual and organization would not make much sense psychologically; it would be an exchange with the self. Any influences that would first and foremost be seen as inputs in an exchange relationship would therefore be more weakly related to desired outcomes the higher an individual's identification. Vice versa, the less there is a sense of oneness with the organization, the more one will experience the employment relationship as one between two distinct entities, and the more the quality of the exchange relationship with the organization will be a key determinant of one's willingness to exert oneself on behalf of the organization. In support of this analysis, van Knippenberg et al. (2007) showed that perceptions of organizational and supervisor support interacted with organizational identification in predicting withdrawal cognitions and behavior, such that the influence of the one was weaker the higher the levels of the other.

What this would mean then from an applied perspective is that leaders and organizations may be better off investing in either building identification or building a social exchange relationship rather than in both, because successful efforts to build the one may reduce the effectiveness of efforts to build the other. This is no academic point either, as organizational identification is associated with other determinants than social exchange quality (e.g., Ashforth & Mael, 1989; Wayne et al., 1997), and the desire to build employee identification therefore would suggest different actions than the wish to invest in high-quality exchange relationships with employees.

The quality of social exchange is understood as contingent on the magnitude of inputs in the relationship as well as reciprocity in the relationship (e.g., Blau, 1964). Accordingly, organizational inputs and fairness in the employment relationship are important predictors of the quality of the social exchange relationship (Rhoades & Eisenberger, 2002). Organizational identification as self-conception is contingent on perceived similarity with the organization and on the influence the organizational membership may have on the valence and distinctiveness of one's sense of identity; individuals value both a positive identity (Tajfel & Turner, 1986) and distinctiveness of identity (i.e., something that lends uniqueness to the group or organization; Brewer, 1991). Accordingly, organizational identification is contingent on such influences as organizational prestige and organizational distinctiveness (Dutton et al., 1994; Mael & Ashforth, 1992).

Leadership is not only an important influence in shaping perceptions of the exchange relationship with the organization, but also in shaping organizational identification (van Knippenberg, 2012b; van Knippenberg et al., 2004), but the specific form this is proposed to take to achieve that end is quite different from that advanced in social exchange analyses. Because of the important role social identification plays in motivating individuals to pursue the collective rather than the self-interest (e.g., De Cremer, van Knippenberg, van Dijk, & van Leeuwen, 2008), a variety of leadership analyses have pointed to the importance of leadership building follower identification with the team or organization (Conger & Kanungo, 1987; Lord, Brown, & Freiberg, 1999; Shamir, House, & Arthur, 1993; van Knippenberg & Hogg, 2003; cf. Tyler & Blader, 2000). Studies in charismatic and transformational leadership for instance have advanced the conclusion that building identification with the collective (i.e., team, organization) is an important aspect of leadership that mobilizes followers for collective goals and missions (Conger & Kanungo, 1987; Shamir et al., 1993).

In counterpoint to the social exchange analysis, this leadership influence is seen as flowing from a sense of self that includes the collective and its interests rather than from catering to individuals' self-interest (Bass, 1985), even when that self-interest is recognized to be served by also attending to the collective's interest (cf. Sparrowe & Liden, 1997). This may express itself in visionary communication emphasizing collective goals and mission (Shamir et al., 1993), appeals to the collective interest (Platow, van Knippenberg, Haslam, van Knippenberg, & Spears, 2006), and actions that serve the collective interest (Hogg & van Knippenberg, 2003; van Knippenberg & Hogg, 2003), potentially even at the leader's expense (i.e., self-sacrifice; Conger & Kanungo, 1987; De Cremer & van Knippenberg, 2002), but also in more general reference to the shared team or organizational membership that may render it more salient, such as reference to the collective's history (Shamir et al., 1993).

Leader visions for the collective may build identification through a combination of several elements. When formulated and communicated effectively, they can paint a picture of the organization and the leader's vision for the organization as strongly aligned with follower values, thus suggesting similarities between followers and organization on important aspects (Shamir et al., 1993). Moreover, such visions can present the organization and its mission as valuable and attractive. This may invite identification because membership in a valued collective reflects positively on the self, and individuals value positive self-evaluation (Ashforth & Mael, 1989; Tajfel & Turner, 1986). When leaders emphasize the organization's interest in word and deed, they similarly convey that the organization and its mission are valuable. Moreover they establish the leaders' dedication to work in the organization's best interest. This may invite identification both because it adds to the credibility of the vision (Conger & Kanungo, 1987) and because leader group-serving behavior in and of itself conveys the message that the collective represents a valued social identity (De Cremer & van Knippenberg, 2004).

What all these leadership actions have in common is that they revolve around the team or organization and not around the leader's relationship with the follower or around benefits to the individual follower (cf. Hogg et al., 2005). Thus, where a social exchange analysis ultimately understands leadership to build psychological linkages between employees and organization as revolving around what followers get out of their relationship with the leader (as representative of the organization) vis-à-vis their own contribution to the relationship, building identification through social identity–based leadership is understood to follow from quite different leader actions.

The social identity and social exchange perspectives thus differ both in how they conceptualize the psychological relationship between the individual and the organization and in how they conceive of leadership's role in building a psychological bond with the organization. The implication of this is that leadership and managerial actions to strengthen the psychological bond between employees and the organization should take different forms when targeted at organizational identification versus when targeted at the quality of the social exchange relationship between employee and organization. This then gives rise to the question of whether there is reason to prefer the one over the other.

At first blush, it would appear it is a wash. Research in the consequences of perceived organizational support, organizational commitment, and organizational identification would seem to suggest that these are pretty similar both in terms of the outcomes they are related to and in terms of the magnitude of these relationships (e.g., Riketta & van Dick, 2005). Yet, research in leadership from a social exchange perspective as compared with charismatic and transformational leadership with its implicit (Bass, 1985) or explicit (Shamir et al., 1993) social identity basis would suggest that there is added value in social identity–based leadership over social exchange–based leadership. Indeed, Bass's (1985) conceptualization of transformational leadership as leadership that invites taking the collective's interest to heart (i.e., the *transformational* quality lies in this shift from self-interest to collective interest) explicitly presents transformational leadership as superior to the arguably more widespread transactional leadership that is targeted at followers' self-interested motivations. Bass's proposition is well supported in subjective ratings of leadership effectiveness at least (Lowe, Kroeck, & Sivasubramaniam, 1996). More in general, it is charismatic and transformational leadership that is credited with exceptional leadership outcomes much more than exchange-based leadership (Bass & Riggio, 2006; Conger & Kanungo, 1998), and collective identification is seen as a key mediating construct in establishing these outcomes (Shamir et al., 1993; van Knippenberg et al., 2004).

Leadership analyses and analyses of the bond between employee and organization thus seem to lead to somewhat diverging conclusions as to whether social exchange–based employee–organization relationships are differently related to outcomes than social identity–based relationships. I propose that this difference between conclusions from leadership research and conclusions from research on the employment relationship points to an issue that is important to consider for theory, research, and practice in the employee–organization relationship: employees' understanding of the organizational identity, objectives, and mission. Leadership research in contrast to research in the employment relationship suggests that there is value in focusing on social identity rather than on social exchange, and I propose that this is because in leadership research, leadership to build organizational identification is understood to be closely tied to leaders' role in shaping perceptions of organizational identity, objectives, and mission. This is an issue I discuss in the next section.

ADVANTAGES OF SOCIAL IDENTITY–BASED LEADERSHIP

Who are we, and what is our purpose? Social exchange analyses typically do not ask the question of what exactly employees perceive the organization to be and to pursue in terms of its mission, objectives, and goals. Whereas this may not be a question that social identity analyses ask on a regular basis either, it is a question that does come more naturally from a social identity perspective (e.g., Dutton et al., 1994). In addition, a social identity perspective is also better positioned to address this question and outline its importance, given the emphasis put on mental representations of social groups and group norms within the social identity perspective (Haslam et al., 2003; Hogg & Terry, 2000; Turner et al., 1987).

The social identity perspective outlines how collectives are mentally represented as prototypes—fuzzy sets of characteristics that capture what unites the members of the collective and differentiate the collective from others (Hogg, 2001; Turner et al., 1987). Identification with a group or organization thus implies at least a certain degree of similarity to that prototype. Moreover, identification also invites ascribing prototypical characteristics to the self: The more someone identifies with a group, the more that person sees the self in terms of group-typical characteristics. For instance, if being Scottish is an important part of how you see yourself, you are likely to see yourself as possessing typically Scottish characteristics. That is, subjective similarity to the collective is not only cause but also consequence of the identification process (Turner et al., 1987). This is no minor point because it means that through a process of identification, group-defining characteristics become internalized in the subjective experience of the self. In a sense, identification thus is an influence process where group-defining characteristics come to inform group member attitudes and behavior to the extent that they identify with the group (Turner et al., 1987).

This observation is key to understanding the influence of organizational identification. Identification does not just breed a generic motivation to serve the organization's interests—its effects are intimately tied to individuals' understanding of what that interest is (van Knippenberg, 2000a). In understanding how organizational identification informs attitudes and behavior, it therefore is important to realize that prototypes also capture what is group normative—what the collective values, believes important, and sees as appropriate—as well as collective objectives and mission—what the collective deems worthy of pursuit (Turner et al., 1987; van Knippenberg, 2000b). Identification with the organization thus not only invites individuals to pursue the organization's interests, but also includes a subjective understanding of what these interests are. Applied to the outcome variables typically of interest in research in the employment relationship, identification does not necessarily or specifically motivate performance or extra-role behavior or inhibit withdrawal behavior (i.e., lateness, absenteeism, turnover).

Rather, organizational identification motivates pursuing the organization's best interest, and perceptions of what this interest is are going to determine whether and how identification expresses itself in employee behavior (van Knippenberg, 2000a).

By means of an illustration, consider a study by James and Greenberg (1989). James and Greenberg experimentally manipulated the salience of students' identification with their university before they engaged in a performance task. Salient identity did not motivate task performance across the board. It only did contingent on the other experimental manipulation: whether the cover story suggested the study would include a comparison with the performance of a rival university or not. Only when high performance would serve the university in this interuniversity comparison did the salience of one's university identification motivate higher performance. (Note that comparison alone did not motivate performance either; this was contingent on identity salience.) That is, only when task performance was perceived as contributing to a subjectively important outcome for the collective (i.e., looking good in intergroup comparison) did social identity motivate performance (also see Worchel, Rothgerber, Day, Hart, & Butemeyer, 1998).

Identification thus does not necessarily inspire outcomes strongly desired by the organization, but it may do so contingent on employees' perception of the organization's interests. Leadership is of critical importance here, because a key function of leadership is to articulate a vision for the collective and to communicate a sense of purpose for the collective. From the perspective of the social identity analysis outlined earlier, leadership would gain in effectiveness if it not only builds identification, but also links this to a sense of identity that would inform desirable expressions of that identification. Put differently, if leadership aims to build identification in an attempt to inspire high performance, leadership should also aim to shape an image of the organizational identity to which high performance is core; if leadership hopes to inspire creativity and innovation through identification (cf. Hirst, van Dick, & van Knippenberg, 2009), leadership should also convey an image of the collective's identity and mission as intimately tied to creativity and innovation.

The challenge for leadership here is to communicate an understanding of the organizational identity and its purpose in a way that it is embraced by followers, either as a change-oriented vision or as capturing the organizational identity and mission in the here and now. Either way, it is important that this vision or mission is not just perceived as the leader's vision or understanding of identity but as "our" collective mission and a shared sense of "we." Effective vision communication should thus include building a sense of collective identity for which the vision is articulated (Conger & Kanungo, 1987; Shamir et al., 1993). Indeed, the one is at best of modest use without the other: A vision needs to be shared as a collective vision to mobilize followers, and identification without a strong sense of purpose is unlikely to yield the outcomes alluded to in research in transformational and charismatic leadership. Putting aside the notion of vision (i.e., which is by definition change oriented), the same point can be made for communications regarding the organizational identity and mission: An understanding of the mission of the organization gives direction to identification-based motivation but is of modest use at best without identification to fuel the efforts required to realize the mission. Thus, I propose that building organizational identification as opposed to high-quality exchange relationships can yield superior outcomes fueled by employees' psychological bond with the organization provided it is done in conjunction with a clear statement of purpose and mission that is consistent with the shared organizational identity.

This perhaps begs the question of whether visionary leadership or leadership conveying a clear sense of mission could not also be combined to the same effect with the building of high-quality social exchange relationships? Whereas this of course is a fair question, it would appear there is a disconnect here in that visionary leadership is tied to the collective identity (i.e., leaders and organizations typically do not convey visions and missions targeted at the employee's self-interest), whereas social exchange–based leadership is tied to the individual self-interest (i.e., to "I" rather than "we"). Such leadership could still mobilize followers in pursuit of the collective vision or mission out of a felt obligation to reciprocate (i.e., "this is what you as an individual get out of contributing to the collective mission"). Indeed, this would be completely consistent with how the employment relationship is understood from a social exchange perspective. The difference, however, would be that in contrast to successful social identity–based leadership the combination of social exchange–based and visionary leadership would not foster an internalization of the organization's interest and an intrinsic motivation to realize the organization's mission.

Intrinsic motivation is important here because it renders employee efforts more sustainable and less contingent on continuous reciprocity as well as breeds more creativity in pursuit of the vision (Amabile, 1988). Indeed, the notion of internalization and sustainable effort is especially important in the realm of inspiring visions, as these more or less by definition entail demanding, high-risk endeavors that require persistence, high effort, and creativity and innovation to move into less explored territory (Bass, 1985; Bryman, 1992; Conger & Kanungo, 1987; Shamir, Arthur, & House, 1994). That is, inspiring visions do not suggest business-as-usual performance; they suggest extraordinary efforts to break away from the old and move to something new. Moreover, if realizing the vision requires exceptional efforts, it would require organizational reciprocity of a magnitude that may neither be feasible nor sustainable in the long run (unless one is willing to advance the proposition that immaterial goods like recognition and appreciation will be enough to sustain exceptional efforts through a process of social exchange, which currently is not a proposition backed up by empirical evidence). For that reason too, social identification–based motivation may be more sustainable in pursuit of exceptional outcomes.

In sum, a comparison of social exchange and social identity perspectives on the psychological relationship between the employee and the organization suggests that organizational identification to a substantial degree is contingent on different influences than the quality of the social exchange relationship between employee and organization. Moreover, provided organizational identification is accompanied by organizational leadership that conveys a clear sense of organizational mission and purpose rooted in the organizational identity, a focus on organizational identification may be better suited to the pursuit of highly ambitious organizational goals (e.g., change and innovation) than a focus on social exchange. Related to this, there is also a case to be made that social identity–based leadership is especially suited (i.e., as compared with exchange-based leaderships) for "hard times" characterized by uncertainty and change. Such contexts invite people to rely more strongly on their social identities as a reassuring source of shared social reality (Hogg, 2000, 2007), and thus also increase the influence and effectiveness of social identity–based leadership (Pierro, Cicero, Bonaiuto, van Knippenberg, & Kruglanski, 2005; van Knippenberg & Hogg, 2003; van Knippenberg, van Knippenberg, & Bobbio, 2008).

As well rooted in theory and research as these conclusions may be, it is important to note that the empirical basis for these propositions largely derives from indirect comparisons across studies. Exceptions are the research in the outcomes of transactional and transformational leadership that can be interpreted as suggesting superior outcomes for social identity–based as compared with social exchange–based leadership (albeit with a rather "material" understanding of the goods exchanged in social exchange), and the van Knippenberg et al. (2007) study showing that social identity and social exchange processes attenuate each others' influence. The remainder of this analysis relies on cross-study comparisons. Inevitably, this to some extent also implies comparing apples and oranges, and more than as a set of definite conclusions based on a large body of research, I forward the current propositions as a roadmap for future research. Even so, these propositions warrant a closer consideration of leaders' role in shaping shared social identity within the organization.

LEADERS AS ENTREPRENEURS OF IDENTITY: MOTIVATING BY SHAPING WHO WE ARE

Whereas there is a good empirical basis to support the mediating role of social identification in leadership effectiveness, the work underlying the analysis of leaders' role in conveying an understanding of the collective identity that gives direction to identification-based motivation is conceptual and case based. In the following, I outline and develop this conceptual and case-based analysis under the understanding that further empirical research is needed here and with the hope that this discussion and the research agenda it implicitly holds may function as a call to arms in this respect.

In recognition of the social identity basis of many instances of exceptional leadership, Reicher and Hopkins (2001, 2003) noted that highly effective leaders often are *entrepreneurs of identity* mobilizing and motivating followers by shaping followers' sense of shared identity (cf. Shamir et al., 1993) and establishing a link between their envisioned ends and that sense of identity. As an illustrative example, consider the following quotes from a speech given in the summer of 1962 by President John F. Kennedy at Rice University, Houston, Texas (transcript retrieved from Space-Video. info, n.d.), regarding the ambition for a manned flight to the moon, and my interpretations of some of the social identity dynamics involved:

> We meet at a college noted for knowledge, in a city noted for progress, in a state noted for strength, and we stand in need of all three, for we meet in an hour of change and challenge, in a decade of hope and fear, in an age of both knowledge and ignorance…
>
> …So it is not surprising that some would have us stay where we are a little longer to rest, to wait. But this city of Houston, this state of Texas, this country of the United States was not built by those who waited and rested and wished to look behind them. This country was conquered by those who moved forward…
>
> …Those who came before us made certain that this country rode the first waves of the industrial revolution, the first waves of modern invention, and the first wave of nuclear power, and this generation does not intend to founder in the backwash of the coming age of space. We mean to be a part of it—we mean to lead it.

At the time, President Kennedy was mobilizing public support for the space program that would, for the first time in history, send men to the moon—a very expensive and not undisputed space program. What these excerpts illustrate is how President Kennedy established a link between this ambition and American identity and history, epitomized by the "local" identity of his public at Rice, Houston, Texas. While presumably many in his audience could agree with President Kennedy's rendering of American identity, it is unlikely that many would have quoted these traits themselves unprompted before the Kennedy administration launched their space plans. President Kennedy's articulation of these aspects of identity likely brought them to the fore for some and created them for others. The reference to the country's history (cf. Reicher & Hopkins, 2003; Shamir et al., 1993) moves these claims away from any associations with a fad of the day and roots the ambitions for space travel firmly in a stable aspect of national identity. The bottom line is that President Kennedy's speech suggested that given the choice between boldly going forward into space or holding off at least for a while, it should be obvious what would be "the American thing to do."

Leadership that establishes an understanding of the shared social identity in alignment with the vision, mission, or objectives advocated by the leader may thus mobilize and motivate followers to great ends. Achieving this may be easier said than done, however. It is one thing to realize that leadership may mobilize followers by conveying an understanding of the shared identity that motivates the actions envisioned by the leader, but quite another to actually do so. In many groups, teams, organizations, and other collectives such as nations, what exactly is the shared social identity is ill-defined. It is this very lack of clarity of identity that offers leaders the degrees of freedom to be entrepreneurs of identity and to suggest a reading of the shared identity that aligns well with the own envisioned course of action. Yet, this is not to say that leaders can just make whatever claims they wish in regard to the collective identity or that each and every leader can make such claims with equal success. Two issues at least are important here: first, the extent to which the leader is seen as *group prototypical*—as representing the collective identity (Hogg & van Knippenberg, 2003); and second, the extent to which the image of the shared identity the leader projects is aligned with group members' understanding of that identity (even if ill-defined).

A formal leadership position does not necessarily mean that a leader is perceived to speak with authority about organizational identity. Indeed, claims about "who we are" might easily come across as presumptuous and most likely require substantial "identity credibility." From a social identity perspective, this requires authority and legitimacy as a group member within the context of the shared social identity much more than formal authority. This points to the influence of leader group prototypicality highlighted in the social identity analysis of leadership (Hogg, 2001; van Knippenberg & Hogg, 2003; van Knippenberg, 2012b). The notion of group prototypes was introduced previously, and in the social identity analysis of leadership, the concept of group prototypicality (i.e., similarity to the prototype) is used specifically in reference to leaders. Group leaders, like all group members, may differ in their group prototypicality—in the extent to which they are representative of the shared social identity. The more leaders are seen to embody the shared identity, the more they are seen to speak with authority about what is group normative and indeed about what the group identity itself is. In groups with which people identify and thus in which the shared identity is a source of influence, group prototypicality renders leaders more effective in influencing followers. Although group prototypicality has typically been studied in reference to such outcomes as leadership evaluations (e.g., Hogg, Hains, & Mason, 1998) and follower performance (e.g., van Knippenberg & van Knippenberg, 2005), Reicher and Hopkins's (2001, 2003) qualitative analyses suggest that prototypicality also plays an important role in leaders' ability to assume the role of entrepreneur of identity.

Reicher and Hopkins (2001, 2003) focused on political leadership and describe how highly successful political leaders like Ghandi, Sukharno, and Thatcher all projected an image of themselves as the embodiment of national identity—as highly prototypical of the shared national identity. They thus were able to establish a link between the shared social identity, themselves, and the course of action they advocated. Gandhi, for example, adopted a sober lifestyle closer to the lives of many of the people he represented, thus conveying an image of himself as truly Indian and as distinctly not British, which was the imperial power India was facing at the time. The analysis of Reicher and Hopkins (2001, 2003) outlines how leaders may present an image of themselves in ways that suggest they embody the shared social identity and present this image in such a way that the courses of action they advocate are perfectly aligned with characteristics that are central and important to the shared identity. The fact that social identities may be negotiable in this respect is nicely illustrated by the example Reicher and Hopkins (2003) offer from the Scottish elections in which both the left and the right described Scottish identity in such a way that their party and party program represented what was valued and true about Scottish identity; the left claimed communal as a quality core to Scottish identity, whereas the right claimed entrepreneurial as a quality at the heart of Scottish identity, and both party programs nicely aligned with these respective claims to Scottishness.

Thus, the analysis by Reicher and Hopkins (2001, 2003) points to three issues that successful social identity–based leadership would need to align: the image the leader conveys as a group member (i.e., of group prototypicality), the understanding of the organizational identity the leader conveys, and the shared identity basis of the course of action advocated by the leader (i.e., mission, vision, objectives). These three issues need to be aligned so group prototypicality gives the leader the credibility and legitimacy to make claims about group identity and the identity consistency of the advocated organizational mission, and the understanding conveyed of organizational identity and its mission is closely connected. Clearly, what leadership communicates about the one directly feeds into the other, and there are constraints to what the leader can claim about self and shared identity. Effective social identity–based leadership as described by Reicher and Hopkins (2001, 2003) thus requires a keen sense for the degrees of freedom one has as a leader in presenting an image of self and conveying an understanding of shared identity.

An important complicating factor in this respect probably is that one typically is not the only leader that might make such identity claims. Ghandi, Sukharno, and Thatcher emerged as illustrative cases in the analysis of Reicher and Hopkins through their ultimate success, but this is not to say that their leadership was undisputed or that there were no alternative readings of the national identity. The analysis by Reicher and Hopkins (2003) of the Scottish elections nicely illustrates this, with left- and right-wing parties both presenting claims strongly rooted in national identity, but claims that were diverging and evidently could unite some but not all of the electorate. Voss, Cable, and Voss (2006) similarly describe how leaders of the same company may diverge in the understanding of the shared identity they convey and how this may have disruptive consequences for employee functioning. Although such opposing readings of "who we are" may be far more typical of the political arena than of organizations, they do indicate that leaders in organizations are constrained, at least to some extent, by the leadership of others within the organization. The chief executive officer (CEO) of an organization would clearly have the greatest leeway here as the leader best positioned to stake claims as to representing the company as a whole, and other (i.e., lower level) leaders within the organization would have to carve out their social identity–based leadership roughly within the degrees of freedom offered by the CEO's leadership. Because many CEOs are far from outspoken when it comes to shared organizational identity, these constraints may, in many situations, be far more hypothetical than the current discussion may suggest. Even so, as illustrated by the Voss et al. (2006) case study, social identity–based leadership would ideally be studied and practiced with a consideration of the broader leadership context in which it plays out.

Another issue to consider here is that conveying an image of group prototypicality probably is not best accomplished by straightforward verbal claims to that effect. In contrast to claims about shared organizational identity and shared mission, claims to one's own group prototypicality put oneself center stage and may therefore lie more sensitive with one's audience. As I observed earlier, to establish their credibility and to role model the implications of their message, leaders need to "walk the talk" (Conger & Kanungo, 1987; van Ginkel & van Knippenberg, in press). This perhaps is particularly true for claims to group prototypicality. Reicher and Hopkins's (2003) example of Ghandi is illustrative here, as are Choi and Mai-Dalton's (1998) example of a general eating with his troops (although they interpreted this as a sign of self-sacrifice) and Shamir, Dayan-Horesh, and Adler's (2005) discussion of the late Israeli Prime Minister Yitzhak Rabin's leadership as rooted in his personal history of service to Israel in combination with his presence at many defining moments in Israeli history.

These examples of leaders who convey an image of group prototypicality and communicate an understanding of the shared identity that is aligned with both their own public image and the mission they advocate show that the leadership implications of the social identity analysis of the employee–organization relationship are implications that can and are enacted in practice. Even so, this is not to say that it is easy to do so, and one might argue that in comparing the social identity and social exchange perspectives on the employment relationship, the potential advantages of a social identity approach might be difficult to achieve. Indeed, one might argue that social identity–based leadership is more demanding, that it is more difficult to do it right, and that, therefore, for many leaders social exchange–based leadership may be more sustainable and easier to develop. This proposition has an interesting parallel in Bass's (1985) observation that transactional leadership is the norm and transformational leadership the exception. Even so, transformational leadership can be developed (Dvir, Eden, Avolio, & Shamir, 2002), and there is no reason to believe that the same would not hold for social identity–based leadership.

For many leaders, their sense of organizational identity is likely to be as ill-defined as it is for many followers, and most leaders will be less than fully aware of the social identity dynamics that impact their effectiveness as a leader. In that sense, an important first step in developing social identity–based leadership is to establish an awareness and understanding of these identity dynamics. Leaders need to develop their own thinking about organizational identity—about "who we are"—as well as about their own identity in relationship to the shared organizational identity. Specifically, they need to identify ways to establish their group prototypicality. There is a growing awareness that the development of one's identity as a leader (i.e., a leader role identity) is a core part of leadership development (Day, Harrison, & Halpin, 2009; DeRue, Ashford, & Cotton, 2009; Kramer, 2003; Lord & Hall, 2005). The present analysis suggests that this leader identity ideally should be tied to the shared collective identity (cf. van Knippenberg, 2012b). The next step in leadership development would then be to develop the skills to convey this sense of identity—both organizational identity and leader identity as tied to this organizational identity—in word and deed and to articulate how a shared mission or objective is intertwined with this shared identity.

WHERE DO THE CULTURAL UNIVERSALS STOP AND THE CULTURAL SPECIFICS BEGIN?

Research in organizational behavior is increasingly aware of the cultural contingencies of many processes studied, and it would seem advisable to also consider to what extent cultural differences posit boundaries to the applicability of the current analysis. Clearly, a substantial part of the current analysis has the form of conceptual propositions to be tested in future research, and accordingly, there is as yet no empirical answer to this question. Taking one step back to the conceptual basis of the current analysis in the social exchange and the social identity perspectives on leadership and the employment relationship, however, we may note that the evidence generally supports the conclusion that these are quite fundamental human processes that tend to hold across cultures. In a recent review of research in the social identity theory of leadership, for instance, I conclude that the social identity theory of leadership is consistently supported in research in a host of countries from all continents with the exception of Africa and Antarctica (van Knippenberg, in press), and the social identity approach more broadly similarly relies on multicontinent evidence (e.g., Haslam et al., 2003).

Social exchange research likewise seems to suggest that these are pretty universal processes, even when social exchange processes like those captured by leader–member exchange may have stronger effects in more collectivistic organizational cultures (Erdogan & Liden, 2006; Erdogan, Liden, & Kraimer, 2006). Although this work concerns organizational culture and not national culture, it does point to the possibility that there are cross-national differences in the importance of social exchange–based leadership. A study by Hogg et al. (2005) speaks against this suggestion, however. These authors pitted social exchange and social identity leadership against each other and replicated findings over Indian and United Kingdom samples, suggesting no cultural differences in the importance or effects of social identity–based or social exchange–based leadership. As this arguably is research that more directly speaks to the current issue than the studies by Erdogan and colleagues, there does not seem to be a case for cross-cultural differences here. The bottom line is that systematic research in these matters is essentially missing and, thus, it would seem advisable to keep an open mind and an open eye for cross-national differences even when there currently is no strong theory to predict that these will exist.

CONCLUSION

Developing the current analysis conceptually, empirically, and in practice is the obvious challenge that is now on the table. This is not to say that the current analysis consists of tentative developments only. There is a firm basis for the conclusion that social identity dynamics deserve careful consideration in research and practice in the employee–organization relationship to complement the current dominance of social exchange considerations. Although this as a more general observation is not necessarily a shocking new insight, it is the current emphasis on the consideration of "who we are" and leadership's role in negotiating that understanding that warrant particular attention both in the science and practice of the employment relationship.

Although I have argued that, particularly for high-ambition levels or in uncertain times, social identity–based leadership may be superior to social exchange–based leadership, in more uneventful circumstances, the one may not have a clear advantage over the other, and I would posit the social identity analysis first and foremost as complementing the social exchange analysis rather than as contending with it. Indeed, an interesting and important question from the current perspective would be as follows: In relatively stable times, what are the contingencies of the relative effectiveness of social exchange– and social identity–based leadership?

The answer to this question might involve employee dispositions (e.g., exchange ideology as predicting sensitivity to social exchange–based leadership; cf. Eisenberger et al., 1986; need to belong as predicting sensitivity to social identity–based leadership; cf. Steinel et al., 2010) but also organizational contingencies such as the extent to which the nature of the organization allows it to present a strong image of an esteemed and distinct identity (cf. Dutton et al., 1994) that would be conducive to effective social identity–based leadership. In sum then, this chapter is clearly not intended to advance a number of conclusions based on a substantive body of research, but instead, is meant to advance a series of propositions regarding the role of leadership in the employment relationship that hopefully have the potential to excite researchers in the field into action.

REFERENCES

Amabile, T. M. (1988). A model of creativity and innovation in organizations. *Research in Organizational Behavior, 10*, 123–167.

Ashforth, B. E., & Mael, F. (1989). Social identity theory and the organization. *Academy of Management Review, 14*, 20–39.

Bass, B. M. (1985). *Leadership and performance beyond expectations*. New York, NY: Free Press.

Bass, B. M., & Riggio, R. E. (2006). *Transformational leadership*. Mahwah, NJ: Erlbaum.

Blau, P. M. (1964). *Exchange and power in social life*. New York, NY: Wiley.

Brewer, M. B. (1991). The social self: On being the same and different at the same time. *Personality and Social Psychology Bulletin, 17*, 475–482.

Bryman, A. (1992). *Charisma and leadership in organizations*. London, UK: Sage.

Choi, Y., & Mai-Dalton, R. R. (1998). On the leadership function of self-sacrifice. *The Leadership Quarterly, 9*, 475–501.

Conger, J. A., & Kanungo, R. N. (1987). Towards a behavioral theory of charismatic leadership in organizational settings. *Academy of Management Review, 12*, 637–647.

Conger, J. A., & Kanungo, R. N. (1998). *Charismatic leadership in organizations*. Thousand Oaks, CA: Sage.

Day, D. V., Harrison, M. M., & Halpin, S. M. (2009). *An integrative approach to leader development*. New York, NY: Routledge.

De Cremer, D., & van Knippenberg, D. (2002). How do leaders promote cooperation? The effects of charisma and procedural fairness. *Journal of Applied Psychology, 87*, 858–866.

De Cremer, D., & van Knippenberg, D. (2004). Leader self-sacrifice and leadership effectiveness: The moderating role of leader self-confidence. *Organizational Behavior and Human Decision Processes, 95*, 140–155.

De Cremer, D., van Knippenberg, D., van Dijk, E., & van Leeuwen, E. (2008). Cooperating if one's goals are collective-based: Social identification effects in social dilemmas as a function of goal transformation. *Journal of Applied Social Psychology, 38*, 1562–1579.

DeRue, D. S., Ashford, S. J., & Cotton, N. C. (2009). Assuming the mantle: Unpacking the process by which individuals internalize a leader identity. In L. M. Roberts & J. E. Dutton (Eds.), *Exploring positive identities in organizations* (pp. 217–236). New York, NY: Routledge.

Dutton, J. E., Dukerich, J. M., & Harquail, C. V. (1994). Organizational images and member identification. *Administrative Science Quarterly, 39*, 239–263

Dvir, T., Eden, D., Avolio, B. J., & Shamir, B. (2002). Impact of transformational leadership on follower development and performance: A field experiment. *Academy of Management Journal, 45*, 735–744.

Eisenberger, R., Armeli, S., Rexwinkel, B., Lynch, P. D., & Rhoades, L. (2001). Reciprocation of perceived organizational support. *Journal of Applied Psychology, 86*, 42–51.

Eisenberger, R., Huntington, R., Hutchison, S., & Sowa, D. (1986). Perceived organizational support. *Journal of Applied Psychology, 71*, 500–507.

Eisenberger, R., Stinglhamber, F., Vandenberghe, C., Sucharski, I., & Rhoades, L. (2002). Perceived supervisor support: Contributions to perceived organizational support and employee retention. *Journal of Applied Psychology, 87*, 565–573.

Erdogan, B., & Liden, R. C. (2006). Collectivism as a moderator of responses to organizational justice: Implications for leader-member exchange and ingratiation. *Journal of Organizational Behavior, 27*, 1–17.

Erdogan, B., Liden, R. C., & Kraimer, M. L. (2006). Justice and leader-member exchange: The moderating role of organizational culture. *Academy of Management Journal, 49*, 395–406.

Gerstner, C. R., & Day, D. V. (1997). Meta-analytic review of leader-member exchange theory: Correlates and construct issues. *Journal of Applied Psychology, 82*, 827–844.

Gouldner, A. W. (1960). The norm of reciprocity: A preliminary statement. *American Sociological Review, 25*, 161–178.

Graen, G. B., & Uhl-Bien, M. (1995). Relationship-based approach to leadership: Development of leader-member exchange (LMX) theory of leadership over 25 years: Applying a multi-level multi-domain approach. *Leadership Quarterly, 6*, 219–247.

Haslam, S. A., van Knippenberg, D., Platow, M., & Ellemers, N. (2003). *Social identity at work: Developing theory for organizational practice.* New York: Psychology Press.

Hirst, G., van Dick, R., & van Knippenberg, D. (2009). A social identity perspective on leadership and employee creativity. *Journal of Organizational Behavior, 30*, 963–982.

Hogg, M. A. (2000). Subjective uncertainty reduction through self-categorization: A motivational theory of social identity processes. *European Review of Social Psychology, 11*, 223-255.

Hogg, M. A. (2001). A social identity theory of leadership. *Personality and Social Psychology Review, 5*, 184–200.

Hogg, M. A. (2007). Uncertainty-identity theory. In M. P. Zanna (Ed.), *Advances in experimental social psychology* (Vol. 39, pp. 69–126). San Diego, CA: Academic Press.

Hogg, M. A., Hains, S. C., & Mason, I. (1998). Identification and leadership in small groups: Salience, frame of reference, and leader stereotypicality effects on leader evaluations. *Journal of Personality and Social Psychology, 75*, 1248–1263.

Hogg, M. A., Martin, R., Epitropaki, O., Mankad, A., Svensson, A., & Weeden K. (2005). Effective leadership in salient groups: Revisiting leader-member exchange theory from the perspective of the social identity theory of leadership. *Personality and Social Psychology Bulletin, 31*, 991–1004.

Hogg, M. A., & Terry, D. J. (2000). Social identity and self-categorization processes in organizational contexts. *Academy of Management Review, 25*, 121–140.

Hogg, M. A., & van Knippenberg, D. (2003). Social identity and leadership processes in groups. *Advances in Experimental Social Psychology, 35*, 1–52.

James, K., & Greenberg, J. (1989). In-group salience, intergroup comparison, and individual performance and self-esteem. *Personality and Social Psychology Bulletin, 15*, 604–616.

Kaiser, R. B., Hogan, R., & Craig, S. B. (2008). Leadership and the fate of organizations. *American Psychologist, 63*, 96–110.

Kottke, J. L., & Sharafinski, C. E. (1988). Measuring perceived supervisory and organizational support. *Educational and Psychological Measurement, 48*, 1075–1079.

Kramer, R. M. (2003). The imperatives of identity: The role of identity in leader judgment and decision making. In D. van Knippenberg & M. A. Hogg (Eds.), *Leadership and power: Identity processes in groups and organizations* (pp. 184–196). London, UK: Sage.

Levinson, H. (1965). Reciprocation: The relationship between man and organization. *Administrative Science Quarterly, 9*, 370–390.

Lord, R. G., Brown, D. J., & Freiberg, S. J. (1999). Understanding the dynamics of leadership: The role of follower self-concepts in the leader/follower relationship. *Organizational Behavior and Human Decision Processes, 78*, 1–37.

Lord, R. G., & Hall, R. J. (2005). Identity, deep structure and the development of leadership skill. *The Leadership Quarterly, 16*, 591–615.

Lowe, K. B., Kroeck, K. G., & Sivasubramaniam, N. (1996). Effectiveness correlates of transformational and transactional leadership: A meta-analytic review of the MLQ literature. *Leadership Quarterly, 7*, 385–425.

Mael, F., & Ashforth, B. E. (1992). Alumni and their alma mater: A partial test of the reformulated model of organizational identification. *Journal of Organizational Behavior, 13*, 103–123.

Meyer, J. P., & Allen, N. J. (1997). *Commitment in the workplace.* Thousand Oaks, CA: Sage.

Meyer, J. P., Stanley, D. J., Herscovitch, L., & Topolnytsky, L. (2002). Affective, continuance, and normative commitment to the organization: A meta-analysis of antecedents, correlates, and consequences. *Journal of Vocational Behavior, 61*, 20–52.

Mowday, R. T., Porter, L. W., & Steers, R. M. (1982). *Employee-organization linkages.* New York, NY: Academic Press.

Pierro, A., Cicero, L., Bonaiuto, M., van Knippenberg, D., & Kruglanski, A. W. (2005). Leader group prototypicality and leadership effectiveness: The moderating role of need for cognitive closure. *The Leadership Quarterly, 16*, 503–516.

Platow, M. J., van Knippenberg, D., Haslam, S. A., van Knippenberg, B., & Spears, R. (2006). A special gift we bestow on you for being representative of us: Considering leader charisma from a self-categorization perspective. *British Journal of Social Psychology, 45*, 303–320.

Pratt, M. G. (1998). To be or not to be? Central questions in organizational identification. In D. A. Whetten & P. C. Godfrey (Eds.), *Identity in organizations: Building theory through conversations.* Thousand Oakes, CA: Sage.

Reicher, S., & Hopkins, N. (2001). *Self and nation.* London, UK: Sage.

Reicher, S., & Hopkins, N. (2003). On the science and art of leadership. In D. van Knippenberg & M. A. Hogg (Eds.), *Leadership and power: Identity processes in groups and organizations* (pp. 197–209). London, UK: Sage.

Rhoades, L., & Eisenberger, R. (2002). Perceived organizational support: A review of the literature. *Journal of Applied Psychology, 87*, 698–714.

Riketta, M. (2005). Organizational identification: A meta-analysis. *Journal of Vocational Behavior, 66,* 358–384.
Riketta, M., & Van Dick, R. (2005). Foci of attachment in organizations: A meta-analysis comparison of the strength and correlates of work-group versus organizational commitment and identification. *Journal of Vocational Behavior, 67,* 490–510.
Rousseau, D. M., & McLean Parks, J. (1993). The contracts of individuals and organizations. *Research in Organizational Behavior, 15,* 1–43.
Shamir, B., Arthur, M. B., & House, R. J. (1994). The rhetoric of charismatic leadership: A theoretical extension, a case study, and implications for research. *The Leadership Quarterly, 5,* 25–42.
Shamir, B., Dayan-Horesh, H., & Adler, D. (2005). Leading by biography: Towards a life-story approach to the study of leadership. *Leadership, 1,* 13–29.
Shamir, B., House, R., & Arthur, M. B. (1993). The motivational effects of charismatic leadership: A self-concept based theory. *Organization Science, 4,* 577–594.
Shore, L. M., & Tetrick, L. E. (1991). A construct validity study of the Survey of Perceived Organizational Support. *Journal of Applied Psychology, 76,* 637–643.
Shore, L. M., Tetrick, L. E., Taylor, M. S., Coyle-Shapiro, J., Liden, R., McLean Parks, J., ... Van Dyne, L. (2004). The employee-organization relationship: A timely concept in a period of transition. In J. Martocchio (Ed.), *Research in personnel and human resources management* (Vol. 23, pp. 291–370). Greenwich, CT: JAI Press.
Sluss, D. M., & Ashforth, B. E. (2007). Relational identity and identification: Defining ourselves through work relationships. *Academy of Management Review, 32,* 9–32.
Sluss, D. M., & Ashforth, B. E. (2008). How relational and organizational identification converge: Processes and conditions. *Organization Science, 19,* 807–823.
Sluss, D. M., Klimchak, M., & Holmes, J. J. (2008). Perceived organizational support as a mediator between relational exchange and organizational identification. *Journal of Vocational Behavior, 73,* 457–464.
Sluss, D. M., Ployhart, R. E., & Cobb, M. G. (2010, August). *Converging newcomer's relational and collective identification: Prototypicality as moderator.* Paper presented at the Annual Meeting of the Academy of Management, Montreal, Quebec, Canada.
Space-Video.info. (n.d.) John F. Kennedy's Rice Stadium moon speech. Retrieved from http://www.space-video.info/speech/19620912-jfk-rice-text.html
Sparrowe, R. T., & Liden, R. C. (1997). Process and structure in leader-member exchange. *Academy of Management Review, 22,* 522–552.
Steinel, W., van Kleef, G. A., van Knippenberg, D., Hogg, M. A., Homan, A. C., & Moffit, G. (2010). How intragroup dynamics affect behavior in intergroup conflict: The role of group norms, prototypicality, and need to belong. *Group Processes & Intergroup Relations, 13,* 779–794.
Tajfel, H., & Turner, J. C. (1986). The social identity theory of intergroup behavior. In S. Worchel & W. Austin (Eds.), *Psychology of intergroup relations* (pp. 7–24). Chicago, IL: Nelson-Hall.
Turner, J. C., Hogg, M. A., Oakes, P. J., Reicher, S. D., & Wetherell, M. S. (1987). *Rediscovering the social group. A self-categorization theory.* Oxford, UK: Blackwell.
Tyler, T. R., & Blader, S. L. (2000). *Cooperation in groups. Procedural justice, social identity, and behavioral engagement.* Philadelphia, PA: Psychology Press.
van Ginkel, W. P., & van Knippenberg, D. (in press). Group leadership and shared task representations in decision-making groups. *The Leadership Quarterly.*

van Knippenberg, B., & van Knippenberg, D. (2005). Leader self-sacrifice and leadership effectiveness: The moderating role of leader prototypicality. *Journal of Applied Psychology, 90*, 25–37.

van Knippenberg, D. (2000a). Work motivation and performance: A social identity perspective. *Applied Psychology: An International Review, 49*, 357–371.

van Knippenberg, D. (2000b). Group norms, prototypicality, and persuasion. In D. J. Terry & M. A. Hogg (Eds.), *Attitudes, behavior, and social context: The role of norms and group membership* (pp. 157–170). Mahwah, NJ: Erlbaum.

van Knippenberg, D. (2012a). Leadership: A person-in-situation perspective. In K. Deaux & M. Snyder (Eds.), *Oxford handbook of personality and social psychology* (pp. 673–700). New York, NY: Oxford University Press.

van Knippenberg, D. (2012b). Leadership and identity. In D. V. Day & J. Antonakis (Eds.), *The nature of leadership* (2nd ed. pp. 477–507). London, UK: Sage.

van Knippenberg, D. (in press). Embodying who we are: Leader group prototypicality and leadership effectiveness. *The Leadership Quarterly*.

van Knippenberg, D., & Hogg, M. A. (2003). A social identity model of leadership effectiveness in organizations. *Research in Organizational Behavior, 25*, 243–295.

van Knippenberg, D., & Sleebos, E. (2006). Organizational identification versus organizational commitment: Self-definition, social exchange, and job attitudes. *Journal of Organizational Behavior, 27*, 571–584.

van Knippenberg, D., van Dick, R., & Tavares, S. (2007). Social identity and social exchange: identification, support, and withdrawal from the job. *Journal of Applied Social Psychology, 37*, 457–477.

van Knippenberg, D., van Knippenberg, B., & Bobbio, A. (2008). Leaders as agents of continuity: Self continuity and resistance to collective change. In F. Sani (Ed.), *Self-continuity: Individual and collective perspectives* (pp. 175–186). New York, NY: Psychology Press.

van Knippenberg, D., van Knippenberg, B., De Cremer, D., & Hogg, M. A. (2004). Leadership, self, and identity: A review and research agenda. *The Leadership Quarterly, 15*, 825–856.

van Knippenberg, D., & van Schie, E. C. M. (2000). Foci and correlates of organizational identification. *Journal of Occupational and Organizational Psychology, 73*, 137–147.

Voss, Z. G., Cable, D. M., & Voss, G. B. (2006). Organizational identity and firm performance: What happens when leaders disagree about "who we are?" *Organization Science, 17*, 741–755.

Wayne, S. J., Shore, L. M., & Liden, R. C. (1997). Perceived organizational support and leader-member exchange: A social exchange perspective. *Academy of Management Journal, 40*, 82–111.

Worchel, S., Rothgerber, H., Day, E. A., Hart, D., & Butemeyer, J. (1998). Social identity and individual productivity within groups. *British Journal of Social Psychology, 37*, 389–413.

5

Resource Commensurability and Ideological Elements of the Exchange Relationship

Judi McLean Parks
Washington University in St. Louis

faye l. smith
Missouri Western State University

> Thomas Jefferson captured the recalibration of work's standing when he described the young American nation as "an aristocracy of talent and virtue." Ever since, *what each of us does for a living has been an expression of identity and a measure of worth.*
>
> —The Week, *June 19, 2009, p. 25 (emphasis added)*

INTRODUCTION

Part of our very identity and our sense of self-worth may be derived from our work. As part of the larger exchange relationship, ideological exchanges are characterized by perceived obligations to support specific causes or ethical principles (Blau, 1964; Thompson & Bunderson, 2003). For example, in 2002 Professor Bernard Amadei started Engineers Without Borders USA (EWB-USA) after he and eight engineering students, working with a local community, installed a sustainable and low-cost clean water system in San Pablo, Belize. In 8 years, EWB-USA has grown to 12,000 members with more than 350 projects in more than 45 developing countries (Engineers Without Borders, 2011). The work that is done by the many engineers and other professionals (e.g., anthropologists, sociologists) provides a source for ideological elements that enhance their identity and sense of self-worth. It is the ideological elements of exchange relationships that are the focus of this chapter.

Exchange relationships typically have been seen in terms of one of three currencies between worker and organization: economic or transactional currencies, socioemotional or relational currencies (McLean Parks, Kidder, & Gallagher, 1998; McLean Parks & smith, 1998; Rousseau & McLean Parks, 1993), and more recently, ideological currencies (Thompson & Bunderson, 2003). Yet these three currencies are not created equal(ly), not only in terms of what resource it is that comprises the exchange, but also in terms of their implications for employee attitudes and behaviors. This chapter focuses primarily on exchanges involving ideological currencies and incorporates their key elements into our theoretical framework:

1. We develop a categorization of the *sources of the exchange elements*. These elements have implications for exchange relationships and ideological exchanges in particular. These sources are *pecuniary, task, role, relational, organizational*, and *occupational* and form the foundation of the inducements of the work relationship.
2. Based on these sources, we build the logic of *pivotal ideological space* that is created by the ideological resources that are exchanged.
   a. Further, pivotal space can be described in terms of *depth* and *breadth*, indicating how embedded the ideology is within the work relationship. Although certainly pivotal space can transcend ideological exchange, it is in the context of ideological elements that we frame our discussion.
   b. We extend the framework further to address *ideological incompatibility, ideological crystallization*, and *meta-ideological exchanges*.
3. We refine the notion of *resource commensurability* in exchange relationships (McLean Parks, 1997; Shore et al., 2004), refining Pruitt's (1981) classification of *specific, homologous*, and *substitute* forms of compensation as well as Sparrowe, Dirks, Bunderson, and McLean Parks (2004) specification of *isomorphic compensation* (see also McLean Parks & smith, 2006; Shore et al., 2004).

We focus on these aspects of the relationship as we believe they are important for ideologically based exchange, representing thorny issues and complexities beyond those found in exchanges based primarily in economic or socioemotional currencies. Perhaps more than any other form of exchange, ideological currency is important because it gets at the very soul of the worker. As a result, ideological exchanges can enhance and affirm a worker's identity in terms of the value the worker places on the cause that the ideology supports. The ideologically infused relationship can be one of the most effective mechanisms for binding workers to an organization, encouraging effort over withdrawal (e.g., Kidwell & Bennett, 1993), identification (e.g., Ashforth & Mael, 1989; Dutton, Dukerich, & Harquail, 1994), extra-role behavior (e.g., Van Dyne, Cummings, & McLean Parks, 1998), and other positive contributions to the organization and its outcomes. Paradoxically, the ideological exchange also can result in perhaps the highest levels of disaffection if the organization's support of the ideology diminishes, severing the relationship and resulting in withdrawal behaviors (e.g., Kidwell & Bennett, 1993), a sense of violation (e.g., Morrison & Robinson, 1997), or even moral outrage (e.g., Bies, 1987).

This conundrum can, in part, be understood in terms of the ideological work elements that are incorporated into ideological currencies. Building on McLean Parks and smith's (2000, 2002) identity frames, we present a model of ideological elements by which the ideological currency of the exchange is provided by pecuniary, task, role, relational, organizational, and occupational work elements. To the extent that each of these ideological elements is jointly affirmed by one another, a pivotal ideological space is created, which strengthens and deepens the ideological exchange.

THEORETICAL DEVELOPMENT

Exchange Elements: Pecuniary, Task, Role, Relational, Reputational, Organizational, and Occupational

March and Simon (1958) argued that the workers' decisions to participate is based on a balance of payments to members for participation in the organization. These payments comprise inducements exchanged by the company in return for the workers' contributions (effort, skills) to the organization, whereby the worker continues to contribute so long as the inducements received are greater than their contribution. However, this perspective has been largely silent on what *actual resources* might comprise those inducements. The literature on psychological contracts has helped to fill this theoretical gap with the delineation of transactional/relational and economic/socioemotional (e.g., MacNeil, 1985; Rousseau & McLean Parks, 1993) categories for the exchanges embedded in these relationships.

In this section of the chapter, we delineate and define different types of inducements found in the relationship between workers and their organizations. We argue that organizational inducements include a number of different elements and that these elements can be generally categorized by their *source*. The elements are resources that the organization controls through decisions and policies, whether formal or informal. For example, a work area may be furnished with ergonomic furniture and equipment, or it may be furnished with out-of-date, dilapidated furnishings. In the first scenario, the resource of office furnishings communicates caring and respect, whereas in the second, the resource provided elicits the suggestion that people are not valued. Similarly, organizational policies are designed to provide standardized criteria and processes for organizational decisions, and when the policies are designed and applied in a fair and consistent manner, the socioemotional resource of "respect" may be part of the set of inducements.

The general sources of the elements in the exchange relationship—the collection of perceived inducements—that we have identified include pecuniary, task, role, relational, organizational, and occupational sources. Note that it is possible that a given element may have characteristics of more than one source. In other words, these sources are not mutually exclusive. For example, task and role elements may have aspects that spill over into the relational domain (e.g., status conferred by role elements). Further, although we believe that the sources we have identified are among the primary sources, our list may not be exhaustive but is a starting point for further development of the actual types of resources found in exchange relationships.[1] We use these elements to refine our understanding of the

---

[1] These element sources apply to exchange relationships more generally. We are focused on the inducements as idiosyncratically perceived by the worker. For parsimony, we have not included the "contributions" side of the equation, although certainly workers can contribute to organizations through contributions derived from each of these sources as well. For example, the reporter whose story wins a Pulitzer Prize contributes a relational element to the organization in terms of a positive reputation (McLean Parks & smith, 2000, 2002).

interaction of resource inducements, in particular, as it applies to ideological exchange.

In the context of the exchange relationship, these elements, to a greater or lesser extent, can create and enhance the identity of the worker. While in the transactional exchange, identity creation/enhancement is largely irrelevant (McLean Parks & smith, 1998), in the relational, socioemotional exchange, the role of identity may be relatively minor or an important aspect of the relationship (McLean Parks & smith, 1998). Ideologies by nature are particularistic (Foa, 1971; Foa & Foa, 1975); in other words, they are uniquely nonsubstitutable. Thus in the ideological exchange, identity is paramount, not only from the perspective of the worker's personal identity, but also the identity of the organization. For example, the motto of Origins, a cosmetic company that eschews animal testing, is "powered by nature, proven by science" and its mission statement notes, "…our long-standing commitment to protect the planet, its resources and all those who populate it is reaffirmed by our earth and animal friendly practices, packaging and policies" (Origins, 2010). Here the values associated with animal rights are reflected in the identity of the company in their "animal friendly practices" and lack of animal testing. Continuing the example, the causes valued by workers may become part of their personal identities—*who* they are as a person. Perhaps a worker at Origins sees herself as a mother, a chemist, and an animal rights advocate. These are all aspects of her identity. In this case, these three respective identities mirror one another and are mutually enhancing and reinforcing. However, if, in response to a personal injury lawsuit over one of their products, Origins were to begin animal testing, their (original) goals have become displaced (Blau, 1964; Merton, 1957; Thompson & Bunderson, 2003). As a result, our chemist's ideological contract has been breached, and her identity is no longer enhanced by that of her employer.[2]

In this way, ideological exchange elements, which comprise inducements through which workers choose to participate, can be identity affirming (Steele, 1988) or disconfirming. Possibilities and potential also are components of one's identity: what might be or who one might become in the future (Christiansen, 1999). For example, someone who joins the

---

[2] As noted by Thompson and Bunderson (2003), the ideologies that workers value may or may not be normatively positive, providing the example of targeted hatred as an ideology (e.g., the ideology of organizations such as the Ku Klux Klan).

Peace Corps is likely to share organizationally espoused and enacted values, including the value of future peaceful and developmental opportunities that can result in positive contributions to countries in need. This future focus may be important in ideological exchange, where the causes themselves focus on a potential for a better future (e.g., for children, animal rights, peace on earth, the environment). We further argue that the extent to which these elements contain ideological aspects and to which the elements are jointly affirmed by one another creates a *pivotal ideological space*, which can be described in terms of two dimensions: breadth (the degree of overlap among elements) and depth (number of sources that contribute to the pivotal space). Within this framework, we also discuss ideological *incompatibility* and ideological *crystallization*. The depth and breadth of the pivotal space, as well as ideological incompatibility and crystallization and associated *meta-ideological exchanges*, have implications for *commensurability* in the execution, fulfillment, and violation of the work relationship grounded in ideological exchange. We now turn to the definitions of each of these constructs.

Pecuniary elements are characteristically economic resources. These are the resources typically ascribed to the transactional exchange and can include wage/salary, bonuses (or penalties/fines), benefits, and other monetized inducements (Rousseau & McLean Parks, 1993). Pecuniary elements typically are fungible and, hence under some circumstances, may be substituted for other elements. However, pecuniary elements can take on the mantle of other elements. For example, if workers believe that they are underpaid (pecuniary) relevant to referent others, the inequity also may communicate that they are less valued, and if known to others, the pecuniary element of underpayment may impact their standing in the organization and the respect conferred (relational) on them by colleagues. Pecuniary elements that have overtones of ideological currency might include matching contributions by the company to the specific cause valued by the worker.

Task elements are specific actions (behaviors) needed to execute one's job at work. How an organization constructs its tasks and communicates their value (to the organization and society at large) is another resource element that can provide an exchange inducement. Hackman and Oldham's (1976) Job Characteristics Model specifies that workers experience meaningfulness when tasks use a variety of their skills (task variety), are significant (task significance), and help create a "whole" (task identity), rather than just one cog in a wheel. Meaningful tasks communicate that workers are valued and hence may induce full participation in the organization. Further, in ideological exchange, meaningfulness may be paramount. Specifically, in ideological exchanges, ideologies are permeated with meaning, and in part, it is that meaning itself that attracts the worker. When the task's meaningfulness is congruent with the meaningfulness of the ideology, this relationship is strengthened.

Role elements are rules and norms that create expectations held both by individuals and by others. They include rules or norms that comprise a blueprint or script that guides behavior and choices (Biddle, 1979), implicitly or explicitly specifying appropriate goals, tasks to be executed, and the like. Roles contain both prescriptions and proscriptions (Kahn, Wolfe, Quinn, Snoek, & Rosenthal, 1964) and delineate mechanisms through which objectives are achieved. The blueprints provided by role elements represent ascriptions or characteristics that shape the workers' personal identities (Allen & van de Vliert, 1982), even though the role elements may be outside the parameters of the workers' direct control (Linton, 1936). Regardless of whether or not they have control, when workers view the role ascriptions as constructive and legitimate, they will not only incur costs to conform to role norms, prescriptions, and proscriptions, but they also will incur costs to punish those who do not conform (Biddle, 1986; Goffman, 1959, 1961). Willingness to incur these costs will be increased when the exchange is ideological.

Relational elements are social and interpersonal aspects of the work environment and thus are socioemotional in character. As noted by McLean Parks and smith (1998), relational exchanges "encompass the full range of resources, including those which are unobservable" (p. 133). Relational elements may include opportunities to form friendships and trusting relationships at work, contributing to workers' formation of relational identities (Andersen & Chen, 2002; Sluss & Ashforth, 2007). Relational elements of the exchange provide reflected appraisals, which enhance self-esteem (Cooley, 1902; Mead, 1934). Relational elements can produce positive interactions with other workers and supervisors, customers, or suppliers, endowing workers with respect of peers and contributing to a positive self-image and reputation. Further, relational elements can be particularistic, where identity becomes paramount. When particularistic resources are involved, they represent more of the individual. As a result, "if the contract is breached, then the loss felt will be more salient and personal" (McLean Parks & smith, 1998, p. 134). For example, relational elements affecting ideological currency might include one's reputation enhancing or tarnishing fellow workers' reputations because of the company they keep.

Organizational elements are the implicit and explicit benefits derived from one's membership or association with the company. As the organizational identity literature attests, workers' identities can be enhanced or damaged through their organization. During the height of the controversy over genetically modified foods, Monsanto, the agri-pharmaceutical giant, found its previously positive reputation damaged. Protestors in Europe shouted "Ban Frankenfood" and "Die Monsatan" (Schurman, 2004), virtually bringing an entire industry to a complete halt (Miller, 2004; Schurman, 2004). At the time of the protests, especially at its European locations, being an employee of Monsanto carried significant costs, and the spillover to one's personal identity was negative. More recently, British Petroleum's (BP) Deepwater Horizon oil spill in the Gulf of Mexico not only tarnished the reputation of BP, but also cast a shadow over its employees (Gnau, 2010). In each of these examples, the organizational element had a direct effect on the ideological exchanges with workers whose valued causes were environmentally focused.

In sum, organizational elements can be a source of self-esteem or identity or, when negatively evaluated, of disidentification (e.g., Dukerich, Kramer, & McLean Parks, 1998; Elsbach & Bhattacharya, 2001) and alienation. In the case of ideological currency, elements related to the ideology or cause are key to the exchange. If viewed positively or as supporting/enhancing that ideology, it will strengthen the work relationship, increasing commitment and the willingness on the part of the worker to go beyond role requirements. In contrast, if viewed negatively or as lacking support or detracting from the cause, it may result in greater turnover, a lack of motivation, and even sabotage (McLean Parks, 1997).

Occupational elements are benefits derived from one's work specialty or profession. Research on occupational prestige has found that different occupations provide different levels of prestige (Nakao & Treas, 1994; Spaeth, 1979) and being able to ply one's trade in the professions may be one inducement for a worker to join a specific organization. Any given organization may involve a number of different occupations (e.g., scientist, secretary, accountant, and janitor). Thus, although clearly related, we regard the occupational and organizational elements as distinct and separable, with potentially different effects. Logically, we can imagine situations where they are distinct. For example, working as an *accountant* (occupational element) for Tom's of Maine after the Enron fiasco may have been associated with negative spillover from the accounting profession. However, working for a *firm* known for its development of earth-friendly personal care products such as those produced and sold by Tom's of Maine may have been a positive inducement (organizational element). Thus, if accountants at Tom's of Maine focused on their occupation, they may have become disaffected. However, if their focus was on environmental issues, their tie to the organization may have enabled them to withstand the negative spillover from the Enron accountants' actions.

In summary, the six sources of resource elements provide an initial context from which inducements contribute to ideological currency and can be exchanged to form a strong relationship between worker and organization. The elements are the source of the actual resources contributing to one's formulation of an ideological exchange. As argued earlier, the elements are not mutually exclusive and are not necessarily comprehensive, but they do provide a basis from which scholars can enrich their understanding of the actual resource elements that create and enhance exchange relationships. Based on these elements, we now turn to the development of the concept of a pivotal ideological space (see Table 5.1).

Features of the Resource Elements

Pivotal Ideological Space

Viewing the content of inducements exchanged in work relationships through the lens of multiple elements suggests that these elements may be "layered," juxtaposed, and overlapped. In this way, alternative ways of supporting ideological values from pecuniary, task, role, relational, organizational, and occupational domains may be positioned against one another, revealing that these elements may be congruent or incongruent. If the former is the case, they provide complementary information concerning the organization's support for the ideology; in the latter case, a single note of incongruence may render cognitive dissonance such that the ideological exchange is breached (McLean Parks, 1997). By incorporating Schein's (1980) notion of pivotal norms, as well as earlier work (Crooker,

TABLE 5.1

Sources of Resource Elements

Source	Definition	Sample Resources	Example
Pecuniary	Economic or monetized	Wages, bonuses, benefits	Salary of $100,000
Task	Specific actions within roles	Pride, identity	Astronaut's "bragging rights" for having worked aboard the Space Station
Role	Rules/norms that guide behavior and choices	Rules, norms, prescriptions, proscriptions	Authorization to sign for expenditures
Relational	Socioemotional and interpersonal connections	Friendships, mentors, trust, respect	Mentor to junior colleagues
Organizational	Derived from membership	Reputation, identity	Being an IBMer
Occupational	Recognition from work specialty	Prestige, earnings potential	Respect and prestige derived from being a physician

smith, & Tabak, 2002; McLean Parks & smith, 2000, 2002), we now define pivotal ideological space as the *overlap* among and within ideological elements. It is in this overlap where elements are interpreted or perceived as compatible and congruent with the salient ideology. The extent to which they overlap may be large, small, or nonexistent. This overlap may be layered across all the elements (large pivotal space) or a subset of them (small pivotal space). Consistent with McLean Parks and smith's (2000, 2002) identity frames, these elements provide information such that they can be characterized as (a) conjunctive (some degree of overlap); (b) disjunctive (no overlap but also no incongruence); (c) equivalent (complete overlap); or (d) incompatible (inconsistent and contradictory).[3]

At the extremes, elements can overlap 100% (equivalent) or be disjunctive. In the latter case, the pivotal space does not exist. *Pivotal ideological space is the ideology that is jointly affirmed by the content of multiple elements.* For example, contributions to a shelter for abused children and

---

[3] Conjunctive, disjunctive, equivalent, and incompatible elements conceptually parallel set theory; for example, disjunctive (no intersection) with no common elements could be denoted $B \cap C = \{\ \}$.

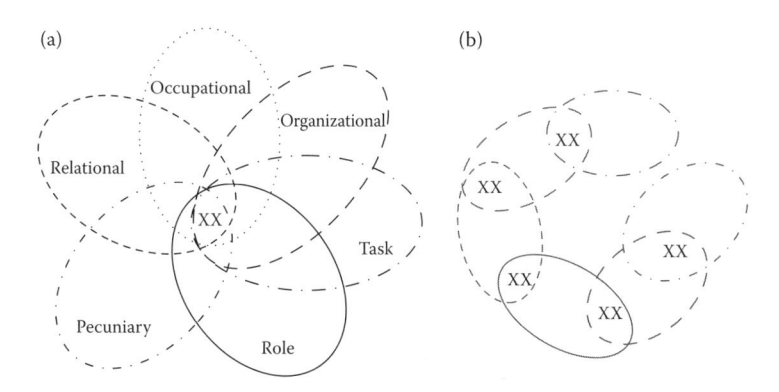

FIGURE 5.1
(a) Pivotal ideological space. (b) Multiple pivotal spaces and absence of pivotal space. XX, pivotal space.

allowing workers to volunteer at the shelter 1 hour a week on company time are two different resource elements (inducements) that both support the same ideological value that is important to one or more workers. Pivotal ideological space can be conceptualized along two dimensions: breadth and depth (McLean Parks & smith, 2000, 2002). The *breadth* of the pivotal space is the degree of overlap across the elements—the number of common or congruent elements that reinforce the ideology. In contrast, *depth* of pivotal space is the number of sources of inducements (pecuniary, task, role, relational, occupational, organizational) that contribute to the pivotal space. Breadth provides inducements from multiple sources, whereas depth parallels the strength of the ideological components. Thus, all of the sources may overlap in one pivotal space that is broad and deep, or one or more of the sources may contribute to pivotal spaces, such that multiple pivotal spaces that are narrow and shallow may accumulate. Each of the multiple pivotal spaces represents separate ideologies. Although not identical, different ideologies can be related to one another (energy sustainability and clean air) or unrelated (energy sustainability and disease eradication). See Figure 5.1.

The greater the pivotal ideological space(s), the stronger is the ideological tie for the worker with emerging self-reinforcing cycles across the ideological elements. However, if support for the ideology is withdrawn by the organization, the disaffection and violation caused will be more pervasive and impact more aspects of the relationship between the company and the worker.

Ideological Incompatibility

In addition to the notion of the pivotal ideological space, ideological incompatibility enhances our understanding of ideological exchange. The pivotal ideological space implies agreement or consistency among elements, whereas no overlap results in the absence of a pivotal space. Yet the ideology communicated by each of the elements also may conflict with one another or be incompatible. Hence a subcategory of disjunctive elements (no pivotal space) is *ideological incompatibility*. Incompatible ideological elements are logically inconsistent with one another and in direct conflict. Yet incompatibility isn't simply the absence of a pivotal space. Lack of a pivotal space is a necessary but not sufficient condition for incompatibility. At one extreme, incompatibility implies antithetical ideologies—polar opposites. Incompatibility is the degree to which an element of the exchange "repels" another, where the elements are perceived as mutually exclusive. Because ideologies are infused with specific values (Thompson & Bunderson, 2003), it follows that ideological incompatibility parallels the incompatibility of values, accounting for their potential irreducibility and distinctiveness. Thus ideologies are value specific, irreducible, nonfungible, and distinctive. To fail to support the valued ideology may be absolutely unacceptable or a nonnegotiable in exchanges involving ideological currency (Thompson & Bunderson, 2003).

Ideological Crystallization

Chatman (1989) has extended the concept of norms (Jackson, 1966) as being more or less crystallized when there is agreement across individuals in terms of what is or is not appropriate behavior. Similarly, and parallel to their development, McLean Parks and smith (2000, 2002) applied crystallization to organizational identity frames in terms of the degree of agreement among perceivers about who the organization is. We now extend crystallization to the notion of exchange relationships. Within an organization, multiple workers may hold similar shared meanings about the resource elements that contribute to each person's exchange relationship, thus making them more or less crystallized. Thus, *ideologically crystallized exchanges are those in which there is a high degree of convergence of shared meaning across individuals about the resource elements that contribute to each person's ideological exchange.* We suggest that such shared meaning may be the basis for strong organizational cultures where individuals mutually and collectively understand the resource elements, resulting in a high degree of consistency from one exchange to another.

Meta-Ideological Exchange

Not only can there be a high level of convergence regarding the ideology across individuals (ideological crystallization), but this crystallized ideology also can contribute to *meta-ideological exchanges*. Crystallization (defined earlier) represents the shared value, whereas meta-ideological exchange occurs when those sharing the ideology collectively act in coherence with the crystallized ideologies. As noted by Simon (2004), "to be is to do and to do is to be" (p. 187). Meta-ideological exchanges can become self-reinforcing, strengthening the ties and implicitly enhancing the value of the ideological currency. Yet, when these meta-ideological exchanges are tightly coupled, violation can rapidly diffuse through the entire network.

Meta-ideological exchange occurs not only because of identification with ideology, but also through the process of identity affirmation as part of the ideological group (Simon, Trötschel, & Dähne, 2008). By sharing ideological values, parties to the meta-ideological exchange strengthen social ties through their collective and mutually supported actions taken to promote the reflected values. In this way, their action reinforces not only the ideology but also the shared identity associated with the ideologically defined social group (Simpson & Macy, 2001). In other words, *meta-ideological exchanges are collective actions affirming the shared ideologies. These collective actions in turn are comprised of multiple exchange relationships embedded within the larger fabric of the ideological exchange.* Further, in an organization, a tipping point or threshold (Granovetter, 1978) can be reached precipitating a chain reaction that spreads throughout the ideological group. Just as a single audience member leaving a boring concert may encourage others similarly bored to exit, so too can meta-ideological exchanges result in collective actions that affirm the ideology. For example, in 2008, several hundred faculty and students at a Midwestern university wore armbands, carried signs, and turned their backs on a controversial honorary degree recipient at the spring commencement ceremony. The degree recipient had actively fought the equal rights amendment and built a lifelong career speaking out against women in the work force. The recipient's actions sparked the protests from faculty and students who strongly believed in the ideology of gender equality and fair treatment for all (Biemiller, 2008).

In summary, resource elements from the different sources (pecuniary, task, role, relational, organizational, and occupational) each contribute to the ideological exchange, potentially creating pivotal ideological space and ideological crystallization, which ultimately can contribute to a meta-ideological exchange. To the extent that the pivotal ideological space is large, that there is ideological crystallization, and that the ideology shared by members results in actions to affirm the ideology and ideological elements, then the ideological exchange or meta-ideological exchange is more likely to be quite durable and strong.

Together, the constructs discussed so far identify "what" it is being exchanged, but do not yet address "how" the exchange occurs. By exploring the commensurability of resource elements, we are able to identify how elements can be exchanged for one another. We now address the commensurability of the resources in each of these sources and develop the notion that resource elements that have common characteristics and attributes can be exchanged more easily within the ideological exchange relationship. In other words, one element from one type of resource may be exchanged for another element in another type of resource when certain attributes are held in common. We first address resource characteristics and attributes.

Resource Commensurability and Characteristics

Foa and Foa (1975) suggested most resources could be characterized along two dimensions[4]: (a) the extent to which they are abstract/concrete, and (b) the extent to which they are particularistic/nonparticularistic. Concrete resources are those that can be interpreted unambiguously by outside others (Foa, 1971; Foa & Foa, 1975), such as when $1.00 is exchanged for 100 pennies (McLean Parks & smith, 1998). In contrast, abstract resources are ambiguous and difficult to interpret, even within the exchange relation-

---

[4] Depending on their positioning along these two dimensions, Foa and Foa (1975) suggested that resources could be categorized into one of six categories. Although tangential to our discussion, as modified by McLean Parks and smith (1998, p. 131) in an application to transactional/relational exchanges, these categories are standardized exchange units (such as money), tangible goods (such as task outcomes), services (such as tax preparation), information (such as organizational policies), status (such as role or occupational titles), and affiliation (such as friendships).

ship. In terms of the particularism dimension, particularistic resources are those where the identity of the exchange partner matters (Foa, 1971; Foa & Foa, 1975), such as affiliation where trust is connected to a particular individual. Nonparticularistic resources, in contrast, are fungible and can be substituted for one another, where the identity of the exchange partner or resource is not important (McLean Parks & smith, 1998). For example, dollars and pennies are both concrete and nonparticularistic, making their exchange value clear, and hence, they are easily substituted. In contrast, ideological currency is specific and abstract. Because a specific cause (e.g., renewable energy) cannot be calibrated easily against another (e.g., gender equality), substituting support for the one with the other will not be satisfactory.

These classifications and attributes of individual resources have implications for the commensurability of the resources when they are exchanged. We illustrate how ideological currencies may be more or less easy to exchange (commensurable) depending on how resource elements exemplify our classifications and attributes. For example, pecuniary elements, which typically can be quantified easily, are less likely to be exchanged for relational elements, which are particularistic (e.g., friendship for money). In part, this is because assigning specific values or rankings to a particularistic resource is inherently difficult. Likewise, ambiguous resources are unlikely to be exchanged for concrete resources, as determining the metric of exchange also will be difficult at best. Thus, the identity and characteristics of the resource elements, as well as their concrete and particularistic attributes, suggest different degrees of commensurability among resources exchanged. Ideological exchanges, where a very specific cause is valued, characteristically are both particularistic and ambiguous. We now turn to the related issue of commensurability.

The difficulty in assessing the specific worth of an ideological element that is both particularistic and ambiguous requires an enrichment of our understanding of commensurability.[5] Further, evaluating the worth of ideological elements suggests that elements may or may not be more or less interchangeable. Trading support for animal rights for recycling

---

[5] The literature on person–environment fit has addressed commensurability in terms of measurement (e.g., Caplan, 1987; Edwards & Cooper, 1990). For example, Edwards and Cooper (1990) discuss the need for measures of components to be commensurate with theoretical dimensions. Our focus is not on how ideologies are measured, but rather on how individuals perceive resource elements from the various sources to determine the extent to which elements are interchangeable.

paper products may not be seen as a fair exchange of ideologies. At least in part, this is because the underlying ideological values (humane treatment of animals versus saving trees) are not commensurate with each other. We enhance our understanding of potential substitution across ideologies (or not) by exploring the theoretical foundations of commensurability (or lack thereof) in ideological elements.

In the context of exchange relationships in general and ideological exchange in particular, there has been a relative paucity of research exploring commensurability in the organizational literature.[6] This has been an unfortunate oversight, as it has implications for the potential for perceived violation in the exchange. We turn to the domains of law and philosophy where the commensurability of resources has long been of interest.

Resources that are commensurable can be precisely quantified or measured using a single metric, such as dollars, inches, or beaver pelts.[7] Whatever the metric, the presumption is that if commensurable, the resource technically is infinitely divisible. Whereas rational choice models argue that only choices made between alternatives on the basis of commensurability are economically rational (Edgeworth, 1881),[8] others note that some resources cannot be ranked along a single metric or divided by the lowest common denominator. They argue that no single metric can capture the richness of all types of resources and their potentially unique attributes; neither can a single metric capture the diversity in how attributes of those resources are valued in the eye of the beholder.[9]

In law, the commensurability or incommensurability of resources has been the subject of debate, resulting in a dichotomization of the concepts into "either/or" perspectives—that resources either are or are not com-

---

[6] For exceptions, see McLean Parks (1997), McLean Parks and smith (2006), Pruitt (1981), and Shore et al. (2004).

[7] In New Netherland in November 1658, a beaver pelt was equivalent to 16 guilders or 2,240 white or 1,120 black wampum beads.

[8] Bix (1998) makes note of the inherent paradox of this view: "it is incommensurability that makes rational choice possible. If all options were reducible to units of some good an individual sought to maximize, there would be no need for 'choice'.... Any automaton can choose $500, when the alternative is $100; and similarly if one way of life 'equals' 5000 'units of happiness/contentment' while an alternative way of life 'equals' only 1000 units (p. 1651)."

[9] It also may be the case that using utilitarian calculus to rank choices or resources according to a single metric is tantamount to "diminish[ing]" our humanity (Hadefield, 1998). Perhaps less extreme, some lament the monetization of possibly incommensurable resources (Salzman & Rhul, 2000), noting that monetization has adverse effects (Salzman & Rhul, 2000), as actions are imbued with social meaning (Lessig, 1995; Sunstein, 1996). For example, emissions trading can make clean air seem like any other commodity with a price set by the market (Sunstein, 1996).

mensurable (cf. Leiter, 1998). For our purposes, a more fruitful perspective is that resources, *to a greater or lesser extent*, have characteristics that are both commensurable and incommensurable. In this sense, we follow the logic of the philosopher, Hegel (1881/1969), who framed the argument as one of quantity (commensurable) versus quality (incommensurable). Hegel argued that quantitative changes require qualitative changes (and vice versa). Using male pattern baldness as an example, Hegel addressed this paradox. In some cultures, a qualitative distinction is made between baldness and having a full head of hair. A change in the number of hairs on a man's head does not necessarily result in a qualitative change; however, at some point, the loss of hair does become a qualitative differentiation where the man would be considered "bald." The transition point from quantitative (losing a hair or two) to qualitative (being seen as bald) likely is subjective, but this transition demonstrates the simultaneously quantitative and qualitative aspects of the resource (in this case, hair).

The duality of Hegel is, we believe, a good one from which to understand resource commensurability of ideological elements in exchange. By recognizing that at least some resources may have characteristics *both* of commensurability and incommensurability, we avoid forcing the straitjacket of commensurability on all resources by attempting to fit the diversity of resources and their rather thorny attributes into one form or metric of exchange, be it money or "utils." Quite simply, some resources can be neither effectively quantified nor easily rank ordered against other resources. It is these resources and their thorny attributes that are the most likely candidates for subjective and idiosyncratic interpretations, and hence more prone to perceived violation in the exchange relationship (Mclean Parks, 1997; McLean Parks & Kidder, 1994; McLean Parks et al., 1998; McLean Parks & Schmedemann, 1994; McLean Parks & smith, 1998, 2006; Rousseau & McLean Parks, 1993; Schmedemann & McLean Parks, 1994). We now address the types of compensation (currencies) and their attributes to develop how ideological elements may be exchanged.

The currencies in the exchange relationships identified are not created equal(ly). A critical way in which the currencies may differ is in terms of their commensurability. Pruitt (1981) introduced the idea of commensurability to the organizational literature in discussing compensation in negotiations. He argued that there are three general types of compensation in an exchange, including specific, homologous, and substitute, and that further, these compensation types could be differentiated in terms of the *need* each fulfills and the *domain* in which the need is manifest. Specific compensation consists of alternative ways of resolving the same need, such as the busy professional who hires a cleaning service. The need for a clean home has been fulfilled, but the coin used has been different (money for service in order to gain time). Homologous compensation is an exchange in which the domain of the resources is the same, but the need that the resource fulfills is different. In the domain of transportation, a homologous exchange might be trading a Porsche for a Prius, where the needs are different (speed versus fuel efficiency). Finally, Pruitt's last classification was that of substitute compensation, where neither the need fulfilled nor the domain is the same. For example, on March 3, 1863, President Abraham Lincoln signed into law the first effective military draft in the United States. Males between 18 and 45 were to be enrolled in local militias and available for service. Yet draftees could gain an exemption by paying a fee of $300 or by hiring a substitute to take their place. The needs fulfilled by these exchanges were different (national security, personal safety, and using wages to provide for one's family), as was the "coin."

Yet, as noted by McLean Parks and smith (2006), "the absence of a form of compensation in which both the need and the coin are identical is a glaring omission" (p. 152). Sparrowe et al. (2004) suggested a fourth type of compensation: isomorphic compensation. Isomorphic compensation is when like resources are exchanged that both satisfy the same need, typical of quotidian exchanges such as changing dollars for euros when traveling. Determining the resources for the like-to-like match can be complex, where it is essential to understand the *meaning* of the resource *to the parties themselves* from their vantage points. For example, if a dean requests that a faculty member teach an extra course in return for course release the following semester, the exchange would be isomorphic if the extra course represented only the time allocation to the faculty member. But if the overload course prevented the faculty member from attending an important career-enhancing conference, then it is no longer isomorphic.

Pecuniary exchanges, which tend to be monetized and easily compared, may be characterized more easily as utilizing specific compensation, satisfying the same need and exchanged easily across domains. Relational resources, on the other hand, may be more socioemotional and are likely to be particularistic and abstract, thus requiring isomorphic compensation. In the case of ideological currencies, substitutions for addressing the specific needs fulfilled by the ideological currency are unlikely to be satisfactory and to lack isomorphism. This will lead not only to the violation of the psychological contract, but also to disidentification—identifying oneself as *not* part of the organization—because a sense of identity violation may be the result.

Cross-Cultural Ideological Exchange

We have developed a framework of ideological exchange, including sources of resources and characteristics and attributes of those resources along with their commensurability. Cultures are themselves akin to ideologies, and whereas specific ideologies may have greater or lesser appeal given that culture's values, the idea of ideologies, the elements exchanged, and the sources of those elements in the work relationship, as well as the commensurability of those elements, will apply across cultures. Yet the meaning of different elements and their sources may vary. For example, in collectivist cultures, pay may be simply a pecuniary, economic resource with pay differentials between the top and bottom of the organizational hierarchy minimized. In more individualistic cultures, however, pay may carry with it implicit knowledge of how much one is valued by the organization for their contributions, and hence may confer status and be more relational in focus. In this way, our framework can be generalized across cultures, yet specific ideologies and the meaning conferred by different elements and their sources may be imbued with different meanings and interpretations. In an increasingly global environment, these cultures and associated ideologies may mean that within organizations there are fewer overlapping ideologies. To capitalize on potential benefits of ideological attachment (e.g., Etzioni, 1988; Katz & Kahn, 1966) in exchange relationships, organizations will need to offer more diverse portfolios of ideologically grounded elements to attract a more diverse workforce.

Implications and Conclusions

When organizations assume the mantle of champion for causes valued by workers, the exchange is at least partially based on ideological currency. Organizations can benefit from ideological exchanges, in which contributions by the worker to the organization are likely to take the shape of forms of extra-role activities (e.g., Van Dyne et al., 1995) including organizational citizenship behaviors (e.g., Organ, 1988), where the worker goes beyond role requirements to benefit the organization (when the ideological norms are upheld by the company). However, if violated, these ideological exchanges may result in cases of disaffected workers who engage in organizational deviance (McLean Parks, 1997; McLean Parks & Kidder, 1994; Robinson & Bennett, 1995). Workers whose ideological contract has been violated may withhold effort or engage in sabotage to punish the organization. Thus consequences of reaffirming or disconfirming the ideological elements of the exchange relationship are nontrivial. In this chapter, we have attempted to enrich our understanding of such ideological exchanges and their consequences.

We defined ideological incompatibility as elements that are perceived as logically inconsistent. If logically inconsistent, some elements militate against the ideological cause. If pivotal ideological space is broad (many elements shared), then reactions to the perceived incompatibility perhaps will be more pronounced than if the ideological exchange were not such a large component of the work relationship. In contrast, when the ideological currency is not as pervasive (pivotal space is narrow and shallow), then it is possible that there will be an active and ongoing renegotiation of the exchange through the worker's "rebalancing" of incompatible elements (Festinger, 1957; Heider, 1958), augmenting or discounting the importance of different aspects of the relationship. Which of the incompatibilities will be dismissed or disbelieved will depend on their commensurability and the motivations, expectations, and ideological involvement of the worker (perceiver; Fiske & Taylor, 1991).

Incompatibility provides a motivation to attempt to restore internal equilibrium. Perceivers will resolve minor incompatibility by moderating (Heider, 1958) or discounting (Festinger, 1957) incompatible elements. Yet incompatibility, especially if significant, is unlikely to go unnoticed by the organization, which may generate credible excuses or justifications (Bies & Sitkin, 1991) or attempts to engage in image management (Elsbach, 1994; Gioia & Thomas, 1996) or labeling processes (Ashforth & Humphrey, 1997). Such activities could moderate one or more of the incompatible elements in the perceiver's eyes. Whether or not the incompatible elements are moderated will depend in part on their level of commensurability. If incommensurable, it will be nonnegotiable, potentially severing the relationship. Further, if pivotal space is broad and deep, it is even more likely that the result of incommensurability will be violation of the ideological contract. If these attempts by the organization are regarded as disingenuous, then these effects may be magnified.

In summary, we have examined ideological exchange, articulating the sources of resources that may contribute to the exchange, as well as the characteristics and attributes of those resources and their commensurability. We have identified six sources of resource elements (pecuniary, task, role, relational, occupational, and organizational) that serve as inducements for workers in their ideological exchange with their organization. We acknowledge that the six sources of resource elements we presented are not mutually exclusive and are not exhaustive.

By viewing the content of exchange relationships through the lens of multiple elements, we have identified pivotal ideological space as that which is jointly affirmed by the content of multiple elements. This pivotal space can be characterized in terms of depth and breadth. When pivotal ideological space is maximized in terms of these dimensions, the strength of inducements will be enhanced. Paradoxically, if organizations fail to support the ideology, the contract is violated, and the reaction of the worker in terms of disidentification (e.g., Dukerich et al., 1998; Elsbach & Bhattacharya, 2001) and disaffection (Etzioni, 1988) is likely to be magnified, relative to a violation when the depth and breadth of the ideological space are weaker. Also, we have recognized that there may be an absence of pivotal space or that the content of the elements may be incompatible.

We have extended the concept of crystallization from the literature on organizational culture (Chatman, 1989) and organizational identity (McLean Parks & smith, 2000, 2002) to suggest that when multiple members of an organization hold shared meanings about ideological resource elements and pivotal space, then ideological crystallization occurs. The more crystallized the ideology, the more pervasive it is across workers, and the more they affirm one another's ideological involvement. However, when the ideology is crystallized, if the organization's commitment to the ideology waivers, reactions also will be stronger and more pervasive. Similarly, meta-ideological exchanges may occur when crystallized ideologies lead to spontaneous or planned actions by those who share ideological elements.

Finally, in an ideological exchange, elements range from commensurable to incommensurable, and we expand three types of currency (economic, socioemotional, and ideological) (Pruitt, 1981) and four types of compensation (specific, homologous, substitute, and isomorphic) (Sparrowe et al., 2004) to explain how exchanges are facilitated between the types of resources. Through these currencies and types of compensation, we provided the means through which the process of exchange can occur.

We believe our framework provides a basis from which further research can be developed as scholars continue to refine the construct associated with ideological exchange relationships, enriching our understanding of the work relationship. If work relationships are to be understood more completely, it is imperative that we employ a more nuanced view of the nature and sources of the elements of exchange, and rather than assuming commensurability in resources exchanged, we need to recognize their complexity and richness, as well as the conundrums that complexity presents.

REFERENCES

Allen, V. L., & van de Vliert, E. (1982). A role theoretical perspective on transitional processes. In V. L. Allen & E. van de Vliert (Eds.), *Role transitions: Explorations and explanations* (pp. 3–18). New York, NY: Plenum Press.

Andersen, S. M., & Chen, S. (2002). The relational self: An interpersonal social-cognitive theory. *Psychological Review, 109,* 619–645.

Ashforth, B., & Humphrey, R. (1997). The ubiquity and potency of labeling in organizations, *Organization Science, 8,* 43–58.

Ashforth, B., & Mael, F. (1989). Social identity theory and the organization. *Academy of Management Review, 14,* 20–39.

Biddle, B. J. (1979). *Role theory: Expectations, identities, and behaviors.* New York, NY: Academic Press.

Biddle, B. J. (1986). Recent development in role theory. *Annual Review of Sociology, 12,* 1267–1292.

Biemiller, L. (2008). Chronicle of Higher Education. *At Washington U., protesters turn their backs on Phyllis Schlafly.* Retrieved November 26, 2010, from http://chronicle.com/article/At-Washington-U-Protesters/40987/.

Bies, R. (1987). The predicament of injustice: The management of moral outrage. In L. L. Cummings & B. M. Staw (Eds.), *Research in organizational behavior* (Vol. 9, pp. 289–319). Greenwich, CT: JAI Press.

Bies, R., & Sitkin, S. (1991). Explanation as legitimation: Excuse making in organizations. In M. McLaughlin, M. Cody, & S. Read (Eds.), *Explaining one's self to others: Reason-giving in a social context* (pp. 183–198). Hillsdale, NJ: Erlbaum.

Bix, B. (1998). Dealing with incommensurability for dessert and desert: Comments on Chapman and Katz. *University of Pennsylvania Law Review, 146,* 1651–1670.

Blau, P. (1964). *Exchange and power in social life.* New York, NY: Wiley.

Caplan, R. (1987). Person-environment fit theory & organizations: Commensurate dimensions, time perspectives and mechanisms, *Journal of Vocational Behavior, 31*, 248–267.

Chatman, J. (1989). Organizational research: A model of person-organization fit. *Academy of Management Review, 14*, 333–349.

Christiansen, C. (1999). Defining lives: Occupation as identity: An essay on competence, coherence, and the creation of meaning. *The American Journal of Occupational Therapy, 53*, 547–558.

Cooley, C. H. (1902). *Human nature and the social order.* New York, NY: Charles Scribner's Sons.

Crooker, K., smith, f., & Tabak, F. (2002). Creating work-life balance: A model of pluralism across life domains. *Human Resource Development Review, 4*, 387–419.

Dukerich, J., Kramer, R., & McLean Parks, J. (1998). Identification with organizations: Tales from the dark side. In D. Whetton & P. Godfrey (Eds.), *Identity in organizations: Developing theory through conversations* (pp. 245–256). Thousand Oaks, CA: Sage.

Dutton, J., Dukerich, J., & Harquail, C. (1994). Organizational images and member identification. *Administrative Science Quarterly, 39*, 239–263.

Edgeworth, F. Y. (1881). *Mathematical psychics: An essay on the application of mathematics to the moral sciences.* Charleston, SC: Nabu Press.

Edwards, J., & Cooper, C. (1990). The person-environment fit approach to stress: Recurring problems and some suggested solutions. *Journal of Organizational Behavior, 11*, 293–307.

Elsbach, K. (1994). Managing organizational legitimacy in the California cattle industry: The construction and effectiveness of verbal accounts. *Administrative Science Quarterly, 39*, 57–88.

Elsbach, K., & Bhattacharya, C. (2001). Defining who you are by what you're not: Organizational disidentification and the National Rifle Association. *Organization Science, 12*, 393–413.

Engineers Without Borders. (2011). Our story. Retrieved from http://www.ewb-usa.org/about-ewb-usa/our-story

Etzioni, A. (1988). *The moral dimension.* New York, NY: Basic Books.

Festinger, L. (1957). *A theory of cognitive dissonance.* New York, NY: Harper & Row.

Fiske, S., & Taylor, S. (1991). *Social cognition.* New York, NY: McGraw-Hill.

Foa, U. (1971). Intrpersonal and economic resources. *Science, 171*, 345–351.

Foa, U., & Foa, E. (1975). *Resource theory of social exchange.* Morristown, NJ: General Learning Press.

Gioia, D., & Thomas, J. (1996). Identity, image and issue interpretation: Sensemaking during strategic change in academia. *Administrative Science Quarterly, 41*, 370–403.

Gnau, T. (2010). BP employees in Ohio feel weight of Gulf spill. *Dayton Daily News*, June 9, 2010.

Goffman, E. (1959). *The presentation of self in everyday life.* New York, NY: Anchor Books.

Goffman, E. (1961). *Encounters: Two studies in the sociology of interaction.* New York, NY: MacMillan Publishing Co.

Granovetter, M. (1978). Threshold models of collective behavior. *American Journal of Sociology, 83*, 1420–1423.

Hackman, J. R., & Oldham, G. R. (1976). Motivation through design of work. *Organizational Behavior and Human Performance, 16*, 250–279.

Hadefield, G. K. (1998). An expressive theory of contract: From dilemmas to a reconceptualization of rational choice in contract law. *University of Pennsylvania Law Review, 146*, 1235–1285.

Hegel, G. W. F. (1969). *The science of logic* (A. V. Miller, Trans.). New York, NY: Humanity Books. (Original work published in 1881)

Heider, F. (1958). *The psychology of interpersonal relations.* New York, NY: Wiley.

Jackson, J. (1966). A conceptual and measurement model of norms and roles. *Pacific Sociological Review, 9,* 35–47.

Kahn, R., Wolfe, D., Quinn, R., Snoek, J., & Rosenthal, R. (1964). *Organizational stress: Studies in role conflict and ambiguity.* New York, NY: John Wiley & Sons.

Katz, D., & Kahn, R. (1966). *The social psychology of organizations.* New York, NY: Wiley.

Kidwell, R., Jr., & Bennett, N. (1993). Employee propensity to withhold effort: A conceptual model to intersect three avenues of research. *Academy of Management Review, 18,* 429–456.

Leiter, B. (1998). Incommensurability: Truth or consequences? *University of Pennsylvania Law Review, 146,* 1723–1731.

Lessig, L. (1995). The regulation of social meaning. *University of Chicago Law Review, 943,* 943–1007.

Linton, R. (1936). *The study of man.* New York, NY: Appleton-Century.

MacNeil, I. R. (1985). Relational contract: What we do and do not know. *Wisconsin Law Review, 1985,* 483–525.

March, J., & Simon, H. (1958). *Organizations.* New York, NY: Wiley.

McLean Parks, J. (1997). The fourth arm of justice: The art and science of revenge. In R. Lewicki, B. Sheppard, & B. Bies (Eds.), *Research on Negotiation in Organization* (pp. 113–144). Greenwich, CT: JAI Press.

McLean Parks, J., & Kidder, D. (1994). Trends: Till death us do part: The changing nature of organizational contracts and commitments. *Journal of Organizational Behavior, Trends, 1,* 111–136.

McLean Parks, J., Kidder, D., & Gallagher, D. (1998). Fitting square pegs into round holes: Mapping the domain of contingent work arrangements onto the psychological contract, *Journal of Organizational Behavior, 19,* 697–730.

McLean Parks, J., & Schmedemann, D. (1994). When promises become contracts: Implied contracts and handbook provisions on job security. *Human Resources Management, 33,* 403–423.

McLean Parks, J., & smith, f. (1998). Organizational contracting: A rational exchange? In J. Halpern & R. Stern (Eds.), *Debating rationality: Nonrational aspects of organizational decision making* (pp. 168–210). Ithaca, NY: Cornell University Press.

McLean Parks, J., & smith, f. (2000, August). *Organizational identity: The ongoing puzzle of definition and redefinition.* Paper presented at the Academy of Management Meeting, Managerial and Organizational Cognition Division, Toronto, CA.

McLean Parks, J., & smith, f. (2002). *Creating organizational identity: The dynamic processes of communication and articulation.* Invited paper and presentation, Organizational Identity Conference, Boston, MA.

McLean Parks, J., & smith, f. (2006). Ghost workers: New organizational realities. In P. Taylor & M. Shams (Eds.), *Developments in work and organizational psychology: Implications for international business* (Vol. 20, pp. 131–162). Amsterdam, The Netherlands: Elsevier, Ltd.

Mead, G. H. (1934). *Mind, self and society: From the standpoint of a social behaviorist.* Chicago, IL: The University of Chicago Press.

Merton, R. K. (1957). *Social theory and social structure.* New York, NY: Free Press.

Miller, H. (2004). *The frankenfood myth: How protest and politics threaten the biotech revolution*. Westport, CN: Praeger.

Morrison, E., & Robinson, S. (1997). When employees feel betrayed: A model of how psychological contract violation develops. *Academy of Management Review, 22*, 226–256.

Nakao, K., & Treas, J. (1994). Updating occupational prestige and socioeconomic scores: How the new measures measure up. *Sociological Methodology, 24*, 1–72.

Organ, D. W. (1988). *Organizational citizenship behavior: The good soldier syndrome*. Lexington, MA: D.C. Heath and Company.

Origins. (2010). *Origins mission statement*. Retrieved November 27, 2010 from http://www.origins.com/customer_service/aboutus.tmpl#/Mission.

Pruitt, D. (1981). *Negotiation behavior*. New York, NY: Academic Press.

Robinson, S., & Bennett, B. (1995). A typology of deviant workplace behaviors: A multidimensional scaling study. *Academy of Management Journal, 38*, 555–572.

Rousseau, D., & McLean Parks, J. (1993). The contracts of individuals and organizations. In L. L. Cummings & B. Staw (Eds.), *Research in organizational behavior* (Vol. 15, pp. 1–43). Greenwich, CT: JAI Press.

Salzman, J., & Rhul, J. (2002). Currencies and the commodification of environmental law. *Stanford Law Review, 53*, 607–694.

Schein, E. (1980). *Organizational psychology*. Englewood Cliffs, NJ: Prentice Hall.

Schmedemann, D., & McLean Parks, J. (1994). Contract formation through employee handbooks: Legal, psychological and empirical analyses. *Wake Forest Law Review, 29*, 647–718.

Schurman, R. (2004). Fighting frankenfoods: Industry opportunity structures and the efficacy of the anti-biotech movement in Western Europe. *Social Problems, 51*, 243–268.

Shore, L. M., Tetrick, L. E., Taylor, M. S., Coyle-Shapiro, J., Liden, R., McLean Parks, J., … Van Dyne, L. (2004). The employee-organization relationship: A timely concept in a period of transition. In G. R. Ferris & J. Martocchio (Eds.), *Research in personnel and human resources management* (pp. 291–370). Greenwich, CT: JAI Press.

Simon, B. (2004). *Identity in modern society: A social psychological perspective*. Oxford, UK: Blackwell.

Simon, B., Trötschel, R., & Dähne, D. (2008). Identity affirmation and social movement support. *European Journal of Social Psychology, 38*, 935–946.

Simpson, B., & Macy, M. (2004). Power, identity & collective action in social exchange. *Social Forces, 82*, 1373–1409.

Sluss, D. M., & Ashforth, B. E. (2007). Relational identity and identification: Defining ourselves through work relationships. *Academy of Management Review, 32*, 9–32.

Spaeth, J. L. (1979). Vertical differentiation among occupations. *American Sociological Review, 44*, 746–762.

Sparrowe, R., Dirks, K., Bunderson, S., & McLean Parks, J. (2004). *Reinventing the wheel and spinning our wheels: Social exchange and discretionary attitudes and outcomes in organizations*. Unpublished manuscript, Washington University at St. Louis.

Steele, C. M. (1988). The psychology of self-affirmation: Sustaining the integrity of the self. In L. Berkowitz (Ed.), *Advances in experimental social psychology* (Vol. 21, pp. 261–302). San Diego, CA: Academic Press.

Sunstein, C. (1996). On the expressive function of law. *University of Pennsylvania Law Review, 44*, 2021–2053.

Thompson, J., & Bunderson, J. S. (2003). Violations of principle: Ideological currency in the psychological contract. *Academy of Management Review, 28*, 571–586.

Van Dyne, L., Cummings, L. L., & McLean Parks, J. (1995), Extra role behaviors: A critical analysis and theoretical interpretation (a bridge over muddied waters). In B. Staw & L. L. Cummings (Eds.), *Research in organizational behavior* (Vol. 17, pp. 215–285). Greenwich, CT: JAI Press.

6

Perceived Organizational Cruelty: An Expansion of the Negative Employee–Organization Relationship Domain

Lynn M. Shore
San Diego State University

Jacqueline A-M. Coyle-Shapiro
London School of Economics & Political Science

Research on the employee–organization relationship (EOR) has primarily drawn upon social exchange theory and the norm of reciprocity (Blau, 1964; Gouldner, 1960) and the inducements–contributions model (March & Simon, 1958) as the bases for describing and categorizing different EORs and their consequences for organizationally desired employee attitudes and behaviors. The key finding emerging from this research supports the contention that social exchange relationships (e.g., perceived organizational support, psychological contract fulfillment, overinvestment and mutual investment employer approaches to the EOR) yield positive benefits for individuals and organizations. An area of the EOR literature that has garnered much less theoretical and empirical attention is negative relationships in which employees perceive that their relationship with the organization is harmful. Two exceptions are psychological contract breach and violation (Robinson, 1996; Rousseau, 1995), consisting of employee perceptions of and emotional reactions to broken promises, and underinvestment and quasi-spot contract using the inducements–contributions employment relationship framework (Tsui, Pearce, Porter, & Tripoli, 1997). In the case of breach and violation, the focus is on lack of organizational fulfillment of promises, a reflection of the norm of reciprocity, and expectations of exchange of favors. In the latter case, the focus is on imbalance of inducements by the organization and contributions by the employee. These literatures provide a starting point for developing a model of negative EORs by highlighting the key roles of reciprocation and balance in establishing and maintaining positive EORs.

Although there is a great deal of research on the deleterious mental, physical, and behavioral effects on employees of abusive treatment in the workplace (Griffin & O'Leary-Kelly, 2004), less attention has been given to the role of the EOR as an intervening variable in situations of mistreatment in contrast to its well-established role in positive organizational treatment (Rhoades & Eisenberger, 2002; Zhao, Wayne, Glibkowski, & Bravo, 2007). Favorable organizational and managerial treatment serves as a signal to employees about the degree to which they have a social exchange relationship with the employer, which determines the employee's degree of commitment, turnover intentions, job performance, and citizenship behavior. We argue that current literature does not reflect the most negative kinds of EORs in which employees perceive egregious harm-doing by the organization and its agents. Likewise, limited attention has been given to understanding the situational and psychological mechanisms that link severely harmful organizational treatment to employee perceptions of the EOR. Thus, in this chapter, we develop a model of perceived organizational cruelty (POC) to address this gap in the literature.

We describe the concept of POC and how it differs from established concepts in the negative EOR domain, including psychological contract breach and violation (Montes & Zweig, 2009; Robinson & Brown, 2004) and quid pro quo and underinvestment employment relationships (Tsui et al., 1997). Subsequently, we present a model of antecedents and outcomes of POC and conclude with implications for research, practice, and cross-cultural issues.

DEFINITION OF PERCEIVED ORGANIZATIONAL CRUELTY

To begin our construction of the POC construct, we first considered the many concepts related to mistreatment by organizations that already exist. A very large body of literature has been established on unfair treatment, including topics such as justice and discrimination (Colquitt, 2001;

Goldman, Gutek, Stein, & Lewis, 2006; Raver & Nishii, 2010); abusive supervision (Tepper, 2007); and aggression, violence, and victimization (Aquino & Thau, 2009; O'Leary-Kelly, Griffin, & Glew, 1996). In the edited volume *The Dark Side of Organizational Behavior* (Griffin & O'Leary-Kelly, 2004), two chapters focused on the EOR; specifically, Rousseau's chapter on under-the-table deals, and Robinson and Brown's chapter on breach and violation. Both are noteworthy for discussing the dark side of EOR issues between employees and employers (negative EORs). However, neither focuses on the more extreme negative views that employees may hold about their relationship with the employer—that is, when an employee perceives their employer to be intentionally callous and malicious.

To aid in developing the concept of POC, we first consulted two dictionary sources. Webster's Online Dictionary (n.d.) definition of cruelty is "The attribute or quality of being cruel; a disposition to give unnecessary pain or suffering to others; inhumanity; barbarity." The Wordnet dictionary (Princeton University, 2010) definition of cruelty is "a cruel act; a deliberate infliction of pain and suffering." A key aspect of cruelty is the distress experienced. Equally important features are the references to "unnecessary" and "deliberate." Thus, when organizations treat employees poorly, employees judge the necessity of and the intentions behind such acts (Skarlicki & Folger, 2004). When treatment is perceived as deliberate, unnecessary, and harmful, employees are likely to view the organization as cruel. Thus, we define POC as the employee's perception that the organization holds him or her in contempt, has no respect for him or her personally, and treats him or her in a manner that is intentionally inhumane.

COMPARISON OF POC AND OTHER NEGATIVE EOR CONCEPTS

Although organizations typically consist of multiple agents representing organizational perspectives and interests, the employee often views the organization as a single entity with human-like characteristics. POC involves employee attributions of a "personified" organization. Levinson (1965) was one of the first scholars to point out that employees personify their employing organization. Levinson's (1965) reasoning as to the basis for personification was due to the following aspects of organizations:

(1) The organization is legally, morally, and financially responsible for the actions of its members as organizational agents. (2) The organization has policies which make for great similarity in behavior by agents of the organization at different times and in different geographical locations. (3) These policies are supplemented by precedents, traditions, and informal norms as guides to behavior. (4) In many instances the action by the agent is a role performance with many common characteristics throughout that organization regardless of who carries it out. (pp. 378–379)

These elements of organizations create perceptions among employees of a unified entity with human-like qualities facilitating employees' characterization of organizations in a manner akin to the characterizations of individuals.

Eisenberger and colleagues (cf. Eisenberger, Huntington, Hutchison, & Sowa, 1986; Eisenberger & Stinglehamber, 2011) built on Levinson's (1965) theorizing to argue that employees have perceptions of organizational support based on inferences that the organization has benevolent or malevolent intentions toward them. Eisenberger and colleagues' studies of perceived organizational support (POS) have focused on benevolent organizational intentions, whereas the present chapter develops a model of perceived cruelty that spotlights employee perceptions of malevolent organizational intentions. Thus, POC can be considered a mirror opposite of POS in the sense that the organization is viewed as malevolent rather than benevolent, and some of the favorable experiences that contribute to POS (e.g., fair treatment, supervisor support, and investment by the organization; Rhoades & Eisenberger, 2002) could in a *negative* form contribute to POC. For example, unfair treatment by the organization, supervisor abuse, or employee investment of time and effort in the organization with no return may all contribute to the development of POC. However, as we will argue later, there are also defining features of POC that are not elements of the POS literature. In particular, the manner in which the agent delivers harmful actions may determine whether the organization is perceived as cruel by the employee.

Psychological Contracts and POC

An important issue is how POC is distinct from other negative EOR constructs such as breach and violation of the psychological contract.

Several defining features are central to psychological contracts: (1) they reflect employee perception; (2) they involve a sense of obligation between employee and employer; and (3) they involve ongoing exchange in the EOR (Robinson & Brown, 2004). Breach and violation both refer to situations whereby the employee views an obligation in the psychological contract as unfulfilled. Morrison and Robinson (1997) distinguished breach, the cognitive evaluation that something promised has not been received, from violation, the emotional experience resulting from the interpretation of that breach.

Breach and violation within the psychological contracts literature have a substantially different focus from POC. Whereas psychological contracts center on perceptions of the degree of fulfillment of promises and obligations, POC focuses on the personified employer as a harmful and cruel entity. Breach could be a contributing factor in POC but is likely somewhat distal, because not just any unfulfilled obligation would create such perceptions. Violation, on the other hand, would more likely be associated with POC because it "not only means that one is not getting something one desired or expected but, moreover, that a trusted other betrayed a trust and failed to live up to norms of reciprocity and goodwill that one expects in an ongoing relationship" (Robinson & Brown, 2004, p. 313). Rousseau (1989, p. 129) likewise argued that "violation is an intense reaction of outrage, shock, resentment, and anger, similar to that described by Cahn (1949) in his treatment of injustice. These hot feelings suggest uncontrollability, a quasi-irreversible quality where anger lingers and 'victims' experience a changed view of the other party and their interrelationship (Bies, 1987)." Although we expect contract violation to be one contributor to POC, we argue that there are also situational and interpersonal determinants of POC that are outside the bounds of psychological contracts.

The Employment Relationship and POC

The employment relationship model developed by Tsui et al. (1997) also includes negative EOR elements, but ones that are quite different than POC. Their model builds on March and Simon's (1958) framework in which the EOR is viewed as an exchange of organizational inducements for employee contributions. Tsui et al. (1997) outline four types of employment relationships that differ on two dimensions: the degree of balance/

imbalance in each party's contributions and whether the focus of these contributions is economic or social. Of relevance here is that a balanced economic exchange (quasi-spot contract) occurs when the employer offers short-term, purely economic inducements in return for highly specified outcomes and the underinvestment approach occurs when the employer expects open-ended commitment and long-term investment from employees in return for short-term economic inducements. In their empirical study, Tsui et al. (1997) found that quasi-spot contracts and underinvestment models were negatively associated with employee attitudes and performance.

Unlike POC, the employment relationship model is based on the exchange offered to groups of employees, either work groups (Hom et al., 2009) or organizations (Song, Tsui, & Law, 2009). The employment relationship model is quite different from POC in that it is focused on the contributions of both parties to the exchange itself, and not on employee perceptions of the personified organization. Thus, although both concepts are within the EOR domain, Tsui's model is less personal and specific to the employee, and unlike POC, it does not focus on individual employee perceptions of intentional organizational harm-doing. Rather, the employment relationship spotlights the nature of the exchange itself as balanced or unbalanced and as economic or social. The underinvestment and quasi-spot contract employment relationships may contribute to POC by creating a setting in which poor organizational treatment is more likely.

Psychological Mechanisms Underlying POC

The psychological contract and POS literatures are based on social exchange theory and the norm of reciprocity (Blau, 1964; Gouldner, 1960), and both of these concepts, along with POC, are perceptual in nature. This raises questions as to the role of norm of reciprocity in relation to POC. Gouldner (1960) argued that "a norm of reciprocity, in its universal form, makes two interrelated, minimal demands: (1) people should help those who have helped them, and (2) people should not injure those who have helped them" (p. 171). According to Norm Violation Theory (DeRidder & Tripathi, 1992), norms serve to sanction the actions of group members, and it is assumed that these norms are commonly known and followed. When violated, such actions are viewed as illegitimate and inspire sanctions for noncompliance as a means to enforce norms and ensure future compliance. In the case of the EOR, employees may be less likely to apply sanctions for noncompliance to the norm of reciprocity given their likely greater dependence on the organization (Shore & Shore, 1995) and fear of reprisals. This creates a dilemma for employees of how best to respond to nonreciprocity from the organization.

Research on the employment relationship model (Tsui et al., 1997) provides evidence that employees prefer and seek balance in the exchange of inducements and contributions with the employer, as shown by the superiority of the mutual investment as compared with the underinvestment model (Hom et al., 2009). Thus, when an employee perceives that she is underrewarded relative to her efforts, she may be challenged as to how to restore a sense of balance, especially if she is not very marketable. Research by Siegrist (1996) provides support that such imbalance is harmful to the employee's health. His Model of Effort–Reward Imbalance at Work proposes that employees compare their efforts and rewards, and if they are in a high cost/low gain condition, this creates a situation of high stress. Recent research on his model showed that "the risk of incident stress-related disease, such as coronary heart disease or depression, is about twice as high in men and women scoring high on effort-reward imbalance compared to non-exposed people" (Siegrist, 2009, p. 305). Thus, in addition to being viewed as unfair and counternormative, an unbalanced EOR challenges the employee's health and well-being.

Disregard of reciprocation by the organization is likely to lead to a loss of trust in the organization and fear of future nonreciprocation. Taking ill treatment a step further, a malevolent and injurious organization is operating in an antinormative manner when directly harming an employee who is helpful to the organization. How might such detrimental treatment be dealt with by the employee? Employees who espouse the negative reciprocity norm, the belief that retaliation, or an "eye for an eye," is an appropriate response to wrongdoing (Eisenberger, Lynch, Aselage, & Rohdieck, 2004), may comfortably act in ways that restore balance in the exchange with the employer when faced with POC by directly harming the organization. By comparison, employees who do not believe in negative reciprocity may be more conflicted as to how best to restore balance in the exchange so that they do not feel victimized by such treatment. Retaliatory behavior can cause employee feelings of guilt, anxiety, and stress (Skarlicki & Folger, 2004), and this may be especially likely for those who are highly conscientious or who would normally frown upon such behavior. Self-regulation impairment may be another reason why abused employees retaliate. That is, the experience of abuse undermines the employee's ability to regulate their own behavior by depleting their emotional resources (Thau & Mitchell, 2010). As argued by Thau and Mitchell (2010), "The experience of abuse challenges victims to process, interpret, and understand the causes and consequences of being harmed" (pp. 1009–1010).

In sum, a key principal that underlies both positive and negative EORs is balance in exchange. Although social exchange and the norm of reciprocity provide a basis for predicting employee attitudinal and behavioral responses when the EOR ranges from neutral to positive, when the EOR is negative due to nonreciprocation by the organization or involves more actively harmful treatment of the employee, other types of norms as well as psychological processes, such as the negative reciprocity norm or self-regulation impairment, may operate. When organizational agents engage in antinormative behavior, employees are challenged as to how to respond given their lesser power and the risks associated with engaging in aggressive actions or with passively accepting ill treatment in light of the negative health consequences. Employees who do not believe in the negative reciprocity norm or fear the consequences of acting in a retaliatory manner will still seek ways to create balance in the exchange, such as through actively seeking ways to create or reinstate a positive relationship (e.g., voicing concerns, asking for changes, or engaging in influence tactics such as ingratiation) or through more subtle harmful behavior (e.g., gossiping, extended breaks). If the stress of being victimized is too great, some employees will behave in ways considered inappropriate (e.g., losing their temper, behaving unprofessionally), which may further enable the transgressor to justify the ill treatment. Employees who view the relationship as irretrievably broken will likely seek jobs outside the current employer or suffer either emotionally or by engaging in self-destructive behavior if changing jobs is not a possibility.

A MODEL OF POC

Our model depicted in Figure 6.1 is an early-stage model of antecedents and outcomes that is intended to guide future empirical research on POC. Unlike models of malevolent supervisors (cf. Tepper, 2000) that focus on

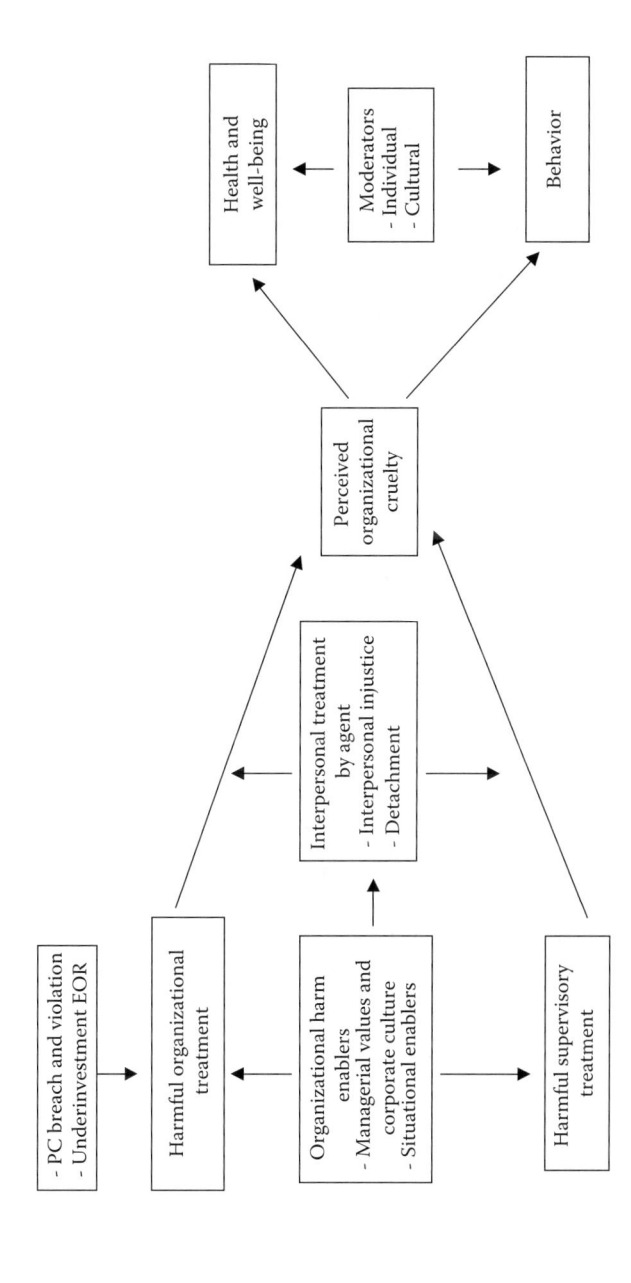

FIGURE 6.1
Model of perceived organizational cruelty. PC, psychological contract.

acts of single individuals, we argue that POC is based on employee perceptions of the participation, either direct or indirect, of multiple organizational agents. Unethical acts within organizations often involve knowing cooperation among numerous employees (Anand, Ashforth, & Joshi, 2005). When managers in positions of power engage in malevolent acts toward individual employees or toward groups of employees, these acts may in fact be viewed as reasonable either because of a business justification or because the recipient(s) may be seen as deserving mistreatment due to their own behavior (Scott, Colquitt, & Paddock, 2009). Such complicit behavior is likely to increase the frequency of harmful acts and the ease of individuals in observing or engaging in destructive treatment of others. Thus, a critical element of POC is the inference by the employee that the organization is involved in his or her mistreatment.

ANTECEDENTS OF POC

We propose that organizational practices deemed to be harmful to the individual and persistent exposure to negative managerial behaviors are likely to lead to the perception that the organization is a cruel one. Although many types of organizational and supervisory treatment could be considered harmful by employees, they may not lead to perceptions of organizational cruelty. Acts deemed to be cruel require organizational conditions that facilitate a level of mistreatment that is perceived as intentionally harmful. We refer to these conditions as "organizational harm enablers," including corporate culture and managerial values, along with organizational processes that increase the likelihood that transgressors do not take personal responsibility for harm-doing, such as legitimizing harm, initial small acts of minor harm-doing, and displaced responsibility. In addition, as part of the sensemaking process, targets of harm assess the degree of organizational cruelty by making attributions of the responsibility, intentionality, and justification for the harm, and also by considering the interpersonal treatment associated with the destructive event. The enactment of organizational harm and its delivery, coupled with an individual's sensemaking of the harmful treatment, are likely to lead to an evaluation that the organization is cruel.

Organizational Harm Enablers

Corporate Culture and Managerial Values as Enablers

Kanter (1987) argued that "Symbols are an important part of organizational culture, and they can send positive or negative messages" (p. 23). The actions of organizational leaders are scrutinized by employees as they seek to understand the culture of their organization. Fraud, insider trading, and giving executives bonuses while employees are getting laid off would all be examples of organizational actions that provide a negative message to employees about the values of their leaders. Such negative symbolic acts may also increase the likelihood that other destructive behaviors involving mistreatment of employees may be allowed or even condoned.

There are a number of ways in which organizations can portray a negative regard for employees' contributions and a disregard for their well-being. Exploitive and cruel practices that are enacted by destructive leaders are in all likelihood a reflection of the values of top management. Destructive leadership assumes that the leader's intentions are bad and certain behaviors are inherently vicious (Padilla, Hogan, & Kaiser, 2007). However, Kellerman (2004) contends that negative leader behaviors can include both incompetence and evil behaviors, and it is the latter that is of relevance here. Zimbardo (2004) defines evil as "intentionally behaving—or causing others to act—in ways that demean, dehumanize, harm, destroy, or kill innocent people" (p. 3). Padilla et al. (2007) argue that destructive leadership may be based on an ideology of hate. This type of leadership can also be seen in the case of Enron, where leaders created a culture of intimidation. For example, chief financial officer (CFO) Andrew Fastow had a desk cube with the inscription "When ENRON says it's going to 'rip your face off' … it means it will rip your face off" (Raghavan, 2002, p. A1, cited in Padilla et al., 2007). Although a drastic symbolic act, the inscription signals a disregard for the well-being of employees through managerial coercion and dominance. Consequently, we would expect that the presence of destructive leadership at the top of organizations will increase the likelihood of organizational practices and policies that employees deem as abusive.

Nishii, Lepak, and Schneider (2008) argued that human resource (HR) practices motivated by a management philosophy based on exploitation or getting the most out of employees would be negatively associated with employee attitudes. Empirically, the authors found that employee attributions of HR practices reflecting a managerial philosophy focused on employee exploitation were negatively related to employee commitment and satisfaction. This is similar to what Storey (1992, p. 26) terms a hard utilitarian approach that views employees as a resource that management should exploit to the fullest and places little value on the concerns of workers. Likewise, we anticipate that employees would perceive the practices implemented as part of a cost-reduction strategy to be potentially exploitative and hence harmful to their needs. Drago (1996) found the effects of high-performance practices for workers to be negative in what was termed "disposable workplaces" where workers were coerced to cooperate because the employer had the power to relocate.

Situational Enablers

Although destructive leadership may at times be intentional, at other times it may be due to elements of the organizational context. Managers who behave ethically in most of their life spheres (e.g., family, community) may nonetheless, within a particular organizational context, behave in corrupt and harmful ways. O'Leary-Kelly et al. (1996) argued that social learning is one reason for harmful behavior. Specifically, when organizational leaders do not punish aggression but rather reward individuals who engage in the behavior, or model the behaviors themselves, employees may increasingly engage in such behavior.

Milgram's studies (1974) on obedience to authority make clear the importance of organizational environments in creating conditions for harmful treatment. Using authority to legitimize the actions, disguising the harmful treatment as somehow appropriate or even helpful, escalating harmful acts by increasing their destructiveness gradually, displacing responsibility for harm to authority figures, and dehumanizing labels and stereotypes of potential victims all increase the likelihood that individuals will engage in harmful treatment of others (Zimbardo, 2000).

Anand et al. (2005) argue that harmful actions in organizations are facilitated by rationalization tactics such as denial of responsibility, denial of injury to the victim, and economic pressures. Likewise, employees can be socialized to accept corrupt practices through rewards and acts of compromise that appear to solve pressing organizational problems but that eventually cause them to "back into" corrupt behavior. As harmful treatment of employees becomes more common, such actions become part of the fabric of the organizational culture through a set of organizational norms.

Harmful Supervisory Treatment

Although harmful practices are likely to be primarily determined by actions and decisions made by upper management as described earlier in terms of organizational enablers, we expect that supervisory treatment will also be important in creating perceptions of POC. The supervisor, as an agent of the organization, is viewed as representing the organization in most interactions with their direct reports (Coyle-Shapiro & Shore, 2007). As such, a supervisor who is perceived as behaving in an intentionally harmful manner will likely contribute to POC.

There are a number of existing constructs that capture supervisory negative behavior toward employees including abusive supervision (Tepper, 2000), hierarchical abuse of power (Vredenburgh & Brender, 1998), petty tyranny (Ashforth, 1997), supervisor aggression (Schat, Frone, & Kelloway, 2006), and supervisor undermining (Duffy, Ganster, & Pagon, 2002). Tepper (2000, p. 178) defines abusive supervision as "subordinates' perceptions of the extent to which supervisors engage in the sustained display of hostile verbal and non verbal behaviors, excluding physical contact." Sharing some conceptual ground, Ashforth (1997, p. 126) defines petty tyranny as the superior's use of power "oppressively, capriciously, and perhaps vindictively." These constructs capture a range of negative behaviors that may or may not be intended to cause harm to the recipient. For example, Tepper's (2000) definition of abusive supervision suggests that supervisors may engage in those behaviors not to cause harm but rather to achieve some other goal such as higher performance, whereas supervisor aggression specifically refers to the intention to cause harm. Putting aside the intention behind such behaviors, all these definitions involve a supervisor "including" the employee in negative interactions.

However, exclusion may be even more damaging from the employee's viewpoint. Ostracism captures the degree to which an individual perceives that he or she is ignored or excluded by others (Williams,

2001) and represents a form of "social death" (Sommer, Williams, Ciarocco, & Baumeister, 2001) because it gives the individual an experience of what it is like not to exist. Social exclusion has been shown to result in harmful cognitive, emotional, behavioral, and health outcomes (Baumeister, DeWall, Ciarocco, & Twenge, 2005; Blackhart, Nelson, Knowles, & Baumeister, 2009; DeWall, Maner, & Rouby, 2009). This form of negative behavior is different from abusive behaviors because despite the aversive nature of such acts on the recipient, there is an acknowledgment through the negative interactions that the recipient exists. According to Williams (2001), long-term targets of ostracism suggested that they would prefer to have verbal or physical abuse than be ostracized.

Employee Sensemaking of Harmful Treatment

Although most harmful treatment occurs at an interpersonal level (supervisor to subordinate), we argue that these actions will in many instances be viewed as reflecting the organization's actions rather than as a result of an organizational agent acting simply as an individual. As Eisenberger and Stinglhamber (2011, p. 41) note, "employees at various levels in the organizational hierarchy tend to experience the organization as a unitary force whether benevolent or malevolent." Such malevolent actions by the supervisor will be interpreted by employees as reflecting the organization's negative evaluation of them. This is more likely to hold true when an individual perceives the supervisor as embodying the values of the organization (referred to as supervisor organizational embodiment), when employees attribute the behavior to the purposeful intentionality of the supervisor, and when it is within the supervisor's control (Stinglhamber & Vandenberghe, 2004). If the employee feels he or she has been singled out for harmful treatment, this represents a personalized form of malevolent treatment and so will be particularly impactful on employee perceptions of organizational cruelty.

Employees' attribution of responsibility for supervisory mistreatment will also affect whether they perceive the organization as a cruel entity. A central premise of attribution of responsibility is that an entity can be held accountable for an event. Heider (1958) argued that attributions involve judgments regarding the responsibility of the entity versus that of the environment, resulting in three attributions: (1) intentionality, indicating the extent to which the outcome is a deliberate action by the organization—in this situation, the extent to which the organization hired and promoted the supervisor and gave the supervisor free rein to act malevolently with employees; (2) foreseeability, indicating the extent to which the organization is held accountable because it should have anticipated the actions of the supervisor; and (3 justifiability, indicating the extent to which the organization's actions are justifiable. Employee attributions of intentionality and foreseeability are likely to strengthen the relationship between negative supervisory behavior and POC, whereas attributions of justifiability are likely to weaken that relationship.

Another way in which employees determine whether the organization is cruel is by the interpersonal treatment they receive when a harmful action is being administered by an organizational agent. There are several forms of interpersonal treatment that are likely to increase employee perceptions of organizational cruelty, including lack of interactional justice and psychological disengagement. Callous, unethical, or disrespectful behavior directed at an employee by a supervisor or another organizational agent generates strong feelings of anger because such treatment signals how little the employee is valued and respected by the organization (Bies, 2001). Thus, harmful treatment that is lacking in interactional justice increases POC. In addition, the employee is more likely to perceive that the organization is cruel when the agent appears to be psychologically disengaged from the harm that they are inflicting (Folger & Pugh, 2002). A study by Clair and Dufresne (2004) showed that employees who administered layoff decisions used humor, depersonalization of the victim, and avoidance of personal contact with layoff victims to psychologically disengage. In a qualitative study by Margolis and Molinksy (2008) on "necessary evils" (i.e., harmful acts required by an individual's work role, such as layoffs and firing), disengagement was reflected in several ways: "(1) denial of any experience of prosocial emotion; (2) active dissociation from the target's experience, through dehumanizing the target or minimizing the task's negative impact; or (3) dehumanizing the self through either deindividuation or attribution of one's personal actions to the role, job or organization rather than to one's private, personal agency" (p. 853). In sum, the manner in which the agent delivers the harmful treatment to the employee will also determine whether the employee perceives the organization as cruel.

OUTCOMES OF POC

Employees are likely to respond in a number of ways to perceiving the organization as cruel, and we focus on two categories of responses: employee health and well-being and behaviors.

Health and Well-Being

Treating individuals in an inhumane and cruel way is a violation of their dignity and self-respect, and this is likely to invoke stress-related reactions. Therefore, POC is likely to be positively associated with metabolic syndrome (a cluster of synergistic risk factors predictive of heart disease/diabetes), stress, anxiety, and depression. Siegrist (2009) reviewed 12 prospective epidemiological studies and showed support for the health-adverse effects (e.g., coronary heart disease, depression, type 2 diabetes) of effort–reward imbalance at work due to potential damage to an individual's self-esteem as a result of failed reciprocity. De Vogli, Brunner, and Marmot (2007) found that self-reported unfairness predicted metabolic syndrome and its components (waist circumference, serum triglycerides, high-density lipoprotein, fasting serum glucose, and blood pressure). The authors speculated that frequent experiences of unfair treatment may produce psychological distress in the form of inward-focused or outward-focused emotions dependent on the attributions for injustice. Inward-focused emotions may include feeling devalued, which can lead to anxiety and depression, whereas outward-focused emotions such as anger and hostility occur when blame is externalized. Likewise, MacDonald and Leary (2005) argue that social pain defined as "an emotional reaction to the perception that one is excluded from desired relationships or being devalued by desired relationship partners or groups" (p. 202) may contribute to pain-related disorders. This body of work suggests that unfairness, failed reciprocity, and devaluation of the relationship have adverse consequences for an individual's physical heath.

Individuals are also likely to experience fear and anger when perceiving that their relationship with the organization is a cruel one. Acts of perceived cruelty could trigger what Kane and Montegomery (1998) call disempowerment, defined "as a process whereby a work event or episode is evaluated by the individual as an affront to his/her dignity; hence a violation of a fundamental norm of consideration and respect" (p. 264). The authors also argue that there is likely to be a strong cumulative effect if allowed to amass over time. Employees who perceive their organization as cruel are likely to experience fear in speaking up about the treatment received. In particular, "quiescent" silence (Pinder & Harlos, 2001) captures the withholding of verbal comments due to the anticipation of negative consequences for the individual. Kish-Gephart, Detert, Trevino, and Edmondson (2009) argue that fear of authority is a prepared fear that helps explain the pervasiveness of silence at work as speaking up risks angering those in higher status, which could lead to negative ramifications.

The feeling of anger that is "associated with the sense that the self (or someone the self cares about) has been offended or injured" (Lerner & Tiedens, 2006, p. 117) is liable to be triggered by experiences such as public humiliation, disrespectful or unjust treatment, or violation of moral standards (Bies & Moag, 1986; Cropanzano, Goldman, & Folger, 2003; Harlos & Pinder, 2000). The nature of employees' anger is likely to be both inward focused and outward focused, with the former directed at the self for acquiescing to a harmful relationship with the employer and the latter directed at the source of the harmful treatment. Kish-Gephart et al. (2009) note that anger and fear may occur simultaneously in reaction to the same event, whereby the intensity of each may influence whether silence or voice is enacted.

In view of the empirical evidence, we argue that POC will have adverse effects on an individual's health and well-being. Being in a relationship with a destructive and demeaning organization is likely to invoke perceptions of relational devaluation and unfairness and is also likely to thwart an individual's basic needs. The violation of justice norms and needs of self-esteem, belonging, control, and meaningful existence as a result of organizational cruelty may explain the resultant effects on employee health and well-being.

Behavior

Behavioral responses to POC can be categorized as passive, such as silence, learned helplessness, and neglect, or as active, including retaliation and exit. Silence is multidimensional, and of relevance here is acquiescent silence, which is the withholding of relevant ideas, information, or opinions based on resignation—disengaged behavior (Van Dyne, Ang, &

Botero, 2003). Acquiescent silence is passive and uninvolved behavior; employees "are resigned to the current situation and are not willing to exert the effort to speak up, get involved, or attempt to change the situation" (Van Dyne et al., 2003, p. 1366). Pinder and Harlos (2001) focused on employee silence as a response to injustice, and similar arguments could be made in terms of employee responses to POC.

Learned helplessness "is the notion that after repeated punishment or failure, persons become passive and remain so even after environmental changes that make success possible" (Martinko & Gardner, 1982, p. 196). An attributional framework was incorporated into learned helplessness theory to explain the link between noncontingent reinforcement situations and the expectation of future noncontingency (Abramson, Seligman, & Teasdale, 1978). The two attributional dimensions capture internal/external and stable/unstable—the degree to which individuals attribute causes to themselves, to others, or to circumstances, and the extent to which individuals attribute causes to a temporary or permanent event (Weiner, 1972). These attributions help predict when individuals will experience helplessness; specifically, when individuals attribute the experience of organizational cruelty to themselves (e.g., because they are not worthy) and when they view the cause as stable (the organization's cruelty is enduring or recurrent), employees are more likely to experience helplessness.

Neglect refers to "passively allowing conditions to deteriorate through reduced interest or effort, chronic lateness or absences, using company time for personal business or increased error rate" (Rusbult, Farrell, Rogers, & Mainous, 1988, p. 601). The authors argue that neglect can capture very passive responses, such as reduced interest, and also reactions that are moderately passive, such as intentionally missing work. Employees in relationships deemed as cruel are likely to have low investment in that relationship given the lack of resources they receive and hence engage in neglect as a response to such treatment. Rusbult et al. (1988) speculate that there may be a temporal element to how individuals respond, and drawing on this, we speculate that neglect may be a temporary response progressing to exit in the longer term.

Individuals may also engage in active responses such as retaliation or exiting the organization. Although there are a number of terms used to reflect negative employee behaviors, Skarlicki and Folger (1997) argue that the term retaliation has less of a pejorative connotation than deviance, and whereas deviance presumes wrongful and negative employee conduct, retaliation can be a legitimate response to mistreatment by managers. In view of the perceived purposeful intention of organizational cruelty as we have defined it, retaliation seems a probable employee response.

There is considerable empirical support for the contention that when employees are mistreated, they respond in a negative way (Aquino, Tripp, & Bies, 1998; Mitchell & Ambrose, 2007; Skarlicki & Folger, 1997). Hollinger and Clark (1983) reported that employees who felt exploited by the organization engaged in acts of theft as a way of correcting the injustice. Two explanations may explain this: restoration of justice and reestablishment of personal control. Gouldner's (1960) negative norm of reciprocity explains why individuals who feel mistreated are motivated to retaliate (an eye for an eye, tooth for a tooth), and according to Bies and Tripp (2001), this negative reciprocity can restore a sense of justice. In addition, Mitchell and Ambrose (2007), drawing on reactance theory, argue that retaliation can restore an individual's sense of control following harmful treatment.

In the social psychology literature, rejection is defined as being excluded from or being devalued by a desired person, group, or relationship (MacDonald & Leary, 2005). POC is a form of rejection in that it signifies a devaluation of the employee and is likely to lead to intentions to leave and turnover. Empirical evidence found that participants rejected by their workgroup were less likely to want to remain with the organization than accepted participants (Hiltan, Kelly, Schepman, Schneider, & Zarate, 2006). Rejection by organizational agents is likely to violate belongingness needs as well as norms of fair treatment and thus motivate an employee to leave the relationship with the organization if at all possible.

MODERATORS

Individual

Although there are potentially numerous moderators that come into play in terms of understanding how individuals respond to POC, we focus on three moderators that have a relational focus: hardiness, dependence, and the employee's belief in the negative norm of reciprocity. Hardiness describes an individual's predisposition to be "resistant to the harmful effects of stressors and effectively adapt and cope with a demanding environment" (Eschleman, Bowling, & Alarcon, 2010, p. 277). It is a multidimensional construct consisting of commitment, control, and challenge. Commitment captures the extent to which an individual is engaged in a variety of life domains and results in the development of social relationships that can act as social support. Control reflects the extent to which an individual believes that he or she can control events and challenge the extent to which difficult situations are seen as challenges or threats (Eschleman et al., 2010). Hardiness has been found to moderate the relationship between stressors and strains by acting as a buffer (Kobasa, 1979), and a recent meta-analysis (Eschleman et al., 2010) provides support for the moderating effect of hardiness: Hardy individuals experience less strain in the presence of stressors than less hardy individuals. We would expect hardy individuals to respond less negatively to POC in terms of anxiety, depression, and stress due to the buffering effect of social support provided by their commitment to a number of life domains. Because hardy individuals have a greater perception of control over their environment, they will be more likely to engage in active responses such as retaliation and exit in response to POC than silence, learned helplessness, and neglect, as the former responses allow the individual to proactively control his or her environment. The challenge subfacet of hardiness is likely to influence an employee's emotional response in terms of diminishing the likelihood of fear of speaking up because the employee would interpret the situation as a challenge rather than a threat.

The extent to which an individual reacts passively or actively depends on the individual's perceived dependence/power imbalance in their relationship with the organization. Rusbult and Van Lange (2003) define dependence situations as those involving "need" or "reliance on" another (p. 363). The authors argue that dependence explains why individuals remain in abusive relationships and endure continuing abuse when they are relatively dependent—high investments and poor alternatives. Molm (1988) argues that in relationships that are characterized by power imbalance, the weaker party is dependent on the more powerful for resources. The more dependent one party is on the other, the more constrained they will be to act in ways that serve their interests. As a result, highly dependent employees who have imbalanced or harmful EORs will view engaging in acts of retaliation as too risky because these acts might provoke the threat of further harmful organizational treatment. Silence is a more probable response due to their dependency on the organization. Conversely, individuals with low dependency might be more likely to engage in retaliation or leave the organization because they will have viable alternatives.

The extent to which individuals subscribe to negative norms of reciprocity is likely to influence the extent to which they respond outwardly to the source of the cruelty. Eisenberger et al. (2004) found that individuals who more strongly endorsed negative reciprocity were more likely to engage in retribution following unfavorable treatment. Mitchell and Ambrose (2007) found that negative reciprocity beliefs moderated the relationship between abusive supervision and deviance directed at the supervisor such that it was stronger for those who endorsed negative reciprocity compared to those who did not. Therefore, we would expect employees who more strongly endorse negative reciprocity beliefs to engage in quid pro quo behaviors directed at the organization (i.e., neglect, retaliation, and exit) following an evaluation that the organization is cruel.

Cultural Influences

Drawing on Hofstede's (1980) work on cultural values, we argue that two cultural values, power distance and masculinity–femininity, are likely to affect how individuals respond to POC. Whereas Hofstede (1980) argued that these cultural values are meaningful at the societal level, Kirkman, Lowe, and Gibson (2006) found that more studies examined cultural values at the individual level than at the societal level, and Clugston, Howell, and Dorfman (2000) found that Hofstede's cultural dimensions capture large variation across individuals in society. We recognize that although cultural values vary across the societal level, there will be variation within a particular society regarding the extent to which individuals subscribe to those values.

Power distance captures "the extent to which a society accepts the fact that power in institutions and organizations is distributed unequally" (Hofstede, 1980, p. 45). Waldman et al. (2006) found that high-level managers in high–power distance cultures are "more self-centered or lacking in concern for shareholders/owners, broader stakeholder groups, and the community/society as a whole.... thus, in such societies, there may be more tendencies toward the manipulative use of power" (p. 834). This suggests that high–power distance managers may be less attuned to the occurrence of the kind of treatment that may be associated with POC within their organization and that there may be greater tolerance for harmful treatment of employees when high-level managers engage in this behavior. Furthermore, as Farh, Hackett, and Liang (2007) argue, employees high on power distance are deferential to authority figures and display respect, loyalty, and dutifulness due to their conformance to role expectations. Thus, in high–power distance cultures, it is unlikely that employees would respond actively (by engaging in retaliation or exit) because this would be seen as a challenge to authority. Managers in high–power distance cultures are more likely to endorse conformity among subordinates and will be less tolerant of variability, suggesting subordinate neglect is unlikely to be tolerated. Given the deferential relationship with authority figures expected in high–power distance cultures, engaging in neglect is likely to create cognitive dissonance in the subordinate and therefore an unlikely response to POC. We anticipate that employees in high–power distance cultures are more likely to adopt silence in response to POC because this would be consistent with the value attached to conformity and hierarchy. On the contrary, individuals in low–power distance cultures are more likely to engage in neglect, retaliation, and exit in response to POC contingent upon an individual's dependence with the organization.

Masculinity–femininity values capture the extent to which the culture emphasizes values of assertiveness, ambition, aggression, achievement orientation, and competitiveness (masculine) or values of quality of life, interpersonal relationships, and concern for the weak (feminine; Hofstede, 1980). We speculate that employees in high-masculine cultures will respond more actively to POC and those in high-feminine cultures will respond more passively. The emphasis on ambition and achievement orientation is likely to promote an individual's self-interest, whereas assertiveness and aggression are likely to provoke action toward resolving the situation to further an individual's self-interest. In view of this, employees in highly masculine cultures may be more likely to engage in retaliation and exit the organization in response to POC. In feminine cultures, the emphasis on benevolence (Gordon, 1976) may translate into doing things for others and being generous, and this might involve a degree of self-sacrifice. Given the emphasis on "what is given to a relationship," employees may be more accepting of being party to a cruel relationship, provoking silence as a response.

Research by Dorfman et al. (1997) comparing leadership behavior cross-culturally (United States, Japan, Taiwan, Korea, and Mexico) also has implications for our model of POC. Specifically, whereas supportive, contingent reward, and charismatic leadership behavior had universally positive effects, directive, participative, and contingent punishment behavior had differential effects across cultures. For example, contingent punishment where managers provided negative feedback in response to poor performance "had a completely desirable effect only in the United States, but equivocal or undesirable effects in other countries" (Dorfman et al., 1997, p. 262). This implies that perceptions of organizational cruelty may be precipitated by varied managerial behaviors in different cultural settings, suggesting the need for future cross-cultural research.

CONCLUSION AND FUTURE RESEARCH

Considerable research has been conducted on the positive EOR, yet few scholars have sought to develop the negative EOR domain. In this chapter, we set forth a new concept of POC, including antecedents and outcomes. As yet, it is unclear how common such perceptions are and the potential long-term impact POC may have. We suspect, in light of the burgeoning literature on workplace aggression and victimization (Aquino & Thau, 2009), that POC might occur more frequently than would be expected at first glance. However, going forward, an important starting point would be to determine the base rate for POC in normally functioning organizations. Although breach of the psychological contract has been established as common (cf. Robinson, 1996), we would expect the more extreme treatment reflected in perceptions of organizational cruelty to be less frequent than breach. Yet, we anticipate that POC would have a much stronger impact on employees' well-being than has been observed with psychological contract breach or with underinvestment employment relationships.

Thus far, research on workplace aggression and victimization has not studied the harmful impact of such treatment on employee perceptions of the EOR, but rather has focused on the buffering effect of positive employment relationships on demanding or taxing work settings. For example, there is evidence that POS can have a buffering effect on workplace stresses (George, Reed, Ballard, Colin, & Fielding, 1993). Our model suggests that at the other end of the EOR continuum, POC is likely to interfere with the employee's ability to cope with stressful work environments by adding to the employee's stress load. POC may be particularly harmful in light of the negative effects on emotions, by undermining the recipient's ability to maintain positive relations with coworkers who might normally provide the social support that would buffer workplace strains (Aquino & Thau, 2009). Even if social support is forthcoming, POC may also weaken the individual's ability to reciprocate because of stress created by high levels of POC. In fact, Nahum-Shani and Bamberger (2011) showed that social support may actually increase stress if the recipient cannot return the favor (underreciprocating). Specifically, they argue that social support that cannot be reciprocated is a violation of reciprocity norms, resulting in a negative self-image and a weaker sense of control over the situation. Exceedingly harmful treatment leading to high levels of POC may decrease the individual's ability to maintain positive workplace relations including repaying social support, which may have a knock-on effect on their capacity to cope.

Models of workplace aggression have not incorporated employee perceptions of the employment relationship that result from such treatment. We view this as an important omission in the literature, especially because there is overwhelming evidence that employees interpret organizational treatment in relational terms and respond accordingly (Eisenberger & Stinglhamber, 2011). Going forward, it will be important to understand the environmental challenges that increase the likelihood of POC. In a globally competitive economy, POC may be more common as companies seek to deal with the associated economic challenges by expecting employees to work longer hours and take on more responsibilities, particularly in tight labor markets where employees may be viewed as more replaceable but themselves are less able to exit. In addition, future research needs to focus on factors that increase the likelihood that managers create high levels of POC beyond those identified in this chapter. We argued for the important role of situations for creating conditions that precipitate organizational cruelty, but it is also possible that individual differences among organizational founders and leaders set the stage for cruel employee treatment. For example, narcissism has been associated with amorality as shown by the lack of hesitation of narcissistic leaders to commit violent and gruesome acts (Horowitz & Arthur, 1988).

This chapter provides a model of POC and supplies some evidence of links that can be made between the workplace aggression literature and the EOR literature. Illustrating these links can provide a useful new lens for understanding negative EORs and for further development of the workplace aggression literature. Employee sensemaking of harmful treatment as reflecting the EOR and associated employee responses have important implications for the development, maintenance, and dissolution of employment relationships. This chapter establishes the connections between organizational and managerial mistreatment, POC, and emotional and behavioral outcomes, but the task of empirical testing and refinement of these ideas is needed to fully understand the negative EOR domain.

REFERENCES

Abramson, L. Y., Seligman, M. E. P., & Teasdale, J. D. (1978). Learned helplessness in humans: Critique and reformulation. *Journal of Abnormal Psychology, 87*, 49–74.

Anand, V., Ashforth, B. E., & Joshi, M. (2005). Business as usual: The acceptance and perpetuation of corruption in organizations. *Academy of Management Executive, 19*, 9–23.

Aquino, K., & Thau, S. (2009). Workplace victimization: Aggression from the target's perspective. *Annual Review of Psychology, 60*, 717–741.

Aquino, K., Tripp, T. M., & Bies, R. J. (2006). Getting even or moving on? Power, procedural justice, and types of offense as predictors of revenge, forgiveness, reconciliation and avoidance in organizations. *Journal of Applied Psychology, 91*, 653–668.

Ashforth, B. E. (1997). Petty tyranny in organizations: A preliminary examination of antecedents and consequences. *Canadian Journal of Administrative Sciences, 14*, 126–140.

Baumeister, R. F., DeWall, C. N., Ciarocco, N. J., & Twenge, J. M. (2005). Social exclusion impairs self-regulation. *Journal of Personality and Social Psychology, 88*, 589–604.

Bies, R. J. (1987). The predicament of injustice: The management of moral outrage. In L. L. Cummings & B. M. Shaw (Eds.), *Research in organizational behavior* (pp. 289–319). Greenwich, CT: JAI.

Bies, R. J. (2001). Interactional justice: The sacred and the profane. In J. Greenberg & R. Cropanzano (Eds.), *Advances in organizational justice* (pp. 89–115). Stanford, CA: Stanford University Press.

Bies, R. J., & Moag, J. F. (1986). Interactional justice: Communication criteria of fairness. In R. J. Lewicki, B. H. Sheppard, & M. H. Bazerman (Eds.), *Research on negotiations in organizations* (Vol. 1, pp. 43–55). Greenwich, CT: JAI Press.

Bies, R. J., & Tripp, T. M. (2001). A passion for justice: The rationality and morality of revenge. In R. Cropanzano (Ed.), *Justice in the workplace: From theory to practice* (Vol. 2, pp. 197–208). Mahwah, NJ: Lawrence Erlbaum Associates.

Blackhart, G. C., Nelson, B. C., Knowles, M. L., & Baumeister, R. F. (2009). Rejection elicits emotional reactions but neither causes immediate distress nor lowers self-esteem: A meta-analytic review of 192 studies on social exclusion. *Personality and Social Psychology Review, 13*, 269–309.

Blau, P. M. (1964). *Exchange and power in social life.* New York, NY: John Wiley & Sons.

Clair, J. A., & Dufresne, R. L. (2004). Playing the grim reaper: How employees experience carrying out a downsizing. *Human Relations, 57*, 1597–1625.

Clugston, M., Howell, J. P., & Dorfman, P. W. (2000). Does cultural socialization predict multiple bases and foci of commitment? *Journal of Management, 26*, 5–30.

Colquitt, J. A. (2001). On the dimensionality of organizational justice: A construct validation of a measure. *Journal of Applied Psychology, 86*, 386–400.

Coyle-Shapiro, A.-M., & Shore, L. M. (2007). The employee-organization relationship: Where do we go from here? *Human Resource Management Review, 17*, 166–179.

Cropanzano, R., Goldman, B., & Folger, R. (2003). Deontic justice: The role of moral principles in workplace fairness. *Journal of Organizational Behavior, 24*, 1019–1024.

DeRidder, R., & Tripathi, R. C. (1992). *Norm violation and intergroup relations.* New York, NY: Clarendon Press/Oxford University Press.

De Vogli, R., Brunner, E., & Marmot, M. G. (2007). Unfairness and social gradient of metabolic syndrome in the Whitehall II Study. *Journal of Psychosomatic Research, 63*, 413–419.

DeWall, C. N., Maner, J. K., & Rouby, D. A. (2009). Social exclusion and early-stage interpersonal perception: Selective attention to signs of acceptance. *Journal of Personality and Social Psychology, 96*, 729–741.

Dorfman, P. W., Howell, J. P., Hibino, S., Lee, J. K., Tate, U., & Bautista, A. (1997). Leadership in Western and Asian countries: Commonalities and differences in effective leadership processes across cultures. *Leadership Quarterly, 8*, 233–274.

Drago, R. (1996). Workplace transformation and the disposable workplace: Employee involvement in Australia. *Industrial Relations, 35*, 526–543.

Duffy, M. K., Ganster, D., & Pagon, M. (2002). Social undermining in the workplace. *Academy of Management Journal, 45*, 331–351.

Eisenberger, R., Huntington, R., Hutchison, S., & Sowa, D. (1986). Perceived organizational support. *Journal of Applied Psychology, 71*, 500–507.

Eisenberger, R., Lynch, P. D., Aselage, J., & Rohdieck, S. (2004). Who takes the most revenge? Individual differences in negative reciprocity norm endorsement. *Personality and Social Psychology Bulletin, 30*, 787–799.

Eisenberger, R., & Stinglhamber, F. (2011). *Perceived organizational support: Fostering enthusiastic and productive employees.* Washington, DC: American Psychological Association.

Eschleman, K. J., Bowling, N. A., & Alarcon, G. M. (2010). A meta-analytic examination of hardiness. *International Journal of Stress Management, 17*, 277–307.

Farh, J.-L., Hackett, R. D., & Liang, J. (2007). Individual level cultural values as moderators of perceived organizational support-employee outcome relationships in China: Comparing the effects of power distance and traditionality. *Academy of Management Journal, 50*, 715–729.

Folger, R., & Pugh, S. D. (2002). The just world and Winston Churchill: An approach/avoidance conflict about psychological distance when harming victims. In M. Ross & D. Miller (Eds.), *The justice motive in everyday life* (pp. 168–186). Cambridge, UK: Cambridge University Press.

George, J. M., Reed, T. F., Ballard, K. A., Colin, J., & Fielding, J. (1993). Contact with AIDS patients as a source of work-related distress: Effects of organizational and social support. *Academy of Management Journal, 36*, 157–171.

Goldman, B. M., Gutek, B. A., Stein, J. H., & Lewis, K. (2006). Employment discrimination in organizations: Antecedents and consequences. *Journal of Management, 32*, 786–830.

Gordon, L. V. (1976). *Survey of interpersonal values–revised manual*. Chicago, IL: Science Research Associates.

Gouldner, A. W. (1960). The norm of reciprocity: A preliminary statement. *American Sociological Review, 25*, 161–178.

Griffin, R. W., & O'Leary-Kelly, A. (2004). *The dark side of organizational behavior*. San Francisco, CA: Jossey-Bass.

Harlos, K. P., & Pinder, C. C. (2000). Emotion and injustice in the workplace. In S. Fineman (Ed.), *Emotion in organizations* (pp. 255–276). Thousand Oaks, CA: Sage Publications.

Heider, F. (1958). *The psychology of interpersonal relations*. New York, NY: John Wiley & Sons.

Hitlan, R. T., Kelly, K., Schepman, S., Schneider, K. T., & Zarate, M. A. (2006). Language exclusion and the consequences of perceived ostracism in the workplace. *Group Dynamics: Theory, Research and Practice, 10*, 56–70.

Hofstede, G. (1980). *Culture's consequences: International differences in work-related values*. Beverly Hills, CA: Sage.

Hollinger, R. C., & Clark, J. P. (1983). *Theft by employees*. Lexington, MA: Lexington Books.

Hom, P. W., Tsui, A. S., Wu, J. B., Lee, T. W., Zhang, A. Y., Fu, P. P., & Li, L. (2009). Explaining employment relationships with social exchange and job embeddedness. *Journal of Applied Psychology, 94*, 277–297.

Horowitz, M. J., & Arthur, R. J. (1988). Narcissistic range in leaders: The intersection of individual dynamics and group processes. *The International Journal of Social Psychiatry, 34*, 135–141.

Kane, K., & Montgomery, K. (1998). A framework for understanding dysempowerment in organizations. *Human Resource Management, 37*, 263–275.

Kanter, R. M. (1987). From the information age to the communication age. *Management Review, 76*, 23–24.

Kellerman, B. (2004). *Bad leadership: What it is, how it happens, why it matters*. Boston, MA: Harvard Business School Press.

Kirkman, B. L., Lowe, K. B., & Gibson, C. B. (2006). A quarter century of culture's consequences: A review of the empirical research incorporating Hofstede's cultural value framework. *Journal of International Business Studies, 37*, 285–320.

Kish-Gephart, J. J., Detert, J. R., Trevino, L. K., & Edmondson, A. C. (2009). Silence by fear: The nature, sources, and consequences of fear at work. *Research in Organizational Behavior, 29*, 163–193.

Kobasa, S. C. (1979). Stressful life events, personality and health: An inquiry into hardiness. *Journal of Personality and Social Psychology, 37*, 1–11.

Lerner, J. S., & Tiedens, L. Z. (2006). Portrait of the angry decision maker: How appraisal tendencies shape anger's influence on. *Cognition Journal of Behavioral Decision Making, 19*, 115–137.

Levinson, H. (1965). Reciprocation: The relationship between man and organization. *Administrative Science Quarterly, 9*, 370–390.

MacDonald, G., & Leary, M. R. (2005). Why does social exclusion hurt? The relationship between social and physical pain. *Psychological Bulletin, 131*, 202–223.

March, J. G., & Simon, H. A. (1958). *Organizations*. New York, NY: Wiley.

Margolis, J. D., & Molinsky, A. (2008). Navigating the bind of necessary evils: Psychological engagement and the production of interpersonally sensitive behavior. *Academy of Management Journal, 51*, 847–872.

Martinko, M. J., & Gardner, W. L. (1982). Learned helplessness: An alternative explanation for performance deficits. *Academy of Management Review, 7*, 195–204.

Milgram, S. (1974). *Obedience to authority*. New York, NY: Harper & Row.

Mitchell, M. S., & Ambrose, M. L. (2007). Abusive supervision and workplace deviance and the moderating effects of negative reciprocity beliefs. *Journal of Applied Psychology, 92*, 1159–1168.

Molm, L. D. (1988). The structure and use of power: A comparison of reward and punishment power. *Social Psychology Quarterly, 51*, 108–122.

Montes, S. D., & Zweig, D. (2009). Do promises matter? An exploration of the role of promises in psychological contract breach. *Journal of Applied Psychology, 94*, 1243–1260.

Morrison, E. W., & Robinson, S. L. (1997). When employees feel betrayed: A model of how psychological contract violation develops. *Academy of Management Review, 22*, 226–256.

Nahum-Shani, I., & Bamberger, P. A. (2011). Explaining the variable effects of social support on work-based stressor-strain relations: The role of perceived pattern of support exchange. *Organizational Behavior and Human Decision Processes, 114*, 49–63.

Nishii, L. H., Lepak, D. P., & Schneider, B. (2008). Employee attributions of the "why" of HR practices: Their effects on employee attitudes, and behaviors, and customer satisfaction. *Personnel Psychology, 61*, 503–545.

O'Leary-Kelly, A. M., Griffin, R. W., & Glew, D. J. (1996). Organization-motivated aggression: A research framework. *Academy of Management Review, 21*, 225–253.

Padilla, A., Hogan, R., & Kaiser, R. B. (2007). The toxic triangle: Destructive leaders, susceptible followers, and conducive environments. *The Leadership Quarterly, 18*, 176–194.

Pinder, C. C., & Harlos, K. P. (2001). Employee silence: Quiescence and acquiescence as responses to perceived injustice. In K. M. Rowland & G. R. Ferris (Eds.), *Research in personnel and human resources management* (Vol. 20, pp. 331–369). New York, NY: JAI Press.

Princeton University. (2010). WordNet search. *WordNet*. Retreived from http://wordnetweb.princeton.edu/perl/webwn?s=cruelty&o2=&o0=1&o8=1&o1=1&o7=&o5=&o9=&o6=&o3=&o4=&h=

Raghavan, A. (2002, August 26). Full speed ahead: How Enron bosses created a culture of pushing limits. *Wall Street Journal*, p. A1.

Raver, J. L., & Nishii, L. H. (2010). Once, twice, or three times as harmful? Ethnic harassment, gender harassment, and generalized workplace harassment. *Journal of Applied Psychology, 95*, 236–254.

Rhoades, L., & Eisenberger, R. (2002). Perceived organizational support: A review of the literature. *Journal of Applied Psychology, 87*, 698–714.

Robinson, S. L. (1996). Trust and breach of the psychological contract. *Administrative Science Quarterly, 41*, 574–599.

Robinson, S. L., & Brown, G. (2004). Psychological contract breach and violation in organizations. In R. W. Griffin & A. O'Leary-Kelly (Eds.), *The dark side of organizational behavior* (pp. 309–337). San Francisco, CA: Jossey-Bass.

Rousseau, D. M. (1989). Psychological and implied contracts in organizations. *Employee Responsibilities and Rights Journal, 2,* 121–139.

Rousseau, D. M. (1995). *Psychological contracts in organizations: Understanding written and unwritten agreements.* Thousand Oaks, CA: Sage Publications.

Rusbult, C. E., Farrell, D., Rogers, G., & Mainous, A. G. (1988). Impact of exchange variables on exit, voice, loyalty, and neglect: An integrative model of responses to declining job satisfaction. *Academy of Management Journal, 31,* 599–627.

Rusbult, C. E., & Van Lange, P. A. M. (2003). Interdependence, interaction, and relationships. *Annual Review of Psychology, 54,* 351–375.

Schat, A. C. H., Frone, M. R., & Kelloway, E. K. (2006). Prevalence of workplace aggression in the U.S. workforce: Findings from a national study. In E. K. Kelloway, J. Barling, & J. J. Hurrell (Eds.), *Handbook of workplace violence* (pp. 47–89). Thousand Oaks, CA: Sage.

Scott, B. A., Colquitt, J. A., & Paddock, E. L. (2009). An actor-focused model of justice rule adherence and violation: The role of managerial motives and discretion. *Journal of Applied Psychology, 94,* 756–769.

Shore, L. M., & Shore, T. H. (1995). Perceived organizational support and organizational justice. In R. Cropanzano & K. M. Kacmar (Eds.), *Organizational politics, justice, and support: Managing social climate at work* (pp. 149–164). New York, NY: Quorum Press.

Siegrist, J. (1996). Adverse health effects of high-effort/low reward conditions. *Journal of Occupational Health Psychology, 1,* 27–41.

Siegrist, J. (2009). Unfair exchange and health: Social bases of health related diseases. *Social Theory and Health, 7,* 305–317.

Skarlicki, D. P., & Folger, R. (1997). Retaliation in the workplace: The role of distributive, procedural and interactional justice. *Journal of Applied Psychology, 82,* 434–443.

Skarlicki, D. P., & Folger, R. (2004). Broadening our understanding of organizational retaliatory behavior. In R. W. Griffin & A. O'Leary-Kelly (Eds.), *The dark side of organizational behavior* (pp. 373–402). San Francisco, CA: Jossey-Bass.

Sommer, K. L., Williams, K. D., Ciarocco, N. J., & Baumeister, R. F. (2001). When silence speaks louder than words: Exploration into the intrapsychic and interpersonal consequences of social ostracism. *Basic and Applied Social Psychology, 63,* 175–182.

Song, L. J., Tsui, A. S., & Law, K. S. (2009). Unpacking employee responses to organizational exchange mechanisms: The role of social and economic exchange perceptions. *Journal of Management, 35,* 56–93.

Stinglhamber, F., & Vandenberghe, C. (2004). Favorable job conditions and perceived support: The role of organizations and supervisors. *Journal of Applied Social Psychology, 34,* 1470–1493.

Storey, J. (1992). *Developments in the management of human resources.* Oxford, UK: Basil Blackwell.

Tepper, B. J. (2000). Consequences of abusive supervision. *Academy of Management Journal, 43,* 178–190.

Tepper, B. J. (2007). Abusive supervision in work organizations: Review, synthesis, and research agenda. *Journal of Management, 33,* 261–289.

Thau, S., & Mitchell, M. S. (2010). Self-gain or self-regulation impairment? Tests of competing explanations of the supervisor abuse and employee deviance relationship through perceptions of distributive justice. *Journal of Applied Psychology, 95,* 1009–1031.

Tsui, A. S., Pearce, J. L., Porter, L. W., & Tripoli, A. M. (1997). Alternative approaches to the employee-organization relationship: Does investment in employees pay off? *Academy of Management Journal, 40*, 1089–1121.

Van Dyne, L., Ang, S., & Botero, I. C. (2003). Conceptualizing employee silence and employee voice as multidimensional constructs. *Journal of Management Studies, 40*, 1259–1392.

Vredenburgh, D., & Brender, Y. (1998). The hierarchical abuse of power in work organizations. *Journal of Business Ethics, 17*, 1337–1347.

Waldman, D. A., Sully de Luque, M., Washburn, N., House, R. J., Adetoun, B., Barrasa, A., ... Wilderom, C. P. M. (2006). Cultural and leadership predictors of corporate social responsibility values of top management: A GLOBE study of 15 countries. *Journal of International Business Studies, 37*, 823–837.

Webster's Online Dictionary. (n.d.). Retrieved August 25, 2011 from http://www.webster-dictionary.org/definition/cruelty

Weiner, B. (1972). *Theories of motivation: From mechanism to cognition*. Chicago, IL: Rand McNally.

Williams, K. D. (2001). *Ostracism: The power of silence*. New York, NY: Guildford Press.

Zhao, Z., Wayne, S. J., Glibkowski, B. C., & Bravo, J. (2007). The impact of psychological contract breach on work-related outcomes: A meta-analysis. *Personnel Psychology, 60*, 647–668.

Zimbardo, P. G. (2000, Fall). The psychology of evil. *Eye on Psi Chi*, 16–19.

Zimbardo, P. G. (2004). A situationist perspective on the psychology of evil: Understanding how good people are transformed into perpetrators. In A. G. Miller (Ed.), *The social psychology of good and evil* (pp. 21–50). New York, NY: Guilford Press.

7

Assumptions in Employee–Organization Relationship Research: A Critical Perspective From the Study of Volunteers

Jone L. Pearce
University of California, Irvine

A FEW THINGS VOLUNTEERS CAN TEACH US ABOUT EMPLOYEE–ORGANIZATIONAL RELATIONSHIPS

> If you are paid, you probably don't question it, you assume you are doing it for a living, volunteers don't know why they are working; they don't know the answer. I guess they assume they do it because they want to do good. These assumptions lead to different ways of doing things. Not that paid people aren't cheerful; it's just that it's not needed.
>
> *—Volunteer in a nonsectarian food distribution program, Pearce, 1993, p. 3*

Employees are not the only people who work for and have relationships with organizations. Volunteers, like contract workers, governing board members, and employees, labor for organizations. Yet, we know little about the relationships between such people and their organizations. There is growing research on contract or contingent workers (temporary or part-time) and their organizations (see Ashford, George, & Blatt, 2007; Gallagher & Connelly, Chapter 10, this volume), and our understanding of the organizational behavior of members of governance boards is in its infancy (for an example, see Westphal & Stern, 2006). This chapter will address what we can infer from the available research about relationships between volunteers and their organizations and what this may mean for our understanding of employee–organization relationship (EOR) theory and research.

Research on volunteers' relationships with their organizations spans the past several decades, although this work has rarely been framed as volunteer–organization relationships. Yet, much of it does reflect on EOR theorizing, reflections that are introduced here. This chapter seeks to contribute to future research on EORs in two ways. First, research on EORs makes a series of implicit assumptions—assumptions that are clearer when framed in the context of the relationships between volunteers and their organizations. The EOR assumptions addressed here include: EORs are clear to the participants, the relationships are primarily driven by how the organization treats the participants, participants are dependent on their organizations, the organizations are not understaffed, and the participants perceive their organizational involvement in inducement-contribution terms. For each of these five assumptions, I will describe how volunteers' relationships with their organizations violate these assumptions in ways that surface these assumptions in EOR theorizing—assumptions that do not apply to many employees in their organizational relationships. Second, EORs are said to be characterized by both economic and social exchange, yet the social component of EOR research has not been as well developed as have the economic or utilitarian inducements. I will suggest that one reason for this imbalance has been the neglect of the complexity of social exchange reflected in the differing theories of what social exchange is and does in participant–organization relationships. An examination of volunteer–organization relationships helps clarify the differing facets and meanings of social exchange in participant–organization relationships. This chapter concludes with a discussion of what violations of these five assumptions mean for future research on EORs. Before exploring these ideas, participant–organization relationships will be briefly defined, and then what is meant by an organizational volunteer is clarified.

Dictionaries define relationships as the ways two parties are connected, or states of being connected, or ways the parties behave or regard one another. The EOR has been defined quite broadly in the organizational behavior literature. It includes employee perceptions of the organization's policies and actions and the employers' formal policies toward employees (Shore et al., 2004). Further, the EOR has been framed as a blend of both an economic and social exchange (Shore et al., 2004; Tsui, Pearce, Porter, & Hite, 1995). It is an economic exchange because the relationship is expected to be a quid pro quo inducements–contributions relationship (March & Simon, 1958). That is, employees evaluate the relationship by whether the inducements they receive from the organization are commensurate with the contributions they provide. However, many have argued that EORs are not purely economic ones, but they include features of a more open-ended social relationship (e.g., Shore et al., 2004). In social exchanges, the exchange is valued for the relationship it symbolizes (Blau, 1964) or the community the exchanges support (Ekeh, 1974), not what is exchanged in itself. In social relationships, the exchange is not expected to be completed with each transaction; instead, the exchange is expected to be ongoing, and the relationship is kept in balance over time rather than with each exchange.

VOLUNTEER–ORGANIZATION RELATIONSHIPS

Volunteers contribute their labor at no charge to nonprofit and, occasionally, for-profit and governmental organizations. Volunteer labor is a major component of the U.S. economy and workforce. In 2010, 63.4 million Americans (27% of adult Americans) volunteered labor worth $169 billion (Corporation for National & Community Service, 2010). Although North America is traditionally known for high levels of volunteering, volunteering is international; volunteers contributing valuable services are present in all but the most autocratic and centralized states. Yet the term "volunteers" is inherently ambiguous (Pearce, 1993); many workers receiving low pay are called "volunteers," as in the U.S. Government's Peace Corp Volunteers. Similarly, some who receive no pay for their work, like members of nonprofit boards of directors, are rarely called volunteers. In addition, to further complicate matters, some volunteers receive token payments for their services, and some student volunteers are required to work a certain number of volunteer hours as a school or course requirement. The volunteers who are the focus of this chapter are those who receive no pay for organizational work in jobs under the supervision of an organizational agent. That is, they do work within a hierarchy of authority subject to dismissal if they do not carry out their assignments in ways the organizational agents deem to be acceptable.

Volunteers are a very heterogeneous category of organizational participants. They may work for small collectives delivering food to the needy, write for their university's student newspaper, fight fires in their township, lead tours of museums, renovate homes for the poor, and stack the shelves of their local library, among many other services they perform. Volunteers range from those providing highly skilled and licensed services, as physicians do for free clinics, to teenagers standing around a soup kitchen waiting for someone to tell them what to do. Volunteers also are more demographically heterogeneous than employees, including young teenagers too young to legally work for pay and the elderly long since retired from their paid employment. All of this heterogeneity contributes great ambiguity in how volunteers should be viewed (are they gifting their services or workers?) and why they work, among many other uncertainties, with important implications for their organizational relationships, as will be detailed below.

Volunteers share some features with employees but also differ from employees (Pearce, 1993). Volunteers are unlike employees because they are not paid wages or salaries for their organizational work, but some volunteers may be like employees in that they expect to receive some inducement for their work (e.g., experience to build a resume or the opportunity to meet people who may become clients of their investment businesses). Volunteers are like employees because they work for a formal organization, under its authorities' supervision, providing a service or product to outside clients or customers; however, volunteers' work is usually structured differently than is employees' work: Volunteering is a leisure activity, and so this means that volunteers usually work part time, sometimes working only a few hours a year. This implies that either the organization will accomplish less work or the organization must have many more individual volunteers to do the same work as full-time employees. Usually, volunteers require comparatively more management than employees because their tasks need to be divided into smaller part-time pieces, done by those who may have less experience and skills than employees can develop over time. Finally, because volunteers are all unpaid there is no need to create fine occupational distinctions or status hierarchies among them, except as might be required by governmental licensing requirements (e.g., only licensed registered nurses can provide certain patient services). So, although it may take more managerial time to coordinate and monitor volunteers' work, it takes less managerial time to manage the emotions and resentments that can be engaged by the unfavorable comparisons inherent in employees' differential pay and titles. In any case, there are enough similarities between employees and volunteers to justify exploring what insights volunteer–organization relationships may provide about these volunteers in their own right, as well as EORs.

ASSUMPTION 1: THE EOR IS CLEAR TO EMPLOYEES

To date, scholars of EORs have assumed that employees have a clear idea of their relationships with their organizations. However, research on volunteer–organization relationships casts doubt on this assumption for volunteers and probably for many employees as well. The inducements–contributions schema is so powerful in North America that the research on the organizational behavior of volunteers has been centered on one question: Why do they do it? Volunteers appear to present a mystery—all of us feel they must be getting something out of the relationship. The pioneer in this work is Sills (1957), who studied the large nationwide U.S. nonprofit organization that raised money for research and provided services for those suffering from polio and their families. His basic findings about what induces volunteers to work have not been fundamentally contradicted in the ensuing decades. Volunteers volunteer for several primary reasons. In his study, Sills (1957) found that 10% volunteered on their own, 52% of the volunteers were brought to their volunteer job by a friend, 20% were introduced to the organization by a member of the community, and 18% came because a colleague from their paid job suggested it. Although the mix of reasons for joining will vary somewhat with the size and mission of the organization, subsequent research confirms that only a minority of volunteers come to their organizations on their own initiative or through a mass media advertisement (e.g., Gallup Organization, 1978; Haski-Leventhal & Bargal, 2008; Yeung, 2004). As the volunteer quoted at the beginning of this chapter reports, most volunteers do not really know why they do it, because the vast majority of volunteers are persuaded, charmed, or dragged into their volunteer jobs by someone they know. This means that a surprisingly large proportion of volunteers do not volunteer for any inducement the organization provides, but to get someone they know off their backs.

In earlier work, I argued that this meant that many volunteers were faced with a problem of insufficient justification for their organizational work. Staw (1976) and others (de Charms, 1968; Deci, 1975) argue that when both extrinsic and intrinsic organizational rewards are abundant, participants can experience overjustification for their participation and so will devalue the less tangible intrinsic inducements they receive from their organizational relationships. By the same logic, when participants have few inducements for their work, they will tend to believe that the less tangible intrinsic rewards of the work are more important to them than they would be if the tangible extrinsic rewards are plainly sufficient.

In a large empirical study of matched pairs of volunteer-staffed and employee-staffed organizations doing the same work, I found that volunteers doing the same community service work as employees (e.g., fire fighting, child care, orchestra musician) reported significantly more intangible inducements of social and service motivation compared to employees (Pearce, 1983). This was the case despite volunteers and employees working in jobs providing the same community services and with the same socializing opportunities in their workplaces. Interestingly, volunteers did not report that their work was more intrinsically motivating than did the employees, the original intangible inducement for which the sufficiency of justification hypothesis was developed and tested by Deci (1975). That is, employees doing valuable work for others working with congenial colleagues did not report these as inducements for their organizational relationship as often as did volunteers. This suggests the employees had oversufficient justification and so did not attend to these more abstract attractions, whereas the volunteers' insufficient justification leads them to attend to these inducements for their organizational relationships.

This has implications for our understanding of participant–organization relationships. Organizational participants do not necessarily focus their attention on the inducements the organization offers but will selectively attend to some, but not all, of the organization's possible inducements. For volunteers, we can easily determine how they arrived at their workplaces (as Sills, 1957, first documented), but it is more difficult to say with certainty what their inducements for remaining with the organization are. Earlier (Pearce, 1993), I called this the inherent ambiguity of volunteers' organizational behavior. Yet, because society expects volunteers to have a reason for what they do, they justify what they do by the socially appropriate reasons of "make a contribution" or "working with a fun group of people." The volunteer–organization relationship is simply not clear to many volunteers.

Clarity in volunteers' and employees' reports of organizational relationships may be exaggerated because they are put on the spot by being asked to justify their workplace involvement. Employees appear to have a less problematic public rationale for remaining with their organizations: "I need to support myself and my family." However, the fact that their organizational relationship is potentially overjustified (they may also be making a contribution and working with fun coworkers) doesn't necessarily mean that the financial inducement of a salary is at the core of their relationships with their organizations.

This has implications for EOR scholarship. Employees may not be as clear about their inducements as we tend to assume. Like volunteers, some employees may stumble into jobs and then retroactively seek to rationalize what their inducements are because that is what society expects. Work by Shore et al. (2004) introduces the idea of dynamism in EORs but still assumes that it is a change in an understood relationship over time, rather than that the relationship itself may be inherently unclear and unstable. Current empirical approaches to assessing employees' perceptions of their EORs (asking them) may have inadvertently led to perceptions of greater employee clarity about their organizational relationships than employees really have. Asking people a question creates demands for an answer. Future research might make fewer assumptions about the clarity of employees' perceptions of their relationships with their organizations, perhaps by introducing participant observation assessment approaches, ones that center on seeking to understand employees' own ways of understanding their EORs.

ASSUMPTION 2: THE EOR IS DRIVEN BY HOW THE ORGANIZATION TREATS PARTICIPANTS

If EORs are more ambiguous to employees than we have assumed, how do employees determine what their relationships with their organizations are? Much of the focus of EOR research has been on how different organizational human resources management practices signal different organization-expected EORs to employees (examples from this volume include Chapter 9 by Kossek and Ruderman and Chapter 17 by Lepak and Boswell). Most notably, Tsui et al. (1995) queried human resources executives about the organizations' investments in employees via such practices as training and providing job security. They found that employees had better supervisor-rated job performance and were more committed when their organizations invested more in the EOR by, for example, providing training and job security. So how organizations treat their employees seems to matter, but is it the most important factor in employees' perceptions of their relationships with their organizations? Organizations' investments in employees tend to apply to all employees in the organization or job, and it is not clear that all participants value the same things.

EOR scholars recently have begun to address the strength of the relationships between organizational inducements and employees' perceptions of their organizational relationships with studies of the impact of employees' immediate social environments on their understanding of their relationships with their organizations. Generalizing from Salancik and Pfeffer's (1978) claim that employees understand their jobs and form job attitudes largely based on how their peers understand these jobs and attitudes (see also Felps et al., 2009; Vardaman, Hancock, Allen, & Shore, 2009), we might suppose that employees' understanding of their EOR is highly influenced by the views and opinions of others in their social environments. Salancik and Pfeffer (1978) proposed that when employees answer questions about their needs or attitudes they, at least partially, report a shared definition of their workplaces. Yet EOR researchers have not found social effects on employees' perceptions of their EORs. In contrast to Salancik and Pfeffer's (1978) argument, Rousseau and Tijoriwala (1998) find little evidence of within–work unit agreement on employees' reports of their own EORs. If employees' perceptions of their relationships with their organizations were socially derived perceptions, we would expect some degree of consensus among those who interact the most at work.

One key to this puzzle comes from understanding volunteers' relationships with their organizations. First, volunteers come to work for many different reasons (cf. Clary et al., 1998; Pearce, 1993). For example, if some hospital volunteers come to the job seeking to make a meaningful contribution while volunteer coworkers are interested in building job skills, supervisor and client contact can represent differential inducements to these different volunteers. More client contact may make for a more meaningful volunteer–organization relationship for the former volunteers who want concrete evidence that they are making a difference. In contrast, more contact with supervisors that provide training and career advice can make the organizational relationship more meaningful for the career-oriented volunteers. If volunteers want different things from their organization, they will evaluate what the organization provides differently. That volunteers come to their jobs for different reasons is widely assumed among those who work with them, but seems not to have merited much attention by those studying EORs. Certainly, going as far back as the Hawthorne Studies (Roethlisberger & Dickson, 1939), we have known that employees are not homogeneous in what they seek from their organizations. That is, a lack of within-workplace consensus on the nature of the EOR does not imply that there is no social influence on participants' EORs, but it can reflect the fact that different people develop relationships with organizations for different reasons.

If volunteers and employees want different things from their organizations, company- or job-wide human resources management practices would not necessarily be the most important influence on employee perceptions of their organizational relationships. If employees work in jobs for which training is irrelevant, we would not expect the provision of training to make them more committed to the relationship. More attention to matching what employees want from their organizational relationships with the inducements they personally value might help us to better understand the most powerful drivers of employee perceptions of their EORs.

ASSUMPTION 3: PARTICIPANTS ARE DEPENDENT ON THEIR ORGANIZATION

An implicit assumption in virtually all research on EORs is that employees are dependent enough on their organizations to make leaving difficult. (In this volume, Chapter 15 by Hom on employee turnover nicely represents this assumption of dependence on the organization.) If there is not at least some dependence on the organization, there would not be much variance in EORs because those with unsatisfactory relationships with their organizations would just leave. We cannot make this assumption about volunteers.

Most volunteers are much less dependent on their organizations than are the employees assumed by EOR theorizing. Volunteers do not depend on their organizations for their livelihoods, and leaving is very easy for most of them. Even those who work for social contact and care a great deal about their social standing among others in the organization can easily find an acceptable excuse to leave. These volunteers discover they have become too busy or find that family demands have escalated. It would be unusual for a particular organization to provide the only possible setting for volunteers to make a contribution, socialize, or gain relevant work experience. Dissatisfied volunteers are rare in organizations because there is virtually no lag between becoming dissatisfied and leaving the organization (Pearce, 1993).

The weak volunteer dependence on their organizations draws attention to the possibility that some employees also may have very limited dependence on their organizations. This may be because these employees have skills in great demand by other organizations, because the employees are wealthy, because temporary or contract workers may have other clients, or because of any number of other reasons. With participant dependence on the organization no longer assumed to be high and constant, this raises a host of questions about the relationship between relative participant dependence and the EOR.

For example, participant dependence on the organization may have an inverse curvilinear relationship with whether the participant sees the relationships with his or her organization as positive or negative. It is possible that those employees, like volunteers, who are not dependent on their organizations would view the relationship favorably (otherwise they would leave). As their dependence increases, those employees who do not view the relationship positively might find they are forced to remain with the organization. This means that participants with moderate dependence would be expected to have a range of different relationships with their organizations, from very positive to very negative. However, the theory of sufficiency of justification suggests that those who are very dependent, the ones who have no alternative organizational options, might be better able to tolerate their situations if they viewed the organization more favorably.

To justify their participation, they may look more favorably on intangible inducements such as interaction with their coworkers or a favorable location. In other words, employees who are very dependent or not at all dependent on their organizations would have little variance in their EOR perceptions. A mix of positive and negative EORs may occur only at moderate levels of employee dependence on the organization. Variance in employee dependence on the organization may be an important driver of the perception of the EOR, making the influence of relative employee dependence worth exploring.

ASSUMPTION 4: THE ORGANIZATION IS NOT UNDERSTAFFED

One of the great challenges faced by organizations that rely on volunteer staffing is the constant risk of understaffing, or insufficient numbers of people willing and able to do the tasks the work demands. Because volunteers are not paid, organizations must work hard to find sufficient inducements to attract enough volunteers to meet their goals. This is because volunteering is a leisure activity, and because volunteers are not dependent on their organizations, it is easy for them to quit, leaving the organization understaffed. For example, a food distribution program was chronically understaffed and ran a regular recruitment program in local churches and service groups to maintain staffing levels (Pearce, 1993).

Decades ago, Barker and Gump (Barker, 1968; Barker & Gump, 1964) proposed that the relative under- or overstaffing (what they called under- or overmanning) of social settings has important implications for how these settings functioned. They argued that all settings, such as workplaces, have an optimal number of occupants to fulfill their demands. When there are fewer participants than the setting demands, the setting is understaffed. An understaffed setting has the following characteristics: (a) there is more pressure on everyone to fully participate rather than lurk as spectators; (b) standards of performance are lowered to reduce barriers to joining; and (c) the participants are more interested in overall setting performance than are participants in optimally or overstaffed settings. In Barker and Gump's (1964) classic study of large and small high schools, they found that the overstaffed large high schools had highly contested elections for student government and varsity athletic positions, and many students were indifferent to school achievements. By contrast, in the understaffed small schools, students had to be begged to serve in student government or on school teams, and most cared a great deal about their schools' successes.

Pearce (1993) found that the volunteer-staffed organizations in her study were understaffed settings. For example, the friends and family members of volunteers were frequently pressed into service—the roommate of the sports page editor in the college student newspaper was asked to cover certain games, and husbands and siblings were asked to deliver for the food distribution program when too few regular volunteers were scheduled at high-demand times. Certainly, the entrance requirements for the volunteer fire department and orchestra were without a doubt lower than for their employee-staffed counterparts. And in all these organizations, volunteers experienced lower performance pressure than did their employee counterparts. Volunteers kept their jobs as long as their performance did not cause direct harm, and absenteeism was tolerated in all of the volunteer-staffed organizations. Overstaffed settings would face the opposite set of these pressures; in overstaffed settings, performance standards are set very high (because more are clamoring for desirable positions), and participants report being less invested in the organization's performance and goals (because the crowded setting is more alienating and allows more lurking rather than demanding active participation).

Although most volunteers find themselves working in understaffed organizations, employees could expect to find themselves in a wide range of settings, ranging from understaffed nonprofits without the money to hire needed workers, to optimally staffed and even overstaffed settings (where money is no object). For example, attractive organizations (because they are glamorous and well-funded), such as Hollywood production studios, tend to be overstaffed. This is reflected in performance standards that demand long internships for participations, such as highly educated employees working without wages as interns doing menial tasks like fetching the refreshments for members of performers' entourages. It would seem that the EOR would be affected by relative staffing levels. For example, in understaffed settings, the selection and performance standards may be so low that some participants have no psychological sense of a relationship with the organization at all. They are working because they support the organization's goals, and the organization, as such, may not be salient to them. By contrast, in overstaffed organizations, the organization, and its agents, may be extremely important to participants. Research on how desirable the jobs are, and thus how under- or overstaffed the organization may be, promises to be influential for employees' relationships with their organizations.

ASSUMPTION 5: PARTICIPANTS UNDERSTAND THEIR PARTICIPATION AS AN INDUCEMENT–CONTRIBUTION EXCHANGE

Rarely do volunteers see their participation in quid pro quo inducement–contribution exchange terms. Volunteer–organization relationships more often are dominated by social exchange normative expectations, helping to illuminate the relative lack of attention to the social exchange aspects of EORs. EOR scholarship, despite formally including both economic and social exchange, has focused largely on inducements and contributions to understand these relationships. Only recently have scholars begun to address social exchange, usually within the context of research reporting that Chinese employees have a longer term orientation in exchange (a feature of some definitions of social exchange) than cultures such as the Dutch, who focus more on whether immediate exchanges have been reciprocated (see Shore, Coyle-Shapiro, Chen, & Tetrick, 2009, for a review). This increasing attention to social exchange is a positive trend, one that can be furthered by attention to the ways differing definitions of social exchange have been limiting its study in EOR research. Clarifying the definitional distinctions in social exchange and drawing on examples of volunteers' varying types of social exchange relationships with their organizations can help bring social exchange more completely into EOR scholarship.

Pearce and Peters (1985) proposed that normative expectations for EORs were characterized by contradictory normative expectations: profit maximization, equity (in which participants receive inducements commensurate with their contributions), equality (all participants receive the same inducements regardless of their contributions), and need (in which participants receive the inducements they need, regardless of their contributions). What EOR scholars call economic exchange would encompass profit maximization and equity normative expectations. Pearce and Peters (1985) proposed that despite the overwhelming scholarly framing of EORs as economic or equity exchanges in the organizational behavior literature, many employee–organization exchanges also had characteristics of equality and need-based exchanges. For example, health care benefits are usually offered equally to all employees and not based on equity (their relative contributions) or need (those who have more health problems receive more generous coverage). In the transition from communism, many companies took care in these countries not to lay off both a husband and wife, which was a decision based on employees' needs, not on their relative contributions or on an equality normative expectation like seniority (Pearce, 2001). In summary, social exchange in organizations can include equity, equality, and need normative expectations.

Blau (1964) is the most widely referenced social exchange theorist in EOR research, but his definition of social exchange has been criticized as overly narrow by other exchange scholars. Blau assumed that social exchanges are governed by equity-based expectations, an assumption that has continued to dominate EOR research. He built on what Malinowski (1922) called a gift exchange; in gift exchanges, the exchange objects symbolize the nature of the relationship, a relationship that can be damaged if one partner treats the exchange as a quid pro quo or economic exchange. In Blau's famous example, when one couple rushes too quickly to reciprocate a dinner invitation, the too-quick couple signals that they want to discharge the obligation in order to avoid an open-ended social relationship with the other couple. Placing an emphasis on the dinner as an economic exchange that must be reciprocated in kind signals that the reciprocating couple sees the relationship as an economic one, not a relationship valued in its own right.

Certainly, many volunteers have relationships closer to Blau's (1964) pure social exchange than to the pure inducements–contributions exchange that dominates EOR research. Yet it is not just that volunteers may be more concerned with the exchange of symbols, but that the normative expectations governing the exchanges are broader than simple profit maximization or equity exchange. Volunteers often recoil from framing their relationships to their organizations as economic arrangements. They were most likely to join because of a prior social relationship and often see their work in terms of those relationships or the community services they provide. That does not mean that there are never any inducements; Starnes and Iyer (2009) found that volunteers do see their relationships with their organizations as having economic exchange features. Volunteers who perceived that their organizations had breached their psychological contracts or were inequitable reduced the hours they worked for the organizations in subsequent months. It is not that volunteers are unconcerned with equity (and in some cases, with economic gain) but that these features present too narrow a picture of their exchange relationship with their organizations.

Goffman (1961) characterizes social exchanges somewhat differently than does Blau (1964), by emphasizing need-based exchange rather than equity. His notion of social exchange is one where what is offered in exchange is what the other party needs (Goffman, 1961, pp. 275–276). Certainly, volunteers who work because they believe the organization needs them to achieve its goals seem to fit more with Goffman's conception of social exchange than Blau's equity-based version. In fact, Pearce (1993) reported that a volunteer-staffed organization that collapsed during data collection (the college student newspaper) did so because volunteers felt that no one even noticed whether or not they showed up for work. The organization did not appear to need them, and that, not any lack of inducements, ill treatment, or betrayal, was what led these volunteers to quit the organization en masse.

Finally, Ekeh (1974) argued that the social exchange of Homans (1961) and Blau (1964) was too individualistic, focusing on the relationship between the two exchange parties alone. Ekeh proposed that Malinowski's (1922) insight was that exchange could support a larger set of community relationships, rather than the particular two parties to the exchange. That is, exchange can take place not solely in the interests of the individual parties directly involved in the exchange, but as between representatives of communities, with the exchanges intended to symbolize and support the relationship between the communities and not the individuals themselves.

Ekeh's (1974) conceptualization of social exchange is reflected in what Sills (1957) terms "joiners," who are volunteers active in many community activities. They saw themselves in a relationship with their communities, not responding to any inducement offered by a particular organization. There are many examples of volunteers who contribute their labor to organizations not because of personal inducements or even to meet a need, but as representatives of a community. For example, many religious groups send members to nonprofits to help with contributions such as soup kitchens or building houses for the poor. These volunteers do not see their relationships as with the organization supervising their work, but instead see themselves as representatives of their religious group and its support for the community. In this case, their religious identity overshadows their organizational one.

In many circumstances, the organization and the inducements the organization provides for volunteers' relationships with it are not in the foreground of volunteers' participation. The organization may be a means to an end, it may be a gathering place for people with whom the volunteers want to socialize, or it can be a vehicle for demonstrating something important about the volunteers' relationships with other organizations or their communities. A surprisingly large number of volunteers think very little of their organizations as entities with which they have relationships. For example, many of the volunteers interviewed for the Pearce (1993) study described earlier could not give the correct name of the organization, but thought of it as an extension of work they did for another group (e.g., their church or school), or could identify it only by the name of the organization's leader. This is consistent with the argument of Ashforth and Rogers (Chapter 2, this volume) that employees may see themselves more in relation to the "tribes" to which they belong, tribes that may be within or across organizational boundaries.

Peters and Pearce (1985) argued that framing EORs as either an economic or equity exchange can be dysfunctional. The ambiguity of many of the contributions required of employees and uncertainty about what might be required in the future make the rigid use of economic and equity exchanges between organizations and their employees difficult. I would propose that, following Goffman (1961) and Ekeh (1974), viewing EORs as primarily inducement–contribution relationships, with an emphasis on what inducements the organization needs to provide, is dysfunctional for both these relationships and our understanding of them. Each of their perspectives on social exchange illuminates some aspect of volunteers' relationships with their organizations, relationships that may well characterize many EORs. Social exchange appears to be more complex than economic exchange, and reducing social exchange to its individualistic quid pro quo components risks misunderstanding this important component of many EORs.

CONCLUSIONS

This brief discussion of volunteer–organization relationships is intended to draw attention to and, I hope, to make more problematic five assumptions implicit in much of the EOR literature. First, many volunteers are often unclear about their relationships with their organizations. Very few volunteers have actively sought out and chosen their particular organizations; most are brought in by family members or friends. As the volunteer quoted in the beginning of this chapter noted, volunteers do not know why they volunteer, so they make assumptions that may be artificially reified by direct questions about their relationships with their organizations. This at least raises the question of how clear employees may be about their relationships with their organizations; those studying early EORs may be assuming rationality that may not be there. The long history of research on Expectancy Theory (Vroom, 1964) has demonstrated that employees are rarely hyperrational calculating machines, and a good number of employees, like volunteers, may simply not have thought much about their organizational relationships until a researcher asks them a question that requires a socially acceptable response. Research in EOR might benefit from seeking to understand to what extent employees do perceive that they have an EOR, rather than assuming it.

Second, volunteers arrive at their organizations for many different reasons, and so even coworkers doing the same work will evaluate what the organization provides in quite different ways. Much EOR research has studied the average responses of large groups of employees, linking these average responses to job or organizational policies and practices. The extreme heterogeneity of volunteers' reasons for working reminds us that employees also have different reasons for working. We may all assume that they are doing it because they have to make a living, but their motives and expectations may be more variable and inchoate than that. It simply is not clear how important the organization and its policies and practices are to all employees' participation. Research in EORs might benefit from a more careful examination of what matters most to employees.

Third, volunteers are rarely very dependent on their organizations and so may have very little psychological relationship with it. Many employees, too, may be only lightly dependent on their organization, and this has implications for their relationships with their organizations. Many EOR scholars assume that employees are the weaker, dependent party and must tolerate the situation (or undertake a costly job search) if they do not like what the organization provides. Looking at volunteer–organization relationships reminds us that employees also vary in their relative dependence on their organizations, and this can have important EOR implications that have not yet been explored.

Fourth, volunteer-staffed workplaces usually are understaffed, resulting in low barriers to entry and weak performance demands. For some volunteers, this can result in organizational participation so slight and undemanding that the organization virtually disappears as an entity with which they have a psychological relationship. While understaffing is stark in volunteer-staffed organizations, under- and overstaffing does occur in employee-staffed workplaces. Here I proposed that relative staffing levels can have significant effects on volunteer–organization relationships, something that may well generalize to EORs.

Finally, EOR research is dominated by an inducements–contributions framing of the relationship. A purely economic exchange is starkly inappropriate for volunteers, and so the various normative expectations at play in their relationships help to illustrate the value of a more complete understanding of social exchange. Many volunteers see their relationships as primarily with their coworkers, their communities, or the mission they work to support. Very few volunteers sought out their organizations and are much more likely to be working there because of preexisting social relationships. Many employees also take jobs without rationally weighing the inducements and contributions and then remain because it is not intolerable or their attention is focused elsewhere. A better understanding of the nonutilitarian aspects of their relationships with their organizations would seem to be a promising area of research.

It is clear that most of the data on which this argument has been based is from North America, but it is unclear how much of it extends to other cultures. Much of the work on volunteers' organizational relationships has occurred in the individualistic cultures of Northern Europe, and certainly the meaning of volunteer work can vary a great deal in different cultures. For example, recruitment via friends and family, which is so dominant in North America, may be less common elsewhere. This argument's emphasis on differences in dependence, and equality and need-based normative expectations, may be particularly welcome in more collectivistic cultures. For example, Chinese guanxi has been described as a complex relationship with both utilitarian and social relationship features (Xin & Pearce, 1996), making the conventional individualistic inducements–contributions framework particularly inappropriate there.

Although this chapter has addressed EOR scholars, it has notable practical implications. For example, much of EOR attention has focused on organization-wide inducements like training or benefits. Yet, the differing motives and more complex organizational relationships of volunteers suggest that an important feature of the EOR for employees may be out of the organization's control. For example, supervisors will have more detailed knowledge of what their subordinates value in their employment relationships and can try to make those differing inducements available to their employees. Similarly, supervisors usually are acutely aware of those situations when key subordinates are not dependent on the organization and often get very frustrated trying to allocate compensation or opportunities in ways that centralized human resources staff members would prefer be allocated in more egalitarian ways. In general, this examination of volunteers' relationships with their organizations suggests a less centralized, more particularized approach to employees.

In conclusion, an examination of volunteer–organization relationships suggests several important moderators that have not been considered in EOR research. The degree to which employees actually perceive and attend to their relationships with their organizations as something meaningful in their workplaces, their dependence on the organization, and the relative staffing levels of the workplace all show promise in helping us to better understand EORs. In addition, the relative emphasis on the economic aspects of the employee–organization exchange to the neglect of the social aspects can be redressed with a clearer understanding of the differing perspectives on social exchange. Volunteers do a lot of organizational work, and attention to their organizational relationships is valuable in its own right, as well as for how it helps us see EORs from a new perspective.

REFERENCES

Ashford, S. J., George, E., & Blatt, R. (2007). New work, old assumptions. *Academy of Management Annals*, *1*, 65–117.
Barker, R. G. (1968). *Ecological psychology*. Stanford, CA: Stanford University Press.
Barker, R. G., & Gump, P. V. (1964). *Big school, small school*. Stanford, CA: Stanford University Press.

Blau, P. M. (1964). *Exchange and power in social life*. New Brunswick, NJ: Transaction.
Clary, E. G., Snyder, M., Ridge, R. D., Copeland, J., Stukas, A. A., Haugen, J., & Miene, P. (1998). Understanding and assessing the motivations of volunteers: A functional approach. *Journal of Personality and Social Psychology, 74*, 1516–1530.
Corporation for National & Community Service, Office of Research & Policy Development (2010). *Volunteering in America 2010*. Washington, DC: Author.
De Charms, R. (1968). *Personal causation*. New York, NY: Academic Press.
Deci, E. L. (1975). *Intrinsic motivation*. New York, NY: Plenum.
Ekeh, P. P. (1974). *Social exchange theory*. Cambridge, MA: Harvard University Press.
Felps, W., Hekman, D. R., Mitchel, T. R., Lee, T. W., Harman, W. S., & Holtom, B. C. (2009). Turnover contagion: How coworkers' job embeddedness and coworkers' job search behaviors influence quitting. *Academy of Management Journal, 52*, 545–561.
Gallup Organization. (1978). *The Gallup study of public awareness and involvement with non-profit organizations*. Princeton, NJ: Gallup.
Goffman, E. (1961). *Asylum*. Garden City, NY: Anchor.
Haski-Leventhal, D., & Bargal, D. (2008). The volunteer stages and transition model. *Human Relations, 61*, 67–102.
Homans, G. C. (1961). *Social behavior*. New York, NY: Harcourt, Brace and World.
Malinowski, B. (1922). *Argonauts of the western Pacific*. London, UK: Routledge and Kegan Paul.
March, J. G., & Simon, H. A. (1958). *Organizations*. New York, NY: Wiley.
Pearce, J. L. (1983). Job attitude and motivation differences between volunteers and employees from comparable organizations. *Journal of Applied Psychology, 68*, 646–652.
Pearce, J. L. (1993). *Volunteers: The organizational behavior of unpaid workers*. New York, NY: Routledge.
Pearce, J. L. (2001). *Organization and management in the embrace of government*. Mahwah, NJ: Lawrence Erlbaum.
Pearce, J. L., & Peters, R. H. (1985). A contradictory norms view of employer-employee exchange. *Journal of Management, 11*, 19–30.
Roethlisberger, F. J., & Dickson, W. J. (1939). *Management and the worker*. Cambridge, MA: Harvard University Press.
Rousseau, D. M., & Tijoriwala, S. A. (1998). Assessing psychological contracts. *Journal of Organizational Behavior, 19*, 679–695.
Salancik, G. R., & Pfeffer, J. (1978). A social information processing approach to job attitudes and task design. *Administrative Science Quarterly, 23*, 224–253.
Shore, L. M., Coyle-Shapiro, J. A.-M., Chen, X.-P., & Tetrick, L. E. (2009). Social exchange in work settings: Content, mixed and process models. *Management and Organization Review, 5*, 289–302.
Shore, L. M., Tetrick, L. E., Taylor, M. S., Coyle-Shapiro, J. A.-M., Liden, R. C., McLean Parks, J. M., … Van Dyne, L. (2004). The employee-organization relationship: A timely concept in a period of transition. In G. R. Ferris & J. Martocchio (Eds.), *Research in personnel and human resources management* (pp. 291–370). Greenwich, CT: JAI Press.
Sills, D. L. (1957). *The volunteers*. Glencoe, IL: Free Press.
Starnes, B. J., & Iyer, U. J. (2009, April). *Psychological contract perceptions and volunteer contributions*. Paper presented at the Society for Industrial and Organizational Psychology Annual Conference, New Orleans, LA.
Staw, B. M. (1976). *Intrinsic and extrinsic motivation*. Morristown, NJ: General Learning Press.

Tsui, A. S., Pearce, J. L., Porter, L. W., & Hite, J. P. (1995). Choice of employee-organization relationship: Influence of external and internal organizational factors. *Research in Personnel and Human Resources Management, 13*, 117–151.

Vardaman, J. M., Hancock, J. B., Allen, D. G., & Shore, L. M. (2009, April). *Impact of collective perceptions of organizational support on individual outcomes.* Paper presented at the Society for Industrial and Organizational Psychology Annual Conference, New Orleans, LA.

Vroom, V. H. (1964). *Work and motivation.* New York, NY: Wiley.

Westphal, J. D., & Stern, I. (2006). The other pathway to the boardroom. *Administrative Science Quarterly, 51*, 169–204.

Xin, K., & Pearce, J. L. (1996). Guanxi: Connections as substitutes for formal institutional support. *Academy of Management Journal, 39*, 1641–1658.

Yeung, A. B. (2004). The Octagon Model of volunteer motivation. *Voluntas, 15*, 21–46.

Part 2

Putting the "R" Back in the EOR

8

Can the Organizational Career Survive? An Evaluation Within a Social Exchange Perspective

David E. Guest
King's College London

Ricardo Rodrigues
Kingston University London

INTRODUCTION

Research on careers has a long and distinguished history. However, contemporary research on organizational careers can usefully be traced back to the work of a group of scholars based at the Massachusetts Institute of Technology (MIT) and Harvard in the mid-1970s. During this time, three seminal books were published by Hall (1976), Van Maanen (1977), and Schein (1978) integrating previous work focusing on careers within organizational contexts and setting the cornerstone of the popular view of careers as a "sequence of promotions and other upward moves in a work-related hierarchy during the course of the person's work life" (Hall, 1976, p. 2). These might be played out in a single organization or sometimes across a number of organizations.

According to Arthur (1994), the growing interest in careers within organizations can be explained by two factors. First, between the postwar period and the 1970s, it was assumed that the large corporations that dominated advanced industrial economies were here to stay. The effective management of organizational careers was viewed as a key factor in the success of these corporations. Second, by the 1970s and 1980s, there was a growing interest in Europe and America in the Japanese style of management, particularly in how the organization of work, the culture of cooperation and continuous improvement, and policies of job security and lifetime employment contributed to the success of Japanese firms (Pascale & Athos, 1981).

Managing the traditional career exchange to ensure a good match between individual and organizational goals and needs at different stages in their relationship has been a widely debated topic from the 1970s onward (Ornstein & Isabella, 1993). Elements of this discussion can be found in the literature on internal labor markets (see, for example, Osterman, 1994) that has discussed how internal organizational rules ensured the conditions for vertical career progression and long-term attachment between workers and organizations. Researchers have described how large organizations divided work to create hierarchies and job ladders, often beyond what was technically required, in order to offer workers formal structures of career opportunity and status gradations (Baron & Bielby, 1986). Academics have also explored the formal practices organizations use to plan and develop people's careers, such as communicating job opportunities, providing formal career counseling, clarifying career pathways and criteria for progression, and offering extensive training, performance appraisal, and regular feedback (Baruch & Peiperl, 2000; Gould, 1979); and they have discussed the impact of these practices on organizational identification and performance (Albert, Ashforth, & Dutton, 2000).

The traditional organizational career is perhaps a classic example of a mutually beneficial exchange. In return for good performance and appropriate displays of commitment, the employee receives job security and the possibility of promotion onward and upward in the organizational hierarchy. Despite the apparent benefits to both individuals and organizations, the organizational career of the kind captured in the definition provided by Hall (1976) is frequently described as being under threat. There is a rhetoric about the new career (Arthur, Inkson, & Pringle, 1999), "the boundaryless career" (Arthur, 1994), "career self-management" (King, 2004), and even "the end of the career" (Cappelli, 1999). The central aim of this chapter is to analyze and evaluate this threat. We do so within the context of an analytic framework that draws upon exchange theory and the resource-based view of the firm and by using a range of empirical sources. However as a first step, we need to elaborate on the meaning of the career and outline some of the distinctive features of the exchange implied in the organizational career.

THE CAREER FROM A SOCIAL EXCHANGE PERSPECTIVE

The progressive organizational career enjoyed by managers and some professionals was only ever available to a minority of staff. As Osterman (1994) and others have observed, firms have typically employed a range of internal labor markets. Only those in managerial and sometimes professional internal labor markets are likely to have the opportunity to experience a traditional organizational career. Furthermore, not everyone seeks an upwardly mobile career. Therefore, we need a broader, more encompassing definition of a career if we are to capture the range of career experiences. Arnold (1997), for example, describes a career as "a sequence of employment-related positions, roles, activities and experiences encountered by a person" (p. 16). This broader definition can apply to all workers and is worth keeping in mind while we focus more narrowly on the careers of the managerial and professional staff.

We have suggested that the traditional organizational career represents a classic form of exchange. Closer inspection suggests that this is a highly complex and in some respects unusual exchange. If we consider the exchange in terms of the psychological contract (Rousseau, 1995; Taylor & Tekleab, 2004), it is highly relational and long term. It relies heavily on what might be termed a "career promise," whereby a heavy investment over a period of time by the employee is offered in the expectation of a return at some future date in the form of promotion. It therefore entails a strong element of postponed gratification. The challenge for the organization is to devise ways to retain the probability in the mind of staff that the promise will be kept. Yet, inevitably, in a typical pyramid-shaped organization structure, not everyone will be able to rise up the hierarchy. In this context, we can use aspects of exchange theory to explore how this challenge can be addressed. The key components are trust, fairness, perceived organizational support, and delivery of sufficient promises within the psychological contract. We will examine each in turn.

Trust is a central feature of any successful exchange model. At the point of recruitment, those embarking on what they hope will be progressive organizational careers—notably graduates entering junior management posts—may believe that a "career promise" has been made to them, even if the language in which it was couched was somewhat ambiguous, leaving the "promise," at best, implicit. In responding to this promise, they are trusting the organization and its agents to deliver on the promise. Coyle-Shapiro and Conway (2004) note "one party needs to trust the other to discharge future obligations (i.e. to reciprocate) in the initial stages of the exchange and it is the regular discharge of obligations that promotes trust in the relationship" (p. 7). However, in the case of the career promise, there is considerable uncertainty about when the delivery will occur, and in practice, both parties are making an investment in the hope of a future return. The new entrants therefore need to demonstrate their potential, and the organization needs to provide evidence to reinforce the trust about future delivery of promotion. The organization may achieve this by pointing to the experience of previous cohorts of graduates, by providing development opportunities, by direct feedback on progress, and by renewal of promises. However, trust in delivery of advancement is likely to diminish over time, particularly if other managers seem to be making swifter progress within what has been described as the career tournament (Rosenbaum, 1979). It has also been suggested (Smola & Sutton, 2002) that contemporary graduates are less patient and less prepared to wait. Furthermore organizations are eager to identify key talent at an ever earlier stage to ensure that they are developed and retained. The scope for a number of young managers within a particular intake to fall by the wayside, reflecting a breakdown in trust, is therefore high. Indeed, in their meta-analysis of the consequences of psychological contract breach, Zhao, Wayne, Gliboswki, and Bravo (2007) found evidence to support the role of trust as a mediator between breach and outcomes such as reduced commitment and increased intention to quit.

One way in which trust might be maintained is by demonstrating high levels of organizational support. Shore and Shore (1995) highlight the career challenge by suggesting that employees are inherently disadvantaged in their exchange with the organization because they have less power, because they have to deal with a variety of agents of the organization, who may communicate different messages, and because of the typical delay in the delivery of promises and obligations. To overcome this disadvantage, Eisenberger, Jones, Aselage, and Sucharski (2004) have argued that the organization needs to demonstrate its support for employees.

> In many cases, promises may lack specificity, leading to uncertainty about whether the organization has fulfilled its obligations. For instance, organizations may promise prospective employees *substantial* future pay raises or *frequent* promotions. In subsequently evaluating whether the organization has fulfilled such qualitative promises, employees with high POS may be inclined to give the organization the benefit of the doubt in determining whether the contract has been fulfilled. (p. 215)

There is evidence (Rhoades & Eisenberger, 2002) that support will be perceived as more valuable when it is voluntary rather than required and when it is distinctive to the individual rather than general. Support can come in the form of words but, at some point, will need to be translated into action.

The gains made by some indication of personalized support may reinforce the commitment of one manager but, unless carefully handled, can do so at the expense of others, raising the question of fairness of treatment. Shore and Shore (1995) suggested that although both substantive and procedural fairness are essential to a positive exchange, procedural fairness will be more important for maintaining a sense of perceived organizational support, partly because substantive rewards in the context of careers are much rarer. However, there is potential ambiguity concerning fairness because although both parties can recognize the importance of procedural fairness, organizations will wish to be selective in identifying talent and individuals will be pleased to be selected out of the pack. Therefore, in the context of a scarcity of the key distributive reward of promotion, there is considerable potential for perceptions of unfairness and an increased need for transparent procedural fairness.

The final relevant component of the exchange model is the psychological contract. The psychological contract addresses the reciprocal promises and obligations between the individual and the organization (Rousseau, 1995). A conceptual distinction is often made between transactional and relational psychological contracts (Rousseau, 1989). Although the operational distinction between these two types of psychological contract has proved difficult to sustain, particularly when defining the boundary between them (Roehling, 2004), the distinction has conceptual and analytic value in the present context. Transactional contracts are explicit, often relatively short term, and easy to monitor, whereas relational contracts are less clear-cut or specified, more long term, and much less straightforward to monitor. As a result, there is more scope for misinterpretation and consequently for breach of the deal.

The promise of a career is an extreme example of a relational psychological contract. It implies long-term exchange in which the outcomes are uncertain and cannot be specified at the outset. The contributions from the employee are usually unclearly specified and may become tied to a set of normative obligations about issues such as working hours and travel that are embedded in the organizational culture. In general, therefore, the content, specificity, and timing of the delivery of organizational careers are highly uncertain. This uncertainty applies to both parties. The employee can be uncertain about how much time she has to demonstrate her potential, about the criteria for high potential performance, and about who makes the key judgment about that performance. As noted earlier, the organization faces uncertainty in its attempts to identify the high potential managers and to do so in a timely fashion that enables it to develop and reward those it particularly wishes to retain. Although rewards can take the form of pay rises, development opportunities, and positive feedback, the key reward is promotion. Promotion is distinctive because it typically brings with it a bundle of additional rewards such as increased pay, higher status, more power, more autonomy, and more responsibility. The essentially ambiguous and uncertain nature of the predominantly relational content of the career dimension in the psychological contract leaves plenty of scope to believe that promises have not been kept.

Lambert, Edwards, and Cable (2003) and Montes and Irving (2008) have demonstrated that breach of relational features of the psychological contract is much more serious than breach of the transactional components. Breach of perceived career promises can be particularly serious because of the bundle of outcomes associated with career advancement and may precipitate an intention to leave the organization. If organizational changes are eroding opportunities for career advancement, then the viability of the traditional organizational career, involving a long-term commitment to the organization in exchange for career progress, is likely to be under increasing threat.

In summary, the traditional organizational career represents a distinctive, highly complex and highly uncertain form of exchange. For both individuals and organizations, there are considerable mutual gains from successful organizational careers, which helps to explain why they have persisted. There are also considerable risks engendered by the complexity of the exchange that can result in at least one party perceiving that the exchange has failed. Despite the potential benefits of the traditional career model for both employees and organizations, it is has come under increasing critical scrutiny in recent years, with some observers even claiming that it is unlikely to survive.

The challenge to the organizational career can be understood and analyzed at two levels. First, there is a general argument about the changing context within which organizations operate and that may be making it less feasible to offer traditional organizational careers. Second, there is a more specific argument about the human resource strategies and especially the career and development strategies that firms need to apply in order to thrive that provides a more selective approach to the conditions under which organizational careers are desirable. These potentially contrasting perspectives then provide a context within which to explore relevant empirical evidence. We start by analyzing the wider context.

THE CHANGING CONTEXT OF CAREERS AND CAREER MANAGEMENT

Commentators have identified a range of global trends affecting the way in which organizations are forced to operate if they wish to survive. These include the growth of the knowledge-based and global economy, the impact of technology, migration, the growth of the professions, and changes in work values in advanced industrial societies. We briefly review these broad trends before focusing more specifically on how they might affect the ability of organizations to offer traditional careers.

The Knowledge-Based Economy and Globalization

Industrial restructuring in the United States and Europe in recent decades is associated with globalization and the shift toward a knowledge-based economy (Mirvis & Hall, 1994). The economy of hardware is being replaced by the economy of software, where economic wealth is grounded on "the creation, production, distribution and consumption of knowledge and knowledge-based products" (Harris, 2001, p. 22). The shift toward a knowledge-based economy, compounded by the increasing pace of globalization, has undoubtedly shaped the competitive environment, fueled uncertainty among workers and organizations, and placed additional pressures on the traditional career model. Globalization and its opening up of a more international labor market seem to be intensifying the war for talent in developed countries and forcing companies to fight to attract and retain the most skilled workers (Chambers, Foulon, Handfield-Jones, Hankin, & Michaels, 1998). The growth of an international labor market for staff in fields such as finance can distort internal labor markets as organizations vie with each other to attract and retain those they regard as key to their future success. One possible consequence of engaging in the war for talent, as Pfeffer (2001) observes, is that companies may be downplaying their own talent to the detriment of newcomers and therefore encouraging workers to seek career progression through interorganizational mobility rather than through internal promotion.

Commentators have also warned that the premium placed on knowledge, associated with higher educational levels of the workforce in developed countries and uncertainty fostered by large firm decentralization, frequent restructuring, and delayering (Littler, Wiesner, & Dunford, 2003), may boost a "hired gun" career mindset among those who possess valuable and rare human capital (Barley & Kunda, 2004). For these people, selling their skills in the market to the highest bidder on a short-term basis may be more appealing than long-term commitment to an organization. All these factors have affected the nature of work, the traditional employment relationship, and thus it is argued, the viability of careers within organizations.

Technology

The widespread use of information and communication technologies may also be contributing to changes in the nature of employment and the traditional career exchange. Technological change destroys old jobs and creates new ones, usually having a positive effect on employment in the long run (Freeman, Soete, & Efendioglu, 1995). However, the newly created jobs may be of a different nature and involve different sets of promises and expectations when compared with traditional organizational career jobs.

Flexible employment arrangements seem to have become more common in some industries and geographical locations where new technologies are more prevalent. Perhaps the epitome of new employment relations can be found in locations like Silicon Valley (Saxenian, 1996), where information technology (IT) professionals frequently move between competing firms in a process that allows them to acquire marketable skills and gives organizations access to talent that drives innovation. The employment patterns of Silicon Valley have been considered by many as "a trendsetter, both for the United States and for the world" (Carnoy, Castells, & Benner, 1997, p. 28). If this is the case, the short-term transactional employment relations that are the norm in these industries may be a sign of things to come.

Migration

In tandem with economic globalization, immigration flows from developing countries have created pressures on traditional career arrangements. In particular, immigration has generated apprehension that a vast reservoir of inexpensive labor would be made available to employers in developed countries, threatening natives' job stability and bidding down salaries (Borjas, 2006). Even though there is evidence that immigration significantly affects the supply of skills in locations with a high concentration of migrants and, consequently, occupation-specific wages and employment rates (Card, 2001), its impact on employment and career patterns is complex and to a large extent dependent on national policy and the profile of migrants. Aydemir and Borjas (2007) have recently compared the impact of immigration on wage rates in different countries between 1980 and 2000. For instance, immigration to the United States is disproportionally low skilled and therefore tends to create pressures at the low end of the income distribution. In contrast, in Canada, where migrants are mainly high-skilled workers, immigration seems to be affecting mostly those at the high end of the labor market. An influx of high-quality but potentially cheaper managers and professionals into organizational hierarchies can distort internal labor markets.

Professionalization

Professional occupations have codified areas of knowledge, specified training, and in some cases, control over access to work (Tolbert, 1996).

The value system of traditional professions, such as medicine and law, is now resonating among other groups of workers such as engineers, nurses, pharmacists, accountants, psychologists, and teachers (Evets, 2003). The growth of professional bodies places the organizational career model under pressure in a number of ways. Because most professionals are currently employees in professional or bureaucratic organizations, instead of self-employed, they must manage loyalties toward their employer and their profession (Wallace, 1995). There is an ongoing debate about whether organizational and occupational value systems are compatible. For instance, in a study with accountants, Sorensen and Sorensen (1974) found that perceived conflict between professional and organizational loyalties resulted in job dissatisfaction and turnover. Because a profession is based on a distinctive body of knowledge, it can be easily transferable across organizations so that an occupational career becomes an alternative to the traditional organizational career. It seems that for a growing proportion of the workforce, the occupation or profession is an increasingly salient locus of careers that will help to shape people's expectations of the employer–employee relationship.

Changing Work Values

There is an extensive literature analyzing generational differences in work values and suggesting that the meaning of work is changing for younger generations, who give a higher priority to achieving a healthy work–life balance rather than a traditional organizational career. Although some of these studies are cross-sectional and therefore need to be treated with caution, Smola and Sutton (2002) replicated a study on work values previously conducted in the United States in 1974. Their evidence suggests that in comparison with Generation X (born between the early 1960s and the mid-1970s), the Millennials (born between 1979 and 1994), who are now entering the labor market, are less loyal to their organizations and more committed to their own personal goals. They also consider work to be a less important part of their lives and are more willing to stop working if they win a large amount of money. All this suggests that those who in the past would have become the stereotypical "company men" seem to be more reluctant to accept the traditional exchange of long working hours and loyalty and commitment to their organizations in return for job security and hierarchical promotion. This attitudinal change may be fostered by changing underlying work values, as the literature suggests, or by workers reacting to fewer career opportunities.

Consequences of Changes for Internal Labor Markets

It is suggested that internal labor markets are more permeable to the external environment in a number of ways (O'Mahoney & Bechky, 2006). First, it has been argued that wages seem to be more sensitive to the value of skills in the market and individual performance than to internal organizational principles (Osterman & Burton, 2005). Second, it has been suggested that companies are more reluctant to invest in training and seem to be emphasizing workers' responsibility for the development of their own human capital (Peiperl & Baruch, 1997). Third, some commentators have linked the growth of the temporary work industry in the United States and Europe from the 1970s onward (Kalleberg, 2000) to the idea that a stable and committed workforce is no longer a priority for companies, who are turning to the external market in search for skills and just-in-time workers (DeFillippi & Arthur, 1994). These trends seem to be associated both with an individualization of employment relations (Rousseau, 2005) and a decline in trade union membership and collective bargaining (Brown, Deakin, Nash, & Oxenbridge, 2000). In summary, the argument is that multiple pressures are making it less feasible for organizations to offer the traditional organizational career. At the same time, it is also argued that changes in values among those entering the labor market mean that they are less enthusiastic about pursuing the traditional organizational career. Therefore, the traditional organization career seems to be under pressure from both partners to the exchange.

THE CASE FOR RETAINING THE ORGANIZATIONAL CAREER

Despite the argument that a range of pressures are making it more difficult to provide careers and keep "career promises," many organizations continue to recruit graduate cohorts and some other staff with the promise of a career. Why do they do this? Part of the answer can be found within an analysis using the resource-based view of the firm (Barney, 1991). This highlights the importance for the competitive advantage of organizations of acquiring and retaining human resources that are rare, valuable, inimitable, and nonsubstitutable. Barney and Wright (1998) have shown how these relate to human resource practices, emphasizing the importance of investing in critical human capital. Lepak and Snell (1999) have developed a framework within which organizations can classify the various types of human resource, identifying those staff who are considered to be central to the firm's success and for whom the firm might wish to provide an organizational career.

The Lepak and Snell model has two dimensions concerned with whether staff are high or low with respect to the uniqueness and the value of their human capital. They suggest that those high on both dimensions are the staff that firms should seek to attract and retain by providing an organizational career. For others, such as, for example, certain kinds of lawyers and consultants who are required only occasionally, they would advocate some form of alliance relationship. In the case of other staff, whose contribution is less valuable and who are easily replaceable, Lepak and Snell suggest there is no case for a long-term investment. The implication is that even among the managerial and professional group within an organization, only a minority have the kind of distinctive and valuable human capital that justifies the full investment in their career. Lepak and Snell (2002) and Peel and Boxall (2005) have demonstrated some validity for the types and patterns of investment implied by the framework, and Lepak, Takeuchi, and Snell (2003) reported higher performance among firms that adopt human resource strategies that align with the framework.

The resource-based view of the firm justifies the case for investing in human resources, and the Lepak and Snell model helps to explain why organizations might wish to adopt a selective approach to career management. However, it is directed toward the whole workforce and is not sufficiently focused on career issues for our present purposes. To develop an analytic framework to explore contemporary organizational careers, we can draw on three perspectives. The first is transaction cost economics (Williamson, 1975), which heavily influenced the resource-based view of the firm and which highlights a core choice, mirrored in the Lepak and Snell model, about whether to "make" or "buy" staff. The second perspective, reflected in exchange theory, concerns the kind of relationship that the organization seeks with its staff. This can most usefully be analyzed in terms of the psychological contract and the distinction, noted earlier, between relational and transactional contracts. Finally, Schein (1978) has shown how workers have different career preferences, reflected in what he terms career anchors, that can lead them to pursue different kinds of career paths. He distinguishes between the general progressive hierarchical career, where progress is reflected in promotion, which can occur across various parts of an organization; the professional or technical/functional career, where progress will occur within a narrow professional hierarchy or take the form of greater depth rather than promotion, reflected in increased expertise and autonomy; and what he describes as movement toward the center of the organization. This can occur among managers who are not considered as high potential but through their tacit knowledge become an essential cog in the smooth operation of the organization. They form a kind of backbone of middle management. These dimensions provide an opportunity to distinguish the types of managerial personnel and the associated careers, illustrated in Figure 8.1.

Figure 8.1 shows four types of career. In the first quadrant, at the top right-hand corner, is the traditional organizational career, geared toward high potential (HiPo) managers who will be developed by and promoted within the organization. They are identified as potential organizational leaders, key to the success of the organization, and with whom the organization will have a broad, highly relational exchange.

In the second quadrant, at the bottom right-hand corner are what we have termed the backbone managers. These may have started out as part of the high potential cadre but have fallen back in the career tournament. They are a moderately valuable resource because they have accumulated a lot of specific inside knowledge of the sort associated with Schein's third

	Relational		
External labor market (buy)	Professional managers (autonomous career)	HiPo managers (traditional career)	Internal labor market (make/develop)
	"Free" managers (boundaryless career)	Backbone managers (constrained organizational career)	
	Transactional		

FIGURE 8.1
A model of managerial career types. HiPo, high potential.

type of career. They are the middle managers who keep the wheels oiled. They may stay in an organization because their specific skills make it difficult to move to other organizations, and they may rise to the middle ranks of the hierarchy, but from an organizational perspective, they are dispensable because they are neither rare nor particularly valuable. They fit in the right-hand side because the organization will have been largely responsible for their development and because they possess specific rather than general knowledge and skills. The psychological contract will be more limited and more transactional than that of the HiPo managers in so far as organizations invest less in the exchange. In practice, it may come closer to what Rousseau (1995, p. 98) has termed a "balanced" rather than a purely transactional exchange.

The third quadrant, in the top left-hand corner, includes professional managers, those who have developed a strong professional knowledge base, typically linked to recognizable qualifications. Within the management group, they would typically include finance and accountancy experts. Some will move into the top right-hand quadrant, but many will retain their specialism. This category also includes the professional workers in public sector and not-for-profit organizations such as hospitals. Their knowledge and skills are developed outside the organization, but their expertise can become invaluable to the organization and some can be very hard to replace. The professional expertise gives them considerable autonomy, and their careers will often take the form of gaining greater depth in their distinctive expertise. Therefore, they will have a highly relational contract reflected in the autonomy and the high level of trust inherent in that autonomy. Growth of professional autonomy rather than hierarchical promotion often represents the development of their career.

The final category, in the bottom left-hand corner, represents what has come to be known as the "new" career. This has been described in terms of the "free worker" (Knell, 2000), free in the sense that the worker is not tied to any organization. Their loyalty is to themselves and their career rather than to any organization. When they work in organizations, the relationship is transactional and conditional. In this context, one can think of certain kinds of bankers and technology experts. Organizations may wish to retain them, but they will remain with an organization only so long as it suits them.

The broad argument within "the new career" model is that there is pressure to move away from the other types of career toward a boundaryless career. The implication in much of the writing is that this is driven by individual preferences as much as, if not more than, by organizations, more particularly because these free workers may be highly talented knowledge workers of the sort organizations would wish to retain. Given their centrality to the contrast between the "old" organizational career and the "new" career, we need to explore this category in more detail.

THE NEW CAREER

The new career involves a shift from a relationship based on the exchange of loyalty and commitment for long-term employment security and career progression to a relationship based on the exchange of performance for the opportunity to develop marketable skills and benefit from competitive wages over a short period of time (Arthur, 1994; Sullivan, 1999). The old career deal was based on mutual interests built around the traditional long-term career exchange. The new deal is typically a more short-term exchange between organization and individual requiring the organization to provide meaningful work experiences and scope for development in exchange for a commitment to work toward organizational goals (Briscoe & Hall, 2006). Hence, under the new deal, success is no longer measured by one's position in a structured organizational hierarchy, power, and income, but rather by one's own self-defined notion of achievement that may encompass, for instance, achieving a satisfactory work–life balance, doing work that contributes to society, or applying one's ideas to creating a new business (Hall & Mirvis, 1995). In this context, three concepts that have been widely associated with this new perspective are the boundaryless career, the protean career, and career self-management. We briefly explore and then evaluate each in turn.

The idea of the boundaryless career, coined after the metaphor of the boundaryless organization, is frequently associated in the literature with mobility across jobs, functions, and organizations, as well as the demise of rigid job structures and hierarchical career paths (Arthur, 1994; Briscoe & Hall, 2006). The concept is, however, broader and richer. Arthur (1994) has highlighted several distinctive aspects of physical and psychological boundarylessness, including how such careers draw validation from outside the present employer, are sustained by extraorganizational networks or information, and reflect a perception of a career without structural constraints and that is, therefore, boundaryless.

The concept of the protean career focuses mainly on the "internal" career, highlighting changes in people's career values and attitudes. A protean career is "one in which the person, not the organization, is in charge, the core values are freedom and growth, and the main success criteria are subjective (psychological success) vs. objective (position, salary)" (Hall, 2004, p. 4). The protean career is driven by a predisposition to act according to one's values and beliefs (Briscoe & Hall, 2006), involves a renegotiation of the psychological contract (Hall & Mirvis, 1995) based on the individual's values, and involves commitment to personally meaningful work experiences as the main route to achieving psychological success.

The boundaryless career and the protean career both reflect the idea that organizational boundaries have become more permeable (Arnold & Cohen, 2008) and, as a result, that membership of an organization or department is more transient and ambiguous (Miner & Robinson, 1994). The suggested demise of organizational careers does not imply the end of job opportunities or career advancement, but rather that these are to be found in career paths that involve frequent moves between different organizations (DeFillippi & Arthur, 1994). To navigate the new career landscape successfully, people are being advised to consider careers as their own property and to take responsibility for managing their own careers (King, 2004) through developing what have been described as intelligent career competencies (DeFillippi & Arthur, 1994). People are encouraged to decouple their identities from their jobs and work settings and advised to build their identity around their occupation, personal interests, or other nonwork activities. By the same token, it is suggested that developing marketable skills and abilities, rather than firm-specific skills, and participating in networks that allow access to work opportunities beyond the boundaries of one's current employer might contribute to career success in the boundaryless career era (DeFillippi & Arthur, 1994).

Although the idea of "the new career" is well established within the career lexicon, both the protean and the boundaryless career concepts have attracted criticism on conceptual, empirical, and operational grounds (Arnold & Cohen, 2008; Inkson, 2006; Pringle & Mallon, 2003). In this section, we briefly outline three conceptual issues raised by the current view on the new career. The next section discusses in greater detail the extent to which the evidence supports the demise of organizational careers.

The first issue that needs further discussion is the assumption that the context in which companies operate is causing the demise of organizational careers. The basis for the new career "acknowledges the unpredictable, market-sensitive world in which so many careers now unfold" (Arthur, 1994, p. 297), echoing some of the core arguments of literature on globalization and technological change previously outlined in this chapter. But are these trends really forcing organizations to lose their role as the main locus of people's careers? A number of economists have argued for some time that the impact of contextual and organizational changes on wages, employment stability, and careers has been exaggerated (Krugman, 1994). The rhetoric of change has not been systematically linked to the reality of contemporary organizational career practice, and there is therefore a need to explore in more detail the link between the changes in the competitive environment and any evidence supporting the rise of the new career.

The second issue concerns the conceptualization and operationalization of the new career with its focus on the permeability of, and movement across, organizational boundaries. The primacy ascribed to organizational boundaries is reflected both in the conceptualization (Sullivan & Arthur, 2006) and in the operationalization of the boundaryless and the protean career (Briscoe, Hall, & DeMuth, 2006). If organizational boundaries have become permeable, does that mean that careers are unfolding in an unstructured environment? Or are careers embedded in other domains, which may then be becoming more salient and impermeable? These questions are difficult to answer within the current framework of the new career. A more complete elaboration and operationalization of the concept needs to consider the nature of boundaries and to discuss how potentially salient boundaries such as the organization, the occupation, the type of employment contract, the divide between work and nonwork, and geographical boundaries shape people's career choices and trajectories (Rodrigues & Guest, 2010).

The final issue that has been largely overlooked in the literature is the breadth of the new career, both in terms of where and to whom the concept applies. Thus far, the discussion on the empirical basis of the new career has been mostly located in the United States (see, for instance, Cappelli, 1999; Jacoby, 1999). Even though several aspects of career boundarylessness have been researched in a number of countries, such as

New Zealand (Pringle & Mallon, 2003), France (Cadin, Bailly-Bender, & Saint-Giniez, 2000), and Germany (Stahl, Miller, & Tung, 2002), the literature has not consistently debated whether this is predominantly an American phenomenon or more widespread. By the same token, the literature has not fully discussed whether the new career can be generalized to all workers or whether it applies only to particular segments of the working population. For instance, Arthur (1994) uses the stereotypical Silicon Valley career and the careers of academics, carpenters, and real estate agents as examples of career boundarylessness, whereas Cappelli suggests that the new career is limited to "white-collar and managerial jobs, the ones that truly were protected under the old model" (Cappelli, 1999, p. 148). Given these questions about the new career concept, there is a need for a fuller empirical exploration of how far it has become established or whether the traditional organizational career appears to have survived.

HAVE ORGANIZATIONAL CAREERS SURVIVED?

In this section, we will explore the validity of the new career in two ways. First, because the new career model is permeated by the idea that employment no longer means holding a permanent job within an organization, but is instead defined as "a temporary state, or the current manifestation of long term employability" (Arthur & Rousseau, 1996, p. 374), one should expect an overall growth of temporary employment. Second, if people are moving across rather than within organizations, we would expect to see a growth in interorganizational movement and an associated reduction in organizational tenure. To explore these two issues, we used Organization for Economic Co-operation and Development (OECD) data for a number of countries, such as the United States and Japan, and major European economies such as the United Kingdom, Germany, and France.

The OECD Employment Outlook of 2002 shows that the cumulative employment growth in the whole OECD area during the 1990s was 11.6%, of which 4.2% was accounted for by temporary employment (OECD, 2002). There are, however, significant differences between countries. In the United Kingdom, Japan, and more particularly the United States, the growth of total employment was mainly attributable to permanent employment. In contrast, in Germany and France, temporary employment accounted for most job growth. In general, the evidence indicates that permanent employment is still the dominant pattern of employment creation in the OECD area. Differences between countries are more readily explained by the strictness of employment protection on permanent contracts in Germany and France, when compared to the United States and the United Kingdom (OECD, 2006), than by the changing nature of employment and careers.

A similar pattern is found when analyzing recent trends in the use of temporary employment. The share of temporary work within overall employment has increased in France, Germany and, more moderately, Japan between 1989 and 2009 (Table 8.1). In contrast, the percentage of temporary employment in the United Kingdom increased in the 1990s but declined between 2001 and 2009, whereas in the United States, temporary employment declined slightly from the mid-1990s onward.

The evidence on temporary work does not support the view that employment is becoming increasingly short term and transactional in nature. Organizations may be outsourcing some of their noncore activities, but there is no clear trend indicating that organizations are seeking a more outsourced or temporary workforce. Although there is evidence to suggest that up to two thirds of temporary workers would ideally prefer permanent contracts (Guest, Isaksson, & De Witte, 2010), there are good reasons why certain categories of workers may prefer temporary employment. For instance, women and older workers, who often prefer flexible work arrangements, have increased their participation in the labor force (Kalleberg, 2000). The service sector, where jobs are more seasonal and temporary, has grown significantly in developed economies (Smith, 1997). Temporary work can also provide an opportunity for young workers to explore distinct occupational identities (Ibarra, 1999) at an early career stage. Research suggests that temporary work is an important route into permanent employment with, on average, between one third and two thirds of temporary workers moving into a permanent position within 2 years (OECD, 2002). In fact, temporary employment seems to have become a common recruitment strategy for organizations (Jacoby, 1999). In summary, several factors, other than organizations' declining interest in maintaining a committed workforce or individuals' motivation to pursue independent careers, can account for any small growth of temporary work.

TABLE 8.1

Percent Share of Temporary Employment 1987–2009 (Dependent Employment)

Country	1989	1991	1993	1995	1997	1999	2001	2003	2005	2007	2009
France	8.5	10.2	10.9	12.3	13.1	14.0	14.9	13.4	13.3	13.7	13.5
Germany	11.0	10.1	10.3	10.4	11.7	13.1	12.4	12.2	13.7	14.2	14.5
Japan	10.6	10.4	10.3	10.5	11.0	11.9	12.8	13.8	14.0	13.9	13.7
United Kingdom	5.4	5.3	5.9	7.0	7.4	6.8	6.7	5.9	5.5	5.8	5.7
United States	n.a.	n.a.	n.a.	5.1	4.6	4.5	4.0	n.a.	4.2	n.a.	n.a.

n.a., not available.
Source: Organization for Economic Co-operation and Development, *OECD Employment Statistics Database*, http://www.oecd.org/statisticsdata/0,3381,en_2649_37457_1_119656_1_1_37457,00.html, 2011. Own tabulation.

In previous work (Rodrigues & Guest, 2010), we reviewed the evidence on job tenure in a number of countries between the 1980s, the period about which the new career was being proposed as the dominant form of employment, and the mid-2000s. This revealed that in the United States, the evidence overall suggests that from the 1980s onward job instability affected particularly men, blacks, younger workers, and less skilled workers. In contrast, well-educated U.S. staff of the sort found in management do not display any marked reduction in organizational tenure of the sort we would expect if the boundaryless career had taken hold. In Europe, the evidence clearly suggests that both workers and organizations still value and retain traditional careers. In the large European economies of the United Kingdom, France, and Germany, overall job tenure has been increasing since the early 1990s. This trend seems to be led by a slight increase in job tenure among women, whereas job tenure among men seems to be essentially stable over the entire period. Updated evidence to 2009 suggests that the recent economic recession has not had a deleterious impact on traditional employment and career patterns. This shows that even at a time when organizations could afford to attract workers from a wider pool of talent, due to the recent waves of bankruptcies and increasing unemployment rates (OECD, 2010), both employers and employees seem to value the benefits of a long-term traditional exchange.

Overall then, and returning to our model of managerial career types, the evidence suggests that the different forms of career exchange proposed should be viewed as developing alongside rather than competing with each other for a dominant career model. Our analysis shows that organizational tenure has not changed significantly since the 1990s and temporary employment has not grown greatly, suggesting that traditional organizational careers are surviving and that the rhetoric of change seems to have underestimated the strength of the mutual commitment between individuals and organizations. Although the free worker ethos may be pervasive in specific contexts, such as Silicon Valley, it is highly unlikely that this model will ever apply to the majority of workers. Traditional organizational careers are likely to persist in the future and be offered to a minority of managerial and professional workers possessing valuable and rare human capital. By the same token, most workers will continue to have access to limited possibilities of promotion. Where we are likely to see some growth, fostered by the increasing professionalization of the workforce, is in the autonomous career type. Our model is therefore useful to address diversity in career exchange and may constitute a basis to discuss trends in the career deal of different types of worker.

SEPARATING THE RHETORIC FROM THE REALITY: THE FUTURE OF ORGANIZATIONAL CAREERS THROUGH THE LENS OF EXCHANGE THEORY

Our analysis has shown that the traditional career exchange is particularly complex and potentially highly fragile. It has been argued by a number of observers that a range of global trends are presenting a serious challenge to the organizational career and to the desire of organizations to perpetuate it. This has encouraged these same observers to anticipate the end of the organizational career and its replacement by a more protean, boundaryless career and a career that is managed by individuals rather than by organizations. When this pronouncement of changes to the nature of careers is coupled with sometimes loose discussion about "old" and "new" careers, the rhetoric of the new career can be appealing. The empirical evidence challenges this rhetoric. The new career and claims for the end of the organizational career are usually allied to assumptions about increased mobility and a growth in temporary work. The empirical evidence about job tenure and temporary employment shows high levels of stability over quite long periods of time including the period when the advent of the new career was proclaimed. This evidence confirms that there has been no significant trend on the part of organizations to reduce tenure or to shift from permanent to temporary workers.

A further challenge to the rhetoric comes from the logic of the resource-based view of the firm, which, as Barney and Wright (1998) suggest, points to a need for organizations to attract and retain those key staff who are likely to provide competitive advantage. This results in a strong case for retaining the traditional organizational career. This case is reinforced by the desire of organizations to win the "war for talent" on the assumption, despite a continuing increase in the supply of well-qualified graduates, that such talent is scarce.

The other side of the coin concerns the workforce. The rhetoric suggests that values have changed, resulting in an increasing reluctance to engage in traditional organizational careers. The numbers applying to enter graduate careers in large organizations challenge this assumption because they remain as robust as ever. Yet the workforce is changing. There are more women in the labor force, and there are more professional and knowledge workers with potentially transferable skills. There is also quite good evidence of some generational change in values. However, these values may not be deeply embedded. Sturges and Guest (2004) present evidence suggesting that many of those who enter organizations giving a high priority to work–life balance get drawn into an organizational career and sacrifice other aspects of their life. At the same time, they maintained at least an illusion of control over the career. Therefore, a common response was to accept that work–life balance was currently out of kilter but that once the current project or job was completed, they would restore the balance.

From a different perspective, the work of Hochschild (1997) is insightful in revealing how some organizations are succeeding in creating attractive work environments where individuals feel they have autonomy. Indeed, sometimes a regimented home life, with a sequence of family and other commitments, can make the work organization appear a relatively peaceful haven. Research is beginning to reveal how job embeddedness, reflected in fit with both the organization and the environment outside work, can help to increase retention (Lee, Mitchell, Sablynski, Burton, & Holtom, 2004). Evidence is also accumulating about the benefits for organizations and their staff of pursuing a high-commitment human resource strategy (Combs, Liu, Hall, & Ketchen, 2006). In other words, the exchange process to retain the commitment of contemporary employees extends beyond the traditional domain of the career.

Our analysis suggests that there are likely to be increasingly diverse organizational patterns of career management both between and within organizations. Banks provide an example of this and also of the inherent problems in such an approach. They offer traditional careers for a significant proportion of their staff; but most large banks have quite separate human resource policies and practices for the key financial experts who deal in the more esoteric but potentially highly profitable aspects of banking. For this second group, the exchange is highly transactional, based on high salaries and more particularly high performance-related financial rewards. However, as we have seen, these potential bonuses encourage risk taking and a focus on personal transactional outcomes that may not be in the long-term interests of banks. These bankers are examples of free boundaryless workers within the new self-managed career; however, with the freedom comes responsibility, and they are also the new mercenaries of organizational life that banks and even governments are struggling to control.

The foregoing analysis presents a strong case for retaining a relational career contract for a significant proportion of managers. However the career-related exchange has become more complex, and the risk that it will not always be possible for organizations to deliver their side of the exchange may have increased. The alternatives seem to be either to restrict the promises or to risk breaching the psychological contract with its probable negative consequences (Montes & Irving, 2008). The former may result in failing to attract key talent; the latter may risk losing them once they have joined. The evidence from experience in the United Kingdom is that as much as half the graduate intake leaves organizations within 3 years, mainly because they feel that they have not received the kind of development that they had been led to expect (Sturges & Guest, 2001). However, if organizations provide a degree of autonomy to encourage job crafting (Wrzensniewski & Dutton, 2001), then individuals may create their own development opportunities. As Nicholson and West (1988) have shown, many jobs into which people move are newly created jobs, and the scope to "craft" their jobs to fit both organizational and personal aspirations is considerable.

The evidence suggests that it is a combination of fulfilling career promises within the psychological contract, maintaining a sense of fairness in procedures, and maintaining trust in the organization that will be crucial to retain key staff. The antecedents to this will include a strong sense of perceived organizational support, which can be reinforced through personalized exchanges. Reinforcing this exchange perspective, it is essential to have in place a set of high-commitment human resource policies and practices (Pfeffer, 1998) and to ensure that they are effectively implemented (Khilji & Wang, 2006). Bowen and Ostroff (2004) have presented a convincing case for a strong human resources system reflected in a climate that supports consistent implementation of human resources and, in so doing, builds a sense of trust, fairness, and support.

What all this suggests, in practical terms, is that organizations should continue to seek to retain the commitment of their staff and that the career promise, in suitably modified and cautious form, is one way of pursuing this. Yet the career exchange is becoming more complex and more challenging to manage. External pressures and market turbulence mean that organization structures and hierarchies are in a state of semipermanent flux, rendering career promises highly risky. Organizations have to seek commitment yet promise flexibility to accommodate a more diverse and increasingly feminized workforce. They have to promise opportunities for career self-management while seeking to manage careers in the organization's best interests. In addition, most organizations have to develop their in-house talent while operating in the external labor market to buy in key human resources to enhance their competitive advantage. One consequence may be the growth of what Rousseau (2005) has labeled as idiosyncratic deals. All this presents a distinct challenge to career management and in particular to the management of fairness. A further implication for managers is that they should be cautious in accepting the rhetoric of "the new"—in this case, "the new career"—without first scrutinizing the evidence on which it is based.

In conclusion, we have analyzed the status of the traditional career within the context of exchange theory. This has confirmed that exchange theory has considerable utility as an analytic framework. In particular, we have drawn upon various components of exchange theory including the psychological contract, fairness, trust, and social support. This rich array of elements helps to deepen the analysis and also to highlight a range of policy issues and choices. Our analysis demonstrates that the traditional organizational career has proved to be remarkably resilient and announcements of its death have proved to be premature. There have been some shifts in the balance of the exchange that underpins the career, as workforce values shift and increasing numbers of key staff possess transferable knowledge and skills. Successful organizations have found ways of modifying the career exchange to the mutual advantage of the organization and its key staff. As long as they continue to succeed in this, the organizational career will survive.

REFERENCES

Albert, S., Ashforth, B., & Dutton, J. (2000). Organizational identity and identification: Charting new waters and building new bridges. *Academy of Management Review*, 25, 13–17.

Arnold, J. (1997). *Managing careers into the 21st century*. London, UK: Sage.

Arnold, J., & Cohen, L. (2008). The psychology of career in industrial and organizational settings: A critical but appreciative analysis. *International Review of Industrial and Organizational Psychology, 23*, 1–44.

Arthur, M. (1994). The boundaryless career: A new perspective for organizational inquiry. *Journal of Organizational Behavior, 15*, 295–306.

Arthur, M., Inkson, K., & Pringle, J. (1999). *The new careers: Individual action and economic change*. London, UK: Sage.

Arthur, M., & Rousseau, D. (1996). Introduction: The boundaryless career as a new employment principle. In M. Arthur & D. Rousseau (Eds.), *The boundaryless career: A new employment principle for a new organizational era* (pp. 3–20). New York, NY: Oxford University Press.

Aydemir, A., & Borjas, G. (2007). A comparative analysis of the labor market impact of international migration: Canada, Mexico and the United States. *Journal of the European Economic Association, 5*, 663–708.

Barley, S., & Kunda, G. (2004). *Gurus, hired guns and warm bodies: Itinerant experts in a knowledge economy*. Princeton, NJ: Princeton University Press.

Barney, J. (1991). Firm resources and sustained competitive advantage. *Journal of Management, 17*, 99–120.

Barney, J., & Wright, P. (1998). On becoming a strategic partner: Examining the role of human resources in gaining competitive advantage. *Human Resource Management Journal, 37*, 31–46.

Baron, J., & Bielby, W. (1986). The proliferation of job titles in organizations. *Administrative Science Quarterly, 31*, 561–586.

Baruch, Y., & Peiperl, M. (2000). Career management practices: An empirical survey and implications. *Human Resource Management, 39*, 347–366.

Borjas, G. (2006). Native internal migration and the labor market impact of immigration. *Journal of Human Resources, 41*, 221–258.

Bowen, D., & Ostroff, C. (2004). Understanding HRM–performance linkages: The role of the "strength" of the HRM system. *Academy of Management Review, 29*, 203–221.

Briscoe, J., & Hall, D. (2006). The interplay of boundaryless and protean careers: Combinations and implications. *Journal of Vocational Behavior, 69*, 4–18.

Briscoe, J., Hall, D., & DeMuth, R. (2006). Protean and boundaryless careers: An empirical exploration. *Journal of Vocational Behavior, 69*, 30–47.

Brown, W., Deakin, S., Nash, D., & Oxenbridge, S. (2000). The employment contract: From collective procedures to individual rights. *British Journal of Industrial Relations, 38*, 611–629.

Cadin, L., Bailly-Bender, A., & Saint-Giniez, V. (2000). Exploring boundaryless careers in the French context. In M. Peiperl, M. Arthur, R. Goffee, & T. Morris (Eds.), *Career frontiers: New conceptions of working lives* (pp. 228–255). Oxford, UK: Oxford University Press.

Cappelli, P. (1999). Career jobs are dead. *California Management Review, 42*, 146–167.

Card, D. (2001). Immigrant inflows, native outflows, and the local market impacts of higher immigration. *Journal of Labor Economics, 19*, 22–64.

Carnoy, M., Castells, M., & Benner, C. (1997). Labour markets and employment practices in the age of flexibility: A case study of Silicon Valley. *International Labour Review, 36*, 27–48.

Chambers, E., Foulon, M., Handfield-Jones, H., Hankin, S., & Michaels, E., III (1998). The war for talent. *The McKinsey Quarterly, 3*, 44–57.

Combs, J., Liu, Y., Hall, A., & Ketchen, D. (2006). How much do high performance practices matter? A meta-analysis of their effects on organizational performance. *Personnel Psychology, 59*, 501–528.

Coyle-Shapiro, J., & Conway, N. (2004). The employment relationship through the lens of the psychological contract. In J. Coyle-Shapiro, L. Shore, S. Taylor, & L. Tetrick (Eds.), *The employment relationship: Examining psychological and contextual perspectives* (pp. 5–28). Oxford, UK: Oxford University Press.

DeFillippi, R., & Arthur, M. (1994). The boundaryless career: A competency-based perspective. *Journal of Organizational Behavior, 15*, 307–324.

Eisenberger, R., Jones, J., Aselage, J., & Sucharski, I. (2004). Perceived organizational support. In J. Coyle-Shapiro, L. Shore, S. Taylor, & L. Tetrick (Eds.), *The employment relationship: Examining psychological and contextual perspectives* (pp. 206–250). Oxford, UK: Oxford University Press.

Evets, J. (2003). The sociological analysis of professionalism. *International Sociology, 18*, 395–415.

Freeman, C., Soete, L., & Efendioglu, U. (1995). Diffusion and the employment effects of information and communication technology. *International Labour Review, 134*, 587–603.

Gould, S. (1979). Characteristics of career planners in upwardly mobile occupations. *Academy of Management Journal, 22*, 530–550.

Guest, D., Isaksson, K., & De Witte, H. (2010). *Employment contracts, psychological contracts and employee well-being: An international study*. Oxford, UK: Oxford University Press.

Hall, D. (1976). *Careers in organizations*. Santa Monica, CA: Scott Foresman & Co.

Hall, D. (2004). The protean career: A quarter-century journey. *Journal of Vocational Behavior, 65*, 1–13.

Hall, D., & Mirvis, P. (1995). The new career contract: Developing the whole person at midlife and beyond. *Journal of Vocational Behavior, 47*, 269–289.

Harris, R. (2001). The knowledge-based economy: Intellectual origins and new economic perspectives. *International Journal of Management Reviews, 3*, 21–40.

Hochschild, A. (1997). *The time bind: When work becomes home and home becomes work*. New York, NY: Metropolitan Books.

Ibarra, H. (1999). Provisional selves: Experimenting with image and identity in professional adaptation. *Administrative Science Quarterly, 44*, 764–791.

Inkson, K. (2006). Protean and boundaryless careers as metaphors. *Journal of Vocational Behavior, 69*, 48–63.

Jacoby, S. (1999). Are career jobs headed for extinction? *California Management Review, 42*, 123–145.

Kalleberg, A. (2000). Nonstandard employment relations: Part-time, temporary and contract work. *Annual Review of Sociology, 26*, 341–365.

Khilji, S., & Wang, X. (2006). "Intended" and "implemented" HRM: The missing linchpin in strategic human resource management research. *International Journal of Human Resource Management, 17*, 1171–1189.

King, Z. (2004). Career self-management: Its nature, causes and consequences. *Journal of Vocational Behavior, 65*, 112–133.

Knell, J. (2000). *Most wanted: The quiet birth of the free worker*. London, UK: The Work Institute.

Krugman, P. (1994). Does third world growth hurt first world prosperity? *Harvard Business Review, 72*, 113–121.

Lambert, L., Edwards, J., & Cable, D. (2003). Breach and fulfillment of the psychological contract: A comparison of traditional and expanded views. *Personnel Psychology, 56*, 895–934.

Lee, T., Mitchell, T., Sablynski, C., Burton, J., & Holtom, B. (2004). The effects of job embeddedness on organizational citizenship, job performance, volitional absences and voluntary turnover. *Academy of Management Journal, 47*, 711–722.

Lepak, D., & Snell, S. (1999). The human resource architecture: Toward a theory of human capital allocation and development. *Academy of Management Review, 24*, 31–48.

Lepak, D., & Snell, S. (2002). Examining the human resource architecture: The relationships among human capital, employment and human resource configurations. *Journal of Management, 28*, 517–543.

Lepak, D., Takeuchi, R., & Snell, S. (2003). Employment flexibility and firm performance: Examining the interaction effects of employment mode, environmental dynamism, and technological intensity. *Journal of Management, 29*, 681–703.

Littler, C., Wiesner, R., & Dunford, R. (2003). The dynamics of delayering: Changing management structures in three countries. *Journal of Management Studies, 40*, 225–256.

Miner, A., & Robinson, D. (1994). Organizational and population level learning as engines for career transitions. *Journal of Organizational Behavior, 15*, 345–364.

Mirvis, P., & Hall, D. (1994). Psychological success and the boundaryless career. *Journal of Organizational Behavior, 23*, 365–380.

Montes, S., & Irving, G. (2008). Disentangling the effects of promised and delivered inducements: Relational and transactional contract elements and the mediating role of trust. *Journal of Applied Psychology, 93*, 1367–1381.

Nicholson, N., & West, M. (1988). *Managerial job change: Men and women in transition.* Cambridge, UK: Cambridge University Press.

O'Mahoney, S., & Bechky, B. (2006). Stretchwork: Managing the career progression paradox in external labor markets. *Academy of Management Journal, 49*, 918–941.

Organization for Economic Co-operation and Development. (2002). *Employment outlook.* Paris, France: Author.

Organization for Economic Co-operation and Development. (2006). *Employment outlook.* Paris, France: Author.

Organization for Economic Co-operation and Development. (2010). *Employment outlook.* Paris, France: Author.

Ornstein, S., & Isabella, L. (1993). Making sense of careers: A review 1989–1992. *Journal of Management, 19*, 243–267.

Osterman, P. (1994). Internal labor markets: Theory and change. In C. Kerr & P. Staudohar (Eds.), *Labor economics and market relations: Markets and institutions* (pp. 303–339). Boston, MA: Harvard University Press.

Osterman, P., & Burton, D. (2005). Ports and ladders: The nature and relevance of internal labor markets in a changing world. In S. Ackroyd, R. Batt, P. Thompson, & P. Tolbert (Eds.), *The Oxford handbook of work and organization* (pp. 425–447). Oxford, UK: Oxford University Press.

Pascale, R., & Athos, A. (1981). *The art of Japanese management.* New York, NY: Simon and Schuster.

Peel, S., & Boxall, P. (2005). When is contracting preferable to employment? An exploration of management and workers perspectives. *Journal of Management Studies, 42*, 1675–1697.

Peiperl, M., & Baruch, Y. (1997). Back to square zero: The post-corporate career. *Organizational Dynamics, 25*, 7–22.

Pfeffer, J. (1998). *The human equation*. Boston, MA: Harvard Business School Press.

Pfeffer, J. (2001). *Fighting the war for talent is hazardous to your organization's health* (Stanford University Research Paper No. 1687). Stanford, CA: Stanford University.

Pringle, J., & Mallon, M. (2003). Challenges for the boundaryless career odyssey. *The International Journal of Human Resource Management, 14*, 839–853.

Rhoades, L., & Eisenberger, R. (2002). Perceived organizational support: A review of the literature. *Journal of Applied Psychology, 87*, 698–714.

Rodrigues, R., & Guest, D. (2010). Have careers become boundaryless? *Human Relations, 63*, 1157–1175.

Roehling, M. W. (2004). Legal theory: Contemporary contract law perspectives and insights for employment relationship theory. In J. Coyle-Shapiro, L. Shore, S. Taylor, & L. Tetrick (Eds.), *The employment relationship: Examining psychological and contextual perspectives* (pp. 65–93). Oxford, UK: Oxford University Press.

Rosenbaum, J. (1979). Tournament mobility: Career patterns in a corporation. *Administrative Science Quarterly, 24*, 220–241.

Rousseau, D. (1989). Psychological and implied contracts in organizations. *Employee Responsibilities and Rights Journal, 2*, 121–139.

Rousseau, D. (1995). *Psychological contracts in organizations*. Thousand Oaks, CA: Sage.

Rousseau, D. (2005). *I-deals: Idiosyncratic deals employees bargain for themselves*. New York, NY: M.E. Sharpe.

Saxenian, A. (1996). Beyond boundaries: Open labor markets and learning in Silicon Valley. In M. Arthur & D. Rousseau (Eds.), *The boundaryless career: A new employment principle for a new organizational era* (pp. 23–39). New York, NY: Oxford University Press.

Schein, E. (1978). *Career dynamics: Matching individual and organizational needs*. Reading, MA: Addison Wesley.

Shore, L., & Shore, T. (1995). Perceived organizational support and organizational justice. In R. Cropanzano & K. Kazmar (Eds.), *Organizational politics, justice and support: Managing social climate at work* (pp. 149–164). Westport, CT: Quorum Press.

Smith, V. (1997). New forms of work organization. *Annual Review of Sociology, 23*, 315–339.

Smola, K., & Sutton, C. (2002). Generational differences: Revisiting generational work values for the new millennium. *Journal of Organizational Behavior, 23*, 363–382.

Sorensen, J., & Sorensen, T. (1974). The conflict of professionals in bureaucratic organizations. *Administrative Science Quarterly, 19*, 98–106.

Stahl, G., Miller, E., & Tung, R. (2002). Toward the boundaryless career: A closer look at the expatriate career concept and the perceived implications of an international assignment. *Journal of World Business, 37*, 216–227.

Sturges, J., & Guest, D. (2001). Don't leave me this way: A qualitative study of influences on the organizational commitment and turnover intentions of graduates early in their career. *British Journal of Guidance and Counselling, 29*, 447–462.

Sturges, J., & Guest, D. (2004). Working to live or living to work? Work/life balance early in the career. *Human Resource Management Journal, 14*, 5–20.

Sullivan, S. (1999). The changing nature of careers: A review and research agenda. *Journal of Management, 25*, 457–484.

Sullivan, S., & Arthur, M. (2006). The evolution of the boundaryless career concept: Examining physical and psychological mobility. *Journal of Vocational Behavior, 69*, 19–29.

Taylor, S., & Tekleab, A. (2004). Taking stock of psychological contract research: Assessing progress, addressing troublesome issues, and setting research priorities. In J. Coyle-Shapiro, L. Shore, S. Taylor, & L. Tetrick (Eds.), *The employment relationship: Examining psychological and contextual perspectives* (pp. 312–331). Oxford, UK: Oxford University Press.

Tolbert, P. (1996). Occupations, organizations, and boundaryless careers. In M. Arthur & D. Rousseau (Eds.), *The boundaryless career: A new employment principle for a new organizational era* (pp. 331–349). New York, NY: Oxford University Press.

Van Maanen, J. (1977). *Organizational careers: Some new perspectives*. New York, NY: Wiley.

Wallace, J. (1995). Organizational and professional commitment in professional and non-professional organizations. *Administrative Science Quarterly, 40*, 228–255.

Williamson, O. (1975). *Markets and hierarchies*. New York, NY: Free Press.

Wrzesniewski, A., & Dutton, J. (2001). Crafting a job: Revisioning employees as active crafters of their work. *Academy of Management Review, 26*, 179–201.

Zhao, H., Wayne, S., Glibowski, B., & Bravo, J. (2007). The impact of psychological contract breach on work-related outcomes: a meta-analysis. *Personnel Psychology, 60*, 647–680.

9

Work–Family Flexibility and the Employment Relationship

Ellen Ernst Kossek
Michigan State University

Marian N. Ruderman
Center for Creative Leadership

A growing body of scholarly literature has accumulated on the changing employee–organization relationship (EOR) (Shore et al., 2004). Relatively little of this body of research has been integrated with changing work and family relationships, which are also undergoing a period of unprecedented transformation. It is critical to incorporate research on the changing work–family relationship into the employment relationship literature. Having positive work–family relationships has critical social meaning for the changing employment social contract of working life. From the employee perspective, a key question is: "Is the current employment deal a favorable social exchange of an individual's time, energy, and psychological capital in relation to personal and work–family well-being and economic return?" From the organizational perspective, the key question is: "When is it in the organization's interests to support positive work and family relationships?" And from an exchange perspective, key questions are: "What are the social expectations of organizations regarding their roles in supporting employees' management of work and family relationships?" and "What are the social expectations of employees regarding support of work and family relationships?" Are these views in alignment?

The main goal of this chapter is to draw from EOR theory to understand changes in work and family relationships as well as add to the integration of these literatures. This analysis will strengthen EOR research by improved consideration of changing work–family dynamics as a growing critical component of the employment contract. Similarly, work–family research will be enhanced by integrating concepts from the EOR literature, such as the importance of alignment between employee needs and preferences and organizational perspectives on the work–family interface. We begin with a brief overview of the transformation of work and family life followed by discussion of commonalties between changing EOR and work–family relationships. Because voluntary workplace flexibility policies and practices help span the boundaries between rising work and home demands, in the second half of this chapter, we argue that formal and informal boundary-blurring practices can be used as a lens for understanding how social exchange theory and its related constructs inform work and family relationships. We develop propositions for future research, some of which are linked to employee preferences for blurring and the EOR. Examples of organizational practices include *formal flexibility policies*, such as telework, flextime, and part-time work, and *informal boundary-blurring practices* through use of technological tools (e.g., laptops, smart phones) to control work location, timing, or load. Examples of employee customization preferences include integration (blending work and family tasks), separation (focusing on each separately), and volleying (cycling back and forth) with patterns of high integration and separation (Kossek & Lautsch, 2008; Kossek, Ruderman, Hannum, & Braddy, 2011).

GROWING DIVERSITY AND INTENSITY OF WORK–FAMILY DEMANDS

In this chapter, we use the term "family" broadly. Our assumption is that even single employees have nonwork and personal concerns related to family, such as social ties to unmarried partners, close friends, siblings, parents, or grandparents. Household and caregiving demands are trending upward with unprecedented levels of labor force participation of individuals who possess significant nonwork responsibilities (Bureau of Labor Statistics, 2010). This expansion is from a significant rise in the employment of single-parent, dual-career, or sandwiched (caring for elders and children) families. Less than 20% of families today with children under 18 years old are composed of two parents with a single breadwinner and a stay-at-home parent (Kossek, 2006). Growing numbers of employees have their own or a family member's health disabilities to manage while working. A combination of trends, including the economic recession, the aging population, and the rise in children and young adults with special needs, has resulted in more working caregivers. There is also a delay in economic and psychological self-sufficiency of many current and post college students. Many students have become accustomed to the regular parental support of daily living and face difficulties transitioning to adulthood. The number of single-person households is increasing, as more working adults are delaying marriage, staying unmarried, or divorcing than ever before. Greater geographic dispersion of nuclear families is making it more difficult for employees to have local family support systems.

The shift in family configurations and demands is accompanied by growing work–family pressures (Kossek, Baltes, & Mathews, 2011). For example, trends from the National Study of the Changing Workplace, a nationwide representative sample surveying U.S. employees, suggests blurring boundaries and rising multitasking and job stress are major concerns (Galinsky, Aumann, & Bond, 2008). One third of employees surveyed report they are contacted by a work colleague outside of their scheduled work hours at least once a week. Over half of employees state that "they often or very often worked on too many tasks and multi-tasked too much" (Galinsky et al., 2008). There are also growing problems with job stress and the health of workers. For example, a third of individuals responding indicated that they "often or very often" felt overwhelmed by their workload over the last several months. One third of employees in the national survey have depressive symptoms, and one fifth have high blood pressure.

These growing work and family demands are pressuring governments to respond at a societal level. The European Union, for example, has made the reconciliation of work and family life a key priority for enhancing the quality of the labor pool. Although the European Commission has no direct influence over the field of child care, it has encouraged nonbinding targets for child care for the member nations (European Commission, 2010). The national government of Australia is also trying to develop policy influencing work and family with a sponsored paid parental leave plan started in 2011. National governments are becoming stakeholders in the relationships between work and family. The Dutch government has started an initiative called 24 and More to encourage more women to work 24 hours a week or more as a way to spur national economic growth. Overall, the trends discussed in this section suggest work and family aspects relevant to the EOR are undergoing a revolution and need increased linkage.

COMMONALITIES IN THE TRANSFORMATION OF WORK, FAMILY, AND THE EMPLOYMENT RELATIONSHIP

Just as new organizational structures, changing work systems, and heightened economic pressures have led to a "new deal" in the social exchange between employee and the organization (Cappelli, 1999), several parallels exist suggesting a similar transformative "new deal" in work and family relationships. These relate to similarities in cultural assumptions reflecting historical paradigm shifts toward more (a) boundarylessness, (b) customization, (c) self-direction, and (d) transactional and shorter term relationships. Given these changes occurring in tandem, it is increasingly important to study work–family and employment relationships together.

Boundarylessness

Both the EOR and the work–family literatures share the assumption of a trend toward boundarylessness, a paradigm shift from seeing organizational roles as specified, formal, and narrowly defined to seeing them as more open-ended, less formal, and with loose definitions. For example, the EOR literature refers to "boundaryless" careers as increasingly the norm. This is the concept of multiemployer employment relationships reflecting the traditional approach of careers unfolding in a single organizational boundary or employment setting (Arthur & Rousseau, 1996).

Boundarylessness in the EOR is also increasingly reflected in employer assumptions toward more open-endedness and expansiveness in job duties, which has critical linkages to work–life balance. Known as "job creep" (Van Dyne & Ellis, 2004, p. 180), boundarylessness in job design can result in the gradual and often subtle expansion of employee job duties that are not necessarily highly valued or formally recognized by the employer. Job creep often changes the employment relationship by resulting in the prevailing belief that an employee will take responsibility for an extra role behavior that is not recognized as part of his or her job and not rewarded (Van Dyne & Ellis, 2004). This trend is more likely to occur when job demands are unclear.

Job creep is also occurring as employees face rising workloads from understaffing due to the global economic downturn in the past few years. Many are also working longer and harder out of fear of losing their jobs as work continues to either move overseas or layoffs occur. The movement away from rigid organizational structures means that people are consistently seeking out new information. In sum, job creep has important implications for the social exchange of work and family relationships. For many employees, work comprises a larger part of life space, shifting the employment deal to tilt toward greater investment in work over leisure. To date, employers have had the upper hand in controlling work–life boundaries to give the work role primacy.

There is also growing boundarylessness in work and family relationships. Work and family roles are increasingly enacted outside the boundaries of work or home. This shift has partially occurred due to societal changes in technological use toward increased blurring of work and home boundaries. This has led to escalation of opportunities for employees to shape behaviors regarding work–family boundary blurring temporally, physically, or mentally (Nippert-Eng, 1996). This development is due not only to the trends noted earlier but also to the proliferation of mobile communication and data technological tools. The rise in use of smart cell phones, laptops, and other portable personal digital assistants (PDAs) increasingly enables employees in all walks of life to have some availability to texts, e-mails, data, and calls of a work *or* personal nature 24 hours a day, 7 days a week. Global work schedules, the increased intensification of workloads, and the diffusion of work into more hours of the day and night have also heightened the boundarylessness of personal time. The working hours of 9 AM to 5 PM are an artifact of the past in today's globalized, technology savvy world. Employees are increasingly sacrificing family life and working longer hours in order to keep their jobs.

Similar to job creep, family creep is occurring. We define family creep as the notion that the employee will take increasing responsibility for family or personal needs informally during work time. Family creep is growing under the radar as more and more employees are taking responsibility for nonwork demands during work time. Examples include an employee getting a text message at work from her child indicating that the child has just gotten home off the bus or managing the scheduling of an elder's medical appointments during working time. More employees lack a nonworking spouse who can handle these issues, compared to the numbers of employees in traditional single-breadwinner families of the past. Given this trend, family demands also have a growing boundarylessness. So from the employer perspective, a firm may see family creep as negatively affecting the employment bargain.

Customization

Building on the psychological contract literature of the unwritten expectations the employer and employee have of each other, a growing theme is the concept of more customization in employment relationships. Increasingly, "one size does not fit all" (Boswell, Colvin, & Darnold, 2008, p. 365). Rousseau (1995, 2005) refers to the growing trend toward nonstandard individualized work arrangements as idiosyncratic deals (I-Deals). Individuals can negotiate an I-Deal that may deviate from standard practices if the individual has a high value in the labor market. For example, employees might receive a higher salary or other perquisites than counterparts in a similar job if they have a highly valued skill set that would result in loss of a strategic asset of rare knowledge or skills if the employee left the firm (Slay & Taylor, 2007). Under EOR theory, such customized inducements lead to increased enactment of discretionary behaviors that meet the employers' interests. I-Deals usually increase within group heterogeneity of employment relationship conditions from pay to benefits to job tasks to work schedules, as they are used as behavioral inducements to attract, retain, or motivate employees with diverse talents and psychological and economic needs (Slay & Taylor, 2007). I-Deals are also often the first step for more standardized practices and can be wins for the employee, the organization, and the employee's coworkers. Thus, work-life arrangements such as flexible work schedules or telecommuting can be viewed as an I-Deal.

The growing trend toward customization of work and family relationships is a departure from the historical roots of organizational support for this nexus. Traditionally, most large organizations and employees have had relatively little customization of work and family relationships. Most professional and managerial workforces were relatively homogenous and unduly devoted to putting energies into careers to climb the corporate ladder. Iconically depicted in the 1950s book, *The Man in the Grey Flannel Suit* (Wilson, 1955), a corporate manager was socialized to divide household labor traditionally in his family. As prototypically edified in the novel, society expected a breadwinner to commute each day into New York City from the far suburbs, leaving behind his stay-at-home wife caring for their three children. With such cultural and actual distance from the domestic realm, the employee (usually male) culturally gave uninterrupted attention to work. When women did work in the firm, they often were socialized to give up marriage for a career. Those few who were married when they began working ended up quitting their jobs once they had a child. Or, if they had to work due to divorce or finances, they usually worked part time or in lower level positions that allowed for higher control over work hours. Those women who stayed in the workplace after childbirth typically had fewer children than their male counterparts in order to prevent family interference with work demands. After work, many went home to work "a second shift" (Hochschild, 1989) taking care of all of the household domestic chores, making culturally invisible their family demands and "competing devotions" to their jobs (Blair-Loy, 2003).

Understanding these historical roots is important because these cultural remnants remain in place today, reinforcing the culturally separate spheres of work and family life (Kanter, 1977). A prevailing workplace assumption is that most employees do not expect or need much organizational family support, let alone differentiated support. Until relatively recently, work–family policies were fairly standardized by the organization in an almost paternalistic manner dictated by the employer such as providing a one-size-fits-all basic family health care package. Most employees worked the same hours set by the organization. Work and family programs and policies were not viewed as inducements in the employment relationship but as a standard benefit an individual received simply for being a member of the organization. Organizational support of work and family was not assumed to motivate discretionary behavior. Pay has traditionally been seen as the most important motivational tool in the workplace.

Today, however, customization is increasingly needed *and* socially expected because most workers are *not* 100% focused on breadwinning and disconnected from domesticity. For example, the professional and managerial workforce is now over half female. Men are more involved in domestic tasks and child care, although U.S. census time use data show they have not yet caught up with women in sharing household labor equally. Thus, customization has begun in part to respond to the increased feminization in values of the workforce, as more workers are juggling gendered roles of domesticity with high engagement in work.

However, customization of work–family relationships is occurring more than just to support caregiving involvement. Younger workers do not expect to have a job for life with one employer and expect customization of working life as part of the social exchange for lessened job security. These Generation X and Y workers are much more interested in having more discretion over when, where, and how they work (Kossek & Distelberg, 2009). It is also important to note that demographics alone do not fully predict customization preferences in work–family relationships. Within demographic group segments, there is increasing variation in why people work and the work and family relationships they seek. Instead of coasting to retirement, some older workers want to remain highly engaged in career. For example, one study (Winkelmann-Gleed, 2009) found that there were two main segments of older employees. One group works mainly for financial reasons, and the other works mainly because they enjoy their career and feel a strong sense of social responsibility to work. This second group of older employees especially values a flexible environment as an inducement. Flexible work arrangements can be one important motivator for this group to remain working in the organization.

Overall, increasing numbers of employees want to work in different ways to match growing variation in preferences for flexibility in the hours worked, the load or amount of work done, and the scheduling of work (Kossek & Michel, 2011). Standardization of work and family relationships, particularly for professionals in terms of the timing and location of work, is on the decline in organizations. One employee may want to work 4 days a week for 10 hours a day. Another may wish to work part time. Still another would like to take a self-funded sabbatical to be able to focus on renewal or a leave of absence to become a stay-at-home mom or dad beyond the boundaries of a typical maternity or paternity leave. Unfortunately, research shows most of these voluntary customized work and family policies are underused by career-oriented workers who fear stigma from use (Kossek, 2005). This gap between availability and use suggests that despite the increased formal adoption of policies, organizational adaptation to changing work and family demands and increased need for customized work and family arrangements are not yet fully integrated in organizational cultures regarding expected EOR relationships.

Self-Direction

Management of the employment relationship and the work–family relationship has changed to move increasingly away from being organizationally driven and paternalistic to employee-directed and characterized by personal responsibility and choice. Employees cannot expect to have their employer take care of their careers and ensure job security for life (Cappelli, 1999). They are expected to self-manage their career; seek feedback, learning, and education; and network to increase their employability (Kossek, Roberts, Fisher, & DeMarr, 1998).

Similarly, employees increasingly cannot assume their organization will be paternalistic and can be counted on to help employees manage and take care of their personal and family needs. It is up to employees to figure out what child care provider is best because companies do not want the liability of recommending a provider. Many maintain a "hands off" and "it is a personal choice" rhetoric on the difficult challenge that many parents or caregivers face in finding quality child or elder care. Organizations usually would not dream of taking steps to ensure that employees do not overwork, until maybe they have a heart attack or a mental health breakdown. If an employee chooses to work during nonwork hours to the extent that it is interfering with their health or their family relationships, the organization generally does not step in. It is up to many employees, especially professionals and managers, but increasingly employees in many occupations, to schedule their work hours and manage and direct how they use their time and energy. The organization will almost always want more investment.

Besides more self-direction in the scheduling of work hours via use of formal human resource policies, there is also a cultural shift in informal work–family boundary management, particularly involving employee self-direction of technology use (Kossek & Lautsch, 2008). Employees can customize how they use their time 24 hours a day, 7 days a week. Many professionals are socialized to have high involvement with their careers. They may choose to check e-mail or text a work colleague on the weekends and evenings. However, if they have a boss who expects a work e-mail to be answered within 24 hours, then is the employee decision to monitor e-mail during their day off discretionary or expected behavior? Similarly if an employee has high psychological investment in family life, he or she may choose to allow children, family members, or friends to electronically contact them via working hours. However, if an employee is a single parent or has a partner who is not able to monitor caregiving issues during the work day, how much of this employee's decision to ask a child to contact them at work to let them know their homework is done or that they got home safely after school is a "choice" or a necessity?

Transactional and Short Term

Most writers in the EOR literature note that the employment relationship has changed in many firms to become more *transactional* and short term, focused on the classic short-term economic exchange Karl Marx once wrote about: the capitalistic purchase of labor's time for money as a short-term transactional economic issue. Tsui, Pearce, Porter, and Tripoli (1997) note that under a pure economic exchange, the organization is focused on the quasi-spot employment relationships with employees. Here the employment relationship is short term, closed ended, and limited to the immediate exchange. They contrast this with more *relational* approaches to the employment relationship. Under relational approaches, there is both an economic and a social exchange relationship, where the organization not only offers a short-term financial reward but also cares about employees' well-being and their careers. Unfortunately, the current global economic downturn has led many firms to shed jobs and move away from seeing the employment relationship as a long-term social exchange.

This similar trend away from relational to transactional social exchange has occurred in work and family relationships. Early work and family policies were adopted in the 1990s by larger organizations based on the idea of a long-term social exchange. The rhetoric was that despite their cost, there is a long-term benefit to the employer. The assumption was that if an employer built an on-site child care center, for example, users of the center would be grateful for this support. Employees' performance might increase, and they would have greater loyalty and be less likely to exit from the firm (cf. Kossek & Nichol, 1992). Another benefit was increased extra-role behavior because users of work–life benefits would be more likely to make additional contributions. However, given rising labor costs and the rapid technological obsolescence occurring in many fields (e.g., information technology and engineering), a long-term investment in work and family support to enable workers to be retained is becoming less and less in the employer's interest. Employers are trying to do all they can to take actions to reduce labor costs by increasing copays and cutting investments in benefits, including costly work–family programs. Evidence of this is based on the fact that employer investment in on-site child care and infant care has not increased in the United States in the past decade (Kossek, 2006).

Although we believe that employer direct support of work and family relationships, such as increasing the quality and availability of child and elder care, is still vital, because there is a shortage of quality child and elder care, we do not see major growth in organizational support for direct support of employee caregiving, given the cost constraints. However, we do see increased employer interest in improving the implementation of formal (e.g., human resources [HR] policies) and informal (e.g., technology-enabled) boundary-blurring flexibility policies and informal practices, because we see these practices as having potential for closer alignment of organizational and employee interests on work–family issues; we focus the rest of this review on this area.

We also see increasing use of work–family flexibility policies and practices as changing the nature of work and family experiences to be more transactional and short term on a daily basis. The growth of boundary-blurring practices and policies has increased the fragmentation and frequency of work and family interactions. In the past, people would go to work and focus on work with few interruptions. Or they would focus on family and take a complete break from work on several-week vacations, during the weekends, or at night or go on a several-year leave of absence for infant care. Now we have more daily interruptions in work and family experiences. One can switch back and forth between a work text and a family text, resulting in fragmented and short-term attention to both. The quality of our work or family relationships, our attention, and our social experiences are more fragmented, with constant interruptions and demands. Technology has made the once solid boundaries between work and personal life more porous and permeable.

Summary

Flexible workplace policies (e.g., flextime, telework) and informal technological practices provide a good lens through which to understand transforming work, family, and employment relationships. These policies and practices capture the themes of boundarylessness, customization, self-direction, and transactional or fragmented relations. Workplace flexibility was defined by Kossek and Michel (2011) as (a) constructed as "different" from standard work hours, yet culturally integrated; (b) regarded as part of a mutual agreement between employee and employer either through use of recognized HR policy or informal supervisory work practice; and (c) experienced as being voluntary and employee initiated. Flexible work schedules have several design conditions related to schedule control: (a) flexibility to control the timing of work; (b) flexibility to control the place or location of work; (c) flexibility to control the amount of work or workload; and (d) flexibility to control the continuity of work. Although these types of flexibility are often studied separately, these design features are sometimes overlapping and used in tandem. For example, someone who teleworks often has increased control over both the timing and the location of work. Similarly, some practices such as telecommuting can involve use of a formal HR policy with informal boundary blurring.

WORK–FAMILY BOUNDARY-BLURRING FLEXIBILITY PRACTICES

Given that there are a lot of flexibility practices and policies, in order to develop our hypotheses on how they relate to the social exchange relationship of employment, we briefly define these attributes. The dimensions we focus on are (a) HR policy or job design feature; (b) types of flexibility available or used; (c) whether use is employer or employee driven; and (d) relation to boundary-blurring preferences.

Formal HR Policies and Informal Job Design Feature

Flexibility policies and practices vary in the degree to which they influence the nature of employee control over boundary blurring. The research on boundary blurring aspects of flexible work practices is organized into two main streams. One stream sees boundary blurring as related to use of a *formal HR policy* such as flextime, and the other sees it as a job design feature (Kossek & Michel, 2011). For example, a flextime practice gives one ability to control the timing of when work is done and restructure work for family time. Telework affects the physical blurring of boundaries over where work is done. Reduced load or part-time work affects the amount of work done and the time one is engaged in the work role in terms of overall life space.

The other stream views flexible work schedules as a *job design characteristic* in terms of perceived flexibility control: the degree to which one perceives they have job autonomy or control over work schedule flexibility. Researchers refer to this measure as perceived *flexibility control* or *control over work time* (Kossek, Lautsch, & Eaton, 2006). This perception is likely a function of job design features. For example, professional workers often have job independence built into the job as a feature, unlike blue color workers. The ability to have access to a personal cell phone at work, to receive personal or family texts at work, or to bring a work smart phone or laptop home is another job design feature.

Organizational or Employee Initiated

Flexibility policies and practice vary in the degree to which the invoking of their use is organizational or employee driven. Sometimes organizations do move to these flexible arrangements as a standardized work pattern and not as a customized work–family endeavor. A well-known example is that of IBM, which in the 1990s moved to a mobile workforce for its Global Services Division where more than half its employees worked out of their homes or out of the clients' location as a business mobility and workplace costs savings strategy and to develop a global mobile workforce.

More often, an employee may request to work at home to be able to reduce the commute or have greater involvement in family or personal life roles. Which party initiates the use of flexibility will influence the degree to which flexibility use is an inducement or seen as a benefit to motivate the worker. We assume that when the use of a voluntary flexibility policy is employee initiated to meet a personal need or preference, it will be more likely to be a positive inducement or motivator to enhance commitment and loyalty in the employment relationship. When it is initiated to save the company office space or building costs, it is less likely to be seen as a positive inducement or motivator.

In countries where there is formal legislation mandating access to or right to request flexible work policies (e.g., the United Kingdom, Australia), the effectiveness of flexibility as an inducement might be different than in countries where organizations are not encouraged by the government to offer flexibility. If a high level of flexibility is common in the country (e.g., Sweden's nurturing of family life), flexibility itself might be less effective as an inducement to commit to the organization than in a country where schedule flexibility is less common or not widely encouraged by society (e.g., Japan's over-work achievement culture mandating separation). Thus, cultural contexts regarding work–family flexibility may affect the EOR differently.

Idiosyncratic Deals Versus Standardized Flexibility

More often than not, assessing positive effects on the employment relationship of flexibility use has become increasingly difficult. There are often many grey areas in capturing the availability of flexibility use and the degree to which the employer actually supports flexibility use. For example, organizations vary in corporate cultural support for flexibility. In some, they view flexibility as an idiosyncratic customized deal. Employees are rarely given flexibility access unless visible work–family needs are requested. For example, the only woman in the finance department might work part time to be able to have more involvement in her child's school. In other firms, work–family flexibility is normative. It is viewed as a normal way of working, as in the IBM example, where over half of the workforce was teleworking in a particular division. In the second example, perhaps flexibility is less of an inducement for performance because people do not see the flexibility as special support and its use is not motivationally linked. However, it may be an inducement to help retention as workers move toward an organization that has a teleworking option.

Policy Availability and Awareness and Use

One other key aspect of assessing the impact of flexibility on the employment relationship involves unpacking the gap between policy availability and awareness and use. From the employer perspective, this means the employer is even willing to formally or informally *offer the opportunity* for employees to work flexibly. From the employee side, a key issue is that many employees lack awareness or understanding of available policies and practices, or if they are aware of them, they may not perceive the policies as "usable" (Eaton, 2003)—that is, they may feel that their supervisor will hold it against them if they use the flexibility policy. An example would be a professor who takes a maternity leave but then gets a lower pay raise because the department chair held it against the professor that the department had to find someone to cover the individual's previously scheduled class. So from the employee side, use or lack of use must be assessed taking into account whether the use can be done without hurting employability status or rewards. From the employer side, there is a usability issue too. The employer may question whether use of a flextime policy can be done without hurting productivity. Will it be harder to schedule meetings? Will the employee really work a full 8-hour day if the manager does not see the employee arrive and leave work? Does the infrastructure support work at nontraditional times? Will the employee use telework as a means of avoiding conversations that must take place in person?

Besides productivity implications of use, there are customization aspects as well. From the employee side, is the use of flexibility "standardized flex," or are employees truly able to adapt flexible work policies to their needs? Some companies have inflexible flexibility policies. An example would be flextime policies that workers can only use if they plan ahead and workers who have family needs characterized by unpredictability. In this case, flexibility practices are less likely to have a large a motivational impact because the design features do not fit the employee needs. Customization also occurs from the employer perspective. Is flexibility standardized throughout the organization? Or are different supervisors allowed and even encouraged to customize the flexibility policy to department needs? One may expect that customization may enhance the influence of the flexibility policy or the employment relationship.

We focus our theorizing in the following section on only work–family flexibility policies and practices where the availability or use is voluntary or particularistic to meet employee needs and preferences. Such flexibility practices are not necessarily something that is given to all members in exactly the same way simply for being a member of the organization. Thus, our discussion is not focused on general practices such as established vacation and sick time policies that are available to all employees and similar by job group.

EOR LINKAGES TO WORK–FAMILY FLEXIBILITY: THEORY AND HYPOTHESES

Two main social exchange theoretical frameworks underlie EOR research and are relevant to organizational support of work–family flexibility: (1) the inducements–contributions framework (March & Simon, 1958), and (2) organizational and supervisor social support (Eisenberger, Huntington, Hutchison, & Sowa, 1986; Singlhamber, Vandenberghe, Sucharski, & Rhoades, 2002). Seminal research on social exchange theory (Blau, 1964) argues that when one party bestows a benefit on the other, the party receiving the benefit may choose whether or not to reciprocate a benefit in return or reciprocate equally. Organizational work–family support such as offering flextime adds a social exchange based on trust and risk to EOR power dynamics.

Inducement and General and Specific Social Support Theories

The inducement–contributions model (March & Simon, 1958) is based on the notion that the organization offers inducements in the employment exchange in return for employee contributions (Coyle-Shapiro & Shore, 2007). From a work–family perspective, employees may be motivated to stay with an employer and work harder if the access or use of a work–family inducement is something they value and motivates more positive employment attitudes and behaviors. An employee may be less likely to turnover if he or she is a user of workplace flexibility or other work–family supports like child care (Kossek & Nichol, 1992). Studies do show users of work–family benefits are more likely to make suggestions on how to improve the workplace (organization citizenship behaviors) (Lambert, 2000). Flexible work arrangements, especially scheduling flexibility, are a boundary-spanning resource (Hill et al., 2008) and a particularly important type of organizational support and empowerment because employees have autonomy to decide when and where to complete the tasks. The employer is likely to benefit from flexibility if the consequence of employee access or use of flexibility results in attitudes or behaviors the employer values. Currently, we assume that most organizations perceive they are generally overinvesting in the employment relationship and social exchange by supporting voluntary employee-initiated work–family flexibility programs. The reason for this is that as currently implemented, work–family flexibility policies are being offered as a general benefit or policy that any employee can use simply by virtue of being an employee or member of the firm. Use of the flexibility is not linked to discretionary performance or other behaviors the employer values such as the degree they are valued and trusted. It is currently not being effectively implemented as an inducement.

> **Proposition 1:** *The more that an organization can ensure that the employee's access to a customized work–family flexibility practice is linked to their being valued and trusted, the more likely the flexibility practice use will be more strongly linked to serving the employer interests (e.g., productivity).*

Perceived organizational support is the extent to which members see the organization as caring about them and valuing their contributions (Eisenberger et al., 1986). Supervisor support is the degree to which members see their supervisor as supportive (Eisenberger et al., 2002). A recent meta-analysis of dozens of studies showed that in regard to work and family, organizational and supervisor support (e.g., perceived organizational support [POS], perceived supervisor support [PSS]) must be work–family specific (e.g., family supportive organizational perceptions [FSOP], family supportive supervisory perceptions [FSS]) (cf. Allen, 2001) to relate to lower work family conflict (Kossek, Pichler, Bodner, & Hammer, 2011). FSOP is the idea that the organization specifically cares about positive work–family support. The Kossek et al. (2011) meta-analysis showed that general organizational support or supervisor support is not as strongly related to lower work–family conflict as family-specific organizational or supervisor support. These findings suggest that in the EOR relationship, employers and supervisors who are specifically focused on providing resources targeting work and family role integration, such as workplace flexibility practices, are likely to be seen as supportive of the work, family, and employment relationship. The meta-analysis also found a mediating relationship showing that supervisors are the mechanism through which

POS operates. To enhance work–family relationships, supportive supervisors are key actors.

> **Proposition 2:** *Perceptions of availability and usability.* The link between individual perceptions of their ability to use available formal flexibility policies that enable boundary blurring without negatively impacting the employment relationship will be stronger when the perceived quality of the relationship with the supervisor is positive.
>
> **Proposition 3:** *Actual use.* Individuals with more supportive supervisors are more likely to benefit from using flexibility policies and are less likely to turnover from the organization.
>
> **Proposition 4:** Individuals with higher POS and FSOP will be more likely to use available flexibility policies. They will also be more likely to perceive their organizations as valuing positive work–life relationships as part of the employment relationship.

The reason for Proposition 2 is that employees who have supportive supervisors who exhibit caring attitudes and behaviors regarding work–family flexibility will be more aware of existing policies and feel freer to be able to actually use needed flexibility without jeopardy. Research shows that supervisors are the mechanisms through which employees develop family supportive perceptions (Kossek, Pichler, et al., 2011). The leader–member exchange relationship with the supervisor will moderate this relationship, such that those employees with more positive leader–member exchange relations will have built up more idiosyncratic credits, which Rousseau (1995, 2005) views as I-Deals. They will feel freer to be able to work in different ways because they are more likely to perceive that their supervisor values their work contributions and their family and personal well-being overall. The rationale for Proposition 3 is that employees with more supportive supervisors will feel more positive support from their supervisor, which will lead to higher POS. Employees will perceive they have more psychological and tangible resources to manage work–family conflict, which will result in lower turnover. The rationale for Proposition 4 is that employees are more likely to perceive that they work in organizational cultures supportive of work and family when they perceive they work for supervisors who are supportive of work–family balance. Research consistently shows that supervisors are the mechanisms through which employees perceive organizational support for work and family, which ultimately affects work–family conflict (Kossek et al., 2011).

A key assumption of EOR research is that inducements or supports to foster more discretionary behaviors lead to higher benefits in the social exchange. For flexibility policies to be an inducement, they must be valued by the employee as attractive in the employment exchange relationship. Research increasingly shows that workers vary in their preferences for use of formal flexibility policies (Rothbard, Phillips, & Dumas, 2005), informal boundary-blurring job design (Kossek et al., 2006), and work styles (Kossek, Ruderman, et al., 2011). If flexibility is attractive to the worker, then access or use will result in greater motivation to reciprocate rewards to the organization, assuming the organization sees higher job satisfaction or increased loyalty and organizational citizenship behaviors as a true benefit.

Overall, work–family flexibility is increasingly an important inducement and support in the EOR relationship. It can serve many roles from social support to reduced work–family strain; it is a reward bestowed on the best workers as part of a social exchange of loyalty. Flexible work arrangements also provide a means for employees to self-regulate boundaries and determine and control when, where, and how they work. It can also allow workers to be able to adapt work schedules and location to fit their working preferences or preferences for boundary management—the degree to which work–life roles are separated or integrated—and vary these conditions as job and family demands wax and wane. However organizations and individuals must take into account power and social dynamics when implementing new ways of working.

Implementation Gap

Applying EOR theory to the rewards and consequences of the social exchange (Shore & Shore, 1995), the organization has far greater power to control the offering of rewards (access and use of flexibility policies) and outcomes (organizational trust and consequences of using policies) than the employee. What the organization cannot fully control is the extent to which the employee reciprocates access to work–family flexibility with increased behaviors and attitudes that benefit the organization. This imbalance is symbolized in the persistence of a critical HR implementation effectiveness gap, due to cultural resistance and EOR power dynamics (Kossek, 2005). Our review of work–family research with an EOR lens leads us to surmise that the mere offering of flexibility is a necessary but insufficient condition to result in a positive social exchange for either organizations or individuals. A positive EOR interaction occurs when there is some balance between employer and employee interests.

Here lies most of the challenges with work–family flexibility and EOR. There has generally not been a highly favorable EOR investment–benefits ratio for either organizations or individuals for several reasons. First, most flexibility policies have an implementation problem where some policies such as telecommuting or part-time work or flextime are underused due to organizational cultural resistance. Many organizations do not see themselves as truly benefiting from giving more support to enable employees to give more time to the family role. The ability to allow individuals to be able to restructure the work role to accommodate personal or family life is not seen as serving employer interests. Managers often do not support use because they face productivity problems such as not knowing how to manage with reduced face time or increased coordination and equity issues among coworkers or not knowing how to redesign work systems to make them work well (Van Dyne, Kossek, & Lobel, 2007). Overall, from the organization perspective, the benefits of the policy (e.g., better job satisfaction, lower turnover, increased engagement) must be seen as outweighing the economic, administrative, and social costs.

A second factor related to implementation issues is that employees do not necessarily receive sufficient benefits either from mere access or use of flexibility. From the individual perspective, the existing research shows that work–family flexibility policies often have greater benefit to the organization than to the employee. This is particularly true in terms of their public relations value than in terms of actually helping employees solve work and family conflicts (Kossek et al., 2011). Career-oriented employees are often afraid to fully use flexible policies for fear of losing jobs, receiving lower pay, or losing promotions. Some studies even suggest that if employees use flexibility policies, their work–family conflict is not reduced because flexibility policies may actually increase work–family conflict by promoting more involvement in caregiving without reducing work involvement (Hammer, Neal, Newsom, Brockwood, & Colton, 2005). One study found that teleworkers had slightly higher work–family conflict than nonteleworkers (Kossek et al., 2006). Perhaps some flexibility policies such as telework merely enable more work–family conflict by bringing all the stresses of work into the home. Overall, from the employee perspective, the use of a work–family flexibility policy must result in real benefits. These include real schedule control, lower work–family conflict, the ability to use a policy without backlash or career stigmatization, and the ability to keep up with job demands.

A third factor is that some flexibility policies such as part-time work are seen as neither affordable nor practical. They are not economically feasible for employees who need the income (part time). From an employer perspective, many employers face legal barriers in prorating benefits and do not know how to restructure work systems to allow for part-time work (Kossek, 2006), or employers may not be able to structure the interdependence of the work so it can be engaged in during nonstandardized hours.

Power Dynamics of Formal and Informal Boundary-Blurring Flexibility

Besides the fact that organizations generally do not see themselves as benefiting from flexibility policies, many do not want to give employees more power in the employment relationship. From the organizational perspective, greater cultural support of work–family flexibility policies may change the power dynamics and truly give employees more control over working hours—an increasingly "contested terrain" (Edwards, 1979). Implementing flexibility policies in ways that allow employees to control when they work would substantially change the dynamics in the power relations between employee and employer. Because employers generally have the upper hand in the employment relationship, employers often resist full implementation because many do not want to give up power and see working conditions as a management right. They do not see a positive cost–benefit rationale. Allowing employees to have greater control over work schedules is seen by employers as overinvesting in the social exchange relationship (cf. Tsui et al., 1997) with employees, where the employee receives more benefit than the employer.

Ironically, unlike formal flexibility policies, technology-based boundary blurring such as through cell phones or laptops may be a power dynamics game changer to give more power to the individual. This assumes technology is implemented in ways that the employee can control. Informally, boundary blurring through technology use, such as with a smart phone that allows an employee to receive a text message from a family member, may be much harder for employers to control. Employees can use these tools to enable more family interruptions to work, and it is harder for employers to monitor and delineate whether the employee is really working. For these reasons, it is possible that technology use to blur boundaries may allow employees to benefit more than formal flexibility policies.

> **Proposition 5:** *Informal flexibility boundary blurring through personal hand-held display devices may offer employees more control to manage work–family relationships in ways that meet individual interests than formal flexibility policies, the use of which is employer determined.*

Work Style Preferences for Boundary-Blurring Preferences and the EOR

We argue that increasingly employer and employee flexibility influences and boundary preferences are overlapping and interacting. One research study (Kossek & Lautsch, 2008) conducted on employees in different organizational settings, from teleworkers in professional financial services and information technology (IT) consulting firms to individuals working in a manufacturing plant, found that employee perceptions of control were critical for well-being and determinants of how people viewed flexibility as working in the employment relationship. What mattered most for positive perceptions of work and family and employer relationships was whether people felt in control of their work boundaries and whether they were using flexibility in ways that fit their personal values for aligning work and personal life. Three types of individual flexibility preferences were identified: integrators, separators, and volleyers (Kossek & Lautsch, 2008). Integrators hop back and forth from work and family to focus on different tasks all day long. Separators like to separate work and personal life, keeping a clear boundary between the two. Some people are volleyers or cyclers, with periods of sometimes high mixing of work and family at defined times of the year and then periods of high separation with a focus on one role at a time. Under each of the three types, there are high boundary control and low boundary control profiles. Positive profiles have high control over how boundaries are managed in ways that fit values. Under each type, there were happy and unhappy integrators (fusion lovers or reactors), separators (role firsters or captives), and volleyers (quality timers or job warriors). Later work by Kossek, Ruderman, et al. (2011) has provided evidence for this variation in boundary management profiles and shows they are linked to many critical outcomes from depressive symptoms to work engagement to dysfunctional work behaviors like surfing the Internet.

To produce positive EOR outcomes, organizations should not neglect both environmental and personal factors. When the environment and personal factors match well, it can synergize autonomous work motivation, which will lead to a positive EOR. We argue that preferences for boundary blurring can impact the individual's motivation. Individuals want to work in different ways in how they manage work–family relationships. When they are able to work in ways that fit their values for boundary management and they can control work–life boundary management, they are likely to be more motivated and have higher EOR satisfaction because either they feel the social exchange is more balanced or they perceive greater POS for work–life demands. Overall, we believe that the preceding review in this chapter suggests that the more a flexibility policy or practice is an idiosyncratic deal designed to meet employee needs and preferences, the greater the strength of the relation to positive EOR employee attitudes and behaviors.

Proposition 6: *Greater customization by an individual employee to tailor a work–family flexibility practice to meet his or her needs will increase the strength of its relation to employee membership attitudes and behaviors related to the employment relationship (e.g., turnover; work–family conflict).*

Imagine an organization with employees with all different types of personal flexibility preferences, which is likely to be the case in an organization. When implementing a work–life flexibility policy, it is not surprising that different employees will have different reactions to the policy. Take telecommuting as an example. Whereas integrators may be excited about the option, separators may be concerned about "doing it all, all the time" and may not choose to use the work–life flexibility arrangement that the company provided. Not being able to take advantage of the flexible work arrangement may lead to separators having lower motivation based on social exchange theory and lower perceived organizational support. In fact, a recent study by Hammer, Kossek, Bodner, Anger, and Zimmerman (2011) found that individuals with low work–family conflict at time 1 had worse outcomes at time 2 when their supervisors were trained to give greater flexibility support.

However, how different types of flexibility styles interact with each other can form a part of the organizational culture. If a separator works in an integrator-dominated culture, he or she will feel pressured because getting e-mails at 11 PM is not very pleasant for some people. Vice versa, if an integrator works in a separator-dominated culture, he or she will feel frustrated because he or she may not get the support needed during after-work hours. With a good match between environment and individual flexibility preference, employees in the environment will be more motivated to work because they get the support they need. We believe that the greater the fit is between the type of flexibility policy offered and individual preferences for boundary blurring, the more that employees will view the flexibility policy as an inducement to motivate positive work behaviors. For example, separators who have a strong family identity may prefer part-time work because it allows them to focus on work when at work and family when at home without boundary crossing. Integrators will prefer telework and flextime as inducements because these allow them to blur boundaries. Cyclers/volleyers' preferences for telework and flextime use and the degree to which use of these policies acts as an inducement may vary depending on the time of the year. For example, for a businessperson who teleworks, telecommuting may be less attractive if their school-age children are now home for the summer and the house can no longer be used as an office. We believe that there is growing variation in how workers want to manage work and personal life relationships and that employers are not fully supporting this variation. The EOR would be enriched if policies and practices were implemented in ways that met employee preferences at the same time that discretionary performance or positive work behaviors for use were supported.

Proposition 7: *Individual preferences for boundary blurring will moderate the degree to which different types of flexibility will be viewed as an inducement.*

We believe that with employers' greater ability to control the power dynamics of how flexibility policies are implemented to date, flexibility policies have not been implemented with a mutual investment approach. Given this chapter's discussion that people want to work in different ways they can control and the importance of mutual EOR investment, we conclude with several final propositions covering the spectrum of preferences for boundary blurring.

> **Proposition 8A:** *Individual performance will be highest when there is equal respect for times the employer prefers separation and for times the employee prefers separation. Assuming employees perceive that they can control boundaries style enactment, these effects will be strongest for employees favoring a separator style.*

Employee–organization policies that allow for a clear separation between work and family will be preferred by those employees who prefer separation as a boundary management strategy. When both the individual and the organization prefer the same separator strategy, performance will be impacted positively. Similarly, when the organization and the individual have different preferred values regarding separation, there will be negative impacts.

> **Proposition 8B:** *Individual performance is likely to be highest when both the organization and the employee feel they are mutually investing in the work–family flexibility, such that there are generally equal trade-offs of work boundary blurring interrupting family and family boundary blurring interrupting work. Assuming employees perceive that they can control boundary crossings, these effects will be strongest for employees favoring an integration style.*

We argue that employee–organization policies that allow and encourage the blurring of boundaries will be most beneficial for employees who favor this style. It is also important that equal trade-offs are perceived and that the individual feels control over when a blurring style is used. There will be negative impacts when the individual and the organization have discrepant styles regarding integration. A clear example of when this lack of alignment occurs might be when an employee takes a sick child to work thinking that is acceptable to the organization when it is not. Similarly, there is a lack of congruence when a boss in an integrator culture asks a worker valuing separation to unexpectedly prepare a presentation over the weekend.

CONCLUSIONS AND FUTURE DIRECTIONS

Looking across the literatures focusing on the changing EOR and work and family offers several promising avenues for further interweaving of the literatures. Both literatures deal with the very nature of the relationships of individuals to their work and the importance of the processes that help individuals and organizations accommodate to one another. EOR emphasizes specific exchanges between the employee and the organization, whereas the work and family literature focuses specifically on the boundary between the employee and the organization. EOR focuses on the mechanisms of inducements and contributions influencing this relationship, whereas work and family literature looks at the roots of conflicts between roles and practices for regulating transitions between work and family domains. Although there has been some overlap of ideas, these two literatures diverge in focus. Looking at both literatures together yields a better understanding of the relationship between individual requirements and organizational resources and enriches the understanding of how flexible work policies can be used to improve person–organization relationships.

For example, the work–family literature emphasizes the importance of individual preferences for informal flexibility in blurring boundaries. Kossek and Lautsch (2008) have argued that optimal boundary arrangements between work and family are a matter of individual preference. Positive EOR is likely to result when employees can work in ways that suit their values and preferences for informal boundary blurring or separation. The work by Kossek and Lautsch clarifies the many ways preferences in flexibility differ and, as such, how they can be used as inducements in I-Deals. In doing so, it provides organizations with a richer understanding of the many ways flexibility can be used as a reward or a recruitment or retention tool. To be effective as an inducement, flexibility practices must recognize individual differences.

Using the EOR perspective to look at the work–family literature suggests the importance of considering the work–family boundary as a negotiated deal. EOR research does a better job of recognizing that work outcomes are influenced by exchanges of inducements and contributions. The EOR literature offers organizations a rich understanding as to how flexibility can be negotiated. It can provide guidance for organizations looking to use flexibility as a tool of recruitment, reward, and retention. Similarly, it can provide individuals with a better understanding of how to request flexible arrangements—by pointing out how flexibility is an inducement for commitment.

Future trends point to additional research needs. For example, the increase in life spans in many Western countries means that elder care will have a growing impact on both relationships between the employee and the organization and the competing demands of work and family. Similarly, the technology revolution is resulting in a diversity of ways to work and to structure tasks, time frames, and the nature of collaboration, all of which have continued potential to transform the employment relationship, as well as relationships between work and other roles.

The joint investigation of country differences in terms of cultural values and work–family legislation could further enrich integration of the two literatures. Future research should consider examination of cultural influences on the work–life issues relevant to the EOR at many levels: the institutional national public policy level, the organizational level, and the supervisory level. An example of a future research issue at the institutional level comes from Germany. Unlike the United States where flexibility policies are normally codified in formal and informal company policies, in Germany, flexibility can be regulated in the individual contracts in some German organizations (Homung, Rousseau, & Glaser, 2008). Individuals can bargain with the employer on the terms of flexibility that they are going to receive in the contracts. Homung et al. (2008) found that the flexibility in work schedules is negatively related to the work–family conflict. Do work–life outcomes differ if access to policies is regulated by contracts and law or employer policies?

At the organizational level, there is cross-cultural variation in how organizations take up innovative employment practices to support employees as they age, and work–life practices may alter the EOR relationship over the life course. One interesting flexibility practice for older employees who are at least 58 years old comes from Sweden. Some firms offer an 80/90/100 employment model, which means "working 80% of normal working hours for 90% of normal pay and a 100% contribution" (Winkelmann-Gleed, 2009, p. 40). Participating firms found this practice, which was used by 20% of eligible workers, to be cost neutral because it "reduced sick leave and helped lessen rehabilitation costs" (Winkelmann-Gleed, 2009, p. 41).

The role of the supervisor in managing work–life-relevant EOR also varies. For example, compared to the United States, in China, the supervisor's control over employees' personal life is much greater. Traditionally, Chinese supervisors of the nation-owned companies have some control over employees' marriage plans. (In order to get married, employee needs to get approval from their company/supervisors, even though this could be "just perfunctory in some firms.") As China globalizes and adopts some Western practices, will this lessen the supervisory influence on employees' nonwork lives?

In sum, the negotiated reality that is at the heart of the exchange process can be very much influenced by the cultural and national boundary conditions set by governing bodies with regard to labor and family affairs. Flexibility as an inducement can be better understood by looking at the relationship in countries where the governments promote flexibility and in those countries where they do not. Looking at the work–family and EOR perspectives together within and between nations and cultures holds greater promise for helping organizations understand the impact of our changing world than either perspective in isolation.

ACKNOWLEDGMENT

We thank Frances Mai of the Michigan State University School of Human Resources and Labor Relations for research assistance and contributions to this paper.

REFERENCES

Allen, T. D. (2001). Family-supportive work environments: The role of organizational perceptions. *Journal of Vocational Behavior, 58*, 414–435.
Arthur, M., & Rousseau, D. (1996). *The boundaryless career: A new employment principle for a new era.* Oxford, UK: Oxford.

Blair-Loy, M. (2003). *Competing devotions: Career and family among women executives.* Cambridge, MA: Harvard University Press.

Blau, P. (1964). *Exchange and power in social life.* New York, NY: Wiley.

Boswell, W. R., Colvin, A. J. S., & Darnold, T. C. (2008). Organizational systems and employee motivation. In R. Kanfer, C. Gilad, & R. D. Pritchard (Eds.), *Work motivation: Past, present, and future* (pp. 361–400). New York, NY: Routledge/Taylor & Francis Group.

Bureau of Labor Statistics (BLS). (2010, May). *Employment characteristics of families summary.* Retrieved August 28, 2011, from http://www.bls.gov/news.release/famee.nr0.htm.

Cappelli, P. (1999). *The new deal at work.* Cambridge, MA: Harvard Business School Press.

Coyle-Shapiro, J. A.-M., & Shore, L. M. (2007). The employee-organization relationship: Where do we go from here? *Human Resource Management Review, 17,* 166–179.

Eaton, S. C. (2003). If you can use them: Flexibility policies, organizational commitment and perceived performance. *Industrial Relations, 42,* 145–167.

Edwards, R. (1979). *Contested terrain.* New York, NY: Basic Books.

Eisenberger, R., Huntington, R., Hutchison, S., & Sowa, D. (1986). Perceived organizational support. *Journal of Applied Psychology, 71,* 500–507.

Eisenberger, R., Singlhamber, F., Vandenberghe, C., Sucharski, I., & Rhoades, L. (2002). Perceived supervisor support: Contributions to perceived support and employee retention. *Journal of Applied Psychology, 87,* 565–573.

European Commission. (2010). *Report on equality between women and men 2010.* Brussels, Belgium: Author.

Galinsky, E., Aumann, K., & Bond, J. (2008). *National study of the changing workplace.* New York, NY: Families and Work Institute.

Hammer, L. B., Kossek, E. E., Bodner, T., Anger, K., & Zimmerman, K. (2011). Clarifying work-family intervention processes: The roles of work-family conflict and family supportive supervisor behaviors. *Journal of Applied Psychology, 96,* 134–150.

Hammer, L. B., Neal, M., Newsom, J., Brockwood, K., & Colton, C. (2005). A longitudinal study of the effects of dual-earner couples' utilization of family-friendly workplace supports on work and family outcomes. *Journal of Applied Psychology, 90,* 799–810.

Hill, E. J., Grzywacz, J. G., Allen, S., Blanchard, V. L., Matz-Costa, C., Shulkin, S., & Pitt-Catsouphes, M. (2008). Defining and conceptualizing workplace flexibility. *Community, Work, and Family, 11,* 149–163.

Hochschild, A. (1989). *The second shift.* New York, NY: Penguin Books.

Homung, S., Rousseau, D. M., & Glaser, J. (2008) Creating flexible work arrangements through idiosyncratic deals. *Journal of Applied Psychology, 93,* 655–664.

Kanter, R. M. (1977). *Work and family in the United States.* New York, NY: Russell Sage Foundation.

Kossek, E. E. (2005). Workplace policies and practices to support work and families. In S. Bianchi, L. Casper, & R. King (Eds.), *Work, family, health, and well-being* (pp. 97–116). Mahwah, NJ: Lawrence Erlbaum Associates, Inc.

Kossek, E. E. (2006). Work and family in America: Growing tensions between employment policy and a changing workforce. A thirty year perspective commissioned chapter by SHRM Foundation and University of California Center for Organizational Effectiveness for the 30th anniversary of the State of Work in America. In E. Lawler & J. O'Toole (Eds.), *America at work: Choices and challenges* (pp. 53–72). New York, NY: Palgrave MacMillan.

Kossek, E. E., Baltes, B. B., & Mathews, R. A. (2011). How work-family research can finally have an impact in organizations. *Industrial and Organizational Psychology: Perspectives on Science and Practice, 4*, 352–369.

Kossek, E. E., & Distelberg, B. (2008). Work and family employment policy for a transformed work force: Trends and themes. In N. Crouter & A. Booth (Eds.), *Work-life policies* (pp. 1–51). Washington, DC: Urban Institute Press.

Kossek, E. E., & Lautsch, B. (2008). *CEO of me: Creating a life that works in the flexible job age.* Upper Saddle River, NJ: Wharton School Publishing.

Kossek, E. E., Lautsch, B., & Eaton, S. (2006). Telecommuting, control, and boundary management: Correlates of policy use and practice, job control, and work-family effectiveness. *Journal of Vocational Behavior, 68*, 347–367.

Kossek, E. E., & Michel, J. (2011). Flexible work scheduling. In S. Zedeck (Ed.), *Handbook of industrial-organizational psychology* (pp. 535–572). Washington, DC: American Psychological Association.

Kossek, E. E., & Nichol, V. (1992). The effects of employer-sponsored child care on employee attitudes and performance (lead article). *Personnel Psychology, 45*, 485–509.

Kossek, E. E., Pichler, S., Bodner, T., & Hammer, L. (2011). Workplace social support and work-family conflict: A meta-analysis clarifying the influence of general and work-family specific supervisor and organizational support. *Personnel Psychology, 64*, 289–313.

Kossek, E. E., Roberts, K., Fisher, S., & DeMarr, B. (1998). Career self-management: A quasi-experimental assessment of a training intervention. *Personnel Psychology, 51*, 935–962.

Kossek, E. E., Ruderman, M., Hannum, K., & Braddy, P. (2011). *A configurational view of work-family identity and cross-role boundary-blurring: development and validation of high and low control profiles.* Working paper.

Lambert, S. J. (2000). Added benefits: The link between work-life benefits and organizational citizenship behavior. *Academy of Management Journal, 43*, 801–815.

March, J., & Simon, H. (1958). *Organizations.* New York, NY: Wiley.

Nippert-Eng, C. (1996). *Home and work: Negotiating boundaries through everyday life.* Chicago, IL: University of Chicago Press.

Rothbard, N., Phillips, K., & Dumas, T. (2005). Managing multiple roles: Work-family policies and individual's desires for segmentation. *Organization Science, 16*, 243–258.

Rousseau, D. (1995). *Psychological contracts in organizations: Understanding unwritten and unwritten agreements.* Thousand Oaks, CA: Sage Publications.

Rousseau, D. (2005). *I-deals: Idiosyncratic deals employees bargain for themselves.* New York, NY: ME Sharpe.

Shore, L., & Shore, T. (1995). Perceived organizational support and organizational justice. In R. Cropanzano & K. Kacmar (Eds.), *Organizational politics, justice, and support: Managing the social climate of the workplace* (pp. 149–164). Westport, CT: Quorum Books.

Shore, L. M., Tetrick, L. E., Taylor, M. S., Coyle-Shapiro, J., Liden, R., McLean Parks, J., ... Van Dyne, L. (2004). The employee-organization relationship: A timely concept in a period of transition. In G. R. Ferris & J. Martocchio (Eds.), *Research in personnel and human resources management* (pp. 291–370). Greenwich, CT: JAI Press.

Slay, H. S., & Taylor, M. S. (2007). Career systems and psychological contracts. In H. Gunz & M. Peiperl (Eds.), *Handbook of career studies* (pp. 337–398). Thousand Oaks, CA: Sage.

Tsui, A. S., Pearce, J. L., Porter, L. W., & Tripoli, A. M. (1997). Alternative approaches to the employee-organization relationship: Does investment in employees pay off? *Academy of Management Journal, 40,* 1089–1121.

Van Dyne, L., & Ellis, J. (2004). Job creep: A reactance theory perspective on organizational citizenship behavior as over fulfillment of obligations. In J. Coyle-Shapiro, L. Shore, M. Taylor, & L. Tetrick (Eds.), *The employment relationship: Examining psychological and contextual perspectives* (pp. 181–205). Oxford, UK: Oxford University Press.

Van Dyne, L., Kossek, E., & Lobel S. (2007). Less need to be there: Cross level effects of work practices that support work-life flexibility and enhance group processes and group-level OCB. *Human Relations, 60,* 1123–1153.

Wilson, S. (1955). *The man in the grey flannel suit.* London, UK: Four Walls/Eight Windows.

Winkelmann-Gleed, A. (2009) Demographic change and implications for workforce ageing in Europe: Raising awareness and improving practice. *Cuadernos de Relaciones Laborales, 27,* 29–50.

10

Rethinking the Employee–Organization Relationship: Insights From the Experiences of Contingent Workers

Daniel G. Gallagher
James Madison University

Catherine E. Connelly
McMaster University

Our understanding of the employee–organizational relationship (EOR) (Coyle-Shapiro, Shore, Taylor, & Tetrick, 2004), as well as other behavioral theories or frameworks related to the employment relationship, is heavily based on the implicit notion of a "standard" employment arrangement (e.g., Ashford, George, & Blatt, 2007; Gallagher & Sverke, 2005; George & Chattopadhyay, 2005; Pfeffer & Baron, 1988; Rousseau, 1997). The EOR draws upon social exchange theory (Blau, 1964) and the inducements–contributions model (March & Simon, 1958) to explain why workers respond to their employers' actions by engaging in reciprocal behaviors. As such, the EOR forms the foundations of many fundamental theories underlying worker behaviors (e.g., psychological contract, perceived organizational support, leader–member exchange, organizational commitment). However, this begs a theoretical and practical question: What if the worker is not an "employee" per se, and what if the employer is potentially a client or even a series of clients, sometimes found through an intermediary?

As noted by Kalleberg (2000), employment has normally been characterized as work that is performed (a) on a full-time basis (e.g., a 35- to 40-hour work week); (b) with an expectation that the employment could continue indefinitely; (c) at the employer's place of business; and (d) under the employer's direction or supervision. It may also be noted that it is inherently accepted that the assorted "standard" workforce of full-time employees, managers, and executives work within a single identifiable "employer" organization (e.g., Western Electric, Canadian Tire, Nokia, IKEA).

The fact that behavioral researchers have built theories and conducted empirical investigations in the context of permanent employment is understandable. First and foremost, the development of organizational behavior as a field of study coincided chronologically with the transition of employment in developed countries to hierarchical organizations with internal labor markets, based on the principles of training, retention, and advancement (Cappelli, 1999; Doeringer & Piore, 1971; Pearce, 1993). Second, for the past few generations of labor force participants, full-time ongoing employment is still the prevailing working arrangement. Third, behavioral research itself tends to originate through scholars who are based at universities and research centers in more affluent and economically developed countries where permanent employment has prevailed.

Today, many organizations have begun to slowly shift away from retention-based staffing toward more transitory contractual arrangements. This strategy has been widely referred to as the "core–periphery" or "core–ring" model (Atkinson, 1984; Gallagher & Connelly, 2008; Handy, 1989). The "core" is comprised of organizational members who can be characterized as permanent employees with "ongoing" attachments to the organization. In contrast, "the periphery" represents workers with varying degrees of affiliation with the organization—those with part-time or temporary fixed-term (i.e., contingent) contracts. The outer edges of the periphery would include the complete outsourcing of functional areas (e.g., payroll, marketing, security, information processing).

Within this broad framework, the objective of this chapter is to examine the EOR through the vantage point of contingent work. More specifically, there is a need to explore the extent to which existing theoretical frameworks, which have been built in permanent employment contexts, are fully applicable to the understanding of contingent work (Rousseau, 1997). Possible peculiarities will be identified with regard to the parties that are involved in the exchange relationship, as well as consideration of what is being exchanged (Cropanzano & Mitchell, 2005). As part of the discussion, we will also consider how well various well-established EOR concepts (e.g., organizational commitment, perceived organizational support, leader–member exchange, and psychological contracts) apply to the various contingent employment arrangements. This chapter also explores the extent to which insights regarding contingent workers' experiences can help us to understand the attitudes and behaviors of more traditional employees. Some practical suggestions will be offered for workplace application as well as avenues for future research.

DEFINING THE DOMAIN

As noted in the research literature related to contingent work, there is considerable variation in the labels assigned to the different contractual arrangements; several terms are also used to capture the same form of arrangement. In part, much of this labeling is somewhat prescriptive and value driven. As suggested, the use of the term "nonstandard" or atypical assumes the presence of a clearly defined and accepted norm of what is standard or typical. What might be typical employment in Nigeria or the Netherlands might not be typical in Canada or Sweden. As noted by De Cuyper et al. (2007), the proper interpretation of empirical research findings associated with nonstandard and temporary employment arrangements is very much dependent on the ability to have clarity in how the particular forms of nonstandard employment are, in fact, being defined. It is important to emphasize that there is also considerable legal ambiguity about the extent to which contingent workers are attached to or even employed by the organizations with which they are affiliated (Wears & Fisher, 2010).

To achieve the objective of viewing the applicability of EORs in the context of nonstandard employment arrangements, we have chosen to specifically focus on and contrast three different but common examples of what can be termed as "contingent" employment relationships (Connelly & Gallagher, 2004a). This list of contingent employment relationships is not exhaustive, but these three particular forms have been chosen because they represent the diversity of employment structures that are available to organizations and workers. Other work arrangements (e.g., seasonal, casual) are largely analogous to the contingent work relationships that are described next and are therefore not specifically included in our discussion. With all three of these forms of contingent employment there exists a commonality in that these employment relationships are all fixed-term, rather than ongoing, in nature. As such, these forms of contingent work all represent "peripheral" employment relationships, as represented in the Atkinson (1984) core–periphery model.

1. *Direct-hire workers:* One very common form of contingent employment is where organizations directly recruit and hire workers on fixed-term contracts (Figure 10.1). Often such "direct-hire" workers are employed by an organization to meet predictable seasonal demands for goods and services. Organizations may also go about directly hiring workers (e.g., "lumpers") on an ad hoc daily basis (Gallagher & Connelly, 2008). One such form of direct-hire work arrangements is "zero-hour" or roster-based employment, where workers are on an on-call basis and are employed and paid only when employers require additional labor on a short-term basis. A familiar example to most of us would be the substitute or "supply" teacher. As with permanent employees, direct-hire workers perform their jobs under the immediate control of the employing organization and at the employer's place of business. However, the work is "precarious" in nature because there is no guarantee of ongoing employment (Gallagher & Connelly, 2008).
2. *Temporary help services:* A form of fixed-term work can be found in an organization's use of temporary help services firms or agencies (e.g., Adecco, Ranstand, Manpower) to provide workers on an ad hoc basis (Figure 10.2). As with direct-hire temporary employees, the work performed for the organization is done on a fixed-term contract. However, the work is performed within the organization by a worker who is often legally a nonemployee; the worker is assigned or dispatched by the temporary help firm, but the work itself is actually performed by an assigned temporary worker (i.e., temp) at the location of the client organization (Gallagher & Connelly, 2008).
3. *Independent contractors:* The third form of contingent work that is included in our discussion is that of independent contractors

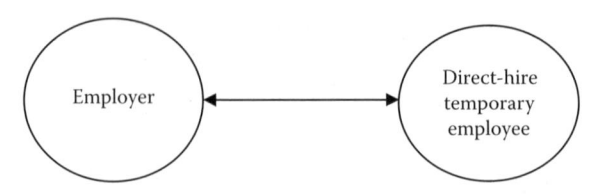

FIGURE 10.1
Direct-hire contingent workers.

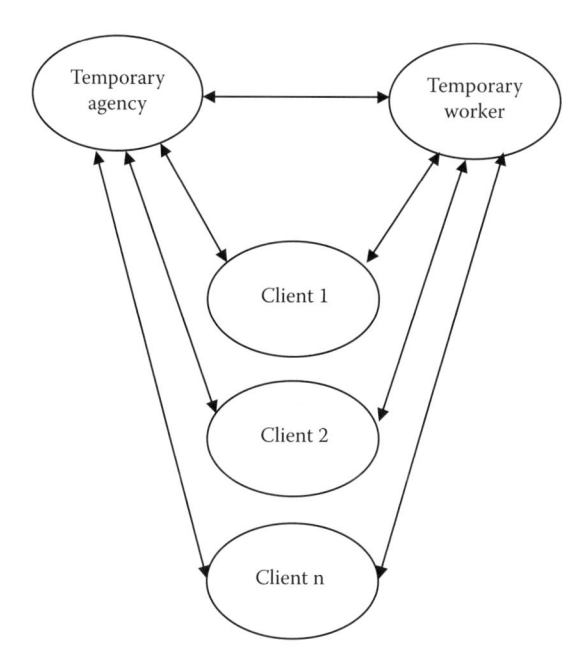

Rethinking the Employee–Organization Relationship • 259

FIGURE 10.2
Temporary agency workers.

(Figure 10.3). Contracting does not involve an employer–employee relationship, but rather a client–contractor arrangement. In situations where contractors rely on intermediaries to secure clients and manage compensation, the arrangement then becomes more akin to that of a temporary staffing service arrangement (Barley & Kunda, 2004). Independent contracting also assumes that, within parameters, it is the contractor and not management who controls how the work is performed (Church & Lambert, 1993; Connelly & Gallagher, 2006). As noted by McLean Parks, Kidder, and Gallagher (1998), independent contractors also have the unusual distinction of being able to simultaneously contract with multiple client organizations. In many respects, independent contractors are technically "self-employed" and are often legally reported as such, but there are instances where workers' status may be legally disputed (Wears & Fisher, 2010).

As a final caveat, it is important to note that workers with these contingent work arrangements may vary in their identification with and

260 • *The Employee-Organization Relationship*

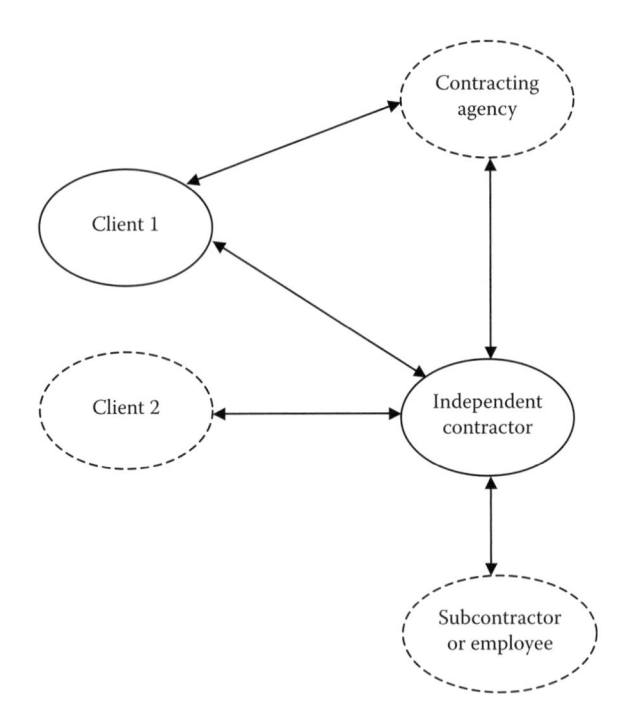

FIGURE 10.3
Independent contractors.

acceptance of the conditions of their employment. For example, some direct-hire temporary workers with long service at an organization may consider themselves to be quasi-permanently employed even though the terms of their contracts specify otherwise. Other workers may be unaware of the technical or legal details of their contracts. Together, these factors may contribute to a further "blurring" of the distinctions between the different forms of contingent employment. For the purposes of this chapter, however, each form of contingent work will be treated as distinct, as we discuss how the forms relate to EORs.

CONTINGENT EMPLOYEE–ORGANIZATION RELATIONSHIPS

Much of the early research about contingent workers assumed there was a weak exchange relationship between the worker and the employer or client. For example, contingent workers' psychological contracts were once said to be necessarily transactional in nature, and it was also originally assumed that contingent workers would not have affective organizational commitment to their clients or engage in organizational citizenship behaviors. Both assumptions have now been shown to be incorrect (Pearce, 1993; Van Dyne & Ang, 1998), but this conjecture of a weak or even nonexistent emotional connection between the worker and the employer was noteworthy because it has formed the bedrock of much of the research in organizational behavior.

Drawing on both social exchange theory (Blau, 1964) and the inducements–contributions model (March & Simon, 1958), the EOR forms the basis for much of the core concepts in organizational behavior (e.g., organizational commitment, perceived organizational support, organizational citizenship behaviors, psychological contracts). Much of the early research about contingent workers' experiences was drawn primarily on the inducements–contributions model. However, on closer examination, it is apparent that contingent workers do have relationships with their employers and clients, although these relationships are necessarily affected by the workers' contingent status and unusual employment structures. Following is a detailed discussion of how three different forms of contingent workers experience the EOR.

DIRECT HIRES

As noted in Figure 10.1, the structural aspects of the use of direct-hire contingent workers is generally the same as the traditional EOR, with an identifiable employer organization to which the direct hire has an administrative attachment. The operational difference rests in the fact that, by definition, direct-hire contingent workers have a temporal attachment that is of a fixed duration or an irregular basis. However, it can reasonably be asserted that virtually all aspects of the EOR have relevance and are readily applicable with minor adaptations of existing constructs and measures.

One immediate illustration of this point rests with the extensive amount of research examining the concept of organizational commitment among contingent workers (e.g., Buch, Kuvaas, & Dysvik, 2010; Connelly, Gallagher, & Gilley, 2007; Coyle-Shapiro & Morrow, 2006).

Along similar lines, there is no reason to suggest that direct-hire contingent workers do not hold perceptions of perceived organizational support or are incapable of structuring a psychological contract. With regard to the latter point, it would be reasonable to assert that workers on fixed-term contracts might have psychological contracts that are somewhat more transactional in nature, but there is no particular reason to suggest that more relational aspects could not, at times, also be emphasized. The question is the *nature* of the exchange relationship, not whether an exchange exists.

Given the relevance of the EOR to the study of direct-hire contingent workers, scholars are on fairly safe ground with a "plug-in" strategy that takes social exchange–based theories and applies them to the study of direct-hire temporaries. However, there may be salient aspects of the contingent work experience that moderate or mediate the relationships between various aspects of the EOR. One particular issue that has surfaced in the temporary worker literature is the importance of the extent to which a worker actually prefers to work on fixed-term contracts, as a deliberate alternative to permanent employment. This issue has been referred to as "volition" (e.g., Ellingson, Gruys, & Sackett, 1998) or, more simply, as "reasons" for working contingently (Moorman & Harland, 2002). As one would expect, workers who are in a particular employment arrangement by choice tend to be more satisfied and committed to the work and organizations where they are employed (e.g., De Cuyper & De Witte, 2008).

Closely related to the issue of volition are questions related to the workers' motivations for applying for and accepting a temporary position within an organization. One motivational factor that might be particularly relevant is the belief that temporary employment (e.g., an internship) will be the doorway into a permanent job within the organization (De Cuyper, Notelaers, & De Witte, 2009). When workers are motivated by the prospect of ongoing employment, they then may be willing to offer greater than expected inputs (e.g., organizational citizenship behaviors) in the hope of future reciprocation in the form of a permanent job. However, a direct-hire temporary worker on a seasonal contract (e.g., summer, holidays) or a temporary worker who is not interested in permanent employment may view the employment relationship as heavily transactional.

At issue is the importance of not treating all forms of contingent work or all forms of direct-hire contingent work as interchangeable; workers' motivations for choosing a particular form of employment relationship may have important consequences for how the workers frame and interpret the EOR. For example, direct-hire temporary workers who are anticipating a continued relationship with the organization may have higher expectations or sensitivity to how they are treated. Perceived organizational support and justice may interact with a worker's motivations for accepting contingent employment to predict their attitudes (e.g., organizational commitment) and behaviors (e.g., organizational citizenship behaviors).

Interpersonal interactions in organizations are said to be governed by an implicit and unspoken social exchange between coworkers. The underlying facilitator of these interactions is trust (Blau, 1964; Homans, 1958), which generally involves one party willing to be vulnerable to the actions of another, due to positive expectations of the other's intentions, even in the absence of monitoring or third-party controls (Mayer, Davis, & Schoorman, 1995; Rousseau, Sitkin, Burt, & Camerer, 1998). Interpersonal trust between coworkers is an integral component of effective social exchanges in organizations and has been linked to both task performance and organizational citizenship behaviors (Chou, Wang, Wang, Huang, & Cheng, 2008; Colquitt, Scott, & LePine, 2007).

Most importantly, in the context of contingent work, trust generally needs time to develop; both parties require the opportunity to observe the other's behaviors (Blau, 1964). The implications for the EORs of direct-hire temporary workers, and indeed for all contingent workers, are therefore potentially serious. These workers may not be at the employer or client for sufficient time for them to be trusted by their supervisors or coworkers. As such, they may find that they are assigned simpler tasks that are easier to monitor (Ang & Slaughter, 2001), which may in turn interfere with their career progression. A lack of interpersonal trust may also interfere with the normal social interactions that ordinarily occur in the workplace and the broader EOR.

There may also be instances, however, where the direct-hire temporary worker may believe that they have a more ongoing relationship with the organization than is warranted by their legal contract. In these situations, the interactions between direct-hire contingent workers and permanent employees may become less distant, with the direct hires engaging in trusting behaviors that, if reciprocated, may result in closer interpersonal ties. Conversely, there may also be instances where the organization considers direct hires to be integral and potentially permanent members of the organization (Stamper, Masterson, & Knapp, 2009). For example, large accounting firms often hire summer interns as part of a long-term recruitment strategy, hoping that these recruits will then work for the firm permanently upon graduation. In these cases, the organization and the direct supervisor may treat these contingent workers particularly well and therefore elicit high levels of perceived support, affective organizational commitment, and organizational citizenship behaviors.

In summary, the direct-hire contingent worker arrangement is a good starting illustration for the simple reason that this employer–employee relationship is structurally simple. Using Pfeffer and Baron's (1988) measures of externalization, direct-hire contingents are primarily distinct from standard workers on the dimension of temporal attachment and are very much like standard workers with regard to administrative and physical attachment. As suggested, we find that aspects of social exchange theory, developed in the context of standard work arrangements, still have applicability to the study of direct-hire temporaries. What is required is not so much the redevelopment of our established theories, but rather greater attention to issues of volition and motivation for accepting this form of employment versus what is typically discussed in the EORs of permanent employees.

Temporary Agency Workers

In contrast to direct hires, the employment of temporary workers through the use of an intermediary introduces a whole series of theoretical issues that have been beyond the scope of past research pertaining to the EOR. As suggested in Figure 10.2, temporary agency workers have relationships with both an agency and a client, and these relationships are based on an expectation that the worker will be moving from one client to the next. This arrangement is especially interesting from an EOR perspective because the worker is not technically an employee of the organization where the job is performed. As noted by Coyle-Shapiro and Conway (2004), there might well be more parties involved in the EOR than initially envisioned.

From both a practical and theoretical perspective, conventional views toward the EOR might be challenged by the simple fact that a clearly defined employer organization does necessarily exist. As noted by

Gallagher and McLean Parks (2001), for temporary help service workers, the fundamental term "organizational commitment" can be confusing. Some workers might assess organizational commitment in terms of the client where they perform their work, whereas others might view the employer as the firm that arranges their placement and signs their paycheck. Given that workers can have multiple foci of commitment, the challenge of measuring temporary worker attitudes (e.g., commitment, perceived organizational support) in this context relates to the need to reconsider how attitude is measured as well as the extent to which client and agency attitudes are interrelated, most notably the degree to which attitudes toward the client are influenced by attitudes to the agency and vice versa (e.g., Connelly et al., 2007; Coyle-Shapiro & Morrow, 2006; Buch et al., 2010). Two such applications of behavioral spillover are organizational citizenship behaviors (Liden, Wayne, Kraimer, & Sparrowe, 2003) and counterproductive work behaviors (Connelly & Gallagher, 2004b).

Similar to direct-hire workers, research on temporary help service–based contingent workers involves a consideration of the importance of both volition and motivation in the understanding of how such workers evaluate their client and agency "employment" relationship. A preference for permanent employment might influence the behaviors such workers have toward the client and agency. As suggested in Figure 10.2, these workers often move from assignments in one client organization to another. From a theoretical perspective, this would suggest that client-based attitudes and the nature of the psychological contracts may change as workers move between assignments. As such, agency-based workers may be particularly prone to contrast effects; the evolution of their EOR might be readily influenced by prior client experiences.

One further aspect of the EOR that has relevance to temporary agency workers and other contingent workers is the issue of time. Many of the aspects of the employer–employee relationship that have been examined by behavioral researchers have assumed that relationships can strengthen or weaken over time. This point has been well demonstrated in the case of psychological contracts and relationships with supervisors and coworkers (e.g., leader–member exchange). As with direct-hire temporary workers, temporary agency workers may face barriers to being trusted by their supervisors and coworkers because of the relatively short duration of their contracts. However, as per social identity theory (Tajfel & Turner, 1986), contingent workers who are affiliated with an agency may also be particularly prone to being considered as outsiders by the permanent employees with whom they work.

One exception to the lack of trust invested in contingent workers, and temporary agency workers in particular, is the phenomenon of "swift trust" (Kasper-Fuehrera & Ashkanasy, 2001; Meyerson, Weick, & Kramer, 1996; Rousseau, 1997). In instances where the temporary agency worker is part of a profession and has been contracted to play a circumscribed role with which the other team members are familiar (e.g., anesthesiologist, accountant), the other organizational members may engage in swift trust. Indeed, the temporary worker's professional commitment, rather than their commitment to their agency or client, may facilitate this process. Temporary agency workers who demonstrate appropriate professional values (e.g., patient care) will more likely be perceived as trustworthy by their new colleagues. It should be noted, however, that swift trust is fragile; once broken, it may be difficult to rebuild (Tomlinson & Mayer, 2009).

There has been a significant level of interest in how the EOR plays out when there is a joint employer or more than one client (Connelly et al., 2007; Coyle-Shapiro & Morrow, 2006). For example, the temporary agency worker may need to develop separate employment relationships with the agency or intermediary as well as several different client organizations. Together, these results suggest that more adapted constructs are needed that are specific to the temporary agency worker context and that capture the complexity inherent in this relationship. For example, it is perhaps more nuanced to refer to a temporary agency worker's attitudes as perceived client support and perceived agency support, rather than as perceived "organizational" support. Similarly, one might refer to agency commitment or client commitment instead of "organizational" commitment, and agency or client justice rather than "organizational" justice. This nomological evolution is somewhat similar to that seen in the literature on perceived union support and union commitment (Gordon, Philpot, Burt, Thompson, & Spiller, 1980; Shore & Tetrick, 1991; Shore, Tetrick, Sinclair, & Newton, 1994). The differentiation between temporary agency workers' commitments to different organizations (i.e., the agency and the client) will enable researchers to determine whether these workers prioritize their relationships with one organization over another, how these relationships are interrelated, and what factors affect these relationships.

As an aside, a competing theory that is sometimes used to explain workers' motivations and behaviors in organizations is "agency theory"

(Eisenhart, 1989). This theory is predicated on the assumption that workers behave in ways that advance their own interests and that the best way to motivate appropriate behavior is to align workers' interests with those of the organization (e.g., introduce profit-sharing plans). Temporary agency workers are therefore a particularly interesting subset of workers to study, in that they provide an illustration of how agency theory cannot fully explain worker behavior because the workers' interests will never be fully aligned with both the agency and the client organization. By definition, the interests of the two organizations are always going to be potentially in conflict. For example, a client will want the assigned tasks to be completed as efficiently as possible (i.e., quickly and with high quality), and the temporary agency will prefer that the assignment generate as much revenue as possible (i.e., speed is not a priority).

Independent Contractors

Of the three broad forms of contingent employment being addressed in this discussion, the status of independent contractors or freelancers is potentially the most complex from a structural and definitional perspective. This complexity is due in part to the fact that independent contracting arrangements can change over time. In its most simple form, independent contracting involves a direct relationship between an individual and a client organization predicated on exchange of particular services for an agreed project or time-based rate. Most importantly, unlike a direct-hire temporary, a true independent contractor is, in most countries, outside the legal definition of "employee." As suggested in Figure 10.3, an independent contractor may work with one client at a time or work simultaneously with multiple clients. Once again referencing Pfeffer and Baron's (1988) levels of detachment, independent contractors tend to be at the outer limits of the core–periphery workforce model. First, although hope may exist for a long-term relationship, these work arrangements are legally fixed term. Second, true "independent" contracting vests administrative control with the independent contractor. Finally, whether or not the work is actually performed "on site" is negotiable rather than required.

Although technically the exchange relationship is not between an *employee* and an organization, exchanges between independent contractors and clients are an important, yet underrecognized, part of the employment landscape. At the most immediate level is the aforementioned exchange of labor (knowledge and skills) for compensation. Such a contractor–client relationship could be viewed as purely transactional. However, as noted by Barley and Kunda (2004), many independent contractors are highly reliant on the ability to attract and retain clients. As a result, it is possible to suggest that the psychological contract with the supervisor at the client organization may broaden over time, as the contractor endeavors to elicit more favorable treatment by engaging in instrumentally motivated extracontract behaviors.

In contrast to temporary agency workers, who are often able to rely on their agencies to procure a series of client assignments, independent contractors usually are responsible for finding their own patrons, either through the extension of a current contract, the renewal of a previous client (e.g., semiannual updating of a website), or positive word-of-mouth that results in a new contract with a new organization. This unique structure, coupled with the fact that independent contractors have fewer legal protections than employees, has implications for the contractor–client relationship, in that independent contractors may be motivated to perform additional tasks (e.g., work overtime not specified in the contract) in the hopes that this will lead to favorable treatment by the client. The resultant dynamic may be different than social exchange because it is not mutual and the underlying intention is instrumental (i.e., to receive additional contracts in the future). Indeed, this aspect of independent contractors' EOR bears more similarity to the inducements–contributions model, although it is enacted somewhat differently than usually conceptualized because the contractor (nonemployee) rather than the organization is the party offering the inducement to receive the added contribution. However, if the relationship continues, the power differential is mitigated (e.g., by both parties being equally dependent on the other), and trust develops sufficiently, then there is a possibility that this relationship could become more of a social exchange.

The fact that independent contractors may be working with a series of clients suggests that the nature of the exchange relationship may differ on a client-by-client basis. Unlike most psychological contracts research, as it generally applies to traditional or single-employer relationships, many contractors are dealing with the possible need to enter into idiosyncratic exchanges with each client organization. Contractor behaviors may be focused not only on client retention, but also on the exchange of services and accommodations with the expectation that such action will be further rewarded by client recommendations and support in securing other opportunities. In effect, what might be generally viewed as primarily economic transactions may evolve into more relational and supportive exchanges over time.

Independent contractors are similar to direct-hire temporary workers in that both types of work involve fixed-term contracts. However, independent contractors are perhaps more similar to temporary agency workers in that there is likely to be a series of clients and client organizations. Indeed, one of the legal requirements of independent contracting in most countries is that the worker is not solely dependent on a single client organization, lest this firm become a de facto employer (Fragoso & Kleiner, 2005). An additional similarity with temporary agency workers arises from the fact that independent contractors sometimes find work through an intermediary.

As noted in Figure 10.3, there are two optional structural characteristics of independent contracting that further contribute to the complexity of exchange relationships in the context of independent contracting. The first is that independent contractors may choose to use a series of contracting agencies in the task of seeking to secure clients. Under such circumstances, independent contract work more closely begins to represent the triangular relationship found in the temporary agency work form of contingent employment. As a result, the contractors' exchange focus extends beyond that of the client organization and involves the contracting agency as well as the other exchange-related issues previously discussed.

Second, an often overlooked aspect of independent contracting and related exchange relationships is the circumstance where the contractor hires workers to provide support services. In such instances, the contractor also assumes a second identity as that of an employer organization. In doing so, there is now the injection of an EOR, which even on a small operational scale fits well with the existing volume of knowledge pertaining to employment relationships. Conversely, rather than embark on an employer–employee relationship, the independent contractor may choose to build his or her own peripheral workforce through the subcontracting of support services (e.g., accounting, marketing, etc.). Such a strategy would again take the business arrangement outside of the traditional EOR.

As is the case with other contingent work arrangements, understanding the attitudes and behaviors of independent contractors requires a consideration of these workers' volition and motivations (Evans, Kunda, &

Barley, 2004; Kunda, Barley, & Evans, 2002). For some workers, the decision to work as an independent contractor may be the result of a lack of traditional employment opportunities, for example, as witnessed by the growing number of workers who have been terminated from their traditional jobs and rehired by the organization as "independent" contractors. The latter case is particularly interesting for the reason that such a transfer of status might not only be involuntary but may also represent to the worker a breach of the preexisting psychological contract. As such, the contractor–client relationship might well be one that operates in an environment of varying levels of trust or distrust.

As with the direct-hire and temporary agency workers previously discussed, it is possible that independent contractors may not work with the organization long enough for interpersonal trust to develop between the contractor and the permanent members of the organization. However, in many instances, independent contractors working at a client organization have a prior employment relationship with the firm. For example, it is not uncommon for an entire department to be "outsourced" or have their employment terminated while an offer of contract work is simultaneously offered (Ho, Ang, & Straub, 2003). Furthermore, many retirees periodically continue working on contract as a form of "bridge employment" that allows them to enjoy some of the advantages of being employed (e.g., social contact, remuneration, a feeling of meaningfulness) with added flexibility (Kim & Feldman, 2000). In these instances, the EOR is likely to be affected by the prior relationship; these independent contractors may have higher expectations for how they will be treated compared with truly independent contractors who have had no prior connection.

In some instances, organizations may become dependent on the services of a particular contractor. For example, the contractor may have expertise or social connections that are unusually rare (e.g., a retired employee who is the only remaining person alive who understands a "legacy" information technology [IT] system, a former politician who is now acting on behalf of a company as a lobbyist). In these cases, the EOR will be affected by the atypical power imbalance between the two parties; the contractor will be able to request preferential treatment over and above what would be expected by an employee.

Finally, an often overlooked component of the "independent" contracting experience that may impact the contractor–client relationship is the level of dependency that the contractor has on the client organization as a source of work. As noted by Connelly and Gallagher (2006), contractors are sometimes heavily reliant on a single client; rather than handling multiple contracts simultaneously, they hope to have their existing contract renewed indefinitely. In these cases, the EOR is again imbalanced; dependent contractors must be on their "best behavior" lest they not have their contracts renewed. It is also difficult for them to demand better treatment, given that they may have few alternative employers and given that the client may have several alternative employees.

RESEARCH IMPLICATIONS

Thus far, the focus of contingent worker research has been on how theories developed in the context of permanent employment can be used to explain contingent workers' attitudes and behaviors and to explain why these workers' experiences differ from those of employees with permanent employment contracts. Although this research is of intrinsic value (Ashford et al., 2007), it may also be fruitful to consider ways in which theories that have been developed in the context of contingent work can be applied to further understanding the experiences of more permanent employees.

One such construct is that of "volition," or the extent to which a worker has voluntarily chosen this form of employment. As noted earlier, this construct has been widely applied to contingent workers and especially to temporary agency workers. However, volition could also be helpful in explaining the attitudes and behaviors of standard or permanent workers. For example, early career entrants may accept jobs that are not in their preferred field of choice (e.g., in sales instead of product development) if they feel they have few viable alternatives and believe that the work experience would be useful. This volition, or lack thereof, may affect the worker's EOR, in a pattern similar to the experiences of contingent workers.

In a similar vein, more emphasis can be devoted to research on the impact of multiple affiliations among permanent employees. For example, a salesperson may be committed to one client, while being relatively indifferent to another one. In this case, both client relationships might affect the worker's attitudes toward the employer. Similarly, it is possible that workers who frequently change jobs (e.g., "job hoppers") may experience attitudinal spillover in that their experiences with one employer may affect their attitudes and behaviors at the next. In these instances, there is more complexity in the EOR than that which would normally be captured with standard measures or cross-sectional research designs.

Despite the recent popularity in research about contingent workers, there are several avenues for research that remain relatively unexplored. For example, given the legal and conceptual similarities between independent contracting and individuals who are self-employed, it may be useful to attempt to reconcile the contingent worker and entrepreneurship literatures. Within the entrepreneurship literature, it may also be useful to apply some of the theoretical advances from research about contingent workers. For example, we now distinguish between different types of nonstandard and contingent workers (e.g., independent contractors versus temporary agency workers); similar distinctions may be made between different types of entrepreneurs.

Although much research exists to explain how personality relates to occupational choice, little research has examined how personality affects broader employment preferences such as the decision to work contingently. One exception is Kolvereid (1996), who has suggested that personality predicts whether an individual will become an entrepreneur or seek employment in an organization. However, much of the existing research about contingent workers has either examined the influence of situational factors (e.g., difficulty finding permanent employment) or ignored the issue altogether. Research is needed to identify how personality and other individual differences affect the likelihood of pursuing contingent work, as well as the preference for one type of contingent work (e.g., independent contracting) over another (e.g., direct-hire temporary work).

One situational factor that has received relatively little attention is the potential impact of industry-wide social norms in moderating contingent workers' job insecurity (e.g., Ashford et al., 2007). For example, in some industries, contingent workers may be less likely to experience the same amount of job insecurity or anxiety because this form of employment may be relatively common, either as a "rite of passage" on the way to permanent employment or as a viable substitute for it. These industry-wide social norms may affect contingent workers' EORs if they heighten or reduce their expectations of how the employer should behave or the consequences of having a fixed-term contract end.

In many respects, one can argue that the distinctions between contingent workers and "traditional" forms of work (i.e., permanent employment) are becoming increasingly less rigid. As noted by Stamper et al. (2009), all organizational members may be viewed as having different "profiles" (i.e., peripheral, associate, detached, and full) based on the rights and responsibilities that are assigned to and assumed by the worker. As noted by Stamper et al., both permanent and contingent workers may have these profiles, depending on the specific experiences of the individual. For example, highly skilled contract workers or permanent employees may be classified as "detached" from the organization. These workers' organizational membership profiles in turn affect their needs as well as whether they believe that these needs are being fulfilled, thereby affecting discretionary and task performance. This theoretical framework is particularly relevant because it includes contingent workers within its conceptualization of organizational members and because it suggests that researchers consider the circumstances of each worker as an individual, rather than as being indistinguishable from his or her employment status. Future research can further consider how such frameworks can similarly encompass both contingent workers and permanent employees.

CULTURAL INFLUENCES

As previously noted, it is important to consider legal variations in how contingent work contracts are stipulated around the world (De Cuyper et al., 2007). In different countries, contingent work arrangements have varying levels of security, stability, and prestige. However, these legal definitions and contextual nuances are often disregarded when research findings are aggregated.

There may also be important cultural differences that will affect how contingent workers experience the EOR. As noted by Henrich, Heine, and Norenzayan (2010), the human participants in much of the world's behavioral research studies are "WEIRD," in that they live in societies that are Western, educated, industrialized, rich, and democratic. Much of the research about contingent workers has been conducted in this context, with the exception of a recent study by Ituma and Simpson (2009). These authors found that contingent workers in Nigeria have a somewhat different focus in terms of the factors they consider when deciding to accept certain jobs; they emphasize ethnic allegiances and personal connections more than Europeans, Australians, and North Americans.

National culture may also play an important role in workers' interest in accepting contingent work arrangements or in workers' preferences for certain types of contingent work. For example, workers with high levels of individualism may be more accepting of independent contracting, whereas people in more collectivist countries may prefer being permanent employees or perhaps direct-hire contingent workers. Future research, with nationally diverse participants, can elucidate these possible differences while taking into account the previously noted differences in the legal definitions of these employment arrangements (e.g., a "temporary agency worker" in Sweden is not legally equivalent to one in Canada).

PRACTICAL IMPLICATIONS

Based on the available research about contingent workers' experiences, it appears that human resources practices may affect the development of an effective EOR between the client (or employer), agency (if applicable), and worker.

At the organizational level, there may be human resource policies that affect how the EOR between the contingent workers and the organization begins; how the relationship is initiated may have long-range effects on its nature and quality. Although many firms use contingent workers specifically to avoid many of the human resources responsibilities that a workforce entails, the engagement of any worker requires some basic groundwork. For example, if the client does not have a prior working relationship with a suitable contractor or temporary worker, the client may choose to work with an intermediary. The temporary agency or contractor's association may then simply send a worker who is (a) available and (b) matches a general description submitted by the client. Alternatively, the client may interview and then select one of a subset of workers who have been nominated by the agency. At the other extreme, some clients recruit and select an appropriate worker but arrange for the payroll to be handled by the agency. The extent of the involvement of the agency and the client has likely implications for the closeness that the worker feels toward each organization.

From the worker's point of view, much more research is needed to identify how contingent workers can best manage their careers. Thus far, there is very little empirical research about how social networks can influence the recruitment and selection of contingent workers, both from the organization's perspective (i.e., finding qualified workers) and the worker's point of view (i.e., securing a steady stream of adequately remunerative and interesting contracts). Future research can specifically examine how social networking sites (e.g., Facebook, LinkedIn) can exacerbate or mitigate the challenges inherent in coordinating contracts.

There is a similar paucity of practitioner-focused research that examines how individuals who are pursuing a "boundaryless" career can effectively balance the positive and negative aspects of different forms of contingent work and permanent employment when they choose a career path. For example, what are the trade-offs involved for early-career entrants who accept a temporary position where the assigned tasks are challenging but there is no internal opportunity for advancement versus a permanent position with less challenge and more security? Advocates of boundaryless careers would suggest that "employment" security accrued through the honing of extensive social networks and up-to-date and in-demand skills will eventually be more valuable than employment offering more traditional job security (e.g., through seniority or a unionized workplace), but longitudinal research is required to see if this bears out.

A related issue that warrants further examination is how workers at various career stages can successfully transition into independent contracting. Many laid-off workers are encouraged to "become their own boss" (witness the old joke: What do you call an unemployed manager? A consultant!), but it is not clear how many are able to use the full set of their abilities and earn a similar salary to what they previously earned. It is equally important to study the process by which temporary workers transition to permanent employment.

From a practitioner standpoint, much remains to be determined in terms of "best practices" or prescriptive guidelines on how to actually manage contingent workers' EORs. An important aspect for managers to consider is the potential for the presence of contingent workers to affect the EORs of the permanent employees who work alongside them because there is some evidence that the presence of contingent workers leads to an increase in permanent employees' withdrawal behaviors (Davis-Blake, Broschak, & George, 2003; Way, Lepak, Fay, & Thacker, 2010).

Managers need to appreciate that the presence of contingent workers may mean that the job design of the permanent employees will need to be adjusted (Ang & Slaughter, 2001) and should anticipate that these employees' attitudes to the employer are likely to change as well. Permanent employees who are taking on additional tasks may feel a sense of injustice if they do not believe that they are fully compensated for these efforts. However, these added responsibilities may represent an opportunity for some permanent employees to improve the quality of their relationships with their supervisors, thereby increasing their leader–member exchange. The additional tasks may also create a more fluid sense of job responsibilities and help to foster a more relational psychological contract.

Because there has been some suggestion that contingent workers are, at times, treated unfairly (Boyce, Ryan, Imus, & Morgeson, 2007; Connelly, Gallagher, & Webster, 2011), there is a possibility that permanent employees who observe such treatment will view their employers negatively. Compared with contingent workers, permanent employees generally have more positive views of their organizations, with more relational psychological contracts (Coyle-Shapiro & Kessler, 2002) and higher levels of affective organizational commitment (Van Dyne & Ang, 1998). However, because people will take into account how well others are treated when they assess the fairness of their own treatment (e.g., Lind, Kray, & Thompson, 1998), positive EORs may be threatened if permanent employees observe that their contingent colleagues are treated unfairly.

CONCLUSION

As noted by Coyle-Shapiro et al. (2004), the EOR is fundamental to our understanding of worker attitudes and behaviors in organizations. However, it is important to recall that not all workers in organizations are employees in the traditional sense. Indeed, a growing cadre of contingent workers (i.e., direct hires, temporary agency workers, independent contractors) is changing how we conceptualize what is meant by "employment" and "organizations" and how workers relate to both. Fortunately, a deeper understanding of the complexities inherent in contingent worker EORs will help us to understand the experiences of all workers, including those of permanent employees.

ACKNOWLEDGMENT

The authors thank Karen Bennington for her assistance.

REFERENCES

Ang, S., & Slaughter, S.A. (2001). Work outcomes and job design for contract versus permanent information systems professionals on software development teams. *MIS Quarterly, 25*, 321–350.

Ashford, S. J., George, E., & Blatt, R. (2007). Chapter 2: Old assumptions, new work. *The Academy of Management Annals, 1*, 65–117.

Atkinson, J. (1984). Manpower strategies for flexible organizations. *Personnel Management, 16*, 28–31.

Barley, S. R., & Kunda, G. (2004). *Gurus, hired guns, and warm bodies: Itinerant experts in a knowledge economy*. Princeton, NJ: Princeton University Press.

Blau, P. M. (1964). *Exchange and power in social life*. New York, NY: Wiley.

Boyce, A. S., Ryan, A. M., Imus, A. L., & Morgeson, F. P. (2007). Temporary worker, permanent loser? A model of the stigmatization of temporary workers. *Journal of Management, 33*, 5–29.

Buch, R., Kuvass, B., & Dysvik, A. (2010). Dual support in contract workers' triangular employment relationships. *Journal of Vocational Behavior, 77*, 93–103.

Cappelli, P. (1999). *The new deal at work*. Boston, MA: Harvard Business School Press.

Chou, L.-F., Wang, A.-C., Wang, T.-Y., Huang, M.-H., & Cheng, B.-S. (2008). Shared work values and team member effectiveness: The mediation of trustfulness and trustworthiness. *Human Relations, 61*, 1713–1742.

Church, P. H., & Lambert, K. R. (1993). Employee or independent contractor? *Management Accounting, 74*, 52–55.

Colquitt, J. A., Scott, B. A., & LePine, J. A. (2007). Trust, trustworthiness, and trust propensity: A meta-analytic test of their unique relationships with risk taking and job performance. *Journal of Applied Psychology, 92*, 909–927.

Connelly, C. E., & Gallagher, D. G. (2004a). Emerging trends in contingent work research. *Journal of Management, 30*, 959–983.

Connelly, C. E., & Gallagher, D. G. (2004b, August). *Temporary workers, permanent consequences: Behavioral implications of triangular employment relationships*. Paper presented at the Academy of Management Meeting, New Orleans, LA.

Connelly, C. E., & Gallagher, D. G. (2006). Independent and dependent contracting: Meaning and implications. *Human Resource Management Review, 16*, 95–106.

Connelly, C. E., Gallagher, D. G., & Gilley, K. M. (2007). Organizational commitment among contracted employees: A replication and extension with temporary workers. *Journal of Vocational Behavior, 70,* 326–335.

Connelly, C. E., Gallagher, D. G., & Webster, J. (2011). Predicting temporary workers' behaviors: Justice, volition, and spillover. *Career Development International, 16,* 178–194.

Coyle-Shapiro, J. A.-M., & Conway, N. (2004). The employment relationship through the lens of social exchange. In J. A.-M. Coyle-Shapiro, L. M. Shore, M. S. Taylor, & L. E. Tetrick (Eds.), *The employment relationship: Examining psychological and contextual perspectives* (pp. 5–28). Oxford, UK: Oxford University Press.

Coyle-Shapiro, J. A.-M., & Kessler, I. (2002). Contingent and non-contingent working in local government: Contrasting psychological contracts. *Public Administration, 80,* 77–101.

Coyle-Shapiro, J. A.-M., & Morrow, P. C. (2006). Organizational and client commitment among contracted employees. *Journal of Vocational Behavior, 68,* 416–431.

Coyle-Shapiro, J. A.-M., Shore, L. M., Taylor, M. S., & Tetrick, L. E. (2004). *The employment relationship: Examining psychological and contextual perspectives.* Oxford, UK: Oxford University Press.

Cropanzano, R., & Mitchell, M. S. (2005). Social exchange theory: An interdisciplinary review. *Journal of Management, 31,* 874–900.

Davis-Blake, A., Broschak, J. P., & George, E. (2003). Happy together? How using nonstandard workers affects exit, voice, and loyalty among standard employees. *Academy of Management Journal, 46,* 475–485.

De Cuyper, N., de Jong, J., De Witte, H., Isaksson, K., Rigotti, T., & Schalk, R. (2007). Literature review of theory and research on the psychological impact of temporary employment: Towards a conceptual model. *International Journal of Management Reviews, 10,* 25–51.

De Cuyper, N., & De Witte, H. (2008). Volition and reasons for accepting temporary employment: Associations with attitudes, well-being, and behavioural intentions. *European Journal of Work and Organizational Psychology, 17,* 363–387.

De Cuyper, N., Notelaers, G., & De Witte, H. (2009). Transitioning between temporary and permanent employment: A two-wave study on the entrapment, the stepping stone and the selection hypothesis. *Journal of Occupational and Organizational Psychology, 82,* 67–88.

Doeringer, P. B., & Piore, M. J. (1971). *Internal labor markets and manpower analysis.* Lexington, MA: D. C. Heath & Company.

Eisenhardt, K. M. (1989). Agency theory: An assessment and review. *Academy of Management Review, 14,* 57–74.

Ellingson, J. E., Gruys, M. L., & Sackett, P. R. (1998). Factors related to the satisfaction and performance of temporary employees. *Journal of Applied Psychology, 83,* 913–921.

Evans, J. A., Kunda, G., & Barley, S. R. (2004). Beach time, bridge time, and billable hours: The temporal structure of technical contracting. *Administrative Science Quarterly, 49,* 1–38.

Fragoso, J. L., & Kleiner, B. H. (2005). How to distinguish between independent contractors and employees. *Management Research News, 28,* 136–149.

Gallagher, D. G., & Connelly, C. E. (2008). Nonstandard work arrangements: Meaning, evidence, and theoretical perspectives. In J. Barling & C. L. Cooper (Eds.), *Handbook of organizational behavior* (pp. 621–640). Los Angeles, CA: Sage.

Gallagher, D. G., & McLean Parks, J. (2001). I pledge thee my troth… contingently: Commitment and the contingent work relationship. *Human Resource Management Review, 11*, 181–208.

Gallagher, D. G., & Sverke, M. (2005). Contingent employment contracts: Are existing employment theories still relevant? *Journal of Economic and Industrial Democracy, 26*, 181–203.

George, E., & Chattopadhyay, P. (2005). One foot in each camp: The dual identification of contract workers. *Administrative Science Quarterly, 50*, 68–99.

Gordon, M. E., Philpot, J. W., Burt, R. E., Thompson, C. A., & Spiller, W. E. (1980). Commitment to the union: Development of a measure and an examination of its correlates. *Journal of Applied Psychology, 65*, 479–499.

Handy, C. (1989). *The age of unreason*. Cambridge, MA: Harvard Business School Press.

Henrich, J., Heine, S. J., & Norenzayan, A. (2010). The weirdest people in the world? *Behavioral and Brain Sciences, 33*, 61–83.

Ho, V. T., Ang, S., & Straub, D. (2003). When subordinates become IT contractors: Persistent managerial expectations in IT outsourcing. *Information Systems Research, 14*, 66–86.

Homans, G. C. (1958). Social behavior as exchange. *American Journal of Sociology, 63*, 597–600.

Ituma, A., & Simpson, R. (2009). The boundaryless career and career boundaries: Applying an institutionalist perspective to ICT workers in the context of Nigeria. *Human Relations, 62*, 727–762.

Kalleberg, A. L. (2000). Nonstandard employment relations: Part-time, temporary and contract work. *Annual Review of Sociology, 26*, 341–365.

Kasper-Fuehrera, E. C., & Ashkanasy, N. M. (2001). Communicating trustworthiness and building trust in interorganizational virtual organizations. *Journal of Management, 23*, 235–254.

Kim, S., & Feldman, D. C. (2000). Working in retirement: The antecedents of bridge employment and its consequences for quality of life in retirement. *Academy of Management Journal, 6*, 1195–1210.

Kolvereid, L. (1996). Organizational employment versus self-employment: Reasons for career choice intentions. *Entrepreneurship Theory and Practice*, Spring, 23–31.

Kunda, G., Barley, S. R., & Evans, J. (2002). Why do contractors contract? The experience of highly skilled technical professionals in a contingent labor market. *Industrial and Labor Relations Review, 55*, 234–261.

Liden, R. C., Wayne, S. J., Kraimer, M. L., & Sparrowe, R. T. (2003). The dual commitments of contingent workers: An examination of contingents' commitment to the agency and the organization. *Journal of Organizational Behavior, 24*, 609–625.

Lind, E. A., Kray, L., & Thomson, L. (1998). The social construction of injustice: Fairness judgments in response to own and others' unfair treatment by authorities. *Organizational Behavior and Human Decision Processes, 75*, 1–22.

March, J. G., & Simon, H. (1958). *Organizations*. New York, NY: Wiley.

Mayer, R. C., Davis, J. H., & Schoorman, F. D. (1995). An integrative model of organizational trust. *Academy of Management Review, 20*, 709–734.

McLean Parks, J., Kidder, D. L., & Gallagher, D. G. (1998). Fitting square pegs into round holes: Mapping the domain of contingent work arrangements onto the psychological contract. *Journal of Organizational Behavior, 19*, 697–730.

Meyerson, D. E., Weick, K. E., & Kramer, R. M. (1996). Swift trust in temporary groups. In R. M. Kramer & T. R. Tyler (Eds.), *Trust in organizations* (pp. 166–195). Thousand Oaks, CA: Sage Publications.

Moorman, R. H., & Harland, L. K. (2002). Temporary employees as good citizens: Factors influencing their OCB performance. *Journal of Business and Psychology, 17*, 171–187.

Pearce, J. L. (1993). Toward an organizational behavior of contract laborers: Their psychological involvement and effects on employee co-workers. *Academy of Management Journal, 36*, 1082–1096.

Pfeffer, J., & Baron, N. (1988). Taking the workers back out: Recent trends in the structures of employment. *Research in Organizational Behavior, 10*, 257–303.

Rousseau, D. M. (1997). Organizational behavior in the new organizational era. *Annual Review Psychology, 48*, 515–546.

Rousseau, D. M., Sitkin, S. B., Burt, R. S., & Camerer, C. (1998). Not so different after all: A cross-discipline view of trust. *Academy of Management Review, 23*, 393–404.

Shore, L. M., & Tetrick, L. E. (1991). A construct validity study of the survey of perceived organizational support. *Journal of Applied Psychology, 76*, 637–643.

Shore, L. M., Tetrick, L. E, Sinclair, R. R., & Newton, L. A. (1994). Validation of a measure of perceived union support. *Journal of Applied Psychology, 79*, 971–977.

Stamper, C. L., Masterson, S. S., & Knapp, J. (2009). A typology of organizational membership: Understanding different membership relationships through the lens of social exchange. *Management and Organization Review, 5*, 303–328.

Standing, G. (2009). Work and occupation in a tertiary society. *Labour and Industry, 19*, 49–72.

Tajfel, H., & Turner, J. (1986). The social identity theory of intergroup behavior. In S. Worchel & W. G. Austin (Eds.), *Psychology of intergroup relations* (pp. 7–24). Chicago, IL: Nelson-Hall.

Tomlinson, E. C., & Mayer, R. C. (2009). The role of causal attribution dimensions in trust repair. *Academy of Management Review, 34*, 85–104.

Van Dyne, L., & Ang, S. (1998). Organizational citizenship behavior of contingent workers in Singapore. *Academy of Management Journal, 41*, 692–703.

Way, S. A., Lepak, D. P., Fay, C. H., & Thacker, J. W. (2010). Contingent workers' impact on standard employee withdrawal behaviors: Does what you use them for matter? *Human Resource Management, 49*, 109–138

Wears, K. H., & Fisher, S. L. (2010, August). *Who is an employer in the triangular employment relationship? Sorting through the definitional confusion.* Paper presented at Academy of Management Meeting in Montreal, Quebec, Canada.

11

Virtual Employee–Organization Relationships: Linking in to the Challenge of Increasingly Virtual EOR

Kathryn M. Bartol and Yuntao Dong
University of Maryland, College Park

Organizations are increasingly using information technology (IT) and digital connections in ways that enable virtual work. Whereas early use of IT by organizations tended to automate routine and labor-intensive processes, the increasing sophistication of software and multiplying memory capacities have allowed the broader availability of information and, in the process, have facilitated possibilities for working virtually. As Zammuto, Griffith, Majchrzak, Dougherty, and Faraj (2007, p. 752) have noted, "IT has become inextricably intertwined with social relations to weave the fabric of organization." For purposes of this chapter, virtual work refers to job activities that are conducted to a substantial degree through computer-mediated means, rather than face to face, often in geographically distributed and time differentiated mode. The increasing integration of computers and communication technology (such as high-quality videoconferencing, online discussion threads, and wireless Internet solutions and products) is continually enabling further growth of the virtual workforce. For example, according to the U.S. Census Bureau (2002), virtual work accounted for more than 15% of the U.S. workforce and was estimated to be growing nearly 30% per year not only in the United States, but globally (Golden & Raghuram, 2010; Ruiz & Walling, 2005; WorldatWork, 2007). A more recent survey of more than 1,000 U.S. adults estimated that the number of Americans involved in virtual work increased from approximately 12.4 million in 2006 to 17.2 million in 2008 (WorldatWork, 2009).

Despite the burgeoning utilization of virtual work and the associated transformation it may portend in terms of the ways in which employees

281

might be connected to their organization (e.g., Golden, 2006), relatively little attention has been paid to the implications for the employee–organization relationship (EOR). EOR is considered to be "an overarching term to describe the relationship between the employee and the organization" (Shore et al., 2004, p. 292). Given the prospects for a distributed workforce and ample evidence regarding the challenges of computer-mediated communication, there are reasons to investigate more closely how the growing virtuality of work might influence EORs. Fewer face-to-face interactions between virtual employees and other organizational members and less exposure to specific features of organizational life (e.g., organizational artifacts, symbols, and ceremonies) threaten to weaken the bonds virtual employees have with their organization (e.g., Golden, 2006; Nardi & Whittaker, 2002). At the same time, Bartol and Liu (2002) raised the possibility that the growing use of digital media might actually present new opportunities for the human resource (HR) function to interface with employees, thereby potentially strengthening the EOR. More specifically, virtual HR systems provide new means to articulate and deliver activities consistent with a mutual investment EOR. Accordingly, the purpose of this chapter is to conceptualize a multilevel EOR virtuality framework (Figure 11.1) that combines EOR, virtual HR, and virtual work literatures, support theories, and notions of psychological connectivity. Such a framework points the way to future research on how organizations might effectively use the growing number of options for virtual work, while also building strong EORs.

The first section of this chapter assesses HR and virtuality architecture of relevance to the issue of EORs and virtual work. The second section addresses an important translating mechanism and two critical psychological states, as well as moderators of these elements. The third section outlines anticipated outcomes of these processes. The final section discusses the theoretical and practical implications of the multilevel EOR virtuality framework, as well as directions for future research, including cultural influences.

HUMAN RESOURCE AND VIRTUALITY ARCHITECTURE

In this section, we focus on three major aspects of HR and virtuality architecture—EOR mutual investment, the virtuality of HR, and the virtuality of jobs.

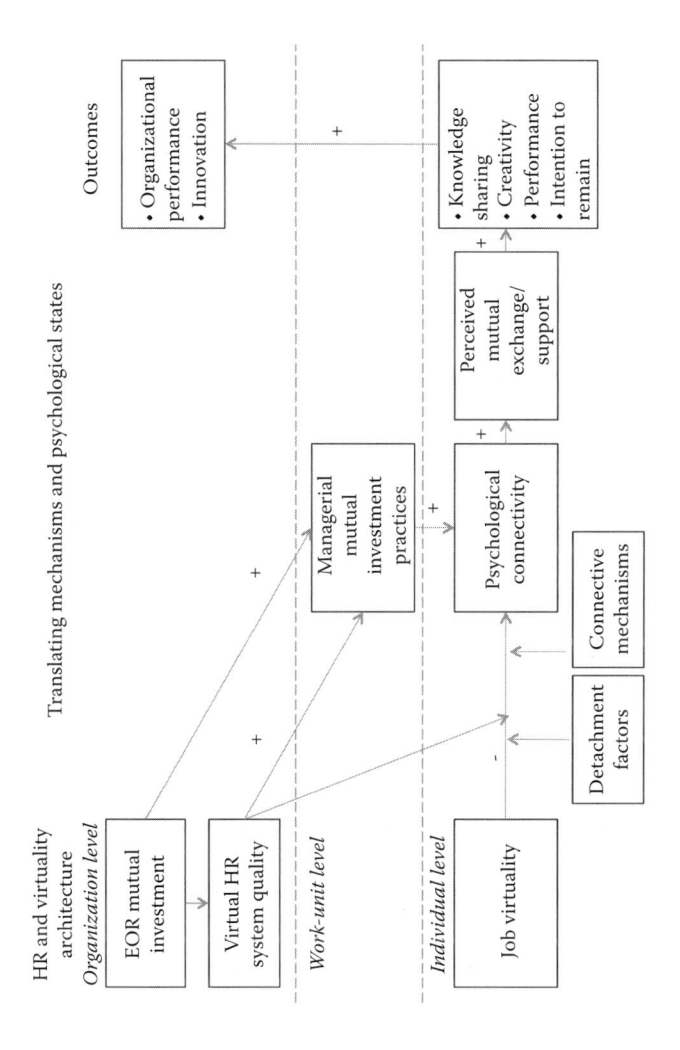

Virtual Employee–Organization Relationships • 283

FIGURE 11.1
The EOR virtuality framework.

EOR Mutual Investment

Tsui, Pearce, Porter, and Tripoli (1997) have created a typology of EORs that includes two balanced and two unbalanced possibilities. Here we consider the balanced mutual investment relationship due to evidence that this approach is most commensurate with the types of outcomes of interest here (Bartol, Liu, Zeng, & Wu, 2009; Tsui & Wu, 2005). According to Tsui et al. (1997), a mutual investment relationship is one that is somewhat open ended and long term, with investments from both the employee and employer. This mutual investment concept builds on the social exchange notions of Blau (1964), which differentiate social exchanges from economic ones because the former type of exchange is characterized by achieving some balance, but over an extended period. With mutual investment, the organization is expected to invest in the career development of employees and generally consider their well-being. In turn, employees are expected to care about the survival and success of the organization, which may entail acquiring skills that are perhaps uniquely relevant to the firm and making other accommodations, such as helping beyond one's job description when it would advance the welfare of the organization (Tsui et al., 1997). The EOR mutual investment approach is consistent with the developing human capital architecture theorized by Lepak and Snell (1999, 2002), in which a commitment-based HR system is often adopted to nurture employee involvement and maximize the firm's return on human capital investments. Amit and Zott (2001) have argued that one critical components of business models in the virtual world is the architectural configuration that specifies linkages among transactions. In a similar manner, it is possible to consider virtuality architecture with respect to virtual influences on relational linkages between employees and the organization. Specifically, we expect that a mutual investment EOR impacts the EOR linkage by positively influencing the quality of its HR systems, including online electronic ones, as well as enabling managerial mutual investment practices. Accordingly, in the next section, we consider the nature of the online electronic HR system (often referred to as "virtual HR"), and we consider managerial mutual investment practices in a later section.

Virtual HR System Quality

Advances in IT have enabled the transformation of work in what some have called the electronic age or digital age (Gephart, 2002). As Zuboff

(1988) has suggested, IT in organizations has tended to go through three stages. The first is automation, in which IT is harnessed mainly to streamline routine processes in pursuit of efficiency. In the next stage, IT "informates" by allowing for the greater distribution of information to various parts of the organization so that work can be coordinated more effectively. In the third stage, the transformational stage, IT is used to redefine processes and practices, opening up prospects for creativity in utilizing knowledge, information, and systems on behalf of competitive advantage. In this latter stage, computer-mediated connections are enabling consideration of the virtuality architecture underlying the various connections among organizational members and functions as well.

Such developments can particularly influence HR systems and practices in organizations. Lai (2001) has argued that HR management is in one of the strongest positions to take advantage of IT to benefit the organization. Along these lines, LeTart (1998) referred to self-service as the "holy grail" of IT use by HR management largely because of the inherent efficiencies to be derived. Bartol and Liu (2002) further noted that the greater connectivity enabled by IT, particularly in the latter stage of IT development, raises new possibilities for the HR management function. A major reason is that the emerging virtuality architecture of many organizations allows the development of virtual HR systems. Such systems combine software, hardware, and systematic procedures to acquire, store, manipulate, analyze, retrieve, and distribute an organization's HR information (Lippert & Swiercz, 2005; Tannenbaum, 1990), as well as to provide organizational members with online real-time HR services based on the electronic database (Brockbank & Yeung, 1995). Often such systems are part of enterprise-wide systems aimed at integrating vast amounts of information across all functions in order to allow maximum rationalization of various activities. In other cases, systems are somewhat stand-alone systems integrated with other technology via organizational intranets, the Internet, or other means. The key factor, however, is the real-time online availability of HR services to managers and employees. To be effective, virtual HR systems must have a reasonable level of quality. Research on online retail marketing coupled with related research on HR systems suggests that value derived from content and functionality is likely to be important in conveying system quality (e.g., Dodds, Monroe, & Grewal, 1991; Parasuraman, Zeithaml, & Malhotra, 2005;

Sirdeshmukh, Singh, & Sabol, 2002). Hence, we define virtual HR system quality as the degree of content value and convenience provided to employee users.

The quality of an organization's virtual HR system can be influenced by the EOR stance taken by the organization. In particular, we argue that EOR mutual investment, with its emphasis on long-term investments to employees, is likely to manifest itself in the form of strong investments in effective virtual HR systems (e.g., Hom et al., 2009; Tsui & Wu, 2005). This is because such systems can enhance the delivery of organizational inducements (e.g., training resources distribution and real-time HR services provision) as well as help communicate expectations of expanded employee contributions (e.g., self-acquisition of new skills for adapting to changes in the work). Therefore, EOR mutual investment in the digital age will have increased capability and capacity to more effectively institute and maintain direct, ongoing connectivity with employees, through high-quality virtual HR systems. Consistent with this view, Lepak, Bartol, and Erhardt (2005) have pointed out that advanced informational technology, including its application such as the high-quality virtual HR systems, provides potential opportunities for HR management to enhance the EOR relationship and the delivery of HR practices.

Job Virtuality

Another important virtual architecture feature relevant to our EOR framework is job virtuality. For purposes here, job virtuality is considered to be the carrying out of job activities, including access to information and coordination with others, primarily via computer-mediated means, rather than face to face. Normally, job virtuality entails some degree of geographical distribution and asynchronous communication (Kirkman & Mathieu, 2005).

Strides in IT have enabled burgeoning methods of computer-mediated connectivity to the point that the relational nature of the workplace is being reconfigured or can potentially be configured. For example, possibilities for computer-mediated connectivity have enabled distributed work in which employees and their tasks can be designed to be shared across venues that are physically, and perhaps also temporally, separated from central business or work locations

(Gajendran & Harrison, 2007). Telecommuting or telework, in which individuals complete all or part of their work away from a traditional work setting, is the most well-known form of distributed work. Other variations, such as virtual teams, are growing in importance also (Bell & Kozlowski, 2002). Various technical means, such as the Internet, intranets, and extranets, along with the growing pervasiveness of Blackberries, iPhones, and iPads, are facilitating the trend toward more virtual work arrangements. Although such technologies have allowed jobs to take on increasing elements of virtuality, there are reasons to be concerned about the implications for EORs inherent in the growing virtuality of work.

One reason for concern is that virtual work's inherent physical separation from others and increased reliance upon technology to interact may result in an employee's perception of isolation (Diekema, 1992; Golden, 2006; Golden, Veiga, & Dino, 2008). More specifically, researchers (e.g., Cooper & Kurland, 2002; Tomaskovic-Devey & Risman, 1993) have indicated that such isolation can manifest itself professionally (e.g., employee's fear of limited promotion and reward opportunities) or socially (e.g., reduced opportunities for informal interactions with colleagues and reduced psychological attachment to the organization).

Another reason for concern about the potential implications for EOR associated with virtual work is evidence regarding challenges with computer-mediated communication (Axtell, Fleck, & Turner, 2004; Martins, Gilson, & Maynard, 2004). For instance, Byron (2008) has pointed out that because emotional content is difficult to transmit accurately in e-mails, e-mail communication may result in a series of negative employee reactions, including lower feelings of connectedness and increased anxiety and insecurity about performance. Although elements such as the use of emoticons to denote specific emotions (such as "smiley faces"), asterisks for emphasis, and capital letters for intensity can provide some nonverbal cues, their use tends to be infrequent, and they can be subject to variable interpretations. Researchers (e.g., Bell & Kozlowski, 2002) also point to challenges associated with establishing common ground or mutual knowledge among distributed workers because of such factors as differences in work context, uneven distributions of information, and difficulties in transmitting and understanding the salience of information.

TRANSLATING MECHANISMS AND PSYCHOLOGICAL STATES

The HR and virtual architecture elements in our framework can influence translation mechanisms and psychological states of particular interest to EOR. In this section, we posit that, at the organizational level, HR architecture in the form of EOR mutual investment and virtual architecture in the form of virtual HR system quality can be expected to impact a major translation mechanism at the work unit level, namely managerial mutual investment practices. This translation mechanism at the work unit level in turn influences psychological connectivity at the individual level. At the individual level, job virtuality is also posited to influence psychological connectivity, which, in turn, can be expected to impact perceived mutual exchange and support. In this section, we consider the nature of these connections, as well as relevant moderating elements.

Managerial Mutual Investment Practices

Because job virtuality entails carrying out one's job duties primarily via computer-mediated means, the manager is likely to play a particularly important role in translating the EOR mutual investment stance of the organization to the employee. As Rousseau and Greller (1994) have suggested, how an organization actually manages its human resources establishes the tone and conditions of the EOR. Moreover, the availability of a high-quality virtual HR system is likely to make the job of the manager easier both because of his or her own access to important HR information, practices, and activities and because of the enhanced access by the virtual worker to HR resources (Bartol & Liu, 2002).

Tsui and Wu (2005) note four areas of HR practices that are particularly important in implementing a mutual investment EOR. With high job virtuality, the manager would be a logical and important mechanism for the delivery of these practices. For example, with the first HR practice area, recruitment and selection, the manager will be an important conduit for emphasizing the long-term loyalty and commitment of the employee, while also conveying to prospective and new employees operating virtually that the organization also expects the loyalty and commitment of employees in return. Second, managers are in a unique position to guide the training and development of virtual workers because they are likely to have the best vantage point for assessing virtual worker training needs and also conveying to the employee the development orientation consistent with a mutual investment EOR. Third, because performance criteria and evaluation with a mutual investment context involves assessing not only individual performance but also broad contributions to the organization, the manager may often be in the only position to determine the bases for such an evaluation and who else should have input. This is because virtual workers are likely to have more limited interactions with organizational members other than their managers due to their job virtuality. Finally, the delivery of compensation and benefits in a mutual investment EOR involves not just meeting economic concerns, but also conveying needed contributions and emphasizing a long-term relationship. It is likely that the provision of job virtuality in many cases may already be reflecting a work arrangement sanctioned by the manager that facilitate employee needs, such as working from home, retaining a job while changing geographical locations, or facilitating development through involvement in virtual teams.

Although managerial mutual investment practices constitute an important EOR translation mechanism at the work unit level, two psychological states are important at the individual level to capture the influence of managerial mutual investment practices and also the direct and indirect impacts of job virtuality. The first is psychological connectivity, which in turn is expected to influence the second state, perceived mutual exchange and support. We first present our conceptualization of psychological connectivity and then consider three categories of moderating factors that can influence the relationship between job virtuality and psychological connectivity. We then turn to the issue of perceived mutual exchange and support.

Psychological Connectivity

Although virtuality has opened up many new possibilities for job configurations, it also brings prospects for negatively influencing, and even substantially undermining, what we conceptualize as employee psychological connectivity with the organization. Psychological connectivity refers to an individual's perception of the adequacy of social ties to the organization. Drawing on social capital theory (Nahapiet & Ghoshal, 1998), we theorize that psychological connectivity encompasses three dimensions, or social network relationships: (1) The structural dimension, addresses the perceived adequacy of ties, or network connections, in terms of basic work flow necessary to function in the job; (2) The relational dimension, refers to perceptions of the sufficiency of ties from which to draw emotional support; and (3) The cognitive dimension, refers to perception of the adequacy of ties from which to draw informational support. Considerable conceptual and empirical research points to the need for individuals in organizations to be in the relevant workflow and have access to relational and advice ties that are capable of providing emotional and informational support (e.g., Farh, Bartol, Shapiro, & Shin, 2010; Morrison, 2002). Yet, due to the communication challenges and prospects for isolation associated with job virtuality discussed earlier, we argue that the extent of job virtuality negatively affects psychological connectivity. The extent of the negative impact is likely to be assuaged by the degree of mutual investment practices carried out by the manager, as noted earlier. However, the potential negative impact of job virtuality is also likely to be acerbated or mitigated by the presence or absence of several moderating circumstances which we delineate next.

Moderating Elements Influencing the Job Virtuality–Psychological Connectivity Relationship

In considering moderators of the relationship between job virtuality and psychological connectivity, we consider three categories of contingency variables. First, we review a set of individual-level moderators that are detachment factors, in that they strengthen the negative impact of job virtuality on psychological connectivity. We next consider a set of connective mechanisms that have the capacity to weaken the negative influence of job virtuality on psychological connectivity. Finally, we focus on how virtual HR system quality can serve as a cross-level moderator.

Detachment Factors

Drawing on the theoretical framework proposed by Bell and Kozlowski (2002) and other research on virtual teams and virtual work (e.g., Gejedran & Harrison, 2007; Golden et al., 2008), we identify a set of contextual factors that may accentuate the disconnectivity, remoteness, and isolation associated with job virtuality. The first detachment element is spatial distribution, which involves working across significant boundaries of space. Extensive geographical distribution makes periodic face-to-face meetings more difficult, which may interfere with developing effective collaborative relationships (Hill, Bartol, Tesluk, & Langa, 2009) and thereby impede psychological connectivity.

Second, large spatial distances often implicate working across boundaries of time (Bell & Kozlowski, 2002). The separation in time zones, as well as the use of some forms of asynchronous communication technology, such as e-mail, will result in delays in information exchange and reactivity in communication between virtual employees and various organization members. Therefore, greater temporal distribution may stimulate a feeling that one lacks the control to actively exchange information and ideas with others in the organization, thus leading to the reduction in psychological connectivity.

Third, related to spatial and temporal distribution, any restrictions in the access to complex and interactive communication technologies are likely to further decrease virtual employees' psychological connectivity (e.g., Gejedran & Harrison, 2007; Maruping & Agarwal, 2004). This is because complex communication technologies, especially those supporting synchronous interactions, maintain the information richness and facilitate reciprocal communication and collaborative decision making (Farmer & Hyatt, 1994; Hollingshead, McGrath, & O'Connor, 1993). Thus, when virtual employees are constrained in accessing these sophisticated communication technologies, they are less likely to actively engage in information sharing and collaboration with other organizational members, and thus are more likely to feel isolated.

Finally, team diversity, particularly in function and culture, has the capacity to accentuate the issue of the lack of psychological connectivity associated with virtual work. One major goal for forming virtual teams is to bring together experts from different functional areas, organizations, and/or cultures (Kirkman, Rosen, Tesluk, & Gibson, 2004). However, the diverse functional and cultural background may make it more difficult for team members to establish shared understanding and emotional attachment (Bell & Kozlowski, 2002). Moreover, such diversity in a virtual environment can also slow the development of trust necessary for knowledge sharing and collaborative efforts (cf. Hill et al., 2009). Consequently, without ample face-to-face interactions and work experience that facilitate shared values and a common set of work procedures, virtual team members are less likely to perceive a psychological connection to others and to the organization.

Connective Mechanisms

Although some contextual factors may constitute challenges to virtual employees' connectivity to their organization, there are other mechanisms (i.e., leadership, coworker relationships, and individual characteristics) that may heighten the positive aspect of virtual work and thereby aid prospects for psychological connectivity. Below we give examples in each category to highlight the role of these connective mechanisms.

First of all, effective leadership can help organizations reap greater benefits from a virtual working environment (Bell & Kozlowski, 2002). Empowering leadership is particularly relevant in the virtual context because it allows the autonomy consistent with virtual work and simultaneously provides the coaching that helps virtual employees cope with difficulties associated with job virtuality. Following previous research (Ahearne, Mathieu, & Rapp, 2005; Kirkman & Rosen, 1999; Zhang & Bartol, 2010), we define empowering leadership as "the process of implementing conditions that enable sharing power with an employee by delineating the significance of the employee's job, providing greater decision-making autonomy, expressing confidence in the employee's capabilities, and removing hindrances to performance" (Zhang & Bartol, 2010, p. 109). Specifically, an empowering leader provides employees with autonomy in regard to how to carry out one's own job (Pearce et al., 2003; Sims & Manz, 1996) while also expressing confidence in employees' competence for high performance (Ahearne et al., 2005). In doing so, the leader not only demonstrates that the organization encourages virtual work but also conveys to employees that they can achieve success in the areas that are recognized and valued by the organization. Therefore, understanding the importance of their contributions to overall organizational effectiveness, virtual employees are less likely to feel isolated.

Second, task interdependence may provide a mechanism that aids employee connectivity in the context of virtual work (e.g., Bell & Kozlowski, 2002; Golden et al., 2008). According to Van de Ven, Delbecq, and Koenig's (1976) typology of interdependence arrangements in teams, high-interdependence tasks require greater levels of synchronous collaboration and information sharing among team members, whereas low-interdependence tasks are static and loosely coupled to the external context and require minimal collaboration with others (Kozlowski, Gully, Nason, & Smith, 1999). As a result, when a virtual employee's tasks require interdependence with others' work, he or she may engage in more frequent formal interpersonal interactions than would be the case generally under conditions of virtual work (e.g., Kirkman et al., 2004). The increased interpersonal interactions, in turn, provide a means to establishing greater psychological connectivity with the organization (Raghuram, Garud, Wiesenfeld, & Gupta, 2001).

Lastly, an individual's characteristics may also positively influence an employee's perceived connectivity to the organization when working virtually. For example, Staples, Hulland, and Higgins (1999) proposed a self-efficacy–based theory for managing remote/virtual employees, in which remote work self-efficacy was defined as employees' "self-efficacy judgments about their abilities to complete relevant remote work tasks" (p. 759). Because one major challenge to virtual employees is that many times they must rely on their own abilities to carry out and complete various tasks, rather than ask for instant help from their leader or coworkers, those with high remote work self-efficacy will be better able to cope with the task-related challenges caused by remote and asynchronous communication (cf. Bandura, 1982; Saks, 1995). As a result, employees with high remote work self-efficacy may tend to feel less isolated and disconnected as a result of the reduction in supervision and in the availability of coworker interaction, may better enjoy the autonomy of the virtual work, and may feel more psychologically connected than counterparts with low remote work self-efficacy.

Cross-Level Impact of Virtual HR

Fewer face-to-face interactions between virtual employees and other organization members and less exposure to specific features of organizational life (such as ceremonies and other manifestations of organizational culture) tend to weaken the bonds virtual employees have with their organization (e.g., Golden, 2006; Nardi & Whittaker, 2002). However, virtual HR systems provide new opportunities to influence organizational interfaces with employees and can reflect an organization's stance toward its employees (e.g., Ferris et al., 1998). Consequently, an organization's high-quality virtual HR system may serve as an important contextual cue suggesting that an individual belongs to the organization and the organization cares about its employees even when they are working out of the office. In this way, a virtual HR system, especially one with high quality, may trigger and reinforce virtual employees' psychological connectivity with the organization (e.g., Gajendran & Harrison, 2007).

Specifically, a high-quality virtual HR system is usually characterized as providing useful HR information and real-time services via a well-functioning HR website, providing employees with the autonomy and convenience to access organizational resources, as well as self-sufficiency in HR-related services (Brockbank & Yeung, 1995; Snell, Pedigo, & Krawiec, 1995). As a result, virtual employees who receive HR information and services from such a system are more likely to perceive that they are central, included, valued, and respected within the organization, which will lead them to view their organizational involvement as self-enhancing and attractive (Luhtanen & Crocker, 1992). Moreover, these aspects are likely to be perceived as discretionary on the part of the organization, thus strengthening their impact (Eisenberger, Huntington, Hutchinson, & Sowa, 1986). Therefore, virtual HR systems may help to attenuate the negative impact of virtual work on psychological connectivity to the organization. In the absence of frequent, traditional contact with other organizational members, a high-quality virtual HR system could provide employees with a more flexible and convenient connection with the organization. In contrast, a low-quality virtual HR system will not help lessen employees' isolation perceptions associated with virtual work and may accentuate them. The impact on psychological connectivity is important because such connectivity is likely to have a positive influence on perceived mutual exchange and support.

Perceived Mutual Exchange and Support

Perceived organization support involves employee global perceptions with respect to the extent to which the organization values their contributions and cares about their well-being (Eisenberger et al., 1986; Shore & Shore, 1995). Within our framework, an individual's perceived mutual exchange and support is directly influenced by the extent of their felt psychological connectivity. Due to the nature of the ties inherent in psychological connectivity, the presence of the three types of connections is likely to be associated with perceived organizational support because their presence signals the availability of task, informational, and emotional resources. Considerable research has demonstrated the importance of these types of resources in eliciting perceptions of support (e.g., Bartol et al., 2009; Farh et al., 2010). Part of the logic behind the importance of exchange and perceived organizational support is that employees will tend to reciprocate when they believe the organization is providing needed resources and support (Rhoades & Eisenberger, 2002). Hence, the nature of the exchange is critical to achieving needed outcomes at two levels, individual and organization.

OUTCOMES

Individual-Level Outcomes

Employees' perceived mutual exchange or organizational support resulting from individual psychological connectivity will influence an array of important individual outcomes. First, for survival, many organizations need outcomes from employees that can be difficult to measure and are somewhat discretionary. One such outcome is knowledge sharing, which is considered to be "individuals sharing organizationally relevant information, ideas, suggestions, and expertise with one another" (Bartol & Srivastava, 2002, p. 65). Knowledge sharing is an important discretionary behavior that might be explained by employees' perception of mutual exchange (e.g., Chen, Eisenberger, Johnson, Sucharski, & Aselage, 2009). As employees reciprocate the organizational investment by showing care for the organization's welfare, they are more likely to offer constructive suggestions to and share critical information with other organizational members to help them better complete their tasks, which will eventually benefit the organization (Rhoades & Eisenberger, 2002).

Second, although empirical evidence of mutual investment and employee creativity has been relatively sparse, there are reasons to believe that mutual investment via psychological connectivity and perceived organizational support will enhance employee creativity. Specifically, an organization that reinforces a mutual investment EOR may provide innovation-related resources, including professional training, diversified task assignments, and developmental feedback (e.g., Madjar, Oldham, & Pratt, 2002; Scott & Bruce, 1994), which enable an employee to rethink work problems from new perspectives and thus to generate novel solutions and ideas. Furthermore, organizational support makes employees feel obligated to reciprocate and to be innovative in return for the resources provided by the organization (Rhoades & Eisenberger, 2002).

Moreover, according to social exchange theory and norms of reciprocity (Blau, 1964; Gouldner, 1960), when an employee perceives psychological connectivity and that the organization sufficiently invests in his or her development, the employee is motivated to reciprocate with correspondingly larger performance contributions (Coyle-Shapiro, Shore, Taylor, & Tetrick, 2004; Eisenberger et al., 1986). In addition, mutual exchange relationships increase employees' performance–reward expectancies, thus motivating them to make greater efforts to achieve task-related goals. Consistently, Rhoades and Eisenberger (2002) found in their meta-analysis that perceived organizational support showed homogeneous relationships with all types of performance (e.g., in-role and extra-role performance).

Finally, perceived mutual exchange will be related to employees' intention to remain, for both institutional and affective reasons (e.g., Maertz, Griffeth, Campbell, & Allen, 2007). On the one hand, as employees receive valuable investments (e.g., developmental opportunities, materialistic rewards, ample resources) from the organization, they feel obligated to remain in the organization to "avoid the psychological discomfort and social stigma of not living up to their end of the bargain as well as to maintain the inflow of resources" (Hom et al., 2009, p. 280). On the other hand, employees' perceived support from the organization can induce a strong emotional attachment to the organization and thus lead them to stay to reciprocate organizational kindness and generosity (Eisenberger et al., 1986).

Organizational-Level Outcomes

Increases in individual-level knowledge-sharing behavior, creativity, performance, and intention to remain will all eventually contribute to the organizational effectiveness and competitiveness. For instance, Collin and Smith (2006) found that knowledge exchange and combination by knowledge workers were positively related to organizational performance measured with revenues and sales growth. Additionally, by definition, creative ideas provided by individual employees may help improve the organizational processes and procedures, as well as the organization's products and/or service quality, thus enabling the organization to outperform its competitors (Amabile, 1988; Madjar et al., 2002; Shalley, Gilson, & Blum, 2000). Lastly, having a high turnover rate, especially voluntary turnover, results in the loss of specific human capital and is detrimental to organizational performance (Cascio, 1998). High turnover leads to reductions in productivity because the organization may lose particularly productive workers and new hires cannot work effectively until they are trained and have adjusted to the new environment. In addition, turnover also reduces tacit knowledge of, for example, service values and norms, the transmission of which to new employees is disrupted (Morrow & McElroy, 2007). The reduction in tacit knowledge, in turn, influences organizational functioning and performance.

Employees' knowledge-sharing behavior and creativity also contribute to an organization's ability to be innovative because individuals are fundamental sources of information that are necessary for an organization to create new knowledge and any original ideas are ultimately offered by individuals. Consistently, as Collins and Smith (2006, p. 547) have stated, "the ability to create new knowledge, which enables firms both to innovate and to outperform their rivals in dynamic environments (Grant, 1996; Kogut & Zander, 1992), results from the collective ability of employees to exchange and combine knowledge (Nahapiet & Ghoshal, 1998)." In addition, there is considerable evidence indicating that employee creativity can fundamentally contribute to organizational innovation and effectiveness (e.g., Amabile, 1996; Shalley, Zhou, & Oldman, 2004).

DISCUSSION

In this chapter, we proposed a multilevel EOR virtuality model explicating how an organization's EOR mutual investment and virtual HR system may function through the translation mechanism of managerial investment practices and jointly with individual job virtuality to influence employee psychological connectivity, which, in turn, impacts perceptions of mutual exchange and support and ultimately important individual-level and organizational-level outcomes. This theoretical framework sets the stage for future research to better understand the influence of virtual practices in organizations and the relevance of the EOR in maximizing the positive impact of virtual work options while minimizing the negative impact.

Although we focused on the mutual investment EOR, other forms of EOR may also have important implications in the virtual work environment. For example, underinvestment of EOR surfaces when organizations furnish few inducements but demand sizeable workforce contributions (Tsui et al., 1997). Researchers (e.g., Sahlins, 1972; Wu et al., 2006) have pointed out that, because underinvestment EOR eschews investment in employees' careers but requires large inputs from them, these exploitative terms tend to impel employees to view this relationship as a temporary arrangement. Hence this type of EOR is unlikely to instill a perception of psychological connectivity. Moreover, limited exposure to organizational life and lack of informal interactions within the organization make it even more difficult to motivate and retain virtual employees by using an underinvestment EOR.

A quasi-spot contract EOR, which exists when employers distribute low or narrow inducements for low or narrow contributions from employees (Tsui et al., 1997), may have more complex impacts for virtual workers. On the one hand, this form of EOR tends to lead to lower employee emotional attachment to the organization because it entails no promise of future employment. On the other hand, it may also help convey clear performance expectations and evaluation criteria that could help virtual employees better direct their efforts while operating out of the sight of their leaders. Consequently, a quasi-spot contract EOR inspires interesting questions regarding how best to design virtual work and how to balance virtual work arrangements with the relational needs of virtual employees.

Although our model is mainly based on EOR and organizational support literature, other theoretical frameworks might be adopted to aid understanding and guide managing increased job virtuality. One promising direction is empowering leadership theory and the empowerment literature. This is because a core conceptual theme of virtual work is psychological control or perceived autonomy (Gejedran & Harrison, 2007), as it is designed to provide employees with choice over the location, scheduling (at least for some), and means of work (e.g., DuBrin, 1991; Standen, Daniels, & Lamond, 1999). Using this framework, it would be valuable to examine which organizational practices and leader behaviors are necessary to enhance virtual employees' perceived empowerment and when job virtuality is more likely to lead to psychological empowerment and subsequent positive outcomes. In addition, social network perspectives may be helpful. Because virtual employees are given more flexibility to work off-site, they may have more opportunities to establish and maintain networks with people outside the organization. As a result, these new connections may simultaneously provide new opportunities in terms of sources of information and new perspectives, but also imply new challenges in terms of reduced identity with and dependence on the organization. In any event, perspectives on EOR will need to accommodate the requirements of an increasingly virtual workforce.

Cultural Influences on Virtual Work

One major advantage of virtual work is that it removes the geographic and temporal barriers and facilitates cooperation among employees from various cultural and national backgrounds (e.g., Connaughton & Shuffler, 2007). As a result, managers need to be aware of the potential impacts of cultural values in coordinating the efforts of cross-cultural virtual employees. In particular, we argue that culture values may interact with job virtuality to impact employees' perceived connectivity to the organization. Culture can be broadly defined as "characteristic ways of thinking, feeling, and behaving shared among members of an identifiable group" (Gibson & Gibbs, 2006, p. 460). Thus, our arguments can be applied not only to the domain of national culture but also to both organizational and group culture.

One cultural dimension that has been studied most often in the virtual work literature is individualism–collectivism (e.g., Jarvenpaa & Leidner, 1999; Paul, Samarah, Seetharaman, & Myktyn, 2005). According to Hofstede (1980), collectivists tend to be more influenced by shared membership and to feel more uncomfortable entering and leaving groups than do their individualist counterparts. Consequently, collectivists will have a stronger need to frequently interact with their coworkers in order to stay connected in their groups and/or organizations. Thus, a virtual work environment may have a stronger impact on perceived isolation for collectivists when they are physically separated from their coworkers. Moreover, studies have shown that individualists may be more likely than collectivists to trust others in computer-mediated communication environments (Jarvenpaa & Leidner, 1999). Hence, it may be easier for individualists, as compared to collectivists, to communicate with others and feel connected to other organizational members even when using computer-mediated methods.

Another cultural difference in communication and behaving that is particularly relevant in the virtual environment is the extent to which people tend to communicate explicitly/directly (such as those in Western cultures) or implicitly/indirectly (such as those in Eastern Asian cultures) (cf. Erez, 2008). Asynchronous, computer-mediated communication is inferior to face-to-face communication in terms of richness and accuracy in information exchange and emotional expression (e.g., Straus & McGrath, 1994). Consequently, virtual employees who tend to communicate in an implicit manner may experience more difficulties in expressing their thoughts and having others understand them when using e-mails, text messages, and telephones. As a result, when working virtually, workers who tend to communicate implicitly may feel more isolated from others in their organizations than is the case for their more explicit counterparts.

Practical Implications

The theoretical arguments in this chapter shed light on three aspects of business practice in virtual environments: virtual HR system quality improvement, mutual investment EOR practices, and effective leadership. First, although we have argued that virtual work has the potential to reduce employees' perceived connection with their organization (e.g., Cooper & Kurland, 2002; Gejendran & Harrison, 2007), our framework also posits that high-quality virtual HR systems may buffer this potential negativity by providing new opportunities for employee–organization interaction. In this way, virtual HR systems can convey positive signals regarding EORs. Therefore, it would be beneficial for organizations that use virtual HR systems to carefully maintain the online HR website, update HR-related information and resources, and provide prompt resolutions for technical problems in order to assure appropriate content and convenience in HR self-service. By doing so, the organization will not only reap the benefits of virtual HR practices per se, such as increased efficiency and employee self-sufficiency, but also help lessen virtual employees' perceived isolation.

Second, by arguing that organizational EOR mutual investment will increase virtual employee psychological connectivity through both unit-level managerial implementations and virtual HR systems, our model highlights the central role of EOR mutual investment in virtual HR practices and, more broadly, in managing work virtuality. Therefore, practices that imply a long-term relationship, such as managers encouraging employee development and offering contingent rewards and providing virtual learning opportunities through virtual HR systems, will be effective in attracting and bonding virtual employees to the organization. Moreover, mutual investment employers expect expanded contributions from employees as a return (Tsui et al., 1997). This emphasis is particularly useful in the virtual environment because the reciprocity norm and social exchange set forth by the organization will constantly signal the value and importance of employees (e.g., Hom et al., 2009), which become less noticeable in virtual work.

Finally, our model points out that some types of leadership (e.g., empowering leadership) and particular functions of leaders (e.g., managing team diversity) may be critical in connecting virtual employees to the organization and increasing virtual work effectiveness. For example, leaders' encouraging and showing faith in employees' ability to decide their own work schedule, goals, and methods, while also providing necessary coaching, will enable virtual employees to better adapt to off-site work. In addition, involving virtual employees in relevant decision-making processes will enhance their perceived connectivity to the organization. Lastly, leaders also need to use advanced technologies to facilitate communication and solve communication difficulties among virtual employees with different functional and cultural background in order to better engage virtual employees (e.g., Bell & Kozlowski, 2002).

Overall, we have provided an EOR virtuality framework that we hope will both offer practical advice to managers and guide future research on developing effective EORs in a world of work that promises to be increasingly virtual.

REFERENCES

Ahearne, M., Mathieu, J., & Rapp, A. (2005). To empower or not to empower your sales force? An empirical examination of the influence of leadership empowerment behavior on customer satisfaction and performance. *Journal of Applied Psychology, 90,* 945–955.

Amabile, T. M. (1988). A model of creativity and innovation in organizations. In B. M. Staw & L. L. Cummings (Eds.), *Research in organizational behavior* (pp. 123–167). Greenwich, CT: JAI Press.

Amabile, T. M. (1996). *Creativity in context.* Boulder, CO: Westview Press.

Amit, R., & Zott, C. (2001). Value creation in e-business. *Strategic Management Journal, 22,* 493–520.

Axtell, C. M., Fleck, S. J., & Turner, N. (2004). Virtual teams: Collaborating across distance. In C. L. Cooper & I. T. Robertson (Eds.), *International review of industrial and organizational psychology.* Chichester, UK: Wiley.

Bandura, A. (1982). Self-efficacy mechanism in human agency. *American Psychologist, 37,* 122–147.

Bartol, K. M., & Liu, W. (2002). Information technology and human resources management: Harnessing the power and potential of netcentricity. *Research in Personnel and Human Resources Management, 21,* 215–242.

Bartol, K. M., Liu, W., Zeng, X., & Wu, K. (2009). Social exchange and knowledge sharing among knowledge workers: The moderating role of perceived job security. *Management & Organization Review, 5,* 223–240.

Bartol, K. M., & Srivastava, A. (2002). Encouraging knowledge sharing: The role of organizational reward systems. *Journal of Leadership and Organization Studies, 9,* 64–76.

Bell, B. S., & Kozlowski, S. W. J. (2002). A typology of virtual teams: Implications for effective leadership. *Group & Organization Management, 27,* 14–49.

Blau, P. (1964). *Exchange and power in social life.* New York, NY: Wiley.

Brockbank, W., & Yeung, A. (1995). Reengineering HR through information technology. *Human Resource Planning, 18,* 24–37.

Byron, K. (2008). Carrying too heavy a load? The communication and miscommunication of emotion by email. *Academy of Management Review, 33,* 309–327.

Cascio, W. (1998). *Managing human resources: Productivity, quality of work life, profits.* Boston, MA: Irwin McGraw-Hill.

Chen, Z., Eisenberger, R., Johnson, K. M., Sucharski, I. L., & Aselage, J. (2009). Perceived organizational support and extra-role performance: Which leads to which? *Journal of Social Psychology, 149,* 119–124.

Collins, C. J., & Smith, K. G. (2006). Knowledge exchange and combination: The role of human resource practices in the performance of high-technology firms. *Academy of Management Journal, 49,* 544–560.

Connaughton, S. L., & Shuffler, M. (2007). Multinational multicultural distributed teams: A review and future agenda. *Small Group Research, 38,* 387–412.

Cooper, C. D., & Kurland, N. B. (2002). Telecommuting, professional isolation, and employee development in public and private organizations. *Journal of Organizational Behavior, 23,* 511–532.

Coyle-Shapiro, J., Shore, L., Taylor, M., & Tetrick, L. (2004). Commonalities and conflicts between different perspectives of the employment relationship: Toward a unified perspective. In J. Coyle-Shapiro, L. Shore, M. Taylor, & L. Tetrick (Eds.), *The employment relationship: Examining psychological and contextual perspectives* (pp. 119–134). Oxford, UK: Oxford University Press.

Diekema, D. A. (1992). Aloneness and social form. *Symbolic Interaction, 15,* 481–500.

Dodds, W. B., Monroe, K. B., & Grewal, D. (1991). Effects of price, brand, and store information on buyers' product evaluations. *Journal of Marketing Research, 28,* 307–319.

DuBrin, A. J. (1991). Comparison of the job satisfaction and productivity of telecommuters versus in-house employees: A research note on work in progress. *Psychological Reports, 68*, 1223–1234.

Eisenberger, R., Huntington, R., Hutchison, S., & Sowa, D. (1986). Perceived organizational support. *Journal of Applied Psychology, 71*, 500–507.

Erez, M. (2008). Social-cultural influences on work motivation. In R. Kanfer, G. Chen, & R. D. Pritchard (Eds.), *Work motivation: Past, present, and future*. Mahwah, NJ: Lawrence Erlbaum.

Farh, C. I., Bartol, K. M., Shapiro, D. L., & Shin, J. (2010). Networking abroad: A process model of how expatriates form support ties to facilitate adjustment. *Academy of Management Review, 35*, 434–454.

Farmer, S. M., & Hyatt, C. W. (1994). Effects of task language demands and task complexity on computer-mediated work groups. *Small Group Research, 25*, 331–366.

Ferris, G. R., Authur, M. M., Berkson, H. M., Kaplan, D. M., Harrel-Cook, G., & Frink, D. D. (1998). Toward a social context theory of the human resource management-organization effectiveness relationship. *Human Resource management Review, 8*, 235–264.

Gajendran, R. S., & Harrison, D. A. (2007). The good, the bad, and the unknown about telecommuting: Meta-analysis of psychological mediators and individual consequences. *Journal of Applied Psychology, 92*, 1524–1541.

Gephart, R. P., Jr. (2002). Introduction to the brave new workplace: Organizational behavior in the electronic age. *Journal of Organizational Behavior, 23*, 327–344.

Gibson, C. B., & Gibbs, J. L. (2006). Unpacking the concept of virtuality: The effects of geographic dispersion, electronic dependence, dynamic structure, and national diversity on team innovation. *Academy of Management Review, 51*, 451–495.

Golden, T. D. (2006). The role of relationships in understanding telecommuter satisfaction. *Journal of Organizational Behavior, 27*, 319–340.

Golden, T. D., & Raghuram, S. (2010). Teleworker knowledge sharing and the role of altered relational and technological interactions. *Journal of Organizational Behavior, 31*, 1061–1085.

Golden, T. D., Veiga, J. F., & Dino, R. N. (2008). The impact of professional isolation on teleworker job performance and turnover intentions: Does time spent teleworking, interacting face-to-face, or having access to communication-enhancing technology matter? *Journal of Applied Psychology, 93*, 1412–1421.

Gouldner, A. W. (1960). The norm of reciprocity: A preliminary statement. *American Sociological Review, 25*, 161–178.

Grant, R. M. (1996). Prospering in dynamically-competitive environments: Organizational capability as knowledge integration. *Organization Science, 7*, 375–387.

Hill, S. N., Bartol, K. M., Tesluk, P. E., & Langa, G. A. (2009). When time is not enough: The development of trust and cooperation in computer-mediated teams. *Organizational Behavior and Human Decision Processes, 108*, 187–201.

Hofstede, G. (1980). *Culture's consequences: International differences in work-related values*. Newbury Park, CA: Sage.

Hollingshead, A. B., McGrath, J. E., & O'Connor, K. M. (1993). Group task performance and communication technology: A longitudinal study of computer-mediated versus face-to-face work groups. *Small Group Research, 24*, 307–333.

Hom, P. W., Tsui, A. S., Wu, J. B., Lee, T. W., Zhang, A. Y., Fu, P. P., & Li, L. (2009). Explaining employment relationships with social exchange and job embeddedness. *Journal of Applied Psychology, 94*, 277–297.

Jarvenpaa, S., & Leidner, D. (1999). Communication and trust in global virtual teams. *Organization Science, 10*, 791–815.
Kirkman, B. L., & Mathieu, J. E. (2005). The dimensions and antecedents of team virtuality. *Journal of Management, 31*, 700–718.
Kirkman, B. L., & Rosen, B. (1999). Beyond self-management: Antecedents and consequences of team empowerment. *Academy of Management Journal, 42*, 58–74.
Kirkman, B. L., Rosen, B., Tesluk, P. E., & Gibson, C. B. (2004). The impact of team empowerment on virtual team performance: The moderating role of face-to-face interaction. *Academy of Management Journal, 47*, 175–192.
Kogut, B., & Zander, U. (1992). Knowledge of the firm, combination capabilities, and the replication of technology. *Organization Science, 3*, 383–397.
Kozlowski, S. W. J., Gully, S. M., Nason, E. R., & Smith, E. M. (1999). Developing adaptive teams: A theory of compilation and performance across levels and time. In D. R. Ilgen & E. D. Pulakos (Eds.), *The changing nature of work and performance: Implications for staffing, personnel actions, and development* (SIOP Frontiers Series). San Francisco: Jossey-Bass.
Lai, V. C. (2001). Intraorganizational communication with intranets. *Communications of the ACM, 44*, 95–100.
Lepak, D., Bartol, K., & Erhardt, N. (2005). A contingency framework for the delivery of HR practices. *Human Resource Management Review, 15*, 139–159.
Lepak, D. P., & Snell, S. A. (1999). The human resource architecture: Toward a theory of human capital allocation and development. *Academy of Management Review, 24*, 31–48.
Lepak, D. P., & Snell, S. A. (2002). Examining the human resource architecture: The relationships among human capital, employment, and human resources configurations. *Journal of Management, 28*, 517–543.
LeTart, J. F. (1998). A look at virtual HR: How far behind am I? *HRMagazine, 43*, 33–35.
Lippert, S. K., & Swiercz, P. M. (2005). Human resource information systems (HRIS) and technology trust. *Journal of Information Science, 31*, 340–353.
Luhtanen, R., & Crocker, J. (1992). A collective self-esteem scale: Self-evaluation of one's social identity. *Personality and Social Psychology Bulletin, 18*, 302–318.
Madjar, N., Oldham, G. R., & Pratt, M. G. (2002). There's no place like home? The contributions of work and nonwork creativity support to employees' creative performance. *Academy of Management Journal, 45*, 757–767.
Maertz, C. P., Jr., Griffeth, R. W., Campbell, N. S., & Allen, D. G. (2007). The effects of perceived organizational support and perceived supervisor support on employee turnover. *Journal of Organizational Behavior, 28*, 1059–1075.
Martins, L. L., Gilson, L. L., & Maynard, M. T. (2008). Team Effectiveness 1997–2007: A review of recent advancements and a glimpse into the future. *Journal of Management, 34*, 410–476.
Maruping, L., & Agarwal, R. (2004). Managing team interpersonal processes through technology: A task-technology fit perspective. *Journal of Applied Psychology, 89*, 975–990.
Morrison, E. W. (2002). Newcomers' relationships: The role of social network ties during socialization. *Academy of Management Journal, 45*, 1149–1160.
Morrow, P., & McElroy, J. (2007). Efficiency as a mediator in turnover-organizational performance. *Human Relations, 60*, 827–849.
Nahapiet, J., & Ghoshal, S. (1998). Social capital, intellectual capital, and the organizational advantage. *Academy of Management Review, 23*, 242–266.

Nardi, B., & Whittaker, S. (2002). The role of face-to-face communication in distributed work. In P. Hinds & S. Kiesler (Eds.), *Distributed work: New ways of working across distance using technology* (pp. 83–110). Cambridge, MA: MIT Press.

Parasuraman, A., Zeithaml, V. A., & Malhotra, A. (2005). E-S-QUAL: A multiple-item scale for assessing electronic service quality. *Journal of Service Research, 7*, 213–233.

Paul, S., Samarah, I. M., Seetharaman, P., & Myktyn, P. P. (2005). Multinational and multicultural distributed teams: A review and future agenda. *Small Group Research, 38*, 387–412.

Pearce, C. L., Sims, H. P., Cox, J. F., Ball, G., Schnell, E., Smith, K. A., & Trevino, L. (2003). Transactors, transformers and beyond: A multi-method development of a theoretical typology of leadership. *Journal of Management Development, 22*, 273–307.

Raghuram, S., Garud, R., Wiesenfeld, B., & Gupta, V. (2001). Factors contributing to virtual work adjustment. *Journal of Management, 27*, 383–405.

Rhoades, L., & Eisenberger, R. (2002). Perceived organizational support: A review of the literature. *Journal of Applied Psychology, 87*, 698–714.

Rousseau, D. M., & Greller, M. M. (1994). Human resource practices: Administrative contract makers. *Human Resource Management Journal, 33*, 385–401.

Ruiz, Y., & Walling, A. (2005, October). Home-based working using communication technologies. *Labour Market Trends*, 417–426.

Sahlins, M. (1972). *Stone age economics*. New York, NY: Aldine de Gruyter.

Saks, A. M. (1995). Longitudinal field investigation of the moderating and mediating effects of self-efficacy on the relationship between training and newcomer adjustment. *Journal of Applied Psychology, 80*, 211–225.

Scott, S. G., & Bruce, R. A. (1994). Determinants of innovative behavior: A path model of individual innovation in the workplace. *Academy of Management Journal, 37*, 580–607.

Shalley, C. E., Gilson, L., & Blum, T. C. (2000). Matching creativity requirements and the work environment: Effects on satisfaction and intentions to leave. *Academy of Management Journal, 43*, 215–223.

Shalley, C. E., Zhou, J., & Oldman, G. R. (2004). The effects of personal and contextual characteristics on creativity: Where should we go from here? *Journal of Management, 30*, 933–958.

Shore, L. M., & Shore, T. H. (1995). Perceived organizational support and organizational justice. In R. Cropanzano & K. M. Kacmar (Eds.), *Organizational politics, justice, and support: Managing social climate at work* (pp. 149–164). Westport, CT: Quorum Press.

Shore, L. M., Tetrick, L. E., Taylor, M. S., Coyle-Shapiro, J., Liden, R., McLean, P. J., ... Van Dyne, L. (2004). The employee-organization relationship: A timely concept in a period of transition. In J. Martocchio (Ed.), *Research in personnel and human resources management* (Vol. 23, pp. 291–370). Greenwich, CT: JAI Press.

Sims, H. P., & Manz, C. C. (1996). *Company of heroes: Unleashing the power of self-leadership*. New York, NY: Wiley.

Sirdeshmukh, D., Singh, J., & Sabol, B. (2002). Consumer trust, value, and loyalty in relational exchanges. *Journal of Marketing, 66*, 15–37.

Snell, S. A., Pedigo, P. R., & Krawiec, G. M. (1995). Managing the impact of information technology on human resource management. In G. R. Ferris, S. D. Rosen, & D. T. Barnum (Eds.), *Handbook of human resource management* (pp. 159–174). Oxford, UK: Blackwell Publishers.

Standen, P., Daniels, K., & Lamond, D. (1999). The home as a workplace: Work-family interaction and psychological well-being in telework. *Journal of Occupational Health Psychology, 4*, 368–381.

Staples, S. D., Hulland, J. S., & Higgins, C. A. (1999). A self-efficacy theory explanation for the management of remote workers in virtual organizations. *Organization Science, 10*, 758–776.

Straus, S. G., & McGrath, J. E. (1994). Does the medium matter? The interaction of task type and technology on group performance and member actions. *Journal of Applied Psychology 79*, 87–97.

Tannenbaum, S. I. (1990). Human resource information systems: User group implications. *Journal of Systems Management, 41*, 27–32.

Tomaskovic-Devey, D., & Risman, B. J. (1993). Telecommuting innovation and organization: A contingency theory of labor process change. *Social Science Quarterly, 74*, 367–385.

Tsui, A. S., Pearce, J. L., Porter, L. W., & Tripoli, A. M. (1997). Alternative approaches to the employee-organization relationship: Does investment in employees pay off? *Academy of Management Journal, 40*, 1089–1121.

Tsui, A. S., & Wu, J. B. (2005). The "new employment relationship" versus the "mutual investment" approach: Implications for human resource management. *Human Resource Management Journal, 44*, 115–121.

U.S. Census Bureau. (2002). Statistical abstract of the United States: 2002. *The National Data Book*, Section 12, Labor Force, employment, and earnings, Table No. 578, Persons Doing Job-Related Work at Home: 2001. Washington, DC: U.S. Census Bureau.

Van de Ven, A. H., Delbecq, A. L., & Koenig, R. (1976). Determinants of coordination modes within organizations. *American Sociological Review, 41*, 322–328.

WorldatWork. (2007). *Telework trendlines*. Press release February 17, 2009. Retrieved August 31, 2011 from http://www.workingfromanywhere.org/news/pr021609.html.

WorldatWork. (2009). *Telework trendlines*. Press release February 8, 2007. Retrieved from August 31, 2011 http://www.workingfromanywhere.org/news/pr020707.html.

Wu, J., Hom, P., Tetrick, L., Shore, L., Jia, L., Li, C., & Song, L. J. (2006). The norm of reciprocity: Scale development and validation in the Chinese context. *Management and Organization Review, 2*, 377–402.

Zammuto, R. F., Griffith, T. L., Majchrzak, A., Dougherty, D. J., & Faraj, S. (2007). Information technology and the changing fabric of organization. *Organization Science, 18*, 749–762.

Zhang, X., & Bartol, K. (2010). Linking empowering leadership and employee creativity: The influence of psychological empowerment, intrinsic motivation, and creativity process engagement. *Academy of Management Journal, 53*, 107–128.

Zuboff, S. (1988). *In the age of the smart machine*. New York, NY: Basic Books.

12

A Relational Perspective on the Employee–Organization Relationship: A Critique and Proposed Extension

Riki Takeuchi
Hong Kong University of Science & Technology

The social exchange relationship is ubiquitous and exists everywhere—for example, between dating couples (Sprether, 2001), between suppliers and distributors (Griffith, Harvey, & Lusch, 2006), and between coaches and athletes (Weiss & Stevens, 1993), not to mention the many types of relationship that exist within the workplace. The social exchange perspective, the conceptual root of which can be traced back to at least the 1920s, has been one of the most influential theoretical paradigms for understanding workplace phenomena (Cropanzano & Mitchell, 2005). Social exchange theory has been instrumental in bridging different disciplines such as anthropology (e.g., Sahlins, 1972), social psychology (e.g., Gouldner, 1960; Homans, 1958), and sociology (e.g., Blau, 1964). However, its influence has been felt most strongly in the fields of organizational behavior and industrial and organizational psychology (e.g., Coyle-Shapiro & Conway, 2004; Cropanzano & Mitchell, 2005; Shore & Shore, 1995) where the social exchange framework has been adopted to conceptualize and examine a variety of topics. To name just a few, these include leader–member exchange (LMX) (e.g., Hofmann & Morgeson, 1999; Masterson, Lewis, Goldman, & Taylor, 2000; Settoon, Bennett, & Liden, 1996; Wayne, Shore, & Liden, 1997), perceived organizational support (POS; e.g., Eisenberger, Huntington, Hutchison, & Sowa, 1986; Hofmann & Morgeson, 1999; Masterson et al., 2000; Settoon et al., 1996; Wayne et al., 1997), organizational justice (e.g., Ambrose & Schminke, 2003; Rupp & Cropanzano, 2002), psychological contract (PC; e.g., Tekleab, Takeuchi, & Taylor, 2005; Turnley, Bolino, & Lester, 2003; Van Dyne & Ang, 1998), organizational commitment (e.g., Settoon et al., 1996; Van Dyne & Ang, 1998), and organizational citizenship behaviors (e.g., Konovsky & Pugh, 1994; Lambert, 2000).

More recently, however, concerns have been expressed in several theoretical reviews regarding social exchange theory and the current state of the literature associated with it (e.g., Coyle-Shapiro & Conway, 2004; Cropanzano & Mitchell, 2005; Cropanzano, Rupp, Mohler, & Schminke, 2001; Shore et al., 2004). For example, Coyle-Shapiro and Conway (2004, p. 22) noted that "research on social exchange is very rarely 'social' in the sense that it seeks to incorporate both parties' perspectives to the exchange, or considers how parties view the social situation and interpret exchange," and recommended a more process-oriented approach. Similarly, Shore et al. (2004, p. 322), in discussing the literature on the employee–organization relationship (EOR), noted that: "The term 'relationship' involves the condition of being connected and associated together. Thus, a focus on the EOR would mean attention to the *interaction* of the two parties." Furthermore, Cropanzano and Mitchell (2005, p. 878) also noted that "by and large, organizational researchers have focused on the social relationships that develop between employees and their employing organization."

Thus, the previous literature on EOR tended to focus on only one party's (typically, the employee's) perception (such as POS, PC, organizational justice, trust in employer, etc.) without considering how each party to the social exchange interacts with each other to influence the quality of the social exchange relationship that develops. Thus, investigating how each party to a social exchange can influence the relationship quality can provide additional insights into the antecedent conditions that lead to higher quality social exchange relationships. In this chapter, first, I briefly review the existing studies that used social exchange theoretical perspective as the primary theoretical perspective to illustrate the tendencies as well as trends in such studies. Then, as a way forward, I develop conceptual arguments for how two parties to an exchange can influence each other, using an individual difference variable (i.e., exchange ideology, defined as "the strength of an employee's belief that work effort should depend on treatment by the organization" by Eisenberger et al. [1986, p. 503]), because Scott and Colquitt (2007) found that exchange ideology acted as a significant moderator of several justice–outcome relationships and its moderating impact was more powerful than Big Five personality traits and equity sensitivity. Thus, I consider exchange ideology to be a more relevant individual difference variable in this context. I adopt a relational perspective by examining both parties to an exchange as well as incorporating multiple stakeholders (supervisors, coworkers, and subordinates) who may develop social exchange relationships with the focal actor (or the focal employee) and impact the quality of such relationships in various ways. More specifically, demography research has adopted the relational perspective in conceptualizing what is called "relational demography." This concept has been advanced initially by Tsui and her colleagues (e.g., Farh, Tsui, Xin, & Cheng, 1998; Tsui, Egan, & O'Reilly, 1992; Tsui & O'Reilly, 1989). Furthermore, Harrison, Price, and Bell (1998) have extended this literature by differentiating deep-level diversity from surface-level diversity. They compared the effects of deep-level diversity (i.e., attitudinal diversity) and surface-level diversity (i.e., demographic diversity). Thus, conceptual advances and empirical findings in the relational demography literature can be applied to examining social exchange relationships within an organization. This chapter, therefore, intends to advance the literature on EORs by adopting a relational perspective at the dyadic (e.g., supervisor–employee and coworker–employee) and group (employee–group) levels.

THEORETICAL OVERVIEWS AND CRITIQUE

Social Exchange Theory

Although there are different extensions/variations of social exchange theory (e.g., Blau, 1964; Homans, 1958; Gouldner, 1960; March & Simon, 1958), the basic premises of social exchange theory are that (a) it involves at least two parties (e.g., Homans, 1958; March & Simon, 1958); (b) social exchange entails unspecified obligations (Blau, 1964); and (c) parties to the exchange strive for balance in their exchanges with their partners even while seeking to maximize their profit from the exchange (Homans, 1958)—that is, "the difference between the value of what is received and the cost of what is given in return" (Coyle-Shapiro & Conway, 2004, p. 8).

Despite the prevalence of studies that use social exchange theory as an overall framework, several scholars have recently noted that social exchange theory has not been articulated and tested as it should be. For instance, Cropanzano and Mitchell (2005, p. 875) stated: "The core ideas that comprise SET [social exchange theory] have yet to be adequately articulated and integrated." Similarly, Coyle-Shapiro and Conway (2004, p. 5) stated that "social exchange still remains theoretically underdeveloped, that some of its key assumptions remain untested, and that the empirical base for social exchange is large in terms of the number of studies, but very narrow in terms of method employed." Along the same lines, Shore et al. (2004) suggested that future research should use the "relationship" metaphor (i.e., to focus on the relationship) at the dyadic level, implying that previous research had looked at the social exchange relationship from the perspective of only one of the parties.

Finally, Cropanzano and Mitchell (2005) noted the existence of three different types of reciprocity or repayment rules: (1) reciprocity as a transactional pattern of interdependent exchanges; (2) reciprocity as a folk belief; and (3) reciprocity as a moral norm. Gouldner (1960, p. 171) suggests two requirements for the norm of reciprocity: "(1) people should help those who have helped them and, (2) people should not injure those who have helped them." In discussing these rules, Cropanzano and Mitchell (2005) emphasize that exchange by definition involves a bidirectional transaction and that although a norm of reciprocity may be a human universal, not all individuals necessarily value reciprocity to the same degree.

Although the idea that social exchange relationship entails exchange partners (at least two individuals, if not more) is well accepted, previous studies that have adopted social exchange relationships have typically treated the other party of an exchange as a "silent" or "invisible" partner and adopted a one-sided view of relationship quality. For example, studies that examine employee perception of LMX or POS typically ask the employee about his or her relationship quality with the other exchange partner/party (e.g., leader in LMX, or an organization in POS) and assume that the other partner or party to an exchange has already provided something of value to the employee. In other words, these studies do not really take into account the other partner/party to this exchange. Of course, I do not intend to criticize these studies because this in and of itself is not a critical flaw. I am merely pointing out that these studies tend to consider the employee's perception of social exchange quality. Next, I briefly review existing studies that have used social exchange theory as the primary theoretical perspective. In this review, I intentionally focus on studies that are published already and have more micro-orientation but do not include studies that used the social exchange theoretical perspective to examine relationships between or among firms (e.g., Castellucci & Ertug, 2010).

Brief Summary of Existing Studies

Given the prevalence of the social exchange theoretical perspective in the organizational behavior literature, a variety of variables have been used as a proxy for the nature or quality of social exchange (except perhaps Shore, Tetrick, Lynch, and Barksdale's [2006] scale that directly measures social exchange quality). Such variables include different types of exchange quality (LMX: Dulac, Coyle-Shapiro, Henderson, & Wayne, 2008; Hofmann & Morgeson, 1999; Masterson et al., 2000; Van Dyne, Kamdar, & Joireman, 2008; Wang, Law, Hackett, Wang, & Chen, 2005; Wayne et al., 1997; team–member exchange [TMX]: Kamdar & Van Dyne, 2007; Major, Kozlowski, Chao, & Gardner, 1995; coworker exchange: Sherony & Green, 2002), justice (Ambrose & Schminke, 2003; Masterson, 2001; Rupp & Cropanzano, 2002), commitment (Settoon et al., 1996; Van Dyne & Ang, 1998), PC (e.g., Tekleab et al., 2005; Turnley et al., 2003; Van Dyne & Ang, 1998), support (POS: Dulac et al., 2008; Hofmann & Morgeson, 1999; Masterson et al., 2000; Settoon et al., 1996; Wayne et al., 1997; supervisory support: Bacharach, Bamberger, & Biron, 2010; coworker support: Bacharach et al., 2010; Settoon & Mossholder, 2002), and trust (leader/supervisor trust: Dirks & Ferrin, 2002; coworker trust: Settoon & Mossholder, 2002), among others.

Table 12.1 provides a very brief summary of what may be considered representative studies that adopt a social exchange theoretical perspective, using different proxies. As the first column shows, the predominant majority of studies include "social exchange" variables, which I would characterize as "employee-centered" (i.e., employee is asked to answer own feelings about different aspects of the social exchange relationship he or she has, such as LMX or POS). For example, one line of research has investigated the different antecedents and outcomes of social exchange quality (LMX and POS: e.g., Masterson et al., 2000; Wayne et al., 1997; Tekleab et al., 2005). For instance, Wayne et al. (1997) examined developmental experiences, promotions, and organizational tenure as antecedents of POS, whereas liking, expectations, and dyad tenure were considered antecedents of LMX. Task performance and organizational

TABLE 12.1

Brief Review of Social Exchange Studies Including Social Exchange Variables Studied

Individual	Relational (Dyadic)	Relational (Social Network)
Dulac, Coyle-Shapiro, Henderson, & Wayne (2008): POS, LMX, PC breach, violation	Engle & Lord (1997): LMX, perceived attitudinal similarity	Flynn (2003): favor exchange between an employee and team members
Erdogan, Liden, & Kraimer (2006): interactional justice, distributive justice, LMX	Phillips & Bedeian (1994): LMX, perceived attitudinal similarity	Lai, Rousseau, & Chang (2009): social exchange quality
Tekleab, Takeuchi, & Taylor (2005): procedural justice, interactional justice, POS, LMX, PC violation	Dose (1999): perceived work value similarity, LMX, TMX	Settoon & Mossholder (2002): network centrality
Janssen & Van Yperen (2004): LMX	Flynn & Brockner (2003)	Zagenczyk, Scott, Gibney, Murell, & Thatcher (2010): POS, similarity, structural equivalence
Flynn (2003): favor exchange, perceived imbalance		
Eisenberger, Armeli, Rexwinkel, Lynch, & Rhoades (2001): POS, affective commitment		
Masterson, Lewis, Goldman, & Taylor (2000): procedural justice, interactional justice, POS, LMX		
Moorman, Blakely, & Niehoff (1998): procedural justice, POS, affective commitment		
Wayne, Shore, & Liden (1997): POS, LMX		
Konovsky & Pugh (1994): procedural justice, trust in supervisor		
Van Dyne, Kamdar, & Joireman (2008): LMX, voice helping		

LMX, leader–member exchange; POS, perceived organizational support; PC, psychological contract; TMX, team–member exchange.

citizenship behaviors were found to be outcomes of both POS and LMX, whereas affective commitment and intentions to quit were considered to be outcomes of POS, and favor-doing was found to be an outcome of LMX. Masterson et al. (2000) considered and found interactional justice to be antecedent of LMX and procedural justice to be antecedent of POS. They also found support for job satisfaction to be an outcome of both LMX and POS, but task performance was only related to LMX (save the indirect effect of POS via LMX). I would characterize these studies as "employee-centered" because only employees' perceptions of social exchange–related variables were examined without taking into account the exchange partners' perceptions. Of course, as I stated before, this is not meant to be a critique of these studies per se, because these studies have provided us with various insights regarding social exchange relationships. My intention is to highlight that it may be time to advance our thinking, given our enhanced understanding of antecedents and consequences of social exchange–related variables from these studies.

The second column of Table 12.1 illustrates some of the studies that considered the other side of the social exchange relationship. For example, there are studies on LMX that consider different types of similarities between the leader and the member (or the subordinate: e.g., Dose, 1999; Engle & Lord, 1997; Phillips & Bedeian, 1994), but I would consider this set of studies to be halfway between pure focus on employees and a "relational" approach because typical studies would ask the employees the extent to which they consider leaders to be similar/dissimilar on various dimensions (such as attitudes, values, and beliefs). Flynn and Brockner's (2003) study may be an exception to this trend. They considered the focal employees as givers as well as receivers of favor-doing/giving and examined whether interactional justice and outcome favorability have a differential impact on the focal employees' commitment to the exchange relationship. Interestingly, they found that interactional justice was strongly related to receivers' commitment to the exchange relationship but not that of the givers, whereas outcome favorability was strongly related to givers' commitment to the exchange relationship but not that of the receivers. Thus, their study considers both sides of the social exchange relationships (as givers and receivers), but the focus is still on the "focal" employees.

Finally, the last column in Table 12.1 illustrates studies that have considered the social exchange theoretical perspective from a social network approach (e.g., Flynn, 2003; Lai, Rousseau, & Chang, 2009; Settoon &

Mossholder, 2002). For instance, Flynn (2003, pp. 543–544) considered an imbalance in favor exchange between the focal employees and their team members by calculating the average of other team members' ratings of "who owes whom" in their relationship with the focal employee, where higher scores meant that "other employees believe a focal employee has given more than he or she has received (that is, is generous)," and found a curvilinear relationship between other-perceived imbalance and productivity, which indicated that the "employee's level of productivity significantly increased as favor exchanges with other employees became more balanced." Settoon and Mossholder (2002) examined and found support for employees' network centrality as antecedents of person-focused and task-focused interpersonal citizenship behaviors.

As this brief review indicates, although there are various approaches to examining social exchange relationships, the majority of studies typically adopt a one-sided view (or employee-centered approach) of social exchange by focusing on the employees. I also recognize that there are studies focusing on the employer perspective (e.g., Tsui, Pearce, Porter, & Tripoli, 1997), but this line of research can still be classified as one-sided. Nonetheless, in this chapter, I focus on extending the employee's perspective by adopting the relational view that takes into account both parties' perspectives and extending it to consider three parties' views on the social exchange relationship, which may fill an important gap between employee-centered and social network approaches.

RELATIONAL VIEW OF SOCIAL EXCHANGE RELATIONSHIPS

As the studies by Flynn (2003) and Flynn and Brockner (2003) illustrate, there are differences between employee giving and receiving. This may be due to the fact that there are individual differences with regard to how one would perceive and respond to exchange currencies being provided. For instance, Cropanzano and Mitchell (2005, p. 878, emphasis added) noted: "Exchange orientation provides an interesting avenue for future research (e.g., relations with supervisors, *coworkers*, outsiders, and among groups)." Hence, I focus on how individual differences in exchange orientation, such as exchange ideology, may influence social exchange relationships that develop with the other party at a dyadic level (i.e., between two individuals) and a triadic level (i.e., among three individuals). I readily admit that the social exchange relationship can also be conceptualized at a group level (i.e., individual member and the group as a collective), but this is outside the purview of this chapter.

Relational Demography

As originally defined by Tsui and O'Reilly (1989, p. 403, emphasis added), relational demography refers to "the comparative demographic characteristics of members of *dyads* or groups who are in a position to engage in regular interactions." Thus, relational demography can be conceptualized as the similarity/dissimilarity of demographic characteristics between one individual and another, such as in the supervisor–subordinate dyad (e.g., Farh et al., 1998; Schaubroeck & Lam, 2002; Tsui & O'Reilly, 1989), or between an individual and another collective entity, such as in the individual member–work team relationship (e.g., Harrison et al., 1998; Shore, Cleveland, & Goldberg, 2003; Tsui et al., 1992).

In general, past studies on relational demography can be considered to have produced mixed, and often contradictory, results (Harrison et al., 1998; Pulakos, Oppler, White, & Borman, 1989; Riordan, 2000). Riordan (2000) lists three factors that he considers to have contributed to these mixed and contradictory findings: (1) differences in the sample characteristics; (2) differences in the referent groups used; and (3) differences in the operationalization of relational demography. More recently, however, scholars have suggested that the surface-level versus deep-level distinction is another factor contributing to these inconsistencies.

Surface-level relational diversity can be defined as the differences between one individual employee and another (who could be a supervisor or a coworker) or between an individual employee and another collective (be it a work team, a business unit, or an organization) in "overt, biographical characteristics that are typically reflected in physical attributes" (Harrison et al., 1998, p. 97), which are not easily changed (Jackson, May, & Whitney, 1995). Deep-level relational diversity, in contrast, refers to the differences between one individual employee and another or between an individual employee and another collective in covert, more mutable characteristics such as values, beliefs, and attitudes (e.g., Harrison et al., 1998; Jackson et al., 1995; Van Vianen, De

Pater, Kristof-Brown, & Johnson, 2004). Some scholars have noted that dissimilarity in relational diversity does not necessarily produce consistently negative effects because demographically dissimilar individuals may hold some values in common and become aware of this over time (e.g., Harrison et al., 1998; Van Vianen et al., 2004). Hence, more recent research, though limited, has started to examine "relational" effects that go beyond the relational demography (i.e., surface-level diversity) effects (e.g., Farh et al., 1998; Harrison et al., 1998). Thus, I seek to illustrate in this chapter the importance of exchange ideology in a social exchange relationship, using a relational lens.

Based on the conceptualization of relational demography, I consider individual differences, such as exchange ideology, defined as "the strength of an employee's belief that work effort should depend on treatment by the organization" (Eisenberger et al., 1986, p. 503), to influence the quality of the social exchange relationship that develops with other parties (employer, supervisor, or coworker; cf. Eisenberger, Armeli, Rexwinkel, Lynch, & Rhoades, 2001). Although exchange ideology was initially conceptualized and used in the employment relationship context (i.e., EOR) as an individual dispositional characteristic, this construct is nonetheless applicable to other exchange relationships in general (cf. Scott & Colquitt, 2007). For instance, Redman and Snape (2005, p. 765, emphasis added) noted: "Those with stronger exchange ideology are predisposed to be more responsive to their perception of how favorably they are being treated by the *exchange partner*." Although exchange ideology as an individual characteristic in a social exchange framework has been examined before (e.g., Eisenberger et al., 1986, 2001; Witt, Kacmar, & Andrews, 2001), most, if not all, of the studies considered it only as a moderator and did not examine the "social" (Coyle-Shapiro & Conway, 2004) or "relational" (Shore et al., 2004) aspects—that is, the interaction between the two parties to the exchange (cf. Cropanzano & Mitchell, 2005). To fill this gap, I developed a conceptual rationale for "relational" exchange ideology (i.e., the interaction between two parties to an exchange regarding their level of exchange ideology).

"Relational" Effect Involving Two Individuals

Extending the relational demography idea and considering exchange ideology to represent one aspect of deep-level diversity, I consider examination of both parties' exchange ideologies jointly to be critical, considering the (interactive) nature of exchange relationships. When considering the influence of two individuals to an exchange (e.g., the leader and the member) jointly, there is a stream of research that is helpful: those studies that examine the similarity or congruence effect within the social exchange framework (e.g., Dose, 1999; Edwards & Cable, 2009). For example, there are studies on LMX that have examined the similarity or congruence effect, which is informative and gives us insights regarding the relational aspects of social exchange relationships (e.g., Liden, Wayne, & Stilwell, 1993; Maslyn & Uhl-Bien, 2001). More specifically, theory of LMX development suggests that similarity (or dissimilarity) in demographic, personality, dispositional, or attitudinal variables can facilitate (or forestall) development of high-quality LMX (Dienesch & Liden, 1986). The underlying premise for this similarity effect is the similarity–attraction paradigm—individuals tend to like others who are similar to themselves (Engle & Lord, 1997), and individuals tend to experience discomfort when there is dissimilarity and seek to reduce this inconsistency (e.g., Festinger, 1957; Heider, 1958).

Similarly, a substantial number of studies have pointed out the importance of value congruence between employees and employers (e.g., Chatman, 1989; Edwards & Cable, 2009; Kristof, 1996; Meglino, Ravlin, & Adkins, 1989). Value congruence refers to the degree to which the employee's values match the values of the organization (Chatman, 1989; Kristof, 1996). The findings from this research suggest that when employees hold values that are congruent with or match with those of their employers, they are more likely to be satisfied with the job, identify with the organization, seek to maintain the employment relationship, reduce deviant behaviors, and succeed in their career (e.g., Brown & Trevino, 2006; Erdogan, Kraimer, & Liden, 2004; Meglino et al., 1989). More recently, Edwards and Cable (2009, p. 670) tested four key explanations (trust, communication, interpersonal attraction, and predictability) why value congruence leads to positive individual outcomes (such as job satisfaction and organizational identification) and found, among others, "the effects of individual and organization values on the outcomes are carried primarily by trust, followed by communication and attraction." As such, their findings also corroborates the similarity or congruence effect, which leads to higher quality social exchange, which, in turn, leads to better employee outcomes. Thus far, these empirical findings lead to the same conclusion that similarity regardless of demographic, personality, or disposition would lead to higher quality social exchange, including but not limited to LMX (cf. Bauer & Green, 1996; Engle & Lord, 1997; Liden et al., 1993). Theoretically, the discrepancy theory of work generally argues that congruence (in which there is no discrepancy) or small discrepancies between people's *values*, interests, or career goals should lead to positive outcomes (Fricko & Beehr, 1992). Thus, I would expect the following:

Proposition 1: *Relational exchange ideology affects the social exchange quality such that dyads similar in exchange ideology develop higher quality social exchange than those that are dissimilar.*

However, I would further argue that examining (deep-level) relational exchange ideology effect more closely reveals a more complex picture than the simple positive effect of demographic (surface-level) similarity (or dissimilarity) on social exchange quality. Specifically, I theorize that differentiating surface- versus deep-level relational diversity can contribute additional insights into the similarity/dissimilarity effect because beliefs, values, and attitudes can have valences associated with them (e.g., being committed is considered good versus not being committed is considered bad). This may be a moot point for relational demography studies because demographic variables do not typically have any values associated them (e.g., being female versus male is neither good nor bad), such that being similar (male leader and male subordinate or female leader and female subordinate) is considered to be qualitatively the same (i.e., similar/congruent or dissimilar/incongruent). However, this is theoretically important in order to examine the effects of deep-level diversity (Harrison et al., 1998; Harrison, Price, Gavin, & Florey, 2002; Phillips & Loyd, 2006). In other words, dyads with exchange partners possessing strong exchange ideologies are considered qualitatively different from dyads with exchange partners having weak exchange ideologies.

I expect that social exchange partners (e.g., an employee and a coworker, a leader and a member, or an employee and an employer) who share weak exchange ideology will develop a higher quality exchange relationship than a leader and member who share strong exchange ideology for the following reasons. First, given that trust is crucial to developing social exchange relationships (e.g., Konovsky Pugh, 1994; Molm, Takahashi, &

Gretchen, 2000), individuals who share weaker exchange ideology (i.e., are more benevolent) are more tolerant of the risk and the uncertainty that may occur during the social exchange process. This mutual tolerance for potential exchange inequity facilitates the long-term development of a higher quality exchange relationship. However, "individuals" with stronger exchange ideology are more sensitive to exchange equity and are less tolerant of imbalance in the exchange. Each party is likely to pay more attention to the other's giving and suspect the intention. This focus on equitable treatment from both parties (e.g., an employer and an employee) is likely to discourage trust building and the long-term orientation necessary for a high-quality social exchange relationship (e.g., Konovsky & Pugh, 1994; Molm et al., 2000).

Second, given that the development of higher quality social exchange requires the cognitive evaluation of the contributions made by oneself and the other, negativity bias (e.g., Rozin & Roysman, 2001) is likely to influence the way both parties to the exchange process information. The basic principle of negativity bias is that negative event/information is more salient, potent, dominant in combinations, and generally efficacious than positive information (Rozin & Roysman, 2001). Thus, when the observer (be it an employer or an employee, for example) to a social exchange is evaluating the amount of contributions made by the other party (the actor), a contribution (positive event) made by the other party is not likely to have the same impact as a lack of contribution (negative event). Individuals who hold stronger exchange ideology are more likely to pay attention to this type of information. Hence, I expect that negativity bias will suppress the impact of the contributions made by the other while enhancing the impact of the lack of contributions. The above arguments lead me to expect that the quality of social exchange will be higher for dyads that share similar exchange ideologies (as opposed to dyads with dissimilar exchange ideologies) but the overall quality of social exchange will be highest for dyads on the benevolent end (i.e., weak exchange ideologies) than a dyad with similarly strong exchange ideologies. Thus, I propose the following:

Proposition 1A: *Relational exchange ideology affects the social exchange quality such that the social exchange quality will be higher for the social exchange partner dyads whose involved parties both have weak exchange ideology than for the dyads whose involved parties both have strong exchange ideology.*

"Relational" Effect Involving Three Individuals

Although a relational perspective and the distinction between surface-level and deep-level diversity enhance our understanding of the complexity associated with social exchange relationship, one party's social exchange relationship is not divorced from other social exchange relationships that the involved parties may also have with others. For example, a "focal" employee may have a social exchange relationship with another employee (a coworker) but both employees are supervised by the same manager. Similarly, a "focal" employee may have a social exchange relationship with a manager and an employer. Thus, conceptualizing and investigating the "relational" aspects of two individuals to an exchange should only be considered to highlight the tip of the iceberg in terms of the socially embedded nature of social exchange relationships in organizations.

When considering how three "individuals" who have social exchange relationships with each other can influence one another, Heider's (1946, 1958) balance theory and related formulations (Newcomb, 1953, 1968; Osgood & Tannenbaum, 1955) appear be useful. In its original formulation, balance theory provides a symbolic language of elements and relations to analyze structures in which three elements (such as individuals) are related to one other. For instance, although a three-element structure need not be comprised of three individuals (i.e., one element can be an "object"), for simplicity sake, I only discuss a three-element structure with three individuals here, designated as Jacqueline, Jacques, and Jack. In essence, Heider (1958) proposed that balance in a three-element structure exists when there are (a) three positive relations or (b) two negative relations and one positive relations (as shown by a, b, c, and d in Figure 12.1) and imbalance to exist when there are (a) three negative relations or (b) two positive relations and one negative relation (as shown in Figure 12.1, e, f, g, and h).

More specifically, if Jacqueline likes or has a favorable evaluation of Jacques and Jack, the relation between Jacques and Jack should also be favorable (Figure 12.1a) for this structure to have balance (i.e., Jacques and Jack also like or have favorable evaluations of each other). Similarly, if Jacqueline likes Jacques but dislikes Jack, the structure is balanced if Jacques also dislikes Jack (Figure 12.1b) or vice versa (Figure 12.1c). Finally, if Jacqueline dislikes both Jacques and Jack but Jacques and Jack like each other, the structure is also balanced (Figure 12.1d) (see also Sherony &

A Relational Perspective on the EOR • 321

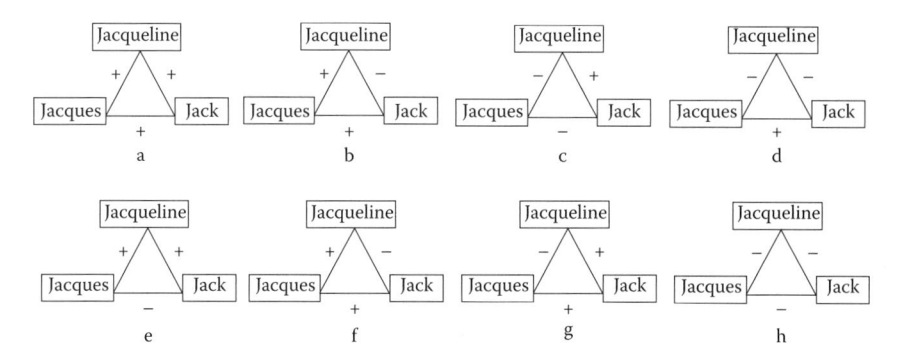

FIGURE 12.1
Balanced/imbalanced triadic structures. (Adapted from Heider, F. *The psychology of interpersonal relations*, Wiley, New York, 1958, except the designation names.)

Green, 2002, for a specific adaptation of balance theory to social exchange context). The other configurations (Figure 12.1, e, f, g, and h) are imbalanced and should not be maintained over time but transformed into one of the four balanced configurations (Figure 12.1, a, b, c, or d) because "unbalanced configurations provoke discomfort and tension" (Sherony & Green, 2002, p. 543). Heider (1958) described three different ways in which imbalanced structures can be converted to balanced ones: (1) attitude change where a person can change his or her liking or disliking toward the other person; (2) distortion or denial where an individual can distort another person's liking or disliking toward the third person as more consistent with his or her own; and (3) cognitive differentiation where an individual can compartmentalize another person into different pieces. Take Figure 12.1e as an example. In this scenario, Jacqueline likes both Jacques and Jack but Jacques dislikes Jack. Accordingly, Jacqueline can (a) change her liking toward Jack by exaggerating his weaknesses (Figure 12.1b) or change her liking toward Jacques (Figure 12.1c); (b) distort the fact that person Jacques dislikes Jack by cognitively distorting or believing that Jacques actually likes Jack (Figure 12.1a; this may entail a reevaluation of his/her dislike as an attraction in disguise, for example); or (c) distinguish person Jacques/Jack into work and nonwork/personal domains such that Jacqueline may like Jacques or dislike Jack personally but not at work (this may entail a statement such as, "I really like Jacques as a friend, but he is a terrible coworker").

Then, this set of logic can also be applied to examining social exchange relationships at work and may be applicable to different types of social exchanges. For instance, Sherony and Green (2002) had discussed this triadic structure in terms of one leader and two members (or subordinates who work for the same leader) and how LMX and coworker exchange (CWX) qualities would be. Thus, if Jacqueline is considered to be the leader who has high LMX qualities with both an employee (Jacques) and another employee (Jack), a high CWX quality between the employees would make this triadic structure stable and sustainable over time (Figure 12.1a). In a similar vein, if the leader has a high LMX quality with one employee but low LMX quality with the other employee, a low CWX quality between the employees will make this structure more stable (Figure 12.1, b or c). Finally, if a leader has low LMX qualities with both of the employees, a high CWX will sustain this triadic structure. Perhaps, both employees perceive the leader as a common enemy, which helps strengthen their bonds to each other.

Applying similar logic, I expect that when a leader possesses weak exchange ideology (more benevolent orientation), which I would consider a more favorable disposition, the leader is likely to develop higher quality social exchange (in this case, LMX) with those employees who also possess weak exchange ideologies and that the social exchange quality (in this case, CWX) between the employees is likely to be high. Thus, it can be argued that when a leader (Jacqueline) and employees (Jacques and Jack) possess weak exchange ideologies, the social exchange qualities among the leader and two employees are likely to be higher (balanced state). It may not be much of a stretch to argue that the leader's (weak) exchange ideology (Jacqueline) and the employees' (weak) exchange ideologies (Jacques and Jack) create positive synergy to enhance the quality of social exchange between the employees (Jacques and Jack).

Perhaps there are two mechanisms through which this occurs: (1) spillover effect, referring to an influence of a variable in one domain affecting another variable in a different domain such as when an employee's experiences at work carry over into the home and when experiences at home affect one's work (cf. Williams & Alliger, 1994); and (b) crossover effect, which refers to the influence of an employee on the attitudes of other (cf. Westman, Vinokur, Hamilton, & Roziner, 2004). Specifically, Jacque may feel good about having a compatible exchange ideology with Jacqueline and is satisfied with this aspect of the job (supervisor satisfaction). This positive feeling may spillover to influence Jacque's satisfaction with another aspect of the job (coworker satisfaction), affecting Jacque's attitudes and behaviors toward Jack in a positive manner (and vice versa). It may also be the case that Jacque's feeling crosses over to Jack because Jacque may talk about the positive aspect of the job, which influences Jack's evaluation of the job as well. Note that the crossover effect is different from the spillover effect in that it is not Jacque's attitude and behavior toward Jack that are affecting Jack. Rather, it is Jacque's feeling providing social cues to Jack about the aspects of the work environment that should be considered important or salient. This is in line with social information processing theory (Pfeffer, 1981; Salancik & Pfeffer, 1978).

> **Proposition 2A:** *Relational exchange ideology between a leader and an employee affects the social exchange quality between employees such that the social exchange quality (CWX) will be higher for the social exchange partner dyads (two employees) who are involved with a third party (leader) with a weak exchange ideology.*
>
> **Proposition 2B:** *Exchange ideologies among a leader and two employees have a synergistic effect such that the highest social exchange qualities (LMX and CWX) can be expected when all three individuals possess weak exchange ideologies.*

Furthermore, I would argue that when there is an imbalance between the triadic structures, there are different ways in which this imbalance will be resolved. In the case of leader and employee triads, there are basically three different possibilities where the leader has developed high LMX qualities (due to weak exchange ideology he or she possesses) with both employees but two employees have a low CWX quality (Figure 12.1e), perhaps due to a prior argument, and I would contend that, over time, their relationship quality will improve (Figure 12.1a). Their CWX quality should improve over time because both employees may compare their social standing with others (or what Henderson, Wayne, Shore, Bommer, and Tetrick [2008] had called relative LMX) in the same workgroup and realize that relative to other employees (who may also serve the same leader), they are being treated better. This realization also increases their behaviors toward each other.

On the other hand, when a leader with moderate exchange ideology has developed a high-quality LMX with one member (with weak exchange ideology) but a low-quality LMX with the other member (with strong exchange ideology; Figure 12.1, f and g), a high-quality CWX between the two employees is likely to diminish over time. This is likely to be the case because the social information provided in this case is likely to focus on the social comparison between the two employees (e.g., in Figure 12.1f, Jack is likely to compare his own standing against Jacques and may perceive that the treatment of the leader is not appropriate), and it may be concluded that the leader's treatment of the other employee is biased (or under favoritism).

Finally, if the leader has low-quality LMX with both of the employees but CWX quality between the two employees is low, perhaps because the leader pitted one employee against the other (Figure 12.1h), over time, I expect the two employees will realize that they have a common enemy (the leader), and this will improve the CWX quality. This assumes, of course, that a leader has more power over the employees.

> **Proposition 3:** *Imbalance in the triadic structure between the leader and the employees will shift toward equilibrium (or steady state) over time.*
>
> **Proposition 3A:** *When the triadic structure between the leader and the employees is imbalanced such that the relationships between the leader and the two employees (or LMX) are positive and negative, the positive relationship between two employees (or CWX) will diminish over time.*
>
> **Proposition 3B:** *When the triadic structure between the leader and the employees is imbalanced such that the relationships between the leader and the two employees are positive, the negative relationship between two employees (or CWX) will improve over time.*
>
> **Proposition 3C:** *When the triadic structure between the leader and the employees is imbalanced such that the relationships between the leader and the two employees (or LMX) are negative, the negative relationship between two employees (or CWX) will improve over time.*

DISCUSSION

This present chapter extends the current thinking on EOR literature that adopts social exchange theory in several different ways. First, I feature the "relational" aspect by investigating how the similarities/differences in the degree of exchange ideology of the two parties to an exchange affect their attitudes and behaviors. Second, it may be argued that this is one of the first conceptual models that underscore the "social" and "relational" aspects of social exchange relationships within a coherent framework. Third, I also feature three social exchange relationships that may exist among three individuals and how the configuration of such relationships would influence the other. Specifically, using similarity or congruence effect, I develop an argument for relational exchange ideology (interaction between an individual's exchange ideology and another individual's exchange ideology), which can be applicable to two employees (i.e., CWX quality between two employees), for example, a leader and a member (i.e., LMX quality perceived by the leader/member) or an employee and an employer (i.e., POS quality perceived by the employee/employer).

In addition, I used LMX and CWX qualities as an example of the social exchange relationships that three individuals can have as a result of their exchange ideologies and illustrated how an imbalanced relationship structure can restore itself over time. This may be another future research direction to examine the dynamics associated with repair or restoration of a damaged relationship. In terms of theoretical implications, this chapter illustrates the importance of incorporating the social context in which social exchange relationship is embedded (cf. Henderson et al., 2008) and underscores the need to include the influence of other stakeholders (e.g., a coworker or coworkers) on the employee or an employee's influence on others. This is also in line with the more recent work by Henderson et al. (2008) that takes a multilevel view of LMX (differentiation). Although Henderson et al. (2008) considered relative LMX as a social comparison between an employee and the average LMX quality for the entire workgroup, not all coworkers may influence the employee in a similar manner. Thus, considering the impact of relational exchange ideology (between two individuals) on the outcomes of interest (such as social exchange quality for the focal employee or the coworker), as well as the impact of relational exchange ideology on the third person, may complement well the approach taken by Henderson and colleagues.

It is also possible that the influence of relational exchange ideology (between the leader and an employee) on the third person (a coworker) may be different across cultures. For example, in some cultures where unequal distribution of power is accepted as a way of life (i.e., high power distance culture), an imbalanced relationship between a leader (Jacqueline) and employees (Jacques and Jack, cf. Figure 12.1, f, g, and h) may not result in an expected move toward equilibrium. Thus, it is also interesting to incorporate cultural context into the equation.

Boundary Conditions

This chapter has certain boundary conditions that should be taken into consideration when considering the future direction for social exchange studies. Although this chapter considers three stakeholders (leader, employee, and coworker/another employee) who are likely to have an impact on the focal actor (employee), I do not specifically consider the influence that significant others (e.g., spouses, children, friends, relatives) can have on the focal employee.

Another limitation is the limited number of variables considered in this chapter. Although it was not my intention to test a comprehensive model of the "social" aspect of social exchange relationships, there may be other relevant variables, such as equity sensitivity, that can be considered. Exchange ideology was used simply for illustrative purposes. Thus, I do not intend to claim that this variable is the most critical and only factor in the social exchange process that should be considered. It is also possible that other individual difference variables, such as negative and positive affectivity and Big Five personality traits, also affect the social exchange relationships under investigation. Perhaps a future research direction would be to examine the relative explanatory power of different deep-level diversity variables. Nonetheless, the findings from this research have many research and practical implications.

In conclusion, this chapter represents, hopefully, a significant step forward by shedding some interesting new light on the social exchange theory through a relational perspective. At the same time, it underscores the need for more theoretical and empirical work in this area.

REFERENCES

Ambrose, M. L., & Schminke, M. (2003). Organization structure as a moderator of the relationship between procedural justice, interactional justice, perceived organizational support, and supervisory trust. *Journal of Applied Psychology, 88*, 295–305.

Bacharach, S. B., Bamberger, P., & Biron, M. (2010). Alcohol consumption and workplace absenteeism: The moderating effect of social support. *Journal of Applied Psychology, 95*, 334–348.

Bauer, T. N., & Green, S. G. (1996). Development of leader-member exchange: A longitudinal study. *Academy of Management Journal, 39*, 1538–1567.
Blau, P. (1964). *Exchange and power in social life*. New York, NY: Wiley.
Brown, M. E., & Trevino, L. K. (2006). Socialized charismatic leadership, values congruence, and deviance in work groups. *Journal of Applied Psychology, 91*, 954–962.
Castellucci, F., & Ertug, G. (2010). What's in it for them? Advantages of higher-status partners in exchange relationships. *Academy of Management Journal, 53*, 149–166.
Chatman, J. A. (1989). Improving interactional organizational research: A model of person–organization fit. *Academy of Management Review, 14*, 333–349.
Coyle-Shapiro, J. A.-M., & Conway, N. (2004). The employment relationship through the lens of social exchange. In J. A.-M. Coyle-Shapiro, L. M. Shore, M. S. Taylor, & L. E. Tetrick (Eds.), *The employment relationship: Examining psychological and contextual perspectives* (pp. 5–28). Oxford, UK: Oxford University Press.
Cropanzano, R., & Mitchell, M. S. (2005). Social exchange theory: An interdisciplinary review. *Journal of Management, 31*, 874–900.
Cropanzano, R., Rupp, D. E., Mohler, C. J., & Schminke, M. (2001). Three roads to organizational justice. In J. Ferris (Ed.), *Research in personnel and human resources management* (Vol. 20, pp. 1–113). Greenwich, CT: JAI Press.
Dienesch, R. M., & Liden, R. C. (1986). Leader-member exchange model of leadership: A critique and further development. *Academy of Management Review, 11*, 618–634.
Dirks, K. T., & Ferrin, D. L. (2002). Trust in leadership: Meta-analytic findings and implications for research and practice. *Journal of Applied Psychology, 87*, 611–628.
Dose, J. J. (1999). The relationship between work values similarity and team-member and leader-member exchange relationships. *Group Dynamics: Theory, Research, and Practice, 3*, 20–32.
Dulac, T., Coyle-Shapiro, J. A.-M., Henderson, D. J., & Wayne, S. J. (2008). Not all responses to breach are the same: The interconnection of social exchange and psychological contract processes in organizations. *Academy of Management Journal, 51*, 1079–1098.
Edwards, J. R., & Cable, D. M. (2009). The value of value congruence. *Journal of Applied Psychology, 94*, 654–677.
Eisenberger, R., Armeli, S., Rexwinkel, B., Lynch, P. D., & Rhoades, L. (2001). Reciprocation of perceived organizational support. *Journal of Applied Psychology, 86*, 42–51.
Eisenberger, R., Huntington, R., Hutchison, S., & Sowa, D. (1986). Perceived organizational support. *Journal of Applied Psychology, 71*, 500–507.
Engle, E. M., & Lord, R. G. (1997). Implicit theories, self-schemas, and leader-member exchange. *Academy of Management Journal, 40*, 988–1010.
Erdogan, B., Kraimer, M. L., & Liden, R. C. (2004). Work value congruence and intrinsic career success: The compensatory roles of leader-member exchange and perceived organizational support. *Personnel Psychology, 57*, 305–332.
Erdogan, B., Liden, R. C., & Kraimer, M. L. (2006). Justice and leader-member exchange: The moderating role of organizational culture. *Academy of Management Journal, 49*, 395–406.
Farh, J. L., Tsui, A. S., Xin, K., & Cheng, B. S. (1998). The influence of relational demography and Guanxi: The Chinese case. *Organization Science, 9*, 471–488.
Festinger, L. A. (1957). *A theory of cognitive dissonance*. Stanford, CA: Stanford University Press.
Flynn, F. J. (2003). How much should I give and how often? The effects of generosity and frequency of favor exchange on social status and productivity. *Academy of Management Journal, 46*, 539–553.

Flynn, F. J., & Brockner, J. (2003). It's different to give than to receive: Predictors of givers' and receivers' reactions to favor exchange. *Journal of Applied Psychology, 88*, 1034–1045.

Fricko, M. A. M., & Beehr, T. A. (1992). A longitudinal investigation of interest congruence and gender concentration as predictors of job satisfaction. *Personnel Psychology, 45*, 99–117.

Gouldner, A. W. (1960). The norm of reciprocity. *American Sociological Review, 25*, 161–178.

Griffith, D. A., Harvey, M. G., & Lusch, R. F. (2006). Social exchange in supply chain relationships: The resulting benefits of procedural and distributive justice. *Journal of Operations Management, 24*, 85–98.

Harrison, D. A., Price, K. H., & Bell, M. P. (1998). Beyond relational demography: Time and the effects of surface- and deep-level diversity on work group cohesion. *Academy of Management Journal, 41*, 96–107.

Harrison, D. A., Price, K. H., Gavin, J. H., & Florey, A. T. (2002). Time, teams, and task performance: Changing effects of surface- and deep-level diversity on group functioning. *Academy of Management Journal, 45*, 1029–1045.

Heider, F. (1946). Attitudes and cognitive organization. *Journal of Psychology, 21*, 107–112.

Heider, F. (1958). *The psychology of interpersonal relations*. New York, NY: Wiley.

Henderson, D. J., Wayne, S. J., Shore, L. M., Bommer, W. H., & Tetrick, L. E. (2008). Leader-member exchange, differentiation, and psychological contract fulfillment: A multilevel examination. *Journal of Applied Psychology, 93*, 1208–1219.

Hofmann, D. A., & Morgeson, F. P. (1999). Safety-related behavior as a social exchange: The role of perceived organizational support and leader-member exchange. *Journal of Applied Psychology, 84*, 286–296.

Homans, G. C. (1958). Social behaviors as exchange. *American Journal of Sociology, 63*, 597–606.

Jackson, S. E., May, K. E., & Whitney, K. (1995). Understanding the dynamics of diversity in decision-making teams. In R. A. Guzzo & E. Salas (Eds.), *Team decision-making effectiveness in organizations* (pp. 204–261). San Francisco, CA: Jossey-Bass.

Janssen, O., & Van Yperen, N. W. (2004). Employee's goal orientation, the quality of leader-member exchange, and the outcomes of job performance and job satisfaction. *Academy of Management Journal, 47*, 368–384.

Kamdar, D., & Van Dyne, L. (2007). The joint effects of personality and workplace social exchange relationships in predicting task performance and citizenship performance. *Journal of Applied Psychology, 92*, 1286–1298.

Konovsky, M. A., & Pugh, S. D. (1994). Citizenship behavior and social exchange. *Academy of Management Journal, 37*, 656–669.

Kristof, A. L. (1996). Person–organization fit: An integrative review of its conceptualizations, measurements, and implications. *Personnel Psychology, 49*, 1–49.

Lai, L., Rousseau, D. M., & Chang, K. T. T. (2009). Idiosyncratic deals: Coworkers as interested third parties. *Journal of Applied Psychology, 94*, 547–556.

Lambert, S. J. (2000). Added benefits: The link between work-life benefits and organizational citizenship behavior. *Academy of Management Journal, 43*, 801–815.

Liden, R. C., Wayne, S. J., & Stilwell, D. (1993). A longitudinal study on the early development of leader-member exchanges. *Journal of Applied Psychology, 78*, 662–674.

Major, D. A., Kozlowski, S. W. J., Chao, G. T., & Gardner, P. D. (1995). A longitudinal investigation of newcomer expectations, early socialization outcomes, and the moderating effects of role development factors. *Journal of Applied Psychology, 80*, 418–431.

March, J. G., & Simon, H. A. (1958). *Organizations*. New York, NY: Wiley.

Maslyn, J. M., & Uhl-Bien, M. (2001). Leader-member exchange and its dimensions: Effects of self-effort and other's effort on relationship quality. *Journal of Applied Psychology, 86*, 697–708.

Masterson, S. S. (2001). A trickle-down model of organizational justice: Relating employees' and costumers' perceptions of and reactions to fairness. *Journal of Applied Psychology, 86*, 594–604.

Masterson, S. S., Lewis, K., Goldman, B. M., & Taylor, M. S. (2000). Integrating justice and social exchange: The differing effects of fair procedures and treatment on work relationships. *Academy of Management Journal, 43*, 738–748.

Meglino, B. M., Ravlin, E. C., & Adkins, C. L. (1989). A work values approach to corporate culture: A field test of congruence process and its relationship to individual outcomes. *Journal of Applied Psychology, 74*, 424–432.

Molm, L. D., Takahashi, N., & Peterson, G. (2000). Risk and trust in social exchange: An experimental test of a classical proposition. *American Journal of Sociology, 105*, 1396–1427.

Moorman, R. H., Blakely, G. L., & Niehoff, B. P. (1998). Does perceived organizational support mediate the relationship between procedural justice and organizational citizenship behavior? *Academy of Management Journal, 41*, 351–357.

Newcomb, T. M. (1953). An approach to the study of communicative acts. *Psychological Review, 60*, 393–404.

Newcomb, T. M. (1968). Interpersonal balance. In R. P. Abelson, E. Aronson, W. J. McGuire, T. M. Newcomb, M. J., Rosenberg, & P. H. Tannenbaum (Eds.), *Theories of cognitive consistency: A source book* (pp. 28–51). Chicago, IL: Rand McNally.

Osgood, C. E., & Tannenbaum, P. H. (1955). The principle of congruity in the prediction of attitude change. *Psychological Review, 62*, 42–55.

Phillips, A. S., & Bedeian, A. G. (1994). Leader-follower exchange quality: The role of personal and interpersonal attributes. *Academy of Management Journal, 37*, 990–1001.

Phillips, K. W., & Loyd, D. L. (2006). When surface and deep-level diversity collide: The effects on dissenting group members. *Organizational Behavior and Human Decision Processes, 99*, 143–160.

Pfeffer, J. (1981). Management as symbolic action: The creation and maintenance of organizational paradigms. In L. L. Cummings & B. M. Staw (Eds.), *Research in organizational behavior* (Vol. 3, pp. 1–52). Greenwich, CT: JAI Press.

Pulakos, E. D., Oppler, S. H., White, I. A., & Borman, W. C. (1989). Examination of race and sex effects on performance ratings. *Journal of Applied Psychology, 74*, 770–780.

Redman, T., & Snape, E. (2005). Exchange ideology and member-union relationships: An evaluation of moderation effects. *Journal of Applied Psychology, 90*, 765–773.

Riordan, C. M. (2000). Relational demography within groups: Past developments, contradictions, and new directions. In G. R. Ferris (Ed.), *Research in personnel and human resources management* (Vol. 19, pp. 131–173). New York, NY: JAI Press.

Rozin, P., & Royzman, E. B. (2001). Negativity bias, negativity dominance, and contagion. *Personality and Social Psychology Review, 5*, 296–320.

Rupp, D. E., & Cropanzano, R. (2002). The mediating effects of social exchange relationships in predicting workplace outcomes from multifoci organizational justice. *Organizational Behavior & Human Decision Processes, 89*, 925–941.

Sahlins, M. (1972). *Stone age economics.* New York, NY: Aldine de Gruyter.

Salancik, G. R., & Pfeffer, J. (1978). A social information processing approach to job attitudes and task design. *Administrative Science Quarterly, 23*, 224–253.

Schaubroeck, J., & Lam, S. S. K. (2002). How similarity to peers and supervisor influences organizational advancement in different cultures. *Academy of Management Journal, 45*, 1120–1136.

Scott, B. A., & Colquitt, J. A. (2007). Are organizational justice effects bounded by individual differences? An examination of equity sensitivity, exchange ideology, and the Big Five. *Group & Organization Management, 32*, 290–325.

Settoon, R. P., Bennett, N., & Liden, R. C. (1996). Social exchange in organizations: Perceived organizational support, leader-member exchange, and employee reciprocity. *Journal of Applied Psychology, 81*, 219–227.

Settoon, R. P., & Mossholder, K. W. (2002). Relationship quality and relationship context as antecedents of person- and task-focused interpersonal citizenship behavior. *Journal of Applied Psychology, 87*, 255–267.

Sherony, K. M., & Green, S. G. (2002). Coworker exchange: Relationships between coworkers, leader-member exchange, and work attitudes. *Journal of Applied Psychology, 87*, 542–548.

Shore, L. M., Cleveland, J. N., & Goldberg, C. B. (2003). Work attitudes and decisions as a function of manager age and employee age. *Journal of Applied Psychology, 88*, 529–537.

Shore, L. M., & Shore, T. H. (1995). Perceived organizational support and organizational justice. In R. Cropanzano & K. M. Kacmar (Eds.), *Organizational politics, justice, and support: Managing the social climate of the workplace* (pp. 149–164). Westport, CT: Quorum Books.

Shore, L. M., Tetrick, L. E., Lynch, P., & Barksdale, K. (2006). Social and economic exchange: Construct development and validation. *Journal of Applied Social Psychology, 36*, 837–867.

Shore, L. M., Tetrick, L. E., Taylor, S. E., Coyle-Shapiro, J. A.-M., Liden, R. C., McLean-Parks, J., ... Van Dyne, L. (2004). The employee-organization relationship: A timely concept in a period of transition. In J. J. Martocchio (Ed.), *Research in personnel and human resources management* (Vol. 23, pp. 291–370). San Diego, CA: Elsevier.

Sprether, S. (2001). Equity and social exchange in dating couples: Associations with satisfaction, commitment, and stability. *Journal of Marriage & Family, 63*, 599–613.

Tekleab, A. G., Takeuchi, R., & Taylor, M. S. (2005). Extending the chain of relationships among organizational justice, social exchange, and employee reactions: The role of contract violations. *Academy of Management Journal, 48*, 146–157.

Tsui, A. S., Egan, T. D., & O'Reilly, C. A. (1992). Being different: Relational demography and organizational attachment. *Administrative Science Quarterly, 37*, 549–579.

Tsui, A. S., & O'Reilly, C. A. (1989). Beyond simple demographic effects: The importance of relational demography in supervisor-subordinate dyads. *Academy of Management Journal, 32*, 402–423.

Tsui, A. S., Pearce, J. L., Porter, L. W., & Tripoli, A. M. (1997). Alternative approaches to the employee-organization relationship: Does investment in employees pay off? *Academy of Management Journal, 40*, 1089–1121.

Turnley, W. H., Bolino, M. C., & Lester, S. W. (2003). The impact of psychological contract fulfillment on the performance of in-role and organizational citizenship behaviors. *Journal of Management, 29*, 187–206.

Van Dyne, L., & Ang, S. (1998). Organizational citizenship behavior of contingent workers in Singapore. *Academy of Management Journal, 41*, 692–703.

Van Dyne, L., Kamdar, D., & Joireman, J. (2008). In-role perceptions buffer the negative impact of low LMX on helping and enhance the positive impact of high LMX on voice. *Journal of Applied Psychology, 93*, 1195–1207.

Van Vianen, A. E. M., De Pater, I. E., Kristof-Brown, A. L., & Johnson, E. C. (2004). Fitting-in: Surface- and deep-level cultural differences and expatriates' adjustment. *Academy of Management Journal, 47*, 697–709.

Wang, H., Law, K. S., Hackett, R. D., Wang, D., & Chen, Z. X. (2005). Leader-member exchange as a mediator of the relationship between transformational leadership and followers' performance and organizational citizenship behavior. *Academy of Management Journal, 48*, 420–432.

Wayne, S. J., Shore, L. M., & Liden, R. C. (1997). Perceived organizational support and leader-member exchange: A social exchange perspective. *Academy of Management Journal, 40*, 82–111.

Weiss, M. R., & Stevens, C. (1993). Motivation and attrition of female coaches: An application of social exchange theory. *Sport Psychologist, 7*, 244–261.

Westman, M., Vinokur, A. D., Hamilton, V. L., & Roziner, I. (2004). Crossover of marital dissatisfaction during military downsizing among Russian army officers and their spouses. *Journal of Applied Psychology, 89*, 769–779.

Williams, K. J., & Alliger, G. M. (1994). Role stressors, mood spillover, and perceptions of work-family conflict in employed parents. *Academy of Management Journal, 37*, 837–868.

Witt, L. A., Kacmar, K. M., & Andrews, M. C. (2001). The interactive effects of procedural justice and exchange ideology on supervisor-rated commitment. *Journal of Organizational Behavior, 22*, 505–515.

Zagenczyk, T. J., Scott, K. D., Gibney, R., Murrell, A. J., & Thatcher, J. B. (2010). Social influence and perceived organizational support: A social network analysis. *Organizational Behavior and Human Decision Processes, 111*, 127–138.

Part 3

Creation, Maintenance, and Completion of the Employee–Organization Relationship

13

Fostering Anticipatory Justice: A New Option for Enhancing the Employee–Organization Relationship?

Debra L. Shapiro
University of Maryland

Mel Fugate
Southern Methodist University

Employee–organization relationship (EOR) research shares the common assumption that the EOR must be *mutually supportive* if desirable organizational outcomes are to occur. This dynamic is described by March and Simon's (1958) inducements–contributions model, wherein inducements or expressions of support by organizations toward employees (e.g., higher compensation and developmental/promotional opportunities) are reciprocated by employee contributions (e.g., productivity and positive citizenship) to the organization. This social exchange is foundational to EOR research and further assumes that the sustainment of positive actions by either organizations or employees requires the presence of positive actions by the other. The quality of this exchange is the focus of EOR and is key to realizing the potential of this relationship from the perspective of each party (cf. Shore et al., 2004).

One implication of EOR is that organizations need to *continually* offer and deliver inducements to employees if employees are to continue contributing their maximal performance to organizations; and conversely, employees need to *continually* offer and deliver maximal contributions (e.g., performance quality) to their organizations if employers are to continue inducing, or rewarding, their employees. These implications suggest that EOR dynamics are highly instrumentally oriented and can vary over time. This also suggests that once there is perceived noninstrumentality, a positive EOR is no longer possible.

Not surprisingly, then, the notion of contracts, or the terms of exchange between the organizations and their employees, is a fundamental EOR concept. When contracts are violated, one or more parties to the contract perceive expected inducements or contributions to be insufficient or lacking. Perceived contract violations, also termed betrayal, have been linked conceptually (cf. Elangovan & Shapiro, 1998) and empirically (Rousseau, 1990) to negative work-related attitudes and behaviors—consequences that are consistent with EOR-related research (see Shore et al. [2004] for a review).

OBJECTIVES AND MOTIVATION FOR INCLUDING ANTICIPATORY JUSTICE IN EOR RESEARCH AND PRACTICE

This chapter has four primary objectives. First, we highlight that despite March and Simon's (1958) inducements–contributions model being foundational to EOR research (Shore et al., 2004), their model poorly explains: (1) the situation where employees remain committed to organizations despite an *absence* of promised inducements (which we call "Situation A"); and (2) the situation where organizations remain committed to employees despite an *absence* of promised contributions (which we call "Situation B"). We describe these situations and posit that the reason they are poorly explained by the inducements-contributions model and other EOR-related concepts (e.g., perceived organization support [POS], leader–member exchange [LMX], team–member exchange [TMX], organizational justice) is because these concepts tend to be focused on past experiences (i.e., how fairly employees perceive they *were* treated) or current experiences (i.e., how fairly employees perceive they *are* treated). As such, much of the theorizing and research pertaining to EOR tends to miss the future-oriented or anticipatory assessments of social exchange (i.e., how fairly employees expect they *will be* treated) that also guide employees' and organizations' decisions about how supportive or continually committed to be toward each other. Importantly, we recognize that there are two EOR-related constructs—namely, the extent to which employees have high levels of POS and LMX—that have been theorized and found to help explain why employees remain committed to organizations despite perceiving a breach between promised versus received inducements (cf. Dulac, Coyle-Shapiro, Henderson, & Wayne, 2008). However, these two EOR constructs, each past oriented, mitigated (and hence moderated) the tendency for perceived breach to be associated with stronger turnover intentions only when the breach was perceived *not* to be reneging. The findings of Dulac et al. (2008) thus do *not* address situations where organizational authorities purposefully decide to delay the timing of initially agreed-upon inducements, as occurs when tough economic times may require salary freezes, hiring freezes, and/or furloughs (pay cuts).

After explaining the benefits of incorporating future-oriented assessments of social exchange, we articulate our second objective and underscore how a more positive EOR is likely when employees expect fair rather than unfair treatment in the future (Figure 13.1). In other words, more rather less *anticipatory justice* in organizations or, conversely, less rather than more *anticipatory injustice* is associated with more positive work-related attitudes and behaviors and trust versus distrust, respectively (see

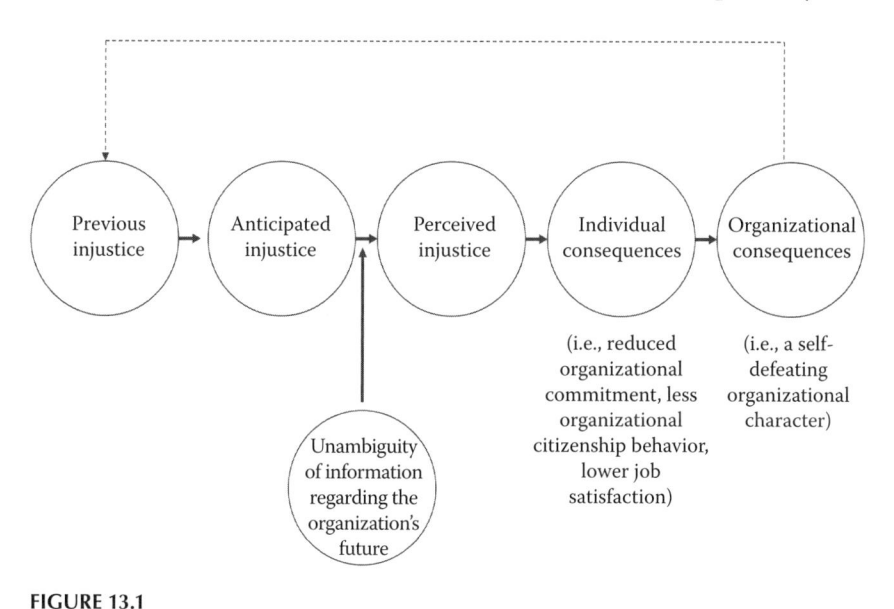

FIGURE 13.1
A model of anticipatory justice. (Reprinted from Greenberg, J., & Cropanzano, R., [Eds.], *Advances in organizational justice*, Stanford University Press, Stanford, CA, 2001. With permission.)

Shapiro and Kirkman [2001] for an elaboration of this view). We review research that suggests that anticipatory justice does indeed enhance inducements and contributions as well as employee attraction and retention. We also describe actions (e.g., communications and other actions geared to generate optimism and hence hope in future positive experiences involving the EOR) that are likely to enhance anticipatory justice. Just as various facets of justice (e.g., aspects relating to procedural qualities, interpersonal treatment-related qualities, and outcome/decision qualities) increase *overall justice* (Ambrose & Schminke, 2009), we posit that various facets of justice perceptions will also likely independently and/or interactively affect the overall assessment of anticipatory justice. For this reason, the hope-generating communications and actions that we identify as likely to enhance anticipatory justice relate to increasing employees' expectation of fair procedures, fair interpersonal interactions, and/or fair decision outcomes (i.e., delivery of promised inducements) in their organization's future. Our discussion of anticipatory justice is not meant to diminish the importance of other past-oriented EOR concepts (e.g., POS, LMX, and organizational justice perceptions); rather, our point is that *complementing* the latter assessments with a measure of anticipatory justice promises to increase the accuracy with which we can predict and explain the quality of EOR. Given the value of positive EOR to the well-being of both employees and their employers (cf. Dulac et al., 2008), it is a matter of practical and theoretical importance to understand antecedents to anticipatory justice.

Our third objective is to examine variables likely to strengthen or weaken the likelihood that actions aimed at fostering anticipatory justice will actually do so (Figure 13.2). The moderating variables we suggest are noncultural as well as cultural in nature. Specifically, as we noted earlier, we include the potentially interactive effects of communications and other actions aimed at enhancing the salience of various justice facets, such as procedural justice, interpersonal justice, and/or distributive justice (see Colquitt [2001] for an elaboration on each of these justice facets). Additional moderating variables we suggest pertain to organizations' degree of cultural diversity. Our focus on this is due to the cultural diversity that characterizes today's workforce (cf. Shapiro, Von Glinow, & Cheng, 2005; Tsui, Nifadkar, & Ou, 2007; Von Glinow, Shapiro, & Brett, 2004) and the fact that more culturally diverse organizations are likely to encounter greater variance in employees' cultural values and, thus also, greater variance

Fostering Anticipatory Justice • 339

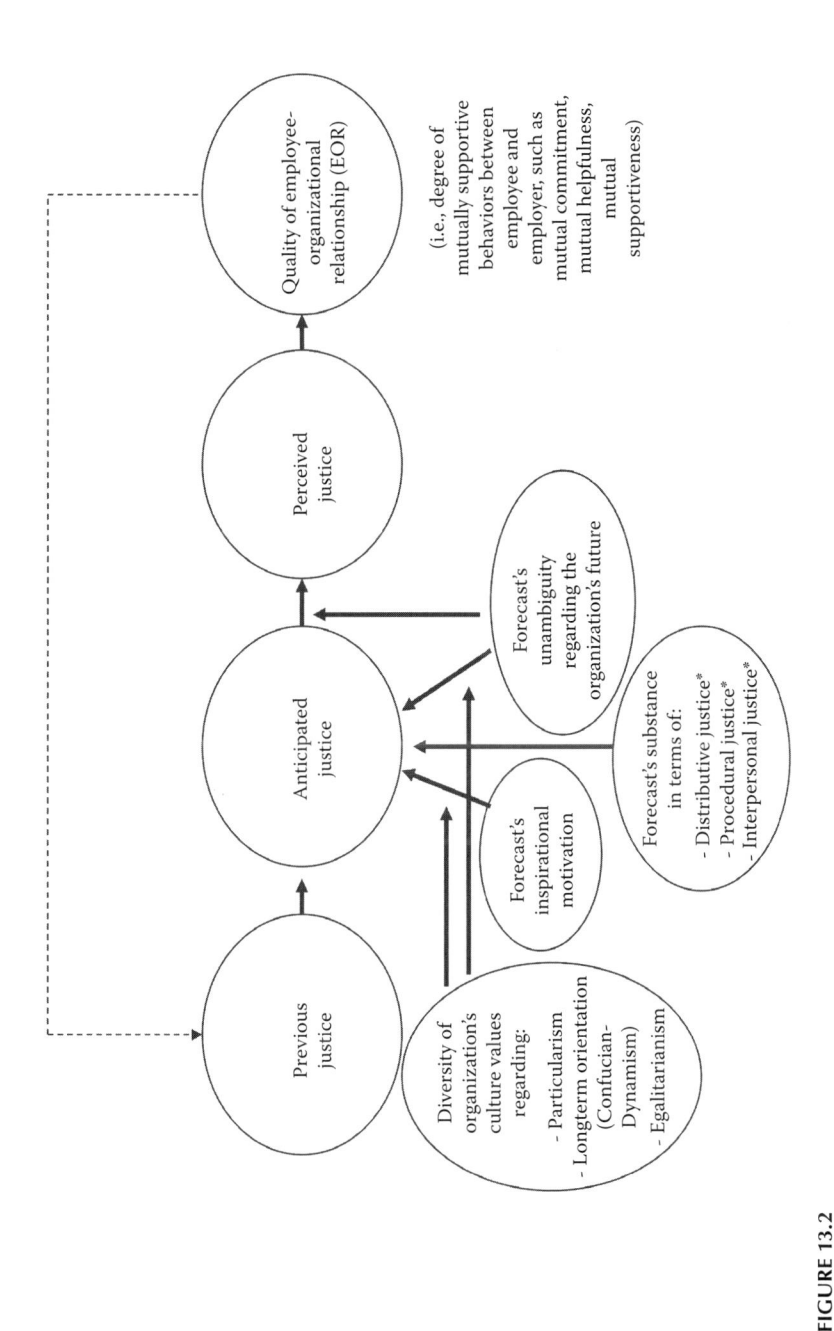

FIGURE 13.2
A model of antecedents to anticipatory justice and their relationships with the employee–organization relationship (EOR). *These justice-facets are likely to interactively affect each other's influence on anticipatory justice.

in receptivity to work practices (cf. Gibson & Grubb, 2005; Kirkman & Shapiro, 2001, 2005; for a review, see Taras, Kirkman, & Steel, 2010). This in turn suggests there is likely to be mixed reactions (rather than uniformly positive ones) to communications and actions that we identify in this chapter as likely to generate optimism or hope in the organization's future in general and in its future fairness in particular. More specifically, we posit that the following cultural values seem more likely than others to strengthen anticipatory justice effects: (a) *particularism* (rather than universalism); (b) *long-term time orientation* (rather than short-term orientation); and (c) *egalitarianism* (rather than authoritarianism, or high power distance); all of these will be defined and described later.

Lastly, we discuss options for increasing the quality of EOR, both conceptually and practically, which are suggested by the anticipatory justice dynamics identified in this chapter. Figure 13.2 visually summarizes suggested EOR-enhancing actions and is offered as an embellishment on some of the relationships depicted in the model of anticipatory justice introduced by Shapiro and Kirkman (2001) (see Figure 13.1). Together, these two models illuminate that anticipatory justice is influenced by previous justice as well as by current actions taken by managers, and that anticipated levels of justice influence the justice that employees see (perceived justice). This in turn influences the extent to which there will be positive work-related consequences (via actions taken by individual employees and the organization), which ultimately become newly experienced justice that then feeds future anticipated levels of justice. This entire justice-assessing process then repeats. As a result, revisions of anticipated and perceived justice are continually being made over time. This is why one of our key conclusions is that EOR-enhancing actions need to be continual too, and *not* treated as one-time or once-per-year events, especially if employees' work environment during the year is high in uncertainty and necessitates sensemaking (see Shapiro and Kirkman [2001] for a supportive view).

To test the veracity of our proposed relationships, we alert scholars to the need for EOR-related studies to include social exchange assessments that are anticipatory in nature *in addition to* the present- or past-oriented assessments that have dominated EOR studies until now. To achieve these objectives, we begin by highlighting situations that poorly match explanations that, until now, seem to have dominated research regarding how to enhance the positive quality of EOR. We hope that illuminating these mismatches may help position anticipatory justice as a concept with theoretical and practical value to the EOR literature.

REVISITING THE INDUCEMENTS–CONTRIBUTIONS MODEL AND OTHER SOCIAL EXCHANGE–BASED CONCEPTS AS EXPLANATIONS FOR THE QUALITY OF EOR

An implication of the inducements–contributions model is that both employees and employers must continually meet the expectations of the other if contributions and inducements are to continue. Yet, this description poorly fits (a) situations where employees remain committed to organizations that fail to deliver promised inducements (Situation A), and (b) situations where organizations remain committed to employees who fail to deliver promised contributions (Situation B). An example of Situation A is the Lincoln Electric Company in the early 1990s. At the time, international expansion-related costs and unexpected challenges associated with attempting to export its incentive system put its bonus program in peril (even for the highest performing employees). Saving this program was possible only by asking employees to give up vacation days and to make other personal sacrifices in order to stop the organization's financial bleeding (Hastings, 1999). An example of Situation B is top managers' continued support of employees, such as beleaguered chief executive officers (CEOs), *long after* their actions and contributions to the company have become ethically questionable, as was well documented for former CEO Ken Lay of Enron and, more recently, for British Petroleum's (BP) then CEO Tony Hayward, whose truth-telling about the gravity of BP's oil leak in the Gulf Coast region of the United States had been questioned for months (from April to July 2010).

Situation A suggests that employees sometimes continue supporting organizations despite the organizations' failure to deliver promised inducements, and Situation B suggests that organizations sometimes continue supporting employees despite the employees' failure to deliver promised contributions. Therefore, social exchange assessments regarding the present or past circumstances *cannot*, at least alone, explain the decisions that employees or their employers make regarding how long to support each other. Instead, these decisions are also likely guided by mutual assessments of how much value each can bring the other in the *future*; hence, they are guided by *anticipatory*, or probability-related, assessments. It is precisely these types of assessments that guide decisions involving uncertainty and risk taking (e.g., Wiseman & Gomez-Mejia, 1998).

Returning to Situation A described earlier, the Lincoln Electric employees had a risky decision to make: Do they reduce commitment to an organization that is failing to deliver promised inducements, or do they instead commit themselves even more to the organization in hopes of strengthening the organization's ability to deliver on its promise? Apparently, the Lincoln Electric employees viewed the probability of faring well to be stronger if they did (rather than did not) attempt to help their organization overcome its financial challenges. Or alternatively, perhaps the Lincoln Electric employees helped their organization during its time of financial crisis because they felt obliged to do so in return for the past benefits they received. This explanation would be consistent with a social exchange perspective of EOR and, more specifically, with Dulac et al.'s (2008) explanation for when employees will respond more positively to undelivered promises or breach. The latter explanation has viability and is indeed part of the speculations offered by Donald Hastings, the CEO of the Lincoln Electric Company, during its troubled times in the 1990s (cf. Hastings, 1999).

However, a yet unexamined explanation also has viability—namely, one that fits Vroom's (1964) Expectancy Theory of Motivation. More specifically, employees' performance, including their choice to make personal sacrifices to help their organization, is guided by their expectation (or "expectancy") that doing so can help their organization survive and, thereby, eventually enable them to enjoy valued rewards such as a place of employment and related privileges. Put another way, descriptions of risk taking–related decision making (cf. Wiseman & Gomez-Mejia, 1998) help explain employees' choices to stay with, rather than abandon, an organization in financial crisis when the employees anticipate that staying (and assisting the organization in righting its course) has greater benefits than costs *over time*.

Returning to Situation B described earlier, when CEOs come under fire, top managers and the boards of directors that advise them have a risky decision to make: Do they reduce commitment to a CEO who is apparently failing to meet expectations (e.g., deliver indisputably high-quality performance), or do they instead commit themselves even more to the CEO in hopes of strengthening his or her ability to deliver the level of performance that he or she was hired and expected to deliver? In instances where beleaguered CEOs receive continued support from their organization, the support providers apparently view the probability of faring well to be stronger if they continue (rather than discontinue) the CEO as leader of the organization. The latter explanation is again consistent with Expectancy Theory because this is essentially saying that the motivation to support beleaguered CEOs is guided by the support givers' expectations that the CEO's continuation will provide more valent rewards for the organization and its stakeholders (including themselves). Also, the theory of rational decision making (Janis & Mann, 1977) helps explain organizational members' choice to support, rather than force out, a beleaguered CEO as likely when greater benefits than costs are expected from the CEO's continuation.

Notice that in both Situations A and B, a decision to commit to the organization or employee who is failing to deliver promised inducements or contributions, respectively, occurs at least partly because of the *future* value that is expected from the other party. It is this anticipatory assessment that is nearly absent from EOR research and from the social exchange–related concepts that Shore et al. (2004) have identified as representative of such work. The one exception is when job applicants are deciding whether to become employees of an organization, which is described by Anderson and Thomas (1996) as an *anticipatory psychological contract* and by Shore et al. (2004, p. 337) as "the initial process of developing the psychological contract." Outside of this preentry moment, we found no mention of anticipatory assessments in the EOR literature, including the descriptions or measures of EOR-related concepts. For example, assessments of POS (cf. Eisenberger, Stinglhamber, Vandenberghe, Sucharski, & Rhoades, 2002), LMX (cf. Scandura & Graen, 1984), TMX (cf. Seers, 1989), and organizational justice (Colquitt, 2001) all ask respondents about previous or current experiences they have had in their organization. Consistent with this observation, Shore et al. (2004, p. 344) note that the social exchange literature "has tended to look at reciprocity and balance in mutual obligations at one point in time." If one considers the time period captured by the measures of many EOR concepts noted earlier, then this time period seems to more accurately reflect past events and not anticipated events in the EOR.

Importantly, we recognize that the expectations held by employees or their organization about the relative costs versus benefits associated with supporting or staying committed to each other, especially during tough times when promised inducements or contributions fail to be delivered, are guided by previous experiences—either direct or vicarious. The importance of past or current experiences in shaping employees' expectations of justice, or anticipatory justice, is consistent with the view of Shapiro and Kirkman (2001). Indeed, this is why the model of anticipatory justice that Shapiro and Kirkman introduced (see Figure 13.1) shows previous injustice as the exogenous variable or "trigger" of injustice-related anticipations. Shapiro and Kirkman phrased their model's construct names with *injustice* in order to alert scholars to the potential harmful consequences to employees as well as the organization when injustice rather than justice is anticipated. They also pointed out that the *seek and you shall find* truism, supported empirically in studies of confirmation bias (cf. Higgins & Bargh, 1987), suggests that present-day perceptions of organizational justice (perceived justice) can be influenced by the degree to which employees expect to be fairly treated. For this reason, Figure 13.1 also shows *perceived injustice* to be a likely consequence of injustice-related anticipations. Shapiro and Kirkman (2001) conceptualized anticipatory (in)justice holistically, as is the case with the recent conceptualization of *overall justice* (Ambrose & Schminke, 2009). However, their model leaves open the possibility, as we will explore later in this chapter, that one or more facets of justice (potentially made salient by managerial interventions) may influence the extent to which employees come to anticipate fairness in the relationship with their organization in the future.

To summarize, our point here is that there is need for anticipatory justice (hence measures of future justice) to *complement* the past- or current-oriented social exchange assessments (e.g., POS, LMX, TMX, organizational justice) that dominate EOR literature specifically and the management literature more generally. Doing so promises to not only increase the accuracy of predicting and explaining differences in the quality of EOR, but also inform the management of this dynamic relationship. Next, we elaborate on what anticipatory justice is and why this concept may potentially broaden interventions for increasing the positive quality of EOR.

ILLUSTRATIONS OF ANTICIPATORY JUSTICE AND HOW IT MIGHT INCREASE EOR QUALITY

The notion of anticipatory justice is supported both conceptually and empirically in numerous streams of research, such as that related to *confirmatory bias* (Snyder & Swann, 1978a, 1978b) and the *halo effect* (Ilgen & Feldman, 1983; Kozlowski & Kirsch, 1987). Both phenomena illustrate the tendency for people to see things they expect to see. Shapiro and Kirkman (2001) echoed this argument and showed that when people expect to be treated fairly, then they are *anticipating justice* and thus also likely, due to the perceptual biases just noted, to see (perceive) justice. Importantly, Shapiro and Kirkman argued that the reverse is also true: Anticipating injustice increases the likelihood that people who expect this will see unfair treatment. They called this justice-specific confirmatory bias the *anticipatory justice effect*. Consistent with this, Sanchez and Brock (1996) found that greater levels of workplace discrimination tended to be reported by minorities whose previous job-related experiences had been more negative rather than positive (e.g., characterized by lower salaries and job rank, among other things). This perceptual difference among the minorities in their study (whose current job situations had similar attributes) may have been due to the employees with more negative (rather than positive) work experiences having lower expectations of fair treatment.

Examples of negative expectations of fairness (anticipatory injustice) are illustrated in the following quotes, taken from Kirkman, Shapiro, Novelli, and Brett's (1996, pp. 56–57) qualitative study regarding employees' expressed concerns associated with self-managing team assignments.

> Concern #1: "How will I be appraised? Will it be fair? How can someone at another location know what I am doing?"
> Concern #2: "Will I work more than others for the same money?"
> Concern #3: "Bullies will ride rough-shod over divergent and valuable ideas."

The first concern is about the fairness of procedures used to appraise one's performance, and hence a concern about the likelihood of *procedural justice*. The second concern is about the fairness of an outcome allocation (i.e., payment), and hence a concern about the likelihood of *distributive justice*. The last concern pertains to the potential for bullying treatment by team members, and thus pertains to a concern about *interpersonal justice* (see Colquitt [2001] for more elaborate descriptions of these various types of justice perceptions). If indeed expectations of (in)justice are positively related to the (in)justice people perceive (see), then those with the team-related concerns noted above ought to experience self-managing teams less positively than those who approach self-managing team assignments without these concerns. This in turn suggests that anticipatory justice is needed if employees are to perceive, or experience, fair treatment and thus ultimately experience positive relationships with their organizations.

Although anticipatory justice and its likely positive influence on perceived justice (described earlier) was theoretically introduced by Shapiro and Kirkman (2001) in the early 2000s, empirical tests of this concept's effects have only recently begun to occur. For example, Bell, Weichmann, and Ryan (2006), via a sample of firefighter applicants, examined the role of justice expectations in the job application process. They found that expectations of fair employment testing procedures influenced applicants' test-taking efficacy and motivation, as well as their intentions to accept the job if offered and to recommend the employer to others. Applicants that had higher expectations of fairness in the employment testing process also perceived this process as more just. Similarly, higher justice expectations amplified applicants' affective and cognitive reactions to the process, such that perceptions of anticipatory injustice intensified negative affect (e.g., frustration) and withdrawal from testing (e.g., letting one's mind wander). Bell et al.'s conclusion that anticipatory justice assists organizations in attracting job applicants is consistent with Anderson and Thomas's (1996) theorizing about anticipatory psychological contracts assisting prospective employees in deciding whether to commit to organizations.

Unlike Anderson and Thomas (1996) who describe anticipatory judgments regarding organizational outcomes as something engaged in by (only) prospective employees, Shapiro and Kirkman (2001) theorized that anticipatory justice is engaged in by current employees, especially during times of uncertainty (e.g., organizational change). As such, they do *not* view the anticipatory psychological contract as relevant solely to pre-organizational entry as described by Anderson and Thomas. Additional support for this position was found in a study involving hospital employees' reactions to a smoking ban at work (Rodell & Colquitt, 2009). These researchers found that employees' support for the smoking ban was significantly greater when they perceived this change to have been implemented fairly and when they anticipated that fair implementation of this change would occur. They also found that employees' expectation of the smoking ban's fair implementation was also positively associated with how fairly they experienced its implementation to be. These findings suggest that EOR can potentially be strengthened by creating *expectations of fairness* and this can ultimately enhance the chance that eventual actions by managers will indeed be perceived as fair. Expectations of fair treatment may thus inoculate employees at all levels, including managers, against future offenses (i.e., future perceptions as unfair actors), which is in fact what Rodell and Colquitt (2009) found.

As noted earlier, confirmation bias research further substantiates the importance of expectations in shaping people's perceptions. This research stream consistently shows that people often attend to, and interpret, situations in ways that are consistent with their expectations or beliefs (e.g., Higgins & Bargh, 1987). Therefore, if employees expect their employers to treat them fairly, it is possible, if not likely, that they will look for supportive information and frame experiences in a manner consistent with their expectations. The converse also makes sense: Expectations of poor or unfair treatment will bias what employees attend to and how they frame their experiences. It then follows that employee behavior is likely to align with these respective expectations and have positive/negative consequences, such as job satisfaction or intentions to quit, respectively, for both the employee and the employer (for elaboration, see Bell et al., 2006; Rodell & Colquitt, 2009; Shapiro & Kirkman, 2001). Because EOR quality is strengthened by job satisfaction and weakened by intentions to quit, these expectation effects are thus likely to also ultimately affect EOR. Shapiro and Kirkman (2001) note that anticipations of positive versus negative treatment (of which expectations of justice/injustice are just one possibility) illustrate trust and distrust, respectively (cf. Deutsch, 1958; Robinson, 1996); and trust in one's organization has been hypothesized and found to be a key determinant of the quality of EOR (cf. Zhang, Tsui, Song, Li, & Jia, 2008). Therefore, the concept of anticipatory justice promises to add predictive and explanatory value to EOR dynamics.

The description of anticipatory justice effects noted earlier suggests that it is keenly necessary, if high-quality EOR is to occur, for employees *and* organizations to expect justice in the future, especially (but not only) if promised inducements or contributions cannot be delivered when initially agreed upon. This argument notwithstanding, there are likely limits or conditions to this contention. Figure 13.1 illustrates a moderating variable that alerts us to the fact that there are probably limits to when employees' (in)justice expectations will lead them to actually perceive more (in)justice. Specifically, the latter confirmatory bias is less likely to occur when *unambiguous* information regarding the organization's future competes with expectations of future justice. For this reason, Shapiro and Kirkman (2001, p. 168) advised those needing to manage employees' perceptions of justice to "make unambiguous information available to organizational members that relates to whatever assurances they receive regarding the organization's future."

To improve on the Shapiro and Kirkman (2001) model of anticipatory justice we offer Figure 13.2, which, unlike the Shapiro and Kirkman model, focuses on antecedents to anticipatory justice and its likely positive effect on the quality of EOR, indicated by mutually supportive actions between employees and their organization. Consistent with the seminal model of Shapiro and Kirkman and with other research findings supporting it (Bell et al., 2006; Rodell & Colquitt, 2009), Figure 13.2 shows previous justice as one antecedent of anticipatory justice. A second predictor variable shown in Figure 13.2 is the unambiguity of information associated with the future state of one's organization. The selection of this predictor is guided by previous findings (reviewed earlier) showing that the confirmatory bias tends to be weakened when unambiguous information contradicts the direction of one's expectation. Illustrations of this include the likelihood of employees more positively versus negatively adjusting their justice expectations (for example, regarding their likelihood of receiving salary raises next year) when they receive unambiguously positive versus negative financial and/or competitive information about their organization's future.

A third predictor variable shown in Figure 13.2 is the extent to which the communication (i.e., forecast) about the organization's future is inspiring. Our reason for choosing this as an additional predictor is due to the fact that the (un)ambiguity of a communication's substance is unlikely by itself to enhance receivers' anticipatory justice. This is because communication effectiveness typically depends on both *style* and *substance*, such as the extent to which communicators seem sincere as well as factually informed (cf. Shapiro, Buttner, & Barry, 1994). For guidance about what style attributes may be key to enhancing anticipatory justice, we posit that much can be learned from leaders who have been described as transformational in general and inspirationally motivating (or charismatic) in particular. For example, a sample item from the inspirational motivation subscale in Avolio and Bass's (1999) larger Transformational Leadership instrument is: "This leader talks optimistically *about the future*" (p. 450, emphasis added). The descriptor "optimistically" is presumably important because positive affect in communications (e.g., passion and warmth) is how charismatic leaders are typically described (cf. Jayakody, 2008). Although the descriptors transformational, inspirationally motivating, and charismatic have been used to describe the communications of *leaders*, these same attributes can describe the communications of *employees* more generally and can characterize the communications between members of self-managing teams specifically (cf. Kirkman & Shapiro, 2001). If employees are to try to enhance their leaders' expectations of future positive performance on the part of employees (for example, when employees' short-term performance has failed to deliver promised contributions), then our theorizing up to this point suggests that employees, too, ought to substantiate positive forecasts with unambiguous facts and in a manner that is inspirationally motivating. This is why Figure 13.2 includes the inspirational quality of information regarding the organization's future as a third antecedent of employees' level of anticipatory justice. The optimism that unambiguous and inspirationally motivating communications ought to raise also likely weakens the tendency for previous injustice to lead its victims to hold on to pessimism. This optimism, or hope, in turn should likely weaken the likelihood that low levels of previous justice will be associated with typically negative-related behavioral correlates such as reduced EOR (cf. Shore et al., 2004). This is why Figure 13.2 shows the three antecedents to anticipatory justice as having interactive as well as direct effects and that anticipatory justice in turn leads to higher quality EOR.

ARE THERE BOUNDARIES OF ANTICIPATORY JUSTICE EFFECTS?

Our theorizing up to this point suggests that organizational members (managers as well as employees) are more likely to perceive organizational justice and thus behave in supportive, EOR-strengthening ways when they *expect* fair treatment—that is, when they more strongly perceive anticipatory justice. This is why understanding antecedents of anticipatory justice is a matter of practical and theoretical importance. We reasoned that organizational leaders may enhance anticipatory justice about their organization's future and that employees may enhance anticipatory justice about their own future contributions to the organization by providing communications about their respective futures in an inspirationally motivating manner that includes unambiguous facts that support the positive forecast being stated. We have posited that the latter communications ought to generate optimism, or hope, that in turn ought to mitigate negative reactions to undelivered promises by the organization or its employees about their respective inducements and contributions.

But what, specifically, might the optimism pertain to if it is to ultimately enhance employees' anticipation of justice in their organization's future? Here is where an understanding of justice facets may be helpful. A meta-analysis by Colquitt (2001) of the organizational justice literature revealed four justice facets that pertain to assessments of fairness related to: (1) the allocation of valued outcomes they have received (e.g., the amounts of a salary raise or bonus, time needed to complete a project, number of personnel needed to do assigned tasks, vacation days, fringe benefits), or *distributive justice*; (2) the criteria or procedural elements used to determine outcome allocations (e.g., the completeness and accuracy of data used to arrive at outcome decisions, the extent to which employees have had input into outcome decisions), or *procedural justice*; (3) the informational qualities used to communicate outcome allocations (e.g., the extent to which employees have had the chance to ask questions and get them answered, the extent to which decision communicators have been truthful), or *informational justice*; and (4) the interpersonal treatment qualities associated with communications of outcome allocations (e.g., the extent to which employees have been treated with dignity and respect), or *interpersonal justice*. Because the latter two categories each involve interpersonal exchange qualities, they are often collapsed in justice studies (see Shapiro & Brett, 2005, for a review). Regardless of whether the justice facets are four or three in number, the point we wish to make here is that managers make these justice facets salient to employees when they communicate (verbally or behaviorally) about them; in so doing, managers manage impressions of fairness (see Bies [1987] and Greenberg [1990] for elaborations of this view). Similarly, then, managers who communicate about the resource allocations, procedures, and/or interpersonal interactions that employees will encounter in their organization's future are managing employees' expectations about these justice facets and thereby influencing the extent to which employees will anticipate justice. Indirect support for this is found in the study of Ambrose and Schminke (2009), in which they found that overall justice perceptions were influenced by each of these justice facets. However, because the justice facets tend to be positively correlated with each other, when any one of these is low, this tends to weaken the overall justice that is perceived. For this reason, we posit that communications aimed at enhancing anticipatory justice are less likely to do so when one or more of the other justice facets is weak. For example, if a manager is attempting to get employees to expect future justice in their organization and, to do so, promises that the employees who have incurred salary freezes this year will be paid next year when the organization's financial situation ought to be improved, the latter communication is less likely to stir high levels of anticipatory justice if the salary-determining procedure seems flawed. This is why Figure 13.2 shows the facet-oriented justice-enhancing communications that managers might make to have interactive, in addition to independent, effects on the degree to which employees anticipate justice in their organization's future.

Because communication rituals are strongly influenced by cultural norms, we now raise the question about the likelihood of positive effects resulting from anticipatory-enhancing (hope-generating) communications in more versus less culturally diverse organizations, especially (but not only) when these communications relate to undelivered promises. Our reasons for questioning this are as follows. First, culturally guided values shape people's sense of what constitutes appropriate versus inappropriate ways of thinking and acting, and these normative preferences in turn shape people's receptivity to the actions of others. For example, people who are *universalistic* tend to believe that rules ought to be uniformly applied and that to do otherwise produces inequity (cf. Leung & Tong, 2004). As a result, universalists will probably see "rule bending" as evidence of procedural injustice. In contrast, Leung and Tong (2004) explain, people who are *particularistic* tend to believe that rules should sometimes be bent— namely, when there are unique situational characteristics that warrant deviating from standard practice. As a result, particularists will probably see rule bending as evidence of interpersonal sensitivity. Consistent with our descriptions here, the relationship-oriented (as opposed to rule-oriented) practice of guanxi has been found to be more acceptable to Chinese rather than U.S. managers (Xin & Tsui, 1996); indeed, people from China versus the United States are generally more particularistic (Leung & Tong, 2004). In summary, less receptivity toward rule bending is likely from universalists than particularists. As a result, universalists are more likely than particularists to be less tolerant of deviations from promised inducements or contributions by organizations or employees, respectively. This in turn suggests that universalists ought to be less positively influenced by anticipatory justice–related communications intended to generate hope or optimism about the delivery of inducements or contributions at a later point in time.

The latter forecast seems likely, also, for people who are more short-term versus long-term oriented—that is, for people who are lower in Confucian Dynamism (cf. Hofstede, 1997). This is because those with a short-term rather than long-term orientation are probably less comfortable with forecasts about a longer time horizon. Consistent with this argument, Hofstede (1997) describes people who are lower in Confucian Dynamism as generally more eager to see quick results, including promised ones. This suggests that employees who are lower in Confucianism ought to be less comforted by anticipatory justice–related communications intended to generate hope or optimism about the delivery of inducements or contributions at a later point in time.

Less receptivity to anticipatory justice–related communications also seems likely to occur on the part of employees who place a lower (rather than higher) value on egalitarianism. This is because, according to Schwartz (1994), egalitarianists generally believe that social interaction, even among people of varying levels of authority, ought *not* be governed by rank, and as such, there is not necessarily a protocol for leaders versus followers to abide by. This description of egalitarianists corresponds well with descriptions by Hofstede (1980) and other cross-cultural scholars (e.g., Kirkman & Shapiro, 2001) of people who are generally low in power distance. In contrast, those who strongly value hierarchy or who are higher in power distance generally believe that organizational leaders ought to receive greater privileges relative to lower level employees, including greater deference and decision-making power (cf. Tinsley,

Brett, Shapiro, & Okumura, 2007). This means that employees who more strongly value egalitarianism are likely to be: (a) more willing to question leaders about the delay in promised inducements (e.g., why a promised bonus may not yet have appeared in a paycheck); (b) more willing to ask leaders to allow delays in promised contributions (e.g., the need for a deadline's extension); and (c) more willing to positively evaluate leaders who explain the need to delay inducements and/or offer deadline extensions or behave in other ways that make employees feel treated as equals. In contrast, the employees who more strongly hold a hierarchical orientation will probably view the making or accepting of such communications as *weak* on the part of leaders and as a failure to show deference on the part of lower level employees.

Consistent with the above rationale, Scandura, Von Glinow, and Lowe (1999) found that employees from Saudi Arabia relative to employees from the United States (where higher versus lower levels of power distance typically exist, respectively; cf. Hofstede, 1980) tended to evaluate leaders as weak when the leaders engaged in more participative leadership (which is one way that egalitarianism gets expressed). The implication is that employees who are lower in egalitarianism are likely to more harshly evaluate leaders who attempt to generate hope or optimism about delayed inducements, such as a promised but postponed pay raise. In contrast, the latter message (or, more generally, the provision of explanations by leaders) is likely to be more appreciated by employees who are higher in egalitarianism.

In summary, culturally guided values, such as the ones described here, shape people's sense of what constitutes appropriate versus inappropriate ways of thinking and acting and, ultimately, people's receptivity to the actions of others. The same applies to employees' receptivity to anticipatory justice–enhancing communications. The values of particularism, long-term orientation (Confucian Dynamism), and egalitarianism ought to increase receptivity to anticipatory justice–enhancing communications. Yet, this is less likely to occur in culturally diverse organizations where these values are likely held by only some, not all, of the organization's members. Therefore, an organization's degree of cultural diversity—specifically with regard to the cultural values of particularism, Confucian Dynamism, and egalitarianism—ought to weaken the tendency for anticipatory justice–enhancing communications to strengthen EOR. This is because people who strongly hold the polar opposites of these three cultural values (universalism, short-term orientation, and hierarchy) are likely to be less receptive to communications intended to generate hope or optimism about inducements or contributions coming at a time that is later than initially promised or agreed upon.

IMPLICATIONS OF BROADENING EOR TO INCLUDE ANTICIPATORY JUSTICE

The implications of adding anticipatory justice to the list of concepts associated with EOR become evident when the following six relationships associated with anticipatory justice (all discussed in this chapter) are illuminated. First, anticipatory justice is future oriented, unlike the concepts and measures associated with the EOR concepts of POS, LMX, TMX, and typical forms of organizational justice. Second, *what people perceive as reality is influenced by people's anticipations about what will occur*, as evidenced by the findings of Bell et al. (2006) regarding the effect of job applicants' expectations about the fairness of upcoming application-related procedures; the finding by Rodell and Colquitt (2009) regarding the effect of employees' expectations about the fairness of an upcoming smoking ban; and by numerous studies documenting the confirmatory bias (Higgins & Bargh, 1987; Snyder & Swann, 1978a, 1978b). Third, people's anticipated and actual justice-related experiences influence attitudes (e.g., how much they can trust the organization/employees) and behaviors (e.g., how committed they will be to the organization/employees) that undoubtedly influence EOR. Fourth, the likelihood of observing a positive relationship between anticipatory and experienced justice, or a confirmatory bias involving justice expectations, suggests that anticipatory justice–enhancing communications may improve the quality of EOR. Fifth, it is both reasonable and practical to consider limits to the effectiveness of EOR-enhancing actions, such as communications aimed at fostering anticipatory justice. Among these limits or moderating conditions are the extent to which communication recipients share the same or different cultural values and the extent to which, for any particular recipient, the effects of the justice facets interact and contribute to their overall sense of organizational justice (cf. Ambrose & Schminke, 2009). Finally, the cultural values that seem likely to increase communication recipients' receptivity to anticipatory justice–enhancing communications include particularism, long-term orientation (Confucian Dynamism), and egalitarianism. Theoretical and practical implications of these six relationships are discussed next.

Theoretical Implications

One theoretical implication of the six anticipatory justice–related points reviewed previously is that employees think about how fairly they *will be* treated in organizations not solely about how fairly they *have been* treated. As such, a future, as well as a past, orientation of justice colors the EOR, including organizational attractiveness and the employee's organizational commitment. Relatedly, current as well as prospective employees engage in anticipatory assessments of organizational life, and thus the dynamics associated with the anticipatory psychological contract described by Anderson and Thomas (1996) ought *not* to be limited to prospective employees. Cumulatively, these observations suggest that future theorizing and empirical tests regarding EOR need to include measures of anticipated, or expected, organizational justice *as a complement* to measures involving evaluations of past organizational experiences. Failure to make such considerations risks proposing and/or testing models of EOR that will be underspecified and yield narrow if not inaccurate conclusions.

A second theoretical implication of the anticipatory justice–related relationships reviewed in this chapter is that more positive attitudes and behaviors toward employees (at all levels of the organization), including perceptions of experienced justice, are more likely to occur when organizational members anticipate being recipients of organizational justice. As such, it probably behooves organizational leaders to run organizations in a manner that creates positive expectations, or hope, for the organizations' future, a view shared by scholars who promote the individual and organizational virtues associated with *positive organizational behavior* (cf. Luthans, Avey, Avolio, & Peterson, 2010). Likewise, employees would be well served to conduct themselves in ways that lead others in the organization to expect positive contributions from them, especially (but not only) when employees have been unable to contribute positively in the short term.

A third theoretical implication for including anticipatory justice in EOR research is that this raises the need to understand what actions, precisely, on the part of organizational leaders and on the part of employees are likely to create expectations of justice or, more broadly, hope in each other. Actions identified in this chapter as possibilities, for which empirical tests are needed, include providing unambiguous information regarding the positivity of whatever future state is being described and doing so in an inspirationally motivating manner.

Until now, our implications suggest that anticipatory justice–related communications are likely to uniformly benefit organizations and employees. Yet, it is important to remember that this chapter also raised the question of how effective anticipatory justice–related communications will be when recipients do *not* necessarily attend to all justice facets in their organization and when they do *not* support the cultural values of particularism, long-term orientation (Confucian Dynamism), and egalitarianism. We also noted the cultural basis of these values and, as such, the improbability that these values will be shared by all employees in culturally diverse organizations (cf. Kirkman & Shapiro, 2005). Thus, the final implication of the anticipatory justice–related theorizing offered in this chapter regards the need for future tests of anticipatory justice–EOR dynamics to include and measure justice facets that employees currently perceive *and/or* anticipate seeing, in addition to the holistic assessment of anticipatory justice and employees' cultural values (and diversity surrounding them). In summary, findings that may seem unsupportive of EOR-related theorizing, or at least its foundational inducements–contributions model, may be easier to explain as well as to predict if future EOR models include: (a) perceptions of anticipatory justice; (b) anticipatory justice–enhancing (hope-generating) communications; and (c) cultural values likely to influence receptivity to these communications.

Practical Implications

There are several practical implications associated with the key relationships illuminated in this chapter. First, managers and employees alike would be well served to recognize that each of these parties ruminates about the future value they will (or will not) receive from each other. Such future-oriented assessments and expectations are in addition to the value they currently see. Recognizing this may motivate both parties to behave in ways that enable each to maintain positive perceptions and expectations of each other, which in turn should foster greater tolerance or even forbearance on occasions when either side is unable to deliver on their promises.

Second, and relatedly, it may behoove both organizations and their employees to give one another hope and optimism for their respective futures. According to Bailey, Eng, Frisch, and Snyder (2007), hope has two fundamental cognitive components—pathways and agency. Pathways describe an individual's belief that a route is available to achieve desired goals, whereas agency describes beliefs that one has the motivation necessary to pursue desired goals. As such, the communications that organizations and employees give each other, if they are to generate hope about positive futures together, likely require two elements. The first element requires a pathway—that is, a description of specific actions that will be taken to reach the future state. Such descriptions possibly need, at a minimum, to refer to the procedures that will be used to guide future decisions (hence procedural justice–enhancing communications). If the procedures that are described are new and if they involve the employees receiving their description, then training to assist employees in using and/or understanding the procedures is also likely to strengthen employees' sense that a pathway with *utility* has been given to them (cf. Brandl & Neyer, 2009).

The second element requires agency—that is, a description of specific reasons leading the communicator to believe that the actions are feasible and that the communicator is fully motivated to realize them. Importantly, Bailey et al. (2007) note that each of the latter elements is more likely to be believed, and hence more likely to generate hope, when the communicator's past or current performance has demonstrated that his or her deeds match his or her words. This view is consistent with Shapiro and Kirkman (2001) who suggest that previous justice (previously received justice in organizations) influences how much justice employees anticipate receiving in the future. However, on the occasions when current justice (e.g., delivery of promised inducements to employees or delivery of promised contributions to organizations) cannot occur, anticipatory justice–enhancing communications may be especially useful. Doing so is likely to foster hope if the communications include both the pathway and agency elements noted and if the messages are substantiated with unambiguous facts or delivered in an inspirational manner (cf. Shapiro & Kirkman, 2001).

A third practical implication pertains to the need for managers and employees to consider when anticipatory justice–enhancing communications will be more or less likely to have their intended effect. Communicators aiming to raise recipients' expectations of future justice are more likely to do so when they can make salient all facets of justice and do so in an inspirationally motivating way that includes reference to unambiguous facts supportive of their message. Such communication skill may require training, as is often provided to leaders who wish to increase the extent to which they are transformational (cf. Munir-Sidani, 2007). Communicators aiming to raise recipients' expectations of future justice are also more likely to do so when receivers have cultural values likely to make them receptive to messages that ask them, essentially, to think long term and to forgive leaders or employees for being unable in the present to deliver on promises. Such values are likely to be, for reasons provided in this chapter, a long-term orientation (Confucian Dynamism), egalitarianism, and particularism. Therefore, it may benefit managers and employees to think about selection and/or training procedures that can facilitate the embracing of these values in their organization. Commonly shared organizational values, especially when organizational identity is strongly shared, can help to overcome any possible deleterious effects associated with differentially held nation-guided values (cf. Gibson & Grubb, 2005).

Finally, the continual revision of justice assessments (past, current, and anticipatory) provides yet another practical implication for managing EOR. As illustrated in Figures 13.1 and 13.2, justice experienced today becomes past oriented and is reflected upon tomorrow, and the past then helps shape what becomes anticipated. Therefore, managers and scholars alike would benefit from considering the inherent feedback loop in the justice process. Although our arguments for including anticipatory justice in the study and management of EOR is clearly not a panacea, it does offer great promise and a new means for shaping the degree to which employees and their managers come to expect positive things from each other, even in instances where circumstances may (temporarily) interfere, such as during dramatic economic hardship. From a practical perspective, this continual justice revision process also suggests that both managers and management scholars need to study via longitudinal research designs how employees go about revising the extent to which they anticipate, as well as perceive, justice in their organizations. It also suggests that periodic "EOR checks" are necessary to capture the revisions that organizational members may (or may not) be making over time.

CONCLUSION

The global economic crisis that started in the fall of 2008 and has yet to end has created numerous situations for employees and organizations to see the *lack* of delivery of promised inducements (e.g., annual pay raises, the absence of furloughs or pay cuts) and promised contributions (e.g., consistently high work performance, potentially challenged by greater work–family stress caused by layoffs of various family members and stress-induced health concerns). The economic tumult associated with these events has provided numerous examples of the potential benefits of *anticipatory justice* for enhancing the quality of the EOR. Hopefully, the ideas presented in this chapter will help managers and management scholars broaden the types of interventions they might try for increasing the quality of EOR, especially, but not only, under challenging circumstances.

REFERENCES

Ambrose, M. L., & Schminke, M. (2009). The role of overall justice judgments in organizational justice research: A test of mediation. *Journal of Applied Psychology, 94*(2), 491–500.

Anderson, N., & Thomas, H. D. C. (1996). Work group socialization. In M. A. West (Ed.), *Handbook of work groups* (pp. 423–450). Chichester, UK: John Wiley & Sons.

Avolio, B. J., & Bass, B. M. (1999). Re-examining the components of transformational and transactional leadership using the Multifactor Leadership Questionnaire. *Journal of Occupational & Organizational Psychology, 72*, 441–462.

Bailey, T. C., Eng, W., Frisch, M. B., & Snyder, C. R. (2007). Hope and optimism as related to life satisfaction. *The Journal of Positive Psychology, 2*, 168–175.

Bell, B. S., Weichmann, D., & Ryan, A. M. (2006). Consequences of organizational justice expectations in a selection system. *Journal of Applied Psychology, 91*, 455–466.

Bies, R. J. (1987). The predicament of injustice: The management of moral outrage. In L. L. Cummings & B. M. Staw (Eds.), *Research in organizational behavior* (pp. 289–319). Greenwich, CT: JAI Press.

Brandl, J., & Neyer, A. K. (2009). Applying cognitive adjustment theory to cross-cultural training for global teams. *Human Resource Management, 48*, 341–353.

Colquitt, J. A. (2001). On the dimensionality of organizational justice: A construct validation of a measure. *Journal of Applied Psychology, 86*, 386–400.

Deutsch, M. (1958). Trust and suspicion. *Journal of Conflict Resolution, 2*, 265–279.

Dulac, T., Coyle-Shapiro, J. A., Henderson, D. J., & Wayne, S. J. (2008). Not all responses to breach are the same: The interconnection of social exchange and psychological contract processes in organizations. *Academy of Management Journal, 51*, 1079–1098.

Eisenberger, R., Stinglhamber, F., Vandenberghe, C., Sucharski, I. L., & Rhoades, I. (2002). Perceived supervisor support: Contributions to perceived organizational support and employee-retention. *Journal of Applied Psychology, 87*, 565–573.

Elangovan, A. R., & Shapiro, D. L. (1998). Betrayal of trust in organizations. *Academy of Management Review, 23*, 547–566.

Gibson, C. B., & Grubb, A. R. (2005). Turning the tide in multinational teams. In D. L. Shapiro, M. A. Von Glinow, & J. Cheng (Eds.), *Managing multinational teams: Global perspectives* (pp. 69–95). London, UK: Elsevier/JAI Press.

Greenberg, J. (1990). Looking versus being fair: Managing impressions of organizational justice. In B. M. Staw & L. L. Cummings (Eds.), *Research in organizational behavior* (pp. 111–157). Greenwich, CT: JAI Press.

Hastings, D. (1999). The Lincoln Electric Company's harsh lessons from international expansion. *Harvard Business Review*. Retrieved from http://hbr.org/1999/05/lincoln-electrics-harsh-lessons-from-international-expansion/ar/1

Higgins, T. F., & Bargh, J. A. (1987). Social cognition and social perception. In M. R. Rosenzweig & L. W. Porter (Eds.), *Annual review of psychology* (pp. 369–425). Palo Alto, CA: Annual Reviews.

Hofstede, G. (1997). *Culture and organizations: Software of the mind*. New York, NY: McGraw-Hill.

Hofstede, G. (1980). *Culture's consequences: International differences in work-related values*. Beverly Hills, CA: Sage.

Ilgen, D. R., & Feldman, J. M. (1983). Performance appraisal: A process focus. *Research in Organizational Behavior, 5*, 141–197.

Janis, I. L., & Mann, L. (1977). *Decision making*. New York, NY: Free Press.

Jayakody, J. A. S. K. (2008). Charisma as a cognitive-affective phenomenon: A follower-centric approach. *Management Decision, 46*, 832–845.

Kirkman, B. L., & Shapiro, D. L. (2001). The impact of cultural values on job satisfaction and organizational commitment in self-managing work teams: The mediating role of employee resistance. *Academy of Management Journal, 44*, 557–569.

Kirkman, B. L., & Shapiro, D. L. (2005). The impact of cultural value diversity on multicultural team performance. In D. L. Shapiro, M. A. Von Glinow, & J. L. Cheng (Eds.), *Managing multinational teams: Global perspectives* (pp. 33–67). London, UK: JAI/Elsevier Press.

Kirkman, B. L., Shapiro, D. L., Noveli, L. Jr., & Brett, J. M. (1996). Employee concerns regarding self-managing work teams: A multidimensional justice perspective. *Social Justice Research, 9*(1), 47–67.

Kozlowski, S. W., & Kirsch, M. P. (1987). The systematic distortion hypothesis, halo, and accuracy: An individual-level analysis. *Journal of Applied Psychology, 72*, 252–261.

Leung, K., & Tong, K. K. (2004). Justice across cultures: A three-stage model for intercultural negotiation. In M. Gelfand & J. Brett (Eds.), *The handbook of negotiation and culture* (pp. 313–333). Stanford, CA: Stanford University Press.

Luthans, F., Avey, J. B., Avolio, B. J., & Peterson, S. J. (2010).The development and resulting performance impact of positive psychological capital. *Human Resource Development Quarterly, 21*, 41–67.

March, J. G., & Simon, H. A. (1958). *Organizations*. New York, NY: Wiley.

Munir Sidani, Y. (2007). Perceptions of leader transformational ability: The role of leader speech and follower self-esteem. *Journal of Management Development, 26*, 710–722.

Robinson, S. L. (1996). Trust and breach of the psychological contract. *Administrative Science Quarterly, 41*, 574–599.

Rodell, J. B., & Colquitt, J. A. (2009). Looking ahead in times of uncertainty: The role of anticipatory justice in an organizational change context. *Journal of Applied Psychology, 94*, 989–1002.

Rousseau, D. M. (1990). New-hire perceptions of their own and their employer's obligations: A study of psychological contracts. *Journal of Organizational Behavior, 11*, 389–400.

Sanchez, J., & Brock, P. (1996). Outcomes of perceived discrimination among Hispanic employees: Is diversity management a luxury or a necessity? *Academy of Management Journal, 39*(3), 704–719.

Scandura, T. A., & Graen, G. B. (1984). Moderating effects of initial leader-member exchange status on the effects of leadership. *Journal of Applied Psychology, 69*, 428–436.

Scandura, T. A., Von Glinow, M. A., & Lowe, K. B. (1999). When East meets West: Leadership "best practices" in the U.S. and Middle East. In W. H. Mobley (Ed.), *Advances in global leadership* (pp. 235–249). Greenwich, CT: JAI Press.

Schwartz, S. H. (1994). Beyond individualism/collectivism: New cultural dimensions of values. In U. Kim, H. C. Triandis, & G. Yoon (Eds.), *Individualism and collectivism* (pp. 85–117). London, UK: Sage.

Seers, A. (1989). Team-member exchange quality: A new construct for role-making research. *Organizational Behavior & Human Decision Processes, 43*, 118–135.

Shapiro, D. L., & Brett, J. M. (2005). What is the role of control in organizational justice? In J. Greenberg & J. Colquitt (Eds.), *Handbook of organizational justice* (pp. 155–177). Hoboken, NJ: Lawrence Erlbaum, Inc.

Shapiro, D. L., Buttner, H. B., & Barry, B. (1994). Explanations: What factors enhance their perceived adequacy? *Organizational Behavior and Human Decision Processes, 58*, 346–368.

Shapiro, D. L., & Kirkman, B. L. (2001). Anticipatory injustice: The consequences of expecting injustice in the workplace. In J. Greenberg & R. Cropanzano (Eds.), *Advances in organizational justice* (pp. 152–178). Stanford, CA: Stanford University Press.

Shapiro, D. L., Von Glinow, M. A., & Cheng, J. L. (2005). *Managing multinational teams: Global perspectives.* London, UK: Elsevier/JAI Press.

Shore, L. M., Tetrick, L. E., Taylor, M. S., Coyle-Shapiro, J., Liden, R. C., McLean Parks, J., … Van Dyne, L. (2004). The employee-organization relationship: A timely concept in a period of transition. In G. R. Ferris & J. Martocchio (Eds.), *Research in personnel and human resources management* (pp. 291–370). Greenwich, CT: JAI Press.

Snyder, M., & Swann, W. B. (1978a). Behavioral confirmation in social interaction: From social perception to social reality. *Journal of the Experimental Social Psychology, 14*, 148–162.

Snyder, M., & Swann, W. B. (1978b). Hypothesis-testing processes and social interaction. *Journal of Personality and Social Psychology, 36*, 1202–1212.

Taras, V., Kirkman, B. L., & Steel, P. (2010). Examining the impact of culture's consequences: A three-decade, multi-level, meta-analytic review of Hofstede's cultural value dimensions. *Journal of Applied Psychology, 95*, 405–439.

Tinsley, C. H., Brett, J. M., Shapiro, D. L., & Okumura, T. (2007). Intervening in employee disputes: How and when will managers from China, Japan, and the U.S. act differently? *Management & Organization Review, 3*, 183–204.

Tsui, A. S., Nifadkar, S., & Ou, Y. (2007). Cross-national cross-cultural organizational behavior research: Advances, gaps, and recommendations. *Journal of Management, 28*, 277–305.

Von Glinow, M. A., Shapiro, D. L., & Brett, J. M. (2004). Can we talk, and should we? Managing emotional conflict in multicultural teams. *Academy of Management Review, 29*, 578–592.

Vroom, V. H. (1964). *Work and motivation.* New York, NY: Wiley.

Wiseman, R. M., & Gomez-Mejia, L. R. (1998). A behavioral agency model of managerial risk-taking. *Academy of Management Review, 23*, 133–153.

Xin, K. R., & Tsui, A. S. (1996). Different strokes for different folks: Influence tactics by Asian-American and Caucasian-American managers. *Leadership Quarterly, 7*, 109–132.

Zhang, A. Y., Tsui, A. S., Song, L. J. W., Li, C. P., & Jia, L. D. (2008). How do I trust thee? The employee-organization relationship, supervisory support and middle managers' trust in the organization. *Human Resource Management, 47*, 111–132.

14

Applicant–Organization Relationship and Employee–Organization Relationship: What Is the Connection?

Ann Marie Ryan
Michigan State University

Applying for a job in today's technologically advanced environment can lead to applicants wondering if "the company even knows I exist." The seamlessness of applying, screening, and receiving rejections via online mechanisms might suggest that the "applicant–organization relationship (AOR)" is not really a relationship at all. On the other end of the spectrum, one can point to cases where applicants have varied interactions with multiple organizational representatives in diverse settings over an extended period of time (via the Internet, at recruiting events, through on-campus interviews and on-site interviews, and over meals), suggesting that meaningful and potentially complex AORs do arise.

The purpose of this chapter is to discuss variations of AORs and how our understanding of the employee–organization relationship (EOR) can enhance and be enhanced by investigation of the AOR. Applicants and organizations do have expectations of one another, and fulfillment of "obligations" does influence individual and organizational decisions regarding engaging in a future employee–employer relationship. The nature of the AOR will be discussed from the lens of research on EOR and social exchange, a perspective lacking in the literature on recruitment and selection. Parties to the AOR, the content and nature of AORs, and influences on the formation of AORs will be covered. Particular attention will be paid to the dynamic nature of AORs, how the AOR serves as signal for a future EOR, and what leads to breach or violation perceptions in AORs.

AOR ELEMENTS

The literature on the EOR provides useful guidance as to what key elements of an exchange relationship are important to consider in discussing AORs, specifically who the parties are to the exchange relationship, the content and nature of the exchange, and influences on how the relationship is formed.

Parties to the AOR

One important term to consider in discussing the AOR is who actually is an applicant. In the United States, the legal definition of an applicant has been set by the Equal Employment Opportunity Commission (EEOC) and differs for in-person versus Internet-based applications. Specifically, the EEOC describes an applicant as "a person who has indicated an interest in being considered for hiring, promotion, or other employment opportunities. This interest might be expressed by completing an application form, or might be expressed orally, depending on the employer's practice" (EEOC, 2008). However, when an individual uses an employer Web page, a job board, or simply e-mails someone at the company to express interest, the individual is only an applicant if three conditions occur: "(a) the employer has acted to fill a particular position; (b) the individual has followed the employer's standard procedures for submitting applications; and (c) the individual has indicated an interest in the particular position" (EEOC, 2008).

Definitions of "applicant" are an interesting place to start a discussion of the AOR because this can be a point of disagreement. That is, an individual who has e-mailed a résumé to the human resources director of a company may view himself as an applicant and will have certain expectations of the organization's obligations (e.g., "They owe me the courtesy of a reply."). However, from the organization's perspective (as well as potentially from a legal perspective), this person might not be viewed as an applicant if there were no jobs open and the procedure for job applications was not followed by the individual. So, disagreements may emerge as to whether or not there is a relationship.

On the organization side, parties to the AOR may be well or ill defined. Organizational agents that are parties to the AOR may include recruiters, test administrators, interview panelists, assessors, potential supervisors, and potential coworkers, and interaction with these agents may vary across time. An Internet applicant is having a relationship with the organization, although the other party is faceless and amorphous. A campus recruiter may be someone an applicant expects to have an ongoing relationship with, only to find he or she never interacts with that person again beyond the half hour on campus, even after being hired. Test administrators may view their role quite narrowly and not see themselves as organizational representatives at all.

Organizational agents affect the nature of the AOR in both positive and negative ways, depending on perceptions of the obligations of each agent in the applicant's view as well as the agreement among the agents as to the organization's obligations in the relationship. Early-in-the-process agents such as recruiters may work hard to establish positive relations with potential recruits (think of armed services recruiters) only to have later agents take a more impersonal approach to screening and interaction that can negatively affect what had been established; conversely, a process that is fairly automated and prescribed in early stages may include more in-depth interactions for those who succeed in passing early hurdles. Shore, Porter, and Zahra (2004) note that there is often great variability in the extent to which agents have a common vision of the organization. They also note that agent activities in the EOR (and thus in the AOR) are influenced by the organization's culture, agent personal interests, and agent understanding of the strategy and available resources.

AORs also can be brokered by third parties (indeed, this is the predominant path to employment in many European countries), which can cause some confusion over obligations. For example, temporary staffing agencies and executive search firms can play a part in attracting and screening applicants and, in that sense, serve a role as organizational agents in the AOR. The potential for disagreement over obligations to applicants between third-party agents and employees of the organization can cause misperceptions, misunderstandings, and negative consequences. For example, Lim and Chan (2001) noted cases where executive search firms failed to define job vacancies accurately for candidates or withheld critical information from applicants about the risks of accepting a job; they also describe failures to present accurate portrayals of candidates to client organizations (see also Guy, 2001). Another example of how third parties can create confusion over obligations and their fulfillment would be that temporary employment firms and their clients are considered coemployers under U.S. law (Ryan & Schmit, 1996). Although client firms can and do dictate the basis and nature of applicant screening, the temporary firm may set many of the terms of employment (i.e., wages, benefits).

In sum, the questions of who has an AOR with the organization and who that AOR is with are not always answered in straightforward ways. From both a practical and theoretical perspective, examining agreement in perceptions of whether relationships exist and who those relationships are with may be important first steps in understanding whether the AOR is a positive one.

Content and Nature

As noted earlier, AORs vary in the amount of interaction an applicant has with the organization (from a "virtual engagement" with a website to extensive time in interviewing and assessments) and the length of the relationship (from only a few minutes completing an application to processes where months are spent as background checks and other screens are conducted). Note that because the point of engaging in AORs is for employers to choose employees and applicants to choose jobs, some applicants and organizations will find the relationship terminated by the other party. Although AORs vary in interaction levels and how long relationships last, many concepts underlying research on EOR can be usefully applied across these variations.

One of the key concepts in the psychological contracts literature is the distinction between *transactional* and *relational* elements of the contract (Coyle-Shapiro & Kessler, 2000; Robinson & Morrison, 1995). Although the transactional elements of EORs are typically in terms of compensation, the exchange in an AOR is not monetized. The essential exchange is that an applicant provides his or her time and information about qualifications in exchange for the organization providing information about the job and an opportunity for employment consideration. The key obligations of both parties revolve around providing accurate and relevant information for mutual decision making—information from the applicant with regard to their qualities and intentions and information from the employer regarding the job and organization and the decision-making process.

There is ample evidence of considerable variability in fulfillment of these transactional obligations associated with the AOR. For example, in providing information to employers, applicants may attempt to impression manage in interviews (e.g., Barrick, Shaffer, & DeGrassi, 2009), fake personal characteristics on personality tests and biodata inventories (e.g., Griffith, Chmielowski, & Yoshita, 2007), commit résumé fraud (Bachler, 1995; Wood, Schmidtke, & Decker, 2007), or just leave answers blank on application forms (Highhouse & Hause, 1995; Stone & Stone, 1987). On the employer side, organizations may provide too positive a portrayal of job duties, earnings, promotion potential, and organizational climate (see Premack and Wanous [1985] for an early review). Information accuracy with regard to hiring process components, decision criteria, and explanations for decisions are employer obligations that also are not always fulfilled (Ployhart, Ryan, & Bennett, 1999; Truxillo, Bodner, Bertolino, Bauer, & Yonce, 2009). Thus, although the obligations of both parties to provide information seem straightforward, the aim of appearing attractive to the other party motivates actions that can result in nonfulfillment of the obligation.

Relational elements or the socioemotional exchange in an AOR may seem minimal, as one would expect in short-term encounters in other business transaction settings (e.g., buyer and seller), and revolve around obligations to treat the other party with courtesy and respect. Nevertheless, perceptions of whether a party is fulfilling relational obligations have proven to be critical to whether the other party continues the AOR and whether the AOR evolves to an EOR. For example, research on applicant attraction has emphasized the importance of interpersonal treatment as a determinant of how applicants react to the hiring process (Bauer, Maertz, Dolen, & Campion, 1998). Ryan and Huth (2008) note, however, that although it is well agreed that employers should treat applicants with respect, specific definitions of what good interpersonal treatment during hiring is may vary depending on individual applicant expectations (e.g., whether a phone call is better than an e-mail, whether a form letter is too impersonal), as well as cultural expectations. As Shore, Porter, et al. (2004) note in discussing strategy and the EOR, a dynamic capability strategic perspective suggests many distinctions among agents and highly individualized relationships (i.e., how an applicant is treated depends on who the recruiter is); a resource-based perspective suggests differences between core and noncore agents (e.g., the human resources department approaches all applicants similarly, but individual hiring managers vary in approaches); and an agency perspective suggests high standardization (i.e., all applicants are treated similarly by all agents). Also, Ryan and Delany (2010) point out that balance between "high-tech" and "high-touch" hiring practices may affect applicant perceptions. On the other hand, because employers do have greater power in the AOR, a failure to meet relational obligations by applicants (e.g., showing up late for an interview, behaving rudely) typically leads to the end of the relationship.

EOR researchers have discussed the importance of mutuality in the exchange. *Mutuality* is how much the two parties agree on obligations (Rousseau, 2011). Unlike the literature that suggests there is often high mutuality on employer obligations in EORs (Atkinson, 2008; Dabos & Rousseau, 2004), mutuality in terms of *employer obligations* is not high in many AORs. Applicants may feel that the organization "owes me" at least an opportunity to "make my case for why I should be hired"; they may feel that organizations that reject applicants on the basis of résumé review or even after some testing have not given them a chance to provide enough information on qualifications. Indeed, research has established the importance of perceived "opportunity to perform" as a key driver of applicant reactions (Schleicher, Venkataramani, Morgeson, & Campion, 2006). Employers, on the other hand, may feel that a valid, standardized, quick screening tool gives ample opportunity for high-quality applicants to distinguish themselves and see this obligation somewhat differently. Ryan and Huth (2008) have suggested that there is a complex relationship in balancing concerns over process efficiency (neither applicants nor employers want a lengthy process) with concerns over opportunity to perform (neither applicants nor employers want a process that does not adequately assess capability). However, mutuality regarding the former may be easier to reach than on the latter.

Mutuality in terms of *applicant* obligations may generally be higher, although there is certainly some variation across relationships. For example, an obligation to provide a truthful portrayal of one's qualifications is generally agreed upon by employers and applicants in principle, but applicants feel (and are often advised by job-seeking self-help books and counselors) that there is no obligation to reveal negative information about oneself (e.g., termination from a position and why) unless directly asked. Applicants are not necessarily lying when engaging in impression management, but presenting their "best self." Also, applicants are advised to treat their résumé as a "marketing tool" (Amare & Manning, 2009), which can lead to practices such as searchbot trickery (i.e., putting words in a résumé that match job ads) where applicants are composing for the search engine that screens résumés. There is likely less mutuality on exactly what information must be presented by applicants than there is on the general principle of providing information.

Cultural influences may play a role in mutuality. For example, in the United States, most employers and applicants would agree that an applicant has an obligation to accept only one job offer at a time. However, in India, accepting multiple offers and then deciding which job to show up for is not uncommon (Cullen, 2007); United States–based multinational companies have had to develop strategies to deal with ways to ensure that applicants who accept offers do indeed become employees, rather than making assumptions about obligations. Another example is that in Western Europe both employers and applicants agree that it is the employer's obligation to provide feedback after psychological testing (Ryan & Tippins, 2009), yet many U.S. companies and applicants would see a letter of acceptance or rejection without specific test score feedback as fulfilling employer obligations. One final example would be that there are cultural differences in whether assertive behavior by applicants in interviews is appropriate (Vance & Paik, 2006), suggesting that relational elements of the AOR may appear violated when individuals with different backgrounds and a lack of cross-cultural competence interact. As more and more organizations engage in cross-border hiring, mutuality may be hard to achieve if employers and applicants apply a global frame to obligations rather than acknowledging cultural influences on obligations.

The psychological contract literature also focuses on balance in obligations or levels of *reciprocity* in the exchange. At first blush, reciprocity may be a hard concept to grasp in terms of the AOR because employers appear to have the upper hand in the exchange. However, although employers have jobs desired by applicants, applicants have aptitudes and skills that employers desire, although the scarcity of that capital varies across job types, industries, and economic cycles. At a broad level, the underlying goal of the AOR is to reach this exchange of individual talent for an employment position; however, the exchanges that are actually part of the AOR are those that are meant to inform both parties as to the feasibility and the desirability of that employment exchange.

The concept of balance may apply more to the applicant's desires than the organization's desires. That is, employers may be seeking an imbalance in their favor (e.g., securing better talent more cheaply through off-shoring). However, in cases of rare talent, employers may be willing to tolerate an imbalance in the AOR for securing an EOR (e.g., extra "wining and dining" and incentives to woo an applicant, or allowing the applicant to name some of the terms of employment).

Interestingly, the shifts in hiring processes due to technology have transferred a lot of the "work" in applying to the applicant. For example, many organizations have gone to the use of computerized applications that require applicants to enter résumé information in a standard format with computerized scoring, making it easier to screen but increasing the applicant's obligation. As another example, an interesting debate point in the literature on unproctored Internet tests is whether the transfer of responsibility for a *good testing environment* from the hiring organization to the test taker is appropriate (Pearlman, 2009). The trade-off here is convenience to the applicant in taking the test when and where they want; the added obligation may not be fully realized by the applicant, and the consequences of not fulfilling that are not apparent (i.e., not turning off the music or minimizing interruptions from others while completing the test can result in a low score and being screened out from the job).

Shore, Tetrick, et al. (2004) note that the employer is generally viewed as having greater power than employees in establishing terms of the psychological contract. Similarly, applicants have less say in the AOR because they cannot determine the nature of hiring tools, the focus of selection (i.e., knowledge, skills, and abilities), the sequence of events, or in many cases, the timing of hiring process hurdles. For example, organizations that lack flexibility in their process (e.g., civil service examinations are often given only once a year or less and only at a specified date in time) may lead to applicants being unable to meet the obligation. In a series of studies, Ryan and colleagues demonstrated that some interested individuals may choose not to continue job pursuit because they did not want to (or were not able to) take a day off from work at their current employer to go through a hiring process hurdle (Ployhart, McFarland, & Ryan, 2002; Ryan, Sacco, McFarland, & Kriska, 2000; Schmit & Ryan, 1997). In a poor job market for job seekers, organizations have even greater power to set the terms of relationships with applicants.

In sum, one can talk about transactional and relational obligations in the AOR, although the specific nature of these is quite different from what is in the EOR. The concepts of mutuality and reciprocity apply to the AOR as well. However, because of the short-term nature of AORs—they either evolve into EORs or become terminated relationships—obligations for both parties should be influenced by the expectations of both parties when they enter into the relationship. Further, although the employer typically has greater influence over the terms of the AOR, labor market conditions can change views as to the obligations of each party and the willingness of each party to invest in the relationship. These two concepts—expectations and investments—are discussed next.

Formation of Relationships

Expectations, or beliefs about a future state of affairs, are a key element in many theories of behavior (Olson, Roese, & Zanna, 1996). EOR research clearly recognizes the preeminent role of expectations; research on applicant–organization exchanges focuses much more heavily on what occurs in the interactions as influencing perceptions of the relationship rather than a priori expectations. However, several researchers have noted the potential importance of applicant expectations, particularly in terms of fair hiring processes and fair treatment during those processes (e.g., Bell, Ryan, & Weichmann, 2004; Bell, Weichmann, & Ryan, 2006; Schreurs, Derous, Proost, Notelaers, & DeWitte, 2008; Schreurs, Derous, Van Hooft, Proost, & DeWitte, 2009).

From an applicant's perspective, Bell et al. (2004) suggested that expectations arise from: (a) past experiences in hiring contexts; (b) indirect information from others, including the organization itself; and (c) enduring beliefs about what is fair. Specifically, research shows that prior experience with a selection procedure influences perceptions of the fairness of that procedure (Kravitz, Stinson, & Chavez, 1994; Ryan, Greguras, & Ployhart, 1996). Gilliland and Steiner (2001) suggested that those lacking experience may be more tolerant of events that others might see as violations of obligations simply because they do not have strong expectations. Social information from family and friends may also influence what one expects of the AOR, as demonstrated by Bazerman, Schroth, Shah, Diekmann, and Tenbrunsel (1994). Most organizations provide advance information regarding the hiring process, and this may influence expectations (e.g., Truxillo, Bauer, Campion, & Parento, 2002). Industry can also play a role in applicant perceptions: When a job seeker attempts to obtain employment in a new field, he or she may have to adjust expectations regarding the basis for hiring, the nature of the hiring process, and the time to hire. As an example, think of someone who moves from an academic to nonacademic position and vice versa; the hiring process in academia occurs almost exclusively on a yearly cycle and involves a "typical" format of vita screen followed by a several-day visit meeting with many people and providing a work sample in the form of a job talk. Alternately, nonacademic positions for similarly credentialed individuals may open up at any time, often involve a phone screening interview prior to a face-to-face one and seldom involve quite so many individuals in the interviewing process. In sum, applicants come to the AOR with expectations of what will transpire and how they will be treated, and these expectations have been formed from both personal experience and contextual influences.

Evidence shows that these expectations of applicants regarding the AOR do influence their attitudes, cognitions, and behaviors during their time as an applicant. Specifically, Bell et al. (2006) found that applicants with higher expectations of just treatment reported higher levels of motivation and more positive job acceptance and recommendation intentions. Justice expectations were also positively related to applicants' perceptions of justice actually experienced in the selection process. Additionally, research on anticipatory justice or expectations of fair treatment in the future (e.g., Shapiro & Kirkman, 2001) suggests that fulfillment of applicant expectations in the AOR may lead to positive expectations for the EOR.

Employer expectations of applicants exist as well, and many of these expectations are outlined in books and workshops targeted to job seekers. For example, Stewart, Dustin, Barrick, and Darnold (2008) noted there are more than a million Internet listings on the importance of the handshake in the interview, and they presented empirical research to support its role in hiring evaluations. Turner-Bowker (2001) highlights how poorer job applicants are challenged to meet interviewer expectations regarding dress (see also Bardack and McAndrew [1985] for empirical links between manner of dress and interview evaluations).

Expectations regarding obligations may not be based so much on a desired relationship as on reality; for example, many employers wishing to use noncognitive measures in hiring may feel that applicants have an obligation to be truthful but find that sufficient numbers of applicants fake or distort their qualifications, rending the measures less useful (Morgeson et al., 2007). Employers are held to an obligation of providing a fair process, and that obligation involves ensuring that those who misrepresent themselves are not taking jobs away from applicants who are honest, at least to the extent it is possible to do so (Berry & Sackett, 2009). Hence, because of a lack of mutuality regarding the obligation of truthfulness, an employer's obligations regarding providing a fair process are affected.

DeVos, DeStobbeleir, and Meganck (2009) note that organizations vary in the extent to which they make employer expectations *after hire* explicit during recruitment and selection and how much is left open to the interpretation of the individual applicant. For example, organizations may provide applicants with a detailed explicit job description that outlines tasks and duties or may only provide a general or generic description of a job category; may provide a very specific look at the work environment (i.e., this would be your desk if you are hired) or only a general tour of the work site; may provide detailed information on policies (e.g., copy from an employee handbook) or talk more generally about work schedules and policies; and may discuss benefits at a general level ("we offer flextime") or give detailed descriptions of benefits. Variability here can be due to many factors (e.g., organizational history, industry norms, cultural context) and may be consciously thought of in a strategic fashion or may just be the process by default.

Employers may engage in deliberate misrepresentation to applicants. Wren, Clark, and Deriso (2006) describe truth in hiring liabilities imposed on employers who do not deliver the employment experiences promised. These can be fraud (misrepresentation of fact), fraudulent inducement (persuading to take a job by misrepresenting factors important to the applicant's decision), or fraudulent concealment (hiding a fact that should be disclosed, such as financial position of the organization). However, even if employers attempt to be clear in communication, applicants may still misconstrue "opportunities" or "potential" as promises (e.g., ability to telecommute seen as being able to work at home whenever desired; moderate travel seen as twice a year rather than twice a month). Robinson, Kraatz, and Rousseau (1994) found that new hire perceptions tend to change considerably during the first year of employment, likely due to gaining clarity regarding what exactly was promised. Further, Buckley, Fedor, Carraher, Frink, and Marvin (1997) pointed out that greater emphasis is placed on the applicant's truthfulness and thoroughness in providing information to the employer than on the equivalent provision by the employer, and that applicants traditionally have less means of verifying the information they receive than do employers (who can use testing and reference and background checks). However, the Internet has greatly enhanced the capabilities of applicants in this regard.

In sum, both employers and applicants have expectations that they bring to the AOR. Perhaps even more so than in the EOR, expectations and their fulfillment play a strong role in shaping the AOR, its continuance, and the eventual likelihood of changing an AOR into an EOR. At a practical level, an organization that promises a "site visit where you can tour our facilities and learn what it is like to work here" may want to consider what applicants expect: Do they expect a day of being "wined and dined" by individuals at the site who will take time out of their day to answer any questions? Do they expect to be meeting with many different employees? Or do they expect a standard visitor's tour? How might an organization manage expectations so that individuals do not feel that an obligation is unfulfilled?

Investments in AOR

In addition to considering expectations, the form of the AOR is influenced by conscious decisions regarding investments in the relationship. Just as with the EOR, employers and applicants make decisions regarding their investment in the relationship, what they are willing to provide, and what they will hence expect in return (Tsui, Pearce, Porter, & Tripoli, 1997). These investments may be thought of from a resource-based view of gaining competitive advantage (Shore, Tetrick, et al., 2004).

Some of the key drivers of AOR investment for today's employers are costs, efficiency, strategy, and context, and these are intertwined. Employers may decide to invest in a detailed, state-of-the-art careers Web page with self-assessment tools for applicants, streaming video profiles of employees and jobs, and similar content for purposes of attracting and informing applicants, or they may go for a less expensive Web portal for applicants. Investment in applicant recruitment activities can be limited to simple job postings or include more expensive and involved activities associated with campus recruiting, sponsorship of events, and advertisement in multiple venues. Employers may embrace a human resource strategy that entails greater investment in screening applicants or one that leads to less time and money on applicants and greater investment in training after hire. Organizations may use off-the-shelf products as selection tools or invest in custom design of their entire screening and selection process. In conjunction with strategy, context affects decisions regarding AOR investment. Recruiting budgets rise and extensiveness of screening falls when unemployment is low, and the inverse is true when the employment cycle reverses. In other words, with all else being equal, many organizations will attend to the attraction aspect of the AOR (i.e., meeting applicant expectations) and less to the selection aspect (i.e., meeting organizational requirements) in low-unemployment contexts.

Applicants also make decisions regarding investment in the AOR. For example, an applicant can decide to tailor each cover letter and resume to the position or to invest less time and use the same materials for all. An applicant can decide whether he or she is willing to obtain credentialing necessary for applying to certain positions, often at his or her own time and expense. An applicant can decide whether he or she is willing to attend test orientation sessions offered by employers for certain positions, particularly civil service ones (Ryan, Ployhart, Greguras, & Schmit, 1998). An applicant can decide whether he or she wants to prepare for a specific job interview through researching an organization thoroughly or superficially. For some highly attractive jobs, such as in policing (Truxillo et al., 2002), applicants may be willing to invest a lot more in order to obtain the job (e.g., pay for training and certification, pay for travel to be interviewed, spend more time being screened, devote more time to networking).

As the AOR evolves, applicants may decide to reduce their investment and self-select out of the process. Kuncel and Klieger (2007) discuss three scenarios where individuals choose not to invest in the AOR or to end their investment: when there are other choices (e.g., in a good labor market for job seekers), when they judge their person–job fit to be low, and when they feel they have little chance of successfully obtaining the job. For example, Kuncel and Klieger (2007) note that in cases where applicants know whether their exact qualifications meet exact requirements of the organization (e.g., Law School Admission Test scores for law school admission, scores on civil service exams) and/or know the selection ratio or acceptance rate of the organization, applicants may make the decision to discontinue (or not even engage in) the AOR if they feel their investment is unlikely to provide a payoff. Others also have noted that anticipated rewards are critical elements of contract beliefs (Coyle-Shapiro, 2002), and thus, applicants' anticipation of obtaining a job will affect what they feel they are willing to do to obtain it.

Culture as an influence in the AOR has been the focus of a growing body of research, and it may be particularly important to consider in terms of both expectations and investments. What employers see as typical and appropriate procedures in different countries (Ryan, McFarland, Baron, & Page, 1999) and what applicants in different countries see as appropriate (Ryan et al., 1998) have both been examined. Of interest, on both the organization and applicant side, there is more similarity than distinctions across cultures in terms of expectations of what an AOR should entail (Anderson, Salgado, & Hulsheger, 2010). However, expectations do differ in certain ways across cultures on both relational obligations (e.g., time spent on building rapport in a selection interview in the Middle East may be much greater than in the United States) and transactional obligations (e.g., timing of new graduate recruitment cycles) (Farndale & Pauuwe, 2007). There is a need, however, to be clear about the *reasons* for differences in AORs across nations. These are often complex and not necessarily driven by cultural value differences, but more often by labor market considerations (Ryan & Tippins, 2010); that is, they are more likely differences in investments than in expectations. For example, Ryan et al. (1998) noted that applicants from countries with fewer economic opportunities react more favorably to testing in the hiring process, presumably because it may allow them access to opportunities they might not otherwise have. Because nationality is linked to educational systems and labor markets, investments in the AOR will vary across countries; this variance is often attributed to a difference in expectations due to cultural values when in reality it is driven by labor pool availability (i.e., investment differences).

In sum, both applicants and employers make decisions about what they are willing to invest into the AOR. Such decisions can be strategic, with employers thinking about how they want to position themselves (e.g., as an employer of choice among minority applicants) and applicants thinking about how to make themselves stand out (e.g., by improving credentials), but can also be highly affected by practical aspects (e.g., on the employer side: what is the budget for a new selection process, how many minutes of testing time can we afford, how can we process applicants efficiently; on the applicant side: how long can I go without employment, how wide a geographic radius will my family allow me to search).

DYNAMIC NATURE OF AORS

Shore, Tetrick, et al. (2004) note that a focus on the dynamic nature of the EOR over time is important; similarly, there have been numerous calls in the applicant perceptions literature for taking a more dynamic look at how views change over the course of the hiring process (Ryan & Ployhart, 2000). Recruitment is a multiphase process, yet recruitment research is often compartmentalized to a single stage (Breaugh, 2008). The influence of information and activities at early stages on later ones has not been fully investigated, although some connections have been shown (Collins & Stevens, 2002; Saks & Uggerslev, 2010).

DeVos (2005) noted that fulfillment of the psychological contract in the past shapes the way the present is interpreted and what is anticipated for the future. The same holds true for the AOR. Suppose an applicant fills out a Web-based application that states "Your materials will be reviewed, and we will be contacting you shortly." The applicant who receives an e-mail update on the status of his or her application within a few days develops a different perspective than one who hears nothing until he or she recontacts the organization. As both individuals proceed through the process, the former may feel more obligated to work to meet the organization's needs (e.g., rearranging his or her work schedule to meet a preferred time for an interview, agreeing to make a decision on an offer promptly), whereas the latter may view obligations quite differently (e.g., being less flexible with regard to times and dates for subsequent screening and interviewing; holding onto an offer longer while considering multiple other offers).

Saks and Uggerslev (2010) discuss changes in applicant views over time in terms of Hogarth and Einhorn's (1992) model of belief updating, which describes how new information is integrated with prior knowledge. (Similarly, Rousseau [2011] has noted various ways in which individuals process information when it is at odds with preexisting contract beliefs.) A belief updating perspective on the AOR would suggest that information received is integrated in with prior knowledge, but more recent and more negative information will receive more weight.

It is important to point out that unlike the singular EOR held by an employee, applicants can simultaneously hold multiple AORs with different organizations. One impetus for changing one's investment level in an AOR is whether one has other AORs and how those AORs compare, especially in terms of what they are signaling about the EOR. A continual criticism of the broader recruitment literature as well as of the more specific applicant perceptions literature is this failure to duly consider the role of available alternatives (Breaugh, 2008; Ryan & Ployhart, 2000).

Shore, Porter, et al. (2004) note that the strategic perspective of the firm affects EOR stability; a similar note can be made regarding the AOR. An agency theory or upper echelon perspective suggests that management has greater control over the AOR and what employer agents say or do with applicants is more consistent over time, whereas resource-based or dynamic capability views suggest that the employer's behavior toward the applicant will change with the external environment.

One final point about the AOR is that some applicants will move from an AOR to an EOR. On the employer side, the decision of who to extend an offer to will be based on criteria defined by job requirements, but also by assessments of organizational fit, by availability of applicants (i.e., selection ratios), and unfortunately, to some extent, by biases and irrelevant factors (see Farr & Tippins [2010] for a comprehensive review). On the applicant side, considerable research has demonstrated that offer acceptance is affected by pay and promotional opportunities (Rynes & Cable, 2003) and organizational characteristics (Chapman, Uggerslev, Carroll, Piasentin, & Jones, 2005) and, to a lesser extent, perceptions of the hiring process and recruiter characteristics. We know that offer timeliness (Rynes, Bretz, & Gerhart, 1991) and inducements (e.g., signing bonuses; Rynes & Barber, 1990) affect decisions to enter into an EOR, as do family and friends (Kilduff, 1990). Thus, there is considerable research on what leads each party to decide that an AOR should advance to an EOR.

In sum, although AORs are typically short in overall duration, they still possess dynamic properties. Candidates that initially look promising to employers and jobs that initially appear ideal to applicants do not always retain their desirability, and as a result, parties to the AOR may feel their obligations have shifted.

AOR AS A SIGNAL OF EOR

The notion that the AOR influences the expectations of the EOR is hardly a new one; signaling theory has long been a focus of recruitment research (see Breaugh & Starke [2000] for a review). However, the psychological contract research has focused on the anticipatory psychological contract (APC), or beliefs predating the employment relationship (DeVos et al., 2009), largely in terms of "future employees" or those who have accepted offers from an organization. The AOR is the relationship with an applicant, who may or may not turn into a future employee. However, like DeVos et al.'s (2009) argument that the APC beliefs during anticipatory socialization are an initial stage of psychological contract formation, the AOR can serve as an influence on those initial psychological contract perceptions.

Casper and Buffardi (2004) introduced the concept of anticipated organizational support, or beliefs of applicants about how much the organization will value and care for them once employed, and suggested that these perceptions are derived from experiencing the selection process. In their research, Casper and Buffardi (2004) found that anticipated organizational support mediated the effects of work–life benefits on job pursuit intentions. Stewart, Mirza, and Campion (2010) found that anticipated organizational support mediated the links between perceptions of the justice of the selection process and applicant attraction to the organization and acceptance intentions. These studies confirm the notions behind signaling theory—that the applicant is receiving and interpreting signals about the future EOR through the AOR.

There are some recurrent themes in research on how the employer sends signals about the EOR through the AOR. At a broad level, whether the organization takes more of a "screening," "recruiting," or mixed orientation in its hiring process (Barber, Hollenbeck, Tower, & Phillips, 1994; Dineen & Soltis, 2011) is a significant strategic choice. A related more specific choice relates to how much realism to provide in signals. Breaugh (2008) reviewed the literature on realistic job previews and noted that realism in recruitment may have a negative impact on applicant attraction even for highly qualified individuals, but the result should be hires with a better understanding of job requirements than those who quit early on.

A specific signal that has been a research focus is how diversity advertising signals the organization's diversity climate and affects recruitment of minorities and women. Avery and McKay (2006) discussed a variety of techniques firms might use to convey a positive diversity climate to minority applicants (e.g., diversity portrayal in ads, placement of ads, sponsoring minority events). Signaling in this area is not necessarily straightforward:

Avery (2003) demonstrated that diversity portrayal in lower level positions only sends a negative rather than a positive signal.

As other examples, many employers regularly update their career Web pages so as to convey to applicants that the organization is on the leading edge of technology and that employees at their organization have positive EORs. Indeed, a glance through some of the streaming video of employee profiles on major company career websites shows many employees with families, engaged in hobbies, or engaged in community service, not just at work—a direct attempt to signal to applicants that the organization is supportive of work–life balance.

In addition to signals sent by the organization, applicants receive information about the AOR and the potential EOR from other sources. Perceptions of the AOR and also applicant anticipatory EOR perceptions are influenced by social networks (Breaugh, 2008; Kilduff, 1990). Further, potential coworkers (Cable & Turban, 2001) and informal Web-based communications about organizations (Van Hoye & Lievens, 2007) affect applicants' perceptions of the organization. For example, one can find information on the Web about individuals' experiences as applicants to an organization detailing the process and how they were treated, and one can garner information on what to expect in terms of an EOR from postings from both current and former employees.

In sum, the AOR is in many ways a key signal of the EOR, interpreted by applicants as to "what it might be like to work here." Organizations recognize this and work to adapt signals to applicants so that they are viewed positively by today's applicants.

BREACH OR VIOLATION

Rousseau (2011) distinguishes between breach and violation, with *breach* being falling short in fulfilling obligations and *violation* being a willful failure to honor commitments. For the AOR, a common breach example would be delays in organizational communication to applicants regarding their status; a failure to get back to the applicant at all would likely be considered a violation. On the other side, an applicant being late to an interview might be considered a breach, whereas cheating on a selection test or résumé fraud typically would be considered a violation. Rousseau notes that the circumstances of a breach affect how it is interpreted, as well as explanations offered for its occurrence. Hence, the employer who explains why an application was "misfiled" or why an interviewee was kept waiting with a scheduled appointment may not see as much damage to the AOR as one who offers no explanation.

Morrison and Robinson (2008) suggested that a lack of agreement between employees and employers in the EOR and consequent perceptions of breach or violation stem from differences in schema regarding what the employment relationship should be like, complexity and ambiguity, and miscommunication. Similarly, agreement between applicants and employers regarding aspects of their relationship might be influenced by these three factors. First, differences in expectations may lead to feelings of breach. Second, ambiguity can enter into the relationship. For example, how long an applicant can "hold onto" a job offer before making a decision is not always clear, or how early in the process an applicant needs to acknowledge "special circumstances" (e.g., "I can't start then because of a contract I'm under") is ambiguous. Employers are also often ambiguous about how various selection criteria will be weighted in deciding who will be hired or how long it will take to reach a decision. Griffin and Ross (1991) suggested that in cases of ambiguity employees and employers will fill in missing information with their own interpretations. Third, miscommunication can be a concern. For example, applicants might assume that certain travel expenses associated with a recruitment visit will be reimbursed, but the employer might have a different interpretation of what is standard and customary (e.g., a job applicant who runs up large charges in long-distance calls or orders an expensive bottle of wine from room service on a hotel bill).

It is also important to note that both the EOR and applicant reactions literatures have recognized that violation is not necessarily an "either/or" proposition, but there is probably some tolerance for minor deviations from expectations (Gilliland, 2008; Gilliland, Benson, & Schepers, 1998; Shore, Tetrick, et al., 2004). One question to explore is what the zones of tolerance are on key attributes of the AOR (e.g., how much of a delay in communication is too much of a delay, when does efficient processing turn into impersonal treatment and rudeness, when are applicant requests in negotiating viewed as beyond reasonable). Here too one should be cognizant of potential cultural differences in zones. Also, just as there is a greater zone of acceptance to changes in the EOR when managers are credible (Shore, Tetrick, et al., 2004), so too is there research to suggest that organizations with good reputations may be able to "get away with more" because they attract more higher quality applicants (Turban & Cable, 2003). Gilliland (2008) has suggested that we need better means of assessing the "tails of the justice distribution," because the vast majority of actions applicants encounter probably are in the middle of a normal distribution of fair treatment.

Deviations from expectations are not likely to be viewed as violations when good explanations are provided (Shore, Tetrick, et al., 2004). The importance of explanations for applicants has been noted earlier, but warrants reemphasis as organizations are often reluctant to provide applicants with more than a form letter in rejection, often on advice of legal counsel. The lack of explanation at the point of rejection may not seem to be particularly important because the AOR is now terminated. However, having this unfulfilled obligation at the end of the relationship may have ripple effects on any future customer–organization relationship with the former applicant, as well as on what they convey to friends, family, and their broader social network about the organization. Similarly, for high-level or specialty positions, unexplained and unusual applicant behaviors can have effects on the individual's reputation in an industry where employers regularly interact and share information.

Turnley and Feldman (1999) suggest that different obligations in a psychological contract have differential importance and hence the effects of violation may vary. Zhao, Wayne, Glibowski, and Bravo (2007) conducted a meta-analysis and reported that breach of relational contracts leads to more negative outcomes than breach of transactional ones. This would suggest that the interpersonal treatment elements would be most important to applicants and employers. For example, Ferguson, Moye, and Friedman (2008) found that interactional justice perceptions regarding the job negotiation process had an impact on turnover intentions after hiring. Overall, although the importance of relational elements is well acknowledged, connection of specific elements of the AOR to subsequent behavior in the AOR and to the EOR is still in need of research.

Shore, Tetrick, et al. (2004) note that it is increasingly important to focus on good employee–employer relations to avoid negative legal consequences, and thus managing the EOR is, in some ways, effective legal risk management. Similarly, some have focused on how violations in the

AOR may lead to legal claiming behavior by applicants (Goldman, Gutek, Stein, & Lewis, 2006), and organizations may invest in aspects of the AOR in an effort to reduce claiming behavior.

PRACTICAL IMPLICATIONS

There are many practical implications for employers that can be drawn from this discussion. Table 14.1 lists suggestions for employers that wish to develop and maintain high-quality AORs.

TABLE 14.1
Implications for Employers

- Ensure individuals are aware of what they must do to be considered an applicant.
- Ensure that organizational agents involved in any aspect of the hiring process understand their obligations and share a common vision.
- Define the obligations of third parties clearly.
- Provide accurate information on job duties, earnings and promotion potential, and organizational climate to applicants.
- Provide accurate information on hiring process components, decision criteria, and explanations for those to applicants.
- Regularly audit the interpersonal treatment applicants are receiving.
- Ensure the process is seen by applicants as providing sufficient opportunity to perform.
- Communicate to applicants the importance of truthful portrayals of qualifications.
- Recognize cultural differences in expected obligations when hiring across borders.
- Communicate clearly to applicants their obligations in technology-enabled application and testing processes.
- Align the level of standardization of AORs with chosen human resources (HR) strategy.
- Gather information on applicant expectations for the AOR and either meet them or work to revise them.
- Clearly convey any expectations of applicants.
- Align the level of investment in the AOR with chosen HR strategy.
- Evaluate what is signaled in the AOR and whether it is what is desired.
- Regularly investigate what other sources are conveying to applicants about your AORs.
- Provide explanations to applicants when breaches occur.
- Avoid violations through clarifying expectations and obligations and through clarity in communication.

CONCLUSIONS

This chapter provides some examples and evidence of connections that can be made between concepts from the literature on EORs to the literature on AORs, as well as noting that the AOR can serve as a signal of what the EOR might be like. Illustrating such links can serve as a useful new lens for looking at traditional recruitment and selection topics. For example, the concept of mutuality has not permeated the applicant perceptions and recruitment literatures and might serve as a springboard for a new basis for connecting applicant perceptions and behaviors. Although the notion of violations has been introduced to the applicant perceptions literature by justice researchers, the concept of breach and its underpinnings has not been well adopted and might serve as a better means of understanding what turns off applicants and employers. This chapter establishes that connections can be made between the AOR and the EOR, but the task of articulating and investigating those connections has only just begun.

REFERENCES

Amare, N., & Manning, A. (2009). Writing for the robot: How search tools affect résumé ethics. *Business Communication Quarterly, 72*, 35–60.

Anderson, N., Salgado, J. F., & Hülsheger, U. R. (2010). Applicant reactions in selection: Comprehensive meta-analysis into reaction generalization versus situational specificity. *International Journal of Selection and Assessment, 18*(3), 291–304.

Atkinson, C. (2008). An exploration of small firm psychological contracts. *Work, Employment, and Society, 22*, 447–465.

Avery, D. R. (2003). Reactions to diversity in recruitment advertising—are differences black and white? *Journal of Applied Psychology, 88*, 672–679.

Avery, D. R., & McKay, P. F. (2006) Target practice: An organizational impression management approach to attracting minority and female job applicants. *Personnel Psychology, 59*, 157–187.

Bachler, C. J. (1995). Resume fraud: Lies, omissions and exaggerations. *Personnel Journal, 74*, 50–59.

Barber, A. E., Hollenbeck, J. R., Tower, S. L., & Phillips, J. M. (1994). The effects of interview focus on recruitment effectiveness: A field experiment. *Journal of Applied Psychology, 79*, 886–896.

Bardack, N. R., & McAndrew, F. T. (1985). The influence of physical attractiveness and manner of dress on success in a simulated personnel decision. *Journal of Social Psychology, 125*, 777–778.

Barrick, M. R., Shaffer, J. A., & DeGrassi, S. W. (2009). What you see may not be what you get: Relationships among self-presentation tactics and ratings of interview and job performance. *Journal of Applied Psychology, 94*, 1394–1411.

Bauer, T. N., Maertz, C. P., Dolen, M. R., & Campion, M. A. (1998). Longitudinal assessment of applicant reactions to employment testing and test outcome feedback. *Journal of Applied Psychology, 83*, 892–903.

Bazerman, M. H., Schroth, H. A., Shah, P. P., Diekmann, K. A., & Tenbrunsel, A. E. (1994). The inconsistent role of comparison others and procedural justice in reactions to hypothetical job offers: Implications for job acceptance decisions. *Organizational Behavior and Human Decision Processes, 60*, 326–352.

Bell, B. S., Ryan, A. M., & Weichmann, D. (2004). Justice expectations and applicant perceptions. *International Journal of Selection and Assessment, 12*, 24–38.

Bell, B. S., Weichmann, D., & Ryan, A. M. (2006). Consequences of organizational justice expectations in a selection system. *Journal of Applied Psychology, 91*, 455–466.

Berry, C. M., & Sackett, P. R. (2009). Faking in personnel selection: Tradeoffs in performance versus fairness resulting from two cut-score strategies. *Personnel Psychology, 62*, 835–863.

Breaugh, J. A. (2008). Employee recruitment: Current knowledge and important areas for future research. *Human Resource Management Review, 18*, 103–118.

Breaugh, J. A., & Starke, M. (2000). Research on employee recruitment, so many studies, so many remaining questions. *Journal of Management, 26*, 405–434.

Buckley, M. R., Fedor, D. B., Carraher, S. M., Frink, D. D., & Marvin, D. (1997). The ethical imperative to provide recruits realistic job previews. *Journal of Managerial Issues, 9*, 468–484.

Cable, D., & Turban, D. (2001). Establishing the dimensions, sources, and value of job seekers' employer knowledge during recruitment. In G. Ferris (Ed.), *Research in personnel and human resource management* (pp. 115–163). Greenwich, CT: JAI Press.

Casper, W. J., & Buffardi, L. C. (2004). Work-life benefits and job pursuit intentions: The role of anticipated organizational support. *Journal of Vocational Behavior, 65*, 391–410.

Chapman, D. S., Uggerslev, K. L., Carroll, S. A., Piasentin, K. A., & Jones, D. A. (2005). Applicant attraction to organizations and job choice: A meta-analytic review of the correlates of recruiting outcomes. *Journal of Applied Psychology, 90*, 928–944.

Collins, C. J., & Stevens, C. K. (2002). The relationship between early recruitment-related activities and the application decisions of new labor-market entrants: A brand equity approach to recruitment. *Journal of Applied Psychology, 87*, 1121–1133.

Coyle-Shapiro, J. A. M. (2002). A psychological contract perspective on organizational citizenship behaviors. *Journal of Organizational Behavior, 23*, 927–946.

Coyle-Shapiro, J. A. M., & Kessler, I. (2000). Consequences of the psychological contract for the employment relationship: A large scale survey. *Journal of Management Studies, 37*, 903–930.

Cullen, L. T. (2007, October 22). The new expatriates. *Time: Global Supplement Section*, 1–4.

Dabos, G. E., & Rousseau, D. M. (2004). Mutuality and reciprocity in the psychological contracts of employee and employer. *Journal of Applied Psychology, 89*, 52–72.

DeVos, A. (2005). The psychological contract of organizational newcomers: An investigation of antecedents and changes over time. *International Journal of Human Resources Development and Management, 5*, 371–388.

DeVos, A., DeStobbeleir, K., & Meganck, A. (2009). The relationship between career-related antecedents and graduates' anticipatory psychological contracts. *Journal of Business and Psychology, 24*, 289–298.

Dineen, B. R., & Soltis, S. M. (2011). Recruitment: A review of research and emerging directions. In S. Zedeck (Ed.), *APA handbook of industrial and organizational psychology* (pp. 43–66). Washington, DC: American Psychological Association.

Equal Employment Opportunity Commission. (2008). Questions and answers: Definition of "job applicant" for Internet and related electronic technologies. Retrieved from http://www.eeoc.gov/policy/docs/qanda-ugesp.html

Farndale, E., & Paauwe, J. (2007). Uncovering competitive and institutional drivers of HRM practices in multinational corporations. *Human Resource Management Journal, 17*, 355–375.

Farr, J. L., & Tippins, N. T. (2010). *Handbook of employee selection*. New York, NY: Routledge/Taylor & Francis Group.

Ferguson, M., Moye, N., & Friedman, R. (2008). The lingering effects of the recruitment experience on the long-term employment relationship. *Negotiation and Conflict Management Research, 1*, 246–262.

Gilliland, S. (2008). The tails of justice: A critical examination of the dimensionality of organizational justice constructs. *Human Resource Management Review, 18*, 271–281.

Gilliland, S., Benson, L., & Schepers, D. H. (1998). A rejection threshold in justice evaluations: Effects on judgment and decision-making. *Organizational Behavior and Human Decision Processes, 76*, 113–131.

Gilliland, S. W., & Steiner, D. D. (2001). Causes and consequences of applicant perceptions of unfairness. In R. Cropanzano (Ed.), *Justice in the workplace: From theory to practice* (pp. 175–195). Mahwah, NJ: Lawrence Erlbaum Associates Publishers.

Goldman, B. M., Gutek, B. A., Stein, J. H., & Lewis, K. (2006). Employment discrimination in organizations: Antecedents and consequences. *Journal of Management, 32*, 786–830.

Griffin, D., & Ross, L. (1991). Subjective construal, social inference, and human misunderstanding. In M. P. Zanna (Ed.), *Advances in experimental social psychology* (Vol. 24, pp. 319–359). San Diego, CA: Academic Press.

Griffith, R. L., Chmielowski, T., & Yoshita, Y. (2007). Do applicants fake? An examination of the frequency of applicant faking behavior. *Personnel Review, 36*, 341–355.

Guy, C. W. (2001). Eroding ethics of executive search. *Consulting to Management, 12*, 51–56.

Highhouse, S., & Hause, E. L. (1995). Missing information in selection: An application of the Einhorn-Hogarth ambiguity model. *Journal of Applied Psychology, 80*, 86–93.

Hogarth, R. M., & Einhorn, H. J. (1992). Order effects in belief updating: The belief-adjustment model. *Cognitive Psychology, 24*, 1–55.

Kilduff, M. (1990). The interpersonal structure of decision making: A social comparison approach to organizational choice. *Organizational Behavior and Human Decision Processes, 47*, 270–288.

Kravitz, D. A., Stinson, V., & Chavez, T. L. (1996). Evaluations of tests used for making selection and promotion decisions. *International Journal of Selection and Assessment, 4*, 24–34.

Kuncel, N. R., & Klieger, D. M. (2007). Application patterns when applicants know the odds: Implications for selection research and practice. *Journal of Applied Psychology, 92*, 586–593.

Lim, G., & Chan, C. (2001). Ethical values of executive search consultants. *Journal of Business Ethics, 29*, 213–226.

Morgeson, F. P., Campion, M. A., Dipboye, R. L., Hollenbeck, J. R., Murphy, K., & Schmitt, N. (2007). Reconsidering the use of personality tests in personnel selection contexts. *Personnel Psychology, 60*, 683–729.

Morrison, E., & Robinson, S. (2008). The employment relationship from two sides: Incongruence in employees' and employers' perceptions of obligations. In J. Coyle-Shapiro, L. Shore, S. Taylor, & L. Tetrick (Eds.), *The employment relationship: Examining psychological and contextual perspectives*. Oxford, UK: Oxford University Press.

Olson, J. M., Roese, N., & Zanna, M. P. (1996). Expectancies. In E. T. Higgins & A. W. Kruglanski (Eds.), *Social psychology: Handbook of basic principles* (pp. 211–238). New York, NY: Guilford Press.

Pearlman, K. (2009). Unproctored internet testing: Practical, legal, and ethical concerns. *Industrial and Organizational Psychology: Perspectives on Science and Practice, 2*, 14–19.

Ployhart, R. E., McFarland, L. A., & Ryan, A. M. (2002). Examining applicants' attributions for withdrawal from a selection procedure. *Journal of Applied Social Psychology, 32*, 2228–2252.

Ployhart, R. E., Ryan, A. M., & Bennett, M. (1999). Explanations for selection decisions: Applicants' reactions to information and sensitivity features of explanations. *Journal of Applied Psychology, 84*, 87–106.

Premack, S. L., & Wanous, J. P. (1985). A meta-analysis of realistic job preview experiments. *Journal of Applied Psychology, 70*, 706–719.

Robinson, S. L., Kraatz, M. S., & Rousseau, D. M. (1994). Changing obligations and the psychological contract: A longitudinal study. *Academy of Management Journal, 37*(1), 137–152.

Robinson, S. L., & Morrison, E. (1995). Psychological contracts and organizational citizenship behavior: The effect of unfulfilled obligations on civic virtue behavior. *Journal of Organizational Behavior, 16*, 289–298.

Rousseau, D. M. (2011). The individual-organization relationship: The psychological contract. In S. Zedeck (Ed.), *AOPA handbook of industrial and organizational psychology* (pp. 191–220). Washington, DC: American Psychological Association.

Ryan, A. M., & Delany, T. (2010). Attracting job candidates to organizations. In J. L. Farr & N. T. Tippins (Eds.), *Handbook of employee selection* (pp. 127–150). New York, NY: Routledge/Taylor & Francis Group.

Ryan, A. M., Greguras, G. J., & Ployhart, R. E. (1996). Perceived job relatedness of physical ability testing for firefighters: Exploring variation in reactions. *Human Performance, 9*, 219–240.

Ryan, A. M., & Huth, M. (2008). Not much more than platitudes? A critical look at the utility of applicant reactions research. *Human Resource Management Review, 18*, 119–132.

Ryan, A. M., McFarland, L. A., Baron, H., & Page, R. (1999). An international look at selection practices: Nation and culture as explanations for variability in practice. *Personnel Psychology, 52*, 359–391.

Ryan, A. M., & Ployhart, R. E. (2000). Applicants' perceptions of selection procedures and decisions: A critical review and agenda for the future. *Journal of Management, 26*, 565–606.

Ryan, A. M., Ployhart, R. E., Greguras, G. J., & Schmit, M. J. (1998). Test preparation programs in selection contexts: Self-selection and program effectiveness. *Personnel Psychology, 51*, 599–621.

Ryan, A. M., Sacco, J. M., McFarland, L. A., & Kriska, S. D. (2000). Applicant self-selection: Correlates of withdrawal from a multiple hurdle process. *Journal of Applied Psychology, 85*, 163–179.

Ryan, A. M., & Schmit, M. J. (1996). Calculating EEO Statistics in the temporary help industry. *Personnel Psychology, 49,* 167–180.

Ryan, A. M., & Tippins, N. T. (2009). *Designing and implementing global selection systems.* West Sussex, UK: Wiley-Blackwell.

Ryan, A. M., & Tippins, N. T. (2010). Global applications of assessment. In J. C. Scott & D. H. Reynolds (Eds.), *Handbook of workplace assessment* (pp. 577–606). San Francisco, CA: Jossey-Bass.

Rynes, S. L., & Barber, A. E. (1990). Applicant attraction strategies: An organizational perspective. *Academy of Management Review, 15,* 286–310.

Rynes, S. L., Bretz, R. D., & Gerhart, B. (1991). The importance of recruitment in job choice: A different way of looking. *Personnel Psychology, 44,* 487–521.

Rynes, S. L., & Cable, D. M. (2003). Recruitment research in the twenty-first century. In W. C. Borman, D. R. Ilgen, & R. J. Klimoski (Eds.), *Handbook of psychology: Industrial and organizational psychology* (Vol. 12, pp. 55–76). Hoboken, NJ: John Wiley & Sons Inc.

Saks, A. M., & Uggerslev, K. L. (2010). Sequential and combined effects of recruitment information on applicant reactions. *Journal of Business and Psychology, 25,* 351–365.

Schleicher, D. J., Venkataramani, V., Morgeson, F., & Campion, M. (2006). So you didn't get the job…Now what do you think? Examining opportunity-to-perform fairness perceptions. *Personnel Psychology, 59,* 559–590.

Schmit, M. J., & Ryan, A. M. (1997). Applicant withdrawal: The role of test-taking attitudes and racial differences. *Personnel Psychology, 50,* 855–876.

Schreurs, B., Derous, E., Proost, K., Notelaers, G., & De Witte, K. (2008). Applicant selection expectations: Validating a multidimensional measure in the military. *International Journal of Selection and Assessment, 16,* 170–176.

Schreurs, B., Derous, E., Van Hooft, E. A. J., Proost, K., & De Witte, K. (2009). Predicting applicants' job pursuit behavior from their selection expectations: The mediating role of the theory of planned behavior. *Journal of Organizational Behavior, 30,* 761–783.

Shapiro, D. L., & Kirkman, B. L. (2001). *Anticipatory injustice: The consequences of expecting injustice in the workplace.* Palo Alto, CA: Stanford University Press.

Shore, L. M., Porter, L. W., & Zahra, S. A. (2004). Employer-oriented strategic approaches to the employee-organization relationship (EOR). In J. Coyle-Shapiro, L. M. Shore, S. Taylor, & L. E. Tetrick (Eds.), *The employment relationship: Examining psychological and contextual perspectives.* Oxford, UK: Oxford University Press.

Shore, L. M., Tetrick, L. E., Taylor, M. S., Coyle-Shapiro, J. A.-M., Liden, R. C., McLean-Parks, J., … Van Dyne, L. (2004). The employee-organization relationship: A timely concept in a period of transition. In J. J. Martocchio & G. R. Ferris (Eds.), *Research in personnel and human resources management* (pp. 291–370). Greenwich, CT: JAI Press.

Stewart, G. L., Dustin, S. L., Barrick, M. R., & Darnold, T. C. (2008). Exploring the handshake in employment interviews. *Journal of Applied Psychology, 93,* 1139–1146.

Stewart, R. W., Mirza, C., & Campion, J. E. (2010, April). *The role of anticipated organizational support in applicant reactions.* Presented at the annual meetings of the Society for Industrial and Organizational Psychology, Atlanta, GA.

Stone, D. L., & Stone, E. F. (1987). Effects of missing application blank information on personnel selection decisions: Do privacy protection strategies bias the outcome. *Journal of Applied Psychology, 72,* 452–456.

Truxillo, D. M., Bauer, T. N., Campion, M. A., & Parento, M. E. (2002). Selection fairness information and applicant reactions: a longitudinal field study. *Journal of Applied Psychology, 87,* 1020–1031.

Truxillo, D. M., Bodner, T. E., Bertolino, M., Bauer, T. N., & Yonce, C. A. (2009). Effects of explanations on applicant reactions: A meta-analytic review. *International Journal of Selection and Assessment, 17*, 346–361.

Tsui, A. S., Pearce, J. L., Porter, L. W., & Tripoli, A. M. (1997). Alternative approaches to the employee–organization relationship: Does investment in employees pay off? *Academy of Management Journal, 40*, 1089–1121.

Tunley, W. H., & Feldman, D. C. (2000). Re-examining the effects of psychological contract violations: Unmet expectations and job dissatisfaction as mediators. *Journal of Organizational Behavior, 21*, 25–42.

Turban, D. B., & Cable, D. M. (2003). Firm reputation and applicant pool characteristics. *Journal of Organizational Behavior, 24*, 733–751.

Turner-Bowker, D. M. (2001). How can you pull yourself up by your bootstraps, if you don't have boots? Work-appropriate clothing for poor women. *Journal of Social Issues, Special Issue: Listening to the Voices of Poor Women, 57*, 311–322.

Vance, C. M., & Paik, Y. (2006). *Managing a global workforce: Challenges and opportunities in international human resource management.* London, UK: M.E. Sharpe.

Van Hoye, G., & Lievens, F. (2007). Investigating Web-based recruitment sources: Employee testimonials versus word-of-mouse. *International Journal of Selection and Assessment, 15*, 372–382.

Wood, J. L., Schmidtke, J. M., & Decker, D. L. (2007). Lying on job applications: The effects of job relevance, commission, and human resource management experience. *Journal of Business and Psychology, 22*, 1–9.

Wren, A. O., Clark, L., & Deriso, M. (2006). Employer beware: Truth-in-hiring may be the new standard in recruiting. *Business Forum, 27*(2), 11.

Zhao, H., Wayne, S., Glibowski, B., & Bravo, J. (2007). The impact of psychological contract breach on work-related outcomes: A meta-analysis. *Personnel Psychology, 60*, 647–680.

15

Employee–Organization Relationships: Their Impact on Push-and-Pull Forces for Staying and Leaving

Peter W. Hom
Arizona State University

Management scholars increasingly focus on how employee–organization relationships (EOR) influence voluntary employee turnover. Historically, turnover researchers examined employees' experiences with their proximal work environment to identify causes impelling them to quit, such as dissatisfying tasks or poor leader–member exchanges (Hom & Griffeth, 1995). During the 1990s, the advent of strategic human resources (Butler & Ferris, 1991; Gomez-Mejia & Balkin, 1992) and radical restructuring of employment relationships (Batt, Colvin, & Keefe, 2002; Cappelli, 2000; Tsui, Pearce, Porter, & Hite, 1995) initiated scholarly inquiry into different EOR forms (Baron & Kreps, 1999). As a consequence, many organizational scientists are documenting how firm-level EORs affect aggregate-level turnover rates (Arthur, 1984; Huselid, 1995), going beyond traditional preoccupation with individual-level antecedents (Griffeth, Hom, & Gaertner, 2000). This escalating avenue of turnover research concludes that certain EOR forms most deter turnover, such as "high-performance" (Huselid, 1995) or "mutual investment" EORs (whereby employees offer bountiful inducements but expect high and broad staff contributions) (Arthur, 1984; Huselid, 1995; Tsui, Pearce, Porter, & Tripoli, 1997). Recently, this research stream investigated mechanisms mediating or moderating EOR effects on attrition or generalized EOR effects across different industries, cultures, and types of turnover (Gutherie, 2001; Hausknecht & Trevor, 2010; Hom et al., 2009; Shaw, Dineen, Fang, & Vellella, 2009; Yalabik, Chen, Lawler, & Kim, 2008). A recent meta-analysis based on 6,105 firms thus estimated a 0.12

correlation between high-performance human resources systems and workforce retention (Combs, Liu, Hall, & Ketchen, 2006).

Although turnover researchers have long advocated firm-level study (Hom & Griffeth, 1995), this emerging macro-level line of inquiry has not kept pace with theoretical and empirical developments in turnover research (Holtom, Mitchell, Lee, & Inderrieden, 2005; Hom, 2010) or fully capitalized on the rich scholarly tradition in this domain (Hom & Griffeth, 1995; Mobley, 1982). All too often, EOR investigators focus on the nature of the exchange between employees and employers to explain how EOR forms affect leaving. To illustrate, Tsui et al. (1997) argue that mutual investment EOR builds organizational commitment and retention because this arrangement induces "social exchange"—relationships based on trust and unspecified obligations whereby employers and employees exchange socioemotional and material resources (Blau, 1964). Because such transactions are long-term and open-ended (Shore, Tetrick, Lynch, & Barksdale, 2006), so Blau's arguments go, employees stay to maintain such beneficial arrangements and to live up to reciprocal obligations (Hom et al., 2009; Takeuchi, Lepak, Wang, & Takeuchi, 2007). Although social (or economic) exchange remains the mainstay explanatory mechanism for EOR theorists (Shore et al., 2006), the quality of employer–employee relationships (and affective attachments thus formed) represents only part of the story according to turnover theory and work. Because "much of the collective turnover literature [including EOR research] is predicated on individual-level theory and rationale" (Hausknecht & Trevor, 2010, p. 360), this chapter integrates modern advances in theoretical views about the psychology of leaving (and staying) to deepen understanding of EOR effects on turnover.

EOR FRAMEWORK ON PUSH-AND-PULL FORCES FOR STAYING AND LEAVING

To more fully clarify how EOR forms induce job loyalty, I describe additional push-and-pull forces for leaving as well as staying based on contemporary frameworks deducing such mechanisms (Hom, Leong, & Golubovich, 2010; Lee, Gerhart, Weller, & Trevor, 2008; Maltarich, Nyberg, & Reilly, 2010; Tharenou & Caulfield, 2010). This organizing framework began with March and Simon's (1958) seminal theory of institutional participation, which identified desirability and ease of movement as proximal antecedents of turnover. These latter constructs (actually, categories of variables) were later construed as job dissatisfaction and job alternatives, respectively (Mobley, 1977, 1982; Price & Mueller, 1981, 1996). Present-day turnover scholars now refer to movement desirability as "push-to-leave" forces and movement ease as "pull-to-leave" forces (Lee et al., 2008; Maltarich et al., 2010; Trevor & Nyberg, 2008) to accommodate additional causes besides dissatisfaction and alternatives.

In particular, Lee and Mitchell (1994) expanded push-to-leave forces by identifying "shocks"—or events precipitating mental deliberations about quitting—as key drivers of leaving. According to research on their "unfolding model" (Lee, Mitchell, Holtom, McDaniel, & Hill, 1999; Lee, Mitchell, Wise, & Fireman, 1996), many, if not most, leavers exit not because they are unhappy or find superior alternatives; rather, they often leave due to shocks, following different turnover paths depending on the nature (e.g., personal versus organizational) of the shocks. To illustrate, some employees harbor preexisting plans to leave ("matching script"), which are activated when certain events occur or a certain time has elapsed (Lee et al., 1996). Lee et al. (1996) thus observed that some nurses exit once they become pregnant; the pregnancy triggered a matching script to exit the labor market when pregnancies occur. EOR investigators have rarely examined shock-driven turnover, although they have noted how certain EOR forms, such as mutual investment EOR (Tsui et al., 2007) can prevent layoffs (a type of shock; Trevor & Nyberg, 2008) or moderate layoff's impact (Zatzick & Iverson, 2006).

By primarily attending to why people leave, EOR authors often neglect how EOR forms can reinforce (or undermine) staying. Inaugurating a paradigm shift in turnover research (Hom, 2010), Mitchell, Holtom, Lee, Sablynski, and Erez (2001) introduced "job embeddedness" to explain why people stay. They contend that prevailing preoccupation with the psychology of leaving fails to explicate the psychology of staying. Just because employees do not quit does not imply that they are intrinsically motivated to stay. Similarly, Meyer, Becker, and Vandenberghe (2004) argue that incumbents who remain because they fear forfeiting ample job investments (e.g., seniority perks) if they leave (*continuance commitment*) do not necessarily feel affectively committed to employing institutions. In particular, Mitchell et al. (2001) theorize that people are bound to jobs by *fit* to the job and community, *links* to workplace and community contacts, and anticipated losses if they quit the job and community (*sacrifices*). In support, studies find that job embeddedness explains unique turnover variance beyond that of job attitudes and job alternatives (Holtom, Mitchell, Lee, & Eberly, 2008; Lee, Mitchell, Sablynski, Burton, & Holtom, 2004). Subsequent research identified additional constraints on leaving, such as embedding leadership (Ballinger, Lehman, & Schoorman, 2010; Carter, Waldman, & Hom, 2011) and human resources management (HRM) practices (e.g., pension, on-site childcare, flextime; Trevor & Nyberg, 2008). Importantly, Hom et al. (2009) found that certain EOR forms sustain job embeddedness, concluding that embeddedness represents a separate but distinct mechanism for building loyalty than social exchange.

Mitchell and Lee (2001) initially attempted to combine their heretofore separate models on leaving and staying to formulate a more comprehensive explanation of organizational participation (March & Simon, 1958). In this vein, Burton, Holtom, Sablynski, Holtom, and Lee (2010) later conceptualized job embeddedness as a pull force for staying, while denoting negative workplace shocks (e.g., organizational injustices) as a push force for leaving. They then demonstrated that highly embedded employees exposed to such shocks do not exhibit diminished performance or organizational citizenship. Only unembedded incumbents behave this way when encountering negative job shocks. Expanding this approach, Tharenou and Caulfield (2010) more fully specified varied push-and-pull forces for staying and leaving to elucidate why "self-initiated" expatriates terminate overseas employment. Their formulation depicts repatriation shocks (e.g., pregnancy may prompt expatriates to return home and rejoin extended families) and host country dissatisfaction as "push forces to repatriate" and home country attractions, such as lifestyle instrumentality and national identity, as "pull forces to repatriate." Moreover, they conceived host country embeddedness, such as having host country friends and relatives, as "pull-to-remain" forces. Their study revealed that each force explained unique variance in expatriates' repatriation intentions, although shocks rather than host country dissatisfaction exhibited unique effects.

In light of this recent trend toward integrated expositions of both staying and leaving forces, I formulate an EOR framework of varied push-and-pull mechanisms for staying and leaving to clarify how different EOR forms affect workforce motivation to stay or leave. For this purpose, the current model builds on Tsui et al.'s (1997) EOR classification scheme. Most EOR perspectives dichotomize EOR systems, such as high- versus low-performance work systems (Becker & Huselid, 1998; Datta, Guthrie, & Wright, 2005; Takeuchi et al., 2007) or high-commitment HRM (Collins & Smith, 2006; Xiao & Bjorkman, 2006), although Baron and Kreps (1999) discerned different "flavors" of high-commitment systems. By comparison, Tsui et al.'s EOR approach differentiates four EOR types: (a) mutual investment; (b) overinvestment (where employers offer abundant inducements to employees for minimal contributions); (c) underinvestment (where firms demand high and broad contributions for subpar investments in employees); and (d) quasi-spot contracts (where firms distribute low or narrow inducements for low or narrow contributions from employees). Importantly, empirical investigations have validated Tsui et al.'s EOR taxonomy (Wang, Tsui, Zhang, & Ma, 2003) and shown that these forms predict aggregate-level quit propensities in America (Tsui et al., 1997) and China (Hom et al., 2009).

By systematically delineating how each EOR form affects varied staying and leaving forces, the present formulation strives to identify not only their full effect but also potentially conflicting effects on turnover. After all, "workplaces often have a mix of HR practices that provide contradictory incentives to workers" to stay as well as to leave (Batt et al., 2002, p. 578). Yet EOR scholars rarely consider countervailing forces on leaving and staying. Nonetheless, self-directed team structures can reduce voluntary turnover (by increasing intrinsic rewards), while contingent pay schemes can increase turnover (invoking uncertainty about employees' ability to meet fixed living expenses; Batt & Colvin, 2011; Hausknecht & Trevor, 2010). Both practices are commonly implemented by mutual investment EOR or high-performance HRM systems (Baron & Kreps, 1999; Tsui et al., 1997). Apart from conflicting effects by a "bundle" of HRM practices, the same HRM practice can differentially affect loyalty of different workforce segments. To illustrate, Shaw et al. (2009) observed that expectation-enhancing HRM practices promulgated by mutual investment EOR promulgates (e.g., variable pay plans) increase poor performer turnover, while diminishing high performer turnover. Figure 15.1 presents this tentative framework of how EOR forms impact the sundry push-and-pull forces for staying and leaving, as well as noting these forces' differential impact on overall turnover and "dysfunctional" turnover (exits among high performers whose attrition is costliest to firms; Hom & Griffeth, 1995). Next, I discuss how each EOR form may influence these forces, which are summarized in Table 15.1 and depicted in Figure 15.1.

TABLE 15.1
Salient Push-and-Pull Forces for Different EOR Forms

EOR Forms	Push-to-Leave Forces	Pull-to-Leave Forces	Pull-to-Stay Forces	Push-to-Stay Forces
Mutual investment	Job dissatisfaction (job insecurity, fewer contingent rewards, job stress)	Movement capital Job-inquiry or job-offer shocks	High job embeddedness Embedding leadership Community embeddedness Family embeddedness	Workplace pressures to stay (closed colleague networks)
Overinvestment			Compensation satisfaction Job security Compatriot attachment Moderate job embeddedness Family embeddedness	Family pressures to stay Workplace pressures to stay (closed colleague networks)
Quasi-spot contracts	Job dissatisfaction (job insecurity) Negative job shocks	Turnover contagion Job alternatives	Pay satisfaction and equity Some job embeddedness	Family pressures to stay
Underinvestment	Job dissatisfaction (low and unfair pay, boring or fatiguing tasks) Negative job shocks (layoffs, dismissals)	Turnover contagion External shocks (script-based quits)	Job sacrifices	Family pressures to stay

Employee–Organization Relationships • 397

Voluntary turnover
- Overall quit rate
- Dysfunctional quit rate

Push-to-leave forces
- Work dissatisfaction
- Constituent dissatisfaction
- Compensation dissatisfaction
- Career dissatisfaction
- Negative job shocks

Push-to-leave forces
- Job opportunities
- Movement capital
- Job-inquiry shocks
- Turnover contagion
- Spousal relocations
- Personal shocks
- Lifestyle instrumentality

Push-to-stay forces
- On-the-job embeddedness
  - Job fit
  - Job links
  - Job sacrifice
- Off-the-job embeddedness
  - Community fit
  - Community links
  - Community sacrifice
  - Family embeddedness

Push-to-stay forces
- Normative pressures
- Closed colleague networks

EOR forms
- Mutual investment
- Overinvestment
- Quasi-spot contracts
- Underinvestment

FIGURE 15.1
EOR push-and-pull forces to stay or leave.

398 • *The Employee-Organization Relationship*

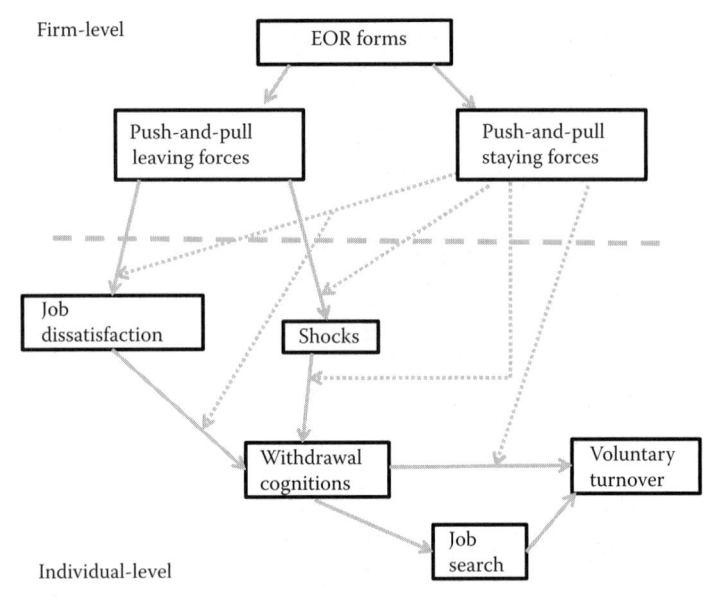

FIGURE 15.2
EOR multilevel mediation and moderation.

Afterward, I elucidate how macro-level EOR forms can impact individual-level attrition (see model in Figure 15.2), supplementing the first focus on content (turnover causes) with another focus on the multilevel process.

MUTUAL INVESTMENT EOR

Push-to-Leave Forces

EOR scholars primarily see mutual investment EORs (or high-commitment work systems) as primarily lessening push-to-leave forces because abundant inducements (attractive compensation) reduce job dissatisfaction, whereas ample investments in training and development enable incumbents to perform skilled or challenging work (earning them more intrinsic rewards and work satisfaction). Moreover, mutual investment EORs promote self-directed teams and other empowering structures (e.g., job enlargement and enrichment) that allow dissatisfied employees to voice their concerns or ameliorate stressful conditions rather than exit (Batt et al., 2002; Hulin, Roznowski, & Hachiya, 1985). Through such means, mutual investment EORs reduce job dissatisfaction, weakening this push-to-leave force (Griffeth et al., 2000; Hom & Griffeth, 1995). By contrast, this particular force is higher in quasi-spot contracts and underinvestment EORs because the former increase job insecurity whereas the latter engender underpayment inequity (Tsui et al., 1997).

Apart from lessening dissatisfaction, mutual EOR employers may proactively manage aversive workplace shocks that can instigate departures (path 2; Lee et al., 1996), such as minimizing layoffs (Trevor & Nyberg, 2008) or applying fair layoff procedures (Datta, Guthrie, Basuil, & Pandey, 2010). Rather than treating workers as disposable, mutual EOR employers encourage long-term workforce employment because they have cultivated "human capital"—a source of competitive advantage—over the years (Guthrie, 2001). To reap investments in worker training, these firms offer inducements to their trained workers to stay—notably, by awarding higher pay for firm-specific skills (Lazear, 1998). At the same, they may craft strategies to strengthen job security and avoid layoffs (and the higher turnover such shocks incur; Trevor & Nyberg, 2008) by maintaining lean workforces (to avoid releasing "surplus" labor during downturns) that assume more responsibilities (given higher training) and emphasizing variable pay (so that they cut bonuses rather than staff during recessions) (Shaw et al., 2009).

While minimizing push-to-leave causes, mutual investment EOR forms instigate more job stress. These organizations expect high and broad workforce contributions and likely deny those failing to live up to expectations financial rewards or recognition. Because this EOR form emphasizes contingent pay (Baron & Kreps, 1999), marginal performers more readily quit due to poorer compensation and higher pay dissatisfaction (Harrison, Virick, & William, 1996; Salamin & Hom, 2005). The predominance of self-managing teams and collective incentives in such workplaces (Baron & Kreps, 1999) also intensify peer pressures on members to expend effort and collaborate to serve the greater good (Xiao & Tsui, 2007). Low performers may readily exit to avoid or curtail intense peer sanctions, which arise when their shirking prevents teams from succeeding or attaining group bonuses. Although mutual investment firms fire fewer people (as their structures for cooperation and mutual learning help those in need; Batt & Colvin, 2011), they may nonetheless expose poor performers to more workplace shocks, such as poor performance reviews, discipline, or potential dismissals (Burton et al., 2010). All told, mutual investment conditions motivate marginal performers to leave (Shaw et al., 2009), increasing functional turnover (exits that advantage firms; Dalton, Todor, & Krackhardt, 1982). Finally, stressful work demands may even induce incumbents performing well under such conditions to exit (or retire) as they grow weary of incessant work pressures—especially when entering different life stages (e.g., Career Disengagement stage; Hom et al., 2010).

Pull-to-Stay Forces

Mutual investment EORs can also promote pull-to-stay forces by increasing job embeddedness through greater on-the-job fit, links, and sacrifice (Mitchell & Lee, 2001). In particular, their hiring and assimilation programs strive to maximize person–organization (in value congruency) and demands–abilities person–job fit (Kristof-Brown & Guay, 2010) so that new hires can fit the culture (Baron & Kreps, 1999) and meet challenging and broad job requirements (Hom et al., 2009; Shaw et al., 2009). Beyond this, mutual investment organizations expand the number of workplace links by demanding extra-role participation in activities supporting teams and the organization as a whole (Hom et al., 2009). To serve other internal constituents, incumbents cooperate and help workmates, offer suggestions to superiors, and participate in quality improvement committees (Tsui et al., 1997). As a result, "people often stay simply because of the number of links," according to Mitchell and Lee (2001, p. 232). Moreover, mutual investment EORs may enhance relationship quality, not just volume of relationships. Given broad—often collective—job duties (spanning functions), employees must learn from multiple developers from varied quarters—not just immediate supervisors—who furnish career (e.g., coaching, sponsorship) and psychosocial (e.g., counseling, role modeling) mentoring (Higgins & Thomas, 2001). High-quality and extensive developmental constellations increase retention (Higgins & Thomas, 2001). As noted earlier, more bountiful inducements by mutual investment firms also foster job sacrifice (Hom et al., 2009), especially among high performers who can satisfy demanding and broad performance requirements (Shaw et al., 2009).

Although overlooked by Mitchell et al.'s (2001) research, supervisors also represent a vital on-the-job embedding link according to leadership research (Ballinger et al., 2010). Mutual investment EOR organizations expect supervisors to empower subordinates and support self-directed teams (Baron & Kreps, 1999; Xiao & Bjorkman, 2006). Leaders in such settings thus share information with subordinates, solicit their suggestions, and delegate authority and broad duties to them. Such leadership actions can help embed followers, forging stronger links and person–job or person–supervisor fit (Kristof-Brown & Guay, 2010). Attesting to this thesis, investigations document that high-quality leader–member exchange (Ballinger et al., 2010; Griffeth et al., 2000) and transformational leadership (Carter et al., 2011)—leadership forms that promote empowerment—do build greater loyalty to superiors (organizational representatives) and thus to organizations (via structurally nested generalization; Sluss & Ashforth, 2008).

Mutual investment institutions (and other EOR types) might also reinforce community embeddedness, although this effect is not clear-cut. Because such employers promote long-term employment, they might indirectly cultivate off-the-job embeddedness as seasoned incumbents and their families develop deeper and wide-ranging community roots. As employees become established within workplaces, their spouses may likewise establish their careers locally. Or else, employees' children—as they age—become increasingly involved in school (e.g., extramural sports) and community organizations (e.g., girl scouts, church). All told, job seniority may indirectly increase "family embeddedness" within the community. In support, research finds that spousal employment and kinship responsibilities deter leaving (Eby & Russell, 2000; Price, 2004).

Push-to-Stay Forces

Mutual investment EORs may invoke "push-to-stay" forces via normative demands to stay from closed networks of colleagues who are mutually connected (Hom & Xiao, 2011). According to Xiao and Tsui (2007), mutual investment EOR promotes clan-like cultures valuing egalitarianism and cooperation. Such cultures inculcate communal values via prolonged employment, collective socialization, and collaborative work designs (and extensive socializing outside work in workplaces in collectivist societies; Hom & Xiao, 2011). Importantly, clan-like firms tend to "close" employees' social networks by encouraging mutual ties among network contacts as such firms value "integrators," "who bring people together to fill structural holes" (Xiao & Tsui, 2007, p. 1). By contrast, "brokers"—employees whose networks comprise disconnected members (Burt, 1992)—may derive more social capital in other organizational cultures (or EOR forms) because they can engage in "calculated or involuntary filtering, distortion, and hoarding of information" (Balkundi & Harrison, 2006, p. 52). Given such potential for hoarding information, clan-like cultures regard brokers as opportunists who can (and might) use structural holes for self-serving rather than collectivist ends (Xiao & Tsui, 2007).

However, closed colleague networks can reinforce loyalty to networks and, by extension, to the larger collectivity (e.g., organizations) in which they are embedded (Hom & Xiao, 2011) due to constituent and normative forces (attachment to workmates and superiors and social pressures to stay or leave, respectively; Maertz & Griffeth, 2004). For one, densely knit networks increase the number and strength of ties among network members. Participants in such networks befriend their friends' contacts to attain cognitive balance (Brass, Butterfield, & Skaggs, 1998) and bond more closely to their contacts when they are mutually attached to other parties (Burt, 2005; Krackhardt, 1998). Moreover, closed networks deliver communal socioemotional and instrumental resources to members because such networks elicit trust among members, who thereby more freely contribute to the pool of resources (Coleman, 1988, 1990). As a result, closed network communities demand fidelity to retain members' resources and ensure that recipients of collective resources repay their debt (Coleman, 1988). Indeed, such networks better enforce the loyalty norms they favor because densely connected members can engage in mutual monitoring and sanctions to deter member defections (Yamagishi, Cook, & Watabe, 1998). Besides pull-to-stay forces from affective attachment to network contacts, people belonging to closed networks also experience more push-to-stay forces from them.

Pull-to-Leave Forces

Mutual investment EOR firms are less likely to encounter "turnover contagion," a phenomenon in which exiting colleagues stimulate others to follow their lead (Felps et al., 2009). Due to social comparisons (Krackhardt & Porter, 1996) or behavioral mimicry, employees may quit as their colleagues' defections make leaving salient and viable (Felps et al., 2009). When supervisors exit, their departure may also diminish followers' career prospects or deprive them of a source of social capital (Ballinger et al., 2010). As discussed earlier, mutual investment EORs reinforce job embeddedness among the entire workforce. When colleagues and superiors are embedded, employees are less likely to experience turnover contagion (Felps et al., 2009).

Conversely, the high investment in training and developing that mutual investment firms offer may upgrade employees' "movement capital"—human capital that enhances job mobility, such as occupational skills and educational attainment (Trevor, 2001). Unless they receive premium compensation (Baron & Kreps, 1999) or promotion to jobs that match rising skills (Benson, Finegold, & Mohrman, 2004), such employees may be recruited away by competitors or exposed to more unsolicited job offers (a form of shock; Lee & Mitchell, 1994). This risk may even be greater when mutual investment firms face financial distress. To illustrate, Zatzick and Iverson (2006) found that mutual investment firms that must lay off staff suffer productivity losses if they fail to maintain high workforce investments. Because they have historically invested in employees, mutual investment firms are obligated to maintain such investment levels even when they have trouble doing so and must lay off personnel (introducing negative shocks; Trevor & Nyberg, 2008). Otherwise, they would break the psychological contract (and implicit job security guarantees; Zatzick & Iverson, 2006) and experience elevated quit rates.

Interactions Between Job Embeddedness and Shocks

By embedding employees (Hom et al., 2009), mutual investment EORs can also attenuate the effects of push-to-leave forces (Mitchell & Lee, 2001). Attesting to such moderation, Burton et al. (2010) noted that highly embedded employees do not exhibit poorer job performance or less citizenship when facing workplace injustices. Less embedded employees, however, do. Further, Carter et al. (2011) determined that employees who develop intentions to quit when enduring unit-level workplace changes are less likely to act on those intentions if superiors are transformational leaders. Presumably, transformational leadership embeds followers by inspiring them to adopt the lofty corporate vision and arousing their intrinsic motivation to pursue the corporate mission (boosting person–firm and person–job fit; Kristof-Brown & Guay, 2010). Finally, Trevor and Nyberg (2008) found that downsizing organizations that implement embedding human resources practices (e.g., on-site childcare, sabbaticals) can lower voluntary quit rates. Without such practices, they face higher turnover rates.

Similarly, mutual investment EORs might weaken the allure of pull-to-leave factors, such as personal shocks (e.g., law school admissions, retirements) or unsolicited job opportunities (Lee et al., 1996). In a preliminary exploratory test, Mitchell and Lee (2001) reported that "across all of the shock attributes [e.g., education-based, family-based, positive, external to the firm], high job embeddedness people had significantly fewer plans to leave the firm than low job embeddedness people" (p. 227). Family migration research (Eby & Russell, 2000; Shauman, 2010) also indicates that employees embedded at work, such as earning higher wages (that increase their family power), are more likely to resist—and even block—spouses' attempts to relocate families to other locales (a common external shock; Lee et al., 1996, 1999). Further, Gerson's (1985) interviews reveal that women's decisions to become full-time mothers reflect not only pull-to-leave (for full-time parenting) but also push-to-leave (e.g., job dissatisfaction) forces. Economically disadvantaged or poorly educated women facing impoverished career opportunities (weak job embeddedness) may thus opt out of work for full-time motherhood (or other unpaid options; Lee et al., 1996; Royalty, 1998).

OVERINVESTMENT EOR

As noted earlier, this EOR form furnishes ample inducements but does not expect commensurate (broad or high) contributions from employees. Overinvestment EORs are common in some societies or industries; they are widely practiced by Chinese state-owned enterprises, quasi-monopolistic corporations, European unionized establishments, and U.S. public sector firms (New York Transit Authority) (Hom et al., 2009; Tsui et al., 1997). However, unionization is not synonymous with overinvestment EORs because some mutual investment firms, such as Southwest Airlines, are actually unionized.

Push-to-Leave Forces

Overinvestment EORs may most alleviate compensation dissatisfaction because people are overcompensated relative to their inputs (eliciting overpayment rather than underpayment inequity). Because many such firms in the United States are also unionized, collective bargaining often induces employers to furnish bountiful inducements to unionized employees (who perform narrowly defined jobs with circumscribed hours). Union contracts also "immunize" employees against various negative organizational shocks (Holtom et al., 2005), such as pay inequity, arbitrary discharges, and layoffs, or can appeal (and reverse) managerial decisions responsible for such shocks (Batt et al., 2002).

Pull-to-Stay Forces

Hom et al. (2009) described how overinvestment EORs increase on-the-job embeddedness more than do underinvestment and quasi-spot contracts, although not as much as mutual investment EOR. By definition, overinvestment institutions offer more inducements than underinvestment EORs and quasi-spot contracts, making leaving costly (greater sacrifices; Mitchell & Lee, 2001). Because they expect less from their workforce, however, they provide less training and development than mutual investment firms. On the other hand, such forms offer stronger employment security due to union or state protections (Tsui et al., 1997) and shield employees from the financial risks of contingent pay (which makes it difficult for them to meet "fixed" living costs, such as mortgages; Batt et al., 2002). Greater job security and more stable (rather than risky) paychecks reduce overall voluntary quits because most employees are risk-averse (Ashford, Lee, & Bobko, 1989; Batt et al., 2002). By comparison, overinvestment EORs likely invoke greater dysfunctional turnover because high performers are insufficiently (and inequitably) rewarded (Shaw et al., 2009).

Overinvestment EOR also embeds employees by increasing fit, links, and sacrifice but to a lesser extent than mutual investment EORs (Hom et al., 2009). Compared to the latter, this EOR form engenders fewer (and narrower) links by not necessitating much team or extra-role obligations. Still, employees stay indefinitely in such employment systems because opportunities for sinecures are scarce during the Great Recession as private and public sector firms cut back labor costs worldwide. Long-term employment promotes stronger links within work units or groups, although these links may not extend beyond the proximal work vicinity. Because individual performance–based incentives are scarce or missing in overinvestment workplaces, workmates also develop more cohesion because they are not competing for financial incentives. Overinvestment

EOR further promotes needs–supplies job fit (by offering bountiful inducements; Kristof-Brown, Zimmerman, & Johnson, 2005), but not demands–abilities (DA) job fit. Given lax (and narrow) performance standards, most employees in this setting—who were neither rigorously recruited nor trained—can perform their jobs. Indeed, a significant segment of the workforce may likely have abilities that surpass those required by jobs (DA misfit) and thus experience boredom (Maltarich et al., 2010). Overqualified incumbents may remain in jobs for which their cognitive abilities exceed the cognitive demands of the job because other job amenities satisfy their broader needs (e.g., flexible hours permit more family time; Maltarich et al., 2010). In short, overinvestment EORs embed incumbents more than do quasi-spot contracts and underinvestment EORs but less so than mutual investment EORs (generating fewer links and weaker person–job DA fit; Hom et al., 2009).

Conceivably, overinvestment EORs may incur community embeddedness in the same way as mutual investment EORs. Due to high job sacrifices, employees stay long term and may develop (along with family members) more robust community ties. More than this, high job inducements may benefit employees' families, such as generous family health coverage (derived from collective bargaining) and housing subsidies (furnished by Chinese state-owned firms; Hom et al., 2009). That is, overinvestment EORs may sustain employees' loyalty by fostering "family embeddedness," which arises when employees' families are proud of their employment at the firm, receive benefits from the firm (housing subsidies; Hom & Xiao, 2011), and have relationships with the employees' colleagues (Ramesh & Gelfand, 2010).

Push-to-Stay Forces

As stated earlier, incumbents' families (or partners) might induce employees to stay because overinvestment EOR supplies broad enticements benefitting families (Ramesh & Gelfand, 2010). Spouses and other relatives may also encourage firm loyalty because overinvestment employment imposes less onerous work responsibilities, allowing employees to more fully participate in family life (and endure less work–family conflicts; Hom & Kinicki, 2001). In addition, colleague networks gravitate toward closure over time when network members stay long term in such bountiful HRM systems, such as Chinese state-owned enterprises (Hom & Xiao, 2011). Closed peer friendship networks, in turn, foster affective bonds (Maertz & Griffeth, 2004) and normative pressures to stay (Hom & Xiao, 2011).

Pull-to-Leave Forces

Unlike mutual investment EOR, overinvestment EOR does not invoke as many pull-to-leave factors. For one, the workforce of such organizations enjoys few work alternatives that would provide abundant investments for minimal or narrow work contributions. According to turnover theory, they stay because they cannot find alternatives offering high inducement utilities relative to their low contribution utilities (Hulin et al., 1985; Mobley, Griffeth, Hand, & Meglino, 1979; Rusbult & Farrell, 1983). They also remain because this EOR arrangement fails to invest in their "movement capital," depriving them of "signals" to the marketplace of their productivity (Maltarich et al., 2010; Trevor, 2001). Further, turnover contagion among colleagues is rare because everyone becomes embedded in this HRM system. As Felps et al. (2009) demonstrated, when incumbents are surrounded by embedded coworkers (and are not exposed to turnover contagion), they remain loyal. Because they embed incumbents less strongly than do mutual investment EORs, overinvestment firms may prove less effective at preventing turnover due to external shocks (e.g., spousal relocations, pregnancies) when they occur (Mitchell & Lee, 2001).

QUASI-SPOT CONTRACTS

In this EOR form, employers primarily furnish economic inducements for well-specified employee contributions. To illustrate, brokerage firms reward stockbrokers for their sales volume, and home builders hire painters for short-term jobs to paint newly constructed homes. Given recessionary periods, this EOR form arguably represents a ubiquitous employment relationship (Cappelli, 2000; Tsui et al., 1995).

Push-to-Leave Forces

Employees may abandon firms practicing this EOR form if they are dissatisfied with economic inducements or the lack of long-term job security (or ongoing contract work) because they are "disposable" workers whose employment ends once their contract is met (Ashford et al., 1989). By the same token, they are free to pursue better "deals" elsewhere once they fulfill their contracts because they have no explicit or implicit obligations to maintain longstanding employment relationships.

Pull-to-Stay Forces

Quasi-spot contracts can produce some job embeddedness, although not as much as overinvestment and mutual investment EORs. After all, these organizations award high financial inducements to stay and produce, which can improve needs–supplies (NS) job fit (especially with regard to pay; Kristof-Brown et al., 2005). Because quasi-spot contracts recruit people for specialized skills or talents, they also embed—if temporarily—personnel by inducing DA job fit. Recruits' abilities can meet job requirements. Further, quasi-spot contracts may also create job sacrifice because employees would forfeit high wages should they leave. In these ways, quasi-spot contracts embed incumbents somewhat (perhaps more so than underinvestment EORs).

Push-to-Stay Forces

If employees earn high compensation (relative to other jobs), their families may encourage them to stay because such income affords them higher standards of living (e.g., better housing or education). Material inducements—that sustain the family's economic well-being—can represent powerful forces for staying in developing countries, where work is primarily a duty to support the family rather than a vehicle for self-fulfillment (Ramesh & Gelfand, 2010). By contrast, employees working for quasi-spot contracts may feel little normative pressures to stay from colleagues whose stint in the firm is also short term and unstable (unless they work together and build densely knit network communities) (Felps et al., 2009).

Pull-to-Leave Forces

Quasi-spot contracts typically forsake inducements such as training or development. After all, these employers treat employees as disposable or contingent staff who are loyal only to their paycheck. These firms may believe it foolhardy to train employees who only join—and remain in—companies offering the highest bid for their services. Firm investments in worker training would surely be lost as such workers may readily leave even for incrementally higher pay elsewhere (Lazear, 1998). Because their relationship is based on economic exchange (Shore et al., 2006), employees feel less obligated to stay and would readily abandon the current job when a better-paid job comes along (Tsui et al., 1997). Thus, incumbents operating under quasi-spot contracts are often scanning or actively seeking higher wages elsewhere (*alternative forces*; Maertz & Griffeth, 2004) and are easily tempted by unsolicited job offers (shocks; Lee & Mitchell, 1994).

UNDERINVESTMENT EOR

Underinvestment employers demand broad and open-ended obligations from workers, while offering primarily monetary rewards but no training or guaranteed employment (Tsui et al., 1997). Economic recessions, intense cost pressures in certain industries (e.g., television or apparel manufacturers), or cost–leadership business strategies (e.g., fast-food restaurants) drive businesses to implement such EOR arrangements (Yalabik et al., 2008). To illustrate, the maquiladora industry, which comprises foreign-owned factories situated along Mexico's northern border with the United States, practice this EOR form (Maertz, Stevens, & Campion, 2003; Miller, Hom, & Gomez-Mejia, 2001). They pay "subsistence" wages to Mexican workers to assemble products for export at competitive prices. Due to peso devaluation (Cravey, 1998), the real maquila wage increased merely 1 cent more per hour in 2000 from $0.41 per hour (in U.S. dollars) in 1996 (Berruecos, 2008), and these wages cannot support families (unless multiple household members work; Cravey, 1998; Fernández-Kelly, 1983; Peña, 1997). Because such (minimum) wages are common across maquila plants (which can engage in wage collusion; Miller et al., 2001), plants vie for workers by offering a menu of benefits, such as meals, bonuses, and health care. Moreover, most factories do not invest in training because workers need few skills to assemble products. For such economic inducements, workers must attend work regularly (6 days a week; aggravating women's work–family conflicts), meet rigorous production standards, and work in hazardous environments (chemical pollutants; Guendelman, Samuels, &

Ramirez, 1998; Maertz et al., 2003; Prieto, 1997; Romero & Cruthirds, 2009; Tiano, 1994). Given the manual nature of assembly work and low education levels of these rural migrants, maquila owners rarely expect workers to creatively solve problems or exercise intellectual abilities. Not surprisingly, most workers respond by leaving in large numbers—often for incremental increases in pay or benefits elsewhere (West, 2004).

Push-to-Leave Forces

Underinvestment EORs often employ workers to do mundane and unskilled labor because they do not invest in human capital development. As a result, workers may find work monotonous and boring (as well as fast paced and grueling; Peña, 1997; Prieto, 1997), increasing work dissatisfaction (and quit propensity). Because work duties require little skill or education, employers implementing this EOR form may feel justified in awarding low wages, invoking pay dissatisfaction. That their workforces assume more onerous tasks also elicits felt pay inequity as well (Tsui et al., 1997). Further, workers anticipate few career opportunities in such workplaces, which offer few career ladders to ascend into high-paying, high-status positions. Finally, underinvestment employers regularly expose workers to layoff or dismissal shocks (Holtom et al., 2005) because workers are easily replaceable by new hires who require little training to perform semi-skilled or unskilled jobs. As Trevor and Nyberg (2008) point out, widespread terminations constitute shocks that prompt even satisfactory workers into contemplating departing because such events signal to other workers that even their own jobs are insecure (cf. Batt & Colvin, 2011; Batt et al., 2002).

Pull-to-Stay Forces

Underinvestment EORs embed incumbents primarily through job sacrifices because they do not promote fit or links (at least not wide-ranging and strong ties). During business downturns, companies may resort to this EOR form (Tsui et al., 2007) and use job sacrifices to retain staff having few available (or better) job opportunities. Similarly, firms in "company towns" (e.g., coal-mining communities) can implement underinvestment EOR because they hold monospony power. Lacking competition, they become the main "buyer" of labor supply and can set prevailing wages in local labor markets. Small-town resident also stay to avoid community sacrifices if they must relocate elsewhere for other employment. Further, export-oriented manufacturing factories in China and Mexico primarily rely on economic inducements to embed their rural migrant workers (Batson, 2010; Miller et al., 2001).

Push-to-Stay Forces

Underinvestment EORs may not induce normative pressures to stay, unless employees' families depend on the source of income that such employers provide (Ramesh & Gelfand, 2010). Having few inducements that prolong staying (e.g., steeply rising pay curves or development opportunities), employees do not stay long. They and their workmates thus do not develop into densely knit network communities from which normative internal pressures to remain can emerge (Hom & Xiao, 2011).

Pull-to-Leave Forces

In such workplaces, employees readily quit once the economy recovers or they have met their short-term financial goals (e.g., accumulated enough savings to return to school—otherwise known as "script-based" leaving; Lee et al., 1996, 1999). Quite often, turnover contagion is rampant in employment settings, such as fast-food restaurants (Krackhardt & Porter, 1986) and low-wage export-oriented factories (Maertz et al., 2003). Widespread coworker defections can generate a turnover culture or norm that legitimizes or endorses leaving, precipitating turnover even among otherwise satisfied incumbents (Bartunek, Huang, & Walsh, 2008; Felps et al., 2009).

Interactions Between Push-and-Pull Leaving and Staying Forces

Because underinvestment EOR engenders the least job embeddedness among all EOR forms (mostly invoking job sacrifices), this EOR may poorly limit the impact of push-and-pull forces to leave (Burton et al., 2010). Employees in such firms readily quit if they are dissatisfied or experience shocks, especially if the economy improves or barriers to leaving (e.g., community sacrifices, such as spousal employment) are lifted (e.g., spouse finds new job elsewhere). In the following sections, this chapter provides a tentative framework for how to explore multilevel EOR influence on individual-level attrition.

EOR MULTILEVEL EFFECTS

Following Carter et al. (2011), I submit a multilevel model describing how EOR forms affect individual-level turnover via direct effects on push-and-pull forces and moderation of those effects (Figure 15.2). As noted earlier, this second model shows that EOR forms directly invoke various push-and-pull forces for staying or leaving. These effects operate—and are depicted in the top of Figure 15.2—at the firm level, whereas how these forces shape individuals' quit propensity are portrayed in an individual-level submodel, shown in the bottom on Figure 15.2. In keeping with theory and research on turnover, this individual-level model specifies job dissatisfaction (Hom & Kinicki, 2001) or shocks (Lee & Mitchell, 1994) as prime stimulants for withdrawal cognitions (global cognitions about leaving). The Hom-Kinicki and Lee-Mitchell formulations also posit that some employees may form withdrawal cognitions and directly leave, whereas others pursue alternative jobs before leaving. Nonetheless, the individual-level submodel presents a simplified version of the process by which employees leave (which Lee and Mitchell [1994] and others elaborate) as this chapter mainly examines how EOR forms drive leaving.

Building on the basic 2-1-1 multilevel mediation model (Zhang, Zyphur, & Preacher, 2009), the framework in Figure 15.2 posits that firm-level forces affect individual-level turnover via various individual-level antecedents. To illustrate, underinvestment EOR invokes greater push-to-leave factors by paying low wages and exposing staff to potential layoffs. These firm-level practices translate into higher pay dissatisfaction and negative job shocks for many—if not most—employees. Yet cross-level effects in our multilevel model do not imply that *all* employees would react the same way (Zhang et al., 2009). For example, working retirees earning minimum wages are not necessarily dissatisfied if their wages supplement retirement incomes, and some layoff victims interpret the shock of losing their jobs as having a "silver lining" (offering an opportunity to engage in more meaningful careers) rather than as threatening or harmful (Fugate, Kinicki, & Prussia, 2008).

Specifying cross-level moderation (Hofmann & Gavin, 1998), this model also submits that staying forces (invoked by EOR forms) moderate how individuals view shocks or dissatisfying conditions. Highly embedded employees may not interpret so-called negative events as shocks or unfavorably appraise disagreeable working conditions (Fugate et al., 2008). As coping perspectives maintain (Sweeney, 2008), whether employees regard events as stressful depends on their perceptions of their severity and their ability to manage the threats. Thus, layoffs of temporary janitorial workers may not pose a threat to the job security of veteran manufacturing workers protected by union contracts (Trevor & Nyberg, 2008). Moreover, staying forces may moderate employees' reactions to job dissatisfaction and shocks. That is, even when embedded incumbents see events or conditions negatively, they may be less prone to form withdrawal cognitions. In support, Mitchell and Lee (2001) observed that highly embedded employees who encounter shocks have fewer plans about leaving than those less embedded who experience shocks. Finally, embedded incumbents who form withdrawal cognitions (when dissatisfied or shocked) are less likely to act on those initial cognitions. Recent studies corroborate this moderation, showing that job embeddedness (Burton et al., 2010) and transformational leadership (an embedding link; Carter et al., 2011) discourage people planning to leave from acting on their plans.

FURTHER MODEL REFINEMENTS

Although advancing understanding of how EOR affects workforce retention, this model nonetheless remains a work in progress. For one, this model only considers two levels of conceptual analysis—firm- and individual-level variables. Yet most employees work in more complex organizations in which their proximal work unit or team is nested within multiple higher order collectives, such multiteam systems (Millikin, Hom, & Manz, 2010). Future research should attempt to model how EOR forms formulated by chief executive officers and top management teams at the firm level impacts individual employee turnover. To what extent do intermediate levels (middle managers and supervisors) effectively translate and transmit top executive strategies to the rank and file.

Moreover, EOR investigators might adapt the current model to the job-level. Indeed, Tsui et al. (1997) noted that many employers adopt different EOR approaches for different workforce subpopulations. For example, organizations often implement mutual investment EORs to strategic employee groups who are vital to their mission (e.g., automotive engineers in auto companies) but deploy quasi-spot contracts with janitorial or cafeteria staff. As a consequence, they might promote greater push-and-pull forces for staying toward core rather than peripheral personnel as well as better insulate the former against push-and-pull forces toward leaving.

Finally, theoretical refinements might identify additional mediators and moderators for the models in Figures 15.1 and 15.2. To illustrate, Hom and Kinicki (2001) identify various steps between the formation of withdrawal cognitions and actual turnover, including work avoidance (other ways to cope with dissatisfaction), search for alternatives, and comparisons of alternatives. Similarly, Lee and Mitchell (1994) describe various paths to turnover activated by different kinds of shocks (personal, unsolicited job inquiries, and negative job shocks) that involve different mediating constructs, such as image violations and job search. Other theorists specified moderators, such as unemployment rates (Hom & Griffeth, 1995) and personality variables (e.g., risk aversion; Allen, Weeks, & Moffitt, 2005), that can prevent withdrawal cognitions from culminating into actual departures in model 2 (see Figure 15.2).

INTERNATIONAL IMPLICATIONS

Although scant, EOR attrition research in other cultures is emerging (Hom et al., 2009; Yalabik et al., 2008). Cross-cultural inquiry is essential because EOR implementations, translating mechanisms, and retention effects are likely culturally dependent (Ramesh & Gelfand, 2010). For one, EOR forms are conceivably expressed or manifested differently across cultures (Hom & Xiao, 2011). To illustrate, unlike mutual investment EORs in the West, top-tier Japanese corporations (e.g., Toyota) mainly recruit cohorts of college or technical-school graduates (who spend entire careers there), base promotions on seniority, and deemphasize individual performance bonuses (Baron & Kreps, 1999). Similarly, overinvestment institutions in China (e.g., state-run enterprises) and the United States (public sector organizations) offer ample nonperformance-based inducements to their workforces. Due to civil service and union protections, however, U.S. workers have more job security and opportunities to voice complaints (including disputing managerial decisions) than Chinese workers (Batt et al., 2002). Although affirming the international generalizability of EOR forms is valuable (Hom et al., 2009), such efforts often downplay *emic* (culture-specific) EOR expressions. After all, Yalabik et al. (2008) documented that mutual investment EOR curbs voluntary quits more effectively in locally owned companies than multinational subsidiaries in East and Southeast Asia, underscoring the efficacy of localized EOR administrations.

In addition, EOR mechanisms (i.e., the pull-and-push forces of EOR forms) may vary across different cultural contexts. For example, Hom et al. (2009) found that job embeddedness is a more stable mechanism conveying EOR influence onto Chinese loyalty than is social exchange. Given that relations (or *guanxi*) are paramount in this collectivist society (Hom & Xiao, 2011), embedding relations may play a dominant role mediating EOR impact on propensity to stay there (Hom et al., 2009). Consistent with this finding, Ramesh and Gelfand (2010) disclosed that organizational links deter leaving more in collectivist India than individualist America. By contrast, job fit did not promote corporate fidelity in India, presumably because family priorities govern quit decisions more than do personal desires for self-fulfillment in collectivist cultures (Ramesh & Gelfand, 2010). Such preliminary findings suggest that push or pull forces involving social ties and obligations (or disrupting the social fabric in the workplace, such as turnover contagion) may constitute paramount EOR mediators in collectivist countries. Accordingly, mutual investment and overinvestment EORs may most reinforce staying among collectivist nationals to the extent they promote more, stronger, and mutually affiliated job links (including family embeddedness; Ramesh & Gelfand, 2010). Conversely, quasi-spot contracts and underinvestment EORs may most induce job departures among collectivist nationals when they engender turnover contagion (Maertz et al., 2003).

Although the discussion above centered on how culture moderates mediating mechanisms, culture might also moderate EOR effects too. Given the prevalence of closed employment systems in collectivist societies (Gelfand, Bhawuk, Nishi, & Bechtold, 2004; Tsui & Wang, 2002; Yamagishi et al., 1998), mutual investment firms—and overinvestment firms to a lesser degree—may better stabilize employment there because they mirror prevailing institutional forms (Baron & Kreps, 1999) and their corporate values of cooperation and communal sharing conform to collectivist values (Xiao & Tsui, 2007). Mutual investment firms may also flourish in low uncertainty avoidance ("extent to which society...relies on social norms, rules, and procedures to alleviate unpredictability" [House, Hanges, Javidan, Dorfman, & Gupta, 2004, p. 30]) and low power distance cultures ("degree to which members of a collective expect power to be distributed equally" [House et al., 2004, p. 30]). Specifically, natives from such cultures are likely more receptive to the broad, open-ended job descriptions, self-directed teams, and flattened hierarchies pervading mutual investment workplaces (Baron & Kreps, 1999; Xiao & Bjorkman, 2006).

PRACTICAL IMPLICATIONS

This integrative perspective may offer several practical implications. First, this model explicitly recognizes that any given EOR form invokes both forces for staying and leaving, as Batt and Colvin (2011) have noted. The current formulation suggests that the same EOR form can drive different kinds of incumbents to leave (e.g., different types of performers; Shaw et al., 2009) but also expose contradictory forces to the *same* incumbents. To illustrate, mutual investment EORs exert more pull-to-stay forces on high-performing or core employees by liberally dispensing greater rewards or benefits. Yet, this EOR form also exposes them to push-to-leave forces by imposing greater or incessant work demands and staffing jobs with contingent workers whose temporary employment signals to core workers that even their jobs are insecure (Batt & Colvin, 2011; Batt et al., 2002). In addition, intensive training offered by such organizations may also increase pull-to-leave forces by cultivating employees' movement capital (Trevor, 2001). That said, employers implementing a particular EOR form must ensure that the forces that they unleash are not working at cross-purposes, undermining their strategic objectives of retaining (or releasing) certain numbers or types of employees (Batt & Colvin, 2011).

Although how mutual investment EOR maximizes retention (or minimizes dysfunctional turnover; Shaw et al., 2009) dominates scholarly inquiry, most businesses practice—by necessity (due to financial distress; Zatzick & Iverson, 2006) or design (to fit business strategy; Wang et al.,

2003; Yalabik et al., 2008)—other EOR forms. Because these alternate EOR forms can be more effective (more so than even mutual investment EORs) under certain circumstances (Wang et al., 2003; Yalabik et al., 2008), it is imperative to consider how these EOR forms can best achieve their "optimal" turnover rates (Glebbeek & Bax, 2004). After all, Zatzick and Iverson (2006) showed that mutual investment EOR firms founder when they fail to maintain workforce investments during layoffs, suggesting that even mutual investment EORs can be executed with varying efficacy. Without a doubt, underinvestment EORs and quasi-spot contracts produce more turnover than mutual investment (or overinvestment) EORs (Hom et al., 2009; Tsui et al., 1997), but some firms implementing these forms may still outperform others deploying the same forms. To illustrate, Miller et al. (2001) observed considerable turnover variation among maquila factories. Although prototypical of underinvestment EORs, some factories better retained Mexican workers—or prolonged their tenure—by offering enticements (e.g., profit-sharing) and better satisfying the economic needs of workers earning subsistence wages.

To ensure that they can retain employees at levels facilitating their strategic objectives, overinvestment institutions might weaken pull-to-stay forces (Table 15.1). Usually, these employers are overstaffed or may find it difficult to maintain bountiful inducements during recessions or intensifying competition in their industry. To diminish job embeddedness (Mitchell & Lee, 2001), these companies might offer severance packages or early retirement to shrink staffing levels, making exits less costly. These firms might offer fewer or diminished compensation to new hires by awarding lower wages or costlier fringe benefits (e.g., demand more employee contributions to pension and health care plans). For newcomers, they might also withhold family benefits that they may have previously granted, lessening family embeddedness (Ramesh & Gelfand, 2010).

Firms implementing quasi-spot contracts may need to retain the services of their contract personnel until a project is completed or for some extended period. To strengthen pull-to-stay forces, these companies might ensure that their compensation inducements are equitable and surpass those competitors offer (improving compensation satisfaction). Financial incentives can help motivate staying until project completion (Cappelli, 2000). These institutions may also increase contingent workers' job embeddedness by promoting DA and NS job fit through targeted recruitment (Cappelli, 2000). To improve DA fit, they can recruit new college or trade-school graduates by offering more opportunities to hone their skills (e.g., apprentices in skilled trades) or accumulate enough work experience to attain professional certifications (e.g., certified public accountants). To illustrate, Cappelli (2000) noted that high-tech firms in Ireland aggressively recruit top talent from universities to achieve better applicant–job matches, although these firms spent little effort to keep college recruits once hired. To enhance NS fit, employers can recruit prospective employees who value compensation—and the opportunity to practice specialized skills—more than job security. For example, JetBlue Airways offers 1-year contracts as flight attendants to college graduates who receive medical coverage and $500 per month of extra pay (instead of other benefits) to help them afford to live in Manhattan (Gittell, & O'Reilly, 2001). Because this job is rarely a long-term career, young people may readily work as short-term flight attendants so that they can freely travel and live in New York. Quasi-spot contracts may also reduce job insecurity (a push-to-leave factor) by offering some guarantees of contract extensions or renewal, assuming these firms can generate or foreshadow client demands for their products (e.g., homebuilders contracting electricians) or services (e.g., universities hiring non–tenure track instructors).

Finally, underinvestment firms prefer to retain staff who are "overworked and underpaid." Obviously, they can maintain such "exploitative" practices if employees are relatively powerless (lacking alternative job options or union representation; Batt & Colvin, 2011). Because organizational injustices invoke so many dysfunctional reactions (Cropanzano, Bowen, & Gilliland, 2007), underinvestment companies might attempt to reduce push-to-leave forces, while initiating pull-to-stay forces. Because procedural and interactional justice can ameliorate negative reactions to poor outcomes, managers might explain how compensation levels are fair relative to the marketplace and that compensation decisions are fairly made (Griffeth & Hom, 2001). Cappelli (2000) observes that some employers (i.e., underinvestment EORs) recruit former addicts, welfare recipients, and ex-cons for low-skill, low-paying jobs. Although costlier to train, such "high-risk" workers might be "grateful and loyal to the company for giving them a chance" (Cappelli, 2000, p. 17) as well as more embedded because they would have trouble finding other employment (sacrifice; Mitchell & Lee, 2001). Further, underinvestment companies may relocate to depressed rural or small-town U.S. communities or developing countries whose countrymen face high unemployment (e.g., Mexico; West, 2004). Like high-risk workers, such workforces feel more pull-to-stay forces because leaving organizations that are the sole or major employers in the community would incur considerable economic sacrifice (Mitchell & Lee, 2001).

In closing, the empirical literature on EOR–attrition relationships is rapidly emerging. Such macro-level research fills a long-standing void in the literature about firm-level determinants of turnover (Hausknecht & Trevor, 2010; Hom & Griffeth, 1995). However, modeling EOR effects on attrition has rarely kept pace with recent developments in theories about leaving and staying. Although extrapolating from psychological models to explain EOR influence may risk the ecological fallacy (Hom, 2010), such applications are often viable (cf. Trevor & Nyberg, 2008) if homology is plausible (Morgeson & Hofmann, 1999). That said, such risks are worth taking if they can stimulate more innovative theory and research about how EOR forms drive workforce retention.

REFERENCES

Allen, D. G., Weeks, K. P., & Moffitt, K. R. (2005). Turnover intentions and voluntary turnover: The moderating roles of self-monitoring, locus of control, proactive personality, and risk aversion. *Journal of Applied Psychology, 90*, 980–990.

Arthur, J. (1994). Effects of human resource systems on manufacturing performance and turnover. *Academy of Management Journal, 37*, 670–687.

Ashford, S., Lee, C., & Bobko, P. (1989). Content, causes, and consequences of job insecurity: A theory-based measure and substantive test. *Academy of Management Journal, 32*, 803–829.

Balkundi, P., & Harrison, D. (2006). Ties, leaders, and time in teams: Strong inference about network structure's effects on team viability and performance. *Academy of Management Journal, 49*, 49–68.

Ballinger, G., Lehman, D., & Schoorman, D. (2010). Leader-member exchange and turnover before and after succession events. *Organizational Behavior and Human Decision Processes, 113*, 25–36.

Baron, J., & Kreps, D. (1999). *Strategic human resources*. New York, NY: John Wiley & Sons.

Bartunek, J., Huang, Z., & Walsh, I. (2008). The development of a process model of collective turnover. *Human Relations, 6*, 5–38.

Batson, A. (2010, June 17). China's shifting jobs keep migrants closer to home. *Wall Street Journal*, p. A.10.

Batt, R., & Colvin, A. (2011). An employment systems approach to turnover: HR practices, quits, dismissals, and performance. *Academy of Management Journal, 54*, 695–717.

Batt, R., Colvin, A., & Keefe, J. (2002). Employee voice, human resource practices, and quit rates: Evidence from the telecommunications industry. *Industrial and Labor Relations Review, 55*, 573–594.

Becker, B. E., & Huselid, M. A. (1998). High performance work systems and firm performance: A synthesis of research and managerial implications. *Research in Personnel and Human Resources Journal, 16*, 53–101.

Benson, G., Finegold, D., & Mohrman, S. (2004). You paid for the skills, now keep them: Tuition-reimbursement and voluntary turnover. *Academy of Management Journal, 47*, 315–331.

Berruecos, L. (2008). The quality of social existence in an Indian community in Mexico due to globalization. *American Behavioral Scientist, 51*, 1694–1712.

Blau, P. (1964). *Exchange and power in social life*. New York, NY: Wiley.

Brass, D., Butterfield, K., & Skaggs, B. (1998). Relationships and unethical behavior: A social network perspective. *Academy of Management Review, 23*, 14–31.

Burt, R. (1992). *Structural holes*. Cambridge, MA: Harvard University Press.

Burt, R. (2005). *Brokerage and closure*. Oxford, UK: Oxford University Press.

Burton, J., Holtom, B., Sablynski, C., Mitchell, T., & Lee, T. (2010). The buffering effects of job embeddedness on negative shocks. *Journal of Vocational Behavior, 76*, 42–51.

Butler, J., & Ferris, G. (1991). *Strategy and human resources management*. Cincinnati, OH: South-Western College Publishing.

Cappelli, P. (2000). Managing without commitment. *Organizational Dynamics, 28*, 11–24.

Carter, M., Waldman, D., & Hom, P. (2011, April). *Buffering against shocks in changing times: How transformational leaders can discourage prospective leavers from quitting*. Paper presented at the Society for Industrial and Organizational Psychology (SIOP), Atlanta, Georgia.

Coleman, J. (1988). Social capital in the creation of human capital. *American Journal of Sociology, 94*, 95–120.

Coleman, J. (1990). *Foundations of social theory*. Cambridge, MA: Harvard University Press.

Collins, C., & Smith, K. (2006). Knowledge exchange and combination: The role of human resource practices in the performance of high-technology firms. *Academy of Management Journal, 49*, 544–560.

Combs, J., Liu, Y., Hall, A., & Ketchen, D. (2006). How much do high-performance work practices matter? A meta-analysis of their effects on organizational performance. *Personnel Psychology, 59*, 501–528.

Cravey, A. (1998). *Women and work in Mexico's maquiladoras*. New York, NY: Rowman & Littlefield.

Cropanzano, R., Bowen, D., & Gilliland, S. (2007). The management of organizational justice. *Academy of Management Perspectives, 21*, 34–48.

Dalton, D., Todor, W., & Krackhardt, D. (1982). Turnover overstated: The functional taxonomy. *Academy of Management Review, 7*, 117–123.

Datta, D. K., Guthrie, J. P., Basuil, D., & Pandey, A. (2010). Causes and effects of employee downsizing: A review and synthesis. *Journal of Management, 36*, 281–348.

Datta, D. K., Guthrie, J. P., & Wright, P. M. (2005). HRM and labor productivity: Does industry matter? *Academy of Management Journal, 48*, 135–145.

Eby, L., & Russell, J. (2000). Predictors of employee willingness to relocate for the firm. *Journal of Vocational Behavior, 57*, 42–61.

Felps, W., Mitchell, T., Hekman, D., Lee, T., Harmon, W., & Holtom, B. (2009). Turnover contagion: How coworkers' job embeddedness and coworkers' job search behaviors influence quitting. *Academy of Management Journal, 52*, 545–561.

Fernández-Kelly, M. (1983). *For we are sold, I and my people: Women in Mexico's frontier*. Albany, NY: State University of New York Press.

Fugate, M., Kinicki, A. J., & Prussia, G. E. (2008). Employee coping with organizational change: An examination of alternative theoretical perspectives. *Personnel Psychology, 61*, 1–36.
Gelfand, M., Bhawuk, D., Nishi, L., & Bechtold, D. (2004). Individualism and collectivism. In R. House, P. Hanges, M. Javidan, P. Dorfman, & V. Gupta (Eds.), *Culture, leadership, and organizations* (pp. 437–512). Thousand Oaks, CA: Sage Publications.
Gerson, K. (1985). *Hard choices*. Berkeley, CA: University of California Press.
Gittell, J. H., & O'Reilly, C. (2001). *JetBlue Airways: Starting from scratch* (Case 9-801-354). Cambridge, MA: Harvard Business School.
Glebbeek, A. C., & Bax, E. H. (2004). Is high employee turnover really harmful? An empirical test using company records. *Academy of Management Journal, 47*, 277–286.
Gomez-Mejia, L., & Balkin, D. (1992). *Compensation, organizational strategy, and firm performance*. Cincinnati, OH: South-Western College Publishing.
Griffeth, R. W., & Hom, P. W. (2001). *Retaining valued employees*. Thousand Oaks, CA: Sage.
Griffeth, R. W., Hom, P. W., & Gaertner, S. (2000). A meta-analysis of antecedents and correlates of employee turnover. *Journal of Management, 26*, 463–488.
Guendelman, S., Samuels, S., & Ramirez, M. (1998). Women who quit maquiladora work on the U.S.-Mexico border: Assessing health, occupation, and social dimensions in two transnational electronics plants. *American Journal of Industrial Medicine, 33*, 501–509.
Gutherie, J. P. (2001). High involvement work practices, turnover and productivity: Evidence from New Zealand. *Academy of Management Journal, 44*, 180–190.
Harrison, D. A., Virick, M., & William, S. (1996). Working without a net: Time, performance, and turnover under maximally contingent rewards. *Journal of Applied Psychology, 81*, 331–345.
Hausknecht, J. P., & Trevor, C. O. (2010). Collective turnover at the group, unit, and organizational levels: Evidence, issues, and implications. *Journal of Management, 37*, 352–388.
Higgins, M., & Thomas, D. (2001). Constellations and careers: Toward understanding the effects of multiple developmental relationships. *Journal of Organizational Behavior, 22*, 223–247.
Hofmann, D., & Gavin, M. (1998). Centering decisions in hierarchical linear models: Implications for research in organizations. *Journal of Management, 24*, 623–641.
Holtom, B., Mitchell, T., Lee, T., & Eberly, M. (2008). Turnover and retention research: A glance at the past, a closer review of the present, and a venture into the future. *Academy of Management Annals, 2*, 231–274.
Holtom, B. C., Mitchell, T. R., Lee, T. W., & Inderrieden, E. J. (2005). Shocks as causes of turnover: What they are and how organizations and management them. *Human Resource Management, 44*, 337–352.
Hom P. W. (2010). Organizational exit. In S. Zedeck, H. Aguinis, W. Cascio, M. Gelfand, K. Leung, S. Parker, et al. (Eds.), *Handbook of industrial/organizational psychology* (Vol. 2, pp. 67–117). Washington, DC: American Psychological Association.
Hom, P., & Griffeth, R. W. (1995). *Employee turnover*. Cincinnati, OH: Southwestern.
Hom, P., & Kinicki, A. (2001). Toward a greater understanding of how dissatisfaction drives employee turnover. *Academy of Management Journal, 44*, 975–987.
Hom, P., Leong, F., & Golubovich, J. (2010). Integrating career theories with turnover models. In J. Martocchio, H. Liao, & A. Josh (Eds.), *Research in personnel and human resources management* (Vol. 29, pp. 115–165). Bingley, UK: Emerald Group Publishing Limited.

Hom, P. W., Tsui, A. S., Wu, J. B., Lee, T. W., Zhang, A. Y., Fu, P. P., & Li, L. (2009). Explaining employment relationships with social exchange and job embeddedness. *Journal of Applied Psychology, 94*, 277–297.

Hom, P., & Xiao, Z. (2011). Embedding social capital: Relational constraints on quits in Chinese high-tech firms. *Organizational Behavior and Human Decision Processes, 116*, 188–202.

House, R., Hanges, P., Javidan, M., Dorfman, P., & Gupta, V. (2004). *Culture, leadership, and organizations*. Thousand Oaks, CA: Sage Publications.

Hulin, C. L., Roznowski, M., & Hachiya, D. (1985). Alternative opportunities and withdrawal decisions: Empirical and theoretical discrepancies and an integration. *Psychological Bulletin, 97*, 233–250.

Huselid, M. (1995). The impact of human resource management practices on turnover, productivity, and corporate financial performance. *Academy of Management Journal, 38*, 635–672.

Krackhardt, D. (1998). Simmelian ties: Super strong and sticky. In R. Kramer & M. Neale (Eds.), *Power and influence in organizations* (pp. 21–38). Thousand Oaks, CA: Sage.

Krackhardt, D., & Porter, L. (1986). The snowball effect: Turnover embedded in communication networks. *Journal of Applied Psychology, 71*, 50–55.

Kristof-Brown, A., & Guay, R. P. (2010). Person-environment fit. In S. Zedeck, H. Aguinis, W. Cascio, M. Gelfand, K. Leung, S. Parker, et al. (Eds.), *Handbook of industrial/organizational psychology* (Vol. 3, pp. 3–50). Washington, DC: American Psychological Association.

Kristof-Brown, A., Zimmerman, R., & Johnson, E. (2005). Consequences of individuals' fit at work: A meta-analysis of person-job, person-organization, person-group, and person-supervisor fit. *Personnel Psychology, 58*, 281–342.

Lazear, E. (1998). *Personnel economics for managers*. New York, NY: John Wiley & Sons, Inc.

Lee, T. H., Gerhart, B., Weller, I., & Trevor, C. (2008). Understanding voluntary turnover: Path-specific job satisfaction effects and the importance of unsolicited job offers. *Academy of Management Journal, 51*, 651–671.

Lee, T. W., & Mitchell, T. R. (1994). An alternative approach: The unfolding model of voluntary employee turnover. *Academy of Management Review, 19*, 51–89.

Lee, T. W., Mitchell, T. R., Holtom, B. C., McDaniel, L., & Hill, J. W. (1999). Theoretical development and extension of the unfolding model of voluntary turnover. *Academy of Management Journal, 42*, 450–462.

Lee, T. W., Mitchell, T. R., Sablynski, C., Burton, J., & Holtom, B. (2004). The effects of job embeddedness on organizational citizenship, job performance, volitional absences, and voluntary turnover. *Academy of Management Journal, 47*, 711–722.

Lee, T. W., Mitchell, T. R., Wise, L., & Fireman, S. (1996). An unfolding model of voluntary employee turnover. *Academy of Management Journal, 39*, 5–36.

Maertz, C., & Griffeth, R. (2004). Eight motivational forces and voluntary turnover: A theoretical synthesis with implications for research. *Journal of Management, 30*, 667–683.

Maertz, C., Stevens, M., & Campion, M. (2003). A turnover model for the Mexican maquiladoras. *Journal of Vocational Behavior, 63*, 111–135.

Maltarich, M., Nyberg, A., & Reilly, G. (2010). A conceptual and empirical analysis of the cognitive ability-voluntary turnover relationship. *Journal of Applied Psychology, 95*, 1058–1070.

March, J., & Simon, H. (1958). *Organizations*. New York, NY: Wiley.

Meyer, J. P., Becker, T. E., & Vandenberghe, C. (2004). Employee commitment and motivation: A conceptual analysis and integrative model. *Journal of Applied Psychology, 89,* 991–1007.

Miller, J., Hom, P., & Gomez-Mejia, L. (2001). The high costs of low wages: Does maquiladora compensation reduce turnover? *Journal of International Business Studies, 32,* 585–595.

Millikin, J., Hom, P., & Manz, C. (2010). Self-management competencies in embedded self-managing teams: Their impact on multi-team productivity. *Leadership Quarterly, 21,* 687–702.

Mitchell, T., Holtom, B., Lee, T., Sablynski, C., & Erez, M. (2001). Why people stay: Using job embeddedness to predict voluntary turnover. *Academy of Management Journal, 44,* 1102–1121.

Mitchell, T., & Lee, T. (2001). The unfolding model of voluntary turnover and job embeddedness: Foundations for a comprehensive theory of attachment. *Research in Organizational Behavior, 23,* 189–246.

Mobley, W. H. (1977). Intermediate linkages in the relationship between job satisfaction and employee turnover. *Journal of Applied Psychology, 62,* 237–240.

Mobley, W. H. (1982). *Employee turnover: Causes, consequences, and control.* Reading, MA: Addison-Wesley Publishing Company.

Mobley, W. H., Griffeth, R. W., Hand, H. H., & Meglino, B. (1979). Review and conceptual analysis of the employee turnover process. *Psychological Bulletin, 86,* 493–522.

Morgeson, F., & Hofmann, D. (1999). The structure and function of collective constructs: Implications for multilevel research and theory development. *Academy of Management Review, 24,* 249–265.

Peña, D. G. (1997). *The terror of the machine: Technology, work, gender, and ecology on the U.S.-Mexico border.* Austin, TX: University of Texas Press.

Price, J. L. (2004). The development of a causal model of voluntary turnover. In R. Griffeth & P. Hom (Eds.), *Innovative theory and empirical research in employee turnover* (pp. 3–32). Greenwich, CT: Information Age Publishing.

Price, J. L., & Mueller, C. W. (1981). A causal model of turnover for nurses. *Academy of Management Journal, 24,* 543–565.

Price, J. L., & Mueller, C. W. (1986). *Absenteeism and turnover of hospital employees.* New York, NY: Elsevier.

Prieto, N. (1997). *Beautiful flowers of the maquiladora.* Austin, TX: University of Texas Press.

Ramesh, A., & Gelfand, M. (2010). Will they stay or will they go? The role of job embeddedness in predicting turnover in individualistic and collectivistic cultures. *Journal of Applied Psychology, 95,* 807–823.

Romero, E., & Cruthirds, K. (2009). Understanding employee turnover patterns in Mexican maquiladoras. *Journal of CENTRUM Cathedra, 2,* 63–72.

Royalty, A. B. (1998). Job-to-job and job-to-nonemployment turnover by gender and education level. *Journal of Labor Economics, 16,* 392–443.

Rusbult, C. E., & Farrell, D. (1983). A longitudinal test of the investment model: The impact on job satisfaction, job commitment and turnover of variations in rewards, costs, alternatives and investments. *Journal of Applied Psychology, 68,* 429–438.

Salamin, A., & Hom, P. (2005). In search of the elusive U-shaped performance-turnover relationship: Are high performing Swiss bankers more liable to quit? *Journal of Applied Psychology, 90,* 1204–1216.

Shauman, K. A. (2010). Gender asymmetry in family migration: Occupational inequality or interspousal comparative advantage. *Journal of Marriage and Family, 72,* 375–392.

Shaw, J. D., Dineen, B. R., Fang, R., & Vellella, R. F. (2009). Employee-organization exchange relationships, HRM practices, and quit rates of good and poor performers. *Academy of Management Journal, 52,* 1016–1033.

Shore, L. Tetrick, L., Lynch, P., & Barksdale, K. (2006). Social and economic exchanges: Construct development and validation. *Journal of Applied Social Psychology, 36,* 837–867.

Sluss, D., & Ashforth, B. (2008). How relational and organizational identification converge: Processes and conditions. *Organization Science, 19,* 807–823.

Sweeny, K. (2008). Crisis decision theory: Decisions in the face of negative events. *Psychological Bulletin, 134,* 61–76.

Takeuchi, R., Lepak, D., Wang, H., & Takeuchi, K. (2007). An empirical examination of the mechanisms mediating between high-performance work systems and the performance of Japanese organizations. *Journal of Applied Psychology, 92,* 1069–1083.

Tharenou, P., & Caulfield, N. (2010). Will I stay or will I go? Explaining repatriation by self-initiated expatriates. *Academy of Management Journal, 53,* 1009–1028.

Tiano, S. (1994). *Patriarchy on the line: Labor gender and ideology in the Mexican maquila industry*. Philadelphia, PA: Temple University Press.

Trevor, C. O. (2001). Interactions among actual ease-of-movement determinants and job satisfaction in the prediction of voluntary turnover. *Academy of Management Journal, 44,* 621–638.

Trevor, C. O., & Nyberg, A. J. (2008). Keeping your headcount when all about you are losing theirs: Downsizing, voluntary turnover rates, and the moderating role of HR practices. *Academy of Management Journal, 51,* 259–276.

Tsui, A., Pearce, J., Porter, L., & Hite, J. (1995). Choice of employee-organization relationship: Influence of external and internal organizational factors. In G. Ferris (Ed.), *Research in personnel and human resources management* (pp. 117–151). Greenwich, CT: JAI Press.

Tsui, A., Pearce, J., Porter, L., & Tripoli, A. (1997). Alternative approaches to the employee-organization relationship: Does investment in employees pay off? *Academy of Management Journal, 40,* 1089–1121.

Tsui, A., & Wang, D. (2002). Employment relationships from the employer's perspective: Current research and future directions. In C. Cooper & I. Robertson (Eds.), *International review of industrial and organizational psychology* (pp. 77–114). Chichester, UK: Wiley.

Wang, D., Tsui, A., Zhang, Y., & Ma, L. (2003). Employment relationships and firm performance: Evidence from an emerging economy. *Journal of Organizational Behavior, 24,* 511–535.

West, M. (2004). Investigating turnover in the international context: A turnover model for the Mexican culture. In R. Griffeth & P. Hom (Eds.), *Innovative theory and empirical research in employee turnover* (pp. 231–256). Greenwich, CT: Information Age Publishing.

Xiao, Z., & Bjorkman, I. (2006). High commitment work systems in Chinese organizations: A preliminary measure. *Management and Organization Review, 2,* 377–402.

Xiao, Z., & Tsui, A. (2007). When brokers may not work: The cultural contingency of social capital in Chinese high-tech firms. *Administrative Science Quarterly, 52,* 1–31.

Yalabik, Z. Y., Chen, S.-J., Lawler, J., & Kim, K. (2008). High-performance work system and organizational turnover in East and Southeast Asian countries. *Industrial Relations, 47,* 145–152.

Yamagishi, T., Cook, K., & Watabe, M. (1998). Uncertainty, trust, and commitment formation in the United States and Japan. *American Journal of Sociology, 104*, 165–194.

Zatzick, C., & Iverson, R. (2006). High-involvement management and workforce reduction: Competitive advantage or disadvantage. *Academy of Management Journal, 49*, 999–1015.

Zhang, Z., Zyphur, M., & Preacher, K. (2009). Testing multilevel mediation using hierarchical linear models. *Organizational Research Methods, 12*, 695–719.

16

Employee–Organization Relationship in Older Workers

Mo Wang
University of Maryland

Yujie Zhan
Wilfrid Laurier University

Demographic projections have shown that by 2012, nearly 20% of the total U.S. workforce will be age 55 or older, up from just under 13% in 2000, leading to a sizable increase in the number of people who will transition into retirement in the next decade (Toossi, 2004). Similarly, 41% of the Canadian working population is expected to be between the ages of 45 and 64 by the year 2021 (Lende, 2005). In the United Kingdom, 30% of workers are already over 50 (Dixon, 2003). These labor force change patterns are also demonstrated by data from other countries and regions (e.g., European Union, Japan, China, and India; Tyers & Shi, 2007), reflecting the fact that the population as a whole is getting older due to several factors, such as the aging of the large Baby Boom generation, lower birth rates, and longer life expectancies (Alley & Crimmins, 2007). Consequently, organizations have to consider older workers' unique characteristics and career development needs when they develop policies and practices to promote the employee–organization relationship (EOR). Given that older workers may expect different types of obligation from the organization compared to younger workers and may use their perception of the EOR to inform mid and late career-related decisions (e.g., early retirement or bridge employment), studying the EOR from the older workers' perspective is extremely important.

To our knowledge, however, few previous studies have investigated EORs among older workers. As such, the existing theories for EOR, such as social exchange theory and the inducements–contributions model, have not been calibrated for applications to older workers. Specifically, although the theoretical mechanisms and principles specified in these theories may hold across older and younger workers, they may be manifested through different constructs that are age specific. Therefore, the purpose of this chapter is to integrate the aging literature with the EOR literature to provide an understanding of EORs for older workers.

To understand the EOR among older workers, we first discuss the meaning of aging to the EOR. Given the different characteristics, needs, and values of older employees from younger employees, we consider what types of benefits or resources received from organizations may be particularly valued by older workers. We also consider what the unique types of reciprocation are that organizations may receive from older workers. In the second half of this chapter, we examine the relationship between EORs and unique career outcomes for older workers, such as retirement intention and decision, early retirement, and bridge employment.

THE MEANING OF AGING TO THE EOR

The EOR literature has drawn upon social exchange theory (Blau, 1964) and the norm of reciprocity (Gouldner, 1960), as well as the inducements–contributions model (March & Simon, 1958), to provide the theoretical basis for understanding the employee and employer exchange relationship. Although the exact focus of these theories may vary, a common theme that emerges in these theories is that EORs can be conceptualized as a resource exchange between the organization and the employee. As such, to understand the meaning of aging to the EOR, it is necessary to take a developmental perspective to analyze the potential changes in terms of the resources that older workers expect from their organizations and the resources that they may offer to their organizations as they age. Specifically, the impact of aging on EORs may depend on the impact of the aging process on employees' physical and mental abilities, work-related functions and activities, and needs and values (Jex, Wang, & Zarubin, 2007; Shultz & Wang, 2008).

The change of the reciprocal relations between older workers and organizations can also be understood from the person–environment (PE) fit perspective. PE fit refers to the congruence or alignment between characteristics of individuals and those of their environment or organization. Fit is dynamic rather than static in nature (Ostroff, Shin, & Feinberg, 2002). As suggested by Feldman and Beehr (2011), older workers may experience a decline of PE fit due to their changes in cognitive ability, physical health, and values. However, the PE fit could be maintained for older workers if their organization implements policies and practices tailoring to older workers' characteristics and needs. The organization itself may also benefit from such implementation given the unique contribution that older workers potentially make.

EOR Benefits Valued by Older Workers

The typical benefits employees may receive from their organizations include, but are not limited to, economic/material benefits, informational benefits, time benefits, and social–emotional benefits (Cropanzano & Mitchell, 2005; Tsui, Pearce, Porter, & Tripoli, 1997). For older workers, four types of resources provided by organizations may be especially valued: aging-related task redesign and training, health care benefits and support, socioemotional support, and family friendly practices.

Aging-Related Task Redesign and Training

As people age, they are exposed to an increasing array of threats to their performance, many of which could be avoided or minimized through improved job design (Fisk & Rogers, 2001). To enhance the EOR for older workers, organizations may want to implement work setting changes that facilitate the performance of older workers. Such implementations can be understood in terms of physical and cognitive aging.

Research has shown a general trend toward decreasing energy and, as a result, reduced capacity for physically demanding tasks with increasing age. For example, with aging, there is a gradual loss of muscle mass and muscle strength, which decreases the maximal exercise capacity (McArdle, Vasilaki, & Jackson, 2002). Aging is also accompanied by the loss of bone tissue throughout the body. Lower bone density may be a risk factor for degenerative arthritis (Sowers, 2001), which is the leading cause of disability among older adults within industrialized countries. Further, metabolism drops as people grow older. With increasing age, mitochondria produce less adenosine triphosphate (ATP), the body's main metabolic source of energy (Jex et al., 2007). The implication is that age-related physical changes may make it more difficult for older workers to perform physically demanding tasks. As such, organizations may promote the EOR by protecting older employees from job tasks that require workers to perform very quickly or require workers to perform physically demanding activities for long periods of time.

In addition to the decline of physical strength, when people grow older, even though their general knowledge remains stable or even increases, they tend to experience a reduction in perceptual and cognitive resources (Fisk & Rogers, 2001; Park, 2000). Specifically, perceptual limitations of older people mainly include vision changes and hearing loss, which may constrain many basic job activities, such as reading and driving. Cognitive aging features declines in processing speed, working memory, inhibition function, and sensations. For example, Salthouse (1996) pointed out that one of the factors accounting for age-related decline in cognitive performance was a general slowing of processing speed of mental operation with aging. Similarly, older adults' working memory capacity (defined as the amount of online cognitive resources that provide simultaneous storage and processing of information) declines, making it more difficult to perform cognitive tasks requiring both processing and storing information (Park, 2000). Hasher and Zacks (1988) also found that, with aging, people have more trouble inhibiting their attention to irrelevant information and concentrating on relevant information, which makes it difficult for older adults to perform tasks that require long periods of mental concentration. Overall, the cognitive aging literature suggests that age-related reduction in cognitive resources may lead to more difficulty for older workers in dealing with high mental load tasks (Shultz, Wang, Crimmins, & Fisher, 2010; Wang & Chen, 2004, 2006).

In this background of physical and cognitive aging, organizations may facilitate EORs by benefiting their older employees via implementing task redesigns to make work settings friendlier for older workers as well as providing training to help them take advantage of new technologies to assist their work (Fisk & Rogers, 2001). For example, organizations are recommended to protect their older employees by avoiding memory demands through provision of familiar cues and minimizing irrelevant or distracting information from work instructions. Applications of new technology (e.g., enterprise resource planning systems) may also relieve workers from excessive information processing by organizing and automating routine productive processes, thereby decreasing the cognitive load imposed on workers. In addition, organizations may want to provide more breaks for older workers to relieve them from the potential negative effects of performing cognitively intense tasks.

Health Care Support

Among the various issues related to aging, health is always viewed as one of the most critical concerns because people are more likely to face health issues during their later life. With physical aging, workers' health care may become an important part of the employment relationship. Entering the 21st century, health care costs have been increasing rapidly in United States, as has the cost for health insurance coverage. Therefore, EORs for older workers may be greatly influenced by the quality of health care benefit provided by the organization, because it has important implications for both older workers' physical and financial well-being.

In addition to health care benefits, organizations may promote the EOR by protecting their older employees from occupational hazards. As people age, they are more vulnerable to threats to their health and safety. For example, research evidence suggests that older adults' immune systems take longer to build up defenses against specific diseases. As a result, older adults become more prone to serious consequences from illnesses that are easily defeated by young adults (Aldwin & Gilmer, 1999). This translates to risks in performing job tasks that may involve exposure to chemicals, being struck by heavy objects, exposure to violence, and repetitive motions. Given the vulnerability of older workers, organizations may implement safety and health care practices to minimize the threats to older employees. In addition, medical care related to schedule flexibility at work may also be greatly valued by older workers.

Socioemotional Support

According to the Socioemotional Selectivity Theory (SST), a basic awareness of passage through different life stages is ubiquitous in all cultures and people, which has implications for people's motivations (Carstensen, 1991). SST also posits that individuals are typically agentic in that they set goals and behave in ways that are likely to help them achieve those goals

(Carstensen, Isaacowitz, & Charles, 1999). Put together, these two principles indicate that where one is in his or her "lifetime" strongly shapes the types of goals an individual will pursue. Specifically, SST posits that when an individual is younger, he or she is closer to the beginning of his or her life cycle and thus views "time" as time since birth. Thus, his or her goals will be future oriented: He or she will aim toward knowledge acquisition, career planning, and the development of new social relationships that will pay off in the future (Carstensen, 1991). Older individuals, by contrast, view "time" as time *left in life*. Thus, they will have more present-oriented goals: They aim toward regulating their emotions to be positive, pursuing emotionally gratifying relationships with others, and engaging in activities that will benefit them relatively immediately (Carstensen, 1991). Overall, according to SST, older adults focus more on socioemotional outcomes, whereas younger adults are more driven by skill, knowledge, and opportunity development and, thus, are more information oriented. Given the focus of older adults on socioemotional outcomes, EORs may play a more important role in older workers' job satisfaction and well-being. EOR literature has shown that social exchange is associated with socioemotional outcomes such as trust, loyalty, and affective commitment (Shore, Coyle-Shapiro, Chen, & Tetrick, 2009; Shore, Tetrick, Lynch, & Barksdale, 2006). Compared to economic exchange, socioemotional support provided by organizations may be perceived to be more valuable for older workers.

Although little research has examined SST in the workplace, several studies do suggest that age-related differences in goals and motivations do manifest themselves in organizational settings. For instance, research has suggested that older workers are less career development oriented and often avoid challenges at work, whereas younger adults tend to have a "learning orientation" and thus use challenges as learning and development opportunities (Kanfer & Ackerman, 2004). In addition, research has shown that compared to older employees, younger employees are typically more competitive rather than cooperative (Wong, Gardner, Lang, & Coulon, 2008), and older adults typically display more affective commitment to their organization, whereas younger employees tend to place more importance on "employability" and opportunity for advancement (D'Amato & Herzfeldt, 2008).

Given that older workers may put more value on regulating their emotions to be positive and pursuing emotionally gratifying relationships with others, organizations should promote a more cooperative and less political work climate among employees. Further, older workers may prefer not to face too many new challenges, especially those of evaluative nature, at the workplace. Accordingly, organizations should pay attention to how they conduct performance evaluation and provide feedback to older workers. When it comes to a feedback event, older workers may be more affected by the quality of the feedback delivery rather than the content of the feedback. As such, interactional justice at the workplace may play an important role in facilitating EORs in older workers. Finally, employment security is obviously preferred by older workers.

Family-Friendly Practices

At present, more and more couples enter the labor force at the same time, creating a large number of dual-earner families. When it comes to older workers, one issue that features the particular need for work–family balance is care-giving responsibility. In today's workforce, the number of workers caring for family members at both ends of the life span—children and elders—is growing quite rapidly. These workers are often referred to as the sandwich generation (Neal & Hammer, 2007). Several social and demographic trends have contributed to the phenomenon of the sandwich generation in the United States, including delayed childbearing, the aging of the American population, the aging of the American workforce, the increasing number of women in the workforce, decreases in family size and changes in family composition, and rising health care costs. Neal and Hammer (2007) found that members from the sandwich generation preferred jobs that allow flexibility either in one's daily work schedule or where the work is performed in order to be able to provide family care. Moreover, members from the sandwich generation also prefer working for organizations that have family-friendly policies so that they can attend to their family care needs.

Given that the typical age of the sandwich generation members ranges from 40 to 55 years, these preferences in terms of jobs and organizations are likely to substantially influence EORs for older workers. Organizations may promote EORs for older workers by providing flexible time schedules that allow people to select their work hours, thereby giving employees flexibility to attend to child and/or elder care needs. Organizations may also set up family leave programs to provide paid or unpaid time off for family issues, such as illness of spouse, children, or parents.

EOR Benefits Offered by Older workers

The typical benefits organizations may receive from their employees include, but are not limited to, productivity, organizational citizenship behaviors, and loyalty (Cropanzano & Mitchell, 2005; Tsui et al., 1997). Although these benefits generally apply to employees across different ages, the unique characteristics of older workers, and their experience and expertise in particular, may change the specific types of contributions they can make.

Experience and Expertise Enhanced by Aging

One thing that we know typically occurs as people age is that they gain experience and often have higher levels of task-related expertise. As one would probably imagine, experience is typically associated with higher levels of work performance. Experience and expertise are also important when complex tasks are performed at work. Although it has been shown that older workers do have more difficulty on physically and cognitively demanding tasks, there have also been studies showing no age-related difference in the performance of such tasks. Scholars have suggested that older employees with higher levels of task-related expertise are able to develop strategies to compensate for their physical and cognitive declines without impairing their task performance. As such, experience and expertise are particularly useful for older workers to continue their careers without having to make a career path change or exit.

Given the experience and expertise of older workers, they may contribute to the EOR not only through their own skilled performance but also through their roles as mentors for younger coworkers. For example, Dendinger, Adams, and Jacobson (2005) have shown that an important work motivation for older workers is to pass their knowledge and skills to younger generations (i.e., generative motivation). Therefore, for organizations, nurturing older workers' expertise and providing them autonomy and opportunities to actively apply it to their work may be important ways to promote EORs in older workers. It may be good for organizations to set up a formal mentoring system that fulfills older workers' generative motivation.

Summary

Aging has particular meanings to the EOR between older workers and their organizations. Beyond the typical benefits and resources involved in the exchange relationship, organizations' obligations to older workers should emphasize aging-friendly work settings, health care benefits and support, socioemotional support, and family-friendly practices. Reciprocally, older workers with extensive experiences are valuable resources for organizations. Also, older workers are the experts who are more motivated to pass their knowledge and skills to younger generations.

Consistent with the reciprocal nature of EORs, according to the PE fit perspective, a reciprocal fulfillment between person and job may prompt employees' job performance and/or psychological well-being. For older workers in particular, although declined cognitive and physical ability may threaten their ability–demand fit in accomplishing some tasks, their experience, expertise, and generative motivation could potentially offer opportunities for fulfilling other job demands such as mentoring. In addition, need–supply fit can be promoted by organizations that take care of older workers' values and needs. It should be noted that few studies have directly examined EORs for older workers, which renders a lack of empirical findings in this area. Future research needs to empirically test the factors theorized here and confirm their roles in promoting positive EORs for older workers.

EORS AND RETIREMENT

Literature has shown that EORs may impact individuals' job-related decision-making process. For older workers, one of the most important career decisions they have to make relates to retirement. As a type of work withdrawal behavior, retirement would occur in different forms sooner or later in one's career life. As such, older workers' decisions regarding when to retire and how to retire could be impacted by EORs. However, because of the aging of the workforce, retirement has become an inevitable issue for organizations. Organizations may strategically influence older workers' retirement process through retirement-related human resource management (HRM) practices that are closely related to EORs.

In this section, we discuss the linkage between EORs and retirement from the perspectives of both older workers and organizations. We believe taking both perspectives will contribute to our understanding of the EOR–retirement relationship because it reflects the two streams of concerns in

EOR research and retirement research. First, further improvement in EOR research requires the consideration of both parties in the relational system (e.g., Coyle-Shapiro & Shore, 2007). As indicated in other chapters of this volume (e.g., Chapter 12), although EOR research has largely been based on social exchange theory (e.g., Coyle-Shapiro & Conway, 2004; Cropanzano & Mitchell, 2005; Shore & Shore, 1995), "research on social exchange is very rarely 'social' in the sense that it seeks to incorporate both parties' perspectives to the exchange" (Coyle-Shapiro & Conway, 2004, p. 22); instead, previous literature on the EOR tended to focus on only one party's perception, in particular employees' perceptions of organizations, such as perceived organizational support and psychological contracts. Therefore, researchers are recommended to involve employees and organizations as well as their interaction in examining the EOR (e.g., Cropanzano & Mitchell, 2005; Shore et al., 2004).

Second, retirement can be viewed as a mutual withdrawal of older workers and their organizations (Adams, Prescher, Beehr, & Lepisto, 2002). It does not exclusively depend on employees' attitudes. In recent literature, retirement has been increasingly conceptualized in multiple ways (Wang & Shultz, 2010). Two conceptualizations, retirement as decision making and retirement as a part of HRM, are especially relevant to EOR research, capturing the perspectives of employees and organizations. The first conceptualization views retirement as a motivated choice behavior of older workers. By making the decision of retirement, employees choose to decrease their psychological commitment to work and behaviorally withdraw from work (Adams et al., 2002; Shultz & Wang, 2008). According to a decision-making model of retirement (Feldman, 1994), organizational factors, especially EOR-related factors (e.g., organizational commitment, perceived organizational support), compose an important set of variables that influence employees' intention and actual decision of retirement. Another conceptualization of retirement concerns organizations' retirement-related HRM practices. Accordingly, organizations are able to manage retirement by designing appropriate HRM practices in order to strategically reach their goals (Wang & Shultz, 2010). Retirement policies and practices, such as early retirement incentives and offering retirement counseling programs, may impact retirement decisions as an important part of EORs for older workers.

Given the dual emphasis on both employees and organizations in both EOR and retirement literature, we organize this section by first discussing the role of EOR in influencing employees' retirement intentions and decisions. We then describe how retirement-related HRM practices may influence older workers' EORs. We draw on social exchange theory as the primary theoretical background.

EOR and Retirement Intentions and Decisions

For individuals, retirement decisions involve a complex evaluation of work, personal, and financial issues. Feldman (1994) has proposed a theoretical model of retirement decision making, defining retirement as an exit taken by older workers from workplaces with a decreased commitment to work thereafter. In Feldman's model, organization-related factors have been explicitly included as a set of antecedents of retirement decision functioning above and beyond traditionally tested demographic information and individual health and wealth.

The quality of the EOR is a part of the decision-making process about retirement. In general, positive perception of EORs may postpone employees' retirement due to three possible reasons. First, social exchange theory suggests that employees who perceive a highly beneficial EOR may feel obligated to reciprocate their organizations by increasing their work input (Coyle-Shapiro & Conway, 2004; Cropanzano & Mitchell, 2005), which may be translated into longer working life for older workers. By contrast, negative perception of EORs may lead to more intention of retirement. Once older workers perceive their organizations to be less supportive and even discriminating against older workers, they will be more likely to withdraw from their organizations as a means of reciprocating to organizations' withdrawal from older workers.

Second, accompanied with the prolonged working life, older workers who perceive highly beneficial EORs may expect better treatment from organizations when they approach retirement. Older workers who are approaching retirement age tend to compare their working status with their expected postretirement life. On the one hand, they value their work role identity; on the other hand, they expect less demands and more personal time during retirement. Compared with older workers with unpleasant relationships with their organizations, workers with more positive EORs are more likely to expect more supportive systems from their organizations, such as flexible work schedules and respect for older workers. Therefore, positive EORs may encourage older workers to continue working in their organizations by satisfying the older workers' expectation of reduced work commitment without losing their work role identity.

Third, older workers may postpone retirement simply because they enjoy working in their organizations. With a higher level of emotional attachment to and identification with the organization, older workers are likely to be willing to stay in their organization for a longer time. In the following sections, we present empirical evidences for the relationship between two EOR indicators, perceived organizational support and organizational commitment, and older workers' retirement intentions and decisions.

Perceived Organizational Support

For employees, the organization serves as an important resource of tangible benefits such as wages and medical benefits, as well as socioemotional support such as respect and caring. Employees who form a positive perception concerning the organizational support would feel attached to their organization and obligated to help the organization reach its goals. In turn, they would expect improved performance to be rewarded (Eisenberger, Huntington, Hutchinson, & Sowa, 1986; Rhoades & Eisenberger, 2002).

Although perceived organizational support has been shown to be negatively related to absenteeism (Eisenberger et al., 1986) and turnover (Baranik, Roling, & Eby, 2010), there is a lack of empirical work directly examining the effect of perceived organizational support in impacting older workers' retirement intention. However, different literatures have paid attention to organizational factors that may impact older workers' retirement through studying perceived socioemotional support from organizations. For example, in some organizations, older workers may face discrimination and negative stereotypes because of possible decline in work capability (Posthuma & Campion, 2009). Experiences of being discriminated against could push older workers out of their employment. For example, Zappala, Depolo, Fraccaroli, Guglielmi, and Sarchielli (2008) tested the effect of firm aging norms in predicting postponing retirement. Their results showed that older workers tended to retire late if the management team in their company displayed special attention to maintain the employability of elderly employees and the supervisors took into account their age, health, and capacity when assigning tasks and conduct evaluations. The effect of aging norms may be explained by a heightened level of perceived organizational support. For older workers, their perceived organizational support is expected to be particularly sensitive to age-related discrimination and negative stereotype. Accordingly, respect and consideration of management teams and supervisors may effectively increase older workers' perceived support.

Organizational Commitment

Organizational commitment is closely related to perceived organizational support and can be viewed as individual perception of the organization's commitment to an employee (Cropanzano & Mitchell, 2005). According to social exchange theory, employees are prone to exchange their commitment for an employer's support (Eisenberger et al., 1986). Many empirical studies have been conducted to examine the relationship between organizational commitment and retirement-related outcomes, such as early retirement intention (e.g., Gaillard & Desmette, 2008), retirement intention (e.g., Adams & Beehr, 1998; Adams et al., 2002), and planned retirement age (e.g., Taylor & Shore, 1995). The effect size of organizational commitment is small to moderate, but organizational commitment is usually a significant predictor of retirement after controlling for individual characteristic variables such as age, personal finances, and health. Furthermore, organizational commitment has been shown to predict retirees' bridge employment intentions. According to a recent empirical study (Jones & McIntosh, 2010), although organizational and occupational commitment both predicted retirement intention, a stronger predictive effect was found for organizational commitment than occupational commitment in predicting bridge employment in the same organization.

Among the studies mentioned above, the commitment construct is typically operationalized by measuring older workers' affective commitment. Nevertheless, researchers have begun to explore the potential differences between specific forms of commitment in impacting retirement decision (e.g., Jones & McIntosh, 2010; Luchak, Pohler, & Gellatly, 2008). For example, Luchak et al. (2008) examined the effects of affective commitment and continuance commitment on planned age of retirement under a defined-benefit pension plan. According to commitment theory, individuals' motivation to stay is experienced as a mind-set that varies depending on the perceived reasons of stay. Specifically, working is a personal choice due to enjoyment for employees with higher levels of affective commitment, whereas working is a necessity to avoid social and economic adversity for employees with higher levels of continuance commitment. Luchak et al. (2008) showed that affective commitment was positively associated with planned age of retirement, whereas a curvilinear relationship was found between continuance commitment and planned retirement age such that employees who had higher levels of continuance commitment tended to retire at the age when their pension benefit reached maximum. As such, the positive effect of affective commitment reflects the emotional reason for stay versus retirement, and the curvilinear effect of continuance commitment reflects the cognitive benefit–cost calculation in the retirement decision-making process.

Economic Exchange

In addition to the influences of sociopsychological exchange relation on retirement, economic exchange also impacts one's decision of retirement. Financial issues are critical to retirement decisions (Wang, Henkens, & van Solinge, 2011). People are more likely to retire when they can afford it. Older workers with financial constraints are expected to be especially sensitive to economic exchange with their organization. For instance, a defined-benefit pension plan is a type of pension plan in which an employer promises a specified monthly benefit on retirement that is predetermined by a formula based on the employee's earnings history and work tenure. Under this plan, older workers tend to retire at the time point when their pension income is maximized (Luchak et al., 2008). A defined-contribution pension plan refers to the retirement plan in which the amount of the employer's annual contribution is specified and retirement benefit fluctuates on the basis of investment earnings. This type of plan provides employees more control and flexibility and is usually viewed as more motivating.

It is necessary to point out that the relationship between the EOR and retirement intentions and decisions is not exclusively negative. Similar to previous findings that demonstrate inconsistent associations between EORs and turnover (see Chapter 15 of this volume), we expect that the impact of EORs on retirement intentions/decisions may also vibrate due to the different strategic goals of organizations. In particular, positive EORs may lead to an increased rather than decreased tendency to retire if organizations strategically encourage employees' retirement. With a more positive EOR, older workers may also tend to expect a satisfying retirement package from their organizations. Therefore, we expect a pleasant retirement process for older workers retiring from organizations with which they have positive relationships. In the next section, we discuss in detail EORs and retirement-related HRM practices.

EORs and Retirement-Related HRM Practices

Within HRM research, Wright, McMahan, and McWilliams (1994) proposed that firms' human resources (HR) practices would shape human capital pool and elicit employee behaviors in line with firm goals. Ostroff and Bowen (2000) further emphasized the role of HRM practices as critical determinants of employee perceptions and behavior that would facilitate organizational effectiveness. Accordingly, retirement-related HRM practices are particularly important indicators of organizations' investment and support to older workers, which may influence the quality of employment relation and employees' attitudes toward their organization.

For organizations, the removal of a compulsory retirement age has introduced uncertainty about staff profiles and financial burden for HR planning. It also requires individuals to take a more active and strategic role in their own retirement planning (Bidewell, Griffin, & Hesketh, 2006). Indicating organizations' investment in EOR, retirement-related HRM practices may serve two different strategic purposes (Wang & Shultz, 2010). First, HRM can be viewed as a subsystem that exchanges resources with the environment to attract, develop, motivate, and retain human capital in order to ensure the effective functioning of the organization (Jackson & Schuler, 1995). By designing appropriate practices providing financial benefits (e.g., generous pension benefit and postretirement medical care benefit) or sociopsychological support (e.g., retirement counseling program [e.g., Shuey, 2004] and mentoring opportunity), organizations are able to show their consideration of older workers and promote positive EORs, resulting in employees' increased commitment to the organization and delayed retirement. Second, HRM may also serve organizations' strategic goals of human capital restructuring or downsizing. Via HRM practices, such as early retirement incentive package (Feldman, 2003) and phased retirement policy (e.g., Greller & Stroh, 2003), organizations invest in the exchange relationships in order to support older workers' withdrawal.

Early Retirement Incentives

In retirement literature in the 1990s when "many organizations were seeking to improve their competitiveness through global manufacturing relocation or outsourcing peripheral services" (Wang & Shultz, 2010, p. 180), one of the most popular retirement-related HRM practices was early retirement incentives. According to Feldman (2003), organizations have much control over the financial incentives offered, but the valence of such incentives varies across organizations with different pension policies (e.g., defined-contribution or defined-benefit pension plan) and workers with different characteristics.

Bidewell et al. (2006) applied the delay discounting perspective to explain the effect of early retirement incentives. According to this perspective, time usually results in a subjective devaluation of the later reward, causing people to prefer a small but early reward to avoid the potential loss during waiting. Further, devaluation of the delayed reward is much greater when the early reward can be collected immediately than when there is a long time to wait before the availability of the early reward. In this scenario, early retirement incentive can be viewed as the small but early reward provided to older workers who are approaching their eligibility to maximized Social Security and pension benefit. Therefore, by providing appropriate early retirement incentives, organizations demonstrate their support to older worker retirement. As shown by Bidewell et al. (2006), retirement age is negatively related to the discounting amount. In addition, early retirement incentives may be accompanied by the organizational support of early retirement counseling program. Because the early retirement decision is usually surrounded by considerable uncertainty and the feeling of involuntariness, a comprehensive preretirement counseling program may help to reduce the ambivalence (Feldman, 1994), as well as the feeling of involuntariness that might be triggered by early retirement (Szinovacz & Davey, 2005).

Bridge Employment Opportunity

When Baby Boomers' retirement starts to lead to labor force shortages, bridge employment will become an increasingly popular research topic (Wang & Shultz, 2010). Bridge employment refers to paid employment taken by older workers after exiting positions or career paths of considerable duration and before their complete work withdrawal (Shultz, 2003). Because older workers are a skilled and experienced workforce, organizations that need to maintain flexible access to such a workforce should communicate their value and provide opportunities for continued work in retirement.

Providing bridge employment opportunity for older workers may also be a good way for organizations to show their commitment to older workers' needs and well-being. For one reason, past studies have shown that many older workers may have not amassed sufficient resources to achieve a desired standard of living at the time they retire (Hershey, Jacobs-Lawson, McArdle, & Hamagami, 2007). In this situation, an opportunity of bridge employment provided by their employers is highly valuable for one's financial transition. Further, previous studies have shown that bridge employment helps retirement transition and adjustment (Kim & Feldman, 2000; Wang, 2007). To mitigate the negative feeling of work role loss, retirees are likely to appreciate a bridge job that helps them to maintain work role identity, social contact, and life pattern. Continued working may increase the perceived organizational membership of retirees, which is a representation of the overall general EOR. Further, Zhan, Wang, Liu, and Shultz (2009) found that bridge employment, especially bridge employment in the same career field as before the retirement, was beneficial for retirees' physical and mental health.

In addition to the needs for financial income, social contacts, and work role identity, a unique reason for older people to work is to pass their knowledge and skills to younger generations (Dendinger et al., 2005). An organization can help older workers to pursue the generative meaning of work by developing mentoring systems embedded in bridge employment that may encourage retirees to mentor and share knowledge with younger workers. These practices not only help older people gain continuity between working and retirement, but also help organizations maintain a flexible access to an experienced workforce as well as smooth the knowledge transfer process from one generation of workers to another.

Given the unique functions of bridge employment, it can be viewed as a special type of EOR for older workers. Applying the meaning of aging to EOR we discussed earlier, bridge jobs are expected to be designed with full consideration of age-related changes in terms of physical and cognitive ability, values, and preferences. Organizations may recruit retirees for certain positions that typically require less physical effort but more professional experiences and expertise, and they reciprocate to reemployed retirees with socioemotional support such as opportunities for promoted sense of self-worth and social acceptance, as well as opportunities to pass their knowledge and skills to younger generations.

Integrating the Organization's and Employee's Perspectives

So far, we have discussed the role of EORs on employees' retirement and organizations' management of EORs through retirement-related HR practices. We now propose a mediation model where the retirement-related HR practices and policies are expected to increase the perceived quality of the EOR, which, in turn, will align employees' retirement decisions with organizations' strategic goals for the workforce (Figure 16.1). Specifically, for older workers, their perception of organizations' resources, practices, and policies provides them information to evaluate organizations' concern and commitment to older workers. Reciprocating to organizations' favorable treatment and expecting more benefit in the future, older workers may increase their work effort by postponing retirement or engaging in bridge employment. For organizations, they design HR practices that are consistent with organizational strategic goals and deliver these practices to employees, which may contribute to the formation of a shared positive perception regarding EORs such that the employer is considerate and supportive. Consequently, a positive EOR increases employees' work well-being and helps organizations to achieve their staffing or downsizing goals.

Nonetheless, several issues need to be discussed regarding the mediating role of EORs between HR practices and retirement. First, the mediation model presented here focuses on a top-down process in which the organization has much control over the development of the EOR. However, EORs can also be developed in a bottom-up process in which employees observe and communicate with each other to infer and attribute the organizations' commitment to their relationship with employees. Employees' perceptions of EORs are not independent of each other for those working in the same organization or work unit; neither is the retirement decision. Coworkers' retirement could prompt others to retire or think about retirement. Observing or hearing about coworkers' unpleasant interaction with the organization may ruin the EOR quality for others. Consequently, employees may be less confident in the mutual exchange relationship

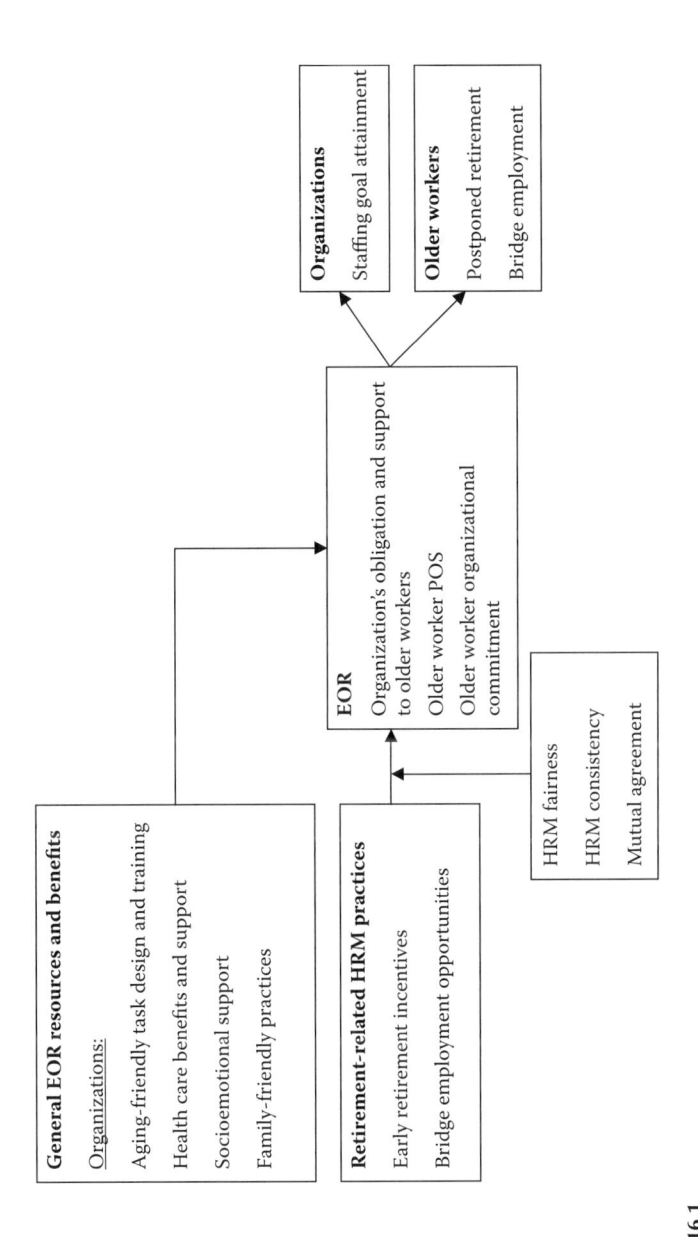

Employee–Organization Relationship in Older Workers • 445

General EOR resources and benefits

Organizations:

Aging-friendly task design and training
Health care benefits and support
Socioemotional support
Family-friendly practices

Retirement-related HRM practices

Early retirement incentives
Bridge employment opportunities

HRM fairness
HRM consistency
Mutual agreement

EOR

Organization's obligation and support to older workers
Older worker POS
Older worker organizational commitment

Organizations

Staffing goal attainment

Older workers

Postponed retirement
Bridge employment

FIGURE 16.1
The mediation role of EOR in older worker–related organizational staffing and retirement decision-making. HRM, human resources management; POS, perceived organizational support.

with the organization. In general, if employees are not exposed to consistent HR practices, it is possible for them to form various perceptions of EORs (Takeuchi, Wang, Marinova, & Yao, 2009). If the EOR perception developed by employees working in the same organization varies across a wide range, it is less likely for the organization to achieve its strategic goal by actively managing its relationship with employees. Therefore, organizations' HR practices should be designed and delivered with full consideration of fairness and consistency (see Figure 16.1; Bowen & Ostroff, 2004). For example, organizations should make sure that all employees are aware of and able to access the resources offered to them. A retirement planning program might be particularly helpful in facilitating communication and seeking feedback.

Second, an underlying assumption in most EOR literature is the mutual agreement between organization and employees of the obligations to each other. However, the two parties do not always agree on the EOR (Shore et al., 2004). Shore et al. (2004) discussed three potential sources of the discrepancies in EOR perceptions: divergent schemata of the employee and employer, the complexity and ambiguity around employment contracts, and miscommunication between the two parties. Given the discrepancy in their understanding of EORs, employees may have difficulties in recognizing the organization's investment in their relationship. At the same time, the organization's practices could not be transferred to corresponding employees' retirement decisions consistent with the organization's strategic goal.

Third, related to the different understanding of EOR by each party, employees and organizations may have a different evaluation of how the other party has fulfilled their obligations. The divergent perceptions will inevitably produce misunderstanding and contract breach. Bennett, Tetrick, Ginter, and McCausland (2010) have applied the unfolding model of turnover to understanding the retirement decision process. According to their model, when an older worker who expects certain rewards for postponing retirement suddenly realizes that his or her organization will not meet this expectation, he or she is likely to experience the violations to his or her values and benefits. Consequently, a retirement decision path may be activated.

Finally, Kuvaas (2008) proposed an alternative model to explain the role of the EOR such that the quality of the EOR can moderate the relationship between perception of HR practices and employee outcomes.

Specifically, when workers perceive an organization's efforts to provide more resources as motivated by self-interest rather than by genuine concern for employees, an organization's HR practices could not lead to positive work outcomes. Supporting this contingency perspective, Tsui et al. (1997) found that employee responses differed under different types of relationships based on the relative investment of organizations. When applied to understand the EOR and retirement relationship, this contingency perspective suggests that when older workers have positive perceptions regarding their relationship with their organization, they are more likely to view the retirement-related HR practices as an organization's investment to improve employees benefit or well-being and to reciprocate to such investment by making more efforts. Therefore, a high-quality EOR may be necessary for older workers to be motivated to respond positively to retirement-related practices in a way that will benefit the organization.

CONCLUSIONS

The purpose of this chapter is to integrate the aging and retirement research literature with the EOR literature to provide an examination of EORs among older workers. It should be noted that the approach taken here is more illustrative rather than exhaustive. Given that few previous studies have investigated EORs among older workers, we contend that our theoretical integration here suggests ways to calibrate theoretical frameworks of EORs for applications to older workers. In particular, when discussing the meaning of aging to the EOR, we emphasized the specific resources exchanged between older workers and the organization, as well as the aspects important for older workers to reach PE fit. When discussing the relationship between EORs and older workers' retirement decisions, we also strived to reach a theoretical balance by drawing perspectives from both older workers and the organizations. Nevertheless, our theoretical development is limited by the social exchange mechanism and the norm of reciprocity. According to Cropanzano and Mitchell (2005), social exchange is one process that leads to the establishment and sustainability of a relationship, but not the only one. Future studies should consider other processes for EOR to form and how they may lead to different implications for older workers.

It should also be noted that culture may be an important boundary condition to consider EORs among older workers. In different societal cultures, older workers may develop different needs and value different things. For example, in Eastern societies heavily influenced by Confucianism, such as Chinese and Japanese societies, older age is typically associated with seniority and higher social hierarchies (Li, Tsui, & Weldon, 2000). Therefore, older workers in those societies may be more sensitive to whether the organization's HR practices demonstrate sufficient respect to them. Such respect may not only be associated with the materialized support they receive from the organization, but also the "good faces" (i.e., positive views from others) they gain from the organization's practice. For example, older workers in those societies may particularly value the opportunity for them to participate in company policy making, even though such practice is only a type of formality (Li et al., 2000). Given that older workers from different cultures may value different resources and benefits they receive from organizations, cultural factors should also be included in considerations when examining EORs in older workers. To our best knowledge, no empirical studies have examined the potential joint effect of culture and age on EORs, which may point to a fruitful future research direction.

This chapter has important practical implications. First and foremost, both employees and organizations should be aware of the age-related physical and cognitive changes and actively manage the reciprocal relation between older employees and organizations to promote EORs. For organizations, they need to recognize the advantages of older employees who have more professional experience and expertise as well as a high generative motivation to deliver their knowledge to colleagues. Also, given the characteristics, values, and preferences of older workers, organizations are recommended to focus more on the health care benefits of older employees, socioemotional support, and family-friendly practices. Second, organizations with specific staffing goals with older workers can take advantage of EORs by implementing retirement-specific HRM practices. On the one hand, organizations that plan to retain older employees are recommended to design appropriate practices providing an older worker–friendly workplace in order to show their consideration of older workers and promote positive EORs. On the other hand, organizations with downsizing plans may implement retirement-supportive practices such as early retirement incentive packages and phased retirement policies. In addition, organizations should pay attention to whether a mutual agreement is established regarding the meaning of EORs for older employees. Third, in the decision-making process about retirement and bridge employment, older workers should take into account the quality of EORs. Considering their declined ability in certain areas and unique motivation for working after retirement, older workers are recommended to assess the organizations' resources, practices, and policies to evaluate the organizations' commitment to older employees.

REFERENCES

Adams, G. A., & Beehr, T. A. (1998). Turnover and retirement: A comparison of their similarities and differences. *Personnel Psychology, 51*, 643–665.

Adams, G. A., Prescher, J., Beehr, T. A., & Lepisto, L. (2002). Applying work-role attachment theory to retirement decision-making. *International Journal of Aging & Human Development, 54*, 125–137.

Aldwin, C. M., & Gilmer, D. F. (1999). Immunity, disease processes, and optimal aging. In J. C. Cavanaugh & S. K. Whitbourne (Eds.), *Gerontology: Interdisciplinary perspectives* (pp. 123–154). New York: Oxford University Press.

Alley, D., & Crimmins, E. (2007). The demography of aging and work. In K. S. Shultz & G. A. Adams (Eds.), *Aging and work in the 21st century* (pp. 7–23). Mahwah, NJ: Lawrence Erlbaum & Associates.

Baranik, L. E., Roling, E. A., & Eby, L. T. (2010). Why does mentoring work? The role of perceived organizational support. *Journal of Vocational Behavior, 76*, 366–373.

Bennett, T. M., Tetrick, L., Ginter, R., & McCausland, T. (2010, April). *Applying job embeddedness and the unfolding model of turnover to understand the retirement decision process*. Paper presented at the 25th Annual Society for Industrial/Organizational Psychology Conference, Atlanta, GA.

Bidewell, J., Griffin, B., & Hesketh, B. (2006). Timing of retirement: Including delay discounting perspective in retirement model. *Journal of Vocational Behavior, 68*, 368–387.

Blau, P. (1964). *Exchange and power in social life*. New York, NY: Wiley.

Bowen, D. E., & Ostroff, C. (2004). Understanding HRM-firm performance linkages: The role of the "strength" of the HRM system. *Academy of Management Review, 29*, 203–221.

Carstensen, L. L. (1991). Selectivity theory: Social activity in life-span context. In K. W. Schaie (Ed.), *Annual review of gerontology and geriatrics* (Vol. 11, pp. 195–217). New York, NY: Springer.

Carstensen, L. L., Isaacowitz, D., & Charles, S. T. (1999). Taking time seriously: A theory of socioemotional selectivity. *American Psychologist, 54*, 165–181.

Coyle-Shapiro, J. A.-M., & Conway, N. (2004). The employment relationship through the lens of social exchange. In J. A.-M. Coyle-Shapiro, L. M. Shore, M. S. Taylor, & L. E. Tetrick (Eds.), *The employment relationship: Examining psychological and contextual perspectives* (pp. 5–28). Oxford, UK: Oxford University Press.

Coyle-Shapiro, J. A-M., & Shore, L. (2007). The employee-organization relationship: Where do we go from here? *Human Resource Management Review, 17*, 166–179.

Cropanzano, R., & Mitchell, M. S. (2005). Social exchange theory: An interdisciplinary review. *Journal of Management, 31*, 874–900.

D'Amato, A., & Herzfeldt, R. (2008). Learning orientation, organizational commitment and talent retention across generations. *Journal of Managerial Psychology, 23*, 929–953.

Dendinger, V. M., Adams, G. A., & Jacobson, J. D. (2005). Reasons for working and their relationship to retirement attitudes, job satisfaction and occupational self-efficacy of bridge employees. *International Journal of Aging & Human Development, 61*, 21–35.

Dixon, S. (2003). Implications of population ageing for the labour market. *Labour Market Trends, 111*, 67–76.

Eisenberger, R., Huntington, R., Hutchinson, S., & Sowa, D. (1986). Perceived organizational support. *Journal of Applied Psychology, 71*, 500–507.

Feldman, D. C. (1994). The decision to retire early: A review and conceptualization. *Academy of Management Review, 19*, 285–311.

Feldman, D. C. (2003). Endgame: The design and implementation of early retirement incentive programs. In G. A. Adams & T. A. Beehr (Eds.), *Retirement: Reasons, processes, and results* (pp. 83–114). New York, NY: Springer Publishing Company.

Feldman, D. C., & Beehr, T. A. (2011). A three-phase model of retirement decision-making. *American Psychologist, 66*, 193–203.

Fisk, A. D., & Rogers, W. A. (2001). Health care of older adults: The promise of human factors research. In W. A. Rogers & A. D. Fisk (Eds.), *Human factors interventions for the health care of older adults* (pp. 1–12). Mahwah, NJ: Lawrence Earlbaum Associates.

Gaillard, M., & Desmette, D. (2008). Intergroup predictors of older workers' attitudes toward work and early exit. *European Journal of Work and Organizational Psychology, 17*, 450–481.

Gouldner, A. W. (1960). The norm of reciprocity. *American Sociological Review, 25*, 161–178.

Greller, M. M., & Stroh, L. K. (2003). Extending work lives: Are current approaches tools or talismans? In G. A. Adams & T. A. Beehr (Eds.), *Retirement: Reasons, processes, and results* (pp. 115–135). New York, NY: Springer.

Hasher, L., & Zacks, R. T. (1988). Working memory, comprehension, and aging: A review and a new view. In G. H. Bower (Ed.), *The psychology of learning and motivation* (Vol. 22, pp. 193–225). San Diego, CA: Academic Press.

Hershey, D. A., Jacobs-Lawson, J. M., McArdle, J. J., & Hamagami, F. (2007). Psychological foundations of financial planning for retirement. *Journal of Adult Development, 14*, 26–36.

Jackson, S. E., & Schuler, R. S. (1995). Understanding human resource management in the context of organizations and their environments. *Annual Review of Psychology, 46*, 237–264.

Jex, S., Wang, M., & Zarubin, A. (2007). Aging and occupational health. In K. S. Shultz & G. A. Adams (Eds.), *Aging and work in the 21st century* (pp. 199–224). Mahwah, NJ: Lawrence Erlbaum Associates.

Jones, D. A., & McIntosh, B. R. (2010). Organizational and occupational commitment in relation to bridge employment and retirement intentions. *Journal of Vocational Behavior, 77*, 290–303.

Kanfer, R., & Ackerman, P. L. (2004). Aging, adult development, and work motivation. *Academy of Management Review, 29*, 440–458.

Kim, S., & Feldman, D. C. (2000). Working in retirement: The antecedents of bridge employment and its consequences for quality of life in retirement. *Academy of Management Journal, 43*, 1195–1210.

Kuvaas, B. (2008). An exploration of how the employee-organization relationship affects the linkage between perception of developmental human resource practices and employee outcomes. *Journal of Management Studies, 45*, 1–25.

Lende, T. (2005). Older workers: Opportunity or challenge? *Canadian Manager, 30*, 20–30.

Li, J. T., Tsui, A. S., & Weldon, E. (2000). *Management and organizations in the Chinese context*. New York, NY: St. Martin's Press.

Luchak, A. A., Pohler, D. M., & Gellatly, I. R. (2008) When do committed employees retire? The effects of organizational commitment on retirement plans under a defined-benefit pension plan. *Human Resource Management, 47*, 581–599.

March, J. G., & Simon, H. A. (1958). *Organizations*. New York, NY: Wiley.

McArdle, A., Vasilaki, A., & Jackson, M. (2002). Exercise and skeletal muscle aging: Cellular and molecular mechanisms. *Aging Research Reviews, 1*, 79–93.

Neal, M. B., & Hammer, L. B. (2007). *Working couples caring for children and aging parents: Effects on work and well-being*. Mahwah, NJ: Lawrence Erlbaum Associates.

Ostroff, C., & Bowen, D. E. (2000). Moving HR to a higher level: Human resource practices and organizational effectiveness. In K. J. Klein & S. W. J. Kozlowski (Eds.), *Multilevel theory, research, and methods in organizations* (pp. 211–266). San Francisco, CA: Jossey-Bass.

Ostroff, C., Shin, Y., & Feinberg, B. (2002). Skill acquisition and person-environment fit. In D. C. Feldman (Ed.), *Work careers: A developmental perspective* (pp. 63–90). San Francisco, CA: Jossey-Bass.

Park, D. C. (2000). The basic mechanisms accounting for age-related decline in cognitive function. In D. C. Park & N. Schwarz (Eds.), *Cognitive aging: A primer* (pp. 3–22). Philadelphia, PA: Psychology Press.

Posthuma, R. A., & Campion, M. A. (2009). Age stereotypes in the workplace: Common stereotypes, moderators, and future research directions. *Journal of Management, 35*, 158–188.

Rhoades, L., & Eisenberger, R. (2002). Perceived organizational support: A review of the literature. *Journal of Applied Psychology, 87*, 698–714.

Salthouse, T. A. (1996). The processing-speed theory of adult age differences in cognition. *Psychological Review, 103*, 403–428.

Shore, L. M., Coyle-Shapiro, J. A-M., Chen, X. P., & Tetrick, L. (2009). Social exchange in work settings: Content, process, and mixed models. *Management and Organization Review, 5*, 289–302.

Shore, L. M., & Shore, T. H. (1995). Perceived organizational support and organizational justice. In R. Cropanzano & K. M. Kacmar (Eds.), *Organizational politics, justice, and support: Managing the social climate of the workplace* (pp. 149–164). Westport, CT: Quorum Books.

Shore, L. M., Tetrick, L. E., Lynch, P., & Barksdale, K. (2006). Social and economic exchange: Construct development and validation. *Journal of Applied Social Psychology, 36*, 837–867.

Shore, L. M., Tetrick, L. E., Taylor, S. E., Coyle-Shapiro, J. A. M., Liden, R. C., McLean-Parks, J., … Van Dyne, L. (2004). The employee-organization relationship: A timely concept in a period of transition. In J. J. Martocchio (Ed.), *Research in personnel and human resources management* (Vol. 23, pp. 291–370). San Diego, CA: Elsevier.

Shuey, K. M. (2004). Worker preferences, spousal coordination, and participation in an employer-sponsored pension plan. *Research on Aging, 26*, 287–316.

Shultz, K. S. (2003). Bridge employment: Work after retirement. In G. A. Adams & T. A. Beehr (Eds.), *Retirement: Reasons, processes, and results* (pp. 215–241). New York, NY: Springer.

Shultz, K. S., & Wang, M. (2008). The changing nature of mid and late careers. In C. Wankel (Ed.), *21st century management: A reference handbook* (Vol. 2, pp. 130–138). Thousand Oaks, CA: Sage Publications.

Shultz, K., Wang, M., Crimmins, E., & Fisher, G. (2010). Age differences in the demand-control model of work stress: An examination of data from 15 European countries. *Journal of Applied Gerontology, 29,* 21–47.

Sowers, M. F. (2001). Epidemiology of risk factors for osteoarthritis: Systemic factors. *Current Opinion in Rheumatology, 13,* 447–451.

Szinovacz, M. E., & Davey, A. (2005). Predictors of perceptions of involuntary retirement. *The Gerontologist, 45,* 36–47.

Takeuchi, R., Wang, M., Marinova, S. V., & Yao, X. (2009). Role of domain-specific facets of perceived organizational support during expatriation and implications for performance. *Organizational Science, 20,* 621–634.

Taylor, M. A., & Shore, L. F. (1995). Predictors of planned retirement age: An application of Beehr's model. *Psychology and Aging, 10,* 76–83.

Toossi, M. (2004). Labor force projections to 2012: The graying of the U.S. workforce. *Monthly Labor Review, 127,* 3–22.

Tsui, A. S., Pearce, J. L., Porter, L. W., & Tripoli, A. M. (1997). Alternative approaches to the employee-organization relationship: Does investment in employees pay off? *Academy of Management Journal, 40,* 1089–1121.

Tyers, R., & Shi, Q. (2007). Demographic change and policy responses: Implications for the global economy. *World Economy, 1,* 537–566.

Wang, M. (2007). Profiling retirees in the retirement transition and adjustment process: Examining the longitudinal change patterns of retirees' psychological well-being. *Journal of Applied Psychology, 92,* 455–474.

Wang, M., & Chen, Y. (2004). Age differences in the correction processes of context-induced biases: When correction succeeds. *Psychology and Aging, 19,* 536–540.

Wang, M., & Chen, Y. (2006). Age differences in attitude change: Influences of cognitive resources and motivation on responses to argument quantity. *Psychology and Aging, 21,* 581–589.

Wang, M., Henkens, K., & van Solinge, H. (2011). Retirement adjustment: A review of theoretical and empirical advancements. *American Psychologist, 66,* 204–213.

Wang, M., & Shultz, K. (2010). Employee retirement: A review and recommendations for future investigation. *Journal of Management, 36,* 172–206.

Wong, M., Gardner, E., Lang, W., & Coulon, L. (2008). Generational differences in personality and motivation: Do they exist and what are the implications for the workplace? *Journal of Managerial Psychology, 23,* 878–890.

Wright, P. M., McMahan, G. C., & McWilliams, A. (1994). Human resources and sustained competitive advantage: A resource-based perspective. *International Journal of Human Resource Management, 5,* 301–326.

Zappala, S., Depolo, M., Fraccaroli, F., Guglielmi, D., & Sarchielli, G. (2008). Early retirement as withdrawal behavior: Postponing job retirement? Psychological influences on the preference for early or late retirement. *Career Development International, 13,* 150–167.

Zhan, Y., Wang, M., Liu, S., & Shultz, K. S. (2009). Bridge employment and retirees' health: A longitudinal investigation. *Journal of Occupational Health Psychology, 14,* 374–389.

Part 4

Organizational and Strategic Implications

17

Strategic Human Resource Management and Employee–Organization Relationship

David Lepak
Rutgers University

Wendy R. Boswell
Texas A&M University

The field of strategic human resource management (HRM) has garnered considerable interest from scholars from a variety of disciplines. Over the past three decades, what might be viewed as a macro view of HRM has evolved into its own research domain often entitled strategic HRM. Within this domain, several issues have received a disproportionate amount of attention from scholars. Perhaps the most prominent issue has been trying to understand how human resource (HR) practices and HR systems relate to organizational outcomes. Indeed, scholars such as Huselid (1995), Delery and Doty (1996), Arthur (1994), Batt (2002), and Guthrie (2001) have provided ample evidence that certain types of HR systems exert a significant impact on organizational outcomes. Predicting firm performance gains (and losses) based on HR initiatives has provided a considerable thrust to this area of research and has helped establish credibility of this domain among practitioner audiences.

More recently, strategic HRM researchers have broadened their focus to explore the specific practices that comprise different HR systems to identify how the parts of the systems work together. For example, there is considerable debate as to whether the practices within HR systems operate in an additive or synergistic manner (e.g., Lepak, Liao, Chung, & Harden, 2006; Macky & Boxall, 2007). There are conceptual rationales for both approaches and little empirical evidence to provide a compelling argument for either perspective. Closely related, researchers have explored which HR practices should be considered as core to these HR systems. For example, is a grievance procedure a core required part of a high-performance work system? Researchers have also explored the nature of these systems and have increased their focus on exploring whether there is a single "best HR system" or whether the best HR system depends on the strategic objectives and/or organizational context (cf. Delery & Doty, 1996; Huselid, 1995).

A third major thrust in the strategic HRM field that has garnered considerable recent attention is an increased emphasis placed on meditational mechanisms linking HR practices to organizational effectiveness. Researchers have focused on mediators such as human capital (Takeuchi, Lepak, Wang, & Takeuchi, 2007), climate (Liao, Toya, Lepak, & Hong, 2009; Takeuchi, Chen, & Lepak, 2009; Zacharatos, Barling, & Iverson, 2005), social capital (Collins & Smith, 2006; Evans & Davis, 2005), organizational justice perceptions (Wu & Chaturvedi, 2009), and various work-related attitudes (Macky & Boxall, 2007) to explore causal models of how HR practices and systems of practices impact individual, group, and ultimately organizational outcomes.

Despite the tremendous progress in the strategic HRM field since the 1980s, we believe that there is a major shortcoming that is fairly typical in most studies in this area. Specifically, most empirical studies and theoretical perspectives in the strategic HRM literature are explicitly or implicitly manager oriented. This is certainly an understandable perspective because HR systems are typically implemented by managers and organizations to encourage certain employee contributions. However, every relationship involves two parties, and the employee–organization relationship (EOR) is in essence an exchange. Yet the research has generally focused on one side of the exchange, with HRM viewed as a managerial initiative to define and facilitate the terms of the inducements–contributions exchange noted by Barnard (1938) and March and Simon (1958). Essentially, HR practices, or at least a number of the practices, are attempts by organizations to induce certain contributions by employees, the argument being that through HR practices particular contributions toward the organization's goals will be induced.

For example, one of the most influential perspectives in the macro HRM literature is the behavioral perspective articulated by Schuler and Jackson

(1987). A key tenet of the behavioral perspective is that HR practices affect firm outcomes through managing employees' displayed behavior (Schuler & Jackson, 1987). Recognizing this, managers strive to identify and elicit different types of behaviors that are more appropriate depending on organizational strategy and other relevant contingencies. By placing emphasis on needed role behaviors, the behavioral perspective recognizes that employee behaviors are instrumental in organizational effectiveness. This perspective also focuses our attention on a key role of HR in organizations—providing clarity regarding desired role behaviors within organizations from employees (Boswell, 2006; Colvin & Boswell, 2007). Researchers such as Arthur (1994), Macduffie (1995), and Tsui, Pearce, Porter, and Hite (1995) have grounded their studies in this perspective. These studies have provided great insights into the HR–performance relationship. However, one challenge of placing primary emphasis on the inducements provided by organizations is the downplaying of variance in the responses of those being induced by those specific practices. Implicitly, individuals are treated as if their response is always as should be expected.

Another dominant perspective within the strategic HRM literature is the resource-based view of the firm (Barney, 1991; Wright, Dunford, & Snell, 2001). Although the behavioral perspective places primary emphasis on the importance of aligning employee behaviors with organizational objectives, the resource-based view of the firm places greater emphasis on the potential that employee talents—individually and/or collectively— may play as a strategic organizational asset. For example, Hitt, Bierman, Shimizu, and Kochhar (2001) found a positive, curvilinear association between human capital and return on sales. Similarly, Pennings, Lee, and van Witteloostuijn (1998) noted that "professionals endowed with a high level of human capital are more likely to deliver consistent and high-quality services" (p. 426) and the contribution of human capital investment to firm survival is critical. Similarly, Snell and Dean (1992) suggested that the higher the level of knowledge, skills, and abilities of employees, the more potential impact of human capital on performance. The key word here is potential, however. Realizing that potential is encouraged by HR practices, but it is only accomplished with the cooperation of employees. In short, much of the strategic HRM literature has emphasized what companies can do to align employee focus, competencies, and motivation with organizational goals. Although these are certainly viable perspectives, it is important to recognize that the research in this area often treats employees as simply responders; they are viewed as demonstrating the appropriate or expected attitudes and behaviors that are solicited by the HR practices. Yet, employees are not robots; they think, they react, they make choices, and they respond. This latter point raises the importance of exchange, a give and take between organizations and employees that goes beyond the more narrowly construed view of employees as mechanical responders to what the organization puts in place.

EVOLVING ISSUES

Although strategic HRM literature has explicitly considered both managerial perspectives and some emphasis on individual-level outcomes, one area that has not received as much attention, but would benefit from more attention, is a greater emphasis on the *exchange* between these two parties. EOR reflects "an overarching term to describe the relationship between the employee and the organization" (Shore et al., 2004, p. 292) including both micro concepts, such as the psychological contract (Rousseau, 1995) and perceived organizational support (POS; Eisenberger, Huntington, Hutchinson, & Sowa, 1986), and macro concepts, such as the employment relationship (Tsui, Pearce, Porter, & Tripoli, 1997). Drawing on social exchange theory (Blau, 1964), the norm of reciprocity (Gouldner, 1960), and the inducements–contributions exchange (March & Simon, 1958), a key point of focusing on exchange is that it emphasizes the importance of the relationship, the reciprocity or the give and take between employees and employers. As we will highlight in this chapter, it also invokes consideration of perceptions of the exchange that may not reflect the actual exchange between the organization and the employee. We believe that incorporating the EOR literature into the strategic HRM literature provides important insights and research opportunities within the broader strategic HRM literature.

It is also important to note that a strategic perspective has begun to emerge within the EOR literature. For example, Shore, Porter, and Zahra (2004) applied theories of organizational strategy to analyze the EOR and specifically the role of the firm in impacting the interaction between individuals and their employers. Similarly, research by Tsui and Wang and colleagues (Song, Tsui, & Law, 2009; Tsui & Wang, 2002; Wang, Tsui,

Zhang, & Ma, 2003) has specifically examined the employment relationship through a strategic management/HRM lens. Again, this "strategic" EOR research tends to focus on the organization's side pertaining to the employee–employer relationship.

In this chapter, we examine the strategic HRM literature from the perspective of the EOR, focusing specifically on how the strategic HRM literature might benefit from taking a more balanced perspective of the exchange that occurs between individuals and their organizations. In doing so, we analyze and discuss what we see as some of the most interesting and important issues within the strategic HRM literature that can be informed by incorporating an EOR perspective. Although there are likely to be many more research issues to consider, we believe that some of the most important issues to address are related to the following topics:

- Why HRM does not work for everyone
- Why HRM does not have stronger effects
- Influencing HRM—who goes first?
- Use versus experience of HRM systems
- Interpretations and attributions of HRM systems
- Temporal nature of HRM systems

Why HRM Does Not Work (Equally) for Everyone

A basic question worthy of some reflection is to ask why HR systems do not have a consistent or uniform impact on employees. As noted earlier, an implicit assumption of much of the strategic HRM literature is that employees will respond to the presence, or absence, of various HRM systems. From a managerial perspective, the implementation of an HR practice should have a direct impact on all exposed to it and, at least implicitly, a universally equal impact on all exposed to it. Yet, some individuals respond in unintended ways (e.g., withholding behaviors), some respond very well, while others remain neutral. Why? By focusing on average improvements, or decrements, in employee attitudes, behaviors, and collective performance based on the use of these HR systems, the role of the EOR perspective in this process is ignored. Focusing on EOR is likely to provide some insights into this variance in reactions. One reason for differences in how employees respond to exposure to HR practices relates directly to different types of exchange relationships that they may find themselves in. At a broad level, we can think of economic (or transactional) versus social (or relational) exchanges as a spectrum on which employees sit. Employees operating in these different exchange relationships hold different expectations for how they are to be managed as well as what they owe their organization. Lepak and Snell (1999) and Rousseau (1995) argued that within the same firm, different groups of employees are treated differently via exposure to distinct HR systems that are consistent with employer views on the nature of these relationships. Given these differences, the presence of a particular HR practice may be consistent with their expectations or inconsistent. Borrowing the terminology of Tsui et al. (1995, 1997), these relationships may be balanced (high or low) or unbalanced in that the practices used to induce contributions are aligned, or not aligned, with what might be expected in the exchange based on their contributions. Given these possibilities, a logical question is whether implementing a single practice that is consistent with what a particular employee group expects, given their contributions, actually motivates them to work harder, or whether it just reinforces their expectations. As an example, what if employees in an economic exchange are exposed to more social-oriented HR practices such as professional development. Perhaps they will respond more positively (even if they are less likely to be exposed to the practices) than employees who have expectations for such social-oriented HR practices.

Another possible explanation for why HR does not always work equally for everyone is that some people within the same group might have different exchange relationships (idiosyncratic deals, or I-deals; psychological contracts). For example, some employees are able to negotiate idiosyncratic employment arrangements that are individually negotiated, are heterogeneous within groups, and vary in scope (cf. Rousseau, Ho, & Greebnerg, 2006). Because of these differences in employment arrangements, individuals within the same group may have different perspectives to exposure to any particular HR practices. The strategic HRM literature often operates at a group level (i.e., department, unit, organization, corporation) and does not place particular emphasis on individual differences and downplays or ignores variations in exchange relationships among individuals within groups. Yet, these differences may be meaningful in their impact on individuals as well as their coworkers. The introduction of a pay for performance plan, for example, may not motivate someone who has already negotiated an accelerated compensation plan. Although it might impact the group, on average, in a positive manner, it might also have different implications than expected for certain individuals within the group. It is also possible, for example, that those without the I-deal may be frustrated that they have to work harder just to earn the same level of compensation. The presence of differences within groups also raises the possibility for dilution of influence of HR practices on individuals.

Extending this point, another possible explanation is that differences in exchange relationships and associated HR practices trigger equity concerns among different groups. Groups that receive lower levels of investment from their organization, although possibly justified from a strategic investment point of view, may experience inequity and display less than desired attitudes and behaviors as a result (Lepak & Snell, 2006). At the same time, treating all employees equally might involve overinvesting in noncritical employees and underinvesting in critical employees. Although such an approach may alleviate equity concerns among noncore employees, it may not be cost effective for the firm and might actually result in expending unnecessary costs without reaping the benefits. These tensions may be magnified in situations where employees in different employee groups (and exposed to different HR systems) perform tasks and activities that are highly interdependent (Boxall, 1998; Rubery, Carroll, Cooke, Grugulis, & Earnshaw, 2004).

Employees may also simply vary in their expectations and ultimately reactions to HR systems due to individual differences created by personal experiences, values, and personality. Such factors play a role in what any one individual is likely to find attractive and/or motivating within the organization. We develop this idea more fully below in discussing an individual's interpretations and attributions of HRM systems.

Why HRM Does Not Have Stronger Effects

A closely related question to the question in the previous section is why HR systems do not have consistently stronger effects than would be expected or have been found. Again, because we are focusing on the actual exchange and perceptions of the exchange between employees and employers, it is important to consider that both parties are active in this exchange. Recognizing this raises issues associated with employee choice and volition, which are often ignored in the strategic HRM literature. What would it mean to consider employee choice? To think that organizations implement HR practices and that the requisite behaviors will automatically come is overlooking the simple assumption that people are predictable in how they respond to those practices.

As noted, although some employees may display desired attitudes and behaviors that are encouraged by HRM practices, this relationship is not automatic. Kidwell and Bennett (1993) noted that there are many circumstances associated with employee propensity to withhold effort that are manifest in behaviors such as shirking, social loafing, and free riding. Thus, although HR practices may be designed to induce certain employee attitudes and/or behaviors, recognizing volition on the part of employees implies that employees do not always respond according to the intentions of organizational decision makers and design of the HRM practices in place. As noted by Shore, Tetrick, et al. (2004), agency theory suggests that employees often have an incentive to misrepresent their abilities, act opportunistically, and possibly shirk their responsibilities. This suggests that when there is room for employee discretion to act, even in response to the presence of a particular incentive or performance management system, some employees may shirk if the opportunity is presented. At the same time, other employees, perhaps due to feelings of affective commitment, may take the opportunity to engage in prosocial behaviors.

The key point is that even when prompted to engage in a certain behavior by HRM practices, even within the same firm, there is likely to be variance in how employees may respond to those HRM practices. Certainly, as discussed earlier, one reason for this might be differences in employment relationships and I-deals. There are other explanations as well. For example, the quality of the exchange over time might have an impact. Because the quality of the exchange between employees and employers is not a one-time assessment, it is reasonable to assume that current practices are couched in the shadow of the past—past positive or negative interactions color employee reactions to current and future interactions. HR practices are thus likely interpreted with an eye to the nature of the exchange relationship over time. In addition, the effects of HR systems might depend on the overall quality of the employment relationship, and in particular, the benefits are likely to be enhanced in a positive EOR. As noted by Tekleab, Takeuchi, and Taylor (2005), high-quality social exchange relationships may foster positive cognitive biases in employees that influence future interpretations to be fairer than they really are. When this happens, an overly positive response to an HR initiative might occur. In contrast, when there is a negative perception of the quality of the relationship, a lower response might be more likely. In effect, the impact of an HR system is likely dependent on the context in which the system occurs.

An additional area of consideration is the impact of other individual and group factors related to EOR that have been shown to play an important role in the HR–organizational outcome relationship. For example, EOR is related to POS (Eisenberger et al., 1986), leader–member exchange (Graen & Cashman, 1975), and psychological contract violations/breach (Robinson, 1996). Although these factors are also associated with HR practices, they have distinct relationships with EOR. Given the multiple relationships among these attitudinal variables and HR practices, it is possible that EOR influences non–HR-related attitudinal factors, which then may attenuate (accentuate) the nature of the HR system influence on individuals' subsequent attitudes and/or behaviors. That is, the extent to which the EOR is associated with POS, for example, may serve as an important contextual factor that might suppress or magnify the influence of HR practices on employees. It is conceivable that factors contributing to the EOR–POS relationship might not be related to HR at all, suggesting that there might be important third-variable effects that impact the influence of HR on employees. Conceptually, what this means is that there are a variety of practices associated with both EOR and HR systems that might work in interactive ways to influence important individual and organizational outcomes. Because HR practices do not work in a vacuum, it is important to recognize that the EOR serves as a critical context that shapes how employees view HR practices but there are also other attitudinal variables that simultaneously influence how employees respond to HR practices.

This relates to the important role of the saliency of HR practices in driving subsequent attitudes and behaviors. In particular, the extent to which HR practices have an impact on individuals is determined by whether those practices are prominent within the general EOR context. The challenge here is that saliency can be viewed from multiple perspectives. For example, in organizations dominated by conditions inconsistent with the intent of the HR practices (e.g., team-based pay implemented in a competitive, individualistic work culture), the influence of such practices is not only likely to be muted but also may not even be salient to employees. From this point of view, saliency might operate as something relevant to the climate or context of the work environment. Relatedly, some practices may be salient because they are particularly visible or prominent. An organization may have an exceptional benefits package, high pay, or generous vacation plan. These practices are salient relative to other practices that are less visible or influential. However, HR practice saliency may also be an individual perspective. At a basic point of view, HR practices may signal to employees their relative importance as being valued or not valued in their organization. From this perspective, salience refers to the message conveyed by the practice. But if we go a step further, saliency may operate at the individual level and reflect individual preferences and tastes. For example, one individual may hold practice A as most salient, whereas for another employee, practice B is most salient. If focusing solely on practice A, its impact might be weaker for those who do not view practice A as particularly salient. Although the saliency of any one practice may be driven by a variety of factors, the key point is that the extent (and nature) of the HR practice effect may be dependent on whether the HR practice is even salient to an individual. The challenge is to understand both what creates these different views of saliency and how to incorporate these individual differences in saliency in a way that fits with the systems thinking logic operating within the strategic HRM literature.

Influencing HRM—Who Goes First?

Another critical issue to consider is who goes first in regard to defining and driving the terms of the EOR. An implicit if not explicit assumption in the strategic HRM literature is that organizations/managers determine the nature of the relationship and employees are simply reactive participants in their relationship with organizations. Yet it is likely that some employees act without being prompted to do so by HRM practices. Indeed, research on prosocial organizational behaviors (Brief & Motowidlo, 1986) and proactive behaviors (Bateman & Crant, 1993) suggests that actions such as helping, sharing, cooperating, and volunteering are fairly pervasive in organizations and are influenced by individual personality traits and values as well as contextual factors such as organizational norms. Similarly, a substantive body of research exists documenting the occurrence of organizational citizenship behaviors (OCBs), which are behaviors displayed by employees without explicit prompting by organizations. These streams of research indicate that employees may display actions that go above and beyond those specifically encouraged by HR practices.

At the same time, employees may also act for instrumental reasons as an attempt to manage others' impressions and their relative standing within their organizations. From an impression management perspective, employees may seek to attain valued outcomes within their organization (e.g., rewards, performance evaluations) or to attain or maintain a positive image (Bolino, 1999). As employees engage in actions to achieve certain workplace benefits, this then helps to shape the terms of the relationship moving forward.

As noted, much of the organization literature has focused on organizational actions such as HR practice as driving the nature of the EOR; that is, the literature typically views the organization as the starting point in influencing the exchange relationship. Indeed, social exchange theory maintains that individuals exchange their contributions for valued resources that the organization provides (Blau, 1964; Homans, 1961; Thibault & Kelly, 1959). Gouldner (1960) referred to the social exchange process as a norm of reciprocity, suggesting that individuals will tend to demonstrate reciprocative behaviors toward those who benefit them. Taking a relational perspective, Sun, Aryee, and Law (2007) found that HR practices were associated with employee citizenship behavior and ultimately improved firm performance by fostering social exchange through the norm of reciprocity. Conversely, poor treatment may trigger negative exchanges because it emphasizes the norm of negative reciprocity (Fehr & Gächter, 2000; Helm, Bonoma, & Tedeschi, 1972; Sahlins, 1965). In applying social exchange theory, research tends to focus on employees reciprocating in exchange for tangible reward or anticipated gain (e.g., influence, security, socioemotional benefit). For example, in a discussion of OCB, a construct associated with social exchange, Bolino noted, "employees engage in OCBs in order to reciprocate the actions of their organizations" (1999, p. 82). This notion is also a fundamental element of POS research (Eisenberger et al., 1986) in that perceived investment and concern on the part of the organization lead to reciprocation (i.e., increased performance, commitment) on the part of the employee. Certain HR practices (e.g., fair reward systems, opportunities for advancement, participation or voice opportunities) are argued to enhance POS by signaling to employees that the organization cares about their well-being and is willing to invest in them (Allen, Shore, & Griffeth, 2003; Wayne, Shore, & Liden, 1997).

Yet must the organization necessarily "act first" in establishing the exchange—offering inducements for *employee reciprocation*—often through HR systems? Although there is certainly an element of reciprocity associated with the exchange relationship employees have with their organization, two parties are involved, both of which are potentially active parties in establishing the exchange. Thus, considering that this is an exchange, it may not be appropriate to assume that organizational actions always precede employee actions. Rather, employees may strive to create or alter the nature of their relationship with their organization through their own actions including effective performance, political behaviors, OCB, and the like. Employees may initiate behavior with the expectation that their actions will be reciprocated in some way by the organization, thus serving as the driver of the exchange to induce action/reciprocation on the part of the organization. Again, the argument is that employees are not necessarily simple reactors to organizational actions/practices but may also seek to define and direct the nature of the exchange themselves.

One interesting question is what motivates whether (or when) employees respond to HR practices in a reciprocal manner or are more proactive in driving the EOR. As noted, when we consider the impression management literature, employees may act instrumentally, engaging in behaviors (tactics) to obtain desired rewards and/or privileges. Researchers have shown that impression management tactics are associated with supervisory liking and performance ratings (Podsakoff, MacKenzie, & Hui, 1993; Wayne & Ferris, 1990) as well as career success (Judge & Bretz, 1994). Given the potential benefits of impression management, it is logical that employees might engage in an opportunistic manner to realize personal gain (Bolino, 1999; Fandt & Ferris, 1990). As noted by Leary and Kowalski (1990), "conveying the right impression increases the likelihood that one will obtain desired outcomes and avoid undesired one" (p. 37). Extending this logic, in some circumstances, it may be more appropriate to view the relationship between organizational practices and employee actions as being initiated by the employee rather than the employer.

The work noted earlier on I-deals (Rousseau et al., 2006) speaks directly to employee-directed EOR. As individualized, nonstandard agreements between an employee and the employer, I-deals are typically sought by the employee directly and granted by the organization due to unique or high-demand human capital possessed by the individual (Rousseau, 2001, 2005). I-deals can help to differentiate among employees by focusing on a broadened employment package to include nonmonetary and particularistic resources such as increased job scope or mentoring (Rousseau et al.,

2006). Such informal and less standardized outcomes can be more easily negotiated by an individual compared to more concrete pay or benefits (Rousseau et al., 2006). In this way, the employee defines and directs the nature and quality of his or her employment relationship with the organization.

Relatedly from a power-dependence perspective, we would expect that employees who possess more valued resources are better positioned to direct the exchange relationship with the organization. Power-dependence theory (Emerson, 1962) argues that actors are dependent on one another for valued outcomes, benefits obtained are contingent on benefits given "in exchange," and exchanges with the same partner recur over time (Molm & Cook, 1995). Accordingly, with the potential for mutual dependency, either partner in the relationship may drive the terms of the EOR. As in I-deals, certain employees will possess greater power, dependent on knowledge, skills, and abilities, to then define the terms of the EOR; yet the relevant point is that organizations are not solely responsible for holding influence over the employees.

Thus, although the research typically views HR practices as being organizationally driven, we recognize the role in which employees can define and drive the exchange. Certainly organizations implement HR practices with the intent to drive employee behavior; yet employees also act on their own volition in the absence of and/or contrary to HR practices. And when displayed without prompting via HR practices, employee work behaviors may be based on altruistic reasons or instrumental reasons to attempt to realize some employment-related benefits or privileges. This is not to argue that there is no (or even a minimal) role for managers or organizations in defining and driving the EOR, but rather explicitly recognizes employee-initiated EOR.

Use Versus Experience of HRM Systems

Recent work within the strategic HRM and related literatures has recognized the critical issue of a potential disconnect between organizational use of HR practices and employee experiences of those intended practices. Nishii and Wright (2008) discussed this issue in terms of the potential variability in practices within an organization in regard to the intended, actual, and perceived employee reactions to HR practices. As noted by others (e.g., Boswell, Colvin, & Darnold, 2008; Gratton & Truss, 2003;

Wright & Boswell, 2002), a first point of variability is that the HR policy as intended by the organization is not necessarily what is implemented in practice by managers, and employees can only experience what has been enacted. Gratton and Truss (2003) argued that the potential "weak translation" of intended policies into practice can stem from a manager's lack of awareness of the intended policy(s) or purposive decision to not implement the intended policy(s). The policy–practice disconnect can also be fueled by managers signaling opposition to stated policies through their behaviors and/or attitudes (e.g., working extended hours contrary to work–life policies, negative statements regarding telecommuting).

Yet even practices fully and consistently implemented by managers may not be perceived or experienced as intended by the organization and/or consistently across individual employees. Nishii and Wright (2008) discussed the variability in employee perceptions across an organization as being a function of differences in cognitive schemas; individual differences in values, personalities, and needs; and the associated fit between those individual differences and the HR practices. The notion that employees react willfully based on their own subjective perception of the environment (Kehoe & Wright, in press; Nishi & Wright, 2008) offers further explanation for a potential disconnect between employee responses and the outcomes hoped for by an organization. Consistent with this, Liao et al. (2009) examined employee and manager "perspectives" of HR practices (i.e., high-performance work practices [HPWS]), finding not only differences between what managers say they are implementing and what employees say they are experiencing, but also differences in perspective across employees. Importantly, what employees reported they experienced in regard to HR practices predicted individual service performance, revealing the criticality of "employees' idiosyncratic experience with the (High Performance Work Practices) HPWS above and beyond management perspective of the HR practices generally implemented for an employee group and the employees' shared perceptions of the HR practices within the group" (Liao et al., 2009, p. 385) in driving important work outcomes.

Along this same vein, but in the specific context of interpersonal treatment at work, Olson-Buchanan and Boswell (2008) discussed how different individuals may have quite similar workplace experiences yet perceive and ultimately respond to the experiences differently. Through the process of sensemaking (i.e., to impose or derive structure or meaning from a situation; Louis, 1980; Volkema, Farquhar, & Bergmann, 1996; Weick, 1995), individuals interpret and reach a conclusion regarding any specific experience (or "trigger"; Olson-Buchanan & Boswell, 2008). An employee, for example, may draw on his or her own prior experiences as well as engage others to reflect on and make sense of the extant situation. Applying this to the EOR more generally, employees may quite distinctly perceive and ultimately react to an organization's HR practices and actions given each will go through a potentially unique process in interpreting those practices. An employee's prior experiences with the present organization or with other organizations and individual differences in preferences, needs, and dispositional traits are likely to shape how that particular individual experiences, interprets, and reacts to HRM practices.

Thus even with the somewhat tenuous assumption that HRM practices are implemented as intended by organizational policy and/or consistently across managers, there remains the issue of any one individual's experiences and interpretations. Indeed, the extensive micro-HRM research focused on individual difference effects offers further evidence to suggest that individuals may react differently to practices such as selection process, reward systems, and work design, even when a practice is similarly implemented. For example, the person–organization fit literature (e.g., Kristof, 1996) specifically recognizes individual differences in employee values, needs, and personality and that these factors influence an individual's attachment to an organization and organizationally directed workplace behavior (cf. Kristof-Brown, Zimmerman, & Johnson, 2005). Just as individuals purposefully and perhaps proactively define and direct the EOR (discussed earlier), we would expect individual differences that lead individuals to "fit" (or not fit) an organization to influence the nature of the exchange experienced between those individuals and their organization and their subsequent reactions.

Taken together, recognizing these potential disconnects in intended policy, implemented practice, and experience of any one employee shifts the focus from simply having and implementing an HR practice to something more complex that balances what management intends and what employees react to. Both are relevant to the exchange relationship and, if out of alignment, yield interesting implications for employee behaviors. The potential disconnects highlight not only how the terms of the EOR may not necessarily be implemented as intended by an organization but also how they may be differentially experienced, interpreted, and reacted to by individual employees.

Interpretations and Attributions of HRM Practices

Related to this discussion of employee perceptions of HRM is the role of employee attributions of organizational actions. It is through interpretation and then the attributions made that employees derive meaning regarding the nature of the exchange. In examining this issue, Nishi, Lepak, and Schneider (2008) explored how employees interpret HR practices and the meanings they attribute to organizational motives for how employees are managed. They found that employees make varying attributions for why management adopts HR practices and that these attributions differentially associate with employee work attitudes and create a shared perspective, ultimately leading to unit-level behaviors and outcomes (e.g., customer satisfaction). For example, attributions that an HR practice reflects quality concerns and/or employee enhancement associated positively with work outcomes, whereas attributions that HR practices reflect cost and/or employee exploitation showed deleterious effects. Relatedly, Eisenberger, Cummings, Armeli, and Lynch (1997) suggest that perceptions of managerial discretion impact how employees view organizational actions. Specifically, they argued that the impact of HR practices on POS is influenced by the degree to which employees perceive managers have discretion in the use of HR practices. Discretionary practices are viewed as having a stronger impact than nondiscretionary behaviors.

A question then is as follows: Where do employees look to derive this meaning? Certainly, expectations are shaped through early interactions (e.g., recruitment) with organizational representatives and as employees "learn the ropes" as new organizational members (e.g., through socialization). Such experiences help to establish the psychological contract that can subsequently be reinforced, reshaped, or perhaps violated (e.g., Robinson, 1996; Robinson & Rousseau, 1994; Robinson, Kraatz, & Rousseau, 1994; Rousseau, 1990) through organizational actions. These organizational policies and practices thus provide initial input for employees to interpret and attribute meaning. This is consistent with HR practices as signals (e.g., Behling, Labovitz, & Gainer, 1968; Shore & Shore, 1995). For example, Boswell, Roehling, LePine, and Moynihan (2003) examined treatment during the recruitment process (e.g., interviewer behavior, arrangements and opportunities, timeliness of follow-up), noting that how one is treated by organizational representatives "for better or for worse, lead job applicants to make inferences about characteristics of the job or the organization" (p. 24). These signals, in turn, provide the impetus for reinterpreting and establishing future expectations in the EOR.

Although employees may make attributions regarding the organization through the words and actions of recruiters, mentors, and coworkers, the immediate manager with the power of reward and rebuke is likely primary to an employee's interpretation of the EOR. The manager in this sense is seen by the employee as the organizational "agent" (Coyle-Shapiro & Shore, 2007; Liden, Bauer, & Erdogen, 2003), representing the organization's end in the dyadic exchange. Although the specification and role of this "agent" in representing the organization to an employee is "underdeveloped in EOR research" (Coyle-Shapiro & Shore, 2007, p. 172), the critical point is that employees are active participants in their exchange with the organization by directing their attention toward and deriving meaning from organizational actions.

Temporal Nature of HRM Systems

The management literature has increasingly recognized the temporal nature of employee–organizational behavior. The general perspective is that individuals do not exist in a vacuum, but rather are influenced by and react based on their prior experiences. These past experiences can serve as input for the sensemaking process (Louis, 1980), discussed earlier, as well as help to shape one's attitudes toward and perceptions of the organization. Recognizing this "baggage" (Shipp, 2006) that employees bring forward highlights how the EOR may evolve or change over time.

The role of time comes into play at multiple avenues in regard to the EOR. First is the role of employees' relationships at other organizations that may then affect the present EOR. This is perhaps particularly germane given the demise of lifetime (i.e., "cradle-to-grave") employment and expectations for significant employee mobility within and across firms. As individuals' experiences in other organizations are brought forward to the present situation, current and future expectations are shaped. In her seminal work on socialization and sensemaking in organizations, Louis (1980) discussed the contrast effect that occurs as individuals enter new settings. In particular, prior jobs often serve as background as individuals experience and make sense of the present situation. Accordingly, the nature of the EOR and experiences in negotiating and managing the EOR with prior employers serve to shape subsequent views of the EOR even with different organizations and managers. As an example, a perceived violation of the exchange relationship by a past employer may direct an employee to expect similar treatment by other employers, perhaps leading the employee to withhold behavior and/or be particularly sensitive to mixed messages or inconsistent policy implementation. Recently, Boswell, Shipp, Payne, and Culbertson (2009) examined how the job attitudes toward the present employer can be influenced by attitudes about the immediate past employer. In particular, Boswell et al. found that particularly negative attitudes toward a past job upon organizational entry may set up high expectations for the new job. The general conclusion was that "employees bring with them and are shaped by their past. These prior experiences are likely to set a standard against which the current job is evaluated" (Boswell et al., 2009, pp. 851–852).

A second role for time in the EOR is the recursive nature of experiences at the present organization in then shaping the EOR moving forward. Ultimately, an individual's experiences with HR systems will affect future perceptions of and reactions to those same systems. Just as experiences with other employers serve as background by which employees experience and make sense of the present situation, the employee's views toward the current organization are revised as he or she moves through the dyadic exchange relationship. Longitudinal research on psychological contract formation and violation, for example, shows how perceived treatment by the organization (e.g., psychological contract breach; that is, underfulfillment of obligations) serves as a signal to the individual of the EOR relationship, including perceptions of trust and support (cf. DeVos, Buyens, & Schalk, 2003; Dulac, Coyle-Shapiro, Henderson, & Wayne, 2008; Kiewitz, Restubog, Zagenczyk, & Hochwater, 2009; Lester, Kickul, & Bergmann, 2007; Robinson, 1996). For example, DeVos et al. (2003) showed how employees' perceptions of an employer's promises changed following organizational entry as employees make sense of employer actions and inducements as well as account for the employee's own contributions to the exchange relationship. As noted by the researchers, it is important to recognize the "psychological contract as a dynamic set of expectation" (DeVos et al., 2003, p. 556), which is shaped and reshaped as individuals experience the EOR and interpret those experiences.

In understanding the effects of HRM, the dynamic nature of the EOR would suggest that employees do not simply react based on any one experience with a practice (e.g., a recent performance review, job assignment, training program, merit pay allocation), but rather that the multitude of their experiences over time accumulate to influence perceptions and reactions. Drawing from the dispute resolution literature as a case in point, one's prior experiences with an organization's remedial voice system (e.g., filing a grievance, use of the "open door" policy) influences an employee's views of the system and decisions to use the system in the future. In addition, one's experience with a particular practice is likely to spill over to influence one's views of other HR practices (Olson-Buchanan & Boswell, 2008). This reinforces the importance of coherence among HR practices within an HR system (i.e., internal fit; e.g., Gratton & Truss, 2003) in creating synergistic effects, yet also suggests how the implementation of HR practices and employee experiences over time should be aligned to facilitate desirable employee responses.

The effect of HR practices and systems at any one time is thus a reflection of the extensive "baggage" brought by an individual—namely, past experiences in other organizations, with the particular practices, and with other organizational practices and systems. A temporal perspective encapsulates many of the considerations discussed earlier. That is, the EORs for employees and any one individual evolve due to the volitional nature of employee action; the potential for different and often unique exchanges; and the individual experiences, interpretations, and attributions of organizational actions.

CONCLUSION AND FUTURE RESEARCH DIRECTIONS

Our primary objective with this chapter was to explore the potential contributions that the EOR perspective might provide for the strategic HRM literature. As noted earlier, we believe that embracing the notion of an exchange between employees and employers, both actual and perceived, is an important step to recognize that employees are active participants in the exchange process, and as active participants, they come with their cognitive perspectives, emotional hurdles, individual differences, and personal opinions. These considerations are not noise but important factors that influence the interpretations employees make, the attributions they form, and the effort they display at work. Embracing these exchange relationship forces strategic HRM researchers to think more carefully about some implicit assumptions regarding human nature in our theorizing about the impact of HR on individual and organizational outcomes.

At the same time, however, we do believe that the EOR literature might also benefit from incorporating aspects of the strategic HRM literature into its theorizing (cf. Shore, Tetrick, et al., 2004). As noted earlier, strategic HRM focuses on more macro-level issues related to how employees are managed to achieve a competitive advantage. Within this research domain, there are a number of areas of focus, but several key themes are: (1) systems thinking, (2) the importance of context, and (3) achieving organizational objectives.

Focusing on the first of these themes, strategic HRM researchers have spent a great amount of time and energy debating the notion of what a system of HR practices is. Although there remains disagreement on many issues, there is some emerging consensus on the notion that employees are exposed to multiple HR practices simultaneously (Delery & Doty, 1996; Lepak et al., 2006; Wright & Boswell, 2002). How they are recruited, the staffing procedures used, and the training content and process shape employees' skills as well as their expectations. However, employees are given external incentives via evaluation and rewards to display certain behaviors at work. Employees are also put into different work settings ranging from isolation to highly interactive teams. The composition of all of these practices together is not necessarily the sum of the parts. Indeed, there is considerable debate about the nature of these interactions, with some scholars suggesting an additive effect of the HR practices within the system and others suggesting more multiplicative effects of the HR practices. In addition, while strategic HRM researchers still struggle with these issues, the notion of systems thinking can help researchers exploring EOR by highlighting how different aspects of the exchange relationship, such as POS, leader–member exchange, and psychological contracts, work in concert, not independently. Focusing on different profiles of these patterns of attitudes might provide interesting insights into the complex nature of the exchange relationship between employees and organizations and how it affects both parties in realizing their own objectives.

The second theme in strategic HRM research that might be particularly useful for EOR research is to continue to explore the role of context. Perhaps the one area of focus within strategic HRM research that has garnered the most attention is focusing on contextual factors that might impact the effectiveness of different HR systems. This research takes a contingency perspective arguing for and examining whether the HR system effects "depend" on some internal or external environmental factor. Whether it is an organization's business strategy (Youndt, Snell, Dean, & Lepak, 1996), customer segments (Batt, 2002), industry (Datta, Guthrie, & Wright, 2005), or other environmental factors (Wright & Snell, 1999), these researchers acknowledge that external factors may impact the appropriateness and effectiveness of different HR systems in different contexts. For example, Youndt et al. (1996) found that commitment-oriented HR systems are effective in manufacturing organizations when paired with a flexibility strategy. However, a control-oriented HR system was effective when used with a cost strategy. One implication is that the same employee, in the same type of job, may be exposed to vastly different HR systems because of the context. One implication of these differences is that they impact the EOR for that employee considerably. For example, although a control-oriented HR system might seem rational in a cost-oriented organization, the effect might be to shift employees' interpretations toward more transactional relationships with their organizations (Tsui et al., 1995; Lepak & Snell, 1999). As such, it could further influence how employees interpret organizational initiatives pertaining to HR, and with a transactional lens, the attributions employees make toward their organization and its initiatives might be more negative in nature. Although speculative, this does highlight that the organizational context that shapes managerial decisions regarding HR investments provides the context for how employees view the EOR and shapes their subsequent attitudes and behaviors.

A third major focus in the strategic HRM literature is an emphasis on organizational outcomes and returns on investments. Given the managerial perspective in this research domain, focusing on the potential return to the organization based on different HR initiatives is a logical focus. This raises a logical question about how adopting this perspective would influence EOR research and thinking. For example, from an organizational point of view, one could imagine that the organization and its employees might be more satisfied and more committed if they had a more positive EOR. Yet in reality, the organization might be able to foster a "better" climate or a more supportive EOR but explicitly chooses not to do so. From a cost–benefit perspective, it might be the case that the returns on creating this type of EOR via HR initiatives might be less than the costs of doing so. The costs of lower satisfaction, diminished motivation, and greater turnover might be reasonable relative to the costs of changing the EOR. From a purely rationale perspective, this might be a logic choice. From an employee perspective, this line of thinking might not always be reasonable or desirable. In addition, some might even argue that from an ethical perspective, organizations have an obligation to provide the best environment possible. We are not suggesting that that would not be a good approach; rather, we are trying to highlight that in this exchange, there are two points of view. The organizational point of view is typically more influential in setting the tone for the nature of the exchange.

Related to this point is the need to recognize that although the employee perspective in the EOR is important, the manager's perspective is important as well and should not be discounted. Indeed, Liao et al. (2009) found disagreement between managers and employees in their assessments of the presence of HPWS in organizations. However, they also found that managerial assessments were related to the human capital of employees. As they noted, even in the context of an exchange relationship, some aspects of employee attributes such as knowledge, skills, abilities, and other characteristics (KSAOs) might be more directly influenced by the presence of HR practices, whereas other aspects of employee attributes such as motivation depend on the interpretation and reaction to those HR practices. What this means is that EORs and employee interpretations of their relationship are clearly important for understanding the impact of HR practices, but some HR practices are still influential regardless of the interpretations of employees. As Liao et al. (2009) noted, "providing training programs may positively influence employee human capital independent of employee's perceptions of the systems…even if they are not aware of or do not perceive those investments as occurring. In contrast, influencing employee motivation to perform is dependent on employee's personal understanding and interpretation of the HPWS practices" (p. 385).

It is also important to recognize the likely role of culture in linking strategic HRM to EOR. As discussed earlier, individuals are likely to bring with them divergent perspectives driven by prior experiences, values, and related individual differences. Certainly, the diversity of the individuals within the organization, including cross-cultural perspectives, again emphasizes potential differences among individuals within an organization in their understanding of and reactions to HR practices. It is possible that individuals from different cultural backgrounds may have distinct perspectives regarding what employees and organizations "owe" one another. In a culturally diverse work environment, these differences may impact the ability of managers to connect to and motivate workers and may also lead to unintended concerns of equity, fairness, or even fair treatment. In addition, the culture (and/or climate) of the organization itself plays a role in setting expectations and ultimately reactions within the EOR. Accordingly, we would expect a complex interplay among national culture, an organization's culture, and an individual's potentially unique experiences and interpretations in defining and driving the EOR. As noted earlier, one of the key features of strategic HRM research is that it tends to be viewed from a group or organizational level. In group contexts, however, differences among individuals in their interpretations and attributions are associated with how they respond to HR practices. The possibility that culture provides additional insights into this process highlights an important avenue for future research.

We believe that focusing on the exchange and strategic HRM research simultaneously highlights several areas of impact for practice. Perhaps the first most direct implication is recognition that the notion of an exchange involves the sharing of information in some form of communication. Often, the strategic HRM literature highlights what HR initiatives organizations have in place and then looks for performance implications. However, the EOR literature highlights that the nature of the exchange itself—the content and process of the exchange (Shore, Tetrick, et al., 2004)—is a critical aspect that influences employees. This would suggest that it is important for organizational decision makers not only to communicate what they are planning on doing, but also to involve employees in the decision process and clearly communicate their rationale for the initiatives. As Nishii et al. (2008) showed, employees will make attributions of organizational motivations. To ensure that those attributions remain positive and help improve company performance, managers should provide information to influence those attributions.

A second area of impact for practice that we believe this blending of EOR and strategic HRM offers is highlighting the importance of trust, time, and relationships over time. This is certainly not a new concept in organizations or in organizational research, yet one theme that consistently emerges is that employees have a memory of past actions and those past actions shape how they respond currently and in the future. The exchange relationship happens over time, not just once. As a result, it is important to think about organizational decisions from a long-term impact perspective. For example, a manager might be able to reduce costs, meet a deadline, or take advantage of an opportunity in the short term by excessive pressure, force, or intimidation. Although the short-term outcome might be realized, the long-term prospects for a healthy and motivated workforce diminish for the next project. As Tekleab et al. (2005) found, past positive interactions provide a positive bias for assessing organizational actions in the future. It only seems reasonable that negative ones do so as well.

In conclusion, we believe that the strategic HRM research domain has provided a number of excellent insights into how HR practices and systems impact individual and organizational outcomes. We also believe that the EOR literature has provided great insights into the nature of the exchange between employees and organizations and sheds light on how these perceptions evolve, as well as their impact on individuals and groups within organizations. However, we are most excited when we think about the research implications and opportunities that emerge when we consider these two domains simultaneously. The managerial perspective within organizations is and will always be an important one. However, placing greater consideration on the individual employee perspective, as well as the nature of the relationship between these two parties provides a more complete lens to understand the dynamic nature of this exchange and how HR practices and systems shape the exchange and impact both individuals and organizations over time.

REFERENCES

Allen, D. G., Shore, L. M., & Griffeth, R. W. (2003). The role of perceived organizational support and supportive human resource practices in the turnover process. *Journal of Management, 29*, 99–118.

Arthur, J. B. (1994). Effects of human resource systems on manufacturing performance and turnover. *Academy of Management Journal, 37*, 670– 687.

Barnard, C. (1938). *Functions of the executive*. Cambridge, MA: Harvard University Press.

Barney, J. (1991). Firm resources and sustained competitive advantage. *Journal of Management, 17*, 99–120.

Bateman, T. S., & Crant, C. J. (1993). The proactive component of organizational behavior: A measure and correlates. *Journal of Organizational Behavior, 14*, 103–118.

Batt, R. (2002). Managing customer services: Human resource practices, quite rates, and sales growth. *Academy of Management Journal, 45*, 587–597.

Behling, O., Labovitz, G., & Gainer, K. (1968). The Herbzerg controversy: A critical reappraisal. *Academy of Management Journal, 11*, 99–108.
Blau, P. (1964). *Exchange and power in social life*. New York, NY: Wiley.
Bolino, M. C. (1999). Citizenship and impression management: Good soldiers or good actors? *Academy of Management Review, 24*, 82–98.
Boswell, W. R. (2006). Aligning employees with the organization's strategic objectives: Out of "line of sight," out of mind. *International Journal of Human Resource Management, 17*, 1489–1511.
Boswell, W. R., Colvin, A. J. S., & Darnold, T. (2008). Organizational systems and employee motivation. In R. Kanfer, G. Chen, & R. Pritchard (Eds.), *Work motivation: Past, present, and future* (pp. 357–393). Mahwah, NJ: Erlbaum.
Boswell, W. R., Roehling, M. V., LePine, M. A., & Moynihan, L. M. (2003). Individual job choice decisions and the impact of job attributes and recruitment practices: A longitudinal field study. *Human Resource Management, 42*, 23–37.
Boswell, W. R., Shipp, A. J., Payne, S. C., & Culbertson, S. S. (2009). Changes in job satisfaction over time: The surprising role of honeymoons and hangovers. *Journal of Applied Psychology, 94*, 844–858.
Boxall, P. (1998). Achieving competitive advantage through human resource strategy: Towards a Theory of industry dynamics. *Human Resource Management Review, 8*, 265–288.
Brief, A. P., & Motowidlo, S. J. (1986). Prosocial organizational behaviors. *Academy of Management Review, 11*, 710–725.
Collins, C. J., & Smith, K. G. (2006). Knowledge exchange and combination: The role of human resource practices in the performance of high-technology firms. *Academy of Management Journal, 49*, 544–560.
Colvin, A. J., & Boswell, W. R. (2007). The problem of action and interest alignment: Beyond job requirements and incentive compensation. *Human Resource Management Review, 17*, 38–51.
Coyle-Shapiro, J., & Shore, L.M. (2007). The employee-organization relationship: Where do we go from here? *Human Resource Management Review, 17*, 166–179.
Datta, D. K., Guthrie, J. P., & Wright, P. M. (2005). Human resource management and labor productivity: Does industry matter? *Academy of Management Journal, 48*, 135–145.
Delery, J. E., & Doty, D. H. (1996). Modes of theorizing in strategic human resource management: Tests of universalistic, contingency, and configurational performance predictions. *Academy of Management Journal, 39*, 802–835.
DeVos, A., Buyens, D., & Schalk, R. (2003). Psychological contract development during organizational socialization: Adaptation to reality and the role of reciprocity. *Journal of Organizational Behavior, 24*, 537–559.
Dulac, T., Coyle-Shapiro, J., Henderson, D. J., & Wayne, S. J. (2008). Not all responses to breach are the same: The interconnection of social exchange and psychological contract processes in organizations. *Academy of Management Journal, 51*, 1079–1098.
Eisenberger, R., Cummings, J., Armeli, S., & Lynch, P. (1997). Perceived organizational support, discretionary treatment, and job satisfaction. *Journal of Applied Psychology, 82*, 812–820.
Eisenberger, R., Huntington, R., Hutchison, S., & Sowa, D. (1986). Perceived organizational support. *Journal of Applied Psychology, 71*, 500–507.
Emerson, R. M. (1962). Power-dependence relations. *American Sociological Review, 27*, 31–41.

Evans, R. W., & Davis, W. D. (2005). High-performance work systems and organizational performance: The mediating role of internal social structure. *Journal of Management, 31*, 758–775.

Fandt, P. M., & Ferris, G. R. (1990). The management of information and impressions: When employees behave opportunistically. *Organizational Behavior and Human Decision Processes, 45*, 140–159.

Fehr, E., & Gächter, S. (2000). Fairness and retaliation: The economics of reciprocity. *Journal of Economic Perspectives, 14*, 159–181.

Gouldner, A. W. (1960). The norm of reciprocity. *American Sociological Review, 25*, 161–178.

Graen, G., & Cashman, J. F. (1975). A role-making model of leadership in formal organizations: A developmental approach. In J. G. Hunt & L. L. Larson (Eds.), *Leadership frontiers* (pp. 143–165). Kent, OH: Kent State University Press.

Gratton, L., & Truss, C. (2003). The three-dimensional people strategy: Putting human resources policies into action. *Academy of Management Executive, 17*, 74–86.

Guthrie, J. P. (2001). High-involvement work practices, turnover, and productivity: Evidence from New Zealand. *Academy of Management Journal, 44*, 180–190.

Helm, B., Bonoma, T. V., & Tedeschi, J. R. (1972). Reciprocity for harm done. *Journal of Social Psychology, 87*, 89–98.

Hitt, M. A., Bierman, L., Shimizu, K., & Kochhar, R. (2001). Direct and moderating effects of human capital on strategy and performance in professional service firms: A resource-based perspective. *Academy of Management Journal, 44*, 13–28.

Homans, G. C. (1961). *Social behavior: Its elementary forms*. New York, NY: Harcourt, Brace & World Press.

Huselid, M. A. (1995). The impact of human resource management practices on turnover, productivity, and corporate financial performance. *Academy of Management Journal, 38*, 635–672.

Judge, T. A., & Bretz, R. D. Jr. (1994). Political influence behavior and career success. *Journal of Management, 20*, 43–66.

Kehoe, R. R., & Wright, P. M. (in press). The impact of high performance human resource practices on employees' attitudes and behaviors. *Journal of Management*.

Kidwell, R.E. Jr., & Bennett, N. (1993). Employee propensity to withhold effort: A conceptual model to intersect three avenues of research. *Academy of Management Review, 18*, 429–466.

Kiewitz, C., Restubog, S. L. D., Zagenczyk, T., & Hochwater, W. (2009). The interactive effects of psychological contract breach and organizational politics on perceived organizational support: Evidence from two longitudinal studies. *Journal of Management Studies, 46*, 806–834.

Kristof, A. (1996). Person-organization fit: An integrative review of its conceptualizations, measurement, and implications. *Personnel Psychology, 49*, 1–49.

Kristof-Brown, A., Zimmerman, R., & Johnson, E. (2005). Consequences of individuals' fit at work: A meta-analysis of person-job, person-organization, person-group, and person-supervisor fit. *Personnel Psychology, 58*, 281–342.

Leary, M. R., & Kowalski, R. M. (1990). Impression management: A literature review and two component model. *Psychological Bulletin, 107*, 34–47.

Lepak, D. P., Liao, H., Chung, Y., & Harden, E. (2006). A conceptual review of HR management systems in strategic HRM research. In J. Martocchio (Ed.), *Research in personnel and human resource management* (Vol. 25, pp. 217–272). Greenwich, CT: JAI Press.

Lepak, D. P., & Snell, S. A. (1999). The human resource architecture: Toward a theory of human capital allocation and development. *Academy of Management Review, 24*, 31–48.

Lepak, D. P., & Snell, S. A. (2007). Employment sub-systems and changing forms of employment. In P. Boxall, J. Purcell, & P. Wright (Eds.), *The Oxford handbook of human resource management* (pp. 210–230). Oxford, UK: Oxford University Press.

Lester, S. W., Kickul, J. R., & Bergmann, T. J. (2007). Managing employee perceptions of the psychological contract over time: The role of employer social accounts and contract fulfillment. *Journal of Organizational Behavior, 28*, 191–208.

Liao, H., Toya, K., Lepak, D. P., & Hong, Y. (2009). Do they see eye to eye? Management and employee perspectives of high-performance work systems and influence processes on service quality. *Journal of Applied Psychology, 94*, 371–391.

Liden, R. C., Bauer, T. N., & Erdogan, B. (2003). The role of leader-member exchange in the dynamic relationship between employer and employee: Implications for employee socialization, leaders, and organizations. In J. Coyle-Shapiro, L. M. Shore, M. S. Taylor, & L. E. Tetrick (Eds.), *The employment relationship: Examining psychological and contextual perspectives* (pp. 226–252). Oxford, UK: Oxford University Press.

Louis, M. R. (1980). Surprise and sense-making: What newcomers experience in entering unfamiliar organizational settings. *Administrative Science Quarterly, 25*, 226–251.

Macduffie, J. P. (1995). Human resource bundles and manufacturing performance: Organizational logic and flexible production systems in the world auto industry. *Industrial and Labor Relations Review, 48*, 197–220.

Macky, K., & Boxall, P. (2007). The relationship between 'high-performance work practices' and employee attitudes: An investigation of additive and interaction effects. *The International Journal of Human Resource Management, 18*, 537–567.

March, J. G., & Simon, H. A. (1958). *Organizations*. New York, NY: Wiley.

Molm, L., & Cook, K. (1995). Social exchange and exchange networks. In K. S. Cook, G. A. Fine, & J. S. Hous (Eds.), *Sociological perspectives on social psychology* (pp. 209–235). Boston, MA: Allyn & Bacon.

Nishii, L. H., Lepak, D. P., & Schneider, B. (2008). Employee attributions of the "why" of HR practices: Their effects on employee attitudes and behaviors, and customer satisfaction. *Personnel Psychology, 61*, 503–545.

Nishii L. H., & Wright, P. (2008). Variability at multiple levels of analysis: Implications for strategic human resource management. In D. B. Smith (Ed.), *The people make the place* (pp. 225–248). Mahwah, NJ: Erlbaum.

Olson-Buchanan, J. B., & Boswell, W. R. (2008). An integrative model of experiencing and responding to mistreatment at work. *Academy of Management Review, 33*, 76–96.

Pennings, J. M., Lee, K., & van Witteloostuijn, A. (1998). Human capital, social capital and firm dissolution. *Academy of Management Journal, 41*, 425–440.

Podsakoff, P. M., MacKenzie, S. B., & Hui, C. (1993). Organizational citizenship behaviors and managerial evaluations of employee performance: A review and suggestions for future research. In G. R. Ferris (Ed.), *Research in personnel and human resource management* (pp. 1–40). Greenwich, CT: JAI Press.

Robinson, S. L. (1996). Trust and breach of the psychological contract. *Administrative Science Quarterly, 41*, 574–599.

Robinson, S. L., Kraatz, M. S., & Rousseau, D. M. (1994). Changing obligations and the psychological contract: A longitudinal study. *Academy of Management Journal, 37*, 137–152.

Robinson, S. L., & Rousseau, D. M. (1994). Violating the psychological contract: Not the exception but the norm. *Journal of Organizational Behavior, 15*, 245–259.

Rousseau, D. (1990). New hire perceptions of their own and their employer's obligations: A study of psychological contracts. *Journal of Organizational Behavior, 11*, 389–400.

Rousseau, D. M. (1995). *Psychological contract in organizations*. Thousand Oaks, CA: Sage Publications.

Rousseau, D. M. (2001). Idiosyncratic deals: Flexibility versus fairness. *Organizational Dynamics, 29*, 260–273.

Rousseau, D. M. (2005). *I-deals: Idiosyncratic deals employees bargain for themselves*. New York, NY: M. E. Sharpe.

Rousseau, D. M., Ho, V. T., & Greenberg, J. (2006). I-deals: Idiosyncratic terms in employment relationships. *Academy of Management Review, 31*, 977–994.

Rubery, J., Carroll, M., Cooke, F. L., Grugulis, I., & Earnshaw, J. (2004). Human resource management and the permeable organization: The case of the multi-client call centre. *Journal of Management Studies, 41*, 1199–1222.

Sahlins, M. D. (1965). On the sociology of primitive exchange. In M. Banton (Ed.), *The relevance of models for social anthropology* (pp. 139–236). London, UK: Tavistock.

Schuler, R. S., & Jackson, S. E. (1987). Linking competitive strategies with human resource management practices. *Academy of Management Executive, 1*, 207–219.

Shipp, A. J. (2006). *The moving window of fit: Extending person-environment research with time*. Unpublished doctoral dissertation, University of North Carolina at Chapel Hill.

Shore, L. M., Porter, L. W., & Zahra, S. A. (2004). Employer-oriented strategic approaches to the employee-organization relationship (EOR). In J. Coyle-Shapiro, L. M. Shore, S. Taylor, & L. E. Tetrick (Eds.), *The employment relationship: Examining psychological and contextual perspectives*. Oxford, UK: Oxford University Press.

Shore, L. M., & Shore, T. H. (1995). Perceived organizational support and organizational justice. In R. S. Cropanzano & K. M. Kacmar (Eds.), *Organizational politics, justice, and support: Managing the social climate of the workplace* (pp. 149–164). Westport, CT: Quorum Books.

Shore, L. M., Tetrick, L. E., Taylor, S. E., Coyle-Shapiro, J. A. M., Liden, R. C., McLean-Parks, J., … Van Dyne, L. (2004). The employee-organization relationship: A timely concept in a period of transition. In J. J. Martocchio (Ed.), *Research in personnel and human resources management* (Vol. 23, pp. 291–370). Greenwich, CT: JAI Press.

Song, L. J., Tsui, A. S., & Law, K. S. (2009). Unpacking employee responses to organizational exchange mechanisms: The role of social and economic exchange perceptions. *Journal of Management, 35*, 56–93.

Snell, S. A., & Dean, J. Jr. (1992). Integrated manufacturing and human resource management: A human capital perspective. *Academy of Management Journal, 35*, 467–504.

Sun, L. Y., Aryee, S., & Law, K. S. (2007). High performance human resource practices, citizenship behavior, and organizational performance: A relational perspective. *Academy of Management Journal, 50*, 558–577.

Takeuchi, R., Chen, G., & Lepak, D. P. (2009). Through the looking glass of a social system: Cross-level mediating effects of high performance work systems on employee attitudes. *Personnel Psychology, 62*, 1–29.

Takeuchi, R., Lepak, D. P., Wang, H., & Takeuchi, K. (2007). An empirical examination of the mechanisms mediating between high performance work systems and performance of Japanese organizations. *Journal of Applied Psychology, 92*, 1069–1083.

Tekleab, A. G., Takeuchi, R., & Taylor, M. S. (2005). Extending the chain of relationships among organizational justice, social exchange, and employee reaction: The role of contract violations. *Academy of Management Journal, 48*, 146–157.

Thibault, J. W., & Kelly, H. H. (1959). *The social psychology of groups*. New York, NY: John Wiley & Sons.

Tsui, A. S., Pearce, J. L., Porter, L. W., & Hite, J. P. (1995). Choice of employee-organization relationship: Influence of external and internal organizational factors. In G. R. Ferris (Ed.), *Research in personnel and human resources management* (pp. 117–151). Greenwich, CT: JAI Press.

Tsui, A. S., Pearce, J. L., Porter, L. W., & Tripoli, A. M. (1997). Alternative approaches to the employee-organization relationship: Does investment in employees pay off? *Academy of Management Journal, 40*, 1089–1121.

Tsui, A. S., & Wang, D. (2002). Employment relationships from the employer's perspective: Current research and future directions. In C. L. Cooper & I. T. Robertson (Eds.), *International review of industrial and organizational psychology* (Vol. 17, pp. 77–114). Chichester, UK: John Wiley & Sons.

Volkema, R. J., Farquhar, K., & Bergmann, T. (1996). Third-party sensemaking in interpersonal conflicts at work: A theoretical framework. *Human Relations, 49*, 1437–1454.

Wang, D. X., Tsui, A. S., Zhang, Y., & Ma, L. (2003). Employment relationship and firm performance: Evidence from an emerging economy. *Journal of Organizational Behavior, 24*, 511–535.

Wayne, S. J., & Ferris, G. R. (1990). Influence tactics, affect, and exchange quality in supervisor-subordinate interactions: A laboratory experiment and field study. *Journal of Applied Psychology, 75*, 487–499.

Wayne, S. J., Shore, L. M., & Liden, R. C. (1997). Perceived organizational support and leader–member exchange: A social exchange perspective. *Academy of Management Journal, 40*, 82–111.

Weick, K. E. (1995). *Sensemaking in organizations*. Thousand Oaks, CA: Sage Publications.

Wright, P. M., & Boswell, W. R. (2002). Desegregating HRM: A review and synthesis of micro and macro human resource management. *Journal of Management, 28*, 248–276.

Wright, P. M., Dunford, B. B., & Snell, S. A. (2001). Human resources and the resource based view of the firm. *Journal of Management, 27*, 701–721.

Wright, P. M., & Snell, S. A. (1999). Toward a unifying framework for exploring fit and flexibility in strategic human resource management. *Academy of Management Review, 23*, 756–772.

Wu, P., & Chaturvedi, S. (2009). The role of procedural justice and power distance in the relationship between high performance work systems and employee attitudes: A multilevel perspective. *Journal of Management, 35*, 1128–1247.

Youndt, M. A., Snell, S. A., Dean, J. W., & Lepak, D. P. (1996). Human resource management, manufacturing strategy, and firm performance. *Academy of Management Journal, 39*, 836–866.

Zacharatos, A., Barling, J., & Iverson, R. D. (2005). High performance work systems and occupational safety. *Journal of Applied Psychology, 90*, 77–93.

18

Emotions: The Glue That Holds the Employee–Organization Relationship Together (or Not)

Lois E. Tetrick
George Mason University

Few people today would dispute the connection between an organization's health and the health of its employees. If an organization's health is measured based on any number of financial indicators such as return on investment, revenue, and profitability, it is clear that the organization's health has implications for employees' health and well-being. The organization's health determines, at least in part, the organization's side of the employee–organization relationship (EOR). That is, the health of the organization is a significant determinant of the investments that an organization can make in employees and the obligations it sets forth in the exchange relationship with employees, either individually or as a group through the policies and practices that can be implemented. These policies and practices affect employees' experience of the work environment and can directly affect employees' health. In addition, the investments and organizational obligations to employees establish a press to reciprocate as evidenced by employees' felt obligations to the organization and the actual contributions that they make to the organization, which affect the organization's health in turn. The ability of employees to reciprocate depends, at least in part, on their individual health. This dynamic cycle of the EOR leads to their experience of positive or negative emotions. Therefore, the health of the organization and the health of employees are inextricably intertwined as shown in Figure 18.1.

One aspect of the EOR that has been insufficiently incorporated in the literature is the role of emotions. It is the thesis of this chapter that the EOR is an important underlying framework for understanding individual

485

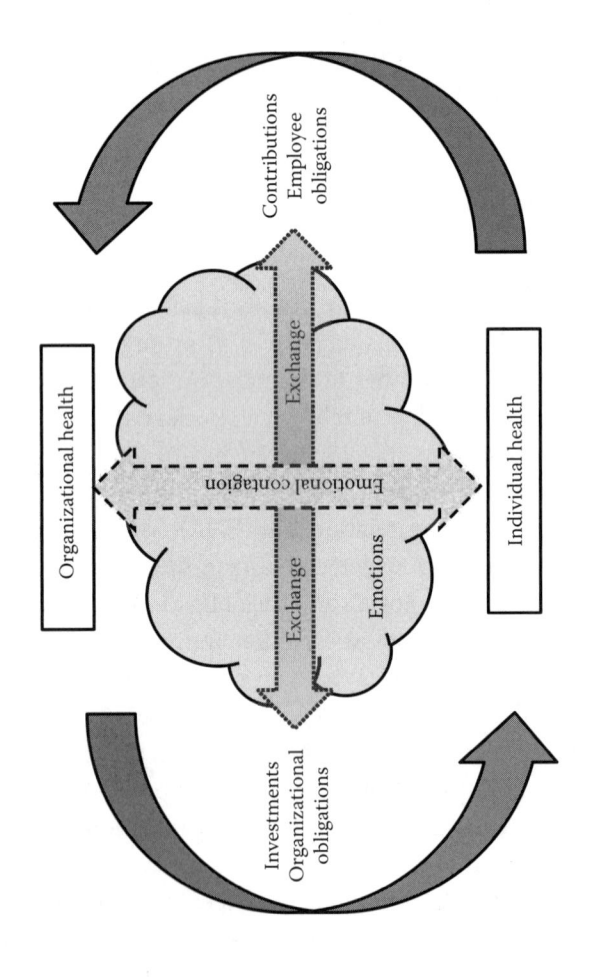

FIGURE 18.1
Interdependence of employee and organizational health.

and organizational health, but only if the role of both positive and negative emotions is more explicitly incorporated. Emotions at both the individual and collective level are central to understanding the EOR and, subsequently, employee and organizational health.

This chapter first gives a brief review of social exchange theory as it relates to the EOR, bringing in the notion of emotional reactions to the exchanges between the employee and the organization. Then this chapter discusses the effect of the organization on the individual and the emotional responses to the exchange by the individual employee. Finally, the circle is completed by linking employees' well-being to the organization's well-being. The premise of this chapter is that emotions are the glue that binds the EOR for better or worse.

SOCIAL EXCHANGE IN THE EOR

Based on the work of Blau (1964), Gouldner (1960), and others, social exchange theory has developed to explain not only the economic exchange that has been characteristic of employee–employer relationships from the outset of paid employment, but also the social exchange. The underlying premise in social exchange theory is that exchanges between two parties function according to the norm of reciprocity whether the resources being exchanged are concrete and more economic in nature or less tangible and more social in nature. As summarized by Cropanzano and Mitchell (2005), economic exchanges typically involve specific obligations, frequently involving tangible resources, with expectations that the obligations will be met within a specific period of time and the parties to the exchange are generally motivated by self-interest. Social exchanges, on the other hand, involve unspecified obligations, frequently involving less tangible resources, with fewer time-specific expectations about when the obligations to reciprocate will be met, and are motivated by interest in the other party. Social exchanges are similar in nature to communal relationships as described by Mills and Clark (1982).

Sparrowe and Liden (1997), drawing on the work of Sahlins (1974), identified three dimensions of reciprocity (immediacy of return, equivalence of resources exchanged, and interest in the other party) that parallel the distinctions between economic and social exchange. Economic exchanges are generally characterized as involving more immediate return and greater emphasis on the equivalence of the resources being exchanged and primarily reflect self-interest. Social exchanges, on the other hand, allow a longer period for return, and this period is often not specified. There is less emphasis on accounting for the equivalence of the resources being exchanged, and there is mutual interest between the parties, if not greater interest in the other party, rather than self-interest.

The literature on social exchange theory makes reference to such concepts as trust, fairness, and gratitude (e.g., Cropanzano & Mitchell, 2005), but the explicit consideration of emotions in social exchange theory has been rare. One exception is the inclusion of anger as a reaction to psychological contract violation (Morrison & Robinson, 1997; Robinson & Morrison, 2000; Rousseau, 1995) in which the employee experiences anger and a sense of betrayal when the organization does not meet its obligations to the employee. Interestingly, even though the literature on occupational health has demonstrated that anger can be detrimental to an individual's health, health has not been included as an outcome of psychological contract violation until relatively recently. For example, Siegrist (2005) reviewed several prospective epidemiological studies and concluded that lack of reciprocity in the workplace resulted in a significant likelihood of stress-related disease, especially cardiovascular disease. He conceptualized lack of reciprocity according to the effort–reward imbalance model of stress (Siegrist, 1996), which is consistent with the literature on social exchange theory and psychological contracts. Essentially, the effort–reward imbalance model posits that employees invest effort in meeting the demands of the organization (the employee's obligations to the organization) in exchange for rewards (the organization's obligations to the employee). If efforts exceed rewards, then the exchange is unbalanced and the employee experiences stress, which leads to ill health including cardiovascular disease.

International Perspectives

Rousseau and Schalk (2000) suggested that the concept of psychological contracts could be generalized across nations to the extent that employees had personal freedom to enter into the exchange and that there was social stability. More recently, the PSYCONES study, an international study, was conducted in Sweden, Spain, the United Kingdom, Germany, Belgium, the Netherlands, and Israel that looked at employment contracts (temporary versus permanent), the psychological contract of the employees, and employees' health and well-being (Guest, Isaksson, & De Witte, 2010). This study also found support for the negative effects of reciprocity failure on employees' work-related well-being and behaviors as well as overall health. Employees who reported that they had fulfilled their obligations to their organization reported better health and life satisfaction as well as work-related well-being, and those employees who reported that their organization had violated their psychological contract reported poorer health and life satisfaction as well as work-related well-being (Guest & Clinton, 2010).

This relation was supported across the countries included in the PSYCONES study, although differences in the scope of the psychological contract were found across countries. Employees in Sweden and the Netherlands reported fewer obligations in their psychological contracts, and employees in Spain and the United Kingdom reported more obligations in their psychological contracts. German employees reported higher levels of psychological contract fulfillment even though their psychological contracts were narrower in scope, including fewer promises compared to the Israeli employees, and the Israeli employees reported lower levels of fulfillment with relatively narrow contracts. Employees in Sweden, the Netherlands, and Belgium reported lower levels of fulfillment than the German employees. Despite these country differences in the scope of employees' psychological contracts, Claes, Schalk, and de Jong (2010) concluded that country does not affect the role of the psychological contract in affecting employee well-being. Failure of organizations to reciprocate by not fulfilling employees' psychological contracts was associated with lower levels of well-being. This supports the proposition that the norm of reciprocity is universal (Sahlins, 1974) in that this relation was observed across the seven countries. Interestingly, organizational characteristics such as size, percentage of nonpermanent employees, and private versus government/nonprofit status were not related to the number of promises and obligations in employees' psychological contracts. However, the data indicated that organizational policies and practices explain most of the variance in the *employers'* view of the psychological contract, not the *employees'* view of the psychological contract (Claes et al., 2010).

Psychological Contract Fulfillment Versus Breach

The PSYCONES study specifically looked at fulfillment of obligations, although the literature on social exchange theory typically has taken a negative perspective, looking almost exclusively at the failure of reciprocity. As Greenberg (2011) discusses, injustice is more salient than justice, so it might be expected that negative exchanges have received more attention in the literature, and in fact, it might be argued that negative exchanges actually may have a greater effect on employees than positive exchanges. Certainly, the effort–reward imbalance model of stress (Siegrist, 1996), described earlier, focuses on failed reciprocity where individuals' efforts are not adequately compensated, resulting in ill health.

This focus on the failure of reciprocity also appears to have been the case in the psychological contract literature. Rousseau's (1995) early description of the psychological contract focused on psychological contract violation, with Robinson and Morrison (2000) subsequently differentiating between psychological contract breach and violation. There was not much attention paid to the consequences of psychological contract fulfillment theoretically or, for that matter, from a measurement perspective. As Lambert, Edwards, and Cable (2003) pointed out, breach has frequently been measured by asking employees if the organization has kept their promises and then simply reverse codes the responses interpreting this as a measure of breach. One study that used a fulfillment measure and interpreted it as fulfillment was the study by Parzefall and Hakanen (2010) that examined the effect of fulfillment on work engagement and health. Work engagement was indicated by vigor, dedication, and absorption, whereas mental health was indicated by the emotions of happy, tired, depressed, nervous, and overstretched as well as life satisfaction (it should be noted that not all scholars would consider all of these to be "emotions" in a strict sense [Warr, 1990]). Parzefall and Hakanen found that psychological contract fulfillment resulted in work engagement and improved mental health.

Another example is Conway and Briner's (2002) diary study in which they measured both broken promises and exceeded promises. In this study, they found that broken promises resulted in feelings of betrayal and hurt, especially for promises that employees saw as important, and exceeded promises resulted in feelings of self-worth and being cared for, again for those promises that employees saw as important. The method of assessing lack of fulfillment of promises and fulfillment of promises and the reactions to these events varied across these previous studies, but despite the different operationalizations, the results are consistent. The effects of broken promises were more robust and qualitatively different from the effects for exceeded promises. This is consistent with the literature on positive and negative emotions to be discussed later. It also suggests value in considering both the positive as well as the negative consequences of the EOR.

The conceptualization and measurement of psychological contract fulfillment needs careful consideration. It may be that the differences between fulfillment and breach mirror those found in the literature on emotions with respect to positive affect and negative affect and the discussion of whether positive affect and negative affect are distinct, orthogonal concepts or ends on a continuum. As Hackman (2009) reminds us, it is important that we clarify conceptually and empirically what the dimensionality of our concepts is. Without this, it is not possible to determine whether observed relations are conceptual overlaps or measurement issues (see, for example, the discussion of unipolar versus bipolar scales by Bagozzi, Wong, & Yi, 1999). Lambert et al. (2003) concluded that the traditional way of measuring both fulfillment and breach is deficient and has not clarified the distinction between breach and fulfillment. Conceptually, it might be that fulfillment and breach are simply opposites of each other; however, it might be that fulfillment is qualitatively different from breach, especially given that there may be fundamentally different reactions to fulfillment versus breach (e.g., positive emotions versus negative emotions).

In summary, social exchange theory does support positive effects on employees' health arising from fulfillment of obligations, at least theoretically, and negative effects on employees' health arising from failure of reciprocity, both theoretically and empirically. The mechanisms by which these effects arise appear to be implicitly through employees' emotional reactions to be discussed later in this chapter. Before turning to a discussion of emotions, it is important to discuss social exchange from a more macro level.

A View From the Top: The Inducements–Contributions Model

The EOR literature has recognized, at least conceptually, that the EOR is a multilevel phenomenon and cannot be fully understood without considering the effects of the organization on the employee and the effects of employees, at least collectively, on the organization. It is acknowledged that the organization can affect individuals by implementing specific policies and practices and that these changes will have an effect on large numbers of people—all employees, certain classes of employees (e.g., managers, workers), and people in specific jobs—whereas a single employee is not likely to make a large impact on the organization as a whole, especially in larger organizations. However, it is acknowledged that collectively employees may be able to have a significant impact on the organization and, in certain instances, specific employees may affect the organization. For example, individuals who hold central positions in internal social networks within the organization may be able to affect the organization more strongly and directly.

From the organizational perspective, the organization offers employees inducements in exchange for their contributions to the organization (Tsui, Pearce, Porter, & Tripoli, 1997). These inducements may be a variety of policies and procedures including training, career development, and employment security. Tsui et al. (1997) found that based on the investments in job incumbents (presumed to be the same for all incumbents) and the organizational emphasis on the unit rather than the individual employee, employees holding specific jobs could be classified as having mutual investment, overinvestment, underinvestment, and quasi-spot EORs. Mutual investment EORs were characterized as balanced, with the employee and organization making some degree of investment in each other with a more long-term orientation. Overinvestment EORs were characterized as unbalanced, with the organization investing more in the employee in the way of a long-term relationship than the employee is expected to reciprocate. The employee narrowly performs the required job functions but benefits from the organization's investments. The underinvestment EOR also was characterized as unbalanced, in that the employee invested in the EOR as if the relationship were a long-term, broadly defined exchange but the organization provided short-term inducements without any indication or expectation of a long-term relationship. The quasi-spot EOR was characterized as short-term, highly circumscribed exchange relationship.

Tsui et al. (1997) found that performance, including core task performance, organizational citizenship behavior, and likelihood of remaining in the organization were higher in the mutual investment and overinvestment EORs compared to the underinvestment and quasi-spot EORs. Job-level performance was higher, and turnover was lower. More recently, Hom et al. (2009) found further support for mutual investment and overinvestment on employees' intention to stay, and this effect was mediated by social exchange. Song, Tsui, and Law (2009) found support for mutual investment on task performance as partially mediated by the social exchange relations. Thus, this supports the notion that the EOR affects organizational health. Performance and turnover are two generally accepted indicators of organizational health (Hofmann & Tetrick, 2003); therefore, these studies support the positive effect of the exchange relationship on organizational health.

Tsui et al. (1997) demonstrated that the EOR exists at the job level and that it can be influenced by organizational policies and practices. The job design literature (Parker, Wall, & Cordery, 2001) also is replete with examples of ways in which jobs can be designed that result in employee well-being. Warr and Clapperton (2010) identified 12 principal job characteristics that affected well-being and positive emotional responses to individuals' jobs. These 12 job characteristics are categorized according to the Vitamin Model to be constant effects characteristics, where more is better, and additional decrement characteristics, where more may not be better and in fact can become harmful. The constant effects characteristics are the availability of money, physical security, valued social position, supportive supervision, career outlook, and equity. The additional decrement characteristics are opportunity for personal control, opportunity for skill use and acquisition, externally generated goals, variety, environmental clarity, and contact with others. Theoretically, these job characteristics can result in "happiness" or "unhappiness" (Warr & Clapperton, 2010). Although happiness may be difficult to define, researchers in positive psychology have defined happiness as containing the three elements of positive emotion, engagement, and meaning (Seligman, 2002) or a composite of life satisfaction, coping resources, and positive emotions (Cohn, Fredrickson, Brown, Mikels, & Conway, 2009). However, most scholars agree that positive emotions are a core component of happiness (Ashby, Isen, & Turken, 1999; Cohn & Fredrickson, 2010), and for many scholars, happiness is essentially the frequency of positive emotions experienced.

In examining Warr and Clapperton's (2010) list of principal job characteristics, it is clear that they are the result of the organization's policies and practices, at least in part. These characteristics may be strategically set to provide inducements/investments as part of the EOR as described by Tsui et al. (1997). They also overlap considerably with the organization's obligations in many measures of the psychological contract (e.g., Rousseau, 1990; Turnley & Feldman, 2000), which typically include such elements as salary, pay raises, bonuses, training, advancement opportunities, career development, overall benefits, retirement benefits, health care benefits, decision-making input, job responsibility, job challenge, feedback on job performance, supervisory support, organizational support, and job security.

It might be useful to conduct a more detailed comparison between principal job characteristics that lead to employee well-being and the specific obligations that are included in the psychological contract. The psychological contract literature suggests that the importance of organizational obligations to individual employees influences the impact of breach, inferring that failure of the organization to meet "important" obligations results in more negative emotional reactions. It may be that there is a common core of important obligations that parallel the principal job characteristics suggested by Warr and Clapperton (2010). If there is a common core of important obligations that are generally agreed upon by individuals, a societal normative set of elemental obligations, then organizations may not have much discretion in meeting these core obligations. Additionally, obligations that are more discretionary based on employees' expectations may be more useful as inducements in enticing extra-role contributions on the part of employees. Much like in the literature on perceived organizational support where it has been shown that organizations' discretionary behaviors signal support but required behaviors do not (Rhoades & Eisenberger, 2002), provision of core obligations and inducements may not be as effective in increasing contributions, although the absence of these core obligations may have negative consequences for organizations. Therefore, the inducements and obligations that organizations provide for their employees based on organizational policies, practices, and job design may not only result in enhanced performance, but they may, in fact, directly affect employees' emotions and hence their well-being.

Tsui et al. (1997) found that balanced, mutual investment EORs were associated with favorable attitudes (affective organizational commitment, perceived fairness, and trust in coworkers) on the part of the employees. These attitudes certainly have an emotional component (Ajzen & Fishbein, 2005; Fishbein & Ajzen, 1974), but the explicit emotions associated with the EOR were not assessed. Interestingly, the PSYCONES study did not find support for the importance of a balanced "deal," but rather, their data suggested that it is the fairness of the exchange relationship that is important (Guest et al., 2010). Guest et al. (2010) argue that general fairness and psychological contract violation may be more critical than assessing the psychological contract itself, at least through the assessment of specific obligations. This parallels the argument of Shore, Tetrick, Lynch, and Barksdale (2006) that it is more useful to assess the social and economic exchange directly rather than the specific elements in the psychological contract.

Based on equity theory and organizational justice theory (Greenberg, 2011), one would predict that different types of the EOR and different levels of mutuality and reciprocity may evoke different emotions. Theoretically, it is plausible that the four types of EOR found by Tsui et al. (1997) may evoke positive or negative emotions. Based on equity theory, organizational justice, and social exchange, one would expect the mutual investment EOR to evoke more positive emotions in that the exchange is likely to be perceived as fair. The overinvestment EOR may also evoke positive emotions given that one has a "surplus." Equity theory would argue to the contrary because by being in an overpayment situation, feelings of guilt or shame might result, although the limited empirical support for the overpayment predictions of equity theory is mixed. The underinvestment EOR would be expected to evoke negative emotions and feelings of injustice because the rewards received do not match the resources expended. It is not clear whether the quasi-spot EOR would be more associated with positive or negative emotions. Because the quasi-spot EOR was conceptualized as balanced, then it may be associated with more positive emotions; however, because it is short term and narrowly focused, it may not be as strongly associated with positive emotions as mutual investment. Clearly, more theoretical development and research are needed to understand the emotional component of the EOR. I suggest that a more complete understanding of the underlying emotions in the EOR will provide a more fine-grained analysis of the effects of the exchange relationship and fulfillment of the obligations to both parties.

EMOTIONS

As indicated earlier, there has been a tendency to focus on the negative effects of failures in the EOR whether viewed from the occupational stress literature such as the effort–reward imbalance model of Siegrist (1996), the psychological contract literature (Robinson & Morrison, 2000; Rousseau, 1995, 2011a, 2011b), or the investments–contributions model (Tsui et al., 1997). Emotions are posited to occur in reaction to an event as well as result in specific behaviors or action tendencies (Fredrickson, 2001, 2005, 2006). For example, fear results in the urge to flee; anger, the urge to attack; and disgust, the urge to expel. Interestingly, positive emotions do not appear to be tied to specific action tendencies. As Fredrickson recounts, some emotions like joy have been described as the urge to do anything and serenity as the urge to do nothing.

The empirical literature on the EOR has implicitly assumed that failures of reciprocity result in negative emotions such as anger or fear, which then result in specific attitudes and action tendencies such as injustice, withdrawal, and counterproductive work behavior. However, the specific emotion that failure of reciprocity evokes has not typically been measured. In the organizational literature as well as the broader literature, the Positive Affect and Negative Affect Schedule (PANAS; Watson, Clark, & Tellegen, 1988) has been most frequently used, although the PANAS has been criticized as not capturing the full structure of affect (Warr, Bindl, Parker, & Inceoglu, 2010). In addition to not including the full structure of affect, the research literature has looked primarily at negative emotions to the relative exclusion of positive emotions (Thoresen, Kaplan, Barsky, Warren, & de Chermont, 2003; but see Kaplan, Bradley, Luchman, & Haynes, 2009; Kaplan, Warren, Barsky, & Thoresen, 2009). Despite the implicit importance of emotions in the EOR literature, theory and empirical research have not adequately examined specific positive and negative emotions or connected them to the occurrence of specific behavioral tendencies and actions. I suggest that the full structure of emotions needs to be explicitly examined to fully understanding the implications of the EOR.

Negative Emotions

Negative affect has been examined much more frequently in the empirical literature, especially in the industrial and organizational psychology and organizational behavior literatures (Thoreson et al., 2003). Negative affect has been implicitly incorporated in major organizational theories such as organizational justice (Barsky & Kaplan, 2007) and occupational stress (Griffin & Clarke, 2011; Perrewé & Zellars, 1999; Spector & Goh, 2001). In general, negative affect (state and trait) has been related to perceptions of unfairness and strains. Although much of the literature has not examined specific negative emotions, Spector and Goh (2001) examined anxiety, anger, depression, and tension, and Perrewé and Zellars (1999) included shame and guilt. The extant literature suggests that different stressors are linked to specific emotions and therefore different outcomes. Therefore, stressors such as organizational injustice (distributive, procedural, and interactional) may evoke different emotions, and then emotions may result in specific behavioral tendencies such as withdrawal, voice, and neglect (see Rusbult, Farrell, Rogers, & Mainus, 1988). Additionally, this literature supports the role of negative emotions in mediating the effects of perceptions of events in the work environment, stressors, on the outcomes of these stressors such as ill-health. Because lack of reciprocity can be described as an organizational injustice (see previous discussion of psychological contract breach, for example), considerable evidence supports emotional reactions to failures of the EOR as the mechanism by which employees' health is negatively affected. The literature on positive emotions is more sparse but growing.

Positive Emotions

George and Brief (1992) provided one of the earliest analyses of positive emotions at work in their review of the mood literature. More recently, Lyubomirsky, King, and Diener (2005) reviewed the literature on positive emotions in the general psychological literature. The existent literature included both field and laboratory studies, with some of the studies focused on the workplace. Most of the studies were cross-sectional, but there were a few longitudinal studies, thus strengthening the results of this meta-analysis. As Warr et al. (2010) observed, the studies included in the Lyubomirsky et al. (2005) meta-analysis primarily used the PANAS (Watson et al., 1988) to assess emotions, which captures only activated feelings (see Watson & Tellegen, 1999). Recognizing this possible limitation, the meta-analysis by Lyubomirsky et al. (2005) found that people who reported higher levels of positive affect were more likely to secure job interviews, to obtain better jobs, to be evaluated positively by their supervisors, to have higher levels of performance and productivity, and to be better managers. They were also less likely to show counterproductive work behavior and burnout and were more satisfied with their jobs. Additionally, positive affect was related to creativity and problem solving (Van Kleef, Anastasopoulou, & Nijstad,

2010). This laundry list of effects provides clear evidence for a connection between positive emotions and individual health.

In addition, Lyubomirsky et al. (2005) found that happy people, those who experience positive emotions, reported higher levels of personal competence and self-esteem, optimism, and a sense of personal mastery. They were more energetic and active and reported more positive health behaviors. Additionally, there was some evidence to support a positive association between positive emotions and immune functioning, although the evidence was stronger for humor and the relation is complex. In addition, positive emotions have been demonstrated to be related to resilience such that the effects of negative events do not impair health as greatly (Tugade & Frederickson, 2004, 2007). These effects suggest that positive emotions may be the mechanism through which individuals gain psychological capital (Avey, Luthans, Smith, & Palmer, 2010; Luthans, Avey, Avolio, & Peterson, 2010) and organizational well-being (Cameron, Dutton, & Quinn, 2003). Taken together, the literature on positive emotions supports the connection between the experience of positive emotions and employees' health. Furthermore, these effects support a positive effect on organizational health at least to the extent that productivity, performance, creativity, and reduced counterproductive work behavior and burnout result in organizational health (see Hofmann & Tetrick, 2003).

Affect Activation

In addition to emotions being described as being positive or negative, emotions have also been described as being active or passive (Russell, 2003; Tellegen, Watson, & Clark, 1999; Warr, 1990, 1994, 2006). According to this conceptualization, emotions vary on the degree of pleasure versus displeasure and on the degree of arousal or activation. Emotions can then be grouped into one of the following four quadrants. High activation–negative affect would include aroused, alarmed, afraid, tense, anxious, uneasy, upset, and discouraged. High activation–positive affect would include alert, excited, energetic, enthusiastic, cheerful, elated, glad, and pleased. Low activation–negative affect would include fatigued, bored, lethargic, gloomy, sad, depressed, miserable, and dejected. Finally, low activation–positive affect would include sluggish, drowsy, tranquil, relaxed, calm, comfortable, contented, and serene. The implication of this conceptualization is that specific emotions may result in different behavioral tendencies and these tendencies will differ based on the level of activity as well as their valence. If an employee experiences contentedness, he or she would be less "active" than if he or she is elated. Similarly, if an individual is anxious, he or she would be expected to be more "active" than if he or she is depressed.

The empirical literature to date has primarily focused on the upper quadrants, which contain positive and negative activation emotions, and has not examined the low level of activation emotions (Warr et al., 2010). One notable exception is Warr et al. (2010), in which the results of six separate studies examining a total of 15 different work behaviors specifically looked at both positive and negative affect as well as high and low activation. Not only did Warr et al. (2010) find that positive emotions were more strongly related to positive organizational behaviors than negative emotions, but they also found that higher activation positive emotions were more strongly related to positive organizational behaviors than were lower activation positive emotions. The findings for negative emotions were somewhat similar in that highly negative emotions were more strongly related to negative organizational behaviors than to positive organizational behaviors; however, lower activation negative emotions were more strongly related to negative organizational behaviors rather than higher activation negative emotions. This latter finding may be the result of the constraints of the employment environment. For example, Warr et al. (2010) suggest that complete withdrawal is not possible in the work environment except for quitting because of role demands. The results of this study support the notion that emotions can drive individual organizational behavior as well as the health of employees, and to the extent that the EOR results in positive and negative emotions, I suggest that emotions serve as the mediating mechanism between the EOR and individual and organizational behavior and health.

AGGREGATION OF INDIVIDUAL-LEVEL EFFECTS TO ORGANIZATIONAL-LEVEL EFFECTS: EMOTIONAL CONTAGION

As mentioned earlier, it is unlikely that a given individual employee's behavior will affect the organization's health. Yet, what we know about multilevel and cross-level effects makes it compelling to argue that the emotions experienced by individual employees may have a direct effect on others in the organization, both at the same level and at other levels in the organization (Rousseau, 2011b). This contagion of emotions can have a direct effect on the emotions and behaviors at other levels in the organization (Barsade, 2002; Hatfield, Cacioppo, & Rapson, 1994).

Emotional contagion refers to the tendency of individuals to experience and express another's emotions (Hatfield et al., 1994). This involves the noticing others' emotional expressions, feeling that one is related to others rather than being independent from others, mimicry of others' emotional expressions, and experiencing a conscious emotional reaction that converges with the other (Dasborough, Ashkanasy, Tee, & Tse, 2009; Kimura, Daibo, & Yogo, 2008). Emotional contagion is a uniquely interpersonal phenomenon that has only recently been examined in organizational behavior and may be affected by several factors. First, it has been demonstrated that people vary in their susceptibility to emotional contagion (Doherty, 1997; Hatfield et al., 1994). In addition, there is evidence that the degree of emotional contagion may be influenced by the valence of the episode (i.e., positive versus negative), the social power in interpersonal relationship, and the degree of affiliation in the interpersonal relationship (Barsade, 2002; Dasborough et al., 2009; Kimura et al., 2008). In fact, Kimura et al. (2008) suggest that there may be cultural differences in emotional contagion based on their findings relative to negative emotions. In their study, they did not find differences in emotional contagion by status, which may have been the result of display rules concerning negative emotions in Japan.

Emotional contagion has been studied or at least theorized as occurring at multilevels of analysis. Barger and Grandey (2006) used emotional contagion as a theoretical mechanism for understanding interactions between employees and customers and found support for the transmission of positive moods through mimicry of displays. However, this study suggested that the effects of emotional contagion through mimicry were mediated by the cognitive appraisal of the service encounter as the quality of service. They argued that perhaps these brief encounters were with customers who were at most acquaintances; this would be consistent with the findings of Kimura et al. (2008) that acquaintances are less likely to evoke emotional responses than friends and people who are of higher or lower social power and who are better known to the individual than mere acquaintances. Similarly, Johnson (2008) found that leaders' positive and negative affect at work was related to followers' affect and that this relation was moderated by the followers' susceptibility to emotional contagion. It also should be noted that follower affect did relate to their attributions of charismatic leadership and organizational citizenship behavior. One note should be made regarding this study; the authors were not specifically assessing emotions per se, but rather general affect at work. Nevertheless, Johnson (2008) is consistent with the proposition being advanced here that emotions are an important component in linking individual and organizational health and may be the key factor in understanding the consequences of the EOR.

The occurrence of emotional contagion in teams has been demonstrated. Ilies, Wagner, and Morgeson (2007), in their study of the linkages between individual team members' positive and negative affect and the team's collective affective state, found support for emotional contagion. As was the case with Johnson (2008), Ilies et al. (2007) measured general affect rather than emotion relative to a specific event, and as they recognize themselves, they only measured overall positive and negative affect rather than specific emotions or affective states. Nevertheless, they did provide support for the notion of emotional contagion in teams. Importantly, they also added support for the moderating effect of susceptibility to emotional contagion as well as introducing the moderating role of individual-level individualism–collectivism in emotional contagion in teams. This latter finding has important implications for cultural (organizational or societal) factors on the effects of emotions within the workplace.

The empirical research that I am aware of tends to take a top-down perspective with respect to emotional contagion within the workplace (e.g., leader to follower, team to individual team member, culture to individual). Dasborough et al. (2009) advanced a model of emotional contagion where micro-level predictors, such as favoritism toward members and affective displays by leaders, result in emotions that subsequently affect not only the leader–member exchange but also the team–member exchange and team climate, which, in turn, affects organizational endorsement of the leader. Following the rationale set out by Dasborough et al. (2009), I believe that a connection between the exchange relationship and the emotions associated with continued reciprocity (or the failure of reciprocity) involved in this relationship not only contribute to individuals' behavior, health, and emotional responses but, through the process of emotional contagion, to the team or workgroup's collective emotional state and ultimately to the organization's collective emotional state. This spreading activation may result in unhealthy organizational climates in the case of negative emotions or healthy and positive climates in the case of more positive emotions. This has yet to be empirically examined in organizational research, to my knowledge, although the organizational climate literature has traditionally included such climate dimensions as warmth and friendliness and climate has been posited to relate to emotions (James et al., 2008; Schneider, Ehrhardt, & Macey, 2011). The development of positive organizational climates through positive emotions, as proposed by Sekerka and Frederickson (2008), has the potential of transforming organizations to organizations that are healthy and thriving.

IMPLICATIONS AND CONCLUSIONS

The basic tenet of this chapter is that the health of organizations and the health of employees are interdependent. Healthy organizations can invest in employees, enhancing employees' health, and employees will contribute to the organization, enhancing the organization's health. This is consistent with the inducements–contributions model and the psychological contract perspective of the EOR. What appears to be missing from the literature based on social exchange theory is the role of emotions in understanding the EOR. Emotions play a pivotal role in translating employees' reactions to their treatment by the organization, serving as the glue that binds the employee to the organization in the case of positive emotions or dissolves the relationship in the case of negative emotions.

The empirical literature, to date, has focused primarily on global positive and negative affect to the exclusion of examining specific core emotions. In addition, the measures of emotions have focused on the activated end of the activation dimension of emotions rather than also examining emotions falling more toward the nonactivated end. Therefore, we know little about the role of such emotions as contented or relaxed. It may be that activated emotions are more important in the work environment because these emotions drive individuals to take action; however, the more passive emotions, especially passive positive emotions, may be more important for creativity and well-being.

I suggest that emotions not only affect the individual employee's health and performance, but through a process of emotional contagion, emotions can affect the health and performance of groups and teams and potentially the climate of the organization as a whole. To the extent that positive emotions spread throughout the organization, the organization will be healthier, and this will translate into financial well-being, enabling the organization to further invest in their employees. On the other hand, negative emotions experienced through such conditions as psychological contract breach or violation and underinvestment may have detrimental effects on employees and ultimately the organization. Therefore, the interdependence between organizational and employee health is cyclical, as depicted in Figure 18.1.

Unfortunately, the literature does not give us much guidance as to the relative effects of different emotions. Are some emotions more potent than others? From the literature, we might conclude that negative emotions may be more potent, but is this the case when one considers the full circumplex of emotions? We also know very little about emotional contagion, especially in the work environment. Are some emotions more contagious than others? Are some individuals more susceptible to emotional contagion than others? The literature is relatively silent on the length of time that specific emotions remain in effect and what the course of emotional contagion might be. Social network analysis may be useful in promoting our understanding of emotional contagion. Given the considerable evidence of the influence of the EOR on attitudes and behaviors, as discussed in other chapters in this volume, and the fact that affect is an element of most definitions of attitudes, emotions are expected to play a key role in the interdependency of employee and organizational health.

REFERENCES

Ajzen, I., & Fishbein, M. (2005). The influence of attitudes on behavior. In D. Albarracín, B. T. Johnson, & M. P. Zanna (Eds.), *The handbook of attitudes* (pp. 173–221). Mahwah, NJ: Lawrence Erlbaum Associates.

Ashby, F. G., Isen, A. M., & Turken, A. U. (1999). A neuropsychological theory of positive affect and its influence on cognition. *Psychological Review, 106*, 529–550.

Avey, J. B., Luthans, F., Smith, R. M., & Palmer, N. F. (2010). Impact of positive psychological capital on employee well-being over time. *Journal of Occupational Health Psychology, 15*, 17–28.

Bagozzi, R. P., Wong, N., & Yi, Y. (1999). The role of culture and gender in the relationship between positive and negative affect. *Cognition and Emotion, 13,* 641–672.

Barger, P. B., & Grandey, A. A. (2006). Service with a smile and encounter satisfaction: Emotional contagion and appraisal mechanisms. *Academy of Management Journal, 49,* 1129–1238.

Barsade, S. G. (2002). The ripple effects: Emotional contagion and its influence on group behavior. *Administrative Science Quarterly, 47,* 644–675.

Barsky, A., & Kaplan, S. A. (2007). If you feel bad, it's unfair: A quantitative synthesis of affect and organizational justice perceptions. *Journal of Applied Psychology, 92,* 286–295.

Blau, P. M. (1964). *Exchange and power in social life.* New York, NY: John Wiley & Sons.

Cameron, K. S., Dutton, J. E., & Quinn, R. E. (2003). Foundations of positive organizational scholarship. In K. S. Cameron, J. E. Dutton, & R. E. Quinn (Eds.), *Positive organizational scholarship* (pp. 3–13). San Francisco, CA: Berrett-Koehler Publishers, Inc.

Claes, R., Schalk, R., & de Jong, J. (2010). International comparisons of employment contracts, psychological contracts, and worker well-being. In D. E. Guest, K. Isaksson, & H. De Witte (Eds.), *Employment contracts, psychological contracts, and well-being: An international study.* New York, NY: Oxford University Press.

Cohn, M. A., & Fredrickson, B. L. (2010). In search of durable positive psychology interventions: Predictors and consequences of long-term positive behavior change. *The Journal of Positive Psychology, 5,* 355–366.

Cohn, M. A., Fredrickson, B. L., Brown, S. L., Mikels, J. A., & Conway, A. M. (2009). Happiness unpacked: Positive emotions increase life satisfaction by building resilience. *Emotion, 9,* 361–368.

Conway, N., & Briner, R. B. (2002). A daily diary study of affective responses to psychological contract breach and exceeded promises. *Journal of Organizational Behavior, 23,* 287–302.

Cropanzano, R., & Mitchell, M. S. (2005). Social exchange theory: An interdisciplinary review. *Journal of Management, 31,* 874–900.

Dasborough, M. R., Ashkanasy, N. M., Tee, E. U. J., & Tse, H. H. M. (2009). What goes around comes around: How meso-level negative emotional contagion can ultimately determine organizational attitudes toward leaders. *The Leadership Quarterly, 20,* 571–585.

Doherty, R. W. (1997). The emotional contagion scale: A measure of individual differences. *Journal of Nonverbal Behavior, 21,* 131–154.

Fishbein, M., & Ajzen, I. (1974). Attitudes towards objects as predictors of single and multiple behavioral criteria. *Psychological Review, 81,* 59–74.

Fredrickson, B. L. (2001). The role of positive emotions in positive psychology: The broaden-and-build theory of positive emotions. *American Psychologist, 56,* 218–226.

Fredrickson, B. L. (2005). The broaden-and-build theory of positive emotions. In F. A. Huppert, N. Baylis, & B. Keverne (Eds.), *The science of well-being* (pp. 217–238). New York, NY: Oxford University Press.

Fredrickson, B. L. (2006). The broaden-and-build theory of positive emotions. In M. Csikszentmihalyi & I. S. Csikszentmihalyi (Eds.), *A life worth living: Contributions to positive psychology* (pp. 85–103). New York, NY: Oxford University Press.

George, J. M., & Brief, A. P. (1992). Feeling good-doing good: A conceptual analysis of the mood at work-organizational spontaneity relationship. *Psychological Bulletin, 112,* 310–329.

Gouldner, A. W. (1960). The norm of reciprocity: A preliminary statement. *American Sociological Review, 25,* 161–178.

Greenberg, J. (2011). Organizational justice: The dynamics of fairness in the workplace. In S. Zedeck (Ed.), *APA handbook of industrial and organizational psychology* (Vol. 3, pp. 271–327). Washington, DC: American Psychological Association.

Griffin, M. A., & Clarke, S. (2011). Stress and well-being at work. In S. Zedeck (Ed.), *APA handbook of industrial and organizational psychology* (Vol. 3, pp. 359–397). Washington, DC: American Psychological Association.

Guest, D. E., & Clinton, M. (2010). Causes and consequences of the psychological contract. In D. E. Guest, K. Isaksson, & H. De Witte (Eds.), *Employment contracts, psychological contracts, and well-being: An international study.* New York, NY: Oxford University Press.

Guest, D. E., Isaksson, K., & De Witte, H. (Eds.) (2010). *Employment contracts, psychological contracts, and well-being: An international study.* New York, NY: Oxford University Press.

Hackman, J. R. (2009). The perils of positivity. *Journal of Organizational Behavior, 30*, 309–319.

Hatfield, E., Cacioppo, J., & Rapson, R. L. (1994). *Emotional contagion.* Paris, France: Cambridge University Press.

Hofmann, D. A., & Tetrick, L. E. (2003). On the etiology of health: Implications for "organizing" individual and organizational health. In D. A. Hofmann & L. E. Tetrick (Eds.), *Health and safety in organizations: A multilevel perspective.* Organizational Frontier Series, Society for Industrial and Organizational Psychology. San Francisco, CA: Jossey-Bass.

Hom, P. W., Tsui, A. S., Wu, J. B., Lee, T. W., Zhang, A. Y., Fu, P. P., & Li, L. (2009). Explaining employment relationships with social exchange and job embeddedness. *Journal of Applied Psychology, 94*, 277–297.

Ilies, R., Wagner, D. T., & Morgeson, F. P. (2007). Explaining affective linkages in teams: Individual differences in susceptibility to contagion and individualism–collectivism. *Journal of Applied Psychology, 92*, 1140–1148.

James, L. R., Choi, C. C., Ko, C. H. E., McNeil, P. K., Minton, M. K., Wright, M. A., & Kim, K. (2008). Organizational and psychological climate: A review of theory and research. *European Journal of Work and Organizational Psychology, 17*, 5–32.

Johnson, S. K. (2008). I second that emotion: Effects of emotional contagion and affect at work on leader and follower outcomes. *The Leadership Quarterly, 19*, 1–19.

Kaplan, S., Bradley, J. C., Luchman, J. N., & Haynes, D. (2009). On the role of positive and negative affectivity in job performance: A meta-analytic investigation. *Journal of Applied Psychology, 94*, 162–176.

Kaplan, S. A., Warren, C. R., Barsky, A. P., & Thoresen, C. J. (2009). A note on the relationship between affect(ivity) and differing conceptualizations of job satisfaction: Some unexpected meta-analytic findings. *European Journal of Work and Organizational Psychology, 18*, 29–54.

Kimura, M., Daibo, I., & Yogo, M. (2008). The study of emotional contagion from the perspective of interpersonal relationships. *Social Behavior and Personality, 36*, 27–42.

Lambert, L., Edwards, J. R., & Cable, D. M. (2003). Breach and fulfillment of psychological contracts: A comparison of traditional and expanded views. *Personnel Psychology, 56*, 893–934.

Luthans, F., Avey, J. B., Avolio, B. J., & Peterson, S. J. (2010). The development and resulting performance impact of positive psychological capital. *Human Resource Development Quarterly, 21*, 41–67.

Lyubomirsky, S., King, L., & Diener, E. (2005). The benefits of frequent positive affect: Does happiness lead to success? *Psychological Bulletin, 131*, 803–855.

Mills, J., & Clark, M. S. (1982). Exchange and communal relationships. *Review of Personality and Social Psychology, 3,* 121–144.

Morrison, E. W., & Robinson, S. L. (1997). When employees feel betrayed: A model of how psychological contract violation develops. *The Academy of Management Review, 22,* 226–256.

Parker, S. K., Wall, T. D., & Cordery, J. L. (2001). Future work design research and practice: Towards an elaborated model of work design. *Journal of Occupational and Organizational Psychology, 74,* 413–440.

Parzefall, M.-R., & Hakanen, J. (2010). Psychological contract and its motivational and health-enhancing properties. *Journal of Managerial Psychology, 25,* 4–21.

Perrewé, P. L., & Zellars, K. L. (1999). An examination of attributions and emotions in the transactional approach to the organizational stress process. *Journal of Organizational Behavior, 20,* 739–752.

Rhoades, L., & Eisenberger, R. (2002). Perceived organizational support: A review of the literature. *Journal of Applied Psychology, 87,* 698–714.

Robinson, S. L., & Morrison, E. W. (2000). The development of psychological contract breach and violation: A longitudinal study. *Journal of Organizational Behavior, 21,* 525–546.

Rousseau, D. M. (1990). New hire perceptions of their own and their employer's obligations: A study of psychological contracts. *Journal of Organizational Behavior, 11,* 389–400.

Rousseau, D. M. (1995). *Psychological contracts in organizations: Understanding written and unwritten agreements.* Thousand Oaks, CA: Sage.

Rousseau, D. M. (2011a). The individual–organization relationship: The psychological contract. In S. Zedeck (Ed.), *APA handbook of industrial and organizational psychology* (Vol. 3, pp. 191–220). Washington, DC: American Psychological Association.

Rousseau, D. M. (2011b). Reinforcing the micro/macro bridge: Organizational thinking and pluralistic vehicles. *Journal of Management, 37,* 429–442.

Rousseau, D. M., & Schalk, R. (2000). Introduction. In D. M. Rousseau & R. Schalk (Eds.), *Psychological contracts in employment: Cross-national perspectives* (pp. 1–28). Thousand Oaks, CA: Sage Publications.

Rusbult, C. E., Farrell, D., Rogers, G., & Mainous, A. G. (1988). Impact of exchange variables on exit, voice, loyalty, and neglect: An integrative model of responses to declining job satisfaction. *Academy of Management Journal, 31,* 599–627.

Russell, J. A. (2003). Core affect and the psychological construction of emotion. *Psychological Review, 110,* 145–172.

Sahlins, M. (1974). *Stone age economics.* New York, NY: Aldine.

Schneider, B., Ehrhart, M. G., & Macey, W. H. (2011). Perspectives on organizational climate and culture. In S. Zedeck (Ed.), *APA handbooks in psychology. APA handbook of industrial and organizational psychology: Building and developing the organization* (Vol. 1, pp. 373–414). Washington, DC: American Psychological Association.

Sekerka, L. E., & Fredrickson, B. L. (2008). Establishing positive emotional climates to advance organizational transformation. In N. M. Ashkanasy & C. L. Cooper (Eds.), *New horizons in management: Research companion to emotion in organizations* (pp. 531–545). Northampton, MA: Edward Elgar Publishing.

Seligman, M. E. P. (2002). *Authentic happiness.* New York, NY: Free Press.

Shore, L. M., Tetrick, L. E., Lynch, P., & Barksdale, K. (2006). Social and economic exchange: Construct development and validation. *Journal of Applied Social Psychology, 36,* 837–867.

Siegrist, J. (1996). Adverse health effects of high-effort/low-reward conditions. *Journal of Occupational Health Psychology, 1*, 27–41.

Siegrist, J. (2005). Social reciprocity and health: New scientific evidence and policy implications. *Psychoneuroendocrinology, 30*, 1033–1038.

Song, L. J., Tsui, A. S., & Law, K. S. (2009). Unpacking employee responses to organizational exchange mechanisms: The role of social and economic exchange perceptions. *Journal of Management, 35*, 56–93.

Sparrowe, R. T., & Liden, R. C. (1997). Process and structure in leader-member exchange. *Academy of Management Review, 22*, 522–552.

Spector, P. E., & Goh, A. (2001). The role of emotions in the occupational stress process. In P. L. Perrewé & D. C. Ganster (Eds.), *Research in occupational stress and well being* (Vol. 1, pp. 195–232). Bingley, UK: Emerald Group Publishing.

Tellegen, A., Watson, D., & Clark, L. A. (1999). On the dimensional and hierarchical structure of affect. *Psychological Science, 10*, 297–303.

Thoresen, C. J., Kaplan, S. A., Barsky, A. P., Warren, C. R., & de Chermont, K. (2003). The affective underpinnings of job perceptions and attitudes: A meta-analytic review and integration. *Psychological Bulletin, 129*, 914–945.

Tsui, A. S., Pearce, J. L., Porter, L. W., & Tripoli, A. M. (1997). Alternative approaches to the employee–organization relationship: Does investment in employees pay off? *Academy of Management Journal, 40*, 1089–1121.

Tugade, M. M., & Fredrickson, B. L. (2004). Resilient individuals use positive emotions to bounce back from negative emotional experiences. *Journal of Personality and Social Psychology, 86*, 320–333.

Tugade, M. M., & Fredrickson, B. L. (2007). Regulation of positive emotions: Emotion regulation strategies that promote resilience. *Journal of Happiness Studies, 8*, 311–333.

Turnley, W. H., & Feldman, D. C. (2000). Re-examining the effects of psychological contract violations: Unmet expectations and job dissatisfaction as mediators. *Journal of Organizational Behavior, 21*, 25–42.

Van Kleef, G. A., Anastasopoulou, C., & Nijstad, B. A. (2010). Can expressions of anger enhance creativity? A test of the emotions as social information (EASI) model. *Journal of Experimental Social Psychology, 46*, 1042–1048.

Warr, P. (1990). The measurement of well-being and other aspects of mental health. *Journal of Occupational Psychology, 63*, 193–210.

Warr, P. (1994). A conceptual framework for the study of work and mental health. *Work and Stress, 8*, 84–97.

Warr, P. (2006). Differential activation of judgments in employee well-being. *Journal of Occupational and Organizational Psychology, 79*, 225–244.

Warr, P., Bindl, U. K., Parker, S. K., & Inceoglu, I. (2010). *An expanded approach to affect-behavior linkages: Activation as well as valence.* Unpublished manuscript, Institute of Work Psychology, University of Sheffield, United Kingdom.

Warr, P., & Clapperton, G. (2010). *The joy of work? Jobs, happiness, and you.* New York, NY: Routledge/Taylor & Francis Group.

Watson, D., Clark, L. A., & Tellegen, A. (1988). Development and validation of brief measures of positive and negative affect: The PANAS scales. *Journal of Personality and Social Psychology, 54*, 1063–1070.

Watson, D., & Tellegen, A. (1999). Issues in dimensional structure of affect—Effects of descriptors, measurement error, and response formats: Comment on Russell and Carroll (1999). *Psychological Bulletin, 125*, 601–610.

19

Managing Diversity Means Managing Differently: A Look at the Role of Racioethnicity in Perceptions of Organizational Support

Derek R. Avery
Temple University

Patrick F. McKay
Rutgers, the State University of New Jersey

Quinetta M. Roberson
Villanova University

More than 25 years have passed since Eisenberger, Huntington, Hutchinson, and Sowa (1986) described the employee–organization relationship (EOR) through the lens of perceived organizational support (POS). Essentially, they believed that (a) an exchange relationship takes place between companies and their workers where the principal concern among the latter is the extent to which they view their employer as supportive, and (b) the magnitude of POS has considerable organizational implications. Subsequent research has borne this out, showing that employees keep tabs on their employer's actions in appraising their supportiveness and that these assessments relate to outcomes such as job satisfaction, organizational commitment, turnover intentions, in-role performance, and organizational citizenship behavior (Ng & Sorensen, 2008; Rhoades & Eisenberger, 2002; Riggle, Edmondson, & Hansen, 2009). It seems that the better organizations are able to create and maintain supportive work environments, the more favorably employees respond with respect to their attitudes and behaviors.

Despite its clear utility in enhancing our understanding of EORs, we believe the POS literature would benefit from greater consideration of diversity and its effects in the workplace. Statistics show that workplaces around the globe are becoming more demographically heterogeneous, particularly with respect to gender, nationality, age, racioethnicity, and religion. Unfortunately, many employees are apt to respond unfavorably to this heightened diversity and the challenges it can produce (Leonard & Levine, 2006; Tsui, Egan, & O'Reilly, 1992). However, little research has explored the influence of diversity on EORs (for exceptions, see Buttner, Lowe, & Billings-Harris, 2010; Chrobot-Mason, 2003; McKay & Avery, 2005). Current findings suggest that (a) perceived organizational obligations differ for minority and majority employees, and (b) many minority employees pay particular attention to what they perceive to be diversity promises and are especially sensitive to their fulfillment; these findings illustrate the need to reconsider EORs in light of the continuing diversification of workplaces around the globe. Consequently, the focus of this chapter is to describe how racioethnic diversity (we limit our focus to racioethnicity due to space considerations) has shaped and will continue to shape the evolution of these relationships.

The remainder of this chapter is structured as follows. First, we describe current trends regarding racioethnic diversity in the workplace. Second, we consider how this type of diversity can influence "employees' general belief that their work organization values their contribution and cares about their well-being" (i.e., POS; Rhoades & Eisenberger, 2002, p. 698). Third, we outline the research implications of integrating diversity and POS to provide an agenda for subsequent empirical study. Finally, we conclude with a discussion of the managerial implications of this chapter, paying particular attention to how organizations can leverage the unique talents of all of their employees.

CURRENT DIVERSITY TRENDS

Numerous statistics indicate workplace demographic diversity is trending upward in settings around the globe. In the United States, for example, the current labor force is older and more gender balanced and contains more racioethnic minorities than in years past (Toossi, 2006). These workplace changes are projected to continue to the point where women slightly outnumber men and there are equal numbers of White and non-White laborers in the year 2050 (Toossi, 2006). In addition to these shifts in domestic forms of diversity, globalization has produced a growing immigrant presence as well. In fact, estimates suggest that immigrants constitute nearly one in seven employees in the United States (Camarota, 2005). Although demographic diversity receives relatively less attention outside the United States, evidence suggests that similar trends are occurring elsewhere in such settings as Europe, Asia, and Australia (e.g., MacGillivray, Beecher, & Golden, 2008; Singh & Point, 2004). Consequently, the importance of considering the influence of such diversity on management practices (and vice versa) is palpable.

As these changes began to occur, a number of authors (e.g., Cox, 1994; Joplin & Daus, 1997) took notice and began documenting the differences between managing a diverse as opposed to a homogenous workforce. Among the various issues they raised are changes to traditional power dynamics, increased diversity of opinions, perceived lack of empathy, tokenism, unequal opportunities for participation, and inertia. Conceptually, these topics are highly similar to Cox's (1994) tripartite definition of diversity climate, which highlights relevant individual-, group-, and organizational-level factors that influence career outcomes and organizational effectiveness. However, because these discussions focused primarily on how (a) organizations should be structured to deal with diversity, and (b) leaders should manage differences, considerably less attention has been devoted to exploring the impact of growing diversity on EORs. Thus, it remains largely unclear how important perceptions of these relationships, such as POS, might be influenced by the rise in demographic heterogeneity.

HOW RACIOETHNIC DIVERSITY INFLUENCES PERCEPTIONS OF ORGANIZATIONAL SUPPORT

From a managerial perspective, one would expect it to be easier to anticipate and meet the desires of a homogenous versus a diverse group of employees. Greater demographic similarity should coincide with less variability in values, wants, needs, and aspirations. Less variability in these attributes allows managers to standardize their methods for dealing with employees and reduces the need for customization of their managerial approaches to accommodate differences among their subordinates. Not only is it simpler to design strategies intended to treat everyone similarly, but doing so also provides a sense of consistency, which is important for ensuring that employees feel they are being treated fairly (Colquitt, Greenberg, & Zapata-Phelan, 2005).

When employees are more heterogeneous, however, it becomes increasingly challenging and even potentially inappropriate to treat them similarly. Take, for instance, an employee who cannot hear. If managers and coworkers embody the belief that everyone should be treated similarly, it makes it difficult (if not impossible) for such an individual to succeed within that environment, irrespective of what other talents he or she might possess. Although the need for accommodating a physical ability is more obvious, making adjustments to include other types of difference also can be important. This may not seem like cause for concern for many readers, but it can become potentially problematic when considered in the context of POS.

Through their day-to-day experiences, employees develop perceptions of the nature of treatment they receive from their employer over the course of an employment relationship. Broadly speaking, these experiences can be classified as pertaining to (a) general fairness, (b) supervisor support, and (c) organizational rewards and job conditions (Rhoades & Eisenberger, 2002). Much of the POS literature builds on organizational justice principles, suggesting that consistency (i.e., treating everyone the same) is a key to fair treatment. Nevertheless, if companies are unwilling or unable to acknowledge and accommodate differences among their employees, they may find it extremely difficult to meet employee expectations and provide a supportive environment for all employees. This is true whether the need for the accommodation is more obvious (e.g., a wheelchair-accessible facility for employees with physical disabilities) or less obvious (e.g., a network group for a newly hired minority employee). In either case, the employee is apt to perceive the organization as unsupportive based on a perceived failure to provide equal employment opportunity.

Because employee perceptions of their employer's provision of equal opportunity are roughly tantamount to diversity climate (Buttner et al.,

2010; McKay, Avery, & Morris, 2009), we believe that managing a company's diversity climate is the key to providing a supportive environment for a racioethnically diverse set of employees (Leveson, Joiner, & Bakalis, 2009). In one of the few studies to examine racioethnic differences in prospective antecedents of POS, Chrobot-Mason (2003) identified five diversity-related promises: (1) diverse representation throughout the organization; (2) consideration of minority input; (3) valuation of different ideas, opinions, and perspectives; (4) the elimination of bias and discrimination; and (5) support/understanding of unique minority issues. We consider each of these in the current discussion and expand on the last of them to include language policies and access to mentors.

Diverse Representation

Organizations vary considerably in their levels of employee demographic diversity. Some contain an abundance of one particular type of diversity (e.g., age), yet very little of other types. Others are comprised of diversity of all types or have virtually none whatsoever. In light of the diversity trends described in the previous section, it is clear that most companies are likely to have more diversity (of many types) in the coming years than they have had in the past. Similarly, employees are likely to experience working with more diverse peers than they have in the past. What is important to the present discussion is that the impact of having more diversity often differs depending on whether or not one is a member of the majority group.

By definition, those in the demographic majority within a geographic context are likely to comprise the demographic majority in firms within that context (e.g., Stoll, Holzer, & Ihlanfeldt, 2000). For instance, White Americans, who represent the racioethnic majority within the United States, are more likely than members of other racioethnic groups to find themselves in the majority within a U.S.-based company. Mathematically speaking, increasing diversity requires either (a) hiring more minorities or (b) replacing members of the majority with members of minority groups (Harrison & Klein, 2007). The offshoot of this notion is that under such circumstances, demographic dissimilarity (i.e., the proportion of individuals belonging to a group other than one's own) will increase for members of the majority and decrease for minority group members. This feature of workforce composition is an important consideration given that racioethnic similarity within organizational settings decreases negative outcomes, such as the likelihood of perceiving discrimination (Avery, McKay, & Wilson, 2008), and increases positive outcomes, such as employee attachment (Leonard & Levine, 2006; Tsui et al., 1992).

As the labor force grows increasingly diverse, many job applicants and employees are likely to form expectations about the demographics of their colleagues. This tendency may be especially pronounced among those working for organizations that presented themselves as diverse during the recruitment process, an increasingly common human resource management strategy (cf. Avery & McKay, 2006). If prospective employees are led to expect diversity or demographically similar coworkers, they may hold their employers accountable to this expectation in their psychological contracts. Thus, the demographic profile of an employer's workforce probably will influence perceptions of organizational support among its personnel in a manner that may not have been expected previously.

In culling the literature for empirical evidence consistent with the preceding conclusion, we discovered a few pertinent findings. First, two studies (Buttner et al., 2010; Chrobot-Mason, 2003) demonstrated that diversity promises, which include diverse representation, influence minority employees' commitment to and intent to remain with their employers. Notably, this was after accounting for variance attributable to the fulfillment of general promises considered to be part of the psychological contract. Second, research has shown that racioethnic dissimilarity with coworkers and prospective customers influences employees' propensity to turnover (e.g., Leonard & Levine, 2006). Perhaps an unexamined mediator of these relationships involves POS, because a lack of racioethnically similar coworkers could reduce coworker support and, consequently, POS (Chattopadhyay, 1999; Ng & Sorensen, 2008). Although not a direct test of our notion that demographic representation is becoming more relevant to POS, these results provide some measure of preliminary support.

Another consequence of increasing diversity is that employees will be expected to communicate and get along with demographically dissimilar others. Although this may sound rather simple, a number of authors have noted that diversity is positively correlated with the level of conflict within a group (see King, Hebl, and Beal [2009] for a recent review of this literature). Because surface-level differences (e.g., race, sex, age) often correspond or are perceived to correspond with deeper level differences (e.g., personality, values, work styles), there are potentially fertile grounds for disagreement to occur along demographic lines. Such diversity-related conflict is often counterproductive for organizations in that it can detract significantly from productivity (Ely & Thomas, 2001; Pelled, Eisenhardt, & Xin, 1999). Consequently, companies will need employees to coordinate and cooperate with other employees, customers, and supervisors who are dissimilar to them if they are to be successful.

Not all employees, however, are equally well suited to work effectively with dissimilar others. Rather, it seems that some may possess "diversity mind-sets" that make them more suitable for this type of work (van Knippenberg & Schippers, 2007, p. 531). According to van Knippenberg and Schippers (2007), diversity mind-sets pertain to the favorability of one's attitudes and beliefs regarding diversity. Although preliminary, they review some evidence suggesting that "diversity mind-sets favoring diversity may thus be expected to prevent intergroup bias as well as to stimulate the integration of diverse information, viewpoints, and perspectives" (van Knippenberg & Schippers, 2007, p. 531). Although further research is needed to develop the mind-set construct, because prior investigations have conceptualized it in a variety of ways (e.g., openness to experience, value of diversity, need for cognition; Homan et al., 2008; Homan, van Knippenberg, van Kleef, & De Dreu, 2007; Kearney, Gebert, & Voelpel, 2009), organizations are likely to expect their employees to possess such mind-sets (or at least be receptive to training designed to help facilitate them). Accordingly, employees are apt to anticipate and desire organizational support for developing and exercising these mind-sets (e.g., training, performance appraisal, compensation).

Consideration of Minority Viewpoints

A common theme among members of traditionally underrepresented demographic groups is that they often feel as though their input does not receive the same level of consideration as majority group members within organizational settings (Blank & Slipp, 1994; Elsass & Graves, 1997). Social identity theory (Tajfel & Turner, 1986) helps to explain why this may occur. According to the theory, individuals classify themselves and others on the basis of readily observable markers (e.g., racioethnicity) and use this classification as the basis for differentiating those who are similar (i.e., in-group) from those who are not (i.e., out-group). Because people are motivated to feel positively about their in-group as a means of feeling positively about themselves, there is a tendency to distort one's perception to the advantage of in-group members (and the disadvantage of out-group members). In practice, this could take the form of ignoring viable ideas presented by out-group members and then praising these same ideas when presented by those in the in-group.

Furthermore, status characteristics theory (Berger, Rosenholtz, & Zelditch, 1980; Ridgeway, 1991) proposes that societies construct status hierarchies based on social identity group membership. In the United States, for instance, some groups (e.g., Whites, men) are accorded greater status and perceptions of competence than other groups (e.g., minorities, women). The result of this status ordering is that in group decision-making contexts, members of high-status groups enjoy higher expectancies of perceived competence, which translates into their input receiving greater consideration than the viewpoints offered by members of low-status groups. Bunderson (2003) showed that in low-tenured groups (contexts wherein visible, demographic characteristics are likely to be used to form initial impressions), racioethnicity had stronger influence on judgments of team members' expertise than more relevant, work-related characteristics like work experience and educational attainment. In addition, patterns of group interactions in which the suggestions of high-status people are lauded while those presented by members of low-status groups are marginalized compel members of the latter group to minimize their contributions to group effectiveness (Cohen, 1982; Ridgeway, 1991). Consequently, prevailing views of low-status group members' relative incompetence are reinforced.

Returning to POS, it is easy to see why the extent that minority viewpoints are considered is relevant in a diverse workforce. Research on employee voice (i.e., having the opportunity to express one's views prior to organizational decisions being made) has illustrated the importance of having one's opinions heard and considered (Shapiro, 1993). In fact, people's perceptions of fairness decline considerably if they offer their perspective only to be ignored by decision makers (Avery & Quiñones, 2002). Most employees likely expect some degree of voice and for their employers to actually to listen to what they have to say. To the extent that this is not the case, it can be expected that many employees will perceive their organizations as unsupportive (Rhoades & Eisenberger, 2002).

Clearly, every worker has a desire to be heard (at least to some extent). The issue here is that the views of employees belonging to certain racioethnic groups may be discounted more often than those of others. This suggests that increasing the presence of underrepresented groups within organizations also means increasing the proportion of individuals whose viewpoints are prone to be ignored because of their social identities. Thus, the inequity of POS discussed in this section is not simply an issue of a lack of voice, which is a more general issue (i.e., equally relevant to members of all demographic groups). Instead, it is a matter of demographic discrimination, which is a diversity-related issue. This could explain why inclusive leadership (i.e., leader–member exchange) appears to be more important when groups are more demographically heterogeneous (Nishii & Mayer, 2009; Stewart & Johnson, 2009).

Valuation of Different Ideas, Opinions, and Perspectives

In the previous section, we focused on reactions and responses to ideas based on who contributes them, with the point being that people in organizations with more inclusive diversity climates will be more open to ideas from everyone and, therefore, less likely to be seen as more supportive of one group of employees than another. In this section, we extend that notion to consider the diversity of the ideas themselves. A key component of a firm's diversity climate involves employees' perceptions of how those in the organization respond to divergent viewpoints (Pugh, Dietz, Brief, & Wiley, 2008; McKay et al., 2009). However, there is often a tendency in organizations to resist the introduction of diverse viewpoints (Thomas & Plaut, 2008). Employees become accustomed to the dominant perspective and view any opinion that differs from it with skepticism and even contempt. As Bowen and Blackmon (2003) noted, this can lead to a "spiral of silence" (p. 1393) wherein individuals become reluctant to speak up if they do not believe their positions are supported sufficiently by others. This process becomes self-reinforcing in that the number of people afraid to dissent from the dominant perspective continues to grow and the prevailing viewpoint remains unfettered by any challenges from holders of divergent viewpoints.

One of the chief reasons organizations claim that they seek diversity is to harness a broader range of perspectives (Cox, 1994; Robinson & Dechant, 1997). It is, therefore, counterintuitive that a company would invest the considerable resources often required to attain a diverse workforce only to expect everyone to think similarly. This inherent contradiction produces a mixed message of sorts (Avery & Johnson, 2008) for employees who probably were led to believe that they were hired to contribute uniqueness, but now essentially are prevented from doing so. Thus, a climate that does not tolerate diverging viewpoints is unlikely to be received well by a diverse group of employees.

Although not many studies have established a link, there is some empirical evidence to support the prediction that diverse groups of employees expect openness to different ideas. For instance, Phillips and Loyd (2006) conducted a study involving three-person groups that varied in their composition. Among their key findings was that groups higher in demographic diversity were more tolerant and accepting of divergent viewpoints than more homogenous groups. In light of that finding, it is not surprising that members of diverse groups also tended to be more confident about voicing dissenting opinions and expressed a greater number of these perspectives than those surrounded by similar others (i.e., groups with low diversity). Admittedly, the authors did not directly assess individuals' expectations of support for voicing divergent viewpoints. Nevertheless, it seems clear from their results that employees working in diverse settings tend to expect such support and may perceive it as a key indicator of how much their employers support them in general.

Due to the growing importance of employee openness to divergent viewpoints, employers are prone to attach greater value to employees being flexible and open-minded. Such tolerance and inclusiveness may be expected to facilitate organizational effectiveness, as coworker and supervisor support for creativity have proven to be important contextual predictors of employees' creative expression (Shalley, Zhou, & Oldham, 2004). Further bolstering this point, a recent meta-analytic study (Byron, Khazanchi, & Nazarian, 2010) showed that social-evaluative threats (i.e., when a person's creative self-identity can be jeopardized) have a curvilinear relationship with creative performance, suggesting that extremely high (or low) exposure to evaluative stress can stifle creativity. Research also has shown dissenting opinions to be significantly more likely to result in innovation if there is a climate that supports employee participation (De Dreu & West, 2001). Thus, although employers may expect employees to be receptive to new and/or divergent ideas and opinions, it is also imperative for organizations to foster work climates in which such viewpoints are encouraged and valued.

Elimination of Bias and Discrimination

It goes without saying that workers expect their employers to treat them equitably and minimize the presence of any bias or discrimination. What is particularly interesting about this diversity-related expectancy, however, is that it is arguably the only one that may be equally important to employees of all demographic backgrounds. In the United States, it is common to think of issues of equal employment opportunity as women or minority issues (Thomas, 2004). Nonetheless, it is vital to recognize that racioethnic majority members also, at times, perceive themselves to be victims of discrimination. In fact, although Black and Hispanic Americans are significantly more likely than White counterparts to report having perceived discrimination (Avery et al., 2008), it is noteworthy that White Americans were responsible for 9% of race discrimination charges filed with the equal employment opportunity commission in 2005 (n = 2,512; Goldman, Gutek, Stein, & Lewis, 2006).

There are clear moral and legal arguments regarding why organizations should work to eliminate bias and discrimination. Chief among them are that it is unethical and potentially quite costly to engage in inequitable employment practices (Demuijnck, 2009; James & Wooten, 2006). It can also induce negative work attitudes among employees who experience or witness it, which can subsequently lead to work inefficiencies (Goldman et al., 2006). Although these residual effects of bias and discrimination may be directly related to organizational productivity and profitability, we posit that the firm-level consequences of unequal treatment may also operate through perceptions of inequitable organizational support.

Human resource management practices that are biased against members of a particular group suggest that transactional exchanges between individuals belonging to that group and the organization are inequitable. Further, indicators of institutional bias can send strong signals to personnel about what is (and is not) valued in the organization. As employees interpret these signals as well as transactional exchanges across the organization, they may manifest behavior consistent with these biases, such as engaging in discriminatory acts against devalued groups (Petersen & Dietz, 2008). This process helps to explain the moderate correlations (mean $r = 0.44$) reported between perceived discrimination attributed to supervisors, coworkers, and the organization as a whole (Ensher, Grant-Vallone, & Donaldson, 2001). Because members of devalued groups can become targets for mistreatment, relational exchanges between these employees and others in the organization also may suffer. Accordingly, those perceiving discrimination are less likely to perceive comparable levels of organizational support relative to those who are not.

Although employees expect their employers to provide a work environment free from discrimination, firms are likely to expect employees to support these efforts. Organizations do not make decisions, people do. This means that discrimination attributed to the employer is a function of bias exhibited by a person or group of people within the company. Those in charge can and should take efforts to ensure that the impact of bias in their decision making is minimal. In conjunction with this directive, they also may expect employees not to engage in discriminatory behavior against one another (e.g., racioethnic harassment or bullying) that might subject the company to legal action or otherwise detract from organizational performance. Overall, employers are likely to support employees who treat one another respectfully and conduct themselves ethically in their dealings, as not doing so may make organizations vulnerable to a number of operational and legal issues.

Support/Understanding of Unique Minority Issues

Language Policies

In most workplaces, there is a dominant language spoken by the overwhelming majority of employees during work hours. From the organization's perspective, having a common language helps to ensure that all personnel are able to communicate with one another. Supervisors can delegate assignments to their subordinates with the certainty that their messages (at least the literal meaning of them) are understood. Additionally, employees can be held accountable for coordinating with their coworkers because management can assume that the common language provides a channel through which communication may occur. As Tange and Lauring (2009) recently put it, "the introduction of a company language has proved helpful to internal and external communication since it provides a common medium for all members of the organisation and offers easy access to official information channels such as company reports or employee magazines" (p. 219). Consequently, many firms deem it a business necessity to have members of their workforce speak the same language while at work.

Although one can see the business rationale for such an approach, restricting the language of employees can have unexpected consequences. For example, employees may be more proficient at communicating in a language other than the one stipulated. In such an instance, the organization's insistence upon restricting business communication to a dominant language could prevent some of its employees from contributing at their fullest potential. As a result, the organization is unable to fully utilize its human capital, which has negative implications for its bottom line (Tange & Lauring, 2009; Teboul & Speicher, 2007). Beyond creating work inefficiencies, attempts to regulate language in the workplace may also be perceived as unsupportive of multilingual employees. Imagine that you speak four languages and are hired by a company that purports to value workforce diversity, but now find yourself restricted to speaking one language when at work. How do you think you would feel about being limited in such a manner? Research indicates individuals in this position commonly experience negative feelings (Blank & Slipp, 1994; Dietz & Pugh, 2004; Teboul & Speicher, 2007). These feelings could be extreme enough to precipitate perceived organizational obstruction by an employee, or a "belief that the organization obstructs, hinders or interferes with the accomplishment of his or her goals and is a detriment to his or her well-being" (Gibney, Zagenczyk, & Masters, 2009, p. 667). Specifically, the employees are apt to question why their skills are being underutilized and wonder why they are subject to potential sanction (i.e., disciplinary action) for speaking another language while their monolingual counterparts are not. They also view such policies as stigmatizing multilingual employees by formally assigning greater value to the chosen language (and those to whom it is native) than to restricted languages (and those to whom these tongues may be native; Aguirre, 2003) and feel unnecessarily limited by these policies, which may encroach on their opportunities for success within the organization.

Mentors

Mentoring is the process of pairing two individuals together for the purpose of one person (i.e., the mentor) helping the other (i.e., the protégé) to learn how to function effectively in the workplace (Kram, 1985). More specifically, mentors provide psychosocial and career-related support that assists protégés in cultivating the skills necessary for career success.

Despite these benefits, research has highlighted a tendency for mentors to select demographically similar protégés, which often makes it difficult for minorities and women to find mentors in organizational settings (e.g., Kilian, Hukai, & McCarty, 2005). Given that mentoring has been shown to be especially relevant to the career success of female and minority employees (Metz, 2009; Thomas, 2001), this unavailability of mentors may obviously hinder their career development. However, we speculate that a lack of mentoring also may be perceived as a lack of organizational support or, worse yet, an organizational obstruction.

Because employees often view developmental relationships as a prerequisite for success, an absence of such a relationship may lead them to feel neglected or unsupported by their employer. This indicates that POS may help to explain why the failure to provide mentoring diminishes job satisfaction and organizational commitment and increases the propensity to turnover (Baranik, Roling, & Eby, 2010; Payne & Huffman, 2005; Ragins, Cotton, & Miller, 2000). Interestingly, supervisors appear cognizant of the importance of mentoring to their subordinates. In fact, research suggests that supervisors will often respond to perceived contract breaches among their subordinates by withholding mentoring (Chen, Tsui, & Zhong, 2008).

Despite considerable variability in individuals' willingness to mentor (Allen, 2003), employers currently expect their more senior personnel to mentor their more junior colleagues. This expectation is almost certain to continue, but its scope can be expected to broaden somewhat. Whereas it may have been acceptable in the past for employees to provide tutelage only to demographically similar protégés, doing so contributes to "homosocial reproduction" (Kanter, 1977, p. 54) and restricts the career development of female and minority employees. Further, as workforces become more diverse in terms of gender and race/ethnicity, the lack of access to mentors for women and ethnic minorities is likely to exacerbate feelings of deprivation where POS is concerned. Consequently, companies will need managers and employees to be open to forming diverse mentoring parings. In addition to a willingness to serve as a mentor to women and minority employees, employers will expect them to provide the support needed to nurture career success. Although such willingness may be difficult to obtain, research suggests that an organization's commitment to diversity mitigates the reluctance to mentor across racioethnic groups (Thomas, 1999). Therefore, the provision of diversified mentoring may be a key signal to minority employees that they are supported by their employer.

RESEARCH IMPLICATIONS

Several research implications follow from our proposed link between racioethnic diversity and POS. Primarily, further study is necessary to better establish the nomological network of the implicit diversity-related cues that minority (but perhaps not majority) employees use as indicators of the firm's level of support for them. Some likely variables include diversity recruitment, organizational demography, and a firm's human resource practices. For example, research on diversity recruitment has indicated that target recruits (e.g., minorities) commonly make inferences about a firm's support of diversity based on (a) the representation of minority personnel in general and in higher level positions (Avery, 2003; Avery, Hernandez, & Hebl, 2004), (b) endorsement of identity-conscious human resource policies (Highhouse, Stierwalt, Bachiochi, Elder, & Fisher, 1999), and (c) the use of recruiters from underrepresented groups (Avery & McKay, 2006; Rynes, Bretz, & Gerhart, 1991). Accordingly, a fruitful addition to such research work would be to examine how the use of such tactics affects job seekers' impressions of anticipated organizational support (i.e., "perceptions of how much applicants expected they would be valued and cared about by the organization if they became employees"; Casper & Buffardi, 2004, p. 394). Because scholars have also theorized that the recruits' initial views of a firm's diversity climate will be confirmed (or disconfirmed) during visits to company premises during later recruitment stages (McKay & Avery, 2006) and initial employment (McKay & Avery, 2005), research is also needed to explore potential changes in implied diversity promises as job seekers move through the selection process.

Organizational research should examine the individual- and firm-level outcomes associated with diversity cues. An immediate outcome of inferences drawn from these cues would seem to be diversity climate and, more distally, POS, job performance, and withdrawal. According to McKay et al. (2009), prodiversity climates are work settings wherein employees have equal opportunity to succeed, and those from underrepresented groups (e.g., racioethnic minorities) are integrated into the social fabric of the organization. Cox (1994) indicated that such climates are likely when there is higher minority representation (especially in high-level positions), a lack of intergroup conflict, and fair human resource policies. Logically, these features are likely to precipitate employee perceptions that their initial diversity expectations are consistent with their subsequent organizational experiences. Consequently, minority employees should perceive comparable levels of support as their majority peers, resulting in smaller differences in satisfaction, productivity, and likelihood to remain with the organization. Cox (1994) further proposes that prodiversity climates should lead to enhanced work attitudes and job performance and enhanced first-level (i.e., attendance, turnover, and work quality) and second-level (i.e., market share, profitability, and achievement of formal organizational goals) outcomes across racioethnic groups. Thus, the fulfillment of implied diversity-related obligations is likely to be related to both (a) smaller demographic differences in individual employee outcomes, and (b) improved organizational performance in general.

Another direction for research in this area is the identification of boundary conditions to the proposed linkages. Because the U.S. workforce is becoming increasingly diverse (Toossi, 2006), it is important to investigate the extent of between-group differences in reactions to diversity-related promises. Recent diversity climate research has revealed that racioethnic minorities are more responsive to the nature of a business unit's diversity climate in regard to job performance (McKay, Avery, & Morris, 2008), absenteeism (Avery, McKay, Wilson, & Tonidandel, 2007), and retention (McKay et al., 2007). Similar work should be extended to the diversity promises construct in regard to women (Gutek, Cohen, & Tsui, 1996), older workers (Redman & Snape, 2007), immigrants (Esses, Dietz, & Bhardway, 2006), sexual minorities (Ragins & Cornwell, 2001), and the disabled (Schur, Kruse, Blasi, & Blanck, 2009). Because firms' diversity cues may be particularly salient to members of these groups, understanding potential differences between their POS and those of the demographic majority could prove insightful.

One boundary condition in particular could be the national or cultural context in which the organizations of interest are embedded. Although racial diversity is relatively limited in many non-U.S. settings, there is considerable ethnic diversity that serves as a powerful basis for social classification and identification. In such scenarios, the pattern of minority–majority differences in POS described here could well apply. That said, there are certainly other dynamics that may be particular to specific settings. For instance, minority–majority differences are likely to be (a) more pronounced in contexts with more extensive histories of intergroup tensions, and (b) less pronounced when there is extensive legislation forbidding racioethnic discrimination. Moreover, in highly collectivist societies, it is possible that organizational membership serves as the superordinate group identity, thereby diminishing the salience and importance of demographic markers. This would reduce the likelihood of detecting any racioethnic differences in POS.

A final research implication is that both the diversity and EOR literatures could stand to benefit from greater integration of the other. Much of the diversity literature focuses on how individuals and organizations respond to increasing diversity in the form of attitudes such as satisfaction and outcomes such as performance. These studies pay considerably less attention to how diversity influences employees' relationships with the organization (other than organizational commitment and turnover). It would be interesting to see research explicitly linking changes in organizational or workgroup composition to EOR constructs such as psychological contract perceptions, POS, and perceived organizational obstruction. Moreover, diversity management practitioners would stand to benefit even more considerably if researchers were to identify prospective situational moderators of those relationships (e.g., diversity climate). From the EOR perspective, it is disappointing to see demographics such as racioethnicity play such a small role in the literature despite reason to anticipate the existence of differences along these dimensions (Coyle-Shapiro & Shore, 2007). We encourage EOR researchers to consider using demographics, demographic dissimilarity, and demographic diversity as prospective moderators of the relationships they study to determine their applicability to today's ever-diversifying workplaces.

MANAGERIAL IMPLICATIONS

There are also a number of practical implications stemming from the link between diversity and POS. On the whole, POS has been associated with positive individual outcomes, such as heightened employee attitudes, performance (in- and extra-role), and retention (Rhoades & Eisenberger, 2002). Consequently, managers would be well served by understanding and attempting to maximize (minimize) the positive (negative) antecedents of employees' perceptions of organizational support, and subsequently improve human resource management. However, because these variables may differ across demographic groups, an accommodative as opposed to assimilative focus may be critical to managing diversity in organizations. For current employees, assessing the degree to which the organization embraces diversity promises can provide insight into whether employee interests are being supported. Further, such information may allow organizations to create initiatives and programs for maintaining inclusive climates in which all employees are treated equally and feel that their viewpoints are encouraged and valued (Shore et al., 2011). Thus, understanding whether the organization is upholding its obligation to support all its employees may help to strengthen employee engagement and retention (Harter, Schmidt, & Hayes, 2002).

For potential employees, querying them about their expectations of employers, diversity-related perceptions of their respective organizations, and anticipated organizational support may provide insight into the diversity-related elements of their relationship with the company should they secure employment there. Consequently, organizations may be able to design recruiting communications tailored to the needs and expectations of specific demographic groups, which may be useful for increasing the diversity of recruitment pools (Highhouse et al., 1999). In addition, by better matching what they can offer employees with the expectations of potential employees, organizations may be able to improve their staffing yield ratios, which may ultimately improve workforce diversity as well.

From a talent management perspective, an understanding of the link between diversity and POS may help employers to identify and manage their expectations of employees. Because increased workforce diversity may bring about changes to the nature of work in many organizations, recognizing what are considered to be employees' obligations may be important for managing their human capital. For example, by identifying the need for employees to value diversity and interact effectively with dissimilar others, employers may be able to look for these characteristics in their selection processes and/or find ways to communicate such values in their on-boarding processes (McKay & Davis, 2007). In addition, employers could assess such competencies in the performance evaluation process and provide training to develop these skills among employees (Dahm, Willems, Ivancevich, & Graves, 2009). Overall, understanding these potential changes may assist organizations in understanding how they can best support their employees to help them to fulfill their evolving workplace responsibilities.

CONCLUSION

In this chapter, we sought to illustrate the role of diversity in employees' perceptions of organizational support. Organizations and the individuals they employ cannot afford to ignore how social identity influences perceptions of the work environment (Roberson & Stevens, 2006). If companies are to attract, develop, and retain the best and brightest personnel, they will need to ensure that they anticipate and meet the broad set of needs among today's multicultural workforce. Likewise, if employees are to fulfill their career potential, they will need to maximize their proficiency at working with and serving dissimilar colleagues and clientele. In sum, diversity is introducing new variance in POS, and recognizing and understanding this trend is a necessary step to facilitating effective employee–employer relationships.

REFERENCES

Aguirre, A. (2003). Linguistic diversity in the workforce: Understanding social relations in the workplace. *Sociological Focus, 36*, 65–80.

Allen, T. D. (2003). Mentoring others: A dispositional and motivational approach. *Journal of Vocational Behavior, 62*, 134–154.

Avery, D. R. (2003). Reactions to diversity in recruitment advertising: Are differences Black and White? *Journal of Applied Psychology, 58*, 672–679.

Avery, D. R., Hernandez, M., & Hebl, M. R. (2004). Who's watching the race? Racial salience in recruitment advertising. *Journal of Applied Social Psychology, 34*, 146–161.

Avery, D. R., & Johnson, C. D. (2008). Now you see it, now you don't: Mixed messages regarding workforce diversity. In K. M. Thomas (Ed.), *Diversity resistance in organizations* (pp. 221–248). New York, NY: Erlbaum.

Avery, D. R., & McKay, P. F. (2006). Target practice: An organizational impression management approach to attracting minority and female job applicants. *Personnel Psychology, 59*, 157–187.

Avery, D. R., McKay, P. F., & Wilson, D. C. (2008). What are the odds? How demographic similarity affects the prevalence of perceived employment discrimination. *Journal of Applied Psychology, 93*, 235–249.

Avery, D. R., McKay, P. F., Wilson, D. C, & Tonidandel, S. (2007). Unequal attendance: The relationships between race, organizational diversity cues, and absenteeism. *Personnel Psychology, 60*, 875–902.

Avery, D. R., & Quiñones, M. A. (2002). Disentangling the effects of voice: The incremental roles of opportunity, instrumentality, and behavior in predicting procedural fairness. *Journal of Applied Psychology, 87*, 81–86.

Baranik, L. E., Roling, E. A., & Eby, L. T. (2010). Why does mentoring work? The role of perceived organizational support. *Journal of Vocational Behavior, 76*, 366–373.

Bell, M. P. (2007). *Diversity in organizations.* Mason, OH: Thomson-South-Western.

Berger, J., Rosenholtz, S. J., & Zelditch, M. (1980). Status organizing processes. *Annual Review of Sociology, 6,* 479–508.

Blank, R., & Slipp, S. (1994). *Voices of diversity.* New York, NY: AMACOM.

Bowen, F., & Blackmon, K. (2003). Spirals of silence: The dynamic effects of diversity on organizational voice. *Journal of Management Studies, 40,* 1393–1417.

Bunderson, J. S. (2003). Recognizing and utilizing expertise in work groups: A status characteristics perspective. *Administrative Science Quarterly, 48,* 557–591.

Buttner, E. H., Lowe, K. B., & Billings-Harris, L. (2010). The impact of diversity promise fulfillment on professionals of color outcomes in the USA. *Journal of Business Ethics, 91,* 501–518.

Byron, K., Khazanchi, S., & Nazarian, D. (2010). The relationship between stressors and creativity: A meta-analysis examining competing theoretical models. *Journal of Applied Psychology, 95,* 201–212.

Camarota, S. A. (2005). *Immigrants at mid-decade: A snapshot of America's foreign-born population in 2005.* Retrieved July 20, 2008, from http://www.cis.org/articles/2005/back1405.pdf.

Casper, W. J., & Buffardi, L. C. (2004). Work-life benefits and job pursuit intentions: The role of anticipated organizational support. *Journal of Vocational Behavior, 65,* 391–410.

Chattopadhyay, P. (1999). Beyond direct and symmetrical effects: The influence of demographic dissimilarity on organizational citizenship behavior. *Academy of Management Journal, 42,* 273–287.

Chen, Z. X., Tsui, A. S., & Zhong, L. (2008). Reactions to psychological contract breach: A dual perspective. *Journal of Organizational Behavior, 29,* 527–548.

Chrobot-Mason, D. L. (2003). Keeping the promise: Psychological contract violations for minority employees. *Journal of Managerial Psychology, 18,* 22–45.

Cohen, E. G. (1982). Expectation states and interracial interaction in school settings. *Annual Review of Sociology, 8,* 209–235.

Colquitt, J. A., Greenberg, J., & Zapata-Phelan, C. P. (2005). What is organizational justice? A historical overview. In J. Greenberg & J. A. Colquitt (Eds.), *Handbook of organizational justice* (pp. 3–56). Mahwah, NJ: Erlbaum.

Cox, T., Jr. (1994). *Cultural diversity in organizations: Theory, research, & practice.* San Francisco, CA: Berrett-Koehler.

Coyle-Shapiro, J. A-M., & Shore, L. M. (2007). The employee-organization relationship: Where do we go from here? *Human Resource Management Review, 17,* 166–179.

Dahm, M. J., Willems, E. P., Ivancevich, J. M., & Graves, D. E. (2009). Development of an Organizational Diversity Needs Analysis (ODNA) instrument. *Journal of Applied Social Psychology, 39,* 283–318.

De Dreu, C. K. W., & West, M. A. (2001). Minority dissent and team innovation: The importance of participation in decision making. *Journal of Applied Psychology, 86,* 1191–1201.

Demuijnck, G. (2009). Non-discrimination in human resources management as a moral obligation. *Journal of Business Ethics, 88,* 83–101.

Dietz, J., & Pugh, S. (2004). I say tomato, you say domate: Differential reactions to English-only workplace policies by persons from immigrant and non-immigrant families. *Journal of Business Ethics, 52,* 365–379.

Eisenberger, R., Huntington, R., Hutchison, S., & Sowa, D. (1986). Perceived organizational support. *Journal of Applied Psychology, 71,* 500–507.

Elsass, P. M., & Graves, L. M. (1997). Demographic diversity in decision-making groups: The experiences of women and people of color. *Academy of Management Review, 22*, 946–973.

Ely, R. J., & Thomas, D. A. (2001). Cultural diversity at work: The effects of diversity perspectives on work group processes and outcomes. *Administrative Science Quarterly, 46*, 229–273.

Ensher, E. A., Grant-Vallone, E. J., & Donaldson, S. I. (2001). Effects of perceived discrimination on job satisfaction, organizational commitment, organizational citizenship behavior, and grievances. *Human Resource Development Quarterly, 12*, 53–72.

Esses, V. M., Dietz, J., & Bhardway, A. (2006). The role of prejudice in the discounting of immigrant skills. In R. Mahalingham (Ed.), *Cultural psychology of immigrants* (pp. 113–130). Mahwah, NJ: Lawrence Erlbaum Associates.

Gibney, R., Zagenczyk, T. J., & Masters, M. F. (2009). The negative aspects of social exchange: An introduction to perceived organizational obstruction. *Group and Organization Management, 34*, 665–697.

Goldman, B. M., Gutek, B. A., Stein, J. H., & Lewis, K. (2006). Employment discrimination in organizations: Antecedents and consequences. *Journal of Management, 32*, 786–830.

Gutek, B. A., Cohen, A. G., & Tsui, A. (1996). Reactions to perceived sex discrimination. *Human Relations, 49*, 791–813.

Harrison, D. A., & Klein, K. J. (2007). What's the difference? Diversity constructs as separation, variety, or disparity in organizations. *Academy of Management Review, 32*, 1199–1228.

Harter, J. K., Schmidt, F. L., & Hayes, T. L. (2002). Business-unit-level relationship between employee satisfaction, employee engagement, and business outcomes: A meta-analysis. *Journal of Applied Psychology, 87*, 268–279.

Highhouse, S., Stierwalt, S. L., Bachiochi, P., Elder, A. E., & Fisher, G. (1999). Effects of advertised human resource management practices on attraction of African American applicants. *Personnel Psychology, 52*, 425–442.

Homan, A. C., Hollenbeck, J. R., Humphrey, S. E., van Knippenberg, D., Ilgen, D. R., & van Kleef, G. A. (2008). Facing differences with an open mind: Openness to experience, salience of intragroup differences, and performance of diverse work groups. *Academy of Management Journal, 51*, 1204–1222.

Homan, A. C., van Knippenberg, D., van Kleef, G. A., & De Dreu, C. K. W. (2007). Bridging faultlines by valuing diversity: Diversity beliefs, information elaboration, and performance in diverse work groups. *Journal of Applied Psychology, 92*, 1189–1199.

James, E. H., & Wooten, L. P. (2006). Diversity crisis: How firms manage discrimination lawsuits. *Academy of Management Journal, 49*, 1103–1118.

Joplin, J. R. W., & Daus, C. S. (1997). Challenges of leading a diverse workforce. *Academy of Management Executive, 11*, 21–31.

Kanter, R. M. (1977). *Men and women of the corporation*. New York, NY: Basic Books.

Kearney, E., Gebert, D., & Voelpel, S. C. (2009). When and how diversity benefits teams: The importance of team members' need for cognition. *Academy of Management Journal, 52*, 581–598.

Kilian, C. M., Hukai, D., & McCarty, C. E. (2005). Building diversity in the pipeline to corporate leadership. *Journal of Management Development, 24*, 155–168.

King, E. B., Hebl, M. R., & Beal, D. J. (2009). Conflict and cooperation in diverse workgroups. *Journal of Social Issues, 65*, 261–285.

Kram, K. E. (1985). *Mentoring at work: Developmental relationships in organizational life.* Glenview, IL: Scott, Foresman & Co.

Leonard, J., & Levine, D. (2006). The effect of diversity on turnover: A large case study. *Industrial & Labor Relations Review, 59*, 547–572.

Leveson, L., Joiner, T. A., & Bakalis, S. (2009). Managing cultural diversity and perceived organizational support: Evidence from Australia. *International Journal of Manpower, 30*, 377–392.

MacGillivray, E. D., Beecher, H. J. M., & Golden, D. (2008). Legal developments: Global diversity and developments impacting workforce management in Asia. *Global Business and Organizational Excellence, 27*, 65–76.

McKay, P. F., & Avery, D. R. (2005). Warning! Diversity recruitment could backfire. *Journal of Management Inquiry, 14*, 330–336.

McKay, P. F., & Avery, D. R. (2006). What has race got to do with it? Unraveling the role of racioethnicity in job seekers' reactions to site visits. *Personnel Psychology, 59*, 395–429.

McKay, P. F., Avery, D. R., & Morris, M. A. (2008). Mean racial-ethnic differences in work performance: The moderating role of diversity climate. *Personnel Psychology, 61*, 349–374.

McKay, P. F., Avery, D. R., & Morris, M. A. (2009). A tale of two climates: Diversity climate from subordinates' and managers' perspectives and their role in store unit sales performance. *Personnel Psychology, 62*, 767–791.

McKay, P. F., Avery, D. R., Tonidandel, S., Morris, M. A., Hernandez, M., & Hebl, M. (2007). Racial differences in employee retention: Are diversity climate perceptions the key? *Personnel Psychology, 60*, 35–62.

McKay, P. F., & Davis, J. L. (2007). Traditional selection methods as resistance to diversity in organizations. In K. M. Thomas (Ed.), *Diversity resistance in organizations: Manifestations and solutions* (pp. 151–174). Boca Raton, FL: Taylor & Francis.

Metz, I. (2009). Organisational factors, social factors, and women's advancement. *Applied Psychology: An International Review, 58*, 193–213.

Ng, T. W. H., & Sorensen, K. L. (2008). Toward a further understanding of the relationships between perceptions of support and work attitudes: A meta-analysis. *Group and Organization Management, 33*, 243–268.

Nishii, L. H., & Mayer, D. M. (2009). Do inclusive leaders help to reduce turnover in diverse groups? The moderating role of leader-member exchange in the diversity to turnover relationship. *Journal of Applied Psychology, 94*, 1412–1426.

Payne, S. C., & Huffman, A. H. (2005). A longitudinal examination of the influence of mentoring on organizational commitment and turnover. *Academy of Management Journal, 48*, 158–168.

Pelled, L. H., Eisenhardt, K. M., & Xin, K. R. (1999). Exploring the black box: An analysis of work group diversity, conflict, and performance. *Administrative Science Quarterly, 44*, 1–28.

Petersen, L., & Dietz, J. (2008). Employment discrimination: Authority figures' demographic preferences and followers' affective organizational commitment. *Journal of Applied Psychology, 93*, 1287–1300.

Phillips, K. W., & Loyd, D. L. (2006). When surface and deep-level diversity collide: The effects on dissenting group members. *Organizational Behavior and Human Decision Processes, 99*, 143–160.

Pugh, S. D., Dietz, J., Brief, A. P., & Wiley, J. W. (2008). Looking inside and out: The impact of employee and community demographic composition on organizational diversity climate. *Journal of Applied Psychology, 93*, 1422–1428.

Ragins, B. R., & Cornwell, J. M. (2001). Pink triangles: Antecedents and consequences of perceived workplace discrimination against gay and lesbian employees. *Journal of Applied Psychology, 86*, 1244–1261.

Ragins, B. R., Cotton, J. L., & Miller, J. S. (2000). Marginal mentoring: The effects of type of mentor, quality of relationship, and program design on work and career attitudes. *Academy of Management Journal, 43*, 1177–1194.

Redman, T., & Snape, E. (2006). The consequences of perceived age discrimination amongst older officers: Is social support a buffer. *British Journal of Management, 17*, 167–175.

Rhoades, L., & Eisenberger, R. (2002). Perceived organizational support: A review of the literature. *Journal of Applied Psychology, 87*, 698–714.

Ridgeway, C. L. (1991). The social construction of status value: Gender and other nominal characteristics. *Social Forces, 70*, 367–386.

Riggle, R. J., Edmondson, D. R., & Hansen, J. D. (2009). A meta-analysis of the relationships between perceived organizational support and job outcomes: 20 years of research. *Journal of Business Research, 62*, 1027–1030.

Roberson, Q. M., & Stevens, C. K. (2006). Making sense of diversity in the workplace: Organizational justice and language abstraction in employees' accounts of diversity-related incidents. *Journal of Applied Psychology, 91*, 379–391.

Robinson, G., & Dechant, K. (1997). Building a business case for diversity. *Academy of Management Executive, 11*, 21–31.

Rynes, S. L., Bretz, R. D., & Gerhart, B. (1991). The importance of recruitment in job choice: A different way of looking. *Personnel Psychology, 44*, 487–521.

Schur, L., Kruse, D., Blasi, J., & Blanck, P. (2009). Is disability disabling in all workplaces? Workplace disparities and corporate culture. *Industrial Relations, 48*, 381–410.

Shalley, C. E., Zhou, J., & Oldham, G. R. (2004). The effects of personal and contextual characteristics on creativity: Where should we go from here? *Journal of Management, 30*, 933–958.

Shapiro, D. (1993). Reconciling theoretical differences among procedural justice research by re-evaluating what it means to have one's views considered: Implications for third party managers. In R. Cropanzano (Ed.), *Justice in the workplace: Approaching fairness in human resource management* (pp. 51–78). Hillsdale, NJ: Erlbaum.

Shore, L. M., Randel, A. E., Chung, B. G., Dean, M. A., Ehrhart, K. H., & Singh, G. (2011). Inclusion and diversity in work groups: A review and model for future research. *Journal of Management, 37*, 1262–1289.

Singh, V., & Point, S. (2004). Strategic responses to the human resource diversity challenge: An on-line European top company comparison. *Long Range Planning, 37*, 295–318.

Stewart, M. M., & Johnson, O. E. (2009). Leader-member exchange as a moderator of the relationship between work group diversity and team performance. *Group and Organization Management, 34*, 507–535.

Stoll, M. A., Holzer, H. J., & Ihlanfeldt, K. R. (2000). Within cities and suburbs: Racial residential concentration and the spatial distribution of employment opportunities across sub-metropolitan areas. *Journal of Policy Analysis and Management, 19*, 207–231.

Tajfel, H., & Turner, J. C. (1986). The social identity theory of intergroup behavior. In S. Worchel & W. G. Austin (Eds.), *Psychology of intergroup relations* (2nd ed., pp. 7–24). Chicago, IL: Nelson-Hall.

Tange, H., & Lauring, J. (2009). Language management and social interaction within the multilingual workplace. *Journal of Communication Management, 13*, 218–232.

Teboul, J. B., & Speicher, B. L. (2007). Regulating 'foreign' language in the workplace: From myths to best practices. *International Journal of Diversity in Organisations, Communities and Nations, 7*, 169–180.

Thomas, D. A. (1999). Beyond simple demography–power hypothesis: How Blacks in power influence White-mentor–Black-protégé developmental relationships. In A. J. Murrell, F. J. Crosby, & R. J. Ely (Eds.), *Mentoring dilemmas: Developmental relationships within multicultural organizations* (pp. 157–170). New York, NY: Lawrence Erlbaum Associates.

Thomas, D. A. (2001). The truth about mentoring minorities: Race matters. *Harvard Business Review, 79*, 98–107.

Thomas, D. A. (2004). Diversity as strategy. *Harvard Business Review, 79*, 98–107.

Thomas, K. M., & Plaut, V. C. (2008). The many faces of diversity resistance in the workplace. In K. M. Thomas (Ed.), *Diversity resistance in organizations* (pp. 1–22). New York, NY: Erlbaum.

Toossi, M. (2006). A new look at long-term labor force projections to 2050. *Monthly Labor Review, 129*, 19–39.

Tsui, A. S., Egan, T. D., & O'Reilly, C. A. III. (1992). Being different: Relational demography and organizational attachment. *Administrative Science Quarterly, 37*, 549–579.

van Knippenberg, D., & Schippers, M. C. (2007). Work group diversity. *Annual Review of Psychology, 58*, 515–541.

20

Why Work Teams Fail in Organizations: Myths and Advice

Eduardo Salas and Stephen M. Fiore
University of Central Florida

The world of work is rapidly changing. The signs of this change are increasingly evident: Work is global and diverse; the workforce is aging; the tasks and processes are technology driven; employees are organized to foster collaboration and teamwork; modern successes require fast learning and adaptation. Given this shift in how organizations function, employee–organization relationships (EORs) matter now more than ever. The mutual dependency that exists among these entities ensures organizational viability and survival so long as this relationship is positive. To this end, some organizations create and manage work teams as a strategy to strengthen the EOR. Work teams have become a way of life in many organizations.

Indeed, promoting teamwork has become a national obsession in both the public and private sectors. Teams are assigned to tasks ranging from those with life-and-death stakes at play to those with decisions affecting thousands of people. Teams are composed and (over) applied at ever increasing rates in organizations. In settings as varied as hospitals (e.g., surgical and emergency teams), corporate boardrooms (e.g., top management teams), airlines (e.g., flight teams), oil rigs (e.g., off-shore and on-shore teams), military operations (e.g., reconstruction teams), and financial entrepreneurs (e.g., research analysts), teams are an overarching mechanism underlying organizational effectiveness. Teams are the agents that work to minimize errors, save lives, and improve livelihoods, and we will argue that the EOR is at the center of this. That is, teams are embedded in organizations and, therefore, influenced by what organizations value and promote. At the end of the day, it is the EOR that will make or break teamwork. Note that by the EOR we mean a form of intraorganizational relationship that is perceptual in nature. We are not specifically envisioning a more formal or contractual relationship. However, we do acknowledge that some organizations do formally implement team-based projects and/or management. As such, there may be a distal connection to a more formal type of EOR.

Given the proliferation of teams in industry, it is gratifying to see the scientific community working to ensure that teams are effective. Concomitant with the growth of teams in industry is research into the science of teamwork. Over the past two decades, the scientific community has generated a wealth of information about teams. We now know about what influences teamwork, how to measure teamwork, how to track teamwork, and what effective teams do (and how they do it). From this, organizations continually assume that teams are serving them well. But how do they know this? Do organizations understand how teams work, how to make them work well, and how to know if they are succeeding? We suggest that, despite the wealth of knowledge about work teams, there are a number of myths and misconceptions about the power of teamwork and that these hinder effective EOR. Following Shore et al. (2004), we define the EOR as "an overarching term to describe the relationship between the employee and the organization" (p. 292). As an umbrella term, this encompasses both micro- and macro-level factors. In this chapter, we emphasize how meso-level factors (specifically, teamwork) can impact the EOR. Developing organizational structures (cf. Grunig, 1992) based on teamwork can provide an important environment for empowering employees (e.g., decentralizing decision making; product/service ownership). Further, within teams, employees are more likely to see the type of symmetrical communications that are argued to support employee satisfaction (Grunig, Grunig, & Dozier, 2002). With this as our stepping off point, in this chapter, we will outline a set of myths about teamwork, discuss why they exist, and detail the realities of teams. First, we will highlight the many theories that guide teamwork research, extracting the main themes that emerge from this body. Next, we will discuss the myths that keep teams from reaching their potential in organizations (Table 20.1). Finally, we will discuss how organizations can foster effective teamwork and work to counter these myths.

TEAMWORK, TEAM THEORIES, AND THE EOR

Teams and teamwork have been extensively studied by the psychology and management research communities. For the most part, the field now agrees on

TABLE 20.1

Best Practices for Training and Supporting Teamwork in Organizations

Best Practice	Area	Relationship	Source
The team to be trained should possess collective efficacy, collective orientation, and positive attitudes toward teamwork.	Teamwork Training	E-T	Holton & Baldwin, 2003
Team training should be relevant, be demonstrative, involve practice, and have feedback.	Teamwork Training	E-T	Cannon-Bowers & Bowers, 2011
The most empirically effective teamwork training interventions are team self-correction training, team coordination and adaptation training, and generic teamwork skills training.	Teamwork Training	E-T	Cannon-Bowers & Bowers, 2011
The organization should periodically "refresh" team training.	Teamwork Training	T-O	Holton & Baldwin, 2003
Organizations should train teamwork KSAs as part of their internal development.	Teamwork Training	E-T	Stevens & Campion, 1994
The organization should encourage a climate of teamwork.	Organizational Policy	T-O	Holton & Baldwin, 2003
Goals for tasks assigned to teams should be phrased in terms of the team.	Organizational Policy	T-O	Holton & Baldwin, 2003
Performance appraisals should emphasize teamwork and collective achievement.	Organizational Policy	T-O	Holton & Baldwin, 2003
Promotion criteria should consider opportunities to develop teamwork skills.	Compensation/ Advancement	E-O	Stevens & Campion, 1994
Teamwork ability should be considered in advancement decisions.	Compensation/ Advancement	E-O	Stevens & Campion, 1994
Compensation should reflect teamwork KSAs	Compensation/ Advancement	E-O	Stevens & Campion, 1994

E-O, employee–organization; E-T, employee–team; KSA, knowledge, skills, attitudes, and abilities; T-O, team–organization.

what teams and teamwork represent. A team is a distinguishable set of two or more people with specific roles or functions to perform who interact dynamically, interdependently, and adaptively in pursuit of a shared goal or outcome, during a limited lifespan of membership (Salas, Dickinson, Converse, & Tannenbaum, 1992). In more simple terms, a team is a group of people who work together toward the same goal while supporting each other. Teamwork, then, is a multidimensional construct that describes how individuals in the team work together. As a rather high-level construct, it is composed of the behavior, attitudes, and cognitions involved in working as part of a team, including mutual monitoring, feedback, back-up behavior, communication, coordination, trust, and planning (Salas, Burke, & Cannon-Bowers, 2000).

Given this definition, it is clear that there is quite a lot to understand about teams. Thankfully, the scientific community has risen to the challenge of illuminating these processes and characteristics. Some of the most fruitful research has been in the area of team mental models. As the EOR is traditionally viewed along the lines of an individual employee's relationship with the organization, team mental model theory provides a potential entry point for conceptualizations of the EOR that consider the employee-team. Team mental model research examines the similarities and differences in how teams conceptualize not only their work and the knowledge they hold and share, but also each other. This line of research is strongly related to team cognition research (Salas & Fiore, 2004), which studies the team almost as though it were an individual itself (e.g., by examining a team's cognitions and behaviors instead of those of the individuals). By studying the communication, coordination, and emergent behaviors of a team, it is possible to characterize the team's performance in depth. Beyond studying how teams work from a cognitive standpoint, a plethora of research has been conducted examining the behaviors teams engage in, the differences between teamwork and taskwork, the relationships between individuals in a team, and the characteristics of a team that lead to successful work. These various research efforts have resulted in a strong core of scientific knowledge on teams. Today, we know what skill dimensions are involved in teamwork (Cannon-Bowers, Tannenbaum, Salas, & Volpe, 1995), the competencies required for effective teamwork (Salas et al., 2000), and have principles for how teams interact successfully (Salas et al., 2000).

Although it is all well and good that the scientific community has produced so much useful knowledge regarding teams, the question for organizations is, "Why do we care?" Naturally, the modern reality of engaging in teamwork necessitates an understanding of teams and teamwork. It is only reasonable that organizations should care about understanding the science of teams for the simple fact that they want their teams to succeed. However, organizations must also integrate this information into their existing knowledge structures and approaches. It is not enough to merely know how teams work. Organizations must transform themselves based on this knowledge. For example, organizations benefit from an understanding of teams when this understanding is integrated into their approach to the EOR. If teams are becoming the primary agents of organizations, then the EOR is no longer simply about the organization and the individual employee. Instead, the "employee" in the EOR can be viewed as the collective of employees—the teams that the organization empowers to accomplish its goals. Essentially, by moving the level of analysis to "teams," we suggest that we can expand how organizational researchers conceptualize the EOR. Indeed, organizational research on EOR has suggested that employees can respond favorably when employers direct them toward group levels of performance (Tsui, Pearce, Porter, & Tripoli, 1997). With this focus, we suggest that it may be possible to examine additional antecedent and consequent factors driving employee satisfaction and organizational performance. Thus, the concept of the EOR must move beyond the employee and the organization and toward a more complex understanding of the employee–team–organization relationship. We suggest that understanding the relationship between employees, teams, and the organization should form the next frontier of EOR research. However, because teams and teamwork are overused concepts in many organizations, we next provide some important insights about them. In particular, to properly work with teams, the organization must consider how it trains, supports, rewards, and otherwise uses teams. Central to a modern understanding of the EOR, then, is an understanding of teams and their relationship to the organization.

THE MYTHS OF TEAMWORK

Unfortunately, despite the considerable scientific knowledge base regarding teams and teamwork, organizations still hold a number of misconceptions about teamwork. These persistent myths continue to plague organizations and impair their ability to effectively harness teams. This, in turn, hinders the development of team-centric EORs—what we have conceptualized as a more meso-level organizational structure. In this context, we suggest that the interconnections within the team moderate the connections to the organization as a whole. In particular, to the degree that teams are allowed to foster a sense of autonomy (e.g., enabled to make decisions) and feel ownership toward their work (e.g., adapt and innovate as they see necessary), their relationship with the organization may improve (e.g., enhanced motivation, greater satisfaction). To support organizations in building their team-centric EOR, we provide an overview of the myths and realities of teamwork.

Myth 1: Organizations Know What Teamwork Is

It is almost ludicrous to ask whether organizations know what teamwork is. Of course organizations know what teamwork is! Teamwork is when you get a group of individuals to work toward the same goal. Except that this really is not the full story. Although this may be a working layperson's definition of teamwork, it actually describes a narrow aspect of the structure that defines a team rather than teamwork. Two or more people working together may be called a team, but the teamwork these individuals use to coordinate their efforts, cooperate over time, and communicate is what determines whether they are good at being a team: "It is equally true that a set of two or more individuals who are expected and required to interact dynamically, interdependently, and adaptively to accomplish their goals but do not are still a team—they are simply an ineffective team" (Stout, Salas, & Fowlkes, 1997, p. 170). So do organizations know what teamwork is? Taking organizations as a whole, the answer is, "not quite."

Although teams are easy to grasp at the most basic level, they are difficult to truly understand. The industrial–organizational psychology literature is full of definitions of what exactly constitutes a team (Salas, Sims, & Burke, 2005). For our purposes, the definition of a team as two or more interdependent individuals striving toward the same goal works well because it encompasses a diverse range of potential team contexts. If we know what a team is, then where does that leave teamwork? As noted earlier, teamwork is a rather complicated construct, encompassing a variety of skills and behaviors. Teamwork includes adaptability, shared situational awareness, performance monitoring and feedback, leadership and management, interpersonal relations, coordination, communication, and decision making (Salas et al., 2000). This multidimensional definition is a far cry from simply "the work that teams do."

Although research has identified what teamwork is, it is not clear that organizations have paid attention to this. Because failure to attend to team "work" can have a cascading effect on other organizational outcomes (e.g., job satisfaction), a team-centric view of the EOR would help the field address how to understand and improve team-based structures. In particular, by emphasizing not just taskwork but also teamwork, organizations may be able to improve the EOR. Examples from the "real world" illustrate how failures to attend to the more interpersonal aspects of teams can have negative consequences. When Volvo implemented a new team-based work plan in its bus plant, it drew on the science of teams to improve its efficiency and profitability. However, the team training program focused on instilling how individuals should work in particular situations rather than training them on how to work in a team (Oudhuis, 2004). By focusing on task-oriented skills in specific situations, this approach was not, in reality, helping trainees to develop the transportable teamwork knowledge, skills, attitudes, and abilities necessary for effective teamwork. Because of the plan's lack of teamwork considerations, it was largely ineffective in improving the organization's productivity.

The implications of subscribing to this myth are straightforward. How can an organization encourage teamwork if it does not understand the knowledge, skills, and attitudes that effective teamwork truly entails? Organizations benefit when teams are properly implemented with effective teamwork training. Just as examples from the "real world" highlight the perils of misappropriating the term "teamwork," they also show how effective use of teamwork can benefit organizations. In the medical domain, the TeamSTEPPS (Team Strategies and Tools to Enhance Performance and Patient Safety) team interaction method (a set of behaviors and tools used to guide teamwork) has been especially successful. Here we have an example of an effective translation from the science of teams to practical applications that are easily adopted by practitioners. For example, the Orange County Kaiser hospital system applied the TeamSTEPPS's SBAR tool (which prompts for descriptions of the situation, background, assessment, and recommendation) to improve its patient handoff, information exchange, and prescription checking (Leonard, Graham, & Bonacum,

2004). Leonard and colleagues further find the positive response from those in complex environments when standardized tools for improvement can be embedded within the organizational context. Similar examples of using teamwork training and applying team interaction paradigms can be found throughout other domains. Through gaining an understanding of teamwork, these organizations have empowered their efforts to enhance teamwork. By providing team members with the methods and tools they need for training and development, organizations are able to delegate responsibility for performance improvement. Teams are then able to determine how and when to implement these methods, providing them with a level of autonomy that can improve the EOR.

Myth 2: Organizations Know How to Manage and Foster Teamwork

Conventional wisdom would suggest that organizations that rely on teams know how to make their teams work well. They would not be team organizations if they did not practice good teamwork, right? Unfortunately, even organizations that are intensely team driven are often deficient in their handling of teams. After all, how can organizations foster teamwork if they do not understand the science thereof? Indeed, organizations that try to support teamwork may shoot themselves in the foot by implementing seemingly useful team programs while failing to change their management principles or neglecting to implement teamwork training.

For example, when StitchCo shifted from a piecework payment system (which rewarded individual output) to a team payment system (which rewarded overall profitability), it encountered drastic problems with teams not communicating and interfacing with each other (Ezzamel & Willmott, 1998). The use of profitability as the sole metric of success resulted in an environment in which teams were striving to reduce costs without regarding the impact their actions would have on other work teams. The pursuit of individual team profitability became more important than good inter-team behaviors. This benefited individual teams but was nearly disastrous for the organization as a whole (Ezzamel & Willmott, 1998). Additionally, StitchCo's use of a team reward structure was inconsistent with the relationship that individual machinists had built up within the organization and resulted in considerable friction. The organization did not properly consider how the notion of the team fit into the existing EOR. Although the intent of these changes was to create self-managing teams capable of mutual monitoring and to reduce "slacking," the end result of StitchCo's changes was that its teamwork initiative disincentivized individual effort and rewarded loafing. Because the organization failed to account for the climate of the organization and its workers, the introduction of teamwork became an imposition rather than an effective reform.

Just because organizations do not always deliver on their attempts to foster teamwork does not mean that teamwork is a flawed approach. As noted earlier, health care is one example where successful teamwork training abounds. The aviation domain has also met with considerable success in its efforts to encourage teamwork. For example, crew resource management (CRM) efforts have been used to train aviation teams to apply more teamwork skills and behaviors than untrained teams (Salas, Fowlkes, Stout, Milanovich, & Prince, 1999). Aviation teams are some of the most safe and successful teams in the world, largely due to their effective team training and teamwork processes. Although it is true that not all organizations know how to foster teamwork, some do. Other organizations are able to mirror these successes by applying team science in supporting and training teams.

Myth 3: Work Teams Are Better Than Individuals

One might expect that, as team researchers, we would espouse teams as the universal solution to all of an organization's problems. Teams are the tools we are in the business of researching and training. However, despite the evidence showing the efficacy of teams in organizations, teams are not always better than individual workers. Teams are organizational tools, a means by which to organize individuals to specific means. The same tool is not appropriate for every job. Although teams are certainly effective agents of organizational work, there are situations where the whole is less than the sum of its parts. For some tasks, such as those that have less demonstrably "correct" answers, teams only achieve the level of their second-best individual workers (Laughlin, Bonner, & Miner, 2002). These tasks include more abstract problem solving, survival problems, and analogy problems. Whereas teams in more concrete problems perform at the level of their best individual contributor, something about these kinds of tasks makes teams less useful for them. This may be the result of group memory being simultaneously helpful and harmful—the collective memory of a team will include both useful information and large amounts of distractor data, failed plans, and aborted strategies (Smith, Bushouse, & Lord, 2010).

In tasks with extremely high cognitive demands, teams may simply not be able to engage in teamwork successfully. For example, when performing a military radar identification task, teams may find it difficult to perform the skills that are part of teamwork; because of the difficulty and stress of the task, feedback, communication, coordination, and other teamwork skills suffer (Hinsz, 2009). Although work teams are a useful way to organize individuals toward different goals, there are situations in which they are not appropriate. Part of knowing how to foster and apply teamwork is recognizing when teams are not warranted.

Myth 4: All Work Teams Are Created Equal

An organization has taken the leap—it has created teams, has put in efforts to train them, and has paid attention to when they are appropriate to use. However, this organization needs to consider the relationship the organization has with these teams. How will it support them? Does it understand the different kinds of support different team types need? Even when individuals are empowered to work in teams and have been trained on how to engage in effective teamwork, their success in any given team is contingent upon external factors. Work teams composed of the same individuals will behave and function in very different ways when their tasks or contexts are changed. In any given organization, teams are likely to fall into a range of potential types including, for example, production, service, management, project, action, and parallel teams, all of which may operate in different ways (e.g., Sundstrom, 1999). These team types are further differentiated based on their level of authority, their lifespan, their degree of specialization and autonomy, and their interdependence (Salas et al., 2000). Given the varied possible combinations of the above factors, organizational support to manage the EOR would vary. For example, production teams with lower authority and a limited lifespan might respond more favorably to incentive-based practices, whereas action teams with a longer lifespan might be encouraged by task enrichment or ownership.

Naturally, the knowledge, skills, attitudes, and abilities (KSAs) required of teams working in different contexts will differ. Some KSAs are task specific, whereas others can be used throughout different kinds of taskwork. Similarly, some KSAs are team specific, whereas others apply to work with any sort of team (Salas et al., 2000). Even the interdependence of teams (and individuals in teams) can be broken down into different modes of interaction (Saavedra, Early, & Van Dyne, 1993). With so many different ways to understand the character of any given team, it is easy to see how comparing two widely disparate teams would be comparing apples to oranges.

What does this mean for an organization? Different teams have different requirements. It is not enough to merely have teams composed of individuals who understand teamwork. Failing to address this can have negative consequences viewed through the lens of team–member exchange. This is defined as an "individual member's perception of his or her exchange relationship with the peer group as a whole" (Seers, 1989, p. 119), where the quality of the relationships, both task and social, can impact team members. To the degree there is a mismatch between, for example, team member KSAs and task needs, this could negatively affect the exchange relationship. For example, inadequate KSAs produce performance asymmetries within the team, thus attenuating the quality of the interaction on both social and task levels. An organization must support and empower teams based on their specific requirements and capabilities. For example, product development teams may perform more effectively when virtually distributed (and supported with collaboration tools) than when working face to face (Schmidt, Montoya-Weiss, & Massey, 2001). By supporting a team based on its characteristics, organizations can improve team effectiveness. Further, organizations moving to team-based structures must take into consideration the capabilities of existing personnel and weigh that against task versus training needs. For example, training investments (cf. Tsui et al., 1997) to move incumbents to a team-based structure must take into account KSA requirements along with existing employee capabilities. If incumbent capability is below some threshold, training may not produce the expected return. However, the situation becomes more complicated when considering complex tasks requiring multifunctional teams. For example, if a team task requires complementary skills, investments in training may be worthwhile in that improvement may be possible for enough members of a team to overcome the limitations of other team members.

Naturally, an organization investing in a team is contingent upon an expectation of return. The primary relationship an organization and its teams share, after all, is one of reciprocal support. An organization empowers a team and provides it with resources so that the team may accomplish the goals of the organization. The characteristics of the team, however, dictate what support a team requires. The relationship between a team and an organization cannot be one-way; the team must provide an organization not only with work but also with requests regarding what the team needs. Thus, teams that take on varying responsibilities are more likely to need to communicate to the organization what their requirements are. Teams that consistently perform the same actions will not require as much support-request communication with the organization. Regardless of the team's context, however, an organization can improve team effectiveness by ensuring that a team's particular needs are met.

Myth 5: Teamwork Is All About Communication, Communication, Communication

Communication is an important component of teamwork (Salas et al., 2005), but that is exactly what it is—a component. There is more to a team than individuals who can effectively communicate to each other, and of course, there is more to fostering teamwork than training communication skills. Indeed, under the "Big Five" conceptualization, communication is merely the coordinative mechanism by which team leadership, mutual performance monitoring, back-up behavior, adaptability, and team effectiveness manifest (Salas et al., 2005). Although you need communication for much of the Big Five to "work," simply having good communication is not what makes teamwork effective. The most generic teamwork skill dimensions and competencies are very much driven by communication (Cannon-Bowers et al., 1995), but other concepts such as interdependence, mutual monitoring, team mental models, and trust define the true character of a team (Salas et al., 2005). In other words, teamwork involves communication but is not defined by it. Indeed, when teams work under high degrees of stress, communication tends to drop off. For teams to be successful under such circumstances, they mostly coordinate their efforts implicitly rather than explicitly communicate intent and status (Kleinman & Serfaty, 1989). Importantly, when considering our team-centric view of the EOR, an important area of inquiry is how inter- versus intrateam communication affects organizational outcomes. In this regard, there are at least four conceptualizations of effective and ineffective communication patterns. For example, there may be effective within-team communications but ineffective communications between the team and the organization as a whole. There may also be ineffective within-team communication, but effective communications between the team and the organization. Although work in "multiteam systems" is beginning to examine some of these forms of communication (see Marks, DeChurch, Mathieu, Panzer, & Alonso, 2005), this remains an underexamined issue in team research. As such, exploring these patterns of communication and their impact on the EOR would strengthen both theory and practice.

Myth 6: Team Players Are Born

The myth of the "natural" team player is perhaps the most insidious piece of team misinformation still coursing through organizations. If team players (i.e., people who work well in teams) were born rather than made, selection would form the core of industrial–organizational psychology. However, we know from the wide team training literature base that it is possible to train teamwork behaviors. Indeed, a major portion of the research into teams has focused on how exactly to ensure individuals are able to exhibit various teamwork skills. The field has investigated the KSAs required for teamwork (Stevens & Campion, 1994). Further, the necessity of a teamwork mental model (i.e., a model of how to engage in teamwork) is echoed throughout the literature base (Smith-Jentsch, Campbell, Milanovich, & Reynolds, 2001).

Because it is possible to train individuals to become effective team members, this myth is especially dangerous. Further, because managerial practices can foster teamwork, organizations can also focus on implementation of particular policies to help teams. This includes, for example, management support for team autonomy (e.g., no micromanagement of a team's work) as well as appropriately devised reward packages recognizing team contributions. Organizations that subscribe to the "natural leader" theory of leadership or the natural team player mentality limit their own growth by denying their workforce the team training they require to become competent team workers.

Myth 7: It Is Easy to Create and Promote Teamwork in Organizations

Many of the myths we have discussed so far deal with organizations that already use teams for various tasks. However, we must also consider organizations that are just beginning to use teams. Despite the complexity of teams as a concept, the organizational approach to establishing teamwork and creating a team environment is often inadequate, especially with regard to using approaches informed by science. For every organizational teamwork success story, there are failures to match. If teamwork were easy to create, high-profile companies would not invest considerable capital only to emerge with an unsuccessful, but implemented, teamwork paradigm.

Creating an effective teamwork environment is not as simple as assigning a group of people to work together. The myths we have discussed thus far have made this more than apparent. As we have noted, each particular instance of teamwork takes place in a potentially unique context. Different teams engage in different kinds of teamwork and taskwork. Creating a teamwork environment, then, cannot be successfully accomplished without considering teamwork alongside the context in which it is taking place (Cannon-Bowers et al., 1995). Thankfully, there are best practices that organizations can follow. The extant base of empirical research has resulted in a number of useful reviews of teamwork interventions. Best practices drawn from these reviews are presented in Table 20.1.

Myth 8: It Is Easy to Measure Teamwork

Teamwork is complicated. Teamwork situated within the context of an organization is even more complex: The relationships between the employees, teams, and organizations create a web of considerations. It is not unexpected, then, that measuring teamwork is a tricky prospect. Although we can train teams to work well and we can investigate how different skills and behaviors manifest themselves in teamwork, these advances have not come easily. Part of this difficulty in reaching a mature team science is the result of the complexity of measuring teamwork. However, organizations today are lucky. The most difficult work of figuring out how to examine and measure teamwork has been done for them. Today, teamwork processes, cognition, communication, and attitude can be measured through established tools. For measuring teamwork processes, tools such as TARGETs (Targeted Acceptable Responses to Generated Events or Tasks) and other behavioral taxonomies can make measuring successful teamwork as simple as checking items on a list (e.g., Fowlkes, Lane, Salas, Franz, & Oser, 1994). Cognitive measures such as concept mapping, card sorting, pathfinder, or SAGAT (Situation Awareness Global Assessment Technique) can be used to probe mental models, situation awareness, and other "in the head" concepts (for a review, see Cooke, 1999; Cooke, Salas, Cannon-Bowers, & Stout, 2000; and Mohammed, Klimoski, & Rentsch, 2000). Measures of collective efficacy or cohesion can be used to examine a team's attitudes (e.g., Paskevich, Brawley, Dorsch, & Widmeyer, 1999). Even traditionally complicated communication analysis is made much more accessible through the development of new tools such as latent semantic analysis (e.g., Kiekel, Cooke, Foltz, Gorman, & Martin, 2002; Landauer, Foltz, & Laham, 1998).

These measurement instruments have been applied in very specific settings. The critical issue is how they can be used to benefit a team-centric view of the EOR. For example, can improved management practices be developed that use such measures? Can more systematically applied team and individual reward systems be put in place through adaptations of these measures? In short, although much research needs to be done, the bottom line is that organizations seeking to measure teamwork need only apply what has already been created by the field.

Myth 9: Culturally Diverse Teams Perform Better or Worse Than Culturally Homogenous Teams

Intuitively, a team whose members share the same culture should perform better, and of course, a team that brings different cultural viewpoints to the table should also perform better. Both of these beliefs cannot be true at the same time; yet, culture in teams remains so misunderstood that these two competing beliefs are pervasive. What is the reality of culture and teams? Well, as with so much of psychology, the relationship depends on context. It is true that culturally homogenous teams perform better. Simultaneously, it is true that culturally heterogenous teams can perform just as well as culturally homogenous teams. How can this be the case? This seeming paradox exists in work teams due to the complexity of culture. Culture cannot simply be defined by the ethnic or national background of a team member. The reality is that a team composed of members from different cultural backgrounds will experience fault lines that reduce performance. However, these problems disappear over time (Watson, Kumar, & Michaelsen, 1993). Once a team has matured, it develops its own culture—a team culture. When all members of a team share the team culture, personal cultural background does not matter. The team monoculture is what is important to understand. Do team members all think similarly about their relationship to the team and the organization? Organizations must consider team culture alongside the more "traditional" concept of culture as nationality, beliefs, and ethnicity. Further, this raises an important research question as to how and when an organization's approach to EOR might lead to the creation of a team monoculture.

ADVICE: FOSTERING EFFECTIVE TEAMWORK

All of these myths paint a bleak picture of teamwork in organizations. That should not be the take-away message of this chapter. After all, the entire reason this chapter can exist is that the field already knows these myths are, well, myths. The research base has already addressed much of what is necessary to work against these myths, which means that there are ways for organizations to properly train, support, and create teams and teamwork. But that is not all—organizations are not the only ones involved in this whole process, after all. Given the hierarchical nature of many organizations, leaders have their own set of responsibilities in making sure their teams are effective. Finally, teams must possess a set of general competencies and capabilities in order to succeed.

What Organizations Need to Do

First, organizations need to consider how their promotion of teamwork, their teamwork policies, and their incentivizing of taskwork and teamwork influence teams. This chapter is, after all, about teams and the EOR—the organization is not only responsible for creating teams and training them, but also for supporting them and fostering their relationship with work teams. Promoting teamwork requires building a true culture of teamwork. An organization that espouses the virtues of teamwork but does nothing to ensure teamwork is actually part of the employee work paradigm cannot be surprised when its teams fail. A culture of teamwork encourages teamwork not because it is an imposed requirement, but because it is viewed as the best way to get things done. Organizations that want to walk the walk need to incentivize teamwork appropriately. Whether these incentives are monetary or through status and recognition, effective teamwork should be encouraged through systems that actually work to promote teamwork. In the aforementioned StitchCo example, "local" teamwork was rewarded to the detriment of interteam teamwork. What can organizations learn from this? There are many ways to reward teams, and structures that seem intuitively effective may end up being counterproductive. In addition, just as there are many ways to reward teams, different teams have different requirements for organizational support.

Next, organizations need to implement effective team training efforts. Fostering teamwork, supporting teams, and incentivizing team performance is of rather diminished usefulness when the teams themselves do not know how to engage in teamwork. As we have noted throughout this chapter, training the individuals in a team on how to interact as a team is an indispensible part of an organization's efforts to have successful team operations. Just as the field has developed a wealth of knowledge on how teams function, so too has it developed a number of best practices for team training. Drawing on the prior successes (and failures) of other organizations, team training is a mature area of study. Today, we know that team training should be contextualized with the specific teamwork competencies appropriate for a given task and context. We know that it is critical to focus on the actual teamwork behaviors, rather than the taskwork the teamwork is in support of, during such training. And we know that this focus on teamwork should not come at the expense of contextualizing the behaviors within the taskwork framework. In addition to these specific teamwork training considerations, organizations seeking to train teams should refer to standard educational best practices. By providing feedback, extending opportunities for practice, evaluating multiple levels of learning outcomes, and providing different modes of learning, organizations can ensure their team training efforts are successful.

What Leaders Need to Do

Whether organizations realize it or not, leaders are not just responsible for setting agendas. Their actions influence how teams operate; even on an implicit level, team members will learn how a leader behaves and alter their own behaviors accordingly. Given this tendency, it is in an organization's best interest to ensure these adaptations support effective teamwork.

Research shows that leadership and team processes are intertwined (Zaccaro & Klimoski, 2002). The functional perspective of leadership suggests a direct link between leadership and a team's actions. Under functional leadership, four main processes describe how leaders interface with their teams: information structuring, information use in problem solving, managing personnel, and managing resources. Leaders support their teams by matching member capabilities to appropriate roles, offering strategy, monitoring for changes in goals, providing feedback, developing shared mental models, and motivating them. Each of these behaviors carries its own considerations and best practices; teams that function in different contexts will respond differently to leaders. However, if there is one take-away point for leaders, it is that effective leadership of teams requires the presence of at least some of these behaviors. If all a leader is doing is setting the team's goals, the leader is not doing much in the way of leading.

Whether leaders are functionally a part of the team or engage in leadership from a more "removed" standpoint, they can influence and support teamwork (Morgeson, DeRue, & Karam, 2010). Indeed, certain behaviors are more effective for leaders "on the inside," whereas others are better applied form the outside. Internally, leaders are well positioned to monitor, support, and work. Externally, leaders are better able to provide training, engage in sensemaking, and distribute resources. Similarly, the level of leadership formality may influence how these behaviors affect teams. Just as team context influences how teamwork functions, so too does leader context influence how leadership affects teamwork.

What Teams Must Have

Finally, we would be remiss in not addressing the highly generalizable set of competencies that a team should possess. Throughout this chapter, we have noted the various forms of support an organization can provide teams. Perhaps the most meaningful way to support teams is to provide them with the basic building blocks of successful team interactions. By training team-generic, task-independent competencies, organizations can ensure that their teams have the general skills and competencies required of any successful team. These transportable skills and competencies can be used by teams of all types in all manner of teamwork tasks (Salas et al., 2000).

What are these general competencies? We have already mentioned some of them throughout this chapter. The first set of general competencies describes dispositions the individuals of a team hold. The very belief in the importance of teamwork is a key component of the effectiveness of a team's interactions. Without this belief, it is unlikely that teams will have the necessary "buy-in" to exhibit more complex team behaviors. Similarly, collective orientation describes the degree to which individuals in the team identify with the team. Individuals whose identity overlaps with the team's identity will be more motivated to ensure the team's success. A team's effectiveness is enhanced when it knows how to build morale and raise motivation for a particular task. Finally, the general level of assertiveness of a team's members will influence how that team interacts. A team with more assertive individuals will see a greater variety of ideas proposed and discussed, which is generally useful to a team's success. An echo chamber is not a good place for innovation!

Beyond these general knowledge and attitude competencies, there are skills and behaviors that are transportable across various team and task types. Given the importance of communication to teamwork, understanding how to exchange information properly is a natural contributor to overall team success. Similarly, knowing how to cooperate and consult with others is essential if team members are to meaningfully interact with each other. Once a team is interacting, conflict will arise sooner or later. Teams that are trained in some form of conflict resolution are not only inoculated against conflict's negative effects but may also be better prepared to benefit from the clash of ideas underlying the conflict.

At a bare minimum, teams should be armed with these transportable competencies. Morale building, conflict resolution, information exchange, task motivation, cooperation, consulting with others, assertiveness, collective orientation, and a belief in the importance of teamwork are applicable to the wide array of potential team and task contexts. Without access to these basic tools, teams are far less capable of tackling team tasks.

CONCLUSION

Although the term EOR suggests a relationship between a sole individual and an organization, the modern organizational reality is one defined by teams. Teams are how things function today. Unless the reality of work changes, understanding how teams fit into the EOR is critical to organizational success. Our intent with this chapter was to provide high-level information that organizations can use to combat the misconceptions that would otherwise prevent them from creating a positive team-focused EOR. The science of teams has provided a fantastic resource for organizations to take advantage of. Our knowledge of teams grows every day. As long as organizations expand their efforts to integrate this team knowledge, their team EORs will remain fruitful.

REFERENCES

Cannon-Bowers, J. A., & Bowers, C. (2011). Team development and functioning. In S. Zedeck (Ed.), *APA handbook of industrial and organizational psychology* (pp. 597–650). Washington, DC: American Psychological Association.

Cannon-Bowers, J. A., Tannenbaum, S. I., Salas, E., & Volpe, C. E. (1995). Defining competencies and establishing team training requirements. In R. Guzzo & E. Salas (Eds.), *Team effectiveness and decision making in organizations* (pp. 333–380). San Francisco, CA: Jossey-Bass.

Cooke, N. J. (1999). Knowledge elicitation. In F. T. Durso (Ed.), *Handbook of applied cognition* (pp. 479–509). London, UK: Wiley.

Cooke, N. J., Salas, E., Cannon-Bowers, J. A., & Stout, R. (2000). Measuring team knowledge. *Human Factors, 42*, 151–173.

Ezzamel, M., & Willmott, H. (1998). Accounting for teamwork: A critical study of group-based systems of organizational control. *Administrative Science Quarterly, 43*, 358–396.

Fowlkes, J. E., Lane, N. E., Salas, E., Franz, T., & Oser, R. L. (1994). Improving the measurement of team performance: The TARGETs Methodology. *Military Psychology, 6*, 47–61.

Grunig, L. A. (1992). How public relations/communication departments should adapt to the structure and environment of an organization—and what they actually do. In J. E. Grunig (Ed.), *Excellence in public relations and communication management* (pp. 467–481). Hillsdale, NJ: Lawrence Erlbaum Associates.

Grunig, L. A., Grunig, J. E., & Dozier, D. M. (2002). *Excellent public relations and effective organizations: A study of communication management in three countries.* Mahwah, NJ: Lawrence Erlbaum Associate.

Hinsz, V. B., & Wallace, D. M. (2009). Comparing individual and team judgment accuracy for target identification under heavy cognitive demand. In D. Andrews, R. P. Hertz, & M. B. Wolf (Eds.), *Human factors issues in combat identification.* Aldershot, UK: Ashgate.

Holton, E. F., & Baldwin, T. T. (Eds.). (2003). *Improving learning transfer in organizations.* San Francisco, CA: Jossey-Bass.

Kiekel, P. A., Cooke, N. J., Foltz, P. W., Gorman, J., & Martin, M. (2002). Some promising results of communication-based automatic measures of team cognition. In *Proceedings of the 46th Annual Meeting of the Human Factors and Ergonomics Society* (pp. 298–302). Santa Monica, CA: Human Factors and Ergonomics Society.

Kleinman, D. L., & Serfaty, D. (1989). Team performance assessment in distributed decision making. In R. Gilson, J. P. Kincaid, & B. Godiez (Eds.), *Proceedings: Interactive networked simulation for training conference* (pp. 22–27). Orlando, FL: Institute for Simulation and Training.

Landauer, T. K., Foltz, P. W., & Laham, D. (1998). An introduction to latent semantic analysis. *Discourse Processes, 25*, 259–284.

Laughlin, P. R., Bonner, B. L., & Miner, A. G. (2002). Groups perform better than the best individuals on letters-to-numbers problems. *Organizational Behavior and Human Decision Processes, 88*, 605–620.

Leonard, M., Graham, S., & Bonacum, D. (2004). The human factor: The critical importance of effective teamwork and communication in providing safe care. *Quality and Safety in Health Care, 13*, i85–i90.

Marks, M. A., DeChurch, L. A., Mathieu, J. E., Panzer, F. J., & Alonso, A. (2005). Teamwork in multiteam systems. *Journal of Applied Psychology, 90*, 964–971.

Mohammed, S., Klimoski, R., & Rentsch, J. R. (2000). The measurement of team mental models: We have no shared schema. *Organizational Research Methods, 3*, 123–165.

Morgeson, F. P., DeRue, D. S., & Karam, E. P. (2010). Leadership in teams: A functional approach to understanding leadership structures and processes. *Journal of Management, 36*, 5–39.

Oudhuis, M. (2004). The birth of the individualised team: The individual and collective in a team based production organisation at the Volvo Bus Plant. *International Journal of Operations & Production Management, 24*, 787–800.

Paskevich, D. M., Brawley, L. R., Dorsch, K. D., & Widmeyer, W. N. (1999). Relationship between collective efficacy and cohesion: Conceptual and measurement issues. *Group Dynamics: Theory, Research, and Practice, 3*, 210–222.

Saavedra, R., Early, P. C., & Van Dyne, L. (1993). Complex interdependence in task-performing groups. *Journal of Applied Psychology, 78*, 61–72.

Salas, E., Burke, C. S., & Cannon-Bowers, J. A. (2000). Teamwork: Emerging principles. *International Journal of Management Reviews, 2*, 339–356.

Salas, E., Dickinson, T. L., Converse, S. A., & Tannenbaum, S. I. (1992). Toward an understanding of team performance and training. In R. W. Swezey & E. Salas (Eds.), *Teams: Their training and performance* (pp. 3–29). Norwood, NJ: Ablex.

Salas, E., & Fiore, S. M. (Eds.). (2004). *Team cognition: Understanding the factors that drive process and performance.* Washington, DC: American Psychological Association.

Salas, E., Fowlkes, J. E., Stout, R. J., Milanovich, D., & Prince, C. (1999). Does CRM training improve teamwork skills in the cockpit? Two evaluation studies. *Human Factors, 41*, 326–343.

Salas, E., Sims, D. E., & Burke, C. S. (2005). Is there a "Big Five" in teamwork? *Small Group Research, 36*, 555–599.

Schmidt, J. B., Montoya-Weiss, M. M., & Massey, A. P. (2001). New product development decision-making effectiveness: Comparing individuals, face-to-face teams, and virtual teams. *Decision Sciences, 32*, 575–600.

Seers, A. (1989). Team-member exchange quality: A new construct for role-making research. *Organizational Behavior and Human Decision Processes, 43*, 118–135.

Shore, L. M., Tetrick, L. E., Taylor, M. S., Coyle-Shapiro, J. A.-M., Liden, R. C., McLean Parks, J., ... Van Dyne, L. (2004). The employee-organization relationship: A timely concept in a period of transition. In J. Martocchio (Ed.), *Research in personnel and human resource management* (Vol. 23, pp. 291–370). Oxford, UK: Elsevier Ltd.

Smith, C. M., Bushouse, E., & Lord, J. (2010). Individual and group performance on insight problems: The effects of experimentally induced fixation. *Group Process Intergroup Relations, 13*, 91–99.

Smith-Jentsch, K. A., Campbell, G. E., Milanovich, D. A., & Reynolds, A. M. (2001). Measuring teamwork mental models to support training needs assessment, development, and evaluation: Two empirical studies. *Journal of Organizational Behavior, 22*, 179–194.

Stevens, M. J., & Campion, M. A. (1994). The knowledge, skill, and ability requirements for teamwork: Implications for human resource management. *Journal of Management, 20*, 503–530.

Stout, R. J., Salas, E., & Fowlkes, J. E. (1997). Enhancing teamwork in complex environments through team training. *Group Dynamics: Theory, Research, and Practice, 1*, 169–182.

Sundstrom, E. (1999). The challenges of supporting work team effectiveness. In E. Sundstrom (Ed.), *The ecology of work group effectiveness: Design guidelines for organizations, facilities, and information system for teams* (pp. 3–23). San Francisco, CA: Jossey-Bass.

Tsui, A. S., Pearce, J. L., Porter, L. W., & Tripoli, A. M. (1997). Alternative approaches to the employee-organization relationship: Does investment in employees pay off? *Academy of Management Journal, 40*, 1089–1121.

Watson, W. E., Kumar, K., & Michaelsen, L. K. (1993). Cultural diversity's impact on interaction process and performance: Comparing homogeneous and diverse task groups. *Academy of Management Journal, 36*, 590–602.

Zaccaro, S. J., & Klimoski, R. (2002). The interface of leadership and team processes. *Group & Organization Management, 27*, 4–13.

21

The Employee–Organization Relationship and the Scholar–Practitioner Divide

Wayne F. Cascio
University of Colorado, Denver

Robert J. Greene
Reward Systems, Inc. & DePaul University

In order for a positive employee–organization relationship (EOR) to exist, employees must believe they are being treated fairly, competitively, and appropriately in the employment relationship. More specifically, the EOR includes both psychological contracts (an individual-level phenomenon) and the employment relationship (a group-level phenomenon) as fundamental building blocks (Shore et al., Chapter 1, this volume). Managers must make decisions, formulate policies, and design and administer workforce-management systems that are prudent and sustainable from a business perspective. They seek certainty about how specific courses of action will work, because deciding which to use involves risk. They may use instinct, past experience, and/or research evidence to decide on appropriate courses of action. If they base their actions on practices that evidence has shown to be sound and effective, they are using evidence-based management. This is the essence of the scientist–practitioner model, which discourages both practice that has no scientific basis and research that has no clear implications for practice (Bass, 1974; Dunnette, 1990; Murphy & Saal, 1990; Rupp & Beal, 2007).

Evidence-based management has become a topic of increasing interest in the last several years (see, for example, Latham, 2009). For scholarly research to be used by practitioners, however, it must be viewed as relevant to the issues they face and as helpful in solving their problems. Researchers,

555

on the other hand, often seek answers to questions that they view as important, whether or not they are of current concern to practitioners. As a result, academics and practitioners live in different "thought worlds," distinct knowledge and practice communities. Academics typically strive to develop and refine theoretically framed, generalizable knowledge (often devoid of context). Practitioners develop and refine knowledge that enables them to solve operational problems that are immersed in context. Both parties have to work hard to appreciate the "mental models" that their counterparts live by, and some just do not want to do so. This difference in focus can result in research that has little or no practical application and in practitioners being left without evidence to use in making decisions. Thus another prerequisite for the practical application of research is that researchers must present their results in a manner that is available to, understandable by, and viewed as relevant by practitioners. The research must speak to them in a manner that acknowledges the contextual constraints they face every day and that scholarly research often ignores.

Of particular relevance to EOR is the reality that even when decision makers use the best available research evidence produced by scholars in making their decisions, we have observed that they are unlikely to share that evidence with employees. As a result, management may be confident in the basis upon which decisions were made, but employees are not presented with evidence they can understand and accept as compelling. This results in employee skepticism about whether they are being treated fairly. The diagram in Figure 21.1 outlines five major challenges in bridging the scholar–practitioner divide: (1) Do researchers make results accessible to practitioners? (2) Do practitioners access the sources and become aware of findings? (3) Do practitioners apply the findings? (4) Do practitioners communicate the basis for their decisions to employees? (5) Do the employees accept the research support as valid, and do they accept the results of applying it?

For example, employees whose self-efficacy is low may reject assigned goals as being unrealistically difficult, despite research evidence that similarly skilled employees working with similar resources have achieved similarly challenging goals in the past. If those same employees had access to evidence that increased their confidence level, practitioners may find that employees are more likely to accept the goals, which increases their motivation to achieve the goals. Further, if practitioners understood the impact of self-efficacy on motivation, they might alter the manner in which goals are set (from assigned to participatory) (Bandura, 1997; Latham, 2007).

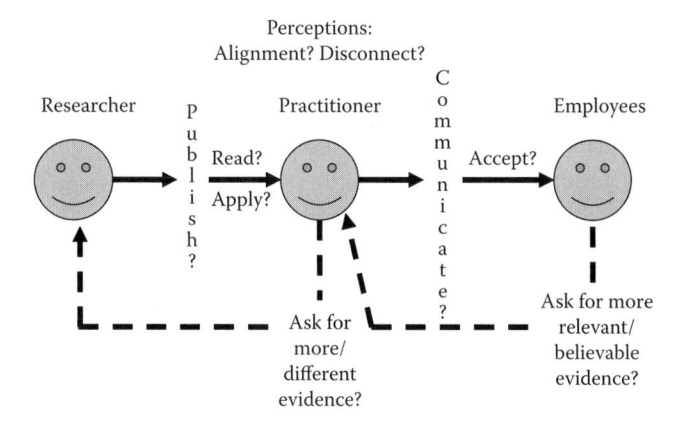

FIGURE 21.1
Major challenges in bridging the scholar–practitioner divide.

One of the difficulties in motivating researchers and practitioners to reach out into the other's world is that there is no specific psychological contract that has been developed between them. Psychological contracts refer to employees' perceptions of what they owe to their employers and what their employers owe to them (Robinson, 1996). More formally, a psychological contract is an individual's system of beliefs based on commitments, expressed or implied, regarding an exchange agreement with another party (Rousseau, 2011).

Researchers whose careers are in the academic world generally have a contract with their employing universities, although the two parties may view the terms of that contract differently. Because it is in the mutual interest of both parties to cooperate, however, a tightly defined contract may not be necessary. There is no such contract between practitioners and researchers, unless of course the practitioners have in some way supported research. When that occurs, it becomes more apparent that the practitioner must identify the issues of interest and that the researcher must propose a methodology that will generate findings relevant to those issues. It is also necessary for the researcher to provide results expressed in terms that are accessible by and acceptable to the practitioner. In our experience, this type of arrangement happens only when the practitioner recognizes a need and believes that it can be addressed by research.

To the extent that the researcher provides evidence that addresses the issue that the practitioner faces and the practitioner finds that evidence to be both accessible and acceptable, the terms of the psychological contract have been fulfilled. To the extent that those conditions do not materialize, there may be a perceived breach of the psychological contract. A breach refers to the extent that one party is perceived to have fallen short in fulfilling its obligations (Robinson & Rousseau, 1994).

The practitioner and the organization's employees have a greater need to fashion an agreement, if not a specific contract, about what employees have a right to know and can expect to know about what evidence underlies management decisions (Tekleab & Taylor, 2003). For example, many organizations decided to freeze pay rates in 2010 because the information available to their human resources (HR) practitioners showed that competitive market rates had not gone up, or had gone up only under certain circumstances. Yet our personal experience has been that many employees viewed this as a ruse to keep costs low and that they perceived the pay freezes as a breach of the psychological contract. When employees perceive a breach of the psychological contract, research indicates that supervisors' and subordinates' attributions regarding the reasons for the breach are likely to differ (Lester, Turnley, Bloodgood, & Bolino, 2002). Specifically, subordinates are more likely to attribute breach to the organization's intentional disregard for the commitments that it had made to employees, whereas supervisors are more inclined to attribute the breach to situations beyond the organization's direct control.

A violation of the psychological contract is a related (Zhao, Glibkowski, & Bravo, 2007), yet different, construct. A violation is the emotional response to what is perceived as a willful failure to honor one's commitments (Rousseau, 2011). Such violations are both more frequent and more intense among managers working in downsizing or restructuring firms, particularly in terms of job security, compensation, and opportunities for advancement (Turnley & Feldman, 1999).

Because the evidence about market rates is rarely shared with employees, at least in detail, this type of suspicion is common even during more favorable economic conditions. This argues for more attention being paid to reaching an understanding between the two parties as to what evidence should be shared when that evidence is used to make decisions that impact the employees. This chapter will discuss the scholar/researcher–practitioner divide and then examine how practitioners can make decisions more effectively and show employees that they are being treated appropriately.

THE SCHOLAR–PRACTITIONER DIVIDE

It can be argued that it is the responsibility of researchers to focus on issues that practitioners often face or are facing. At the same time, however, it is also the responsibility of practitioners to make the effort to find research that is relevant to their particular problems and to understand how it might apply to their issues. Both parties need to make a sincere effort to bridge the divide. Once practitioners are able to access and understand relevant, research-based evidence, they must be able to apply it to their specific operational contexts and be able to use that evidence to help employees understand and accept the bases for their decisions.

Cascio and Aguinis, in a 2008 *Journal of Applied Psychology* article, found that very few HR practitioners contribute to the *Journal of Applied Psychology* or *Personnel Psychology*, which are among the "A journals" that most researchers view as the ideal place to publish their research. Earlier, Rynes (2007), Rynes, Colbert, and Brown (2002), and Rynes, Giluk, and Brown (2007) found that HR practitioners do not read those journals or other leading sources of research evidence. Further, practitioners do not have a good understanding of what research evidence reveals about critical issues such as motivation, turnover, and engagement. As Cascio and Aguinis (2008) and Cascio (2011) suggested, professional associations should do more to connect research and practice. They can offer interactive sessions in which academics and practitioners can work together on important problems (Bartunek, 2007). They can and should offer truly interactive sessions. Rynes (2007) noted that this is probably the single most important thing that our professional associations can do to narrow the academic–practitioner gap. Bridges need to be built, and all parties must participate in the building in order to span the gap between those doing research and those who would benefit from that research.

Practitioners and scholars both rely on criteria to guide their actions. The next section presents some potential criteria that each group may use.

Practitioner Criteria for Using Research-Based Findings

For practitioners to find research-based evidence to be useful, the research should meet the following conditions. It should have an apparent connection to important management decisions in the practitioner's organization.

It also should be accessible and understandable; it should come from a credible source, be supported by evidence, and be targeted to appropriate parties; and it should come to the user via channels that the potential user consults, or at least it should be easily accessible.

To assess whether strategies/methods/processes may have a positive impact on management decisions, the basis for the evidence that supports them should be clear, compelling, and understandable. In addition, the degree of certainty about whether the findings of the research would generalize to the practitioner's context should be understandable and credible. The evidence itself should come with a practical usage guide—that is, with information about how it can be used in making management decisions and how its relevance and credibility can be sold to those who must accept it.

Finally, evidence should be accompanied by an assessment of (a) the consequences of being right or wrong, (b) the probability of being correct, and (c) viable alternatives (along with an objective assessment of their advantages and disadvantages). At the same time, practitioners must be willing to walk part way across the bridge, which entails equipping themselves with the ability to understand research methods and results, together with a willingness to become conversant in the language of research.

Practitioners must also make an honest effort to review the literature relevant to the problems they face and to remain abreast of advances in knowledge on a continuous basis. Researchers can help by identifying a manageable number of resources and perhaps even by providing "translation" services, which may be a summary of findings in publications practitioners do read regularly. At a broader level, the research community could provide periodic summaries of findings that are deemed to have particular relevance to the practitioner community. However transmitted, the target audience should find that the results are understandable.

Criteria for Scholars Who Perform Research

As a general matter, research must be done in a manner that is commonly accepted in one's profession, employing standards that meet professional scrutiny and peer review. Beyond that, scholars should have a clear understanding of the types of decisions that challenge practitioners (along with an understanding of the contextual constraints they face) and the kinds of evidence needed to inform practitioners' decisions. At the same time, researchers should have their intellectual property protected, via the usual channels for doing so (e.g., copyrights, patents), and citations to their work should afford them appropriate credit.

Researchers also should make every effort to determine the generalizability (external validity) of their studies, rather than focusing solely on internal validity. They need to recognize that, from the perspective of practitioners, the transportability of the findings across differing contexts is a critical consideration. Practitioners do not want one organization's success to become their disaster, and researchers can assist them by clearly specifying boundaries on the generalizability of their findings, as well as the contextual characteristics that should exist in order for the research findings to generalize to other settings.

Chapter Outline

The remainder of this chapter focuses on strategies for bridging the scholar–practitioner divide, with particular emphasis on psychological contracts and employment relationships. We will apply relevant practitioner criteria for using research to these topics, and we will provide practical examples and suggestions for ways to make that literature more practitioner-friendly. Our objective is to provide, in concrete terms, ways in which evidence can guide managerial decision making in the EOR.

To be sure, we cannot satisfy all of the practitioner criteria for using research that we described earlier. One approach, however, is to offer actual company examples of psychological contracts that work in practice, that is, where both parties accept and implement their mutual obligations. The following section presents one such example.

Nucor

Much of the material in this section comes from Byrnes (2006). Nucor is the largest steel company in the United States. Its 387% return to shareholders from 2000 to 2005 handily beat almost all other firms in the Standard & Poor's 500 Index during that time period. Despite a difficult year in 2009, when revenues were off 53%, the company still increased its dividend for the 37th consecutive year. As is its custom, the company lists the names of all 20,400 of its workers in its annual report (Nucor Corporation, 2009). This is not a stunt to emphasize that "people are the company's most important assets." Actually, the story began in the late 1980s with the radical insight of its legendary chief executive officer (CEO), Ken Iverson, that employees, even hourly clock punchers, will make an extraordinary effort if you reward them richly, treat them with respect, and give them real power.

At Nucor, the art of motivation, and the essence of the psychological contract, is a laser-like focus on front-line employees; it is about talking to them, listening to them, taking a risk on their ideas, and accepting the occasional failure. This is a hard model to follow because it requires managers to abandon the command-and-control model that has dominated so many businesses for the past century. It requires them to trust their people and to do a much better job of sharing the corporate wealth. Money is where rhetoric meets reality for many employees, and Nucor's radical pay system is the most difficult for outsiders and employees of acquired companies to embrace.

Experienced steelworkers at other companies can easily make up to $21 an hour. At Nucor, the guarantee is closer to $10. A bonus, tied to the production of defect-free steel by an employee's entire shift, can triple the average steelworker's take-home pay. The company uses a true incentive plan, where gains are rewarded and failures are penalized. This is a rarity among incentive plans, because most are success-sharing plans where there is gain for performing well but no penalty or downside risk for performing poorly (Greene, 2011; Milkovich, Newman, & Gerhart, 2011).

Bonuses are calculated on every order and paid out every week. If workers make a bad batch of steel and catch it before it moves on, they lose the bonus they otherwise would have made on that shipment. If the bad batch reaches the customer, however, they lose three times that. Workers are not the only employees who put their pay at risk; managers do too. Department managers typically receive a base pay that is 75% to 90% of the market average. In a great year, however, that same manager might receive a bonus of 75% or even 90%, based on the return on assets of the entire plant.

Relative to other U.S. companies, where the CEO may make 400 times (or more) the salary of the typical factory worker, pay disparities at Nucor are modest. The CEO makes 23 times that of the average steelworker. Executive pay focuses on team building and on working to maximize the performance of the company as a whole. Thus, the bonus of a plant manager, a department manager's boss, depends on the entire corporation's return on equity. The message is that there is no glory in winning at your own plant, if the others are failing.

As Byrnes (2006) noted: "But to focus only on pay would be to miss something special about the culture that Nucor has created. There's a healthy competition among facilities, and even among shifts, balanced with a long history of cooperation and idea-sharing" (p. 62). Plant managers and other employees, such as shipping department supervisors, regularly visit other plants to study their practices and to learn from them. In that sense, Nucor facilities serve as "living laboratories" that facilitate the sharing of internal best practices. Its egalitarian culture, reinforced by the structure of the rewards system, fosters that kind of cooperation.

What can other companies learn from Nucor? At a general level, here are five lessons:

1. Pay for performance. (Nucor uses production bonuses and profit sharing to demonstrate that linkage.)
2. Listen to the front line. (Nucor finds that almost all of the best ideas come from the factory floor and that the newest workers often come up with them.)
3. Push authority down (e.g., from supervisors to line workers, and from plant managers to supervisors).
4. Safeguard your culture (e.g., make cultural compatibility a key criterion for acquisitions of other companies; constantly look for ways to ensure egalitarian treatment of all employees and to promote team spirit).
5. Be willing to take risks, recognizing that some of them will not pay off. This is the essence of learning organizations and entrepreneurial firms.

At Dartmouth College's Tuck School of Business, Professor Vijay Govindarajan teaches Nucor as an example of outstanding strategic execution: "My students say: 'I thought Nucor created steel. And I say: 'No. Nucor creates knowledge'" (Byrnes, 2006, p. 58).

In terms of the practitioner-usage criteria we enumerated earlier, what does the Nucor example tell us? We think there are five key lessons. First, evidence should have an apparent connection to important management decisions in the practitioner's organization. The Nucor example has the potential to inform decisions about organizational design and structure, decisions about reward systems, and decisions about "intrapreneurship" in other firms.

Second, information should be accessible and understandable; many practitioners read the business press, and when stories include key lessons from a company example, in understandable terms, decision makers can decide if those lessons apply to their organizations. As scholars, we pride ourselves on having published literature that uses the scientific method and relies on evidence, but our publications are not always seen as accessible or understandable to those outside of academia.

Third, information should come from a credible source, supported by evidence. Many practitioners find high-end business publications such as *The Economist*, *The Wall Street Journal*, *Bloomberg Business Week*, or *Forbes* to be well documented and well researched and, therefore, possess high credibility. Fourth, information should be targeted to appropriate parties. Although the sources above might be more appealing to higher level executives than to lower level workers, there is no reason why those executives cannot share the information or at least the major lessons they derived from it with their front-line employees. Fifth, and finally, the degree of certainty should be understandable and credible. It is the job of scholars and practitioners to recognize the limits to which results might apply. Specific features of the context in which evidence might or might not apply define those limits. This is where a partnership of scholars and practitioners can be most helpful.

In terms of the psychological contract, Nucor illustrates several important lessons. A psychological contract is an individual-level phenomenon and is struck with each employee. Yet Nucor promotes a team-oriented culture and a sense of "we're all in this together." The two are not in conflict, as each individual employee learns through experience that if he or she contributes to the team, he or she will share in the rewards that flow to the members of that team.

Psychological contracts also entail a set of mutual obligations. These are illustrated nicely through the Nucor example; managers give up their command-and-control approach to relationships with employees, and employees, in turn, feel motivated to contribute because they see their ideas put into practice. Just as importantly, they see the long-term results of those improved practices in terms of the bonuses and profit sharing that they receive. Nucor creates knowledge that is put into practice. Finally, psychological contracts entail explicit descriptions of the exchange relationship between employee and employer. Nucor's pay system and overall approach to rewards make each party's expectations explicit.

The Nucor example also reinforces two principles: (1) employees need to have a reasonable amount of control over results they are expected to produce, and (2) the culture must enable employees to exercise an adequate amount of latitude, which makes it possible for them to innovate and perform well. In order for the Nucor pay systems to motivate high levels of effort and performance, these prerequisites must be in place. Emulation of Nucor's systems is not a wise strategy if an organization's context does not share these characteristics.

Changing Employment Relationships and the Lessons of Nucor

In terms of the literature on broader employment relationships, Shore, Coyle-Shapiro, and Tetrick (Chapter 1, this volume) emphasized that in recent years, and fueled by the Great Recession, employment relationships have undergone dramatic changes. The major changes are the removal of traditional job security by employers, the withdrawal of loyalty by employees, and increased flexibility in dealing with each other (Roehling, Cavanaugh, Moynihan, & Boswell, 2000). Certainly the nature of the jobs in question influences the employment relationship.

Thus, Masters and Miles (2002) argued that firms use permanent employment relationships more often when they need to make repeat hiring for the job, when the job requires firm-specific skills, and when performance in the job is difficult to assess. Their results are consistent with earlier conceptual work by Lepak and Snell (1999) that used the criteria of value (repeated hiring) and uniqueness (firm-specific skills) in determining the different types of employment modes and relationships. Together these studies suggest that the structure of the organization, the nature of the jobs in question, and the quality of human capital are the antecedents or determinants of employment relationships in firms.

Here is how Nucor relates to those findings. In exchange for employee loyalty, Nucor provides a measure of job security for its employees. In 2009, for example, in the depths of the Great Recession, Nucor lost 6% of its employees, relative to 2008, predominately through attrition. It went to considerable lengths to keep its end of the bargain with employees. In return, surviving employees at all levels shared the pain by bringing home smaller paychecks. Structurally, Nucor's pay system facilitates that kind of an approach to the employment relationship: Everyone does well in good years, and in bad years, all share the pain. Nucor uses that flexibility to avoid layoffs and large-scale hiring of contingent employees.

INTEGRATING THE ORGANIZATION'S AND THE EMPLOYEE'S PERSPECTIVES

Shore et al. (Chapter 1, this volume) noted that both employees and employers come to the employment relationship with different mindsets and understandings of their respective obligations. Those understandings shape, guide, and influence what they observe, remember, and interpret in the employment relationship. Not surprisingly, therefore, the amount and quality of communication between the employee and employer can contribute to the degree of misunderstanding between them. Beyond that, coworkers are important sources of information to individuals about the nature of their relationship with the employer. Researchers study EORs differently, depending on whether their focus is on the individual, the supervisor–subordinate exchange, the work group or bargaining unit, or the firm. EOR is therefore a multilevel phenomenon that is likely to be influenced by a number of contextual factors. These may include organizational stresses (e.g., brought on by exogenous factors, such as the general state of the economy), group and organizational norms and culture (endogenous factors), and employees' personal circumstances. EORs also change over time, for example, as a result of changing circumstances or in response to managerial actions (e.g., across-the-board downsizing), and are therefore dynamic.

To illustrate these phenomena, we present information from a real-life case involving managerial actions regarding pay—an issue that can be highly emotional and about which employee perceptions can change easily in response to managerial actions. We begin our treatment by reemphasizing a point made in the introductory section of this chapter, namely, that employees must be convinced that the reasons for management decisions and the implications of implementing them are sound.

As an example, consider an activity that takes place in almost all organizations, comparison of internal pay structures and pay rates to the external "market." Firms do this for a variety of reasons, but principally to establish their budgets for pay increases based on their desired competitive posture. These decisions become the basis for actions regarding employees' pay. If employees are not convinced that the outcomes are fair, competitive, and appropriate, then dissatisfaction with pay will result. Yet many organizations communicate very little about how they measure prevailing market levels and how they decide on pay actions.

Employees will seek information to determine if they are paid fairly and competitively. Many of the commonly used sources, particularly on the Internet, are not reliable. However, that does not mean employees will not believe numbers that agree with what they think is fair, no matter the quality of the information. The following case study summarizes the results of an effort to convince a group of employees with critical skills that their pay was competitive with prevailing market levels.

Case Study

ESTABLISHING THE CREDIBILITY OF RESEARCH

Coauthor Greene managed a large national compensation survey that focused on information technology (IT) jobs. This survey had data from more than 2,000 firms, reporting on some 250,000 IT employees. The survey was the standard for organizations seeking competitive data they could use to establish externally competitive pay structures and pay rates for their IT personnel.

A very large Chicago-based financial organization called Greene to ask for his assistance in convincing its top IT manager and his staff that the organization was paying competitively. Prior to tackling the challenge of convincing employees, Greene determined that the potential of the research included in the survey was not being fully used by the HR practitioners in the organization. They had been basing their decisions on data from the standard reporting categories in the survey (national average, Chicago average, and average for their type of IT system). This had left the door open to challenges by the IT staff, based on their suspicion that a lot of "little, unsophisticated" IT units were included in the data, which resulted in inappropriately low survey averages. Greene conducted an in-depth analysis of the survey database to determine the appropriate comparable sample for the organization and convinced the firm's HR department to use a select sample of participating organizations to produce the most relevant competitive averages.

In anticipation of continued skepticism on the part of IT personnel about the relevance of the numbers, knowledgeable employees were engaged in the process of selecting the competitor list. Based on that dialogue, a select group of about 50 organizations was identified. The decision was based on the location of the organizations, their size and relative sophistication in IT, their industries, and even their reputation "on the street." At the last minute, a group of software designers suggested that perhaps the comparison base should change across organizational specialties (i.e., Systems Analysis, Software Programming, Applications Programming, Computer Operations). They pointed out that some organizations had very large IT installations that were not very sophisticated, because they did primarily data storage and routing processing, whereas other organizations were primarily software designers. To deal with this issue, managers from each of the functional areas within IT reviewed the selected competitor sample and made modifications as they deemed appropriate.

Greene also conducted a short course to familiarize the employee-participants with the quantitative methods used in surveys. Although the IT employees certainly knew the difference between the mean of a sample and the median, they were confused about which was the most appropriate to use as "the going rate" in compensation surveys. Greene converted a frequency distribution of the rates reported in the survey for a job family into a visual, which demonstrated that the rates did not conform to a standard distribution. He explained that the mean was generally higher than the median in a sample of pay rates because rates were much more constrained at the low end than they were at the upper end. (Low rates were constrained due to minimum-wage law and the difficulty of hiring anyone at rates lower than a reasonable level, but people were not resistant to accepting very high pay rates.) Given this reality, high rates increased the mean more than the median and generally made the mean 3% to 5% higher than the median in very large samples.

The participation of employees in this analysis gave them a full understanding of what was behind the numbers reported in the survey, thereby lessening suspicions that there was manipulation involved. The gesture of including employees in the analysis of the pay-survey data also demonstrated a respect for the employees and communicated to them the willingness to conduct an open dialogue about how the organization compared itself to prevailing rates in each relevant labor market. This level of engagement, similar to that discussed in the earlier Nucor case, had a positive impact on employee understanding of the research used by the organization and contributed to their acceptance of survey results.

Now back to the salary survey. The samples that each of the functional areas within IT selected produced numbers that differed only slightly from the results that the HR department had been using, but the acceptance by the IT staff increased dramatically.

This case illustrates the value of the researcher and the practitioner (HR in this instance) collaborating to produce a sound model for competitive analysis. It also illustrates the value of having the practitioner and the affected employees collaborate, to ensure the result is believable and relevant to the context in question.

From an EOR perspective, how effectively and appropriately an organization defines, measures, and rewards performance has a major impact on employee satisfaction. The case study is an example of how an organization can use participation and open communication to increase employee acceptance of the manner in which their employer develops the pay structures. Using market data to establish pay structures, however, is only an attempt to establish external competitiveness. For employees to fully accept their pay levels and pay actions they must also believe the following:

1. Their performance is defined and measured using relevant criteria and standards.
2. They were aware of the criteria and standards at the beginning of the performance period, after having had a say in their establishment.
3. They received feedback that informed them about how they were doing and that enabled them to redirect their efforts, if doing so would improve the manager's perception of their performance.
4. Their performance was appraised in a manner that was fair relative to other employees.
5. Their pay actions were determined using a credible process (procedural justice) and were fair relative to peers (distributive justice), and the employee was treated respectfully (relational justice) (Greenberg, 2009).

Now, we consider several other well-established scholarly findings, relative to the EOR. We focus on some of the key conditions necessary for employees to accept pay levels and reward structures as fair and to motivate high performance.

A fundamental requirement for acceptability and motivation is the clear definition of performance. A manager who defines performance ensures that individual employees or teams know what is expected of them and that they stay focused on effective performance (Bernardin, Hagan, Kane, & Villanova, 1998). Virtually every review of domestic and global performance management systems identifies this crucial component (see, for example, Briscoe, Schuler, & Claus, 2009; Cascio, in press; DeNisi & Sonesh, 2011; Dowling, Festing, & Engle, 2009). Conversely, a meta-analysis of expatriate adjustment and performance (Bhaskar-Srinivas, Harrison, Shaffer, & Luk, 2005) found that uncertainty regarding goals, objectives, and role requirements is the strongest stressor in expatriates' overseas work environments.

Domestically, "knowing what is expected of me" has been found to be the most impactful factor on employee satisfaction and effectiveness in the Gallup research (Buckingham & Coffman, 1999), and although this research is largely anecdotal, it is generally found that while managers believe their employees have a clear understanding of the criteria and standards used to evaluate their performance, employees believe they do not. If employees are to accept that they are rewarded fairly based on their performance, however, this reality poses a problem. As the goal-setting research (Latham, 2007) has suggested, clearly understood and accepted goals have a positive impact on the motivation to achieve them. "Understood" and "accepted" are mandatory prerequisites though. The degree to which employees participate in setting goals will vary across contexts, but even imposed goals must be understood if they are to have an effect.

A well-established finding in applied psychology is that timely and relevant feedback is a necessary condition to motivate employees to maximize their performance (Pulakos & O'Leary, 2011). How the feedback is delivered, however, is likely to vary across cultures (Cascio, in press). Thus in individualistic cultures, such as the United States, Great Britain, and Australia, the feedback is likely to be direct, and typically it is put in writing. Indeed, the ability to communicate good as well as bad news is considered a key skill for a successful manager.

By contrast, in collectivist societies, such as Korea, Guatemala, and Taiwan, discussing a person's performance openly with him or her is likely to clash head-on with the society's norm of harmony, and the subordinate may view it as an unacceptable loss of face. Such societies have more subtle, indirect ways of communicating feedback, as by withdrawing a normal favor or by communicating concerns verbally via a mutually trusted intermediary (Hofstede & Hofstede, 2005). Also, there is extensive research support for only holding employees accountable for things over which they have a reasonable amount of control (Latham, 2009). Practitioners familiar with this research will be more likely to design roles for employees that are effective and that incorporate the research findings.

Perhaps the biggest obstacle to employee acceptance of their performance ratings and the rewards they receive as a result of them is the belief that they are fair, relative to other employees. Equity theory (Adams, 1963) supports the notion that employees cannot decide whether their outcomes are in an appropriate proportion to their inputs without a frame of reference. To do that, they select referent others to whom they compare themselves. Adams's findings also suggest that employees will compare themselves to others about whom they have considerable information and who share similar employment conditions.

The easiest comparator is someone in the same unit with the same job. But employees also form opinions about how they are treated relative to employees in other parts of the organization. Can you relate to this example? Most people suffered as a result of believing that the teacher they had in school was a much stricter grader than the teacher down the hall. They believed that their teacher's high grading standards disadvantaged them compared to those fortunate enough to have the pushover as a grader. Research has established that people tend to distort their performance relative to others in a positive direction (Cascio & Aguinis, 2011). The aggregated research establishes that one of the most difficult challenges for managers is to convince employees that they were treated fairly, that actions affecting their pay were based on a fair appraisal of their performance, and that the appraisal ratings and actions affecting the pay of others were fair, compared to the employee's. These realities should be shared with employees, and employees should be shown the research that demonstrates these tendencies exist in all of us. Telling employees that we all are predisposed to perceptions that positively distort our performance relative to others sets the stage for developing a credible process for minimizing inconsistency across employees and units in the appraisal process.

More on Performance Management

One of the authors consulted with a national research laboratory that relied on a performance management process that produced a high level of acceptance on the part of employees that performance ratings were fair, on a relative basis, across the organization. Once all the supervisors in a unit had done their appraisals, the manager conducted a "calibration session" with all supervisors present. Through discussion and presentation of job-related facts, the ratings of each supervisor were compared to those of all the others. Once the calibrations were done at that level, the next level of management convened a session with all of the direct-report managers. The process continued all the way to the top of the organization.

There was no attempt to force ratings into a normal distribution, a practice that has had very little legal success (Boyle, 2001). Rather, managers were required to produce aggregated rankings and to rely on those ranks to recommend pay actions. The appraisal ratings were adjusted as appropriate to equalize the rigor of the performance standards used by each rater, using whatever method each manager deemed appropriate. Because there was a fixed pool for pay actions, based on competitive analysis and business realities, if the ratings were fair on a relative basis, then the pay actions were as well. Making employees aware of the calibration process and of the reasons for its adoption contributed significantly to dispelling the notion that peers in other units were receiving more advantageous treatment. It also led to employee perceptions that the employer's obligations under the psychological contract were being fulfilled.

CONCLUSION

In summary, there is substantial research evidence that can be useful to HR practitioners in convincing employees that they are being treated fairly and in a manner consistent with the perceived employment relationships they have with their employers. If HR practitioners are not aware of the research or if they do not understand the relevance of research findings to their issues, the potential value of that research will be lost. In addition, if the practitioners do not use the research to guide them in communicating to employees why policies and practices are fair and why they are being used, the true value of the research will not be fully realized. In today's hypercompetitive markets, HR professionals should seize such opportunities to share enlightened, evidence-based management practices. Doing so can reduce the scholar–practitioner divide that has so much potential for improving EORs.

REFERENCES

Adams, J. S. (1963). Toward an understanding of inequity, *Journal of Abnormal Psychology, 67*, 422–436.

Bandura, A. (1997). *Self-efficacy: The exercise of control*. New York, NY: Freeman.

Bartunek, J. (2007). Academic–practitioner collaboration need not require joint or relevant research: Toward a relational scholarship of integration. *Academy of Management Journal, 50*, 1323–1333.

Bass, B. M. (1974). The substance and the shadow. *American Psychologist, 29*, 870–886.

Bernardin, H. J., Hagan, C. M., Kane, J. S., & Villanova, P. (1998). Effective performance management. In J. W. Smither (Ed.), *Performance appraisal: State of the art in practice* (pp. 3–48). San Francisco, CA: Jossey-Bass.

Bhaskar-Srinivas, P., Harrison, D. A., Shaffer, M. A., & Luk, D. M. (2005). Input-based and time-based models of international adjustment: Meta-analytic evidence and theoretical extensions. *Academy of Management Journal, 48*, 257–281.

Boyle, M. (2001, May 28). Performance review: Perilous curves ahead. *Fortune*, 187–188.

Briscoe, D. R., Schuler, R. S., & Claus, L. (2009). *International human resource management* (3rd ed.). London, UK: Routledge.

Buckingham, M., & Coffman, C. (1999). *First break all the rules: What the world's greatest managers do differently*. New York, NY: Simon & Schuster.

Byrnes, N. (2006, May 1). The art of motivation. *Business Week*, 56–62.

Cascio, W. F. (2011). Professional associations: Supporting useful research. In E. E. Lawler & S. A. Mohrman (Eds.), *Doing research that is useful for theory and practice—25 years later* (pp. 251–267). San Francisco, CA: Berrett-Kohler.

Cascio, W. F. (in press). Global performance management systems. In I. Bjorkman, G. Stahl, & S. Morris (Eds.), *Handbook of research in international human resource management* (2nd ed.). London, UK: Edward Elgar Ltd.

Cascio, W. F., & Aguinis, H. (2008). Research in I/O psychology from 1963-2007: Changes, choices, and trends. *Journal of Applied Psychology, 93*, 1062–1081.

Cascio, W. F., & Aguinis, H. (2011). *Applied psychology in human resource management* (7th ed.). Upper Saddle River, NJ: Pearson Prentice-Hall.

DeNisi, A. S., & Sonesh, S. (2011). The appraisal and management of performance at work. In S. Zedeck (Ed.), *APA handbook of industrial and organizational psychology* (Vol. 2, pp. 255–277). Washington, DC: American Psychological Association.

Dowling, P. J., Festing, M., & Engle, A. D., Sr. (2009). *International human resource management* (5th ed.). Mason, OH: Thomson-South-Western.

Dunnette, M. D. (1990). Blending the science and practice of industrial and organizational psychology: Where are we and where are we going? In M. D. Dunnette & L. M. Hough (Eds.), *Handbook of industrial and organizational psychology* (2nd ed., Vol. 1, pp. 1–27). Palo Alto, CA: Consulting Psychologists Press.

Greenberg, J. (2009). Everyone talks about organizational justice but no one does anything about it. *Industrial/Organizational Psychology, 2*, 181–195.

Greene, R. J. (2011). *Rewarding performance: guiding principles, custom strategies*. New York, NY: Routledge.

Hofstede, G., & Hofstede, G. J. (2005). *Cultures and organizations: Software of the mind* (2nd ed.). New York, NY: McGraw-Hill.

Latham, G. P. (2007). *Work motivation*. Thousand Oaks, CA: Sage.

Latham, G. P. (2009). *Becoming the evidence-based manager: Making the science of management work for you*. Boston, MA: Davies-Black.

Lepak, D. P., & Snell, S. A. (1999). The human resource architecture: Toward a theory of human capital allocation and development. *Academy of Management Review, 24*, 31–48.

Lester, S. W., Turnley, W. H., Bloodgood, J. M., & Bolino, M. C. (2002). Not seeing eye to eye: Differences in supervisor and subordinate perceptions of and attributions for psychological contract breach. *Journal of Organizational Behavior, 23*, 39–56.

Masters, J. K., & Miles, G. (2002). Predicting the use of external labor arrangements: A test of the transaction cost perspective. *Academy of Management Review, 45*, 431–442.

Milkovich, G. T., Newman, J. M., & Gerhart, B. (2011). *Compensation* (10th ed.). New York, NY: McGraw-Hill.

Murphy, K. R., & Saal, F. E. (1990). What should we expect from scientist–practitioners? In K. R. Murphy & F. E. Saal (Eds.), *Psychology in organizations: Integrating science and practice* (pp. 49–66). Hillsdale, NJ: Erlbaum.

Nucor Corporation. (2009). *Annual Report*. Retrieved on August 24, 2010, from http://phx.corporateir.net/External.File?item=UGFyZW50SUQ9MzczODg4fENoaWxkSUQ9MzcxODA3fFR5cGU9MQ==&t=1.

Pulakos, E. D., & O'Leary, R. S. (2011). Why is performance management broken? *Industrial and Organizational Psychology: Perspectives on Science and Practice, 4*, 146–164.

Robinson, S. L. (1996). Trust and breach of the psychological contract. *Administrative Science Quarterly, 41*, 574–599.

Robinson, S. L., & Rousseau, D. M. (1994). Violating the psychological contract: Not the exception but the norm. *Journal of Organizational Behavior, 15*, 245–259.

Roehling, M. V., Cavanaugh, M. A., Moynihan, L. M., & Boswell, W. R. (2000). The nature of the new employment relationship: A content analysis of the practitioner and academic literatures. *Human Resource Management, 39*, 305–320.

Rousseau, D. M. (2011). The individual-organization relationship: The psychological contract. In S. Zedeck (Ed.), *APA handbook of industrial and organizational psychology* (Vol. 3, pp. 191–220). Washington, DC: American Psychological Association.

Rupp, D. E., & Beal, D. (2007). Checking in with the scientist–practitioner model: How are we doing? *The Industrial–Organizational Psychologist, 45*, 35–40.

Rynes, S. L. (2007). Let's create a tipping point: What academics and practitioners can do, alone and together. *Academy of Management Journal, 50*, 1046–1054.

Rynes, S. L., Colbert, A. E., & Brown, K. G. (2002). HR professionals' beliefs about effective human resource practices: Correspondence between research and practice. *Human Resource Management, 41*, 149–174.

Rynes, S. L., Giluk, T. L., & Brown, K. G. (2007). The very separate worlds of academic and practitioner periodicals in human resource management: Implications for evidence-based management. *Academy of Management Journal, 50*, 987–1008.

Tekleab, A. G., & Taylor, M. S. (2003). Aren't there two parties in an employment relationship? Antecedents and consequences of organization-employee agreement on contract obligations and violations. *Journal of Organizational Behavior, 24*, 585–608.

Turnley, W. H., & Feldman, D. C. (1999). The impact of psychological contract violations on exit, voice, loyalty, and neglect. *Human Relations, 52*, 895–922.

Zhao, H., Glibkowski, W. S., & Bravo, J. (2007). The impact of psychological contract breach on work-related outcomes: A meta-analysis. *Personnel Psychology, 60*, 647–680.

22

Conclusion and Directions for Future Research

Lynn M. Shore
San Diego State University

Jacqueline A-M. Coyle-Shapiro
London School of Economics and Political Science

Lois E. Tetrick
George Mason University

Our goal for this volume was to expand the boundaries of the employee–organization relationship (EOR) literature by critically examining established viewpoints, forging connections with potentially related but independent literatures, and questioning the utility of EOR concepts for organizational goals. We believe all of these goals have been met and in many ways exceeded. In this chapter, we discuss each of these goals, and then present suggestions for future research directions based on the contributions to this volume.

EXAMINING ESTABLISHED VIEWPOINTS

Social exchange theory (Blau, 1964), the norm of reciprocity (Gouldner, 1960), and the inducements–contributions model (March & Simon, 1958) have dominated the EOR literature. As reviewed in the introductory chapter to this volume, the evidence gathered in support of the application of these paradigms has been overwhelmingly positive. Why then, might the reader ask, question established viewpoints? Our answer is because these simple models of exchange do not fully explain the social, contextual, and complex world of work as experienced by individuals and groups in relation to the EOR. Below are some of the themes pertaining to established viewpoints that emerged across chapters.

Who Is the "O"?

Although a fundamental issue that has been raised in prior research (see, for example, Coyle-Shapiro & Shore, 2007; Shore, Porter, & Zahra, 2004), theorizing about the "O" in the EOR has remained underdeveloped. Particularly noteworthy in the EOR literature is that as yet, there has been little exploration empirically of who represents the organization in the relationship. Likewise, there has been little theoretical development in understanding the basis for employee perceptions of the organization as an entity in a relationship. Many of the chapters in this volume point to ways to enrich and understand how employees develop perceptions of a relationship with the "O" and make evaluative judgments about that relationship. In doing so, new concepts and theories have been introduced to broaden and deepen our understanding of the EOR. Ashforth and Rogers (Chapter 2) argue for the preeminence of the tribe (supervisor and group members) in determining members' perceptions of the EOR. Although they argue that the organization provides the context in which tribes operate, the organization is an abstraction (especially if large), and so individuals look to the tribe (their supervisor especially as their primary organizational agent, and their peers) for formulating an understanding of the organization. Essentially, this is a shared understanding of the organization as an entity that then becomes translated into personal, relational terms as reflected in psychological contracts and perceived organizational support. Several other authors in this volume argue for the key role of the supervisor as the organizational agent who creates employee perceptions of the EOR. Schminke (Chapter 3), van Knippenberg (Chapter 4), Takeuchi (Chapter 12), Bartol and Dong (Chapter 11), and Shore and Coyle-Shapiro (Chapter 6) all highlight the critical role of the supervisor in formulating the EOR. In each of these chapters, different literatures are drawn upon and varied mechanisms of influence are proposed.

van Knippenberg points to the vital role of the supervisor in shaping employees' understanding of a shared organizational identity.

This shared identity is based on the ability of the supervisor to convey an image of him- or herself as embodying the organization. van Knippenberg depicts the supervisor as a proactive organizational agent who can enhance the EOR through identification processes. Bartol and Dong also view the supervisor as an active participant in the EOR, but highlight his or her role as a translator of the organization-level employment relationship for the employee through a trickle-down model. Shore and Coyle-Shapiro view the supervisor as an agent who can treat employees in a harmful manner and thus help shape perceptions that the organization is cruel. However, like Bartol and Dong, they argue that only when the supervisor is viewed by the employee as acting in concert with higher level organizational systems do perceptions of the relationship with "O" get created.

Schminke draws upon the ethics literature, spotlighting the key role of supervisors in influencing ethical behaviors. His chapter thus underlines the potential for the supervisor to influence the EOR through social learning processes. Specifically, employees may make inferences about the EOR by observing the direct supervisor. What the supervisor says and does, how the supervisor treats employees, and the way the supervisor represents the organization to employees may all be key sources of influence. Schminke also sees a role for top managers and coworkers, but argues for the preeminence of the supervisor in formulating perceptions of the EOR.

Like Ashforth and Rogers, Takeuchi points out the value of examining social exchange in the work group setting by concurrently focusing on multiple relationships. Based on relational demography theory, he argues for the greater influence of some relationships than others based on a newly conceptualized form of deep-level similarity—relational exchange ideology. Specifically, Takeuchi conjectures that there are many relationships that can be used to help devise perceptions of the EOR (supervisor, individual coworkers, the work group) but that employees opt to choose others at work for this formulation who hold similar beliefs about the norm of reciprocity (i.e., exchange ideology).

These chapters together underline the criticality of human agents, whether individuals or groups, in influencing employee perceptions of a relationship with "O." The chapters differ in the underlying processes that inform such perceptions to include identification, social learning, relational demography, and various exchange processes. Uncovering additional processes that influence how employees perceive their relationship with "O" and empirically testing the propositions presented in these chapters is an area that merits further work.

And Then There Is Social Exchange

Pearce (Chapter 7) believes that despite the reference to social exchange as the primary theoretical base in the EOR literature, the actual focus has primarily been on economic exchange due to the framing of reciprocity as involving inducements and contributions. She points out that several different types of exchange are used in the EOR in organizations, including equity (in which participants receive inducements commensurate with their contributions), equality (all participants receive the same inducements regardless of their contributions), and need (in which participants receive the inducements they need, regardless of their contributions). As Pearce points out, the focus in the literature on equity, or balance, has limited thinking and understanding of the EOR. Although needs have played a role in the EOR literature (cf. Eisenberger & Stinglhamber, 2011; Masterson & Stamper, 2003), the focus has been on need fulfillment resulting from social exchange rather than need-based exchange.

Shapiro and Fugate (Chapter 13) likewise comment on the instrumental focus of the inducements–contributions and associated social exchange paradigm reflected in the EOR literature. They argue that a chief limitation of existing literature is the emphasis on the past and present (what has been given and received in the EOR), without consideration of the role of the future, specifically, the anticipatory appraisals of social exchange by both employee and employer. Based on a review of empirical research, these authors put forward the view that anticipatory justice does indeed enhance inducements and contributions as well as employee attraction and retention.

McLean Parks and smith (Chapter 5) spotlight another type of exchange—ideological—that has received much less attention in the EOR literature. Although relying on exchange of resources, the authors do not frame these ideas in social exchange terms as per Blau (1964), but rather through identification processes. They develop the concept of ideological crystallization—that is, when multiple members of an organization hold shared meanings about ideological resource elements of the relationship, which can serve to enhance identification with the organization. Conversely, when the organization's commitment to the ideology waivers, employees may react quite negatively (e.g., alienation, disidentification, and turnover), and these effects are likely to be more pervasive than when ideological crystallization is low. These arguments highlight the importance of integrating theories other than social exchange to explain the broader EOR domain, including negative relationships.

Shore and Coyle-Shapiro (Chapter 6) raise questions about whether social exchange theory and the negative norm of reciprocity (Gouldner, 1960) are adequate for explaining relationships within the negative EOR domain. McLean Parks and smith's ideas point to social identity theory and other theories of belonging, as well as literature on alienation (cf. Etzioni, 1975) that may help develop this domain. Likewise, Pearce's arguments highlighted earlier imply that need theories (exchanges based on need) and social justice theories (equity and equality exchanges) may also be meaningful ways of framing negative relationships in the EOR. Research already points to the value of these arguments. For example, Lawrence and Robinson (2007) highlight the role of need frustration in their model of workplace deviance, and many studies in the EOR literature incorporate justice as a key element (see Shapiro & Fugate, Chapter 13). Thwarted and dysfunctional relationships are likely to operate differently than positive relationships that rely on social exchange arguments and point to the necessity of expanding the theoretical bases of the EOR literature.

Changing Nature of Work and Work Arrangements

Several chapters point to the changing nature of work and work arrangements, including Guest and Rodrigues (Chapter 8), Kossek and Ruderman (Chapter 9), Gallagher and Connelly (Chapter 10), and Bartol and Dong (Chapter 11). All of these authors point to the utility of social exchange theory for understanding a variety of formal work arrangements such as temporary and contract employees, part-time and full-time employees, virtual work, and varied (flexible) work hours. The arguments made across chapters suggest the universality of social exchange and the norm of reciprocity for understanding the building and maintenance of relationships between people, regardless of the formalized role (e.g., contract, permanent) held by the individual with the organization.

Guest and Rodrigues focus on career exchange, comparing the old career (based on mutual interests and long-term career exchange) with the new career (a more short-term exchange in which the organization provides meaningful and developmental work experiences in exchange for employee commitment to work toward organizational goals). They conclude that organizational tenure has not changed significantly and temporary employment has not grown greatly since the 1990s, signifying that traditional organizational careers are surviving. As these authors point out, although promotions are likely to be fewer, their data suggest that the strength of the mutual commitment between individuals and organizations remains the same, supporting the utility of the social exchange paradigm for present-day organizations.

Bartol and Dong's model highlights the essential role of a mutual investment approach to the employment relationship for virtual employees and also for managing work virtuality. Key human resources (HR) practices suggested by these authors are those that imply a long-term relationship, such as encouraging employee development and offering contingent rewards, because these will be effective in attracting and eliciting commitment of virtual employees to the organization. Likewise, mutual investment employers expect broader contributions from employees in return. This will signal to virtual employees that they are valued and are in a social exchange relationship. Thus, Bartol and Dong suggest that the development of EORs based on social exchange can be beneficial to both exchange parties—employee and organization—and can help create a positive virtual relationship.

An issue raised by Gallagher and Connelly is the effect of the presence of contingent workers on permanent workers and the inherent challenges this poses. Social comparison theory might suggest that permanent workers would view their relationship with the organization more positively given their permanent status. However, the authors point to evidence that suggests permanent employees engage in withdrawal behaviors perhaps because they worry more about their own job security or because of increased responsibilities. This highlights the importance of the social environment in determining employees' interpretations of organizational signals pertaining to the nature of the EOR. Different employment arrangements in the same work group may have unintended negative effects if not carefully managed, raising questions about organizational motives among permanent employees.

Kossek and Ruderman examine the work–family flexibility research via the social exchange perspective and argue that the "mere offering of flexibility is a necessary but insufficient condition to result in a positive social exchange for either organizations or individuals" (Chapter 9, the section "Implementation Gap"). The balancing of employer and employee interests is critical to the success of flexibility practices. Flexibility practices that are offered are often not used by employees because these practices conflict with the organizational culture, which may, for example, equate long hours with commitment and dedication. Managers may find it challenging to work with employees who are telecommuting or working part time because this provides fewer opportunities for "face time" that is used by managers to assess productivity and effort. Like virtual relationships, the extra effort required in creating and supporting social exchange relationships may challenge managers who work with employees in nontraditional roles. The authors cite evidence that employees may not always benefit from utilizing flexible practices because there may be significant losses experienced both at work and at home associated with doing so. The social exchange paradigm applied in the EOR literature provides insights into how, from a relational perspective, flexibility practices may be problematic for both the employee and the employer.

Forging Connections

Although there is a great deal of literature on entry and dissolution of employment, much of the literature has not incorporated an EOR lens, but rather has tackled these issues from a practical, predictive perspective. For example, which applicants are offered employment or accept jobs in organizations? Which employees retire or quit, and why? How do employees react to fair or unfair treatment? Several authors in this volume developed expanded perspectives of employment processes via the incorporation of the EOR, including Shapiro and Fugate (Chapter 13), Ryan (Chapter 14), Hom (Chapter 15), and Wang and Zhan (Chapter 16).

Shapiro and Fugate argue for the value of examining anticipation of fair or unfair treatment in all stages of the EOR—preentry anticipation, maintenance, and dissolution of the relationship. They argue for the value of these future-oriented perspectives on the EOR because they influence the behavior of employees and the behavior of those serving as organizational agents in the relationship (e.g., the immediate manager, HR managers). Anticipation of future reciprocation or lack thereof becomes important in all stages of the EOR because in social exchange the timing of reciprocation is unspecified (Shore, Tetrick, Lynch, & Barksdale, 2006).

Ryan points out that the applicant views their interaction with the organization in relational terms, which she refers to as the applicant–organization relationship (AOR). Citing a large and growing body of literature on recruitment and applicant attraction, she highlights the potential connections that can be made from the EOR literature to the development of the AOR literature. Ryan also makes an important point about the signaling effect from the applicant's perspective of the AOR for the potential future EOR. Like Shapiro and Fugate, these ideas spotlight the importance of employee anticipation of future treatment as signaling the likely quality of the EOR.

Hom presents a model of turnover that integrates the employment relationship model of Tsui, Pearce, Porter, and Tripoli (1997) with literature on job embeddedness (Mitchell, Holtom, Lee, Sablynski, & Erez, 2001). He links each of the four employment relationship types with push-to-leave forces (e.g., job dissatisfaction), pull-to-leave forces (e.g., job alternatives), pull-to-stay forces (e.g., community embeddedness), and push-to-stay forces (e.g., family pressures to stay). Hom's model provides a thought-provoking foundation for linking the organization-level employment relationship with the individual-level decision to stay or leave the organization. Like other chapters in this volume (cf. Bartol & Dong, Chapter 11; Shore & Coyle-Shapiro, Chapter 6), Hom connects organization-level decisions about the type of EOR provided with individual-level experiences, decisions, and behavior. Testing of such cross-level models will be critical to moving the EOR literature forward.

Building on the cross-level theme, Wang and Zhan present a model of the EOR that focuses specifically on older workers. In their chapter, they argue for the importance of organizations considering the unique perspective and needs of older employees in their policies and practices. Resources and benefits such as health care benefits and support and socioemotional support may encourage older workers to delay retirement, whereas retirement incentives may encourage earlier retirement decisions. In their model, these resources, or inducements, are examined by older employees through the lens of the EOR and their perceptions of organizational support prior to deciding when to retire and what type of retirement approach to take (e.g., bridge employment). This chapter provides an example of theorizing about need-based exchange as recommended by

Pearce (Chapter 7) by focusing on whether organizations meet the needs of older workers and how the degree of need fulfillment contributes to choices pertaining to retirement.

Similarly, Avery, McKay, and Roberson (Chapter 19) focus on the needs of minorities, highlighting this somewhat neglected aspect of exchange. Based on current research, these authors conclude that (a) perceived organizational obligations differ for minority and majority employees, and (b) many minority employees pay particular attention to what they perceive to be diversity promises and are especially responsive to their fulfillment. Given the increasing levels of global diversity, these authors underline the importance that organizations should place on the sometimes differing needs and preferences that may be associated with the EOR.

In sum, this set of chapters all focus on processes pertaining to the development, maintenance, or cessation of employment and how the EOR may influence such processes. In each chapter, there are distinct elements, but the general theme is that the relational processes reflected in the EOR literature influence a variety of employment decisions through employee and employer understanding of the nature of the relationship.

THE EOR AND ITS IMPACT

Each of the chapters in this volume discusses issues pertaining to the EOR that are important for employees, work groups, and organizations. Some of the chapters also tackle broader societal issues. Following is a discussion of the impact of the EOR on each of these focal recipients.

Impact on Individuals

Many of the chapters present ideas or models that specifically pose that the EOR affects individuals. One area that has been highlighted in several chapters is that of emotion. Other than some research on psychological contract breach and violation (cf. Morrison & Robinson, 1997; Rousseau, 1995; Zhao, Wayne, Glibkowski, & Bravo, 2007), the role of emotions in the EOR has received very limited attention. Tetrick (Chapter 18) argues that emotions at both the individual and collective level are central to understanding the EOR and subsequently employee and organizational health.

She points out that emotions play a pivotal role in translating employees' reactions to their treatment by the organization, serving as the glue that commits the employee to the organization in the case of positive emotions or disbands the relationship in the case of negative emotions. Schminke (Chapter 3) argues for the potential role of emotions in the development of the EOR, and Shore and Coyle-Shapiro (Chapter 6) hypothesize that negative emotions such as anger and fear result from perceptions of organizational cruelty.

Many chapters have discussed how the EOR is associated with employee decisions to join, stay, or leave organizations and whether employees choose to have a career in a single organization or multiple organizations. Less often studied are examinations of how different formal work arrangements influence perceptions of the EOR, whether these varied arrangements influence career exchange differently, and how such variability in work arrangements and associated EOR perceptions influences work–family strain, family dynamics, children's health and happiness, and viability of communities. These nonwork outcomes seem very important and yet are virtually ignored in most of the EOR literature.

Impact on Organizations

Tetrick (Chapter 18) argues that individual health and organizational health influence one another because healthy organizations can supply valued individual inducements that have a positive impact on employee health, and vice versa, in a reciprocal exchange of beneficial treatment. Lepak and Boswell (Chapter 17) view the EOR as one means to better link HR practices with firm performance, especially given that HR practices do not seem to have consistent effects. They also note that differences in the EOR among groups within the same organization may dilute the effects of the strategic HR efforts by organizational leaders by raising employee concerns of equity and fairness. Related to this, Avery et al. (Chapter 19) point out that the fulfillment of implied diversity-related obligations is likely to be related to improved organizational performance in general by enhancing perceptions of organizational support to a diverse set of people. Furthermore, Salas and Fiore (Chapter 20) argue for the increasing importance of the EOR in light of the diverse interconnections both inside and outside the organization critical to organizational success. To facilitate this end, some organizations create and manage work teams as a strategy to strengthen the EOR. In fact, they point out that the "employee" in the EOR can be viewed as the collective of employees—the teams that the organization empowers to accomplish its goals—and that such a focus will facilitate greater links between the EOR and organizational performance.

Cascio and Greene (Chapter 21) discuss the scholar–practitioner divide in relation to the EOR. Although scientific evidence about the EOR can support and enhance management decisions, there are often disconnects between researchers and managers and also between managers and employees impacted by the decisions. These authors argue for the importance of closing these gaps. In particular, researchers should specify the practical implications for managers and make research-based evidence accessible to them. In turn, managers should familiarize themselves with the research evidence pertaining to the EOR, incorporate it into their decisions, and share with employees how and why these decisions were made.

FUTURE RESEARCH

Several themes are apparent in these chapters that point to future research needs. Although social exchange theory and the norm of reciprocity are widely supported by research evidence and viewed as essential to EOR research, many authors argue that the theoretical basis of the EOR needs to be broadened. Social identity theory seems a strong contender for enriching our understanding of the EOR, and several chapters highlight its role in understanding, enhancing, and harming the EOR—the latter occurring in cases where the organization acts in ways that are counter to the belief system associated with the organizational identification. Clearly, more research is needed to test these ideas.

Another theme is the emphasis on cross-level and trickle-down models of the EOR. As highlighted across chapters, studies developing and evaluating sources of influence at the organizational, team, supervisory, and individual level concurrently and separately are needed. The view that the EOR is occurring at multiple linked levels is becoming increasingly apparent and is reflected in several chapters in this volume. The complexity associated with such cross-level linking makes it critical for scholars to provide a body of evidence that can be used by organizational leaders to make decisions about the EOR that are conducive to a variety of positive outcomes at the individual, group, and organizational levels, as well as considering outcomes that are important more broadly, such as those affecting families and communities.

Many of the chapters also highlighted the ways that the workforce and the world of work are changing and the associated call for examining the EOR in light of these changes. Assuming a "one size fits all" model of the EOR limits the utility of this body of knowledge. There are core human phenomena, such as fulfillment of basic needs for belonging and esteem, the norm of reciprocity, and treatment that is fair and respectful, associated with the EOR. However, there are many possible ways in which different groups view these core phenomena that need to be integrated into models of the EOR in order to more fully understand relationships at work. Likewise, some of the chapters posit new ways to think about what is essential in positive relationships and aspects of work relationships that are contextualized and varied.

We requested that authors in this volume also discuss their ideas in light of cross-cultural implications. A review across chapters suggests that the EOR is likely to have cultural overtones as well as to reflect the economic and political systems in which particular organizations are embedded. Clearly, some of the essential assumptions of the EOR literature, such as the universality of social exchange and the norm of reciprocity, need examination across nations. Other relational concepts that are more culturally embedded, such as guanxi in China, also deserve attention in the EOR literature to assess whether there are both universal and specific cultural elements to the EOR that require consideration within organizations.

CONCLUSION

The chapters in this volume are varied and reflect a rich array of ideas, theories, and perspectives that hold much promise for the future of the EOR literature. The chapters stimulate new ideas and avenues, drawing upon different literatures that highlight the connections between EOR and other domains. It is our hope that the EOR and these other domains will develop in new and valuable ways, stimulating the next wave of research.

REFERENCES

Blau, P. M. (1964). *Exchange and power in social life*. New York, NY: John Wiley & Sons.

Coyle-Shapiro, A.-M., & Shore, L. M. (2007). The employee-organization relationship: Where do we go from here? *Human Resource Management Review, 17*, 166–179.

Eisenberger, R., & Stinglhamber, F. (2011). *Perceived organizational support: Fostering enthusiastic and productive employees*. Washington, DC: American Psychological Association Books.

Etzioni, A. (1975). *A comparative analysis of complex organizations*. New York, NY: Free Press.

Gouldner, A. W. (1960). The norm of reciprocity: A preliminary statement. *American Sociological Review, 25*, 161–178.

Lawrence, T. B., & Robinson, S. L. (2007). Ain't misbehavin: Workplace deviance as organizational resistance. *Journal of Management, 33*, 378–394.

March, J. G., & Simon, H. A. (1958). *Organizations*. New York, NY: Wiley.

Masterson, S. S., & Stamper, C. L. (2003). Perceived organizational membership: An aggregate framework representing the employee-organization relationship. *Journal of Organizational Behavior, 24*, 473–490.

Mitchell, T., Holtom, B., Lee, T., Sablynski, C., & Erez, M. (2001). Why people stay: Using job embeddedness to predict voluntary turnover. *Academy of Management Journal, 44*, 1102–1121.

Morrison, E. W., & Robinson, S. L. (1997). When employees feel betrayed: A model of how psychological contract violation develops. *Academy of Management Review, 22*, 226–256.

Rousseau, D. M. (1995). *Psychological contracts in organizations: Understanding written and unwritten agreements*. Thousand Oaks, CA: Sage Publications.

Shore, L. M., Porter, L. W., & Zahra, S. A. (2004). Employer-oriented strategic approaches to the employee-organization relationship. In J. A.-M. Coyle-Shapiro, L. M. Shore, M. S. Taylor, & L. E. Tetrick (Eds.), *The employment relationship: Examining psychological and contextual perspectives* (pp. 135–160). Oxford, UK: Oxford University Press.

Shore, L. M., Tetrick, L. E., Lynch, P., & Barksdale, K. (2006). Social and economic exchange: Construct development and validation. *Journal of Applied Social Psychology, 36*, 837–867.

Tsui, A. S., Pearce, J. L., Porter, L. W., & Tripoli, A. M. (1997). Alternative approaches to the employee-organization relationship: Does investment in employees pay off? *Academy of Management Journal, 40*, 1089–1121.

Zhao, H., Wayne, S. J., Glibkowski, B. C., & Bravo, J. (2007). The impact of psychological contract breach on work-related outcomes: A meta-analysis. *Personnel Psychology, 60*, 647–680.

Author Index

A

Abramson, L. Y., 156
Ackerman, P. L., 432
Adams, G. A., 434, 436, 439
Adams, J. S., 571
Adkins, C. L., 317
Adler, D., 104
Agarwal, R., 291
Aguinis, H., 559, 571
Aguirre, A., 521
Ahearne, M., 292
Ajzen, I., 494
Alarcon, G. M., 157
Albert, S., 194
Allen, D. G., 176, 296, 414, 465
Allen, N. J., 42, 88
Allen, T. D., 239, 522
Allen, V. L., 119
Alley, D., 472
Alliger, G. M., 322
Alonso, A., 545
Amabile, T. M., 98, 297
Amare, N., 368
Amit, R., 284
Anand, V., 148, 150
Anastasopoulou, C., 497
Andersen, S. M., 119
Anderson, N., 343, 346, 355, 376
Andrews, M. C., 316
Ang, S., 155, 261, 263, 270, 276, 307–308, 311
Anger, K., 246
Aquino, K., 141, 157, 161, 162
Argyis, A., 5
Armeli, S., 7, 9, 40, 87, 312, 316, 470
Armstrong, R. W., 57
Arnaud, A. U., 68
Arnold, J., 195, 208
Arnold, T. J., 36
Arthur, J. B., 457
Arthur, R. J., 162
Aryee, S., 465
Ashford, S. J., 105, 169, 255, 271, 272, 405, 408
Ashforth, B. E., 11, 14, 23, 24, 27, 28, 29, 31, 33, 36, 39, 40, 44, 46, 85, 86, 87, 89, 91, 92, 115, 119, 132, 148, 151, 184, 194
Ashkanasy, N. M., 57, 266, 500
Athos, A., 194
Atkinson, C., 256, 258
Atkinson, J., 368
Atwater, L., 39
Aumann, K., 225
Avery, D. R., 15, 379, 380, 509, 510, 513, 514, 516, 519, 523, 524, 585, 586
Avey, J. B., 355, 498
Avolio, B. J., 104, 349, 355, 498
Axtell, C. M., 287

B

Bacharach, S. B., 311
Bachiochi, P., 523
Bachler, C. J., 367
Bagozzi, R. P., 75, 491
Bailey, T. C., 357
Bailly-Bender, A., 210
Bakalis, S., 513
Balkin, D., 391
Balkundi, P., 402
Ballard, K. A., 161
Ballinger, G., 394
Baltes, B. B., 225
Bamberger, P. A., 162, 311
Bandura, A., 37, 293, 556
Baranik, L. E., 438, 522
Barber, A. E., 378, 379
Bardack, N. R., 372
Bardes, M., 59

591

Bargal, D., 173
Barger, P. B., 500
Bargh, J. A., 344, 347, 354
Barker, J. R., 36, 38
Barker, R. G., 179
Barksdale, K., 4, 8, 392, 432, 495, 584
Barnard, C. I., 456
Baron, J., 194, 391, 395, 399, 400, 401, 403, 414, 416
Baron, N., 255
Barrick, M. R., 367, 372
Barry, B., 348
Barsade, S. G., 500
Barsky, A. P., 496
Bartol, K. M., 13, 14, 281, 282, 284, 285, 286, 288, 290, 291, 292, 295, 578, 579, 581, 582, 584
Bartunek, J., 411, 559
Baruch, Y., 194, 203
Bass, B. M., 92, 93, 94, 98, 555
Basuil, D., 399
Bateman, T. S., 35, 464
Batson, A., 411
Batt, R., 391, 395, 398, 399, 405, 410, 415, 416, 418, 455, 475
Bauer, T. N., 33, 318, 367, 371, 471
Baumeister, R. F., 152
Bax, E. H., 417
Bazerman, M. H., 371
Beal, D. J., 514, 555
Bechtold, D., 415
Becker, B. E., 395
Becker, T. E., 32, 65, 66, 393
Bedeian, A. G., 312, 313
Beecher, H. J. M., 511
Beehr, T. A., 318, 429, 436, 439, 450
Behling, O., 470
Bell, B. S., 287, 290, 291, 292, 301, 346, 347, 348, 354, 371, 372
Bell, M. P., 309
Bell, S. J., 55, 56
Ben-Hador, B., 33
Benner, C., 201
Bennett, B., 132
Bennett, M., 367
Bennett, N., 115, 307, 462
Bennett, T. M., 446
Benson, L., 381

Berger, J., 516
Bernardin, H. J., 570
Berruecos, L., 409
Bertolino, M., 367
Bhardway, A., 524
Bhaskar-Srinivas, P., 570
Bhattacharya, C., 120, 133
Bhawuk, D., 415
Biddle, B. J., 119
Bidewell, J., 441, 442
Bielby, W., 194
Biemiller, L., 126
Bies, R. J., 115, 132, 143, 153, 155, 157, 351
Billings-Harris, L., 510
Bindl, U. K., 496
Biron, M., 311
Bix, B., 128
Bjorkman, I., 395, 401, 416
Blackhart, G. C., 152
Blackmon, K., 517
Blader, S. L., 86, 92
Blair-Loy, M., 229
Blakely, G. L., 312
Blanck, P., 524
Blank, R., 515, 521
Blasi, J., 524
Blatt, R., 169, 255
Blau, P. M., 1, 2, 3, 72, 85, 87, 91, 113, 117, 139, 144, 171, 182, 183, 238, 255, 261, 263, 284, 296, 307, 309, 392, 428, 458, 465, 487, 577, 580
Bloodgood, J. M., 558
Bobbio, A., 98
Bobko, P., 405
Bodner, T. E., 239, 246, 367
Boisnier, A., 46
Bolino, M. C., 307, 465, 466, 558
Bommer, W. H., 36, 55, 323
Bonacum, D., 539
Bonaiuto, M., 98
Bond, J., 225
Bonner, B. L., 541
Bonoma, T. V., 465
Borman, W. C., 315
Boswell, W. R., 15, 176, 228, 455, 457, 467, 468, 469, 470, 472, 473, 474, 565, 586

Bowen, F., 517
Bowen, S. A., 57
Bowers, C., 535
Bowling, N. A., 157
Boxall, P., 204, 455, 456, 461
Boyle, M., 572
Braddy, P., 224
Bradley, J. C., 496
Brandes, P., 23, 47
Brandl, J., 357
Brass, D. J., 30, 402
Breaugh, J. A., 377, 379, 380
Brender, Y., 151
Bretz, R. D., 378, 466, 523
Brewer, M. B., 45, 91
Brief, A. P., 464, 497, 517
Briner, R. B., 1
Briscoe, J., 207, 208, 209
Brock, P., 345
Brockbank, W., 285, 294
Brockner, J., 312, 314
Brockwood, K., 242
Broschak, J. P., 276
Brown, D. J., 92
Brown, G., 140, 143
Brown, K. G., 559
Brown, M. E., 56, 58, 317
Brown, S. L., 493
Brown, W., 203
Brunner, E., 154
Bryman, A., 98
Buch, R., 261, 265
Buckley, M. R., 373
Buffardi, L. C., 379, 523
Bunderson, S., 114, 516
Burke, C. S., 536, 538
Burt, R. E., 266
Burt, R. S., 263
Burton, J., 215, 394, 399, 403, 411, 413
Bushouse, E., 542
Butemeyer, J., 96
Butler, J., 391
Butterfield, K., 402
Buttner, E. H., 510, 512, 514
Buttner, H. B., 348
Buyens, D., 33, 472
Byrnes, N., 561, 563
Byron, K., 287, 518

C

Cable, D. M., 103, 198, 317, 378, 380, 382, 490
Cacioppo, J., 500
Cadin, L., 210
Camarota, S. A., 511
Camerer, C., 263
Cameron, K. S., 44, 498
Campbell, G. E., 545
Campion, J. E., 379
Campion, M. A., 367, 368, 371, 409, 438, 535, 545
Cannon-Bowers, J. A., 535, 536, 544, 546, 547
Caplan, R., 127
Cappelli, P., 194, 209, 210, 226, 231, 256, 391, 407, 417, 418
Carlson, D. S., 59
Carmeli, A., 33, 39
Carnoy, M., 201
Carraher, S. M., 373
Carroll, M., 461
Carroll, S. A., 378
Carstensen, L. L., 431, 432
Carter, M., 394, 401, 403, 412, 413
Cascio, W. F., 16, 297, 555, 559, 570, 571, 587
Cashman, J. F., 463
Castells, M., 201
Castellucci, F., 311
Cavanaugh, M. A., 449
Chambers, E., 200
Chan, C., 365
Chang, K. T., 13
Chao, G. T., 311
Chapman, D. S., 378
Charles, S. T., 432
Chatman, J. A., 46, 124, 133, 317
Chattopadhyay, P., 255, 514
Chaturvedi, S., 456
Chavez, T. L., 371
Chen, G., 456
Chen, S., 119
Chen, S.-J., 391
Chen, X.-P., 186, 430, 432
Chen, Y., 430
Chen, Z. X., 45, 311, 522

Cheng, B. S., 309
Cheng, J. L., 338
Chiaburu, D. S., 35
Chittipeddi, K., 32
Chmielowski, T., 367
Choi, Y., 104
Chonko, L. B., 59
Chou, L.-F., 263
Chow, C. W., 45
Christiansen, C., 117
Chun, R., 31
Chung, Y., 455
Church, P. H., 259
Ciarocco, N. J., 152
Cicero, L., 98
Claes, R., 489
Clapperton, G., 493, 494
Clark, B. A., 75
Clark, J. P., 157
Clark, L. A., 496, 498
Clark, M. A., 44
Clary, E. G., 176
Claus, L., 570
Clement, R. W., 38
Cleveland, J. N., 315
Clinton, M., 489
Clugston, M., 159
Cobb, M. G., 87
Cochran, P. L., 57
Cohen, E. G., 516
Cohen, J. D., 75
Cohen, L., 208
Cohn, M. A., 493
Colbert, A. E., 559
Colin, J., 161
Collins, C., 297, 377, 395, 456
Colquitt, J. A., 140, 148, 263, 308, 316, 338, 343, 346, 347, 348, 350, 354, 512
Colton, C., 242
Colvin, A. J. S., 228, 391, 395, 399, 410, 416, 418, 457, 467
Combs, J., 215, 392
Conger, J. A., 92, 93, 94, 97, 98, 104
Conn, A. B., 35
Connaughton, S. L., 299
Connelly, C. E., 13, 169, 255, 256, 257, 258, 259, 261, 265, 266, 271, 276, 581, 582

Converse, S. A., 536
Conway, A. M., 493
Conway, N., 1, 8, 196, 264, 307, 308, 309, 310, 316, 436, 437, 490
Cook, K., 402, 467
Cooke, F. L., 461
Cooke, N. J., 547
Cooley, C. H., 119
Cordery, J. L., 493
Corley, K. G., 24, 28
Cornwell, J. M., 524
Cotton, J. L., 522
Cox, T., Jr., 511, 517, 523, 524
Coyle-Shapiro, J. A-M., 1, 8, 9, 12, 23, 24, 30, 31, 32, 56, 64, 75, 139, 151, 181, 196, 238, 255, 261, 264, 265, 266, 276, 296, 307, 308, 309, 310, 311, 312, 316, 337, 366, 375, 432, 436, 437, 471, 472, 525, 565, 577, 578, 579, 581, 584, 586
Craig, S. B., 87
Crant, C. J., 464
Cravey, A., 409
Crawford, M. T., 36
Crimmins, E., 427, 430
Crooker, K., 121
Cropanzano, R., 42, 68, 155, 256, 307, 308, 310, 311, 314, 316, 337, 418, 429, 434, 436, 437, 439, 447, 487, 488
Cruthirds, K., 410
Culbertson, S. S., 472
Cullen, J. B., 68
Cullen, L. T., 369
Cummings, J., 470
Cummings, L. L., 115

D

D'Amato, A., 432
Dabos, G. E., 34, 368
Dahm, M. J., 526
Dähne, D., 125
Daibo, I., 500
Damasio, A., 75
Daniels, K., 298
Darley, J. M., 75
Darnold, T. C., 228, 372, 467
Dasborough, M. R., 500, 501

Datta, D. K., 395, 399, 475
Daus, C. S., 511
Davey, A., 442
Davies, G., 31
Davis, J. H., 263
Davis, W. D., 456
Davis-Blake, A., 276
Dawson, J. F., 46
Day, D. V., 74, 88, 105
Day, E. A., 96
de Chermont, K., 496
de Jong, J., 489
de Oliveira-Souza, R., 75
De Vos, A., 33
De Witte, H., 211, 489
De Witte, K., 262
Deakin, S., 203
Dean, J., Jr., 457
Dean, J. W., 475
Dechant, K., 517
Decker, D. L., 367
DeGrassi, S. W., 367
Delbecq, A. L., 292
Delery, J. E., 455, 456, 474
DeMarr, B., 231
Demuijnck, G., 519
DeMuth, R., 209
Dendinger, V. M., 443
DeNisi, A. S., 570
Depolo, M., 438
DeRidder, R., 144
Deriso, M., 373
Derous, E., 371
DeRue, D. S., 105, 550
Desmette, D., 439
DeSteno, D., 75
DeStobbeleir, K., 373
Deutsch, M., 347
DeVos, A., 373, 377, 379, 472
DeWall, C. N., 152
Dharwadkar, R., 23
Dickinson, T. L., 536
Diekema, D. A., 287
Diener, E., 497
Dienesch, R. M., 317
Dineen, B. R., 56, 379, 391
Dino, R. N., 287
Dirks, K. T., 114, 311

Distelberg, B., 230
Dixon, S., 427
Dodds, W. B., 285
Doeringer, P. B., 256
Dolen, M. R., 367
Donaldson, S. I., 519
Dorsch, K. D., 547
Doty, D. H., 455, 456, 474
Drago, R., 150
Drake, B. H., 58
DuBrin, A. J., 298
Duchon, D., 32
Dufresne, R. L., 153
Dulac, T., 311, 312, 337, 338, 342, 472
Dumas, T., 241
Dunfee, T. W., 57, 69, 70
Dunford, B. B., 457
Dunford, R., 200
Dunnette, M. D., 555
Dustin, S. L., 372
Dutton, J. E., 33, 89, 91, 94, 107, 115, 194, 216, 489

E

Earley, P. C., 45
Earnshaw, J., 461
Eaton, S. C., 235, 237
Eberly, M., 394
Eby, L. T., 401, 404, 438, 522
Eden, D., 104
Edmondson, A. C., 155
Edmondson, D. R., 509
Edwards, R., 243
Efendioglu, U., 200
Egan, T. D., 309, 510
Eichler, D., 75
Einhorn, H. J., 386
Eisenberger, R., 1, 6, 7, 9, 10, 11, 24, 31, 32, 36, 39, 40, 64, 65, 66, 85, 87, 88, 89, 91, 107, 140, 142, 145, 152, 159, 162, 196, 197, 238, 239, 294, 295, 296, 307, 308, 312, 316, 343, 438, 439, 458, 463, 465, 470, 494, 509, 510, 512, 516, 525, 580
Eisenhardt, K. M., 515
Ekeh, P. P., 171, 183, 184
Elder, A. E., 523

Ellingson, J. E., 262
Elsass, P. M., 515
Elsbach, K., 120, 132, 133
Ely, R. J., 515
Emerson, R. M., 467
Enders, J., 46
Eng, W., 357
Engle, E. M., 312, 313, 317, 318
Erdogan, B., 33, 46, 105, 106, 312, 317
Erez, M., 300, 393, 584
Ertug, G., 311
Eschleman, K. J., 157, 158
Esses, V. M., 524
Etzioni, A., 75, 131, 133, 581
Evans, J. A., 269, 270
Evans, R. W., 456
Evets, J., 202

F

Fandt, P. M., 466
Fang, R., 56, 391
Faraj, S., 281
Farh, C. I., 290, 295
Farmer, S. M., 291
Farndale, E., 376
Farr, J. L., 378
Farrell, D., 156, 407, 497
Fay, C. H., 276
Fedor, D. B., 373
Fehr, E., 465
Feinberg, B., 429
Feldman, D. C., 9, 270, 382, 429, 436, 437, 441, 442, 442, 443, 494, 558
Feldman, J. M., 345
Felps, W., 176, 402–403, 407, 408, 411
Ferguson, M., 382
Ferrell, O. C., 56, 60
Ferrin, D. L., 311
Ferris, G. R., 31, 293, 391, 466
Festinger, L. A., 37, 132, 317
Fielding, J., 161
Finegold, D., 403
Fiore, S. M., 16, 536, 586
Fireman, B., 28
Fireman, S., 393
Fisher, G., 430, 523
Fisher, S. L., 231, 257, 259

Fishman, C., 47
Fisk, A. D., 429, 430
Fiske, S., 132
Fleck, S. J., 287
Florey, A. T., 318
Flynn, F. J., 312, 313, 314
Foa, U., 117, 126, 127
Ford, R., 67
Fowlkes, J. E., 538, 541, 546
Fraccaroli, F., 438
Fredrickson, B. L., 493, 496
Friedman, R., 382
Frink, D. D., 373
Frisch, M. B., 357
Fugate, M., 14, 44, 335, 412, 413, 580, 581, 585, 584

G

Gaertner, S., 391
Gaillard, M., 439
Gainer, K., 470
Gajendran, R. S., 287, 294
Galinsky, E., 225
Gallagher, D. G., 13, 114, 169, 255, 256, 257, 258, 259, 261, 265, 271, 276, 581, 582
Gamson, W. A., 28, 42
Ganster, D., 151
Gardner, W. L., 156
Garud, R., 293
Gaudine, A., 75
Gavin, J. H., 318
Gebert, D., 515
Gellatly, I. R., 439
George, E., 169, 255, 276
George, J. M., 161, 497
Gephart, R. P., 284
Gerhart, B., 378, 392, 523, 562
Gerstner, C. R., 74, 88
Ghosh, D., 57
Ghoshal, S., 289, 297
Gibbs, J. L., 299
Gibney, R., 312, 521
Gibson, C. B., 159, 291, 299, 340, 358
Gilley, K. M., 261
Gilliland, S. W., 371, 381, 382, 418
Gilmer, D. F., 431

Gilson, L. L., 287, 297
Giluk, T. L., 559
Gittell, J. H., 47, 418
Glebbeek, A. C., 417
Glew, D. J., 141
Glibkowski, B. C., 1, 34, 75, 140, 585
Glibkowski, W. S., 558
Glibowski, B., 382
Goffman, E., 119, 183, 184
Goldberg, C. B., 315
Golden, T. D., 281, 282, 287, 290, 293
Goldman, B. M., 307, 55, 141, 155, 307, 312, 383, 519
Golubovich, J., 392
Gordon, M. E., 266
Gorman, J., 547
Gould, S., 194
Gouldner, A. W., 7, 68, 79, 87, 139, 144, 296, 307, 309, 310, 428, 458, 465, 487, 577, 581
Graen, G. B., 64, 88, 343, 463
Graham, S., 539
Grant, R. M., 297
Grant-Vallone, E. J., 519
Gratton, L., 467, 468
Graves, D. E., 526
Graves, L. M., 515
Green, R. M., 68
Greenbaum, R. L., 59, 67
Greenberg, J., 96, 337, 351, 490, 495, 512, 569
Greene, J. D., 16, 75
Greene, R. J., 555, 562, 567, 568
Greguras, G. J., 371, 375
Greller, M. M., 228, 441
Grewal, D., 285
Griffin, B., 441
Griffin, D., 381
Griffin, R. W., 35, 140, 141
Grugulis, I., 461
Grunig, L. A., 534
Gruys, M. L., 262
Guay, R. P., 400, 401, 403
Guendelman, S., 409
Guest, D. E., 13, 196, 209, 211, 213, 215, 216, 489, 495
Guglielmi, D., 438
Gully, S. M., 493

Gundry, L. K., 26
Gupta, V., 293, 416
Gutek, B. A., 141, 383, 519, 524
Gutherie, J. P., 391
Guy, C. W., 365

H

Hachiya, D., 398
Hackett, R. D., 160, 311
Hagan, C. M., 570
Hains, S. C., 102
Hall, A., 215
Hall, D., 193, 194, 199, 207, 208, 209
Halpin, S. M., 105
Hamagami, F., 443
Hamilton, D. L., 36
Hamilton, V. L., 322
Hammer, L. B., 239, 242, 246, 433
Hancock, J. B., 176
Hand, H. H., 407
Handy, C., 256
Hanges, P., 416
Hannum, K., 224
Harden, E., 455
Harland, L. K., 262
Harris, R., 200
Harrison, D. A., 35, 56, 287, 290, 291, 294, 298, 300, 309, 315, 316, 318, 399, 402, 513, 570
Harrison, G. L., 45
Harrison, M. M., 105
Harrison, S. H., 24, 33
Harter, J. K., 526
Harvey, M. G., 307
Hasher, L., 430
Haski-Leventhal, D., 173
Haslam, S. A., 89, 92, 95, 105
Hastings, D., 341, 342
Hatfield, E., 500
Hause, E. L., 367
Hausknecht, J. P., 391, 392, 395, 419
Hayes, T. L., 526
Haynes, D., 496
Hebl, M. R., 514, 523
Hegel, G. W. F., 129
Heider, F., 132, 152, 317, 320, 321
Heine, S. J., 273

Henderson, D. J., 36, 37, 311, 312, 323, 325, 337, 472
Henkens, K., 440
Henrich, J., 273
Hernandez, M., 523
Herscovitch, L., 85
Hershey, D. A., 443
Highhouse, S., 367, 523, 526
Hill, J. W., 393
Hill, S. N., 291
Hinsz, V. B., 542
Hirst, G., 96
Hite, J. P., 171, 391, 457
Hitt, M. A., 457
Hochschild, A., 215, 229
Hofmann, D. A., 307, 311, 413, 419, 493, 498
Hofstede, G. J., 45, 69, 159, 160, 299, 352, 353, 571
Hogarth, R. M., 377
Hogg, M. A., 85, 86, 87, 89, 92, 93, 95, 98, 101, 102, 106
Hollenbeck, J. R., 379
Hollinger, R. C., 157
Hollingshead, A. B., 291
Holtom, B. C., 215, 392, 393, 394, 405, 410, 584
Holton, E. F., 535
Holzer, H. J., 513
Hom, P. W., 14, 144, 145, 177, 286, 296, 301, 391, 393, 394, 395, 399, 400, 401, 402, 403, 404, 405, 406, 407, 409, 411, 412, 413, 414, 415, 417, 418, 419, 493, 583, 584
Homans, G. C., 183, 263, 307, 309, 463
Homung, S., 249
Hong, Y., 456
Hopkins, N., 99, 100, 102, 103
Horowitz, M. J., 162
House, R. J., 92, 98, 416
Howell, J. P., 159
Howes, J. C., 42, 46
Huang, M.-H., 263
Huang, Z., 411
Huffman, A. H., 522
Hukai, D., 522
Hulin, C. L., 398, 407
Hulland, J. S., 293
Hülsheger, U. R., 376

Humphrey, R., 132
Huntington, R., 6, 64, 88, 142, 238, 294, 307, 438, 458, 509
Huselid, M. A., 391, 395, 455, 456
Husted, B. W., 60
Hutchinson, S., 294, 438, 458, 509
Hutchison, S., 6, 64, 88, 142, 238, 307

I

Ibarra, H., 211
Ilgen, D. R., 345
Imus, A. L., 276
Inceoglu, I., 496
Inderrieden, E. J., 392
Inkson, K., 194, 208
Irving, G., 198, 216
Isabella, L., 194
Isaksson, K., 211, 489
Isen, A. M., 493
Ituma, A., 273
Ivancevich, J. M., 526
Iverson, R. D., 393, 403, 416, 417, 456
Iyer, R., 58, 60
Iyer, U. J., 183

J

Jackson, J., 124
Jackson, S. E., 315, 441, 456–457
Jacobs-Lawson, J. M., 429
Jacoby, S., 209, 211
James, E. H., 519
James, K., 96
James, L. R., 502
Janis, I. L., 343
Janssen, O., 312
Jarvenpaa, S., 299
Javidan, M., 416
Jayakody, J. A. S. K., 349
Jex, S., 428, 430
Jia, L. D., 56, 347
Johns, G., 27
Johnson, C. D., 518
Johnson, D. J., 46
Johnson, E. C., 30, 316, 406, 469
Johnson, J. L., 9
Johnson, K. M., 9, 295

Johnson, O. E., 517
Joiner, T. A., 513
Joireman, J., 311, 312
Jones, T. M., 57
Joplin, J. R. W., 511
Joshi, M., 148
Judd, C. M., 24

K

Kahn, R. L., 29, 119, 131
Kalleberg, A. L., 203, 211, 255
Kamdar, D., 311, 312
Kane, K., 154
Kane, M. J., 75
Kanter, R. M., 149, 229, 522
Kanungo, R. N., 92, 93, 94, 97, 98, 104
Kaplan, S. A., 496
Karam, E. P., 550
Kashima, Y., 45
Kasper-Fuehrera, E. C., 266
Kearney, E., 515
Keefe, J., 391
Kehoe, R. R., 468
Kellerman, B., 149
Kelloway, E. K., 151
Kelly, H. H., 465
Kennedy, F. A., 46
Kessler, I., 9, 276, 366
Khazanchi, S., 518
Khilji, S., 216
Kickul, J. R., 34, 472
Kidder, D. L., 114, 129, 132, 259
Kidwell, R. E., Jr., 462
Kiekel, P. A., 547
Kiewitz, C., 472
Kilduff, M., 378, 380
Kilian, C. M., 522
Kim, S., 270, 443
King, E. B., 514
King, L., 497
King, Z., 194, 208
Kinicki, A. J., 27, 406, 412, 414
Kirkman, B. L., 159, 286, 291, 292, 293,
    338, 340, 344, 345, 346, 347, 348,
    349, 352, 357, 372
Kirsch, M. P., 345
Kleef, G. A., 497, 515

Klein, K. J., 35, 38, 513
Kleiner, B. H., 269
Kleinman, D. L., 544
Klieger, D. M., 375
Klimchak, M., 31, 88
Klimoski, R., 547, 550
Kline, M. J., 57
Knight, D. B., 29, 42
Knowles, M. L., 152
Kochhar, R., 457
Koenigs, M., 75
Kogut, B., 297
Kolvereid, L., 272
Konovsky, M. A., 308, 312, 318, 329
Kossek, E. E., 13, 176, 223, 224, 225, 230,
    231, 232, 233, 234, 235, 238, 239,
    240, 241, 242, 243, 244, 245, 246,
    248, 581, 582
Kottke, J. L., 88
Kowalski, R. M., 466
Kozlowski, S. W. J., 287, 290, 291, 292, 293,
    301, 311, 345
Kraatz, M. S., 373, 470
Kram, K. E., 521
Kramer, R. M., 105, 120, 266
Kravitz, D. A., 371
Krawiec, G. M., 294
Kreiner, G. E., 44
Kreps, D., 391, 395, 399, 400, 401, 403, 414,
    416
Krettenauer, T., 75
Kriska, S. D., 370
Kristof, A. L., 317, 469
Kristof-Brown, A. L., 30, 316, 400, 401,
    403, 406, 408, 469
Kroeck, K. G., 94
Krueger, J., 38
Kruglanski, A. W., 98
Krugman, P., 209
Kruse, D., 524
Kuenzi, M., 59, 68
Kumar, K., 547
Kurzban, R., 24

L

Labovitz, G., 470
Laham, D., 547

Lam, S. S. K., 315
Lambert, L., 198, 490, 491
Lamond, D., 298
Landauer, T. K., 547
Lane, N. E., 546
Lang, W., 432
Langa, G. A., 291
Laughlin, P. R., 541
Lauring, J., 520, 521
Lautsch, B., 224, 231, 235, 244, 248
Lawler, J., 391
Lawrence, P. R., 28, 36, 581
Leary, M. R., 154, 157, 466
Leonard, M., 539
Leong, F., 392
Lepak, D. P., 15, 149, 176, 204, 276, 284, 286, 392, 455, 456, 460, 461, 470, 474, 475, 565, 586
LePine, J. A., 263
LePine, M. A., 470
Lepisto, L., 436
Lerner, J. S., 155
Lester, S. W., 34, 307, 472, 558
LeTart, J. F., 285
Leung, K., 351, 352
Levi, A., 39
Levine, D., 510, 514
Lewis, K., 42, 141, 307, 312, 383, 519
Li, C., 56, 347
Li, J. T., 448
Liang, J., 160
Liao, H., 455, 456, 468, 476
Lickel, B., 25
Liden, R., 6, 31, 33, 88, 89, 90, 92, 105, 265, 465, 471, 487
Lievens, F., 380
Lim, G., 365
Lind, E. A., 6, 276
Littler, C., 200
Liu, S., 443
Liu, W., 282, 284, 285, 288
Liu, Y., 215, 392
Loi, R., 34
Lord, R. G., 92, 105, 312, 313, 317, 318
Lord, J., 542
Loughry, M. L., 46
Lowe, K. B., 94, 159, 353, 510
Loyd, D. L., 318, 518

Luchak, A. A., 439, 440
Luchman, J. N., 496
Luhtanen, R., 294
Luk, D. M., 570
Lusch, R. F., 307
Luthans, F., 355, 498
Lynch, P. D., 4, 7, 9, 40, 87, 145, 164, 311, 312, 316, 392, 432, 470, 495, 584

M

Ma, L., 395, 459
MacDonald, G., 154, 157
MacKenzie, S. B., 466
Macky, K., 455, 456
MacNeil, I. R., 116
Macy, M., 125
Maddux, W. W., 45
Madjar, N., 296, 297
Mael, F. A., 44, 85, 86, 87, 91, 92, 115
Malinowski, B., 182
Mallon, M., 208, 210
Maltarich, M., 392, 393, 406, 407
Maner, J. K., 152
Mann, L., 343
Manz, C. C., 292, 413
Mao, Y., 34
March, J. G., 1, 2, 4, 115, 130, 139, 143, 171, 238, 255, 261, 309, 335, 336, 392, 428, 456, 458, 577
Margolis, J. D., 153
Marks, M. A., 545
Marmot, M. G., 154
Martinko, M. J., 156
Maruping, L., 291
Marvin, D., 373
Maslyn, J. M., 317
Massey, A. P., 543
Masters, J. K., 565
Masters, M. F., 521
Masterson, S. S., 27, 42, 264, 307, 311, 313
Masuch, M., 79
Mathews, R. A., 225
Mathieu, J. E., 286, 292
Matsuba, M. K., 75
McCarty, C. E., 522
McCausland, T., 446
McElroy, J., 297

McFarland, L. A., 370, 376
McKay, P. F., 15, 379, 509, 510, 513, 514, 517, 523, 524, 526, 585
McLean Parks, J., 11, 12, 75, 87, 88, 113, 114, 115, 116,117, 118, 119, 120, 121, 122, 123, 124, 126, 127, 128, 129, 130, 132, 133, 259, 265, 580, 581
Merton, R. K., 117
Meyerson, D. E., 266
Michaels, E., 200
Michel, J., 230, 234, 235
Milanovich, D., 541, 545
Miles, G., 565
Mills, J., 467
Mirvis, P., 199, 207, 208
Mirza, C., 379
Mobley, W. H., 393, 393, 407
Moffitt, K. R., 414
Mohammed, S., 547
Mohrman, S., 403
Montes, S. D., 140, 198, 216
Moore, A. B., 75
Moorman, R. H., 262, 312
Morgeson, F. P., 276, 307, 311, 368, 372, 419, 501, 550
Morris, M. A., 513, 524
Morrison, E., 9, 36, 37, 115, 143, 290, 366, 381, 488, 490, 496
Morrow, P., 261, 265, 297
Morton, K. R., 75
Mowday, R. T., 88
Munir Sidani, Y., 358
Murphy, K. R., 386, 555
Myktyn, P. P., 299

N

Nahum-Shani, I., 162
Nash, D., 203
Nazarian, D., 518
Neuberg, S., 24
Neyer, A. K., 357
Nichol, V., 232, 238
Nicholson, N., 216
Nifadkar, S., 338
Nijstad, B. A., 497
Nippert-Eng, C., 227

Norenzayan, A., 273
Notelaers, G., 262, 371
Nyberg, A. J., 392, 393, 394, 399, 403, 410, 413, 419
Nystrom, L. E., 75

O

O'Leary-Kelly, A. M., 9, 140, 141, 150
O'Reilly, C. A., III., 315
Ofori, G., 59
Oldham, G. R., 296, 518
Olson, J. M., 371
Organ, D. W., 132
Osterman, P., 194, 195, 203
Ostrosky-Solís, F., 75

P

Paddock, E. L., 148
Padilla, A., 149
Page, R., 376
Pagon, M., 151
Paik, Y., 369
Panzer, F. J., 545
Park, D. C., 430
Parker, S. K., 493, 496
Pascale, R., 194
Patterson, M. G., 26
Pearce, J. L., 4, 12, 56, 139, 169, 171, 172, 174, 176, 178, 179, 180, 181, 182, 183, 184, 187, 232, 256, 261, 284, 292, 314, 374, 391, 429, 457, 458, 492, 537, 580, 584, 585
Pedigo, P. R., 294
Pelled, L. H., 515
Peña, D. G., 409, 410
Pennings, J. M., 457
Perrewé, P. L., 496, 497
Peters, R. H., 181, 182, 184
Peterson, S. J., 355, 498
Phillips, A. S., 312, 313, 318
Phillips, J. M., 379
Phillips, K., 241
Philpot, J. W., 266
Pichler, S., 239, 240
Pierro, A., 98
Platow, M. J., 89, 92

Plowman, D. A., 32
Ployhart, R. E., 87, 367, 370, 371, 375, 377, 378
Pohler, D. M., 439
Posner, B. Z., 35
Posthuma, R. A., 438
Preacher, K., 412
Premack, S. L., 367
Prince, C., 541
Pruitt, D., 128, 129, 133
Prussia, G. E., 412
Pugh, S. D., 153, 308, 312, 318, 319, 517, 521
Pulakos, E. D., 315, 570
Purcell, J., 9

R

Raghavan, A., 149
Ragins, B. R., 522, 524
Ramirez, M., 410
Rapson, R. L., 500
Raver, J. L., 141
Reilly, G., 392
Reingen, P. H., 28
Rhoades, L., 1, 6, 7, 24, 36, 40, 65, 85, 87, 88, 89, 91, 140, 142, 197, 238, 295, 296, 316, 343, 438, 494, 509, 510, 512, 516, 525
Ribeiro-Soriano, D., 56
Ridgeway, C. L., 516
Riggio, R. E., 94
Riggle, R. J., 509
Roberson, Q. M., 527
Roberts, K., 59, 231
Rodell, J. B., 346, 347, 348, 354
Rodrigues, R., 13, 193, 209, 213, 581
Roese, N., 371
Roethlisberger, F. J., 177
Rogers, G., 156, 497
Rogers, K. M., 11, 14, 23, 28, 86, 184, 578, 579
Rogers, W. A., 429, 430
Rohdieck, S., 145
Romero, E., 410
Rosenbaum, J., 196
Rosenholtz, S. J., 516

Rosenthal, R., 119
Rouby, D. A., 152
Rousseau, D. M., 1, 5, 13, 26, 33, 34, 37, 64, 66, 75, 87, 88, 114, 116, 118, 129, 139, 143, 176, 195, 197, 203, 206, 210, 217, 226, 228, 240, 249, 255, 256, 263, 266, 288, 312, 313, 336, 368, 373, 377, 380, 458, 460, 466, 467, 470, 488, 494, 500, 557, 558
Rozin, P., 319
Roznowski, M., 398
Ruderman, M. N., 13, 176, 223, 224, 241, 245, 581, 582
Russell, J. A., 401, 404, 498
Ryan, A. M., 276, 346, 363, 366, 367, 368, 369, 370, 371, 375, 376, 377, 378, 583, 584

S

Sabol, B., 286
Sahlins, M. D., 7, 8, 307, 465, 487, 489
Saint-Giniez, V., 210
Salancik, G. R., 36, 176, 323
Salas, E., 16, 533, 536, 538, 539, 541, 542, 543, 544, 546, 547, 550, 586
Salvador, R., 59
Samarah, I. M., 299
Samuels, S., 409
Sanchez, J., 345
Schat, A. C. H., 151
Schaubroeck, J., 59, 315
Schepman, S., 157
Schippers, M. C., 515
Schleicher, D. J., 368
Schmidt, J. B., 543
Schminke, M., 11, 14, 55, 56, 68, 78, 307, 308, 311, 338, 344, 351, 354, 578, 579, 586
Schmit, M. J., 366, 370, 375
Schneider, B., 149, 470, 502
Schneider, K. T., 157
Schoorman, F. D., 263
Schroth, H. A., 371
Schuler, R. S., 441, 456, 470
Schurman, R., 120
Seetharaman, P., 299

Seidner, R., 47
Seligman, M. E. P., 156, 493
Shaffer, M. A., 367, 570
Shalley, C. E., 297, 518
Shamir, B., 92, 93, 94, 97, 98, 99, 100, 104
Shanock, L. R., 65
Shapiro, D. L., 290, 335, 336, 337, 338, 340, 344, 345, 346, 347, 348, 349, 350, 352, 353, 356, 357, 372, 516, 580, 581, 583, 584, 586
Sharafinski, C. E., 88
Shauman, K. A., 404
Sherman, S. J., 36
Shi, Q., 427
Shore, L. M., 1, 4, 6, 8, 12, 23, 24, 27, 30, 31, 32, 36, 37, 55, 56, 64, 75, 85, 86, 87, 88, 114, 128, 139, 145, 151, 171, 175, 176, 181, 196, 197, 223, 228, 238, 241, 255, 266, 282, 294, 296, 307, 308, 310, 311, 312, 315, 316, 323, 335, 336, 343, 349, 365, 367, 370, 374, 377, 378, 381, 382, 392, 409, 432, 436, 439, 446, 458, 462, 465, 470, 471, 474, 477, 495, 525, 526, 534, 555, 565, 566, 577, 578, 579, 581, 584, 586
Shore, T. M., 6, 145, 196, 294, 307
Singlhamber, F., 238
Sisaye, S., 45
Sitkin, S. B., 132, 263
Skaggs, B., 402
Skarlicki, D. P., 141, 145, 156, 157
Slaughter, S. A., 263, 276
Slipp, S., 515, 521
Sluss, D. M., 30, 31, 33, 34, 39, 46, 87, 88, 90, 119
Smith, A. D., 32
Smith, C. M., 542
Smith, D. B., 35
Smith, E. M., 293
smith, f. l., 11, 12, 113, 114, 116, 117, 119, 120, 122, 123, 124, 126, 127, 128, 129, 130, 133, 580
Smith, K. G., 296, 297, 395, 456
Smith, R. M., 498
Smith, V., 211
Smola, K., 196, 202
Snell, S. A., 204, 294, 457, 460, 461, 475, 565
Snyder, C. R., 345, 354, 357
Soete, L., 200
Song, L. J. W., 4, 56, 144, 458
Sorensen, K. L., 509, 514
Sorra, J. S., 35
Sowa, D., 6, 64, 88, 142, 238, 294, 307, 438, 458, 509
Spaeth, J. L., 120
Sparrowe, R. T., 31, 88, 89, 90, 92, 114, 130, 134, 265, 467
Speicher, B. L., 521
Spell, C. S., 36
Stahl, G., 210
Stanley, D. J., 85
Staw, B. M., 174
Steiner, D. D., 371
Stephens, D., 58
Stern, I., 170
Stevens, C. K., 307, 377, 527
Stevens, M. J., 535, 545
Stierwalt, S. L., 523
Stilwell, D., 317
Stinson, V., 371
Stone, E. F., 367
Stone, D. L., 367
Stout, R., 538, 541, 547
Straub, D., 270
Straus, S. G., 300
Stroh, L. K., 441
Sturges, J., 215, 216
Sucharski, I. L., 10, 24, 31, 65, 88, 196, 238, 295, 343
Swann, W. B., 345, 354
Swiercz, P. M., 285

T

Tajfel, H., 89, 91, 92, 265, 515
Takeuchi, R., 13, 14, 204, 307, 312, 392, 395, 446, 456, 462, 578, 579
Tamkins, M. M., 27
Tange, H., 520, 521
Taras, V., 340
Teasdale, J. D., 156

Tee, E. U. J., 500
Tekleab, A. G., 5, 9
Tellegen, A., 496, 497, 498
Terry, D. J., 85, 86, 89, 98
Tesluk, P. E., 291
Tetrick, L. E., 1, 4, 15, 23, 24, 27, 36, 37, 67, 68, 75, 88, 181, 255, 266, 296, 311, 323, 370, 374, 377, 381, 382, 392, 432, 446, 462, 474, 477, 485, 493, 495, 498, 565, 577, 584, 585, 586
Thakor, A. V., 44
Tharenou, P., 392
Thorne, L., 75
Tiano, S., 410
Tiedens, L. Z., 155
Tijoriwala, S. A., 176
Tinsley, C. H., 352
Tomaskovic-Devey, D., 287
Tonidandel, S., 524
Tower, S. L., 379
Toya, K., 456
Trevino, L. K., 56, 57, 58, 59, 68, 71, 73, 78, 79, 155, 317
Tripathi, R. C., 144
Tse, H. H. M., 500
Tsui, A. S., 4, 8, 9, 10, 14, 45, 56, 77, 78, 139, 140, 143, 144, 145, 171, 176, 232, 243, 284, 286, 298, 309, 314, 315, 338, 347, 352, 374, 391, 392, 393, 394, 395, 399, 400, 401, 402, 404, 407, 409, 410, 415, 416, 417, 429, 434, 448, 457, 458, 460, 475, 492, 493, 496, 514, 524, 537
Tugade, M. M., 498
Tung, R., 210
Turban, D., 380, 382
Turken, A. U., 493
Turnley, W. H., 9, 311, 382, 494, 558
Twenge, J. M., 152
Tyers, R., 427
Tyler, T. R., 6, 86, 92

U

Uhl-Bien, M., 64, 88, 317

V

Van de Ven, A. H., 292
van de Vliert, E., 119
van Dick, R., 30, 39, 46, 86, 93, 96
van Dijk, E., 92
Van Dyne, L., 115, 132, 155, 156, 226, 227, 242, 261, 276, 307, 311, 312, 543
Van Hoye, G., 380
van Kleef, G. A., 497, 515
van Knippenberg, B., 87, 98, 102
van Knippenberg, D., 11, 14, 85, 86, 87, 89, 90, 91, 92, 93, 94, 95, 96, 98, 99, 101, 102, 104, 105
van Leeuwen, E., 92
Van Maanen, J., 193
van Solinge, H., 440
Vandenberghe, C., 24, 65, 88, 152, 238, 343, 393
Vardaman, J. M., 176
Venkataramani, V., 368
Victor, B., 68
Villanova, P., 509, 570
Volpe, C. E., 536
Vredenburgh, D., 151

W

Waldman, D. A., 33, 159, 394
Wallace, A. M., 202
Wang, A.-C., 263
Wang, D., 311, 395, 415, 416, 417, 458
Wang, H., 311, 392, 456
Wang, M., 427, 428, 430, 436, 440, 441, 442, 443, 446, 583, 584
Wang, T.-Y., 263
Wang, X., 15, 216
Warren, C. R., 496
Watabe, M., 402
Wayne, S. J., 1, 6, 34, 36, 75, 88, 91, 140, 265, 307, 311, 312, 323, 337, 382, 465, 466, 472
Weick, K. E., 32, 266, 469
Weiner, B., 156
Weldon, E., 448
Werbel, J. D., 46
West, M. A., 46, 216, 410, 414, 419, 518
Westman, M., 322

Westphal, J. D., 170
Wetherell, M. S., 86
Wheatley, K., 23
White, I. A., 315
Whitney, K., 315
Widmeyer, W. N., 547
Wiesenfeld, B., 293
Wiesner, R., 200
Williams, K. J., 57, 151, 152, 322
Williamson, O., 204
Wood, J. L., 367
Wooten, L. P., 519
Wren, A. O., 373
Wright, P., 204, 214, 395, 441, 457, 467, 468, 474, 475

X

Xiao, Z., 395, 399, 401, 402, 406, 407, 411, 414, 415, 416
Xin, K. R., 187, 309, 352, 515

Y

Yalabik, Z. Y., 391, 409, 414, 415, 417
Yamagishi, T., 402, 415
Yao, X., 446
Yeung, A. B., 173, 285, 294
Yi, Y., 491
Yogo, M., 500
Yonce, C. A., 367
Yoshita, Y., 367
Youndt, M. A., 475
Youngblood, S. A., 57
Yuki, M., 45
Yzerbyt, V., 24

Z

Zaccaro, S. J., 550
Zacharatos, A., 456
Zacks, R. T., 430
Zagenczyk, T. J., 312, 472, 521
Zahra, S. A., 365, 458, 578
Zammuto, R. F., 281
Zander, U., 297
Zanna, M. P., 371
Zapata-Phelan, C. P., 512
Zappala, S., 438
Zarate, M. A., 157
Zarubin, A., 428
Zatzick, C., 393, 403, 416, 417
Zeithaml, V. A., 285
Zelditch, M., 516
Zellars, K. L., 496, 497
Zeng, X., 284
Zey-Ferrell, M., 56, 60
Zhan, Y., 427, 443, 583, 584
Zhang, A. Y., 56, 65, 347
Zhang, X., 292
Zhang, Y., 459
Zhang, Z., 412
Zhao, H., 1, 9, 34, 75, 196, 382, 558, 585
Zhao, Z., 140
Zhong, L., 522
Zhou, J., 297, 518
Zimbardo, P. G., 149, 150
Zimmerman, K., 246
Zimmerman, R. D., 30, 406, 469
Zott, C., 284
Zuboff, S., 284
Zucker, L. G., 44
Zweig, D., 140
Zyphur, M., 412

Subject Index

A

Acquiescent silence, 156
Affect transfer, 39
Aging to EOR, meaning of, 428–429
   EOR benefits offered by older workers, 433–435
   EOR benefits valued by older workers, 429–433
Anthropomorphization, 39
Anticipatory justice, 337, 348
   continual revision of justice assessments, 358
   effects, boundaries of, 349–354
   in EOR research and practice, 336–341
   illustrations of, 345–349
   implications of broadening EOR to include, 354–355
      practical implications, 356–358
      theoretical implications, 355–356
Anticipatory psychological contract (APC), 379
Applicant-organization relationship (AOR), 363–389
   breach or violation of, 380–383
   culture influencing, 376
   dynamic nature of, 377–378
   elements, 364
      content and nature, 366–371
      formation of relationships, 371–374
      investments in AOR, 374–376
      parties to AOR, 364–366
   employer expectations of applicants, 372
   implications for employers, 383
   organizational agents, 365
   practical implications, 383
   relational elements/socioemotional exchange in, 367
   as signal of EOR, 378–380
Assumptions in EOR research
   EOR is clear to employees, 173–175
   EOR is driven by organization's treatment of participants, 175–177
   organization is not understaffed, 179–181
   participants are dependant on their organization, 177–179
   participants understand their participation as inducement-contribution exchange, 181–184
   volunteer-organization relationships, 171–172

B

Backbone managers, 205
Balanced reciprocity, 8
Balanced social exchange, 4. *See also* Mutual investment EOR
Behavioral sensemaking, 39
Bias/discrimination, elimination of, 519–520
Boundarylessness, 226
Boundary-spanning resource, 238
Breach, definition of, 558

C

Career promise, 195, 198
Commensurable resources, 128
Commitment, 158
Commitment and flexibility, organizations assurance of, 217
Communication rituals, 351
Confirmatory bias, 345
Confucian Dynamism, 352
Contingent EOR, 260–261
Contingent work, 263
Control, sense of, 158
Core–periphery model, 258
Core–ring model, 256

607

608 • Subject Index

Coworker ethics-related actions, 62
Coworker exchange (CWX), 322
Coworker influences on employee ethics, 59–61
Cruelty, 141
Crystallization, 124
Cultural influences, 273–274
Customization, 228–231

D

The Dark Side of Organizational Behavior (Griffin & O'Leary-Kelly), 141
Dependence situations, 158
Destructive leadership, 149
Detachment factors, 290–292
Direct-hire contingent workers, 258
Direct-hire workers, 258
Direct supervision, 33–34
Discrimination, elimination of, 519–520
Disempowerment, 154–155
Distributive justice, 350
Diversity and intensity of work–family demands, 224–226
Diversity management, 509–510
  consideration of minority viewpoints, 515–517
  current diversity trends, 510–511
  diverse representation, 513–515
  elimination of bias and discrimination, 519–520
  managerial implications, 525–526
  racioethnic diversity, influences perceptions of organizational support, 511–513
  research implications, 523–525
  support/understanding of unique minority issues
    language policies, 520–521
    mentors, 521–522
  valuation of different ideas, opinions, and perspectives, 517–519

E

Economic exchanges, 3, 440–441
Effective social identity–based leadership, 103

Effort–Reward Imbalance at Work (Siegrist), 145
Emotional contagion, 500
Emotions, 485–487, 495–496
  affect activation, 498–499
  aggregation of individual-level effects to organizational-level effects, 499–502
  EOR, ethics and, 74–76
  negative, 496–497
  positive, 497–498
  social exchange in EOR, 487–488
    inducements–contributions model, 491–495
    international perspectives, 488–489
    psychological contract fulfillment versus breach, 490–491
Employee and organizational health, interdependence of, 486
Employee–organization relationship (EOR), 1, 170–171, 282, 308, 391–392, 458, 534
  creation, maintenance, and completion of, 14–15
  EOR framework on push-and-pull forces for staying and leaving, 392–398
  EOR multilevel effects, 412–413
  and ethics. *See* Ethics, EOR and
  HRM and. *See* Human resource management and EOR, strategic
  international implications, 414–416
  underinvestment, 409–410
    interactions between push-and-pull leaving and staying forces, 411–412
    pull-to-leave forces, 411
    pull-to-stay forces, 410–411
    push-to-leave forces, 410
    push-to-stay forces, 411
  impact of, 585
    on individuals, 585–586
    on organizations, 586–587
  model refinements, 413–414
  multilevel mediation and moderation, 398

Subject Index • 609

mutual investment EOR, 284
  interactions between job
    embeddedness and shocks,
    403–404
  pull-to-leave forces, 402–403
  pull-to-stay forces, 400–401
  push-to-leave forces, 398–400
  push-to-stay forces, 401–402
as mutual obligation, 23
new ways of thinking about, 11–12
overinvestment EOR, 404
  pull-to-leave forces, 407
  pull-to-stay forces, 405–406
  push-to-leave forces, 404–405
  push-to-stay forces, 406–407
practical implications, 416–419
push-and-pull forces for different
  forms, 396
push-and-pull forces to stay or leave,
  397
putting "R" back in, 12–14
quasi-spot contracts, 407
  pull-to-leave forces, 408–409
  pull-to-stay forces, 408
  push-to-leave forces, 407–408
  push-to-stay forces, 408
relational perspective on. *See*
  Relational perspective on EOR
teamwork, team theories, and, 534–537
virtual. *See* Virtual EOR
Employees' knowledge-sharing behavior,
  297
Employee's perspectives and
  organization's, integrating,
  566–567
Employee's view of organization. *See*
  Perceived organizational
  support (POS)
Employee-tribe relationship, 46
Employment, 255
Employment relationship, work–family
  flexibility and, 223–224
  commonalities in transformation of
    work, family, and employment
    relationship, 226
  boundarylessness, 226–228
  customization, 228–231
  self-direction, 231–232

  transactional and short term,
    232–233
  growing diversity and intensity
    of work–family demands,
    224–226
  linkages to work–family flexibility,
    238
  implementation gap, 241–243
  inducement and general and
    specific social support theories,
    238–241
  power dynamics of formal and
    informal boundary-blurring
    flexibility, 243–244
  work style preferences for
    boundary-blurring preferences
    and EOR, 244–248
  work–family boundary-blurring
    flexibility practices, 234
  formal HR policies and informal
    job design feature, 234–235
  idiosyncratic deals versus
    standardized flexibility, 236
  organizational or employee
    initiated, 235–236
  policy availability and awareness
    and use, 236–237
Employment relationship model, research
  on, 145
Employment relationships, 4
Empowering leadership, 292
Enactment, in organizations, 32–33
EOR. *See* Employee–organization
  relationship (EOR)
EOR and scholar–practitioner divide,
  555–558, 559
  case study, 567–569
  criteria for scholars who perform
    research, 560–561
  integrating organization's and
    employee's perspectives,
    566–567
  Nucor, example of, 561–565
    changing employment relationships
      and the lessons of, 565–566
  practitioner criteria for using research-
    based findings, 559–560
EOR in older workers, 427–428

EORs and retirement, 435–437
  EOR and retirement intentions and decisions, 437–441
  EORs and retirement-related HRM practices, 441–444
  integrating organization's and employee's perspectives, 444–447
  meaning of aging to EOR, 428–429
  EOR benefits offered by older workers, 433–435
  EOR benefits valued by older workers, 429–433
EOR mutual investment, 284
EOR research, assumptions in
  EOR is clear to employees, 173–175
  EOR is driven by organization's treatment of participants, 175–177
  participants are dependant on their organization, 177–179
  participants understand their participation as inducement–contribution exchange, 181–184
  that organization is not understaffed, 179–181
  volunteer–organization relationships, 171–172
EOR research, implications for, 64
  cross-cultural effects, 68–70
  role of ethics as foundation for EOR, 67–68
  role of supervisors in EOR, 64–66
  structure of multiple psychological contracts, 66–67
EOR scholarship, 175, 181
EOR theory, current status of, 2
  employment relationships, 4
  perceived organizational support (POS), 6–7
  psychological contracts, 5
  social exchange theory and inducements–contributions model, 2–4
EOR versus perceived organizational cruelty (POC) concepts, 141–142
  employment relationship and POC, 143–144

psychological contracts and POC, 142–143
psychological mechanisms underlying POC, 144–146
EOR virtuality framework, 283
Equal Employment Opportunity Commission (EEOC), 364
ERA. See Ethics-related actions (ERA)
Establishing the credibility of research, 567–569
Ethical behavior, four-component model of, 73
Ethical leadership, 58
Ethics, EOR and, 55–56
  coworker influences on employee ethics, 59–61
  ethics and employment relationship, 77–79
  ethics literature, looking deeper into, 72–73
  implications for EOR research, 64
  cross-cultural effects, 68–70
  role of ethics as foundation for EOR, 67–68
  role of supervisors in EOR, 64–66
  structure of multiple psychological contracts, 66–67
  implications for ethics research, 70
  extending reach of ethics research, 70–71
  insights from building blocks of EOR, 71–72
  multidimensional models of moral behavior, 73–74
  POS, PSS, and ethics, 76–77
  role of emotion, 74–76
  supervisor influences on employee ethics, 58–59
  top management influences on employee ethics, 57–58
  top management/supervisors/coworkers, strongest influence, 61–64
Ethics-related actions (ERA), 62
Ethics Resource Center, 61, 62
Evil, 149
Exchange ideology, 316

Exchange model, 195–197
Exchange relationship
  cross-cultural ideological exchange, 131
  exchange elements, 115–121
  features of resource elements
    ideological crystallization, 124–125
    ideological incompatibility, 124
    meta-ideological exchange, 125–126
    pivotal ideological space, 121–124
    multiple pivotal spaces and absence of pivotal space, 123
    pivotal ideological space, 123
  resource commensurability and characteristics, 126–131
  resource commensurability and ideological elements of, 113–115
  role of identity, 117
  sources of resource elements, 122
  theoretical framework, 114
Exclusion, 152–153
Expanding boundaries and challenging assumptions, 1–2
  creation, maintenance, and completion of EOR, 14–15
  current status of EOR theory, 2
    employment relationships, 4
    perceived organizational support (POS), 6–7
    psychological contracts, 5
    social exchange theory and inducements–contributions model, 2–4
  new ways of thinking about EOR, 11–12
  organizational and strategic implications, 15–16
  outcomes associated with EOR, 9
    attitudes, 9
    behaviors and performance, 9–10
    putting "R" back in EOR, 12–14
    underlying explanatory mechanisms, 7
      level of investment and balance/imbalance, 8–9
      reciprocity, 7–8
Expectancy theory of motivation, 342

F

Family and employment relationship. *See* Employment relationship, work-family flexibility and
Family commitments, 224
Family creep, 227
Family-friendly practices, 433
Flexibility policies and practice, 235–236
Forging connections, 583–585
Formal flexibility policies, 224
Formal HR policies, and informal job design feature, 234–235
Formal leadership position, 101
Fostering anticipatory justice, 335–336
  anticipatory justice, illustrations of, 345–349
  anticipatory justice effects, boundaries, 349–354
  anticipatory justice in EOR research and practice, 336–341
  implications of broadening EOR to include anticipatory justice, 354–355
    practical implications, 356–358
    theoretical implications, 355–356
  model of antecedents to anticipatory justice and their relationships with EOR, 339
  model of anticipatory justice, 337
  revisiting inducements–contributions model, 341–344
    British Petroleum (example), 341–342
    Lincoln Electric (example), 341–342
"Free" managers, 205

G

Generalized EOR, 43
Generalized reciprocity, 8, 89
Gift exchange, 182
Greene (Chicago-based financial organization), 567
Group prototypicality, 101

H

Halo effect, 345
Hardiness, 157
Harmful supervisory treatment, 151–153
Health care support, 431
Heteromorphic reciprocity, 7
Hierarchical organizational culture, 44
High performance (HiPo) managers, 205
Homeomorphic reciprocity, 7
Human resource and virtuality architecture, 282
Human resource management and EOR, strategic, 455–458
    evolving issues, 458–459
    influencing HRM, 464–467
    interpretations and attributions of HRM practices, 470–471
    lack of equality in HRM, 459–461
    lack of strong effects of HRM, 461–464
    temporal nature of HRM systems, 471–473
    use versus experience of HRM systems, 467–470

I

Idealized EOR, 43
Ideological crystallization, 124–125
Ideological exchange element, 117–118
Ideological incompatibility, 124
Idiosyncratic deals versus standardized flexibility, 236
Impact of EOR, 585
    on individuals, 585–586
    on organizations, 586–587
Incompatibility, 124
Independent contractors, 258, 260, 267–271
Individual-level knowledge-sharing behavior, 296
Inducements–contributions model, 2, 238, 336, 491–495
Informal boundary-blurring practices, 224
Informational justice, 350
Information technology (IT), organization using, 281
    self-service as holy grail of, 285

Integrative social contracts theory (ISCT), 69
    principles, 69
Internal labor markets, 203
    consequences of changes for, 203
International implications, of EOR, 414–416
    expansion-related costs, 341
    and social exchange, 488–489
    and volunteering, 171–172
Interpersonal justice, 350
Intrinsic motivation, 98
Investment and balance/imbalance, 8–9

J

Job creep, 227
Job embeddedness, 393–394
Job virtuality, 286–287
Joiners, 183

K

Knowledge-based economy and globalization, 199–200
Knowledge sharing, 295

L

Leader–follower relationships, 88
Leader–member exchange (LMX), 32, 34, 64, 322
Leader relational behavior, 33
Leaders as entrepreneurs of identity, 99–105
Leadership and employment relationship, 86–94
Leadership predicted relational identification, 34
Leader visions, 93
Learned helplessness, 156
Learning orientation, 432
Lepak and Snell model, 204

M

The Man in the Grey Flannel Suit (Wilson), 229
Masculinity–femininity values, 160
Meta-ideological exchange, 118, 125–126

Minority issues, support/understanding of unique
  language policies, 520–521
  mentors, 521–522
Misspecified EOR, 23–25
  boundary conditions, 43
  implications for practice, 46–47
  implications for theory, 41–43
  national culture, 45
  nature of organization, 44–45
  organization as context, 25–27
    tribe as mediator, 27–29
  psychological convergence of tribe and organization, 39–41
  roles of tribe members
    role of focal individual, 29–30
    role of immediate manager, 30–34
    role of peers, 34–38
Moral judgment, 73
Moral sensitivity, 73
Mutual investment EOR, 77–78
  closed colleague networks reinforcing loyalty, 402
  delivery of compensation and benefits, 289
  interactions between job embeddedness and shocks, 403–404
  lessening dissatisfaction, 399
  pull-to-leave forces, 402–403
  pull-to-stay forces, 400–401
  push-to-leave forces, 398–400
  push-to-stay forces, 401–402
  turnover contagion, 402
Mutuality, 368
  cultural influences and, 369

N

National culture, 45
Negative emotions, 496–497
Negative reciprocity, 8, 79
Neglect, 156
Nonparticularistic resources, 127
Nucor, 561–565
  changing employment relationships and the lessons of, 565–566

O

Occupational elements, 120, 122
OECD Employment Outlook of 2002, 210
Older workers, EOR and, 427–428
  EOR and retirement, 435–437
    integrating organization's and employee's perspectives, 444–447
    intentions and decisions, 437–441
    retirement-related HRM practices, 441–444
  meaning of aging to EOR, 428–429
    EOR benefits offered by older workers, 433–435
    EOR benefits valued by older workers, 429–433
Organizational career survival, 193–195, 210–214
  career from social exchange perspective, 195–199
  case for retaining organizational career, 203–207
  changing context of careers and career management, 199
    changing work values, 202–203
    consequences of changes for internal labor markets, 203
    knowledge-based economy and globalization, 199–200
    migration, 201
    professionalization, 201–202
    technology, 200–201
  model of managerial career types, 205
  new career, 207–210
  percent share of temporary employment 1987–2009, 212
  separating rhetoric from reality, 214–217
Organizational citizenship behaviors (OCB), 9, 42
Organizational climate measure, 26
Organizational commitment, 439–440
Organizational culture, 27
  inventory, 26
Organizational elements, 120, 122
Organizational harm enablers, 148
Organizational identification, 95

Organizational support theory (OST), 31
Organization for Economic Co-operation and Development (OECD), 10
Organization's and employee's perspectives, integrating, 566–567
Origins (cosmetic company), 117
Ostracism, 152
Outcomes associated with EOR, 9
    attitudes, 9
    behaviors and performance, 9–10
Overinvestment EOR, 4, 77, 404
    pull-to-leave forces, 407
    pull-to-stay forces, 405–406
    push-to-leave forces, 404–405
    push-to-stay forces, 406–407

P

Particularistic resources, 127
Pecuniary elements, 118, 122
Pecuniary exchanges, 130
Peers, influence, 35
Perceived organizational cruelty (POC), 139–140
    antecedents of, 148
        harmful supervisory treatment, 151–153
        organizational harm enablers, 149–151
    comparison of POC and other negative EOR concepts, 141–142
        employment relationship and POC, 143–144
        psychological contracts and POC, 142–143
        psychological mechanisms underlying POC, 144–146
    definition of, 140–141
    model of POC, 146–148
        psychological contract, 147
    moderators
        cultural influences, 159–160
        individual, 157–159
    outcomes of POC, 154
        behavior, 155–157
        health and well-being, 154–155
Perceived organizational membership, 27

Perceived organizational support (POS), 6–7, 40, 239
    enhancing work–family relationships, 240
    PSS, and ethics, 64, 76–77
    retirement, EOR and, 438
Perceived supervisory support (PSS), 31, 39–40
    POS and ethics, 64, 76–77
Permanent employment, preference for, 211
Personalization, 39
Pivotal ideological space, 118, 121–124
POC. *See* Perceived organizational cruelty (POC)
POC versus EOR concepts, 141–142
    employment relationship and POC, 143–144
    psychological contracts and POC, 142–143
    psychological mechanisms underlying POC, 144–146
Policy availability and awareness and use, work–family benefitting, 236–237
POS. *See* Perceived organizational support (POS)
Positive emotions, 497–498
Power distance, 45, 159
Procedural justice, 6, 350
Professionalization, 201–202
Professional managers, 205
Progressive organizational career, 195
Psychological connectivity, 289–290
Psychological contract, 5, 197, 557
    breach of, 558
    fulfillment versus breach, 490–491
    and POC, 142–143
    structure of multiple, 66–67

Q

Quasi-spot contract EOR, 298
Quasi-spot contracts, 77–78, 407
    pull-to-leave forces, 408–409
    pull-to-stay forces, 408
    push-to-leave forces, 407–408
    push-to-stay forces, 408
Quiescent silence, 155

R

Racioethnic diversity influences perceptions of organizational support, 511–513
Reciprocity, 7–8, 90
Rejection, 157
Relational demography, 315–316
Relational effect
  involving three individuals, 320–324
  involving two individuals, 316–319
Relational elements, 119, 122
Relational perspective on EOR, 307–309
  balanced/imbalanced triadic structures, 321
  brief summary of existing studies, 311–314
  discussion, 324–326
    boundary conditions, 326
  relational view of social exchange relationships, 314–315
  relational demography, 315–316
  relational effect involving three individuals, 320–324
  relational effect involving two individuals, 316–319
  social exchange theory, 309–311
Relationships, 170
Representing organization, 30–32
Resource commensurability and ideological elements of exchange relationship, 113–115
  cross-cultural ideological exchange, 131
  exchange elements, 115–121
  features of resource elements
    ideological crystallization, 124–125
    ideological incompatibility, 124
    meta-ideological exchange, 125–126
    pivotal ideological space, 121–124
    multiple pivotal spaces and absence of pivotal space, 123
  pivotal ideological space, 123
  resource commensurability and characteristics, 126–131
  sources of resource elements, 122
Rethinking EOR, 255–257
  contingent EOR, 260–261
  cultural influences, 273–274
  defining domain, 257–260
  direct-hire contingent workers, 258
  direct hires, 261–264
    independent contractors, 267–271
    temporary agency workers, 264–267
  independent contractors, 260
  practical implications, 274–276
  research implications, 271–273
  temporary agency workers, 259
Retirement, 436
  EOR and, 435–437
    bridge employment opportunity, 442–443
    early retirement incentives, 442
    EOR and retirement intentions and decisions, 437–441
    EOR and retirement-related HRM practices, 441–444
    integrating organization's and employee's perspectives, 444–447
    mediation role of EOR in older worker-related organizational staffing, 445
    perceived organizational support, 438
Role elements, 119, 122

S

Salience, 464
Scholar–practitioner divide, EOR and, 555–558
  case study, 567–569
  criteria for scholars who perform research, 560–561
  integrating organization's and employee's perspectives, 566–567
  major challenges in bridging, 557
  Nucor, 561–565
    changing employment relationships and the lessons of, 565–566
    practitioner criteria for using research-based findings, 559–560

Script-based leaving, 411
Self-direction, 231–232
Senior managers, role of, 47
Situational strength, 44
Social conduct, 68
Social construction, 35
   importance of, 35–36
   process of, 36–38
"Social death." See Exclusion
Social exchange, 56, 71–72
   in EOR, 487–488
      inducements–contributions model, 491–495
      international perspectives, 488–489
      psychological contract fulfillment versus breach, 490–491
   perspective, 87
   process as norm of reciprocity, 465
   quality of, 91
   versus social identity, 93
   and social identity conceptualizations, 86
Social exchange relationships, 3, 307
   relational view of, 314–315
      relational demography, 315–316
      relational effect involving three individuals, 320–324
      relational effect involving two individuals, 316–319
   timing of reciprocation, importance of, 3
Social exchange theory (SET), 3, 309–311
   and inducements–contributions model, 2–4
   social exchange studies including social exchange variables studied, 312
Social identity, 95
   analysis, 86
   dynamics, 100
   versus social exchange, 93
Social identity-based leadership and EOR, 85–86
   advantages of social identity-based leadership, 94–99
   leaders as entrepreneurs of identity, 99–105
   leadership and employment relationship, 86–94
   stopping of cultural universals and beginning of cultural specifics begin, 105–106
Social influence, 39
Social pain, 154
Socioemotional selectivity theory (SST), 431
Socioemotional support, 431–432
Supervisor ERAs, 62
Supervisor influences on employee ethics, 58–59
Supervisor's organizational embodiment (SOE), 65
Surface-level relational diversity, 315

T

Task elements, 118, 122
Task interdependence, 292–293
Team diversity, 291
Team-member exchange (TMX), 34
Teamwork, myths about, 537–538
   all work teams are created equal, 542–544
   creating and promoting teamwork in organizations, 545–546
   culturally diverse teams versus culturally homogenous teams, performance, 547–548
   measuring teamwork, 546–547
   organizations know how to manage and foster teamwork, 540–541
   organizations know what teamwork is, 538–540
   team players are born, 545
   teamwork is all about communication, 544–545
   work teams are better than individuals, 541–542
Temporary agency workers, 259, 264–267
Temporary help services, 258
Top management ERAs, 62
Top management influences on employee ethics, 57–58
Traditional organizational career, 194

Subject Index • 617

Transactional and short term, work/
 family/employment relationship,
 232–233
 relational approaches, 232
Transactional contracts, 198
Transaction cost economics, 204
Transformational leadership instrument,
 349
Transformation of work/family/
 employment relationship,
 commonalities, 226
 boundarylessness, 226–228
 customization, 228–231
 self-direction, 231–232
 transactional and short term,
 232–233
Translating mechanisms and
 psychological states, 288
 managerial mutual investment
 practices, 288–289
 moderating elements influencing
 job virtuality–psychological
 connectivity relationship,
 290–294
 connective mechanisms, 292–293
 cross-level impact of virtual HR,
 293–294
 detachment factors, 290–292
 perceived mutual exchange and
 support, 294–295
 psychological connectivity,
 289–290
Tribe, 24
 endorsement of, 36
 and interpersonal influences, 36
 and organization, psychological
 convergence of, 39–41
Tribe members roles
 role of focal individual, 29–30
 role of immediate manager, 30–34
 direct supervision, 33–34
 enacting organization, 32–33
 representing organization, 30–32
 role of peers, 34–38
 importance of social construction,
 35–36
 process of social construction,
 36–38

Trust, 195–196
2-1-1 multilevel mediation model, 412
Turnover contagion, 402

U

Underinvestment EOR, 4, 77, 409–410
 interactions between push-and-pull
 leaving and staying forces,
 411–412
 pull-to-leave forces, 411
 pull-to-stay forces, 410–411
 push-to-leave forces, 410
 push-to-stay forces, 411

V

Virtual EOR, 281–282
 cultural influences on virtual work,
 299–300
 EOR mutual investment, 284
 human resource and virtuality
 architecture, 282
 job virtuality, 286–287
 outcomes
 individual-level outcomes,
 295–296
 organizational-level outcomes,
 296–297
 practical implications, 300–301
 translating mechanisms and
 psychological states, 288
 managerial mutual investment
 practices, 288–289
 moderating elements influencing
 job virtuality–psychological
 connectivity relationship,
 290–294
 perceived mutual exchange and
 support, 294–295
 psychological connectivity,
 289–290
 virtual HR system quality, 284–286
Volition, 262
Volunteer–organization relationships,
 171–172
Volunteers and EOR, 170
Volunteers versus employees, 172

W

Work and work arrangements, changing nature of, 581–583
Work–family boundary-blurring flexibility practices, 234
    family configurations, shift in, 225
    flexible work arrangements, 230
    formal HR policies and informal job design feature, 234–235
    idiosyncratic deals versus standardized flexibility, 236
    organizational or employee initiated, 235–236
    policy availability and awareness and use, 236–237
    work and family programs/policies, 229
    work–family flexibility policies and practices, 233, 241
Work–family flexibility
    and EOR, 242
    linkages to, 238
        implementation gap, 241–243
        inducement and general and specific social support theories, 238–241
        power dynamics of formal and informal boundary-blurring flexibility, 243–244
        work style preferences for boundary-blurring preferences and EOR, 244–248

Work teams, failure in organizations, 533–534
    best practices for training and supporting teamwork in organizations, 535
    fostering effective teamwork, 548
        necessary action of leaders, 549–550
        necessary action of organization, 548–549
        necessary aspects in team, 550–551
    myths of teamwork, 537–538
        all work teams are created equal, 542–544
        creating and promoting teamwork in organizations, 545–546
        culturally diverse teams versus culturally homogenous teams, performance, 547–548
        measuring teamwork, 546–547
        organizations know how to manage and foster teamwork, 540–541
        organizations know what teamwork is, 538–540
        team players are born, 545
        teamwork is all about communication, 544–545
        work teams are better than individuals, 541–542
    teamwork, team theories, and EOR, 534–537